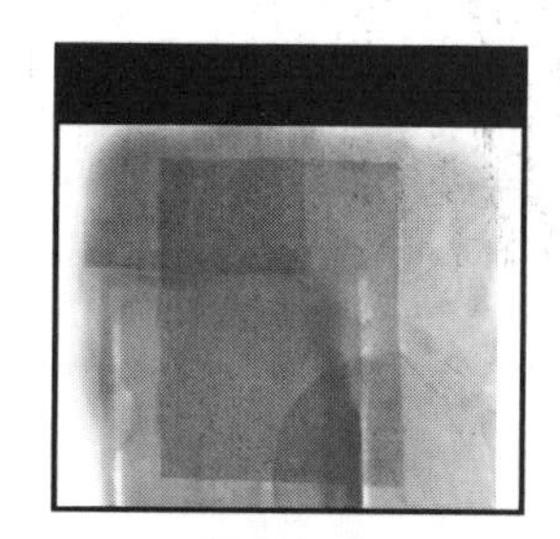

Developing Java™ Enterprise Applications

Stephen Asbury
Scott R. Weiner

Wiley Computer Publishing

John Wiley & Sons, Inc.
NEW YORK • CHICHESTER • WEINHEIM • BRISBANE • SINGAPORE • TORONTO

For my friends and the lessons they taught that were sometimes hard to learn.

—Stephen Asbury

For my wife Susan, who is special in too many ways to list here. For my daughter Emily, who comes to kiss me goodnight right about the time I start to work on the book each night. They both make me smile and I just wanted them to know I appreciate their patience, love and support.

—Scott Weiner

Publisher: Robert Ipsen
Editor: Theresa Hudson
Assistant Editor: Kathryn A. Malm
Managing Editor: Angela Murphy
Electronic Products, Associate Editor: Mike Sosa
Text Design & Composition: Benchmark Productions, Inc.

This book is printed on acid-free paper. ♾

Published by John Wiley & Sons, Inc.
Published simultaneously in Canada.

Library of Congress Cataloging-in-Publication Data:

Asbury, Stephen
Developing Java enterprise applications / Stephen Asbury, Scott R. Weiner.
p. cm
"Wiley computer publishing."
Includes index.
ISBN 0-471-32756-5 (pbk.)
1. Java (Computer program language) 2. Application software--Development. I. Weiner, Scott R. II. Title.
QA76.73.J38A83 1999
005.13'3--dc21 98-55106

Printed in the United States of America.
10 9 8 7 6 5 4 3 2 1

Contents

Acknowledgments

First, we would both like to thank the PRI gang; Alberto, Brad, Eric, Ethan, Glen, John, Karen, Kerry, Nicole, Shrinand, and Tyler. Sometimes writing takes away from work and we appreciate their dedication in our stead. Special thanks to Ethan for his LDAP expertise and Alberto for listening to Stephen complain about another late night, a fouled up example, or basically anything worth commiserating about.

And where would authors be without editors? Many thanks to Terri Hudson, Kathryn Malm, and Gerrie Cho for transforming our sometimes confused expositions into logical explanations.

Finally, unending thanks to our wives Cheryl and Susan. You can only apologize for coming to bed at 3 A.M. and working through the weekend so many times before you realize that the person you keep apologizing to knew long before you did what your decision to write a book entailed. I know from my experience that Cheryl is always two or more steps ahead of me, and although I kick myself for not figuring it out sooner, I wouldn't have it any other way. I bet if you asked Scott about Sue, he would tell you the same thing.

— Stephen Asbury

About the Authors

Stephen Asbury is the Chief Technology Officer for Paradigm Research, Inc. This is Stephen's fourth book on Web technology. He has also authored numerous courses on Java, JavaScript, Active Server pages, HTML and just about everything else that Web programmers need to know. In addition, Stephen has designed and built two Web-based training environments and a number of other commercial applications and frameworks. Stephen lives in Sunnyvale, California with his beloved wife Cheryl.

Scott Weiner is president of Paradigm Research, Inc. He has been involved in consulting with object-oriented design and programming for over ten years. Before founding Paradigm Research, Scott ran a mentoring program for NeXT Computers where he helped Fortune 1000 companies embrace object-oriented techniques for creating mission-critical applications. Today, Scott is leading Paradigm Research on a mission to create the best training for development teams leveraging leading-edge technologies and corporate end-users using the latest productivity applications. Scott lives in Northern California with his wife Susan, his beautiful one-year-old daughter, Emily, and their two dogs, Casey and Jake.

Introduction

Java is steadily becoming the language of choice for new enterprise-wide development projects. A number of factors have lead to this explosion in Java's popularity as a programming language and in particular as a language for large scale development projects. If you are reading this book, we expect that you already have some familiarity with Java as a programming language, and won't bore you with the laundry list of marketing buzz words that are often used to excite folks about Java. Instead, we have focused this book on the enterprise technologies that Sun is standardizing for the Java developers. These technologies, as standards, are motivating numerous companies to move their new projects onto the Java platform.

Our goal for *Developing Java Enterprise Applications* is to provide developers and evaluators alike an opportunity to learn about Java enterprise development at a technology level and from the perspective of a real world project. There are a number of emerging Java technologies and we have taken a snapshot of the available libraries, frameworks, and tools. Certainly, the list of available technologies will grow, but this book should serve as a solid foundation for your Java development.

Currently the main technologies being adopted, or about to be adopted, by enterprise developers include JDBC for database connectivity, the Java Naming and Directory Interface (JNDI) for accessing services, and RMI for Java remote method invocation and distributed objects. On top of this foundation are Servlets, JavaServer Pages, Enterprise Java Beans, Java Messaging Service, and Transaction Management. All of these combine into a feature-rich tool kit for developing Java applications.

What about CORBA?

You may have noticed that in all this discussion, we have made no mention of one of the more pervasive and potential influential technologies in enterprise development, CORBA. In researching and writing this book, we realized that their just wasn't room to do CORBA, and the Java technologies for accessing it, justice. Seeing the number of books that just discuss Java and CORBA, we decided that our time, and your money were better served discussing the other technologies well and leaving CORBA for a separate manuscript. We both realize that it would be short-sighted to expect Java developers to ignore CORBA, and we do not intend that. Rather, we decided to leave it out for the opposite reason, and ensure that your research into CORBA is complete and productive.

How This Book Is Organized

You will find three types of chapters in this book. First, each technology is introduced, the underlying concepts are discussed, and comparable technologies are described. Second, the programming techniques and technical concepts required to use a technology are described using small examples. These chapters provide a framework for studying larger examples. Each technology that this book focuses on has a targeted example provided for it. This example solves a medium size problem and provides a larger context for learning what the technology is for and how it is used. Finally, the book is concluded with two large examples. These tie together numerous concepts from the book and are intended to provide a stepping stone to your real world development projects.

At least that is the general idea. If we look at a specific example, Servlets, we see *Chapter 6: What Are Servlets?* introduces the concept of a servlet as a Web server extension. *Chapter 7: Programming Servlets* discusses the details of creating a servlet, and provides a number of small examples. *Chapter 8: A Servlet-Based Search Engine* demonstrates how servlets can be used to create a Web site search engine. Finally, *Chapter 25: A Four-Tier Online Store* uses a number of servlets in the creation of a small on-line store. And that's just for servlets. RMI, JavaServer Pages, Enterprise Java Beans, and Java Messaging Service all have the same, if not more, coverage. Also, JDBC and JNDI have chapters to introduce them, and describe the basic techniques required to use them. We decided that since these technologies show up in so many other places, it wasn't necessary to provide a single large example for them. One note about JBDC; it is a fairly lengthy topic, and if you are planning extensive database access we suggest that you use a book that focuses on JDBC. Like CORBA we didn't think that we could meet our main goals and do JDBC justice. But we thought that it was necessary to provide the basics here as a foundation for the other examples.

Based on this underlying design template the book is organized into the following chapters:

Chapter 1: An Introduction to Java Enterprise Development introduces the technologies in this book and describes some of the fundamental concepts that these technologies are built on.

Chapter 2: What Is JDBC? introduces the Java Database Connectivity framework (JDBC) and describes the goals and basic architecture for this important library.

Chapter 3: Basic JDBC Programming discusses the basic techniques used to access databases with JDBC. Because JDBC is a large library we have not tried to provide a complete discussion of it. Instead, we introduce the basic techniques used to access data. These techniques are used in numerous examples throughout the book.

Chapter 4: What Is JNDI? introduces what the Java Naming and Directory Interface is and the design goals behind it. The discussion includes information on naming and directory services in general as well as how JNDI accesses them.

Chapter 5: Using JNDI describes and provides techniques for developing Java programs that access naming and directory services. These techniques are used later in the book for accessing Enterprise JavaBeans and Java Messaging Service facilities.

Chapter 6: What Are Servlets? introduces servlets and compares them with other Web server programming tools.

Chapter 7: Programming Servlets describes the techniques used to write servlets and the libraries that support servlets. This chapter also provides a number of example servlets for retrieving data from the user, sending data to the user and communicating between applets and servlets.

Chapter 8: A Servlet-Based Search Engine is the first focused example in the book. This chapter describes a servlet based Web site search engine, including the code for indexing HTML pages.

Chapter 9: What is Server-side Scripting? introduces the concept of server-side scripting for Web pages and compares the different techniques to JavaServer pages.

Chapter 10: Creating JavaServer Pages demonstrates the techniques and syntax used to create JavaServer Pages. Examples are used to highlight each concept.

Chapter 11: A JavaServer Page Online Store discusses a larger JavaServer Page example that defines an online store. This store dynamically provides an interface for a categorized group of products. Advertisements are displayed on pages, and new products can be added without changing the code.

Chapter 12: Overview of Distributed Objects introduces the concept of distributed objects and describes how Java RMI fits in to the distributed object realm.

Chapter 13: Introduction to Java RMI describes the techniques and tools used to create distributed Java applications using RMI. Examples are used to demonstrate important points, like class loading, object passing and distributed garbage collection. A small discussion is included, with an example, on the RMI Object Activation Framework provided with Java 2.

Chapter 14: A Network File Locking Server describes a larger RMI example that demonstrates how a server can be used to implement file locking on a single machine or the network.

Chapter 15: What are Enterprise JavaBeans introduces the powerful new technology called Enterprise JavaBeans. In this first discussion of EJB the various roles involved in creating Enterprise JavaBeans are listed and EJB is motivated as a development technology.

Chapter 16: Programming Enterprise JavaBeans discusses the techniques and libraries that programmers use to create Enterprise JavaBeans. Examples are used to highlight important concepts like Entity beans versus Session beans. Enterprise JavaBeans defines an important standard for developing server side code.

Chapter 17: Deploying Enterprise JavaBeans lists the steps used to deploy an EJB application on an application, or some other server. This chapter is provided as an introduction to the basic issues when deploying EJB applications.

Chapter 18: Enterprise JavaBean Business Rules Engine describes an example Enterprise JavaBean application that uses a configurable rules engine to process check requests. This example demonstrates both the EJB technology and how scripting can be used to create dynamic business rules.

Chapter 19: What is Messaging and the Java Messaging Service? introduces the concept of messaging and how the Java Messaging Service supports this programming paradigm. Messaging is an alternative method for defining network communication and has begun to gain popularity for large, complex enterprise projects, especially for integrated disparate systems. This chapter also defines the basic messaging styles, including point-to-point and publish-subscribe.

Chapter 20: Programming With the Java Messaging Service demonstrates the techniques used to create applications that use JMS to send point-to-point and publish-subscribe style messages. Examples are provided for major concepts, including applications that send and receive messages using both styles.

Chapter 21: A JMS-Based Alarm System defines and describes a larger JMS application. This application uses messages to create an alarm system. Users can define alarms and have them triggered automatically at the appropriate time. This chapter also includes an interesting library for managing timed notifications.

Chapter 22: Transactions, JTA, and JTS introduces the concept of a transaction and discusses the Java libraries being defined to manage them.

Chapter 23: Using Transactions with Enterprise JavaBeans relates transactions to Enterprise JavaBeans and provides examples of how an enterprise bean can manage its transactional context.

Chapter 24: Architecture Review ties many of the concepts in this book together and introduces the two large examples that conclude the book.

Chapter 25: A Four-Tier Online Store discusses an online store implementation. This store uses JavaServer pages and servlets to define a Web page interface. Servlets are used to manage searching and advertisement placements. A servlet is also defined to manage a shopping cart for the user. This servlet works with an Enterprise JavaBean to access data in a database about inventory and credit. Another servlet is provided for creating inventory reports.

Chapter 26: MiniJMS discusses an implementation of the JMS libraries. This JMS provider uses RMI, JDBC and JNDI to implement network messaging.

As you can see, the basic flow for each technology is an introduction followed by details and an example. Finally, two large examples are used to tie the concepts together. We strove for educational clarity and usefulness in our examples, so please do not consider them the end all be all of programming. We have tried to show the tradeoffs we made, but there were tradeoffs. Please keep this in mind as you study the example code.

Who Should Read This Book

This book is designed for two types of readers. First, technical evaluators should be able to use the introductory chapters to learn about each technology at a high level. Then the example chapters can provide demonstrations for what the technology can do. Experienced Java programmers can use the programming chapters to learn the new libraries and classes before diving into the example code to see how these programs really work and get ideas for their own projects. Both types of readers should be able to leverage the rules and guidelines throughout the book in future projects.

This book covers a lot of topics. You may want to read it straight through or jump around. In either case, keep in mind the design template discussed above so that you can jump to a technology without jumping into the middle of it, unless you want to. If you are planning to read the code for the examples, you should already have experience writing Java programs, including basic threads programming. If you have also used the networking libraries, that will help with some of the distributed technologies, although it is not a requirement.

Necessary Tools and CD-ROM Content

One problem we encountered when writing this book is that enterprise programming needs a lot of deployment support. In particular, JDBC needs a database to access, JNDI needs special service providers, Servlets and JavaServer Pages need a Web server, EJBs need a host and JMS requires a service provider as well. For JMS we have written a sample provider that is discussed in *Chapter 26: MiniJMS*. For JDBC we have often discussed ODBC to meet the most commonly available database engines. But we have also provided a demonstration version of Cloudscape's JDMS a pure Java database engine on the CD-ROM. For EJB examples we have included a demonstration version of the BEA WebLogic application server on the CD-ROM. This server also provides some JNDI services, as do the sample providers available from Sun. For servlets, we have included the Servlet Development Kit. Unfortunately, you will need to download a server, possibly from Sun, that supports JavaServer pages to test the examples.

That's quite a list. Each chapter that introduces a new technology will provide specific details for the programs and tools you need to run the examples from that chapter.

All of the examples rely on the standard Java Development Kit, we chose 1.1.6 and 1.2. Many use the Swing user interface library as well. Java 2 is provided on the CD-ROM, while both the 1.1 JDK and Swing can be downloaded from Sun's Web site.

Although we did our testing on Windows NT, Windows95, and Windows98 all of the examples are pure Java and should be easily run on other platforms. Please refer to the Web site for this book at http://www.crl.com./~sasbury/ejava/ for the latest information on these examples. You can also use that site to let us know of any problems you have with a particular version or operating system so that we can let others know about those issues.

Note on Versions

Java is a growing, changing and expanding technology. You will always hear about the next version just when you learn the newest one. As authors this can be especially challenging for us. We have tried to provide the best available information in this book. However, we know of some rumors and releases already and for completeness have listed them here.

At the time we are writing, Enterprise JavaBeans was at version 1.0. Sun has already announced that there will be a "maintenance" release, probably called 1.1, that may appear before this book is published. This release is designed to fix bugs and resolve issues with the JDK security model. Sun is also working with its partners on EJB 2.0. Little information is available on this release at the time of this writing, but indications are that it will build on the 1.0 release, so what you learn here will provide a firm foundation for future versions. Sun has also indicated that they will probably provide a "reference implementation" for an EJB host. This will allow you to test your EJB projects in a product independent environment.

The Java transaction APIs were not finalized at the time of this writing and may change somewhat in early 1999. Please use the latest documentation on your EJB host and Sun's Web site for information on transaction management. Keep in mind that changes to JTA may effect the EJB specification as well.

The Servlet specification is being refined and updated. Like EJB, the content of this book should provide a great foundation for your work with future versions of servlet programming. JavaServer pages are also being updated and the new specification is discussed in some detail in chapter 10.

Things will always be changing, but for enterprise projects you want a stable development platform. We strongly suggest that for at least the first half of 1999 that you stick to JDK 1.1.7 and possibly 1.2 for deployment. Also stay with the earlier versions of the enterprise APIs until the new versions are fully supported by your server vendors. This means EJB 1.0, JDBC 1.0 and the other versions discussed here. Although specifications are being updated it will often take time for the service providers to update their code. A great example of this is JDBC where 2.0 is nearly out but the drivers are not yet supporting it. As a result we have discussed 2.0 features but have not included examples of JDBC 2.0 here.

Summary

Our goal in writing this book was to provide a solid, example rich, introduction to the Enterprise Java Technologies. We can't hope to discuss every issue in enterprise development, despite how hard we tried. We can hope that you will use this book to start your journey into Java enterprise development. Please let us know how you do and what you would like to see in future books so that we can continue to provide a solid programming introduction to new technology.

An Introduction to Java Enterprise Development

Developing enterprise applications requires an understanding of many technologies. In addition to understanding Java, it is important to understand the technologies that support networking, the Web, and database connectivity. Often, the enterprise developer is faced with the task of applying very specific knowledge about a technology to the problem of connecting it with another possibly unknown application.

This chapter introduces some of the concepts that support enterprise Java development. Once these concepts are defined, the main enterprise Java technologies are introduced. The remainder of this book discusses these technologies in detail.

Supporting Concepts

A number of concepts support enterprise Java technologies. These concepts include HTTP, threads, and the Java language itself. Let's take a look at these basic concepts. If you are familiar with these concepts, feel free to jump ahead to the section entitled "Enterprise Technologies."

HTTP

Many of the applications being written today are being deployed on the World Wide Web or in a miniature version of the Web inside a corporate network. Most likely you are familiar with the Web, but you may not have had to deal with the protocols that drive it.

The primary protocol that drives the Web is called the HyperText Transfer Protocol (HTTP). Although the name implies that this protocol is used only to transfer text, it can actually be used for any type of file. HTTP creates a relationship between a resource provider (the server) and a resource requester (the client). All HTTP interactions occur in the form of requests. The client sends a request, and the server replies. Between requests, there is no connection between the client and the server, making HTTP a stateless protocol.

Each HTTP request and reply includes a header and a body. The header contains configuration information such as the resource being requested. The body for a request can contain information relevant to the request; the body of the reply contains the requested information. A number of request types can be used, each indicated in the header. The first, called GET, is used to request a resource. POST requests also ask for a resource but are expected to include information, often from an HTML form, along with the request. PUT requests are used to put data on the server; other, more esoteric request types can be used to query the server and perform other operations.

As far as the content of this book is concerned, the main concepts that you need to understand are that HTTP is stateless, there are several types of HTTP requests, and the requests contain a header and a body.

Java

A number of Java concepts are particularly relevant to enterprise programming. First, enterprise applications often require the use of multiple threads. Second, many of the enterprise technologies require object serialization. Finally, enterprise applications must be deployed to be used.

Perhaps the only one of these concepts that is appropriate to mention in this book is deployment. As Java has matured, a number of important deployment-oriented technologies have been released. First, the Java Run-time Environment (JRE) is a version of the Java interpreter and classes intended for deployment rather than development. The JRE does not include the development tools but does include the classes required to run Java applications. JDK 1.1 uses a separate JRE; JDK 1.2 (now called Java 2) integrates the JRE into the JDK, providing JRE add-ons for development tools.

The second big step in deployment is the Java plug-in, which is available for JDK 1.1 and Java 2. The Java plug-in is a browser extension that works with Microsoft Internet Explorer and Netscape Navigator. Basically, the plug-in is like the JRE for a browser. Users who install the plug-in can run Java applets using the associated version of Java. This is a great leap forward because the browser vendors were hard pressed to keep their Java versions in sync with the versions being released by Sun. Using the Java plug-in, you can release to your customers applets that use the latest technologies, without waiting for customers' browsers to be updated.

Specialized Servers

Enterprise development adds a new layer of servers to the basic Web application. Whereas the Web has Web servers, enterprise applications have databases, application servers, and transaction monitors. You may already be familiar with databases.

Application servers are programs that provide server-type services such as resource management to extensions written by enterprise developers. The goal of application servers is to manage the "hard parts" of client/server programming. Transaction monitors are a special type of server that manages distributed transactions. These transactions are discussed more in Chapter 23, "Using Transactions with Enterprise JavaBeans."

Basic Enterprise Design

Over the past couple years, a number of buzzwords have been coined to describe the basic designs for enterprise applications. In particular, the terms *three-tier* and *n-tier* are used to describe enterprise applications that reside on the client and several servers. This book describes and discusses a number of variations on the tiered application theme. Specifically, two-tier applications, such as the designs pictured in Figure 1.1, are created. These might connect a client to a Web server or database.

Extending a two-tier application to three tiers allows the programmer to leverage other resources. In particular, the server can use a database for storing information or an application server to process information. Several three-tier application designs are pictured in Figure 1.2.

Certainly, four- and five-tier applications are possible. Often these applications are grouped under the heading of n-tier applications because they combine numerous computers into a potentially deep and complex relationship. Figure 1.3 demonstrates a couple of n-tier application designs.

Although these examples provide only the basic design for an enterprise application, they represent an important step in enterprise development. Before you can create an enterprise application, it is important to decide what technologies will be used and to determine the computers that will run them.

Security

Enterprise applications often require some form of security management. The Java security model is undergoing some major changes from JDK 1.1 to Java 2. The new

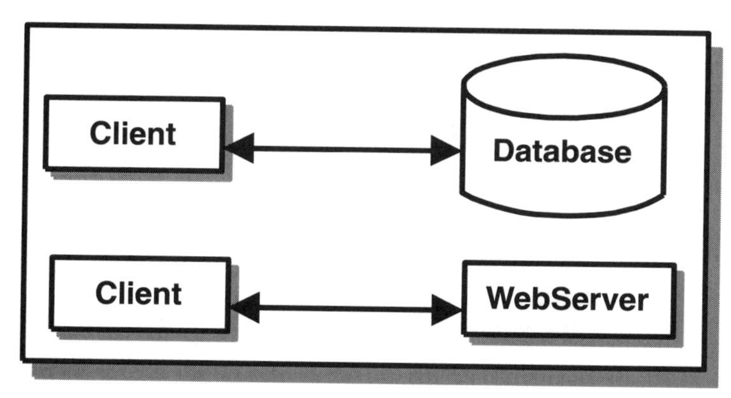

Figure 1.1 Two-tier applications.

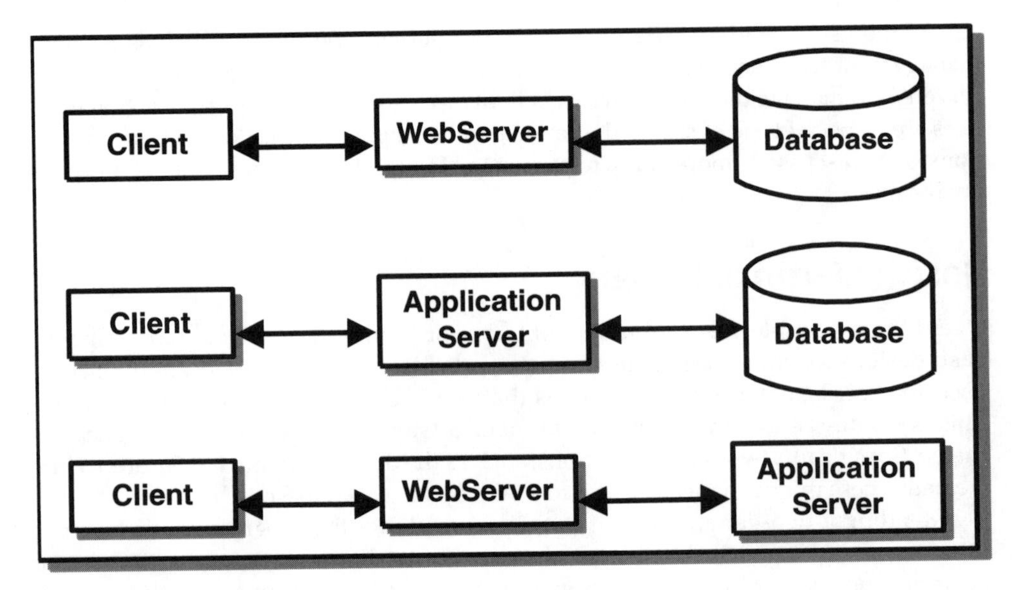

Figure 1.2 Three-tier applications.

model is beyond the scope of this book, but it does define the standard concepts that we will rely on. First, security often uses the concepts of a username and password to

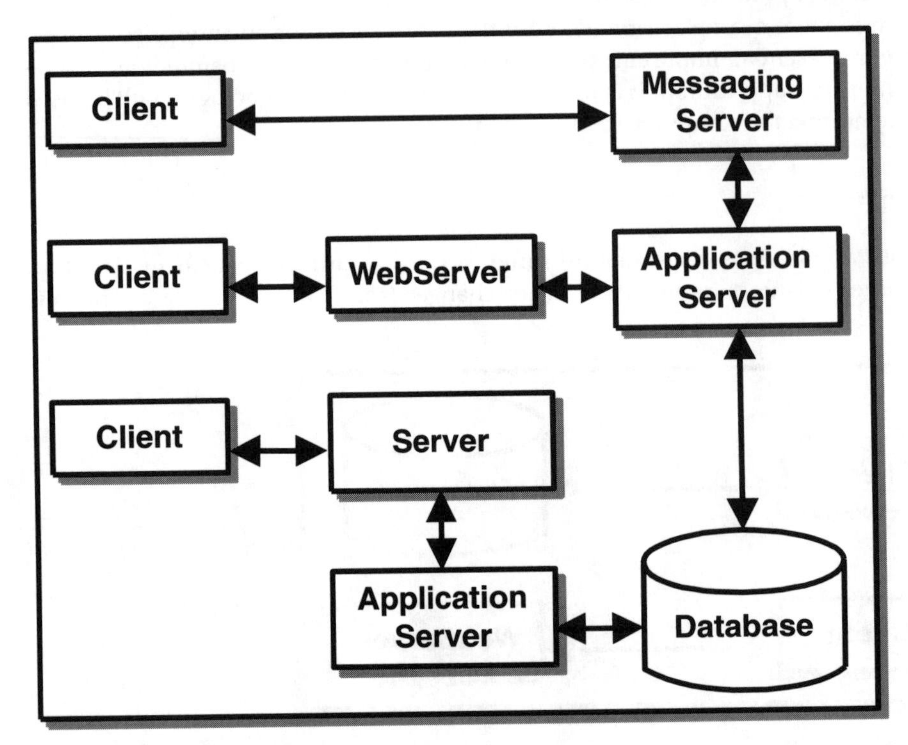

Figure 1.3 N-tier applications.

identify people. The Java enterprise technologies use these concepts as well. Users can sometimes be organized into groups or roles. A role might represent the idea of a manager. All managers, regardless of their usernames, might have the same permissions. For example, perhaps all managers could submit a hiring request, while employees cannot.

Java also relies on the concept of permissions. Permissions indicate what operations a user or role can perform. So, in our example, employees do not have permission to make hiring requests, while managers do. The configuration for these permissions is organized into an Access Control List (ACL). In our examples, we will sometimes use ACLs to control who can use a particular resource, such as an Enterprise JavaBean.

The remaining security concepts such as encryption and digital signatures are not used in this book, although they are supported in JDK 1.1 and Java 2. Please refer to the Sun Web site for more information on the latest security model.

Enterprise Technologies

This book discusses a number of Java technologies:

JDBC. The Java Database Connectivity (JBDC) libraries are used to connect a Java program to a data source. The initial version of JDBC was targeted at relational databases, but JDBC 2.0 extends this model to other types of data sources.

JNDI. The Java Naming and Directory (JNDI) interface, like JDBC, is really an enabling technology more than a library for use all by itself. Many of the technologies discussed in this book rely on JNDI to provide access to objects such as enterprise beans and JMS destinations.

Servlets. Servlets extend Web servers. In an enterprise environment, servlets can be used to solve a number of problems. First, servlets replace CGI in providing server-side processing for HTTP requests. Second, servlets can extend dynamic Web pages using server-side includes or JavaServer Pages. Third, servlets can be used to form a gateway between Web clients and other services such as databases, Enterprise JavaBeans, and JMS. Finally, the servlet interfaces can be used as a generic interface for services. For example, programmers might use the service method as an interface for generic RMI objects or even enterprise beans.

JavaServer Pages. JavaServer Pages (JSPs) are used to create dynamic Web pages using Java as a scripting language. JSPs are primarily used in situations in which a Web page changes with each request.

RMI and distributed objects. Like JDBC, Remote Method Invocation (RMI) is an enabling technology. Many applications and libraries use RMI to form their network connections. Other applications may rely on raw sockets or HTTP connections to interact with servlets and the Web Server. The goal of RMI is to provide a transparent link between two Java applications.

Enterprise JavaBeans. Enterprise JavaBeans (EJBs) are designed to be the standard building blocks for corporate server applications. Whenever your application is implemented on a server, definitely consider using an EJB host server, such as

BEA WebLogic Application Server, and Enterprise JavaBeans. This combination allows you to rely on heavily tested services from the server provider and focus your resources on application-specific programming. The component design of Enterprise JavaBeans makes them a great way to encapsulate business rules and processes. They can also form the foundation of a library that provides standard services that your enterprise applications require, such as data processing or report generation.

Java Messaging Service. The Java Messaging Service (JMS) is designed to act as a front end to messaging providers. Messaging as a technology is a great way to objectify the communication between applications.

Creating an enterprise application involves combining these technologies to create a complete solution to your business problems.

Creating an Enterprise Application with Java

Let's get something clear. This isn't a book on designing applications. There are hundreds of books on that topic, and we couldn't do the topic justice in this small space. However, it is worthwhile to look at the basic steps used to create an application and see how they apply to Java Enterprise development.

The first step for any project is to define the project and its goal. For an enterprise project, this may involve defining functionality across multiple computers or domains. Don't tie yourself to a particular platform at this point. Instead, focus on what the entire application needs to do, then separate the functionality in later steps.

Once you have a list of requirements, analyze them and design a set of components and objects that fulfill the requirements. At this point, start thinking about application boundaries, but don't lock yourself into saying "This is an EJB" or "This is a JMS message." The main goal is to determine a clear set of client applications and the components that support them. For this book, the design of client applications with a user interface is left to the reader. Our focus is on the libraries that the client might use to communicate with the supporting components. The one exception is the use of Web pages as an interface to an application on the server. The book discusses these; you should use good Web page and Web site design techniques to augment the discussion. Keep in mind that some "client" applications may not have a user interface at all. They may be report generators or the like.

Take the components that your programs need, and determine what communication mechanism they should use to interact. Possible choices are HTTP, RMI, CORBA, sockets, and JMS. HTTP is normally used for applications that use a Web page front end, but it can also be useful in situations in which the components are separated by a firewall. With the availability of RMI and CORBA, sockets should be used only when required to support existing protocols or applications. RMI and CORBA both use the concept of distributed objects, discussed in Chapter 12, "Overview of Distributed Objects," to enable interapplication communication. For applications being written in pure Java, RMI provides the most native distributed object choice. Applications that need to connect to programs written in other languages should probably choose

CORBA. As mentioned in the preface, this book doesn't cover CORBA, but the discussions on RMI are relevant. Finally, JMS allows programs to communicate via encapsulated messages. Messages can be sent between Java programs and even to non-Java programs, depending on the provider. More discussion on reasons you might choose JMS is provided in Chapter 19, "What Are Messaging and the Java Messaging Service?"

Given the components and the protocols between them, the next step in the development process is to determine what type of component to implement. JavaServer Pages and servlets can be used to drive a Web page user interface. Servlets can also provide generic services over HTTP or some other protocol. Enterprise JavaBeans are used to define components that live on a server of some type, such as an application server. Using EJBs, you can leverage services provided by the server, such as transaction management and resource optimization. RMI and JMS can be used with EJBs or servlets as well as in applets or applications. For example, you can create an application that provides services by receiving JMS messages and sending JMS messages for the reply.

The final step in this process is to write the client applications and components and, of course, test them. The goal for this book is to not only help you write the applications and components but to provide some ideas and tips for making the decisions we've discussed. In particular, the last three chapters in this book start with a review of the technologies and describe situations in which they should be used. Then two large examples are described in detailed, real-world applications.

Why Use Java for Enterprise Development?

Of course, you may still be asking the question, "Why should I use Java for my enterprise development?" It is certainly a valid question, and we would be hard pressed to argue that Java is perfect for every single programming situation. However, there are a number of great reasons to use Java for enterprise development and development in general. Let's look at the specific advantages of the Java enterprise technologies.

First, despite some hiccups, Java is extremely portable. This doesn't mean solely that the programs can move between computers; it means that components such as Enterprise JavaBeans can be moved between different application servers. Using EJB, you can develop an application on one server and deploy it on another one. This can save cost, because developers don't all need a deployment environment available to them. Of course, you should always test on the deployment environment before actually deploying your enterprise applications. Sun has made "Write Once, Run Everywhere" a mantra and is constantly improving the availability of Java and the enterprise Java technologies. With companies such as IBM, BEA, Oracle, and Sybase on board as well as a host of innovative startups such as Cloudscape, it isn't hard to see how Java will continue to grow and improve.

Second, the standards defined by the enterprise Java technologies reduce education cost. Once you learn the specifications described in this book, you can apply them on multiple servers. Compare this to the old way of doing things, when programmers specialized in a particular database or transaction monitor.

Technologies such as Enterprise JavaBeans and servlets split an application into components and centralize code. With RMI, JNDI, and JMS, it is easy to manage the relationship between components. In other words, you can leverage technologies such as application servers to help break your code into manageable components, both during development and once they are running.

These technologies leverage the advantages of Java. For example, servlets allow you to plug custom code into a Web server, as a plug-in or extension library would. However, servlets have garbage-collection and exception-handling abilities, so a problem in a servlet should not affect the server as a whole. The same is true for Enterprise JavaBeans that may be deployed on a database or application server. In both cases, Java is creating a safety zone around each enterprise application to protect it from naughty neighbors.

And the list goes on. We could spend several pages talking about why you should use these technologies. This list is a great start, though, and once you see what the technologies are and how they work, you will be able to fill in the list for yourself. So let's get started.

Summary

As you work through the concepts and examples in this book, keep in mind the goals you have for your Java applications. Consider where each technology can be used, and think about which one is the right technology to use. Hopefully, as you reach the two final large examples at the end of the book, you will begin to think of new ways to combine the enterprise Java technologies. Ultimately, your success creating enterprise applications is limited only by your ability to choose the right technology for the job and apply it appropriately.

The next two chapters introduce JDBC. This introduction is provided for programmers who have no JDBC experience and is not intended as a complete discussion of the Java database access libraries. If you are already familiar with JDBC, you may want to skip ahead to Chapter 4, "What Is JNDI?"

What Is JDBC?

Java Database Connectivity (JDBC) is an application programming interface (API) that describes a standard Java library for accessing data sources, primarily relational databases, that use the Structured Query Language (SQL). JDBC is JavaSoft's answer to the corporate developer's requirement for database access from an enterprise Java application. Not only does JDBC provide a standard API for accessing data sources such as relational databases, but it also provides a standard architecture for database vendors so they can provide data source drivers. These drivers allow access to the vendor's products directly from your Java applications.

NOTE In May 1998, Sun released the JDBC 2.0 specification. The discussions in this book mostly refer to the JDBC 1.0 specification because few drivers support 2.0 at this time. Where appropriate, JDBC 2.0 features and enhancements are identified.

This chapter describes the goals and architecture of JDBC. It assumes you are familiar with relational database theory and SQL. If you are not familiar with SQL, you may want to read one of the many available SQL books such as *A Visual Introduction to SQL* by J. Harvey Trimble and David Chappell.

Although SQL is an ANSI standard language used to manage relational databases, each database vendor implements its own slightly unique version of SQL to take advantage of database-specific features. In order for application developers to access various databases without having to learn an entirely new database access library each time, standard specifications for database access drivers (sometimes referred to as *bridges*) have emerged. These standards allow developers to build applications that can access, view, and modify data from multiple, diverse databases as well as easily port new and existing applications to new data sources. The bridge acts as a translator that takes generic database access calls and translates them to database-specific calls. The most common driver specification is ODBC, or *Open Database Connectivity.* ODBC is a C- based standard developed by the SQL Access Group (SAG) standards committee and popularized by Microsoft. ODBC is based on the Call Level Interface (CLI) specification of SAG.

NOTE **In 1995, SAG joined with the X/Open Data Management Technical Committee to form the X/Open SQL Access Group. This group is composed of representatives from AT&T, Inprise, Computer Associates, IBM, Informix, INTERSOLV, Microsoft Corporation, Oracle Corporation, Progress, Sybase, Visigenic Software, and other vendors.**

ODBC allows users to access data in a relational database management system. ODBC provides a consistent interface for communicating with a database. However, the standard suffers from several drawbacks. Developers have complained that ODBC is slow and limited in functionality. Another problem is that ODBC drivers are platform specific. This means if you write your application to run on multiple platforms, you will need a separate driver for each platform, which makes your application less portable.

NOTE **You can find more information on ODBC at www.microsoft.com/data/odbc/.**

Like ODBC, JDBC uses drivers to create a bridge to a specific database. Because JDBC drivers are still being developed for many databases, you can use the JDBC/ODBC bridge from JavaSoft to act as your database driver until a native driver is available.

NOTE **For a list of available JDBC drivers and vendors supplying them, check http://java.sun.com/products/jdbc/jdbc.drivers.html.**

ODBC is more mature than JDBC, so there are drivers for accessing most databases through ODBC. The JDBC/ODBC bridge allows you to use a native Java interface to access your database through ODBC without having to learn the ODBC specification. This extra overhead does create some performance issues, and ODBC is not as rich a specification as JDBC; therefore you can't take full advantage of all of JDBC's capabilities with this driver. However, this technique will allow you to get up and running while the vendors continue to develop and deliver database-specific JDBC drivers. For most of the JDBC chapters in this book, we use the JDBC/ODBC bridge in our examples. It is free from JavaSoft and will work with most databases you may have access to, provided you have the appropriate ODBC driver.

Goals for JDBC

JDBC was modeled after the ODBC architecture. The JDBC developers had two high-level goals for its design: adhering to common database standards and keeping the API simple.

Support Common Database Standards

Java programmers use JDBC for most database access calls. The JDBC API is designed to allow application programmers to communicate with any data source that has a JDBC driver implementation. In order to talk to various data sources, the API must remain fairly generic. However, the goal is to replace the functionality of ODBC in C-based applications and specifically provide interaction with SQL databases. This goal is met in three ways:

JDBC provides the ability to pass raw SQL statements directly to the data source. By providing a facility for passing SQL to the database, JDBC allows the application programmer to take advantage of database-specific features. However, this means that the programmer has to be responsible for sending appropriate SQL commands. The drivers provide metadata that can indicate what commands are valid for a particular data source. Metadata is information about or documentation of other data managed within an application or environment. For example, meta-data in a relational database describes the database tables, including the name of each attribute, the type of each attribute, and the size of each attribute. JDBC provides methods to return this information from the driver.

JDBC drivers must at least support the ANSI SQL92 Entry Level standard in order to be considered compliant. Sun has trademarked the term "JDBC Compliant" in order to assure consumers that a vendor's JDBC driver handles a minimum level of SQL support. Just because a driver does not have this stamp does not mean it is not a good driver. It simply indicates that the vendor chose not to conform to the SQL92 standard. In most cases, it is probably worth asking the vendor why it chose not to provide this minimum level of standard SQL support, because the industry expects this minimal level of interoperability.

JDBC architecture must support the functionality of common database bridges such as ODBC. JDBC developers realized it would take time for database vendors to provide native JDBC drivers for all the various data sources developers needed. They ensured that the JDBC API would provide a superset of the ODBC capabilities. JDBC improves on the ODBC standard and is optimized to leverage the strengths of the Java language. In general, Java programmers use JDBC for all database access calls. This way, creating one driver for ODBC, the JDBC/ODBC bridge, enables developers to immediately take advantage of JDBC with virtually any data source.

Supporting common standards enables enterprise developers to take advantage of the latest Java technologies while maintaining a high degree of interoperability with other industry-standard products. JDBC solves most relational database access requirements from Java.

Keep It Simple

Combining database access with an application-level API often results in compromises because the natures of the languages (SQL versus Java, for example) are quite different in their design and common use. If a developer has to master and maintain applications that utilize various combinations of these languages, the whole process becomes quite complex. Emphasis on keeping JDBC simple has resulted in an API that works well with the rest of JavaSoft's Java class libraries. Clearly, the Java philosophy as outlined in Sun's white paper, "The Java Language Environment: A White Paper," written by James Gosling and Henry McGilton, has been considered in the design decisions for JDBC. In order to keep JDBC simple, the designers considered the following guidelines:

Keep the common cases simple by providing specific APIs for standard activities such as selecting data using parameters. By providing methods for common cases, application programmers can write and maintain less code.

Leverage the style and benefits of the Java core classes as much as possible. By consciously keeping Java's strengths in mind while designing JDBC, JavaSoft has created an API that application programmers can easily integrate into their Java projects. This goal is realized in the JDBC 2.0 specification, which is geared toward working with the JavaBeans component model as well as other Java technologies, such as the Java Transaction Services (JTS) discussed in Chapter 22, "Transactions, JTA, and JTS."

Create methods that map to specific functionality rather than relying on a small API with multiple meanings based on parameter values. Rather than trying to keep the API small, it makes more sense to provide a rich API that addresses most of the database tasks with specific method calls. This approach makes it easier for new JDBC programmers to understand the use of each method. Another approach would have been to create a small API with few methods, each taking several parameters that allowed the programmer to configure the method. For example, an execute method could be used for all types of SQL calls, but it would take a parameter to specify whether the SQL call expected a return result. This would have made it easier for a programmer to learn all of the available methods but harder to learn how to use each method. For this reason, a rich API was chosen. This decision is evident in JDBC 2.0, which has a significantly larger API but methods that are relatively simple to understand and use.

Use strong, static typing wherever possible to provide compile-time checking. As part of the Java philosophy, static typing is used wherever possible so that more errors can be caught at compile time rather than run time. The challenge with JDBC is that because raw SQL can be passed to the database and then interpreted at run time, the programmer must contend with SQL being, by nature, a dynamic language. This means that data types are often determined as the result of a query at run time, so warnings and exceptions must be carefully monitored.

One of the best features of JDBC is that it allows Java programmers to quickly develop database access strategies for their applications. With a very small amount of code, a developer can create a connection to a database, query the database, and update values. JDBC even supports a transaction model so developers can make several database modifications and, if necessary, undo all of them as a single transaction. The next section looks at the architecture of JDBC that provides these services.

JDBC Architecture

The basic architecture of JDBC is quite simple. A class called DriverManager provides a service for managing a set of JDBC drivers. The DriverManager class attempts to load the driver classes referenced in the jdbc.drivers system property. You can load drivers explicitly using Class.forName(). For instance, to load the JDBC-ODBC bridge driver, call the following:

```
Connection con = null;
Class.forName("sun.jdbc.odbc.JdbcOdbcDriver");
con = DriverManager.getConnection("jdbc:odbc:myDataSource);
```

Class.forName() loads the driver class. On load, the driver should register itself with the DriverManager. The call DriverManager.getConnection() looks for a registered driver that can handle the data source described by the URL that uses the jdbc: protocol and returns an object from the driver that implements the connection interface. A *connection* represents a session with the data source and includes methods for executing database operations. It provides information about the data source, called meta-data, which includes information about the data source structure.

The protocol used to specify the data source is in the format jdbc:subprotocol:datasourcename, where datasourcename is, in this case, the name of a registered ODBC data source, such as a Microsoft Access database or an Oracle database. The getConnection() method takes an optional username and password for registration with data sources that require these.

Typical Scenarios

There are several typical scenarios for using JDBC. These scenarios differ based on the location of the database, the driver, the application, and the communication protocols used. The main scenarios are:

- Standalone applications
- Applets communicating with a Web server
- Application and applets communicating with a database through the JDBC/ODBC gateway
- Applications accessing remote resources using mechanisms such as the Java Remote Method Invocation (RMI), discussed in Chapter 13, "Introduction to Java RMI."

These scenarios can be grouped into two- and three-tier architectures. In a two-tier architecture, the application resides on the same machine as the database driver. The driver can access the database running on a database server. The database driver is responsible for handling the networked communication. Figure 2.1 illustrates a simple two-tier JDBC architecture. In this example, the Java application running on the client machine uses a JDBC driver residing locally. The local driver, in turn, uses a vendor-specific client library for accessing the database remotely, over the network. The Java application accesses this resource transparently, meaning that it never has to deal with network communication issues.

NOTE **The database may reside on the same machine as the application and still be considered a two-tier architecture because the application resides in a separate address space from the database. The driver must still handle the interprocess communication.**

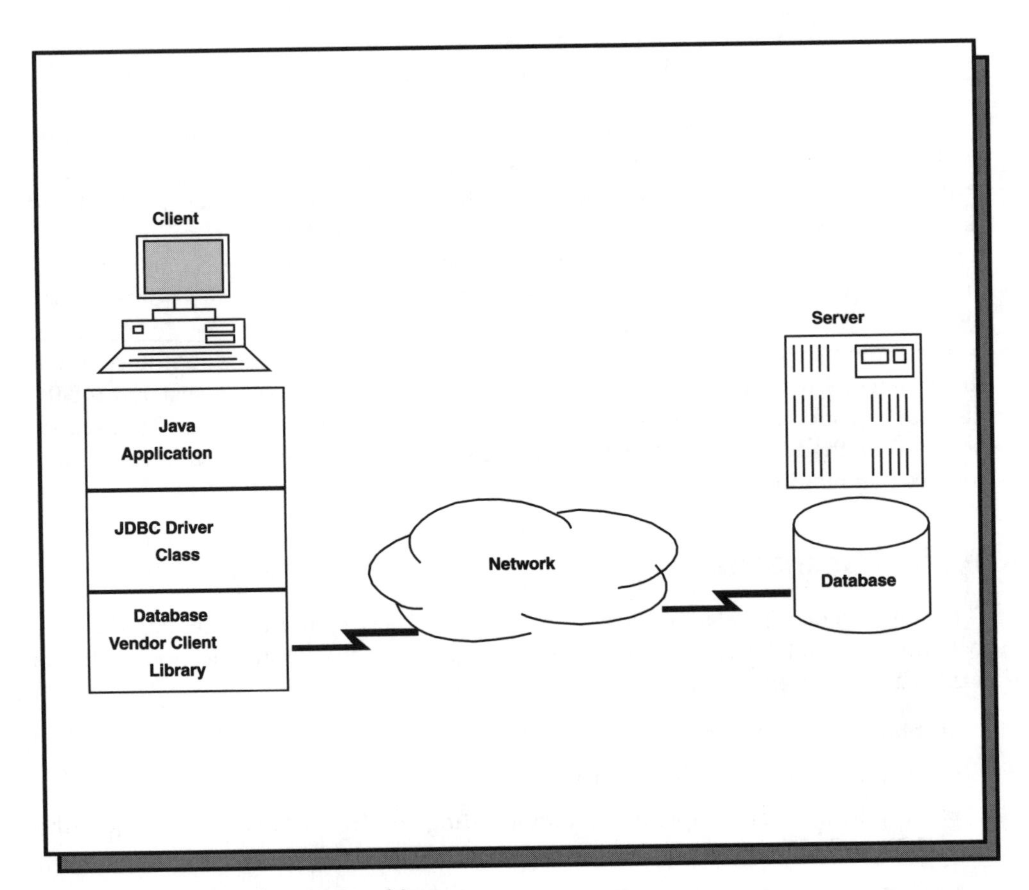

Figure 2.1 A two-tier JDBC architecture.

The three-tier architecture involves an application or applet running on one platform and accessing the database driver on another. The database driver can be accessed through a variety of mechanisms:

- An applet may access the driver through a Web server
- An application may access a remote server program that communicates locally with a database driver
- An application may communicate with an application server that accesses the database for you

Figure 2.2 illustrates a three-tier scenario in which an applet on the client Web browser accesses a server application that accesses a database behind the firewall.

By placing all the database access logic in the JDBC driver, the driver vendor handles the issues of communicating with the database and database vendor's client library. This means you can write applications that function in a two-tier or three-tier

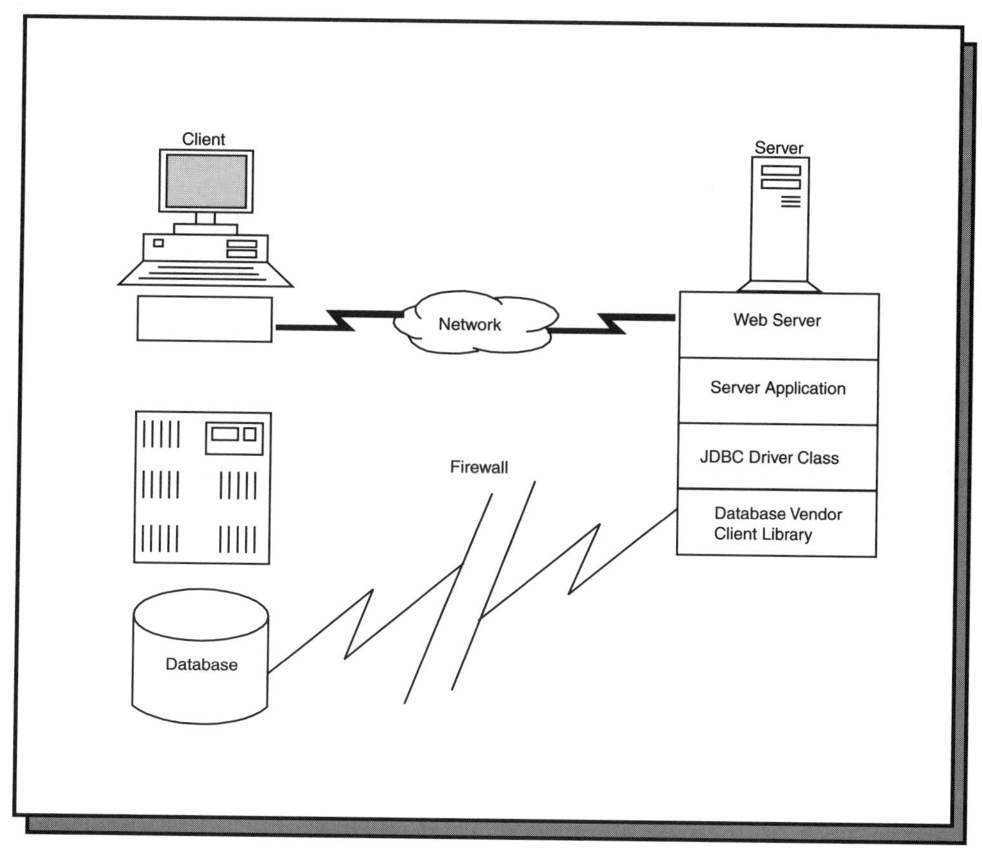

Figure 2.2 A three-tier JDBC architecture.

environment with few or no changes to your code. The JDBC design allows any Java programmer to access a relational database with little or no extra skill.

Summary

JDBC is a standard mechanism and API for Java programs to access relational databases and other data sources. JDBC programs can send queries and updates to a data source as well as ask the data source about information regarding the data source itself or the data it contains. In order to make using JDBC simple and efficient, access to specific databases is managed by drivers that implement a common set of Java interfaces. This allows the database connectivity provider, or driver programmer, to use whatever mechanisms needed to create a high-performance database connection while making it easy for programmers to change databases without changing a lot of code. Chapter 3, "Basic JDBC Programming," looks at the actual JDBC API and builds a simple database application.

Basic JDBC Programming

This chapter covers the basic use of JDBC. The goal of this chapter is to enable you to create database connections and access database values via JDBC. This chapter describes the steps to connect to a data source and query it using the JDBC API. The data source example used in this chapter is a Microsoft Access database called INV.mdb, found on the CD-ROM that accompanies this book. This is a small inventory database with four user tables. The Access database was chosen because it is common and can be accessed through the JDBC-ODBC driver. This means you don't need a special driver for the database, because Access comes with an ODBC driver.

NOTE **If you do not have Microsoft Access for the examples in this chapter, the CD-ROM included with this book includes a build script called Inv.script that can be used and modified to create this schema in most relational databases.**

About the Sample Database

The sample INV database used in the next few examples is a simple inventory database. The tables involved are described in Tables 3.1 through 3.4. Figure 3.1 shows the relationships among the tables. The examples in this chapter perform various queries

Table 3.1 Categories Schema

FIELD	TYPE	NOTES
CategoryID	AutoNumber (integer)	Primary key
CategoryName	Text	

on these tables, such as looking up all the vendors that sell beverages. The tables include the following :

Categories. A list of inventory types, such as Beverage, Produce, or Seafood.

Inventory. A list of inventory items such as Chef Anton's Gumbo Mix and associated information such as unit price.

Supplier. A list of vendors that sell the product in the inventory list.

ProductSuppliers. A list of inventory items provided by each supplier.

NOTE **For this chapter, it is important that you understand SQL and have access to a relational database. If you do not have Microsoft Access, make sure you modify the INV.script so that it creates the appropriate tables on your database. In any event, you will need to set up an ODBC data source called Inventory that refers to your database. Check the documentation that comes with your ODBC driver for information on how to create an ODBC data source. This relationship among the ODBC driver, JDBC, and the ODBC data source should become more clear as you examine the code used to make a database connection. For now, keep in mind that to run the examples, you need a database. If you can't use the one used here, you will need to alter the code provided on the CD-ROM to make it work with this database.**

Table 3.2 Inventory Schema

FIELD	TYPE	NOTES
ProductID	AutoNumber (integer)	Primary key
ProductName	Text	
ProductDescription	Text	
CategoryID	Number (integer)	Foreign key
Price	Currency	
ReorderLevel	Number (integer)	
Discontinued	Yes/No (Boolean)	
LeadTime	Text	
Quantity	Number	

Table 3.3 Supplier Schema

FIELD	TYPE	NOTES
SupplierID	Text	Primary key
SupplierName	Text	
ContactName	Text	
ContactTitle	Text	
Address	Text	
City	Text	
PostalCode	Text	
StateOrProvince	Text	
Country	Text	
PhoneNumber	Text	
FaxNumber	Text	
PaymentTerms	Text	
EmailAddress	Text	
Notes	Memo	

Table 3.4 ProductSupplier Schema

FIELD	TYPE	NOTES
SupplierID	Number (integer)	Primary key
ProductID	Number (integer)	Foreign key
Price	Currency	

JDBC Basics

The process for accessing a database using JDBC is fairly straightforward. This section describes the steps necessary to create a connection to a data source and then access it.

The first step in any enterprise project is to determine the environment in which the project will be deployed. For example, are you writing an applet, an application, servlets, or enterprise JavaBeans? If JDBC is part of the project, you will have a number of JDBC-specific issues to decide. The main configuration issues you need to determine will be:

Which database should you choose? You might need to consider database-specific issues, such as how to map custom data types to Java.

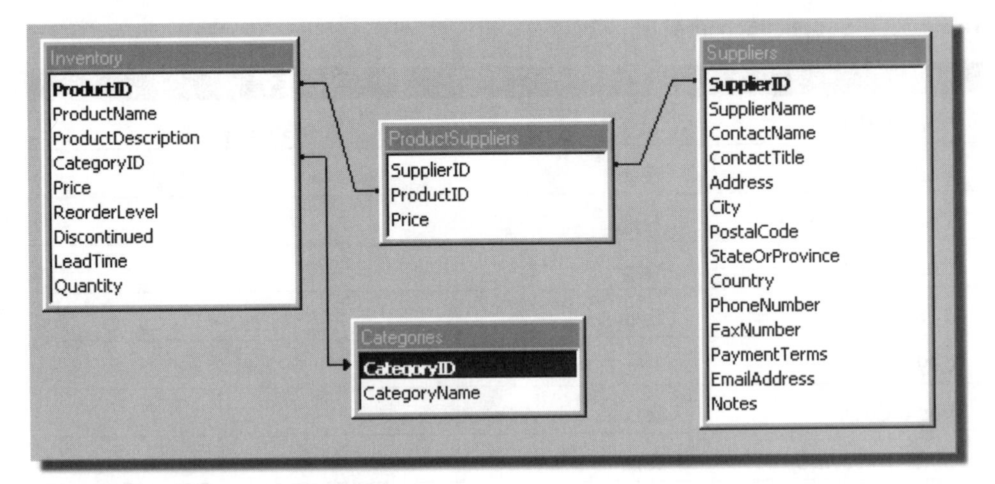

Figure 3.1 INV database schema.

Which driver should you choose? There may be more than one driver available for a given data source. Knowing the benefits of each driver will help you determine which is right for your application. For example, if you choose the ODBC driver, you have more flexibility as to which data source you connect to; however, if you choose a driver specifically designed for Oracle, it may be more efficient for accessing an Oracle database.

Where will the driver be located? Depending on where you locate the driver, you may have performance considerations. For example, if you load the driver from a remote server, you'll need to handle standard Java security issues.

Regardless of the configuration you choose, the steps for accessing and interacting with the data source are almost identical. First, load a JDBC driver. A JDBC driver should implement the java.sql.Driver interface. When a driver class is loaded, it should create an instance of itself and register it with the DriverManager. This means that a user can load and register a driver by calling Class.forName("package.DriverName"). Table A.3 in Appendix A contains a partial list of the drivers currently available. The list is maintained on the Sun Web site at www.javasoft.com/products/jdbc/jdbc.drivers.html.

NOTE **When loading a driver, you must consider certain security issues. For example, if you have an applet in a Web browser that loads a driver over the network, you need to make sure the applet is from a trusted source. For more information on this subject, check out java.sun.com/products/jdk/1.2/docs/guide/jdbc/spec/jdbc-spec.frame5.html.**

Next, create a connection to the data source. Create a URL that describes your data source and call the getConnection() method of the DriverManager. This method searches all the available drivers, looking for one that understands the URL passed in. Once the method finds one that can handle your data source, it returns a connection to that data source, as shown in Figure 3.2.

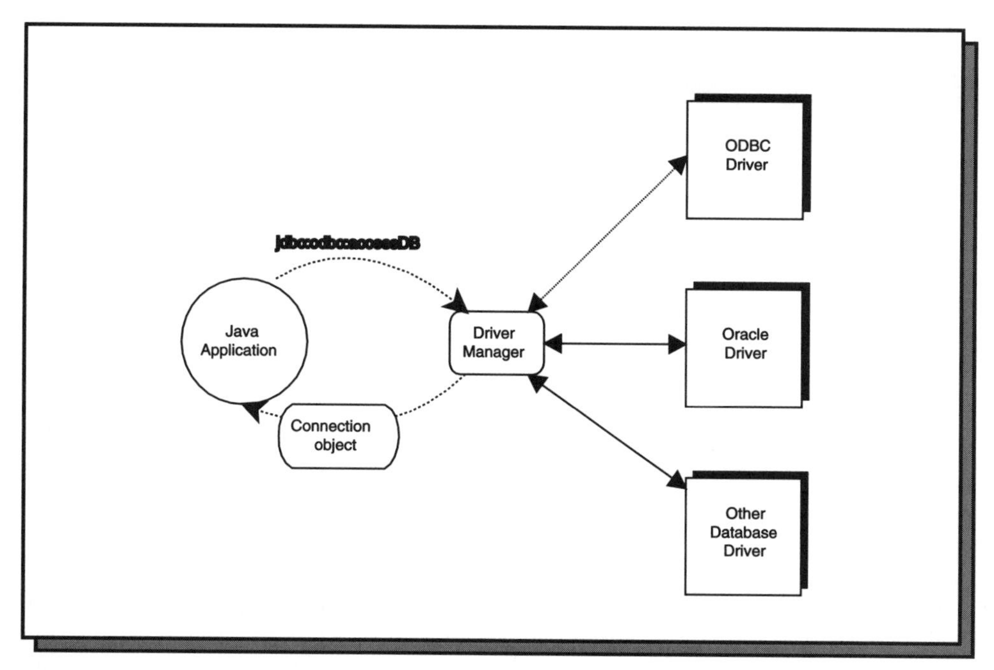

Figure 3.2 Selecting a driver.

If necessary, query the Connection for meta-data about the database structure. The meta-data is returned from the Connections' method getMetaData in an object implementing the interface DatabaseMetaData. This interface contains a large number of methods. The DatabaseMetaData methods are described in detail in Appendix A, "JDBC Information." The metadata is useful for figuring out unique features of a data source, such as a data source's ability to use the GROUP BY clause or whether the database supports transactions.

Once you have your connection, create a SQL statement from that connection. To create a statement, call the Connections method createStatement(). This returns an object implementing the Statement interface. Use this Statement object to execute the query that uses the statement. The Statement object can be used to execute a SQL query by calling one of the methods listed in Table 3.5.

NOTE **JDBC 2.0 adds the method int[] executeBatch(), which can be used to submit a batch of commands to the database for execution. This method returns an array of update counts for each statement executed.**

Once a statement is executed, check for any problems with the query by calling getWarnings(). This returns an instance of the SQLWarning class.

If no warnings occurred or if you can ignore the warnings, process the results from the query. Call getResults() to access ResultSet. Use this object to access all the return values.

Finally, close the database connection. Database connections are usually a limited resource for a database, so close the connection when you are finished.

Table 3.5 Execute Methods of the Statement Interface

METHOD	FUNCTION
`boolean execute(String sql)`	Execute a SQL statement that may return multiple result sets. This usually occurs when you call a stored procedure that returns non-rectangular data. The method returns true if the next result from this statement will be a result table.
`ResultSet executeQuery(String sql)`	Execute a SQL statement that returns a single result set. A result set is an interface that represents a set of data returned from a query.
`int executeUpdate(String sql)`	Execute a SQL INSERT, UPDATE, or DELETE statement. It returns a the number of affected rows.

This is the complete process for accessing a data source with JDBC. The next section looks at the source code for a simple example that demonstrates all of these steps. You can compile and run the version on your CD-ROM; the example is located in the Chapter 3 directory.

A Simple JDBC Example

This small example shows the steps to connect, query, and print the results of a database call. To keep the example simple, little error checking is done. A Microsoft Access database called INV.mdb is used as the data source; it is available on the CD-ROM. The URL for the data source in this example is jdbc:odbc:inventory.

NOTE **You must have the JDBC driver that you are using in your class path. For example, this example uses the sun.jdbc.odbc.JdbcOdbcDriver.**

Our query retrieves all columns from the Inventory table (SELECT * FROM Inventory), so we need to determine the number of columns by looking at the metadata of the result set. Bold lines indicate the typical code used for creating a connection, querying the database, and querying the result set metadata to determine how many rows were returned from the query. Figure 3.3 shows the results.

```
import java.sql.*;

public class Example
{
    public static void main (String args[])
    {
        try
```

```
{
/*
  Load the JDBC-ODBC bridge,
  it will register itself with DriverManager.
*/
  Class.forName("sun.jdbc.odbc.JdbcOdbcDriver");
} catch (Exception e)
{
    System.out.println("JDBC-ODBC driver failed to load.");
    return;
}

try
{
 /*
   Pass the url to the DriverManager.
   It should find our driver and return a database
   connection to an ODBC data source called "inventory."
 */

    Connection con =
      DriverManager.getConnection("jdbc:odbc:inventory","","");

  // Create a statement and use it to execute a query.
  Statement stmt = con.createStatement();
  /*
    This returns a result set.
    We will assume it is not null for simplicity.
  */
    ResultSet rs =
      stmt.executeQuery("SELECT * FROM inventory" +
                        "ORDER BY price");

  /*
    In order to determine the type and amount of data returned
    by our query, we access the metadata of the result set.
  */
    ResultSetMetaData rsmd = rs.getMetaData();

  /*
    From the metadata, we determine how many columns were
    actually returned.
  */
    int numberOfColumns = rsmd.getColumnCount();
    int rowCount = 1;

  /*
    We will loop through the result set, printing out
    values for each row.
  */
    while (rs.next())
```

```
                {
                    for (int i = 1; i <= numberOfColumns; i++)
                    {
                        System.out.print(rs.getString(i)+" ");
                    }
                    System.out.println("");
                    rowCount++;
                }

                // We are done with the statement, so we close it.
                stmt.close();

                // We are done with our connection, so we close it.
                con.close();
            } catch (Exception e)
            {
                System.out.println(e);
            }
        }
    }
```

You can experiment with the SELECT statement by specifying which columns of Inventory you want to retrieve. The next section looks at the specifics of connecting to any data source.

Connecting to a Data Source

The last section provided a simple example of a complete JDBC application. This section provides a detailed look at the process for choosing a driver and connecting to a data source.

Any item with a JDBC driver, such as a database management system (DBMS), a file system, or a text file, can be a data source. To connect to a data source, first identify the

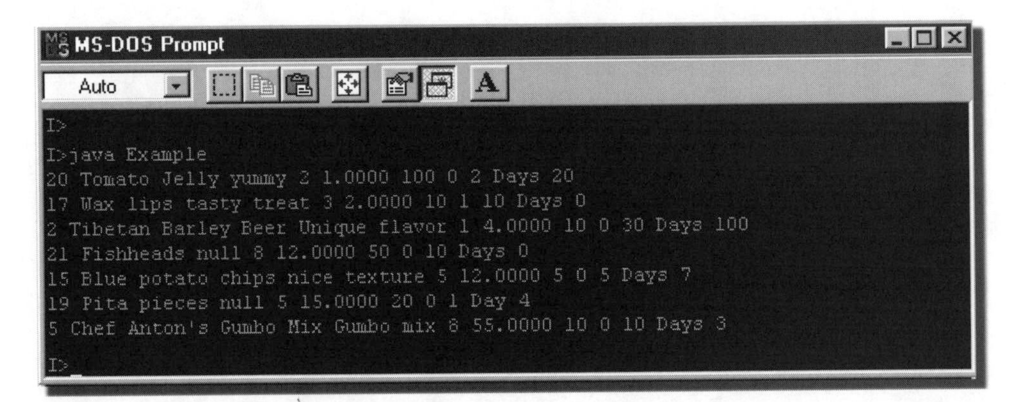

Figure 3.3 Example results.

data source you intend to connect to. For example, is it Oracle? Sybase? Is it another relational database or some other type of data source such as a file system? Next, obtain a JDBC driver for your data source. Typically, the data source vendor will provide the driver; however, you can get a complete list of the registered vendors from the Sun Web site.

Determine if the data source will be local to the application or remotely accessed. If the driver will be remotely accessed, make sure you consider the standard Java security issues involved in loading Java classes over the network, such as loading classes in an applet. There are no unusual security issues for local access. Just make sure the driver is in your CLASSPATH.

NOTE **JDBC tracks the class loader that provides each driver. When the DriverManager class opens a connection, it uses only drivers from the local file system or from the same class loader as the code requesting the connection.**

Load the appropriate driver in your code. One way to load drivers is to put the name of the driver in the jdbc.drivers System property. This will be checked when the DriverManager class is initialized. If you want to load several drivers, define a list of drivers, separated by colons. Your property entry might look something like this:

```
jdbc.drivers= sun.jdbc.odbc.JdbcOdbcDriver:another.typeof.driver
```

Another option is to use the Class.forName() method to load the class explicitly. When a driver is loaded, it is expected to call the DriverManager method registerDriver(). This registers the driver so it can be used later. If you want to know what drivers are available, call the DriverManager method getDrivers().

Once you have loaded the driver, call DriverManager.getConnection() to get a connection to your data source. There are several versions of the getConnection() method; they are listed in Table 3.6. All of these versions take a URL parameter. The URL is a JDBC protocol that specifies the data source to load. The URL takes the form

```
jdbc:sub-protocol:datasource-name;optional-parameter=value
```

Table 3.7 lists the meaning of each URL component.

Each of the getConnection() methods returns a Connection object representing a physical connection to the specified URL.

NOTE **A driver developer can reserve a name to be used as the subprotocol in a JDBC URL. JavaSoft acts as an informal registry for JDBC subprotocol names. To register a subprotocol name, JavaSoft recommends you send e-mail to jdbc@wombat.eng.sun.com.**

Use the Connection returned by DataManager to access the data source. A Connection object represents a session with a data source. Any number of SQL statements can be executed over this Connection, as shown in Figure 3.4. An application can have one or more connections to a single data source, or it can have connections to several databases.

Table 3.6 The getConnection Methods

METHOD	USE
`public static Connection getConnection(String url, Properties info) throws SQLException`	■ url is of the form jdbc:subprotocol:datasourcename ■ info is a list of keys/values that are useful for the driver; the property list contains at least a username and password field
`public static Connection getConnection(String url, String user, String password) throws SQLException`	■ url is of the form jdbc:subprotocol:datasourcename ■ user is the name of the database user making this connection password is the database password used to connect with this user name
`public static Connection getConnection(String url) throws SQLException`	■ url is of the form jdbc:subprotocol:datasourcename

Table 3.7 JDBC Protocol Structure

PROTOCOL COMPONENT	MEANING
`jdbc`	Specifies that we are using a JDBC protocol.
`Sub-protocol`	Indicates the type of data source. For example, the URL could be jdbc:oracle:myDatabase or jdbc:odbc:myDatabase. When DriverManager is looking for a registered driver to connect to your data source, it passes this URL. The driver can then determine if it can handle this data source.
`Datasource-name`	The name your driver or your DBMS uses to identify the data source. For example, with ODBC, the data source name is the name registered with ODBC and could differ from the name of the actual database it maps to; with Sybase, the data source name could be the name of the configuration data used to connect to the database over the network.
`Optional-parameter`	Can be used to pass extra information that is specific to the driver. The protocol can take zero or more optional parameters in the format of key/value pairs. For example, a URL might look like this: jdbc:odbc:Inventory;user=admin;password=xyz

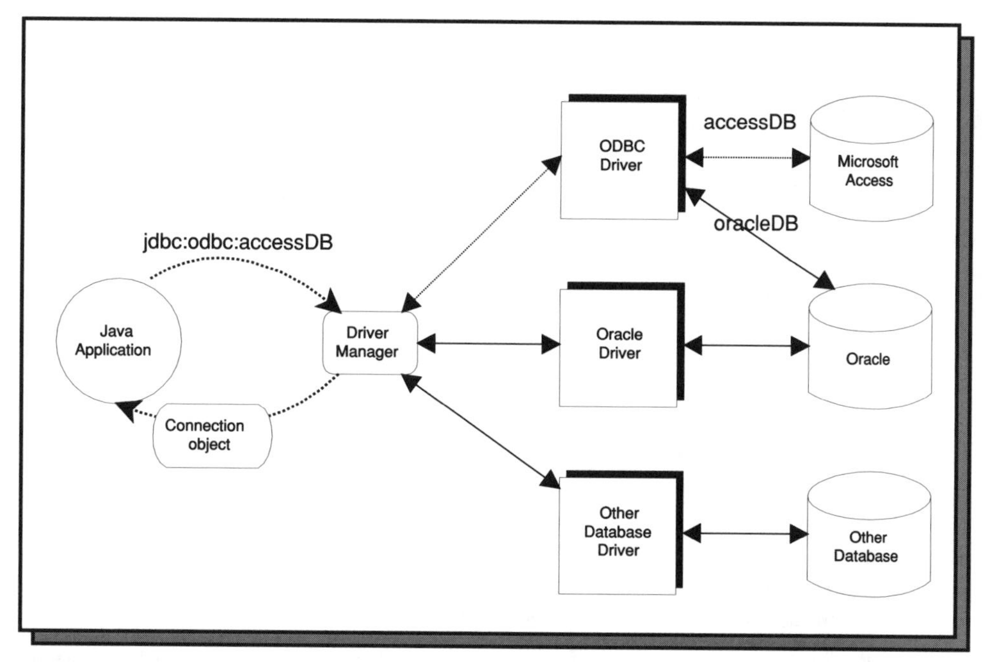

Figure 3.4 Connecting to a data source.

You now have a connection object that can be used to access the database, assuming that you specified the URL correctly and that you have an appropriate driver. There are four types (levels) of drivers today; they are discussed in the following section.

Driver Types

JavaSoft has segmented JDBC drivers into four categories. These categories, referred to as levels, range from platform-specific bridges (level 1) to pure Java database connections (level 4). The four levels are:

- JDBC-ODBC bridge plus ODBC driver
- Native-API partly Java driver
- JDBC-Net pure Java driver
- Native-protocol pure Java driver

JavaSoft believes that over time, most drivers will be level 3 or 4. This means that most drivers should be pure Java and run on most platforms. Let's explore each of the levels in more detail:

1. **JDBC-ODBC bridge plus ODBC driver.** The JavaSoft bridge product provides JDBC access via ODBC drivers. This is a simple JDBC driver that supports the ODBC capabilities and doesn't necessarily support all of the capabilities of a particular data source. It is common that ODBC binary code, and in many cases database client code, must be loaded on each client machine that uses this driver.

If you use this type of driver, you typically are not concerned with installing extra software on your client machines. This type of driver is also useful in a server application that is part of a three-tier architecture. In this case, the ODBC driver software and possibly the database client code are installed on the server. Clients connect to the application running on the middle tier. The application uses the JDBC-ODBC bridge to communicate with ODBC, which in turn communicates with the database running on the third tier. Performance is the main issue in this case. The middle-tier server is hit with client requests that must be transported through the bridge. A pure Java solution should be more efficient.

2. **Native-API partly-Java driver.** Most vendors provide platform-specific libraries for communicating with their databases. These libraries are usually platform-specific compiled libraries that are typically implemented in C or a similar language. These libraries can take advantage of database-specific features. However, they must be installed on client machines. The JDBC driver at this level is written in Java, but it makes calls out to the database client library. Although this solution is not completely portable, at least the JDBC driver can take advantage of all the features provided by the database client library. This level of driver is useful in the same scenarios as level 1 drivers, except that this level can access more database-specific features.
3. **JDBC-Net pure Java driver.** Middleware products that allow you to remotely access enterprise resources, such as databases, are emerging. Components of one new class of middleware are referred to as *application servers*. These products often have their own network protocol. By sending specific instructions to the application server, it can map these database-independent calls to database-specific requests. These products enable you to centralize issues like security, load balancing, and so on, outside your application. The JDBC drivers for these products map JDBC calls to the middleware-specific calls. A demonstration copy of BEA WebLogic Application Server is included on this book's companion CD-ROM. Examples later in this book will show you how to use the application server to access enterprise resources.
4. **Native-protocol pure Java driver.** Database vendors are starting to support network protocols that allow you to directly communicate with the database over the network. The JDBC drivers can be completely implemented in Java and do not need to rely on a specific client library. Rather, they send commands directly over the network to the database. This is a flexible model, but each vendor has its own protocol. To access multiple databases using this technique, you may need multiple drivers, because each vendor may have its own unique driver for leveraging vendor-specific features such as transaction management.

Connection Example

Once you have chosen a JDBC driver, you need to establish a connection to your database. The following example shows the typical process for connecting to a data source using JDBC. The first bolded line loads the JDBC-ODBC bridge. When the driver loads, it registers itself with DriverManager in order to be located when a driver-manageable request to connect to a data source is issued.

After loading the driver class, pass the URL to DriverManager in the getConnection method. DriverManager should find the driver and return a database connection to an ODBC data source called Inventory.

When the connection is no longer needed, close it. Even though the connection would be collected as garbage, it is important to free connections as soon as possible. Because most databases allow a limited number of connections, the connections are a valuable resource.

```
import java.sql.*;

public class ConnectionExample
{
    public static void main (String args[])
    {
        try
        {
            /*
              Load the class for the driver.
              Make sure the driver is in your CLASSPATH.
            */
            Class.forName("sun.jdbc.odbc.JdbcOdbcDriver");
        } catch (Exception e)
        {
            System.out.println("JDBC-ODBC driver failed to load.");
            return;
        }

        try
        {
            /*
               Specify the data source you want to connect to by
               passing in the URL. If a driver is found that can
               connect to this data source, you will get a
               Connection object.
            */
            Connection con =
                DriverManager.getConnection("jdbc:odbc:Inventory",
                                            "","");
            // When you are done, close the connection.
            con.close();
        } catch (Exception e)
        {
            System.out.println(e);
        }
    }
}
```

Connecting with Properties

In the previous example, the driver and data source were "hard-coded" in the code. Although this is a reasonable technique, it misses one of the dynamic features of JDBC. JDBC allows you to determine what data source and driver to use at run time. This could be important for load balancing or for easy configuration and installation of your application in various environments. In order to select a driver and data source dynamically, use a property list loaded from a text file.

Follow these steps to load the text file:

1. Open the text file using an InputStream object.
2. Create a java.util.Properties object.
3. Use the Properties object load() method to enter the values from the InputStream into the Properties object.

NOTE The name of the property file is arbitrary, as are the keys and values stored. These are all programmer defined.

In this example, a connection is made to the Inventory data source; however, the driver name and the data source information are stored in a text file called data-source.config instead of hard coding the information in the class file. The text file has the following values:

```
datasource.driver=sun.jdbc.odbc.JdbcOdbcDriver
datasource.protocol=jdbc
datasource.subprotocol=odbc
datasource.name=Inventory
datasource.username=
datasource.password=
```

The example also uses the ClassLoader method getSystemResourceAsStream to return an InputStream to our datasource.config file. This method searches the entire ClassPath for our file. In most of our examples, we assume "." is in your ClassPath. If it isn't, place the datasource.config file in a CLASSPATH directory.

```
import java.util.Properties;
import java.io.InputStream;
import java.sql.*;

public class PropertyExample
{
    public static void main (String args[])
    {
        String dsDriver="";
        String dsProtocol="";
        String dsSubprotocol="";
        String dsName="";
        String dsUsername="";
```

```
String dsPassword="";

try
{
    // Loads the configuration file
    InputStream is = ClassLoader.getSystemResourceAsStream
        ("datasource.config");
    if(is != null)
    {
        Properties p = new Properties();
        p.load (is);
        dsDriver = p.getProperty("datasource.driver");
        dsProtocol = p.getProperty("datasource.protocol");
        dsSubprotocol =
            p.getProperty("datasource.subprotocol");
        dsName = p.getProperty("datasource.name");
        dsUsername = p.getProperty("datasource.username");
        dsPassword = p.getProperty("datasource.password");
    }
} catch (Exception e)
{
    System.out.println("Unable to read property file");
    return;
}

try
{
    Class.forName(dsDriver);
}
catch (Exception e)
{
    System.out.println("Failed to load  driver.");
    return;
}

try
{
    String theURL = dsProtocol+":"+dsSubprotocol+":"+dsName;
    /*
       Create a connection using the values parsed from
       the configuration file.
    */
     Connection con = DriverManager.getConnection
        (theURL,dsUsername,dsPassword);
    if(con != null)
    {
        System.out.println("Successfully connected to " +
                               dsName);
        con.close();
    }
}
```

```
            catch (Exception e)
            {
                System.out.println("Failed to connect: " + e);
                return;
            }
        }
    }
```

Now either open a connection by hard coding the URL components or load them from a configuration file. If you load the values from the property file, you need to realize that these values may be changed, even though the class file does not. This means you should take more precautions in preparing your query by checking the metadata of the connection to verify that the database is appropriate for your query. For example, suppose the name of the database is changed in the property file and you try to query it. If the tables you expect to have in the database aren't there, your application will fail. Rather than waiting for the application to fail, you could examine the data source first to see what tables are available. We follow this procedure in the next section.

Examining a Data Source

Once a connection has been established with a data source, processing of SQL can begin. However, it is often useful to query the data source for information about its structure, capabilities, and limitations. This will enable you to optimize your query and prevent access errors such as trying to retrieve data that doesn't exist. Before examining the code for this process, let's view the metadata using a tool called JDBCTest.

JDBCTest is a Java application written by Intersolv that loads and interacts with any JDBC driver. It is a useful tool for looking at your data source and testing your JDBC driver's capabilities before you actually use it. After examining the data source with JDBCTest, this section walks through an example program that demonstrates how you might do this in your own code.

JDBCTest

If you do not have JDBCTest installed, you may download and install it from http://java.sun.com/products/jdbc. When JDBCTest starts, the screen in Figure 3.5 appears.

Press the Press Here To Continue button to load the main JDBCTest window. This window, shown in Figure 3.6, has a menu bar that allows you to connect to a data source, explore its metadata, and even execute SQL commands. The main window has four parts: a menu bar, a list of data source connections, result output from the driver, and a box that displays the Java code executed to perform your requests. This last box is valuable in learning JDBC because you can execute a command and then cut and paste the code into your own application. It is a quick technique for learning the library.

Follow these steps to try out JDBCTest:

Figure 3.5 Startup screen for JDBCTest.

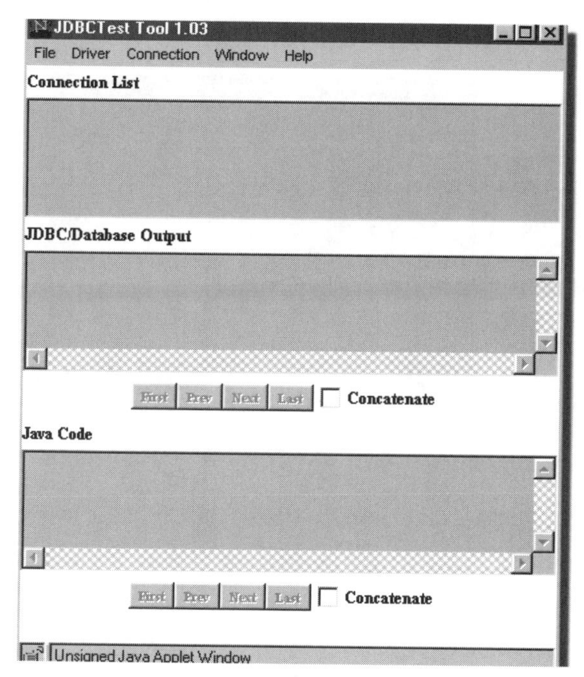

Figure 3.6 JDBCTest main screen.

1. From the Driver menu, select Register Driver. A panel with a text field appears.
2. Type sun.jdbc.odbc.JdbcOdbcDriver and press Return. This registers the JDBC-ODBC bridge driver. The Java code generated is displayed in the Java code text box.
3. Now that you have registered the driver, select Connect to DB from the Connection menu. A panel displays fields for you to type the URL for the data source as well as the login name and password. In the Database field, type: jdbc:odbc:Inventory
   Use the default name and password, so leave those fields blank.
4. Click the Connect button. Assuming you have a registered ODBC data source called Inventory, you now have a connection. If the connection was established successfully, the JDBCTest main screen indicates there were no problems, and the Connection panel for your new connection is displayed. This panel, shown in Figure 3.7, allows you to interact with your data source. It displays feedback from the connection and the Java source code for the executed commands.
5. Now issue a SQL statement on our data source. In the Connection panel, select Create Statement from the Connection menu. Before executing SQL commands, a Statement object to hold your SQL must be created. Observe the Java code generated in the Connection window by executing this command.
6. After creating a statement, fill it with SQL. To do this, select Execute Stmt Query from the Statement menu in the Connection panel. The Execute Query Panel displays. In this panel, type the following query: SELECT * FROM INVENTORY.

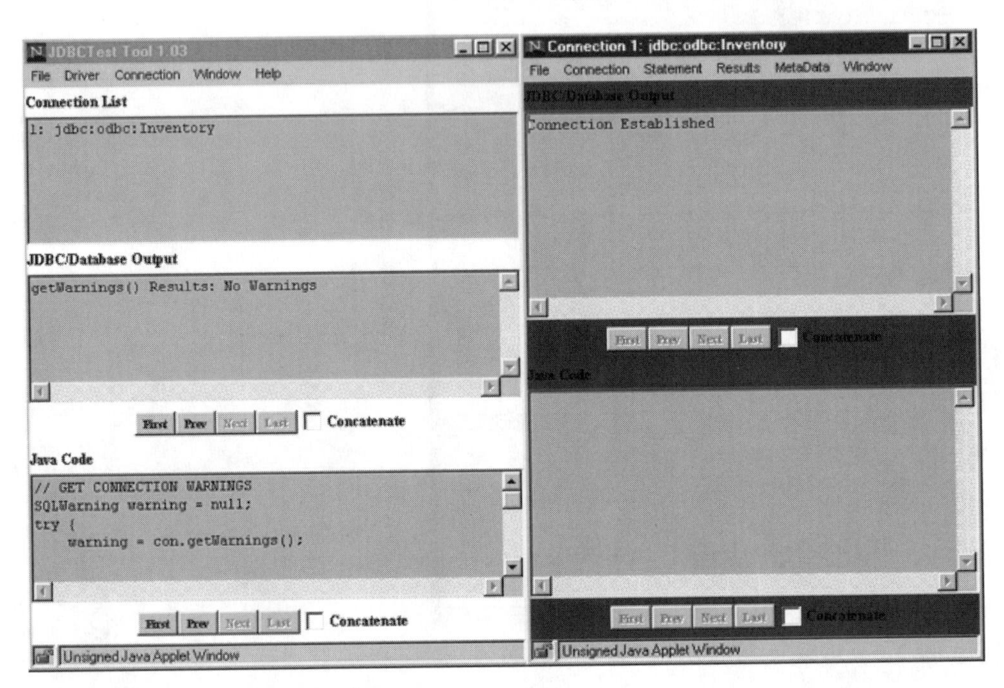

Figure 3.7 JDBCTest connection screen.

Then click the Submit button. In the Connection panel you should see that the statement returned a result set that contains a list of return values.

7. From the Results menu, select Show All Results. Figure 3.8 shows how the Connection panel will look after you do so.
8. Now that you have looked at values in the database, finish by looking at the attributes of the database itself. To do this, select Get DB Meta Data from the Connection menu of the Connection panel. This creates a result set containing information about the database.
9. To view the metadata, select Show Meta Data from the MetaData menu in the Connection panel. In the top text box are all of the attributes of the database that are available through the JDBC driver. In the bottom text box is the Java code used to print these values. These windows are shown in Figure 3.9. Scroll down the list of values to get a feel for the types of information available to you. If you have any questions about the meaning of a value, refer to Appendix A, which lists the DBMetaData methods and their meanings.

As you can see, JDBCTest offers a great deal of information about the data source that you can use to optimize and configure queries. Using this information inside your application allows you to dynamically configure data access routines. For example, knowing if the data source supports the GROUP BY clause can help you configure how to structure your queries. Let's take a look at an example for accessing and processing database metadata in your application.

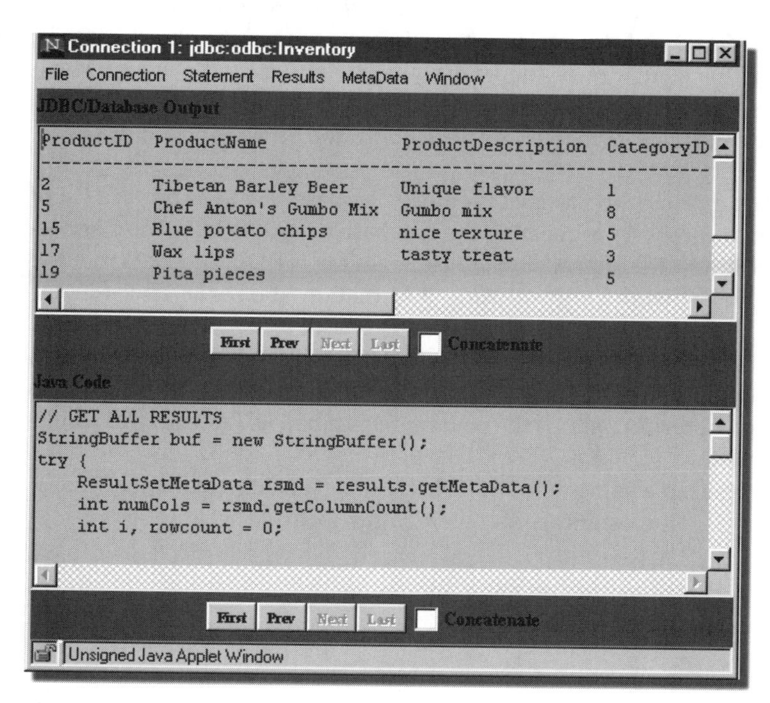

Figure 3.8 JDBCTest displaying results.

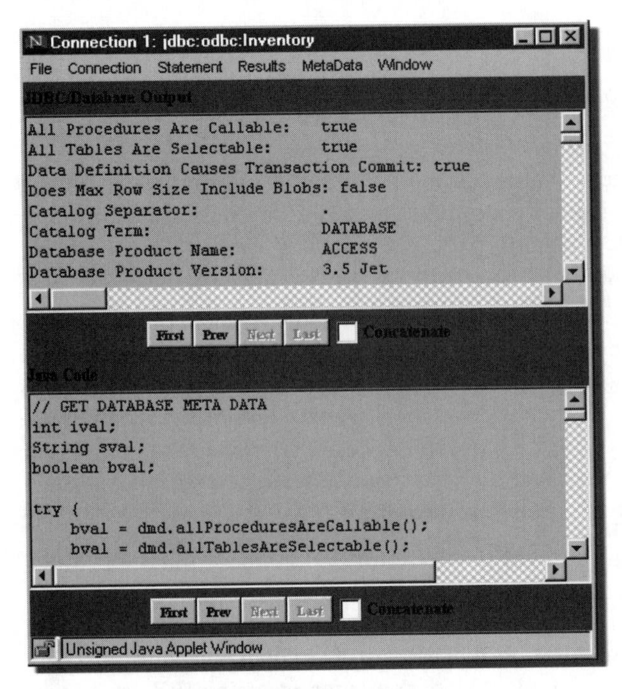

Figure 3.9 JDBCTest displaying metadata.

The Connection object provides you with this information through an object implementing the DatabaseMetaData interface. Once you have a Connection object, query it for information about the structure of the underlying database by calling getMetaData(). This method returns an object implementing the DatabaseMetaData interface. (Appendix A lists the information you can retrieve about the database from the DatabaseMetaData object.)

This example creates a connection to the Inventory database and then prints a list of all the tables and their columns by requesting the database metadata from the Connection object, then requesting a list of available tables by calling the DBMetaData method getTables(). This returns a result set containing information about the tables in the database.

The method getTables takes the parameters listed in Table 3.8. This method returns a result set that consists of values returned from the database query. This result set is described later in this chapter. It contains the columns described in Table 3.9. All results in this result set are strings.

In the next example, the table names and the table types for all tables (columns 3 and 4) are printed to the console. The results are shown in Figure 3.10.

```
import java.sql.*;

public class MetaDataExample
{
    public static void main (String args[])
```

Table 3.8 The getTables() Parameters

PARAMETER	USE
String catalog	"" retrieves those without a catalog; null means drop catalog name from the selection criteria
String schemaPattern	A schema name pattern; "" retrieves those without a schema
String tableNamePattern	A table name pattern
String[] types	A list of table types to include; null returns all types

Table 3.9 The getTables() Result Set Values

COLUMN NAME	VALUE
1. TABLE_CAT	Table catalog (may be null)
2. TABLE_SCHEM	Table schema (may be null)
3. TABLE_NAME	Table name
4. TABLE_TYPE String	Table type such as TABLE, VIEW, ALIAS
5. REMARKS	Comments about the table

```
{
    try
    {
        Class.forName("sun.jdbc.odbc.JdbcOdbcDriver");
    } catch (Exception e)
    {
        System.out.println("JDBC-ODBC driver failed to load.");
        return;
    }

    try
    {
        Connection con = DriverManager.getConnection
                        ("jdbc:odbc:Inventory","","");

        /*
           Once you have a Connection object, use it to get the
           DatabaseMetaData of the Connection (the datasource).
           Use the getTables method to get a list of all tables
           accessible from the datasource.
        */
        DatabaseMetaData dmd = con.getMetaData();

        ResultSet rs = dmd.getTables(null,null,null,null);
```

```
            System.out.println("Table Name\tTable Type");

            while (rs.next())
            {
                /*
                   Print the results by iterating through
                   the result set and printing out the default string
                */
                System.out.println(rs.getString(3) +
                                    "\t" + rs.getString(4));
            }

            con.close();
        } catch (Exception e)
        {
            System.out.println(e);
        }
    }
}
```

Using this technique, you can read all the attributes of the data source. Use this information to determine the capabilities of the data source before you access it. Now that you have this information, you are ready to access the database.

Accessing the Database

The connection with the database is used to send commands and SQL statements to the database. The connection acts as direct link to the database driver. You request a SQL statement object from the connection and put your SQL in this object. Think of the

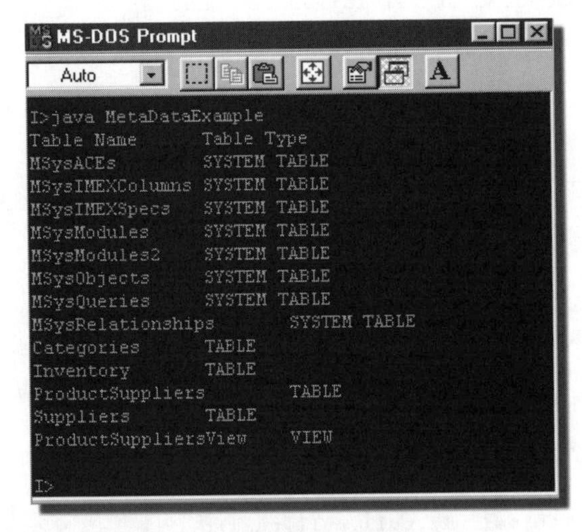

Figure 3.10 Displaying metadata.

Statement object as an envelope into which you put your message. The Connection object is the transport that sends your message. When you pass SQL to the connection, it forwards this information to the driver. The driver forwards the SQL to the database and then returns results. The results come back to you in the form of a result set.

The Connection object has three methods that return objects representing a database call. These methods are as follows:

createStatement(). Returns an object that implements the Statement interface. Use this for executing single SQL calls on the database.

prepareStatement(). Returns a PreparedStatement object that extends the Statement interface. Use this for sending SQL that contains parameterized values (referred to as IN parameters). This type of statement may be more efficient if you plan to call a specific SQL statement multiple times, because it may be precompiled.

prepareCall(). Returns a CallableStatement object that extends the PreparedStatement to handle OUT parameters. Use this to execute stored procedures that have both IN parameters and OUT result values.

A Statement object has three methods for sending SQL to the database and executing database calls:

executeQuery(). Queries the database for a single table of result values. Usually used for simple SELECT statements.

executeUpdate(). Updates values in the database. Usually used for INSERT, UPDATE, DELETE, or data definition commands such as CREATE. This method returns a count of rows affected by the command.

execute(). Queries the database for potentially multiple tables of result values. Use this for calling a stored procedure that returns multiple results. Under some (uncommon) situations, a single SQL statement may return multiple result sets and/or update counts. Normally, you can ignore this method, unless you're executing a stored procedure that may return multiple results or you're dynamically executing an unknown SQL string. If you use this method, call the Statement method getMoreResults() to access subsequent result sets.

NOTE **JDBC 2.0 adds a fourth method: executeBatch(). This method allows you to submit a batch of commands to the database for execution. executeBatch() returns an array of update counts for each command in the batch. The counts are ordered based on the order in which the commands were inserted into the batch.**

In the following example, a new table is created in the database. This example can be run only once because it does not check for the existence of the table before executing the CREATE statement. This means that on subsequent calls, a JDBC exception is thrown that tells us the table exists. The database build script in Chapter 25, "A Four-Tier Online Store," shows how you can handle this exception, allowing the database to be recreated if necessary.

This example creates a new table in our database called SalesHistory. To create the table, first create a statement, then use it to create a new table. The data types NUMBER, CURRENCY, and DATE in the CREATE statement are database dependent. If the table already exists, an exception is thrown so that the success message prints only when we actually add the table. Close the statement when done. Although closing the statement in this case is unnecessary because the program is about to end anyway, in some cases you want to immediately release a statement's resources instead of waiting for this to happen when it is collected as garbage.

```
import java.sql.*;

public class ExecuteExample
{
    public static void main (String args[])
    {
        try
        {
            Class.forName("sun.jdbc.odbc.JdbcOdbcDriver");
        } catch (Exception e)
        {
            System.out.println("JDBC-ODBC driver failed to load.");
            return;
        }

        try
        {
            Connection con =
             DriverManager.getConnection("jdbc:odbc:Inventory","","");

            // Use a connection to create a new statement.
            Statement stmt = con.createStatement();

            // Use this statement to execute a specific SQL statement.
            stmt.execute("CREATE TABLE SalesHistory" +
                         "(ProductID NUMBER," +
                         " Price CURRENCY, " +
                         "TrnsDate DATE)");

            System.out.println("Created Sales History table");

            /*
               As you do for connections, you should close the
               statement when you are done.
            */
            stmt.close();

            con.close();
        } catch (Exception e)
        {
            System.out.println(e);
```

```
            }
        }
    }
```

The Statement object allows you to fetch and modify data. The next section looks at how you can process the results returned from executing a SQL statement.

Fetching Data

Selecting data from a single table is done by using the Statement method executeQuery(). The steps for fetching data are as follows:

1. Create a statement from a connection.
2. Execute the query.
3. Fetch a result set from the Statement object.

For example, the following call returns a list of all inventory items:

```
...
Connection con = DriverManager.getConnection("jdbc:odbc:Inventory",
                                             "","");
Statement stmt = con.createStatement();
ResultSet rs = stmt.executeQuery("SELECT * FROM Inventory");
...
```

A database query returns a result set. If no values are returned, ResultSet will not contain values.

Working with a Result Set

Once you have fetched a result set from a database call, you will want to process it. ResultSet is organized into logical rows and columns of data. It maintains a cursor to the current row. You can instruct ResultSet to move to the next row by calling next().

NOTE **JDBC 2.0 contains methods for traversing to the next, previous, first, and last row of ResultSet. It has methods for deleting current row, jumping to the insert row, and so on. In general, ResultSet is much more feature rich. However, with some work, most of these features can be duplicated in JDBC 1.0.**

The columns of ResultSet can be accessed in any order and as often as needed. Columns can be accessed by their positions in the column list or by name. For instance, if you had the following SQL:

```
SELECT name, address, city FROM Customers
```

you could access the address attribute by name, address, or by index, 2. To get values from ResultSet, use the getXXX methods included in the ResultSet object. Table 3.10 lists these methods.

Table 3.10 ResultSet getXXX Methods

INDEX GETXXX METHOD	NAME GETXXX METHOD	USE
InputStream getAsciiStream(int columnIndex)	InputStream getAsciiStream(String columnName)	Get a column value as a stream of ASCII characters.
BigDecimal getBigDecimal(int columnIndex, int scale)	BigDecimal getBigDecimal(String columnName, int scale)	Get the value of a column as a java.lang.BigDecimal object.
InputStream getBinaryStream(int columnIndex)	InputStream getBinaryStream(String columnName)	Get a column value as a stream of bytes.
Boolean getBoolean(int columnIndex)	boolean getBoolean(String columnName)	Get the value of a column as a Boolean integer.
byte getByte(int columnIndex)	byte getByte(String columnName)	Get the value of a column as a byte.
byte[] getBytes(int columnIndex)	byte[] getBytes(String columnName)	Get the value of a column as an array of bytes.
Date getDate(int columnIndex)	Date getDate(String columnName)	Get the value of a column as a java.sql.Date object. Date is a thin wrapper around java.util.Date.
double getDouble(int columnIndex)	double getDouble(String columnName)	Get the value of a column as a double.
Float getFloat(int columnIndex)	float getFloat(String columnName)	Get the value of a column as a float.
int getInt(int columnIndex)	int getInt(String columnName)	Get the value of a column as an int.
Object getObject(int columnIndex)	Object getObject(String columnName)	Get the value of a column as an Object. The mapping is based on the JDBC spec and is listed in Appendix A.
short getShort(int columnIndex)	short getShort(String columnName)	Get the value of a column as a short.
String getString(int columnIndex)	String getString(String columnName)	Get the value of a column as a String.

Table 3.10 *Continued*

INDEX GETXXX METHOD	NAME GETXXX METHOD	USE
Time getTime(int columnIndex)	Time getTime(String columnName)	Get the value of a column as a java.sql.Time object. Time is a wrapper around java.util.Date that adds formatting and parsing operations to support the JDBC escape syntax for time values.
Timestamp getTimestamp(int columnIndex)	Timestamp getTimestamp(String columnName)	Get the value of a column as a java.sql.Timestamp object. Timestamp is a wrapper around java.util.Date that adds the ability to hold the SQL TIMESTAMP nanos value and provides formatting andparsing operations to support the JDBC escape syntax for timestamp values.

NOTE **If two columns have the same name, the first one matching your column name will be returned. For this reason, it is recommended that you use the position or index to reference the column. This way, programmers can guarantee they are returning the correct column.**

The next example fetches a list of all suppliers and the beverage products they sell from the ProductSuppliersView view in the INV database. Once the list is loaded, the program prints these values. To get data from the database, this example uses the executeQuery method, which returns a ResultSet. Because the names of the returned data are known, the actual column names are used to retrieve the values. Initially, the ResultSet cursor is positioned before the first row of results. Each time rs.next() is called, the ResultSet places its cursor on the next row and returns true until it reaches the end of the results. Then it returns false. Figure 3.11 illustrates what your results will look like.

This example fetches all BEVERAGE products and their associated suppliers as well as the prices charged for the product, then prints this list, sorted by product. The ResultSet rs is returned with its cursor set before the first record. This is convenient for starting a while loop with rs.next().The first time through, the cursor is on the first record. Inside the loop, the values for the associated row columns are referenced by name. Use the getInt() method for the price. We didn't mind losing some data for our simple display purposes. You could have used getFloat() or getDouble() and then formatted the output.

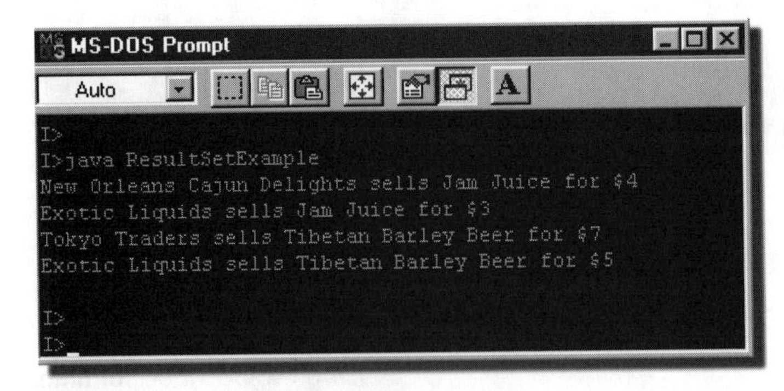

Figure 3.11 ResultSetExample output.

```
import java.sql.*;

public class ResultSetExample
{
    public static void main (String args[])
    {
        try
        {
            Class.forName("sun.jdbc.odbc.JdbcOdbcDriver");
        } catch (Exception e)
        {
            System.out.println("JDBC-ODBC driver failed to load.");
            return;
        }

        try
        {
            Connection con =
              DriverManager.getConnection(
                                            "jdbc:odbc:Inventory",
                                            "","");

            Statement stmt = con.createStatement();

            // Execute a query and retrieve ResultSet.
            ResultSet rs = stmt.executeQuery("SELECT SupplierName," +
                                " ProductName, Price " +
                                "FROM ProductSuppliersView " +
                                "WHERE CategoryName " +
                                "LIKE '%BEVERAGES%' " +
                                "ORDER BY ProductName");

            /*
               Now iterate through ResultSet and print the values
               of each attribute in the row. ResultSet maintains a
               cursor pointing to its current row of data. Initially,
```

```
                the cursor is positioned before the first row. The
                next method moves the cursor to the next row.
              */
              while(rs.next())
              {
                  String supplier = rs.getString("SupplierName");
                  String product = rs.getString("ProductName");
                  //ResultSet has methods to map values to Java types.
                   int price = rs.getInt("Price");

                  System.out.println(supplier + " sells " + product +
                                        " for $" + price);
              }

              stmt.close();
              con.close();
          } catch (Exception e)
          {
              System.out.println(e);
          }
      }
  }
```

The results of a query are returned in a result set. ResultSet stores the results in rows and maintains a pointer to the current row. Each value within a row can be accessed by its name or by its position. For example, instead of the line:

```
int price = rs.getInt("Price");
```

the following could have been used:

```
int price = rs.getInt(3);
```

This works only because we know that Price is the third column in the preceding query. You could also find this out by looking at the metadata of ResultSet. The next section explores the ResultSetMetaData class.

Working with ResultSetMetaData

In the previous example, the query was hard coded, so using the column names was a reasonable choice for fetching the data. However, what happens when you don't know the column names before accessing ResultSet? Each ResultSet can return an object that implements the ResultSetMetaData interface. This object contains information about the returned results, including the number of columns returned and the names and types of the columns. This information can be used to dynamically display values. Table 3.11 lists the ResultSetMetaData values.

In this next example, the user is asked to type in SQL SELECT statements. The program will dynamically make requests against the database and display the results. The program will continue until the user types the word "exit." In this example, only SQL

Table 3.11 ResultSetMetaData Methods

TYPE AND METHOD	USE
String **getCatalogName**(int column)	Returns a column's table catalog name.
int **getColumnCount**()	Returns the number of columns in ResultSet.
int **getColumnDisplaySize**(int column)	Returns the column's preferred maximum width in characters.
String **getColumnLabel**(int column)	Returns the suggested column title for displaying the column.
String **getColumnName**(int column)	Returns a column's name.
int **getColumnType**(int column)	Returns a column's SQL type.
String **getColumnTypeName**(int column)	Returns a column's data source-specific type name.
int **getPrecision**(int column)	Returns a column's number of decimal digits.
int **getScale**(int column)	Returns a column's number of digits to right of the decimal point.
String **getSchemaName**(int column)	Returns the name of a column's table's schema.
String **getTableName**(int column)	Returns a column's table name.
boolean **isAutoIncrement**(int column)	Returns whether this field is automatically generated. If it is automatically generated, it should be considered a read-only set of values.
boolean **isCaseSensitive**(int column)	Returns true if the column's case matters to the data source.
boolean **isCurrency**(int column)	Returns whether the column is a monetary value.
boolean **isDefinitelyWritable**(int column)	Returns whether a write on the column definitely will succeed.
int **isNullable**(int column)	Returns true if you can put a NULL in this column.
boolean **isReadOnly**(int column)	Returns true if the column definitely is not writable.
boolean **isSearchable**(int column)	Returns true if the column can be used in a WHERE clause.
boolean **isSigned**(int column)	Returns true if the column represents a signed number.
boolean **isWritable**(int column)	Returns true if it is at least possible for a write on the column to succeed.

statements that begin with the word SELECT are executed. This example could easily be extended to handle any SQL calls.

The example uses a java.io.BufferedReader to read values from the console, then loops while the variable notDone is true. This variable is set to false when the user types "exit" at the prompt. Assuming the user types a valid SELECT statement, we call executeQuery() because we expect a result set back.

NOTE **The Statement method executeQuery() always returns a result set, even if there are no values returned. In that case, ResultSet would have no rows, but it would contain metadata related to the query.**

To find out what columns are returned, first access ResultSetMetaData, then use that to find the column count. Now iterate through the columns and print each column name. After that, iterate through each row of data, printing the values. As an added example of using metadata, check the data source column type and print a $ if the type of the column is CURRENCY, a Microsoft Access-specific data type. You could also have used the ResultSetMetaData method isCurrency(). This would have been more database independent. getColumnType was used for example purposes only, as shown in Figure 3.12. If the name of a column, but not its index, is known, the method findColumn() can be used to find the column number.

```
import java.sql.*;
import java.io.*;
public class ResultSetMetaDataExample
{
    public static void main (String args[])
    {
        try
        {
            Class.forName("sun.jdbc.odbc.JdbcOdbcDriver");
        } catch (Exception e)
        {
            System.out.println("JDBC-ODBC driver failed to load.");
            return;
        }

        try
        {
            Connection con =
              DriverManager.getConnection("jdbc:odbc:Inventory",
                                          "","");

            Statement stmt = con.createStatement();

            boolean notDone = true;
            String sqlStr = null;
            /* In this example we use a buffered reader to read in an
               SQL statement from the command line. This allows the
               user to type in any arbitrary SQL statement.
```

```
   Try SELECT * FROM INVENTORY
*/
 BufferedReader br = new BufferedReader(
    new InputStreamReader(System.in));

// We iterate until the user types "exit"
while(notDone)
{
    System.out.print("Enter SELECT Statement:");
    sqlStr = br.readLine();

    if(sqlStr.startsWith("SELECT") ||
        sqlStr.startsWith("select"))
    {
        // If this is a SELECT statment, then process
        ResultSet rs = stmt.executeQuery(sqlStr);
        ResultSetMetaData rsmd = rs.getMetaData();

        /* Since we don't know how many columns will come
           back from an abritrary query, we need to check
           the metadata of ResultSet.
        */
        int columnCount = rsmd.getColumnCount();

        // Print all the column names.
        for(int x =1;x<=columnCount;x++)
        {
            String columnName = rsmd.getColumnName(x);
            System.out.print(columnName +"\t");
        }
        System.out.println("");

        // Now print each row of data.
        while(rs.next())
        {
            for(int x =1;x<=columnCount;x++)
            {
                if(
                   /*
                      The metadata returns the data type
                      so we can adjust our display for
                      certain types such as currency.
                   */
                   rsmd.getColumnTypeName(x).
                     compareTo("CURRENCY") == 0
                  )
                System.out.print("$");
                String resultStr = rs.getString(x);
                System.out.print(resultStr +"\t");
            }
```

```
                        System.out.println("");
                    }
                }
                else if(sqlStr.startsWith("exit"))
                    notDone = false;
            }
            stmt.close();
            con.close();
        } catch (Exception e)
        {
            System.out.println(e);
        }
    }
}
```

As this example shows, there is more to fetching data than just retrieving values. You may also need to query the results themselves for metadata. Use this information to determine the validity of your data and its format.

The next section looks at the process of modifying values and sending data to the data source.

Handling Data

Besides fetching information from a data source, you will want to insert, update, delete, and modify the structure of a data source. All these activities can be accomplished using the executeUpdate() method of a Statement object. This method returns the number of rows affected by the call. For example, the following code creates a table and inserts values into it, updates the values, and then deletes the rows and drops the table.

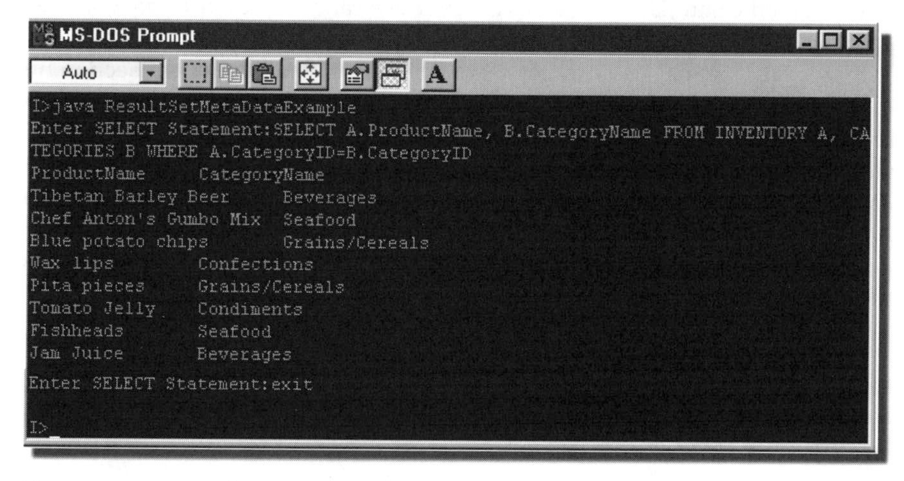

Figure 3.12 ResultSetMetaDataExample output.

```
...
Statement stmt = con.createStatement();

stmt.executeUpdate("CREATE TABLE Temp" +
                    "(id int, name varchar(25), value float)");

int insCount = stmt.executeUpdate("INSERT INTO Temp" +
                                   "VALUES (1,"test1", 5.0)");
System.out.println("Inserted " + insCount + "rows");

insCount = stmt.executeUpdate("INSERT INTO Temp " +
                               "VALUES (2,"test2", 10.0)");
System.out.println("Inserted " + insCount + "rows");

int updateCount = stmt.executeUpdate("UPDATE Temp SET value=1.0");
System.out.println("Updated " + insCount + "rows");

int deleteCount = stmt.executeUpdate("DELETE FROM Temp");
System.out.println("Deleted " + insCount + "rows");

Stmt.executeUpdate("DROP TABLE Temp");

Stmt.close();
...
```

Prepared Statements

As shown in the last example, it is common to execute the same statements repeatedly, with changes to only the value attributes. Each time you construct a statement string, it must be compiled and the driver must map the values in your string to the SQL understood by the underlying database. If you execute enough identical statements, this can become inefficient. JDBC provides an interface called a *prepared statement* that implements the Statement interface. A prepared statement represents a "compiled" statement that is fairly static. You can get a prepared statement from a connection by calling the prepareStatement() method. The only things that change in the PreparedStatement string are the parameters to the SQL string that the statement contains. These parameters are represented in the original string by question marks (?). To set the values for these parameters, PreparedStatement has setXXX methods that take two parameters. The first parameter is the index (starting at 1) of the parameter you want to modify; the second parameter is the value. Consider the previous example. Here is what the PreparedStatement version of that example might look like:

```
...
Statement stmt = con.createStatement();
PreparedStatement pstmt = con.prepareStatement(
    "INSERT INTO Temp VALUES (?,?,?)"
);
```

```
stmt.executeUpdate("CREATE TABLE Temp " +
                   "(id int, name varchar(25), value int)");

//First paramter is index, second is value of specified type
pstmt.setInt(1,1);
pstmt.setString(2,"test1");
pstmt.setFloat(3,5.0);
int insCount = pstmt.executeUpdate();
System.out.println("Inserted " + insCount + "rows");

pstmt.setInt(1,2);
pstmt.setString(2,"test2");
pstmt.setFloat(3,10.0);
insCount = pstmt.executeUpdate();
System.out.println("Inserted " + insCount + "rows");

int updateCount = stmt.executeUpdate("UPDATE Temp SET value=1.0");
System.out.println("Updated " + insCount + "rows");

int deleteCount = stmt.executeUpdate("DELETE FROM Temp");
System.out.println("Deleted " + insCount + "rows");

Stmt.executeUpdate("DROP TABLE Temp");

Stmt.close();
...
```

NOTE **Stored procedures can be called from the Statement and PreparedStatement objects. However, a connection has a method named prepareCall() that returns an object that implements the CallableStatement interface. This interface extends the PreparedStatement interface by adding methods that allow you to get the values coming back from a store procedure. Typically, these values are marked as OUT parameters in the stored procedure declaration. Stored procedure handling is beyond the scope of this section, but the principle is similar to the topics discussed so far.**

PreparedStatement is beneficial when you intend to call the same SQL multiple times. It saves on the time necessary to compile a query. For a one-time query, use the Statement object. In each case, you are handling one SQL statement at a time.

The next section looks at how to control multiple SQL calls in a single transaction.

Managing Transactions

A *transaction* is a collection of consecutively executed database commands that are considered linked as one business process. If any part of a transaction fails, the programmer has the option of retrying the transaction or saving the current state of the transaction as permanent. To retry a transaction, it must be rolled back. *Rollback transaction* is a common term for resetting the state of the database to the point before the transaction was executed. To save the transaction, execute a *commit transaction* function. This saves all the changes made to the database as permanent changes. The important point is that all statements executed as part of a transaction are considered a group. Whatever you do to the transaction affects all statements in that transaction. For example, if you deleted a row, changed the value in another row, and then rolled back the transaction, both the delete and the update would be undone.

By default, a connection is set to auto commit. This means that every statement executed is considered to be in its own transaction. So, if the statement is successful, it is committed. To have several statements executed as a single transaction, turn off auto commit by calling the Connection method setAutoCommit() and passing false. Then use the Connection methods commit() and rollback() to control the status of your transaction. Not all databases support transactions; even the ones that do support them at different levels.

Most JDBC drivers support transactions. In fact, a JDBC-compliant driver *must* support transactions. DatabaseMetaData supplies information describing the level of transaction support a DBMS provides. This level is called the *transaction isolation level.* The higher this level, the more careful the database will be in preventing multiple users from overwriting each other's transactions. However, the higher the isolation level, the slower the database may be. This is due to the degree of locking the database will perform. To find out the isolation level of your database, call the Connection method getTransactionIsolation(). Calling setTransactionIsolation can set level(). Be careful changing the isolation level during a transaction, because this causes the method commit to be called, which will cause any changes up to that point to be made permanent.

The isolation levels are listed and explained in Table 3.12.

Most databases support transactions; however, some do not. In these cases, you may find that the driver ignores your transaction calls. You can usually find out how the driver will handle transactions by checking the metadata and checking the property supportsTransactions. In some situations, an exception may even be raised.

The next section details the error-handling mechanisms of JDBC.

Table 3.12 Transaction Isolation Levels

TRANSACTION LEVEL	MEANING
TRANSACTION_NONE	Transactions are not supported.
TRANSACTION_READ_COMMITTED	Dirty reads are prevented; non-repeatable reads and phantom reads can occur.
TRANSACTION_READ_UNCOMMITTED	Dirty reads, non-repeatable reads, and phantom reads can occur.
TRANSACTION_REPEATABLE_READ	Dirty reads and non-repeatable reads are prevented; phantom reads can occur.
TRANSACTION_SERIALIZABLE	Dirty reads, non-repeatable reads, and phantom reads are prevented.

Exception-Handling /SQL Warning

Notice the previous examples were catching SQLExceptions. This is the generic exception type for JDBC methods. JDBC provides three types of exception handling:

- SQLException
- SQLWarning
- DataTruncation

Let's take a look at each of these in more detail.

SQLExceptions

SQLException is a subclass of exception consisting of a string error message, a string containing the SQL state as defined by the XOPEN SQL state specification, and a driver-specific int used as an additional error code. Here is an example:

```
try
{
    Statement s = con.createStatement();
}catch (SQLException e)
{
   System.println.out(e);
   System.println.out("Database Driver/Source error code: " +
                      e.getErrorCode());
   System.println.out("XOPEN SQL State: " + e.getSQLState());
}
```

If multiple errors were generated, multiple SQLException instances can be chained together. To get access to the next error, call getNextException() on the SQLException object. To add to the chain, call setNextException().

SQLWarnings

The SQLWarning class is a subclass of SQLException, but it is typically used for non-critical errors. Usually, it is not thrown as an exception. Rather, it is typically up to the program to query for SQLWarnings by calling the getWarnings() method of any Connection, Statement, or ResultSet object. Each time these objects are used, they clear out the warnings by calling clearWarnings(). This means that if you do not poll for messages, you will not get them.

Data Truncation

The DataTruncation class is a subclass of SQLWarning. A data truncation occurs when you perform a query and do not or cannot process all of the results. For example, you might get a data truncation warning if you perform a query that returns 15 rows, and you process only the first one with your result set before closing it. DataTruncation warnings are issued as part of a chain of SQLWarning messages. This means that as you process a SQLWarning chain of messages, you must look specifically for DataTruncation objects if you want to call DataTruncation-specific methods. Finding a DataTruncation requires you to perform an instance of DataTruncation check on each SQLWarning.

The following example illustrates this process:

```
SQLWarning warning = stmt.getWarnings();
while (warning != null)
{
    System.out.println(warning.getMessage());
    if(warning instanceof DataTruncation)
    {
        DataTruncation dt = (DataTruncation)warning;
        if(dt.getParameter())
            System.out.print("The parameter had ");

        System.out.print("A trunction error in column: " +
                         dt.getIndex() +
                         "should have tranfered " +
                         dt.getDataSize() + "bytes. " +
                         "Actually transfered " +
                         dt.getTransferSize() + "bytes");

        if(dt.getRead())
            System.out.print(" while reading.");
        else
            System.out.print(".");

        System.out.println("");
    }

    warning = warning.getNextWarning();
}
```

Notice that getWarnings continue to be called until null is returned. Null signifies that there are no more errors.

The next section puts together the concepts discussed in this chapter by demonstrating a larger application.

Putting It Together

The final example for this chapter is a complete Java application. This application uses the Java Foundation Classes (JFC), which are included with Java 2. If you are unfamiliar with JFC, you may want to read our book, *Programming with JFC* (John Wiley & Sons, 1998). This example is not meant to demonstrate the optimal use of all JDBC features. Rather, this is a combination of JDBC features that have been put in one application to demonstrate several capabilities of JDBC 1.0. The example illustrated in Figure 3.13 displays a list of inventory items from our INV database. Some columns are calculated. At the bottom of the main screen is a series of buttons:

Query Database. This button loads the records from the database and displays them.

Delete Current Row. Deletes the row from the database currently selected in the JTable.

Insert Row. Inserts a new row in the JTable.

Start Transaction. Starts a transaction. After this, all operations are in the transaction scope until the transaction is committed or rolled back.

Commit Transaction. Commits the transaction if there is one in progress

Rollback Transaction. Rolls back the transaction if there is one in progress.

The example consists of three classes:

JDBCTable. A subclass of JPanel that displays our UI, including a table of data.

JDBCTableModel. A subclass of AbstractTableModel that implements all of the database access routines and keeps track of the current selection from the database.

WindowCloser. A subclass of WindowAdapter used as a convenience class for quitting the application when the user closes the main window.

Let's look at each of these classes in detail.

JDBCTable

The following code defines the JDBCTable class. The JDCTable class displays the main JPanel and places a JTable and six buttons in the table. JDBCTable handles the action for each button. The JDBCTable main method starts by creating a new JDBCTableModel, which takes a URL, a driver class name, a user name, and a password as parameters. The table uses a JDBCTableModel to connect to the database. Once the model connects to the database, the JDBCTable installs this model in the JTable.

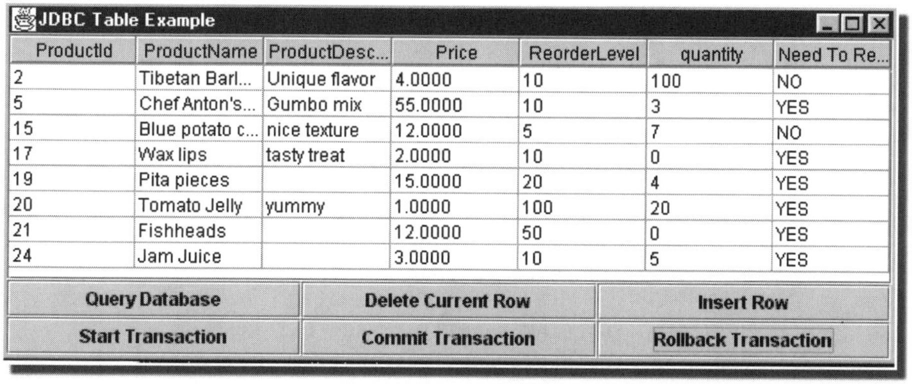

JDBC Table Example

ProductId	ProductName	ProductDesc...	Price	ReorderLevel	quantity	Need To Re...
2	Tibetan Barl...	Unique flavor	4.0000	10	100	NO
5	Chef Anton's...	Gumbo mix	55.0000	10	3	YES
15	Blue potato c...	nice texture	12.0000	5	7	NO
17	Wax lips	tasty treat	2.0000	10	0	YES
19	Pita pieces		15.0000	20	4	YES
20	Tomato Jelly	yummy	1.0000	100	20	YES
21	Fishheads		12.0000	50	0	YES
24	Jam Juice		3.0000	10	5	YES

Query Database
Delete Current Row
Insert Row
Start Transaction
Commit Transaction
Rollback Transaction

Figure 3.13 JDBCTable application.

As part of this example, we check the results of requesting the model commit or rollback transaction because these could fail if the database doesn't support transactions, if the records are locked by someone else, and so on. The start transaction isn't checked because in this case it won't affect much. However, you could easily add that feature.

```
import java.awt.swing.*;
import java.awt.event.*;
import java.awt.*;
import java.io.*;
import java.util.*;

public class JDBCTable extends JPanel implements ActionListener
{
    JDBCTableModel model;
    JTable table;

    static String queryStr = "Query Database";
    static String deleteStr ="Delete Current Row";
    static String insertStr = "Insert Row";
    static String startTranStr = "Start Transaction";
    static String commitTransStr = "Commit Transaction";
    static String rollbackStr = "Rollback Transaction";

    public JDBCTable()
    {
        File root;
        Font f;
        JPanel tmpPanel;

        setLayout(new BorderLayout());

        // Instantiate the model passing in URL for the JDBC driver.
        model = new JDBCTableModel("jdbc:odbc:Inventory"
                                ,"sun.jdbc.odbc.JdbcOdbcDriver"
                                ,""
                                ,"");

        table = new JTable();
        table.setModel(model);
        table.createDefaultColumnsFromModel();
        table.setRowSelectionAllowed(true);
        add(JTable.createScrollPaneForTable(table),"Center");

        // Create set of buttons for controlling the interface.
        tmpPanel = new JPanel();
        tmpPanel.setLayout(new GridLayout(2,3));

        this.addButtonWithTitleToPanel(queryStr,tmpPanel);
        this.addButtonWithTitleToPanel(deleteStr,tmpPanel);
        this.addButtonWithTitleToPanel(insertStr,tmpPanel);
```

```
        this.addButtonWithTitleToPanel(startTranStr,tmpPanel);
        this.addButtonWithTitleToPanel(commitTransStr,tmpPanel);
        this.addButtonWithTitleToPanel(rollbackStr,tmpPanel);

        add(tmpPanel,"South");
    }

    // Convenience method to install button and action.
    private void addButtonWithTitleToPanel(String title,
                                          JPanel panel)
    {
        JButton button = new JButton(title);
        button.addActionListener(this);
        panel.add(button);
    }

    // Handle action based on button pressed.
    public void actionPerformed(ActionEvent evt)
    {
        String ac = evt.getActionCommand();
        if(ac.compareTo(queryStr) == 0)
            model.executeQuery();
        else if(ac.compareTo(insertStr) == 0)
            model.executeInsert();
        else if(ac.compareTo(deleteStr) == 0)
            model.executeDelete(table.getSelectedRow());
        else if(ac.compareTo(startTranStr) == 0)
        {
            model.startTransaction();
            JOptionPane.showMessageDialog(this,
                    "Transaction is now in progress.",
                    "", JOptionPane.INFORMATION_MESSAGE);
        }
        else if(ac.compareTo(commitTransStr) == 0)
        {
            // Make sure commit succeeds first.
            if(model.commitTransaction())
                JOptionPane.showMessageDialog(this,
                    "Transaction has been commited. ",
                    "", JOptionPane.INFORMATION_MESSAGE);
            else
                JOptionPane.showMessageDialog(this,
                     "Transaction could not be commited. ",
                     "", JOptionPane.INFORMATION_MESSAGE);
        }
        else if(ac.compareTo(rollbackStr) == 0)
        {
            if(model.rollbackTransaction())
                JOptionPane.showMessageDialog(this,
                     "Transaction has been rolled back. ",
                     "", JOptionPane.INFORMATION_MESSAGE);
```

```
                else
                    JOptionPane.showMessageDialog(this,
                          "Transaction could not\n be rolled back. ",
                          "", JOptionPane.INFORMATION_MESSAGE);
            }
        }

        public Dimension getPreferredSize()
        {
            return new Dimension(600, 300);
        }

        public static void main(String s[])
        {
            JFrame frame = new JFrame("JDBC Table Example");
            JDBCTable panel = new JDBCTable();

            System.setErr(System.out);

            frame.setDefaultCloseOperation(JFrame.DO_NOTHING_ON_CLOSE);
            frame.setForeground(Color.black);
            frame.setBackground(Color.lightGray);
            frame.getContentPane().add(panel,"Center");

            frame.setSize(panel.getPreferredSize());
            frame.setVisible(true);
            frame.addWindowListener(new WindowCloser());
        }
    }
```

JDBCTableModel

JDBCTableModel class does all the database access. Let's take this class one method at a time. First, initialize some strings and variables, including static variables for the queries used in this example.

```
import java.util.*;
import java.util.*;
import java.sql.*;
import java.awt.swing.table.*;
import java.awt.swing.event.*;


public class JDBCTableModel extends AbstractTableModel
{
    //JDBC objects
    Connection connection;
    Statement statement;
    PreparedStatement delStatement;
```

```
    ResultSet resultSet;
    ResultSetMetaData metaData;

    //Default strings used for accessing the Access databases.
    static String queryStr = "SELECT ProductId, ProductName, " +
                             "ProductDescription, Price, " +
                             "ReorderLevel, quantity, " +
                             "IIf(quantity - reorderlevel > 0," +
                             "'NO','YES') AS " +
                             "[Need To Reorder] FROM Inventory";
    static String insertStr = "INSERT INTO Inventory(ProductName) " +
                              "Values ('New Product')";

    // Table objects
    Vector names;
    Vector types;
    Vector data;
```

JDBCTableModel

The constructor for JDBCTableModel creates a connection with the database. This connection persists until the application ends. By keeping the connection and the associated resources open, database resources are being used up, but keeping them open makes the example shorter. If the connection is not expected to be open long or if you are not concerned about resource constraints, it is reasonable to leave it open for the duration of your application. After creating a connection, create PreparedStatement for deleting records. This object passes a single value, the product id, and deletes the associated row. After creating these resources, executeQuery is called, which initially loads the records from the database and displays them in the table.

```
public JDBCTableModel(String url, String driverName,
String user, String passwd)
{
    data = new Vector();
    names = new Vector();

    try
    {
        //load the driver
        Class.forName(driverName);
        connection = DriverManager.getConnection(url, user, passwd);

    /*
      Create a statement for use in all the methods of this object.
      In general, it would be better to create and close the
      statement more often. However, keeping it open makes
      the example shorter.
    */
        statement = connection.createStatement();
```

```
            // Create a compiled statement for executing deletes.
            delStatement =
             connection.prepareStatement("DELETE FROM "
                   + "Inventory WHERE ProductId = ?");

            // Initialize the table.
            this.executeQuery();
        }
        catch (Exception exp)
        {
            System.out.println("Error connecting: "+exp);
        }
    }
```

executeQuery

The executeQuery method queries the database and returns ResultSet containing Inventory items. These records have some calculated fields. The product id and the calculated fields are not editable, but the rest of the fields are. ResultSet is loaded into a set of internal vectors that represent the data in the JTable. Calling fireTableChanged() notifies the table that the data has changed, and it reloads the data from these vectors.

```
    public void executeQuery()
    {
        int i,max;
        Vector rowData;
        int curType;

        try
        {
            data = new Vector();
            names = new Vector();

            resultSet = statement.executeQuery(queryStr);
            metaData = resultSet.getMetaData();
            max =  metaData.getColumnCount();

            //get the column names
            for(i=0;i<max;i++)
            {
                //adjust for meta data index start at 1
                names.addElement(metaData.getColumnLabel(i+1));
            }

            //load the data
            while (resultSet.next())
            {
                rowData = new Vector();

                for (i=0;i<max;i++)
```

```
                {
                    rowData.addElement(resultSet.getObject(i+1));
                }

                data.addElement(rowData);
            }

            fireTableChanged(null);
        }
        catch (Exception exp)
        {
            System.out.println("Error performing query: "+exp);
            exp.printStackTrace();
        }
    }
```

executeInsert

When the Insert button is pressed, a record is inserted in the underlying database. The UI is updated to reflect the change. This could be made more efficient by not actually fetching the data again, instead keeping track of the inserted records manually until the next fresh query.

NOTE **JDBC 2.0 contains methods for directly manipulating ResultSet. This would more elegantly solve the problem of refetching values.**

```
public void executeInsert()
{
    if(statement != null)
    {
        try
        {
            statement.executeUpdate(insertStr);

            // refresh
            this.executeQuery();
        }catch(SQLException e)
        {
            System.out.println(e);
            return;
        }
    }
}
```

executeDelete

When the Delete Current Row button is pressed, the executeDelete method takes the row id and deletes that row by using a prepared statement that takes one parameter, the product id. Because the index for the JTable starts at 0, you need to offset to 1. This is because JDBC index also starts at 1.

```
public void executeDelete(int row)
{
    if(row > -1)
    {
        // Get the product ID.
        Object id = this.getValueAt(row,0);

        if(statement != null)
        {
            try
            {
            /*
              Set the value of the first paramter in
              this compiled delete statement.
            */
                delStatement.setObject(1,id);

                // Execute the statement.
                delStatement.executeUpdate();

                //Refresh. In JDBC 2.0, there is a refresh method.
                this.executeQuery();
            }catch(SQLException e)
            {
                System.out.println(e);
                return;
            }
        }
    }
}
```

setValueAt

When a user types in an editable table field, the setValueAt method is called. The text the user typed in and the position of the cell are passed in. If the value has changed, determine the type of field in the database, then use the appropriate syntax to store it.

```
public void setValueAt(Object value, int row, int col)
{
    Vector rowData = (Vector)data.elementAt(row);
    Object o = rowData.elementAt(col);

    if(o != value)
    {
        try
        {
            String s = "UPDATE INVENTORY SET " +
                        metaData.getColumnName(col+1) + "=";
```

```
                int curType = metaData.getColumnType(col+1);

                switch(curType)
                {
                    case Types.CHAR:
                    case Types.VARCHAR:
                    case Types.LONGVARCHAR:
                    case Types.DATE:
                        s += "'"+value.toString()+"'";
                        break;
                    case Types.TINYINT:
                    case Types.SMALLINT:
                    case Types.INTEGER:
                    case Types.BIGINT:
                    case Types.FLOAT:
                    case Types.DOUBLE:
                        s += value.toString();
                    break;
                        default:
                        s += "'"+value.toString()+"'";
                }

                s += " WHERE PRODUCTID = " + rowData.elementAt(0)+";";
                statement.executeUpdate(s);

                // refresh
                this.executeQuery();

            } catch(SQLException e) { System.out.println(e);}
        }
    }
```

startTransaction

When the Start Transaction button is pressed, the startTransaction method is called. In order to start a transaction, turn auto commit off. You cannot do this on some drivers if you have an open ResultSet. So, close ResultSet, then reestablish the query after turning on the transaction.

```
public void startTransaction()
{
/*
  Turn off AutoCommit; this makes all commands fall
  into same transaction.
*/
    try
    {
    /*
       Must close existing result set before
       changing transaction state.
    */
```

```
            if(resultSet != null)
                resultSet.close();
            connection.setAutoCommit(false);

            // refresh
            this.executeQuery();
        }catch(SQLException e)
        {
            System.out.println(e);
        }
    }
```

commitTransaction

When a transaction is committed, it saves all current statements to the database. The commitTransaction method in JDBCTableModel handles the case in which a commit may fail, as in the case of no current transaction or if a database error occurs—for example, if someone else locks the record we are trying to change.

```
    public boolean commitTransaction()
    {
        boolean commitIsOk = false;

        try
        {
        /*
            Check if autocommit is on.
            If it is, don't commit manually.
        */
            commitIsOk = !connection.getAutoCommit();

            if(commitIsOk)
            {
                // Commit transaction
                connection.commit();

                // Turn on AutoCommit; this is default.
                connection.setAutoCommit(true);
            }
        }catch(SQLException e)
        {
            System.out.println(e);
            commitIsOk = false;
        }

        //refresh
        if(commitIsOk)
            this.executeQuery();

        return commitIsOk;
    }
```

rollbackTransaction

The rollbackTransaction method works similarly to the commitTransaction() method. If this method is successful, the current transaction rolls back and all changes done within the scope of the transaction are undone.

```
public boolean rollbackTransaction()
{
    boolean rollbackIsOk = false;

    try
    {
        //Check if auto commit is on. If it is, don't roll back.
        rollbackIsOk = !connection.getAutoCommit();

        if(rollbackIsOk)
        {
            // rollback transaction
            connection.rollback();

            //Turn on Auto Commit; this is default.
            connection.setAutoCommit(true);
        }
        }catch(SQLException e)
        {
            System.out.println(e);
            rollbackIsOk = false;
        }

        //refresh
        if(rollbackIsOk)
            this.executeQuery();

        return rollbackIsOk;
    }
}
```

Miscellaneous Table-Related Methods

The following are housekeeping methods required by the JDBCTableModel.

The close method is called to close the connection to the database and all associated resources.

```
public void close() throws SQLException
{
    resultSet.close();
    statement.close();
    connection.close();
}
```

The close method is called from finalize(), which has been overridden to call close.

```
protected void finalize() throws Throwable
{
    close();
    super.finalize();
}
```

The getColumnName method is a convenience method that returns the name of a column based on its positional index.

```
public String getColumnName(int col)
{
    String retVal;

    retVal = (String) names.elementAt(col);

    if(retVal == null)
        retVal = "";

    return retVal;
}
```

The method isCellEditable returns true if the column is one of the first five. This method is a sort of "hack," so we don't have to add too much code for processing the logic of each individual column. The intent is to keep the example straightforward:

```
public boolean isCellEditable(int row, int col)
{
/*
  Only the first four columns after the product id are
  updateable in this example (adjust for index difference).
*/
    return ((col < 6) && (col > 0));
}
```

The getColumnCount method returns the number of columns in the table.

```
public int getColumnCount()

{
    return names.size();
}
```

The getRowCount method returns the number of rows in the table.

```
public int getRowCount()
{
    return data.size();
}
```

The getValueAt method returns the value of a specific cell of the table.

```
public Object getValueAt(int row, int col)
```

```
{
    Vector rowData = (Vector)data.elementAt(row);

    return rowData.elementAt(col);
}
```

WindowCloser

WindowCloser is used to respond to a windowClosing event. It quits the application.

```
class WindowCloser extends WindowAdapter
{
    public void windowClosing(WindowEvent e)
    {
        Window win = e.getWindow();
        win.setVisible(false);
        System.exit(0);
    }
}
```

This example highlights the basic use of JDBC 1.0. Sun has recently released the specification for JDBC 2.0, which is even more powerful. The next section highlights some of the features that will be available when JDBC 2.0 product is released in full.

JDBC 2.0 Features

JDBC 2.0 adds many new features to the overall architecture of JDBC. When drivers start supporting these features, database access activities will be even easier and more flexible. In general, JDBC 2.0 supports the goals of JDBC 1.0, which include ease of use and good integration with the rest of the Java 2 platform, and Java philosophy of software design.

The specific goals of JDBC 2.0 include the following:

Leverage the strengths of the JDBC 1.0 and Java APIs. JDBC 1.0 goals are still important for the further development of JDBC.

Maintain compatibility with JDBC 1.0 applications and drivers. This is an important goal because it ensures that as JDBC improves, your current applications won't stop working. In fact, your application is guaranteed to work with JDBC 2.0 drivers.

Leverage JavaBeans. JavaSoft believes it is important for JDBC as a core data access technology to leverage the JavaBeans component model. JDBC 2.0 supports JavaBeans by implementing a RowSet object capable of tracking a set of records, even when not connected to the data source. This object is a serializable JavaBean, which can be used as a data container in any tool or application that supports JavaBeans.

Provide advanced database features. JDBC 1.0 does a good job of providing capabilities equivalent to ODBC. JDBC 2.0 takes a hard look at database-specific features that add more power and provides mechanism for tapping into these features. Features include more support for Binary Large Objects (BLObs) and scrollable cursors.

JDBC 2.0 is designed so that JDBC 1.0 programmers can easily adopt its functionality. JDBC 2.0 extends the capabilities of JDBC 1.0.

Database Enhancements

There are many improvements in the JDBC 2.0 specification. The most notable improvements include these:

Scrollable cursors. These are implemented using ResultSet, which maintains an internal pointer called a *cursor.* The cursor indicates the row in the *result set that is currently being accessed*. In JDBC 2.0, these cursors may be used to move backward as well as forward. This allows the user to manipulate a record and come back to it later without having to requery the database.

Advanced data type support. JDBC 2.0 provides better mapping support between Java objects and SQL3 data types such as BLObs. Additionally, there is support for user-defined types.

Non-SQL database support. JDBC 2.0 provides some support for non-SQL databases so that drivers for data sources like file systems and non-SQL databases are easier to use.

Batch updates. Batch updates allow you to store several database calls, then execute them all at once. If auto commit is off, these statements can be grouped in a single transaction, or they can be executed as a set of separate transactions.

Persistence of Java objects. Support for type mapping and better object support allow drivers to ease the process of storing Java objects and custom types in a database.

Connection pooling. Connection pooling may be implemented on top of the JDBC driver layer, allowing for a connection cache that works between JDBC drivers used by your application. This is a performance feature that enables you to share a connection to a database, allowing you to avoid the high cost of creating and destroying database connections.

JDBC 2.0 is more powerful because it allows you more flexibility in how you access and manipulate data. It is also easy to use because it simply extends the features of JDBC 1.0, which means everything you have learned here will apply to JDBC 2.0. However, there are some design changes, as discussed in the next section.

Design Changes

In JDBC 2.0, the API has been split into two packages. The first package, java.sql, is referred to as JDBC 2.0 Core API. A new package, javax.sql, is called the JDBC 2.0 Standard Extension. The JDBC 2.0 Core API consists of all of the classes discussed in this chapter plus the list in Table 3.13.

Table 3.13 JDBC 2.0 Core API Class Additions

CLASS/INTERFACE	USE
ArrayLocator	An interface that represents reference during a transaction to an array of values in the database.
BatchUpdateException	A subclass of SQLException that provides information on all statements within the batch being processed.
BlobLocator	An interface that represents a reference to a binary large object in the database.
ClobLocator	Similar to a BlobLocator except for Character Large Objects (CLObs).
Ref	An interface that can be saved to persistent storage and represents a reference to a SQL structured value in the database.
SQLData	A Java class registered for type mapping implements this interface. It enables the driver to populate the object with values from the database or write the class's values to the database.
SQLInput	Streams containing values that represent SQL values implement this interface.
SQLOutput	Streams containing values that represent SQL values implement this interface.
SQLType	This interface provides some information about a SQL type.
Struct	Extends the SQLData interface for mapping of structured data.
StructLocator	This interface represents a reference during a transaction to a structure in the database.

The javax.sql package contains the parts of the JDBC 2.0 API that are related to other Java standard extensions, such as the Java Naming and Directory Interface (JNDI) and the Java Transaction Service (JTS), discussed later in this book. This package includes features such as connection pooling and row sets. At the time of this writing, the specification was not available. For more information on javax.sql, check the Sun Web site at www.javasoft.com/products/jdbc/index.html.

Summary

JDBC provides a solid architecture for accessing a data source in a platform-independent fashion. Most significant is that JDBC leverages the benefits of the Java design philosophy by keeping the API simple and easy to use. As new drivers appear, they will continue to fall more and more into the level 3 and 4 categories, which means vendors of databases, application servers, and other middleware products will have a tendency to provide pure Java solutions. Drivers that will support JDBC 2.0 features will still work with your JDBC 1.0 applications. This means you should develop for JDBC today and think about how the JDBC 2.0 features will help you tomorrow.

When developing applications that access a database, the most critical issues are:

- Accessing the data and features of the specific data source
- Performance of the gateway used to access this database
- Ease of new features that can be added to the application for supporting advanced database calls
- Database resources should almost always be considered limited and valuable in your design

JDBC does a good job of providing a baseline API for accessing your data source and allowing driver suppliers to extend the API so you can access specific database features. However, if the driver you are using is limited, be prepared to make some database calls through other means, such as vendor-specific gateways or libraries. Just make sure you encapsulate these calls in a separate method or class so that as more advanced drivers come out, you can easily move all of your calls to JDBC-only solutions. JDBC-only solutions give you more flexibility and make future enhancements easier because the vendors will update the data access features for you. Most important, remember that connections to the database represent real network and database resources. You should disconnect as soon as possible or at least minimize the number of open connections a client holds, because most databases can only handle a limited number of these. One solution to this problem is to use an intermediate product such as an application server. These products can provide you with access to your database through shared connections to your database.

JDBC provides a standard API for Java developers and makes it possible to write database applications using a pure Java API. An enterprise developer can use JDBC to connect all its heterogeneous database systems. Many of the services provided by Sun enable Java programmers to access standard repositories of information. The next chapter looks at another type of data repository called a naming and directory service. A naming and directory service provides information about resources on the network, such as printer locations, employee e-mail address lookup, and so on. The name of the Java API for accessing these services is called the Java Naming and Directory Interface, or JNDI.

This chapter covered the basics of connecting to a database using JDBC 1.0. For a more comprehensive look at this topic, you may want to consider *JDBC Database Access With Java: A Tutorial and Annotated Reference (Java Series)* by Graham Hamilton, Rick Cattell, and Maydene Fisher, published by Addison-Wesley. Also check out the Sun Web site at www.javasoft.com/products/jdk/1.1/docs/guide/jdbc/getstart/introTOC.doc.html. If you are interested in taking a course on this topic, check www.pri.com for a Java course schedule.

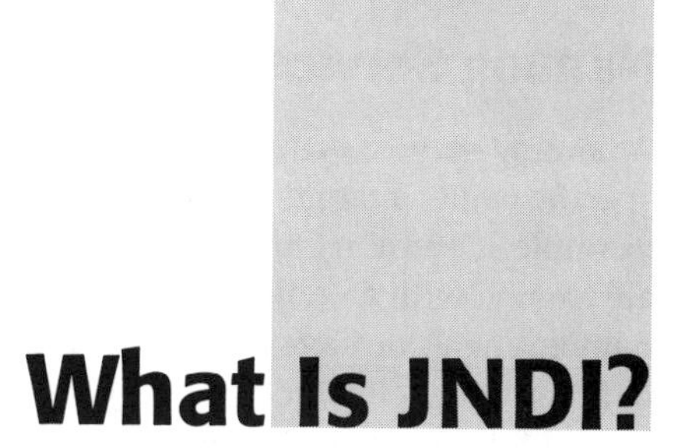

What Is JNDI?

Internet and intranet applications rely heavily on naming and directory services for accessing network resources. These services provide networkwide sharing of information related to users, machines, other network services, and remote applications. Java Naming and Directory Interface (JNDI) is an API that describes a standard Java library for accessing naming and directory services such as Domain Naming Service (DNS), Lightweight Directory Access Protocol (LDAP), Remote Method Invocation (RMI), or even the file system on your computer. JNDI is powerful because it allows various services to be linked through a single API, enabling Java applications that use JNDI to navigate seamlessly across file systems, databases, servers, and so on. For example, you could look up a specific RMI registry by requesting the information from an LDAP server, then use the same JNDI API to request a specific object from the registry and save a reference to the object in your file system using the JNDI file system service provider API.

This chapter describes the terminology, goals, and architecture of JNDI.

Terminology

In order to understand when and how to use JNDI, you must be familiar with the two types of services it supports: directory and naming services. *Directory services* typically provide access to a hierarchical tree of objects, such as the directories in the file system on your computer. A *naming service* allows access to objects by name. For example, a corporate LDAP server could allow you to find an e-mail address by entering the person's last name and department number. DNS, on the other hand, allows programs to look up a computer's IP address by name. JNDI for directory and naming services enables the Java developer to build applications that leverage the features of the Java object model and, at the same time, integrate well with most commercial enterprise applications. In order to use JNDI, you should also be familiar with at least one service provider with which JNDI works, such as LDAP. Both the file system service provider and the LDAP service provider are used in the examples in Chapter 5, "Using JNDI." Table 4.1, which appears later in this chapter, lists the services that are currently available.

Naming Service

A naming service provides a method for mapping unique identifiers, or names with a specific value, a range of values, or an object that is referenced by the name service. For example, Common Object Request Broker Architecture (CORBA) allows you to associate a name with an object so that you can remotely access the object by requesting it by name. When you save a file on your computer, you name the file so that you can refer to it and access it later.

The following terms are important to understand when using a naming service: binding, namespace, compound name, composite name, and service providers. These terms are discussed in more detail in the following sections.

Binding

The mapping between a name and a unique object is referred to as a *name binding*. One obvious computer naming service that performs binding is the file system on your computer. Each file and directory has a name that identifies it. When you create a file, you give it a name. This is the name binding for your data; it can be retrieved by that name later. When you rename a file, you are actually rebinding the file to a new name.

Namespace

A *namespace* is a set of names in which all names are unique. If you think of a directory on your computer as a namespace, you realize each file within the directory must have a unique name. However, you can have two files with the same name if each is in a different directory, or namespace. With multiple namespaces, you can reuse names without conflicts.

Compound Name

A *compound name* is a sequence of names that conform to the naming convention of a namespace. In a file system, you may have a compound name such as /usr/tmp/myfile.txt./, usr, tmp, and mysfile.txt—these are all names of objects in the file system. The symbol, or name /, maps to the root directory; the name usr maps to a subdirectory under /; and the name tmp maps to the subdirectory called tmp under usr. The name myfile.txt maps to a file. Together they create a compound name that is, for example, different from /usr/local/myfile.txt.

Composite Name

Composite names span multiple namespaces. Composite names are common on the World Wide Web. A URL usually consists of at least three parts: protocol name, server name, and resource name. For example, in the URL http://www.wiley.com/index.html, the protocol name is http; the name of the server is //www.wiley.com; and the name of the resource is index.html. Ultimately, it is hoped that JNDI will support highly composite names. For example, you might use the first part of a name as a URL to find an LDAP server, use the next part of the name to find a resource on the LDAP server, and use the results of the LDAP query and the final part of the name to find an object using RMI.

Service Providers

Although JNDI provides a common, unified API for name services, each name service requires a *service provider* that maps JNDI into the specific operations supported by the name service. Name services differ in description of names, organization of the name space, schema description (if any), and the list of operations supported by inserting and searching for objects and values in the service. This mapping of an API to a service provider's code is similar to the mapping between the JDBC interfaces and driver implementations discussed in Chapter 2, "What Is JDBC?" and Chapter 3, "Basic JDBC Programming."

DNS and RMI are good examples of naming services because, although they each organize information differently, they still use unique names in a namespace to identify their objects. A list of currently available service providers appears in Table 4.1.

DNS

The Domain Name System (DNS) is an Internet naming service that maps the Internet address of computer systems, such as 192.42.172.21, with simple names like pri.com. These names allow users direct access to remote computer systems through recognizable names.

RMI

Remote Method Invocation (RMI) is an example of a distributed object management system that provides a naming service for mapping names to objects residing on remote computers. The client could request the service of an object in another address space simply by referring to it by name. For example, your application could request a printing object from an RMI repository to print a specific type of report. The code might look like this:

```
Printer p = (Printer)rmiService.lookup("Report_Printer");
p.print(myReportObject);
```

Naming services provide a good mechanism for mapping objects to identifiable names. There are many mechanisms for organizing and storing these named objects, such as LDAP or RMI or even your computer's file system. JNDI provides a consistent API for accessing all of these types of naming services. JNDI also allows you to manipulate and traverse the organization of more complex services known as directory services.

Table 4.1 Service Providers

SERVICE PROVIDER	DESCRIPTION
LDAP	The LDAP service provider currently supports versions 2 and 3 of the LDAP protocol. For more information on the LDAP protocol, see www.umich.edu/~dirsvcs/ldap/.
NIS	The Network Information Service (NIS) service provider allows access to UNIX machines running NIS.
NIS+	NIS+, an enhanced version of NIS, provides better security, scalability, and dynamic updates.
COS Naming	COS Naming provides access to Common Object Request Broker Architecture (CORBA) naming services through the standard JNDI interface.
File System	The File System service provider uses java.io.File to represent files in your file system. Using this provider, you can access your file system in a platform-independent way and even store object references in your file system.
RMI Registry	The RMI Registry allows you to use JNDI to find objects in a Remote Object Invocation (RMI) Registry.
SLP	The Service Location Protocol (SLP) provides a dynamic framework for selection of network services.
Novell	Novell provides access to NetWare 3X's Bindery, the Novell File Systems, and other Novell services such as Extended NCP.
WebLogic JNDI	The WebLogic JNDI service provider interface is a naming service for Java application server services, including RMI, JDBC, EJB, and so on. WebLogic JNDI includes toolkits for building custom naming and directory providers.

Directory Services

Directory services are types of naming services that provide structure to some set of objects or data values. You can think of a phone book as a sort of directory service that organizes collections of names, phone numbers, and addresses based on region, city, state, or country. Typically, the structure of a directory service is hierarchical. For example, most computer file systems start with a root directory and have a series of subdirectories, each containing files. Although this directory structure is common, other attributes of the resources within a directory service namespace may vary greatly. One directory service may be capable of setting information such as the file access permissions or the modified date, while other directory services, such as LDAP, allow the definition of arbitrary attributes on a resource.

Each node or directory structure can be considered the root of the directory tree below it, hierarchically. Clients of the directory set their focus on the specific subdirectory they are interested in accessing. An example of this would be the act of changing directories in your file system and then accessing a file. If you wanted to access the file /usr/tmp/myFile.txt, you could change directories to /usr/tmp and then access the file by referring to it by its name, myFile.txt. Otherwise, if you were at the root directory, you would have to refer to the file by the name /usr/tmp/myFile.txt. Like files in the file system, contents of directories are referred to by name, relative to the current directory. This current directory is called a context.

Context

Each node of a directory structure can be referred to as a *context*. Directory services allow you to read and modify attributes attached to contexts and have the ability to search a context using those attributes as a filter. For example, you could search an LDAP directory service for all people working in the marketing department named Joe, where Joe is the value of the name attribute of the person you are searching for. In this structure, you could have people listed in your company directory that have the names of their assistants associated with their listing, while others do not even have an assistants attribute.

Service Providers

Each directory service requires a service provider that maps from JNDI into the specific operations supported by the directory service. Directory services may vary greatly in how they organize information, search directories, and modify attributes. However, JNDI provides a consistent interface, so your Java program can retrieve and modify values in a directory with a single API. One of the most prominent directory services that you will want to access in your enterprise will be an LDAP server. This service is discussed in Chapter 5, "Using JNDI," to show how to use the directory features of JNDI. A list of currently available service providers is presented in Table 4.1.

NOTE **For the most recent list of service providers, check the URL http://java.sun.com/products/jndi/serviceproviders.html.**

LDAP

Lightweight Directory Access Protocol (LDAP) directory service provides a lightweight version of X.500 directory service that can run on the TCP/IP protocol stack. This protocol is becoming popular and is a common service integrated in products such as Netscape's Enterprise Server. The protocol allows networked users access to information and resources in a consistent fashion by providing a simple searching facility that allows you to search and modify items based on their position in the directory hierarchy, referred to as a *context*. For example, you could search LDAP for all the people in the marketing department that have a fax number in the 415 area code. Once you located them, you could change their area code to 650. The search could ignore anyone that did not have a fax number attribute associated with their information. The attributes associated with a context are variable, which provides flexibility but does require extra discipline by administrators to adhere to a consistent naming structure. In other words, LDAP does define some standard in how to organize information, but it is fairly free-form, so the administrator must take care when naming attributes and deciding where attributes belong in the directory. For example, one person could have an attribute called telephone while another person could have an attribute called phone. This is legal in LDAP but would make it difficult to search for people by their telephone numbers, because you would need to search for the existence of either attribute.

Goals for JNDI

Understanding the design goals that the architects of JNDI had in mind may help you understand and appreciate how the JNDI designers intended JNDI to be used. This section is based on the JNDI specification from Sun Microsystems and provides a brief insight into these goals.

Keep it consistent and intuitive. One of the design goals for JNDI was to make sure the API made sense. That means that they tried to use classes and methods that added the maximum benefit and didn't overlap too much with services of other APIs. Great effort was taken to avoid duplicating the capabilities of objects in the Java class libraries. By keeping the number of classes to a minimum and leveraging other object classes, the design of JNDI could be made simple yet powerful. Even within JNDI, this principle was followed. For example, the API design for the directory service functionality is simply an extension of the more subset functionality of the naming service API. In this way, the directory service part of the API is easy to learn and use, once you understand the fundamentals of the naming portion of the API.

Pay for what you use. The term "pay for what you use" means that the designers didn't want you to have to learn or use more of the features and API than you needed to do the task at hand. This reduces your learning curve and reduces the overall size and complexity of your program. For example, if you want to look up a file on your computer, you need to use only a few classes and interfaces from the javax.naming package. You don't need to look at the javax.naming.directory package at all to get your job done.

Implementable for common directory and naming service protocols. Obviously, it is important that a standard interface for accessing naming and directory services support the common protocols. However, the designers are making a more significant commitment to keep the API as implementation independent as possible. This means you should not find too many methods that don't apply to your service provider. In other words, the API provides just what you would expect for most services. At the same time, you can still leverage the unique features of a particular service by adding your own functionality or by using a service provider that extends the capabilities of JNDI to access these unique features.

Enable seamless and dynamic services. The goal to enable directory services to seamlessly plug in behind JNDI greatly benefits the programmer using JNDI. By designing JNDI with a dynamic interface for accessing services, you can offload, until run time, choices about which protocol or technique to use for accessing your service. This gives your application more flexibility and lowers the cost of maintaining and enhancing your application over time. For example, today you could access files on your local machine and, with very few or no code changes, access a remote file via some combination of LDAP, RMI, and so on. The ability to seamlessly modify the source of the data without changing your application provides great flexibility and better long-term maintenance of your code, which results in lower total cost.

JNDI Architecture

The JNDI API is a Java extension API and is contained in the packages javax.naming, javax.naming.directory, and javax.naming.spi.

- The package javax.naming is the basic API used typically to look up objects and values in a naming service, such as an RMI object registry.
- The package javax.naming.directory contains a slightly more sophisticated API used for filtered searching and modifying of hierarchical values in directory and naming services such as LDAP.
- The package javax.naming.spi provides a set of interfaces and objects used by service provider developers. Most enterprise developers will not need to use this API, because it is used for mapping JNDI calls to a specific service provider. Typically, you will use the higher-level calls in the javax.naming and javax.naming.directory packages.

Clients of a service provider should be familiar with the JNDI interface. Clients interested in writing a service object class should be familiar with the service provider interfaces and classes in the javax.naming.spi package. Service providers create libraries using the javax.naming.spi package, which contains classes and interfaces that define the behavior of a JNDI service provider. Figure 4.1 illustrates the JNDI architecture.

NOTE **Because most enterprise Java programmers use services rather than creating their own providers, this book does not cover the javax.naming.spi.**

Most application developers will use just the classes and interfaces defined in the javax.naming and javax.naming.directory pages, as shown in Figure 4.1. Refer to Table 4.1 for the available service providers.

NOTE **Service providers exist for many of the major directory and naming services. If you can't find a provider for a service you want to access, you can use SPI to create a JNDI solution that integrates seamlessly with other naming and directory services.**

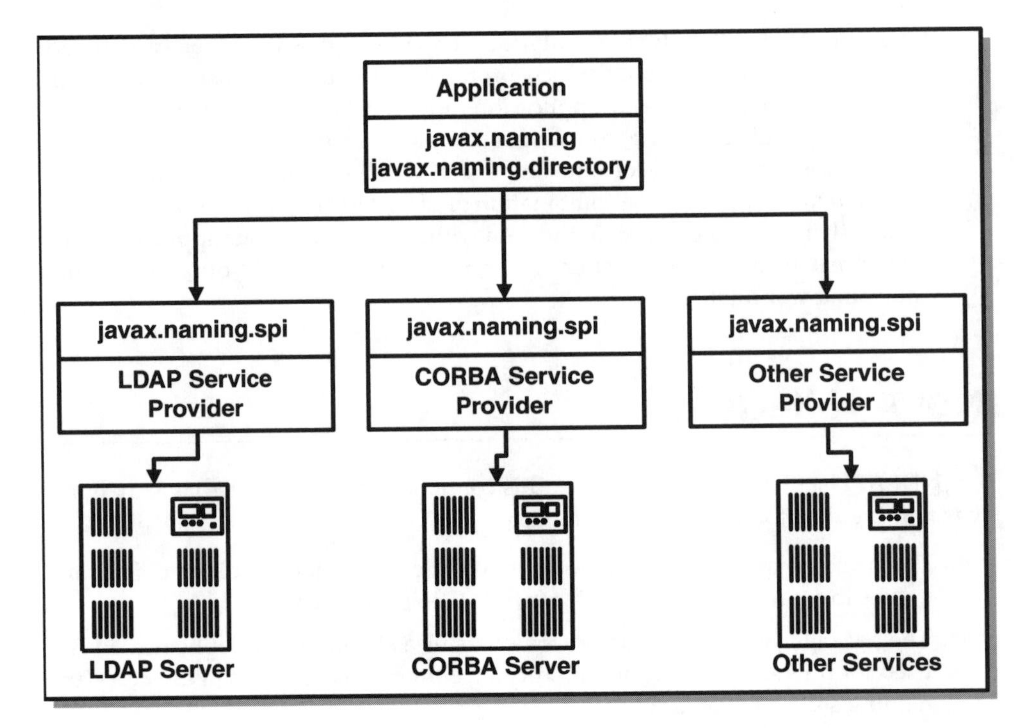

Figure 4.1 JNDI architecture.

Summary

JNDI enables all of the various resources in an enterprise, including files, printers, servers, security services, databases, and business processes, to work together. Most directory services have the ability to manage a set of resources. JNDI allows you to leverage the strengths of many services. Because of JNDI's design, you need to learn a fairly small API that allows your Java application access to a great variety of enterprise resources. The next chapter explores APIs and looks at code examples for using specific naming and directory services.

Using JNDI

This chapter covers the basic use of JNDI. The goal of this chapter is enable you to set up and create directory and naming service connections to access contexts via JNDI. This chapter discusses JNDI 1.1. For information on future versions of JNDI, browse the Sun Web site at http://java.sun.com/products/jndi.

JNDI provides a consistent model for accessing and manipulating enterprise resources such as the file system, CORBA, a directory service, or an application server, through Java. JNDI provides the additional benefit of allowing you to bind a Java object into these services. Figure 5.1 illustrates the JNDI architecture. At the top of the JNDI architecture is the Java application that wants to use JNDI. This application uses the javax.naming and javax.naming.directory packages to access JNDI services. The two client packages use the NamingManager, or DirectoryManager, to create the appropriate JNDI context for an application. A context represents a connection to a JNDI service provider. The code for a context is written by a JNDI service provider and implements the appropriate javax.naming.spi interfaces as well as the required interfaces from the client API. Ultimately, a service provider's implementation talks to a data source, like LDAP, the file system or the RMI registry. Most of these connections are hidden from the user behind a set of properties used to create the context.

This chapter focuses on the services available in the javax.naming and the javax.naming.directory packages. The service provider package is not discussed in detail because it will be used only by the few programmers creating JNDI service providers.

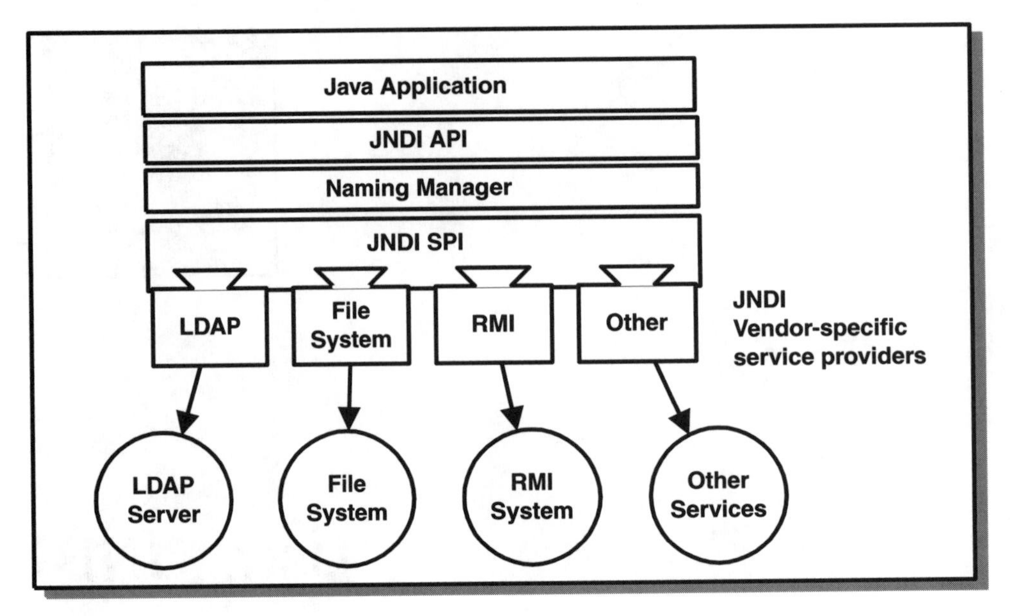

Figure 5.1 JNDI architecture.

Setup Requirements

In order to program with JNDI, you should have the following libraries accessible from your computer:

- JDK 1.1.2 or higher.
- JNDI package—your CLASSPATH should include jndi.jar; otherwise, the path to jndi.jar must be included on the command line for each example in this chapter.
- A service provider package for each service you access through JNDI.

You will need additional resources such as an LDAP server to use some of the later examples in this chapter. The CD-ROM contains the Java components you need to run the examples in this chapter; however, the final versions of the two service providers we have used were not released at publication time. To find a list of available providers and download the latest implementations provided by Sun, browse http://java.sun.com/products/jndi/serviceproviders.html. In addition, an LDAP configuration file is used with this chapter. You don't have to use this configuration file. Using another configuration won't affect the effectiveness of the examples, but it will produce results that differ from the examples discussed in this chapter.

If you intend to use JNDI with other directory and naming services such as CORBA, you will require additional service provider packages. The service provider is created by implementing the interfaces in the javax.naming.spi package for the specific naming service. In order to use any provider, you must put it in your CLASSPATH. For example, to use the file system service provider, you must have fscontext.jar in your

CLASSPATH. The jar fscontext.jar contains the implementation of the javax.naming.spi specifically for accessing the file system.

About the Sample Service Provider

The service provider used for most of the examples in this chapter is the file system provider called FsContext. This provider allows you to access your file system as a set of file system context objects that represent directories and as file objects that represent the files in those directories. Because files are represented with java.io.File, this provider is platform independent and can be used to access the directory structure on any platform on which the Java application runs.

FsContext provides naming services and associated names, file paths, with File objects. After the chapter explores the basic features of the naming services, it examines some of the advanced features of JNDI implemented by directory services, such as attribute manipulation and attribute queries. These features require the use of another provider. We chose the LDAP service provider. If you do not have LDAP, you should be able to follow along with the examples presented here and get an understanding of how directory services can be used.

NOTE **If you do not have access to an LDAP server, you can download one from the University of Michigan Web site at www.umich.edu/~dirsvcs/ldap/ldap.html.**

The goal of this chapter is to provide an overview of JNDI. Because the JNDI interface is consistent across all service providers, little time is spent on LDAP specific issues. Instead, the focus is on general use of JNDI. If you do have LDAP and choose to load the example configuration from your CD-ROM, you should have schema checking turned off for some of the later examples. We recommend turning it off because the schema we built is not necessarily self-consistent; it was designed for educational value and not production use.

The Naming Package

The naming package provides a set of classes and interfaces that are used to access any naming service for which you have a provider. Once you have a provider, you can perform the following functions using the naming package:

- Access a context, including listing and searching
- Rename, move, add, replace, or remove a binding for an object
- Store references to Java objects

This section steps through the components of the javax.naming package necessary to perform the procedures listed above.

Access a Context

The javax.naming package defines the Context interface. A *context* represents a starting point for a naming or directory service. The file system context in the examples for this chapter uses the set of files and directories stored on the local file system as a context. Figure 5.2 shows the directory structure used for the examples in this chapter. Because this structure represents the context in which the following naming examples are written, you should familiarize yourself with it. The CD-ROM contains a script to build the sample directory structure if you want to run the provided examples.

Once created, an object implementing the Context interface represents the root for all naming operations performed. The initial context can be thought of as the root for your file path; however, it is not always the same as the root directory in your file system. For example, it could be a subdirectory in your file system. Figure 5.3 illustrates how the marketing directory could be the root for a context.

To create a Context object, perform the following steps:

1. **Set up the environment.** JNDI uses a set of environment variables to tell it which service providers to access and how to initialize them. If you don't set one of these values, the System properties are used. Table 5.1 lists these properties. The simplest way to assign the environment is to load a property file as described for JDBC in Chapter 3, "Basic JDBC Programming," or create a hash table containing the environment settings. There are many properties that can be used to create a new context; study Table 5.1 carefully. However, as demonstrated in the examples in this chapter, only a few of these properties are required. In particular, the initial factory and provider URL will normally be required to create a context.

2. **Create an initial context.** JNDI requires that you have an initial context for all operations. This context is considered the root of your naming operations. For example, consider the directory structure in Figure 5.2. If an initial context is created at /, the path to report1.txt is /tmp/marketing/reports/report1.txt. However, if an initial context is created at /tmp/marketing/, the path is /reports/report1.txt.

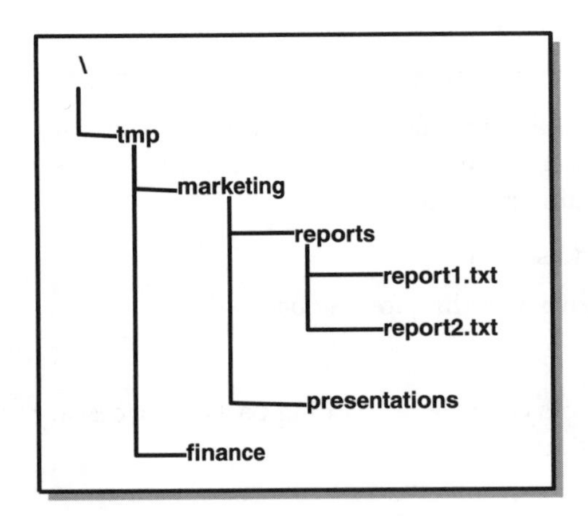

Figure 5.2 Example directory structure.

Table 5.1 Environment Variables for JNDI

ENVIRONMENT PROPERTIES	DESCRIPTION	CONSTANT DEFINED
Program Configuration		
java.naming.factory.initial	Class name of initial context factory to use. When unspecified, determined by the java.naming .factory.initial system property.	Context.INITIAL_CONTEXT_FACTORY
java.naming.factory.object	Colon-separated list of class names of object factory classes to use. When unspecified, determined by the java.naming.factory.object system property.	Context.OBJECT_FACTORIES
java.naming.factory.url.pkgs	Colon-separated list of package prefixes to use when loading in URL context factories. When unspecified, determined by the java.naming.factory.url.pkgs system property.	Context.URL_PKG_PREFIXES
Access Configuration		
java.naming.provider.url	Specifies configuration information for provider to use. When unspecified, determined by the java.naming .provider.url system property. When system property is unspecified, the URL is determined by the provider using its own configuration.	Context.PROVIDER_URL7
java.naming.dns.url	Specifies the DNS host and domain names to use for the JNDI URL context. When unspecified it is determined by the java.naming.dns.url system property.	Context.DNS_URL

Continues

Table 5.1 Environment Variables for JNDI *(Continued)*

ENVIRONMENT PROPERTIES	DESCRIPTION	CONSTANT DEFINED
Service-Related		
java.naming.authoritative	Specifies the authoritativeness of the service requested. True specifies that the most authoritative source is to be used. False specifies that the source doesn't need to be authoritative. When unspecified, defaults to false.	Context.AUTHORITATIVE
java.naming.batchsize	Specifies the preferred batch size to use when returning data via the service's protocol. This is a hint to the provider to return the results of operations in batches of the specified size so the provider can optimize its performance. When unspecified, determined by provider.	Context.BATCHSIZE
java.naming.referral	Specifies that referrals encountered by the service provider are to be followed automatically. If "follow," follow referrals automatically. If "ignore," ignore referrals encountered. If "throw," throw ReferralException when a referral is encountered. When unspecified, determined by provider.	Context.REFERRAL
Security		
java.naming.security.protocol	Security protocol to use for service. When unspecified, determined by provider.	Context.SECURITY_PROTOCOL
java.naming .security.authentication	Use "none," "simple," "strong," or a provider-specific string. When unspecified, determined by provider.	Context.SECURITY_AUTHENTICATION

Continues

Table 5.1 *Continued*

ENVIRONMENT PROPERTIES	DESCRIPTION	CONSTANT DEFINED
Security		
`java.naming .security.principal`	Identity of principal for the authentication scheme. When unspecified, defaults to the identity of user running the application.	`Context.SECURITY_PRINCIPAL`
`java.naming .security.credentials`	Principal's credentials for the authentication scheme. When unspecified, obtained by the provider on behalf of the user. This is done using the security system available to the provider, such as passwords or certificates.	`Context.SECURITY_CREDENTIALS`
Internationalization		
`java.naming.language`	Specifies a colon-separated list of preferred language to use with this service, such as "en-US: ja-JP-kanji". Languages are specified using tags defined in RFC 1766. When unspecified, the language preference may be determined by the provider.	`Context.LANGUAGE`

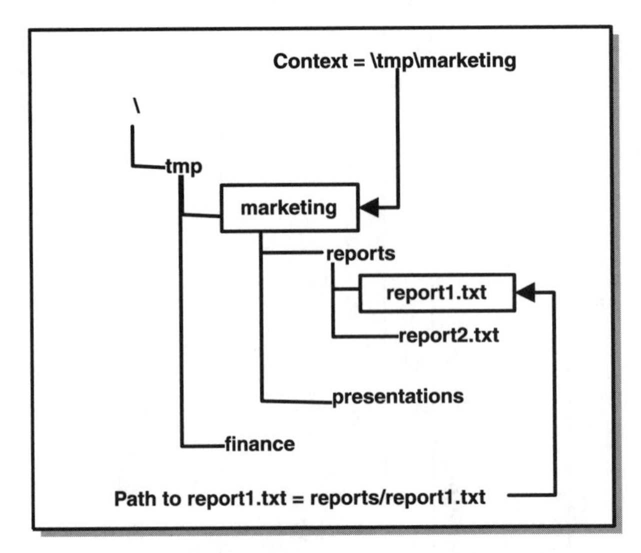

Figure 5.3 Setting a context.

The class java.naming.InitialContext implements the Context interface and can be used to create context objects. The following code defines a method that creates an InitialContext from command line arguments. The code used to create the context and assign the configuration properties is in bold. This example sets the user and password for the context, if one is provided. Later examples in this chapter skip this step to make them more readable. However, the examples using JNDI with Enterprise JavaBeans rely on this name and password to gain access to the application server. The values for these security properties are provider specific. Be sure to read the documentation for your provider to determine the values appropriate for the security parameters and the effects of setting these parameters.

```
static public Context getInitialContext(String[] args) throws
    Exception
{
    Properties p = new Properties();
    String url = "t3://localhost:7001";
    String user=null;
    String password=null;

    if ((args != null) && (args.length > 1))
    {
        for (int i = 0; i < args.length; i++)
        {
            if (args[i].equals("-url"))
                url = args[++i];
            else if (args[i].equals("-user"))
                user = args[++i];
            else if (args[i].equals("-password"))
                password = args[++i];
```

```
                else if (args[i].equals("-start"))
                    start = Long.parseLong(args[++i]);
                else if (args[i].equals("-max"))
                    max = Integer.parseInt(args[++i]);
            }
        }

        p.put(Context.INITIAL_CONTEXT_FACTORY,
                "weblogic.jndi.T3InitialContextFactory");

        p.put(Context.PROVIDER_URL, url);

        if (user != null)
        {
            p.put(Context.SECURITY_PRINCIPAL, user);

            if (password == null) password = "";

            p.put(Context.SECURITY_CREDENTIALS, password);
        }

        return new InitialContext(p);
    }
```

Once a context has been defined, it can be accessed using methods defined in the Context interface. These methods allow you to perform several operations, including listing the contents of a context or searching for a specific entry in the context.

List and Search a Context

The Context interface defines several methods for searching for objects in a naming or directory service. Table 5.2 lists the searching methods provided by a context. These methods allow you to retrieve any type of object located by a naming service, provided the provider can access it. The fsContext provider locates files and maps them to java.io.File. It locates directories and maps them to contexts that can, in turn, be accessed.

Table 5.2 Search Methods of Context

METHOD	USE
`list(Name)`, `list(String)`	Returns a NamingEnumeration of the names and the class names of their bound objects in the named context.
`listBindings(Name)`, `listBindings(String)`	Returns a NamingEnumeration of the names and their bound objects in the named context.
`lookup(Name)`, `lookup(String)`	Retrieves the named object.
`lookupLink(Name)`, `lookupLink(String)`	Retrieves the named object, following links except for the terminal atomic component of name.

Every method in the Context interface that requires a name as an argument has a version that accepts a String name argument and a version that accepts a Name object. Name is an interface that represents an ordered sequence of zero or more components. Name is used by a context to represent a composite name so that you can name an object with a name that spans multiple namespaces. If you intend to manipulate names or deal with multiple namespaces, this ability is a convenient way of referencing multiple namespaces in a single object. For simple operations with services such as the file system, strings are just as useful.

For example, given a context, ctx, for the marketing department files, you can view the available reports to print by specifying:

```
NamingEnumeration ne = ctx.list("Reports");
```

where the result of calling list is a javax.naming.NamingEnumeration containing the objects in the Reports context.

NamingEnumeration extends Enumeration to allow exceptions to be thrown after the enumeration. By calling the NamingEnumeration's hasMore() method instead of the Enumeration method hasMoreElements(), the NamingEnumeration throws an exception when no more elements are available. This allows you to handle exceptions on a list. Suppose you limited the size of a search to 10 elements. If the search returned 11 elements, the exception SizeLimitExceedException would be thrown when you tried to access the 11th element. The method hasMoreElements() would not throw an exception; it would just return false. A complete list of naming exceptions is shown in Table 5.16 at the end of this chapter.

As you can see in Table 5.2, two mechanisms are provided for searching a context: listing and lookups. *Listing* returns a list of the items in the context named in the methods argument. In the previous example, the call to list returned all of the objects in the Reports context. The *lookup* methods return a single object, with the provided name, in the current context.

Listing can be accomplished with one of two methods: list() and listBindings(). The method list() returns a NamingEnumeration containing a list of names and the class names they are bound to. The method listBindings() returns a NamingEnumeration containing a list of names and the objects they are bound to. In each case, you are expected to pass in the name of the context relative to the initial context to search. If you pass in "", the initial context is listed. Passing in null causes a NullPointerException.

When you perform a list operation on a service, the returned NamingEnumeration consists of NameClassPair instances. Table 5.3 lists the methods of this class. NameClassPair contains an object's name and the name of the object's class. Use this information to process the results of a lookup. This is especially handy if you are writing a directory browser because it allows you to get the listing of the names of the files without actually loading all of the objects in the directory.

The listBindings method returns an enumeration of objects of the Binding class. Table 5.4 lists the methods of this object. Binding extends NameClassPair and represents a name to object binding. Although listBindings() provides the same information, it is potentially a much more expensive operation because it actually retrieves the underlying objects. Use list if you only need the name of the object.

Table 5.3 NameClassPair Methods

METHOD	USE
`NameClassPair(String name, String className)`	This constructor creates an instance of a NameClassPair and sets the name and class name associated with it.
`NameClassPair(String name, String className, boolean isRelative)`	This constructor creates an instance of a NameClassPair and sets the name and class name associated with it. If isRelative is set to true, the name is set relative to the target context of the listing. If isRelative is set to false, the name is a complete URL string.
`String getClassName()`	Returns the class name of the object bound to this NameClassPair instance.
`String getName()`	Returns the name of this binding.
`boolean isRelative()`	Returns true if the name of this binding is relative to the target context.
`void setClassName(String name)`	Sets the class name for this binding.
`void setName(String name)`	Sets the name associated with this binding.
`void setRelative(boolean r)`	Sets whether the name of this binding should be considered relative to the target context.

The code listing that follows for a class List demonstrates how these methods work. This example program uses an initial context of /tmp/marketing and lists the contents of the context and the bindings for each object in the context. The JNDI elements of this example are in bold.

```
import javax.naming.*;
import javax.naming.directory.*;
import java.util.Hashtable;
import java.util.Enumeration;
import java.io.*;

// example use: java List

public class List
{
    public static void main(String[] args)
    {
        // Create a list of environment settings for our example.
        Hashtable env = new Hashtable();

        /*
          By specifying we are using refFSContextFactory, we will
          have the ability to access the file system and lookup and
```

Table 5.4 Binding Methods

METHOD	USE
`Binding(String name, Object obj)`	This constructor creates an instance of a binding with specific non-null name relative to the target context and the bound object, which can be null.
`Binding(String name, Object obj, boolean isRelative)`	This constructor creates an instance of a binding with specific non-null name and the bound object, which can be null. If isRelative is set to true, name is considered to be relative to the target context. If isRelative is false, name is considered to be a complete URL.
`Binding(String name, String className, Object obj)`	This constructor creates an instance of a binding with specific non-null name relative to the target context. If className, the class name of object (obj, the possibly null object bound to name) is returned using getClassName(). If obj is also null, getClassName() returns null.
`Binding(String name, String className, Object obj, boolean isRelative)`	This constructor creates an instance of a binding with specific non-null name. If className, the class name of object (obj, the possibly null object bound to name) is returned using getClassName(). If obj is also null, getClassName() returns null. If isRelative is set to true, name is considered to be relative to the target context. If isRelative is false, name is considered to be a complete URL.
`String getClassName()`	Returns the class name of the object bound to the name of this binding.
`Object getObject()`	Returns the actual object bound to the name of this binding.
`void setObject(Object obj)`	Sets the object associated with this binding to obj.

```
  store objects as well.
*/
env.put(Context.INITIAL_CONTEXT_FACTORY,
    "com.sun.jndi.fscontext.RefFSContextFactory");

// Specify the file system to search in this example.
env.put(Context.PROVIDER_URL,"file:/tmp/marketing");

try
{
    // Place holder for items in a context.
    Object item = null;

    // Based on our environment, set an initial context.
    Context initCtx = new InitialContext(env);
```

```
            NamingEnumeration nl = initCtx.list("reports");

            System.out.println("*** Printing context list ***");

            if (nl == null)
                System.out.println("\nNo items in name list");
            else
                while (nl.hasMore())
                {
                    item=nl.next();
                    System.out.println("item's class is " +
                      item.getClass().getName());
                    System.out.println(item);
                    System.out.println("");
                }

            System.out.println("*** Printing context" +
                " list bindings ***");

            nl = initCtx.listBindings("reports");
            if (nl == null)
                System.out.println("\nNo items in name list");
            else
                while (nl.hasMore())
                {
                    item=nl.next();
                    System.out.println("item's class is " +
                        item.getClass().getName());
                    System.out.println(item);
                    System.out.println("");
                }
        }catch(Exception e)
        {
            System.out.println(e);
            e.printStackTrace(System.out);
        }
    }
}
```

Figure 5.4 shows what would so far be returned from our example, assuming the previous code above was executed.

In addition to accessing a list of objects in a context, you can also access a specific object by using the lookup or lookupLink methods. These methods look for a specific object in the current context and return the object bound to the name you provide. Here is the code for an example, Print, that uses the lookup operation to retrieve the file report1.txt based on the directory structure in Figure 5.2 and displays the file.

```
import javax.naming.*;
import javax.naming.directory.*;
import java.util.Hashtable;
```

Figure 5.4 Results of calling list() and listBindings().

```
import java.util.Enumeration;
import java.io.*;

// example use: java Print

public class Print
{
public static void main(String[] args)
{
Hashtable env = new Hashtable();
        env.put(Context.INITIAL_CONTEXT_FACTORY,
"com.sun.jndi.fscontext.RefFSContextFactory");

        env.put(Context.PROVIDER_URL,"file:/tmp/marketing");

        try
        {
            Context initCtx = new InitialContext(env);

            // We assume we are reading in a file.
            File f =(File)initCtx.lookup("reports/report1.txt");

            //Print the file located
            if(f != null)
            {
                BufferedReader br =
new BufferedReader(new FileReader(f));
                String l = null;
                while((l = br.readLine()) != null)
                    System.out.println(l);
            }
        }
        catch(Exception e)
```

```
            {
                System.out.println(e);
                e.printStackTrace(System.out);
            }
        }
    }
```

The bold code above performs the lookup on the current context looking for reports/report1.txt. If the context had been / instead of /tmp/marketing, a lookup would have to explicitly be set to tmp/marketing/reports/report1.txt to perform the same lookup operation. All of these searching operations rely on the concept of object bindings, which we examine next.

Object Bindings

A *binding* is the name of an object, the name of the object's class, and the object itself. Context provides methods for manipulating these bindings. Table 5.5 lists these methods.

The examples in this section revolve around the fsContext service provider, but it is important to keep in mind that these same operations can be used for removing an object from a CORBA repository or adding personal contact information to an LDAP directory server. All the functions described in this section are useful with any provider. How that provider actually implements each function depends on the provider. The documentation on each provider will tell you how these functions work for that specific provider. For example, unbind deletes a file when using the file system provider, but with RMI it simply removes an object reference from the remote registry. Let's look at the unbind function first.

Table 5.5 Binding-Related Methods of Context

METHOD	USE
`bind(Name, Object)`, `bind(String, Object)`	Binds the name to the object in the context. Throws an exception if the name is already in use.
`createSubcontext(Name)`, `createSubcontext(String)`	Creates and binds a new context to the name.
`destroySubcontext(Name)`, `destroySubcontext(String)`	Destroys the named context and removes it from the namespace.
`rebind(Name, Object)`, `rebind(String, Object)`	Binds the name to the object, overwriting any existing binding.
`rename(Name oldName, Name newName)`, `rename(String oldName, String newName)`	Binds newName to the object bound to oldName and unbinds oldName.
`unbind(Name)`, `unbind(String)`	Unbinds the named object from the namespace.

Deleting an Object Binding

To delete report2.txt from the marketing reports directory, execute the command "java Delete report2.txt" to initiate the following code:

```
import javax.naming.*;
import java.util.Hashtable;

// Deletes files from the marketing directory
// example use: java Delete filename

public class Delete
{
    public static void main(String[] args)
    {
        // Define a starting point for operation.
        String initalContextString = "/tmp/marketing/reports";

        if(args.length < 1)
        {
            System.out.println("Usage: java Delete filename");
            System.exit(-1);
        }
        System.out.println("This program assumes the context is " +
            initialContextString);

        Hashtable env = new Hashtable();
  env.put(Context.INITIAL_CONTEXT_FACTORY,
"com.sun.jndi.fscontext.RefFSContextFactory");
        env.put(Context.PROVIDER_URL,"file:" + initalContextString);


        try
        {
            Context initCtx = new InitialContext(env);

            // Delete file or other object...
            System.out.println("Attempting to unbind " + args[0]);

            initCtx.unbind(args[0]);

            System.out.println("Done.");
        }catch(NamingException e)
        {
            System.out.println(e);
            e.printStackTrace(System.out);
        }
    }
}
```

The Delete program sets an initial context of /tmp/marketing/reports and requests that the user enter the name of a file to delete in that directory. The *unbind* method is called to unbind or delete the selected file. The initial context is set for safety as this program deletes files; we wouldn't want you to accidentally delete important files on your computer.

NOTE The fsContext provider will not delete directories, it will only delete files through the unbind method. Other providers may perform differently.

Renaming and Moving an Object

Using the rename method of a context allows you to change the name bound to the object. In the case of the file system provider, this is equivalent to changing the name of a file or directory. However, there is one difference: If the path to the named object differs from the path to the new name, the object is explicitly moved in the context. For example, if you rename /tmp/marketing to /tmp/products, the directory marketing will be renamed products. However, if you rename /tmp/marketing/reports/report1.txt to /tmp/report1.txt, the report1.txt file (object) will be moved into the subcontext /tmp. The program Rename in the code listed below takes two command line inputs: a file or directory name or path and the new path name. Try renaming/moving files and directories to get a feel for how this works.

```
import javax.naming.*;
import java.util.Hashtable;

// Rename filename1 to filename2
// example use: java Rename filename1 filename2
public class Rename
{
    public static void main(String[] args)
    {
        //This program renames any file you access, so be careful!
        String initialContextString = "/";

        if(args.length<2)
        {
            System.out.println(
                "Useage: java Rename filename1 filename2");
            System.exit(-1);
        }

        // Create a list of environment settings for our example.
        Hashtable env = new Hashtable();

        /*
          By specifying we are using refFSContextFactory, we will
          have the ability to access the file system and lookup
          and store objects as well.
```

```
        */
        env.put(Context.INITIAL_CONTEXT_FACTORY,
            "com.sun.jndi.fscontext.RefFSContextFactory");

        // Specify the file system to search in this example.
        env.put(Context.PROVIDER_URL,
            "file:" + initialContextString);

        try
        {
            // Based on our environment, set an initial context.
            Context initCtx = new InitialContext(env);

            System.out.println("Renaming " + args[0] +
                " to " + args[1]);
            initCtx.rename(args[0],args[1]);
            System.out.println("Done.");

        }catch(NamingException e)
        {
            System.out.println(e);
            e.printStackTrace(System.out);
        }
    }
}
```

The boldface code in the preceding listing renames the object bound to the name described by args[0]. The new binding for this object may be in a different part of the directory structure, based on the args[2] parameter. For example, the following code actually moves the reports directory (context) to /reportdir. This is because the initial context defined in the Rename program was set to /. If the initial context had been set to /tmp, reports would have been moved to /tmp/reportdir.

```
java Rename /tmp/marketing/reports reportdir
```

One thing to note is that if the initial context had been /tmp instead of / in the example, it would not have worked. Remember that the file paths are *relative* to the initial context. Because there is no file /tmp/tmp/marketing/reports, you would get an exception. Try various combinations of changing the initial context and the file paths to rename files and directories and move them relative to the initial context.

Replacing and Adding Objects

Another feature of the context is the ability to add objects. By combining the renaming feature and the ability to add objects, you can replace an object in a context. The following code listing describes a program Changes that does this.

```
import javax.naming.*;
import java.util.Hashtable;

// Rename the report directory and create a new report directory.
```

```
// example use: java Changes
public class Changes
{
public static void main(String[] args)
    {
        Hashtable env = new Hashtable();
env.put(Context.INITIAL_CONTEXT_FACTORY,
"com.sun.jndi.fscontext.RefFSContextFactory");

        env.put(Context.PROVIDER_URL,"file:/tmp/marketing");

        try
        {
            Context initCtx = new InitialContext(env);

            // Rename the reports directory.
            initCtx.rename("reports","oldreports");

            // Create new reports directory.
            initCtx.createSubcontext("reports");
        }catch(NamingException e)
        {
            System.out.println(e);
            e.printStackTrace(System.out);
        }
    }
}
```

All the operations in this section equate to simple file operations.

Next, let's look at how to use the binding operations to bind a Java object to the context. It is important to realize that while the file system has been used as the naming service for the examples, you can simply replace the service provider and, with little else, perform the same operations against an LDAP server, an RMI registry, or other service. For example, given a context for an LDAP server, you can store the report file object from your computer in LDAP using the following code:

```
...
ldapCtx.bind("cn=MyFileName", theFile);
//To retrieve the file object from LDAP execute:
File  theFile = (File)ldapCtx.lookup("cn=MyFileName");
...
```

NOTE **cn=MyfileName is a convention of LDAP and has nothing to do with JNDI specifically.**

Because the File class supports serialization, the LDAP service provider serializes the object into the directory server. However, not all services or service providers support serializing. For example, the file system service provider used thus far will not serialize objects. In this case, you can store objects that implement the Referenceable interface using a class called a *reference*. A referenceable object is an object that implements the method public Reference getReference() throws NamingException. This method returns information describing this particular object precisely enough that it could be reconstructed later by a factory class. Before exploring a referencing example, let's look at what a reference actually does for us.

Storing Java Objects as References

Objects are stored in naming and directory services in different ways. Some services can store serialized versions of your Java object. In such a case, you could simply serialize your object and store it for later retrieval. However, some naming and directory services do not support the storing of Java objects. In addition, other applications using the service may not be able to read serialized objects. Therefore, there are cases when a serialized Java object might not be the most appropriate representation of your data.

To handle the cases in which a serialized object cannot be stored, JNDI defines the reference class. A reference contains information on how to construct a copy of your object. JNDI attempts to turn references looked up from the directory into the Java objects they represent. Reference objects provide a way of recording address information about objects that themselves are not directly bound to the naming and directory service. Figure 5.5 illustrates the use of references for retrieving an object. Using references, you can seamlessly store and retrieve objects from your service without focusing on the representation of the data in a particular directory and naming service.

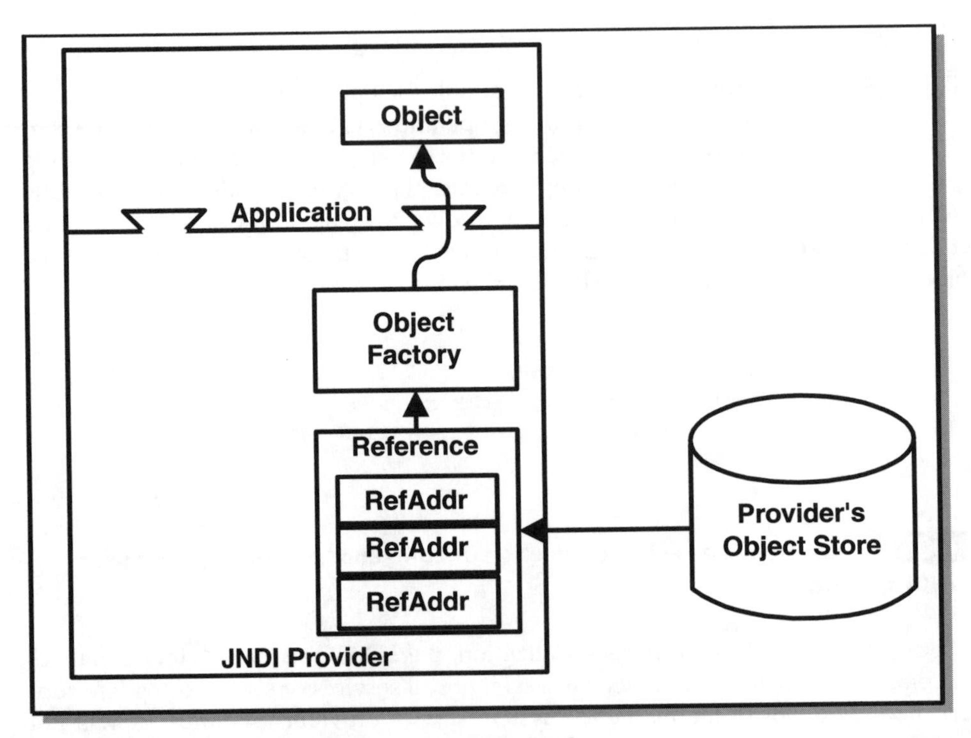

Figure 5.5 Storing and retrieving a Java object reference.

A reference consists of information to assist in creating an instance of the object to which this reference refers. This information includes:

- The class name of the object being referenced
- A vector of RefAddr objects representing the addresses
- The string name of the factory for the object and the location of the factory object

A reference contains the class name of the object as well as the class name and location of a factory object used to reproduce the object. These factories are discussed in detail in this section. Each address in the list identifies a communications end point for the same conceptual object. For example, an address could be a URL pointing at the data necessary to reconstruct the object. The order of the addresses in the list may be of significance to object factories that interpret the reference. Addresses are stored as instances of RefAddr.

RefAddr is an abstract class that defines an association between a string type and an object. This object is called the *content*. To access the type and content, you can use these methods:

```
public String getType()
public Object getContent()
```

The content is used to store information required to rebuild an object; and the type is used to identify the purpose of the content. For example, a reference for a Car object might store the value "red" under the type "color" and the value "Saturn" under the type "make." RefAddr also overrides the equals and hash code methods to ensure that two references are equal if their contents and type are equal.

JNDI defines two concrete subclasses of RefAddr. StringRefAddr stores a string, and BinaryRefAddr stores an array of bytes. These classes provide constructors to create the reference by specifying the content and type as arguments.

References are not synchronized. Threads that need to access a single reference concurrently should synchronize and provide locking.

In the case of the file system service provider, the object references are stored for a specified context in a file named .bindings. In the following example, a set of Car objects are created and bound to the file system. The main class, Bind.java, creates an initial context is set to the presentations subdirectory. Then several Car objects are instantiated, and they are bound into the file system by calling Context's rebind method. By using rebind, we can run the program repeatedly, replacing existing bindings with new ones. If the bind method was used and the example ran twice, an exception would be thrown. Finally, the car belonging to Cheryl is located using the lookup method of Context. The following code defines the Bind class.

```
import javax.naming.*;
import java.util.Hashtable;
import javax.naming.spi.ObjectFactory;

public class Bind
{
    public static void main(String[] args)
```

```
    {
Hashtable env = new Hashtable();
env.put(Context.INITIAL_CONTEXT_FACTORY,
"com.sun.jndi.fscontext.RefFSContextFactory");

        // Specify the filesystem to search in this example.
        env.put(Context.PROVIDER_URL,
            "file:/tmp/marketing/presentations/");

        try
        {
            Context initCtx = new InitialContext(env);
            /*
              Bind each customer into the file system.
              Use rebind in case they are already there.
              This way, earlier entries will be overwritten.
              Otherwise, if we used bind(), an exception would
              be thrown if we run this twice.
            */
            initCtx.rebind("Susan", new Car("Toyota","Camry"));
            initCtx.rebind("Cheryl", new Car("Saturn","Coupe"));
            initCtx.rebind("Nicole", new Car("Ford","Bronco"));

            Car c = (Car)initCtx.lookup("Cheryl");
            System.out.println(c);
        }catch(Exception e)
        {
            System.out.println(e);
            e.printStackTrace(System.out);
        }
    }
}
```

Here is what the /tmp/marketing/presentations/.bindings file contains after running the Bind program:

```
#This file is used by the JNDI FSContext.
#Sun Oct 11 19:50:11 PDT 1998
Susan/ClassName=Car
Nicole/RefAddr/0/Type=Car Description
Susan/RefAddr/0/Type=Car Description
Nicole/RefAddr/0/Encoding=String
Nicole/ClassName=Car
Cheryl/RefAddr/0/Type=Car Description
Nicole/FactoryName=CarFactory
Susan/FactoryName=CarFactory
Cheryl/ClassName=Car
Nicole/RefAddr/0/Content=Ford:Bronco
Cheryl/FactoryName=CarFactory
Cheryl/RefAddr/0/Content=Saturn:Coupe
Susan/RefAddr/0/Encoding=String
Susan/RefAddr/0/Content=Toyota:Camry
Cheryl/RefAddr/0/Encoding=String
```

The information in this file is generated by the service provider and tells the provider what object mappings have been made for the subcontext, presentations. This .bindings file is FSContext specific, but it shows how the context can store reference information for the caller.

The following code example is for the Car object. Notice that the class must implement the Referenceable interface, meaning it must implement a method called getReference(), which returns a Reference object. The Reference object should contain the name of the class, a string representation for reconstructing the object, the name of the factory class that reconstructs the object, and, if necessary, the location of the factory object. In this case, the make and model of the car are used to identify it. This information is stored in a StringRefAddr under the type "Car Description." If the Car class was used to define a remote object, you may want to include the server name where the object resides.

```
import javax.naming.*;

/*
   This class is referenceable class that can be stored by service
   providers like the file system provider.
*/
public class Car implements Referenceable
{
    String make;
    String model;

    public Car(String mk, String md)
    {
        make = mk;
        model = md;
    }

    public Reference getReference() throws NamingException
    {
        String cName = Car.class.getName();
        StringRefAddr cRef = new StringRefAddr("Car Description",
                make + ":" + model);
        String cfName = CarFactory.class.getName();

        Reference ref = new Reference(cName, cRef, cfName, null);

        return ref;
    }

    public String toString()
    {
        return (make+" "+model);
    }
}
```

When the Car object is bound, the service provider stores the reference values in the appropriate format for the service. Calling lookup causes the service provider to load the reference bound to the lookup name and use it to access the factory class responsible for reconstructing the object from the information provided by the reference. The CarFactory class code that follows implements the ObjectFactory interface, which is defined in javax.naming.spi. This interface includes the getObjectInstance method, which returns a newly constructed object based on the Reference object, obj. If a new object can't be reconstructed based on the parameters passed in, the factory is supposed to return null.

```
import java.util.Hashtable;
import javax.naming.*;
import javax.naming.spi.ObjectFactory;

/*
   This is an object factory that when given a reference for a Car
   object, will create an instance of that Car.
*/
public class CarFactory implements ObjectFactory
{
        public CarFactory()
     {
     }

        public Object getObjectInstance(Object obj, Name name,
              Context ctx, Hashtable env) throws Exception
     {
         if (obj instanceof Reference)
         {
              Reference ref = (Reference)obj;
              if (ref.getClassName().equals(Car.class.getName()))
              {
                  RefAddr addr = ref.get("Car Description");
                  if (addr != null)
                  {
                            String s = (String)addr.getContent();
                       int n = s.indexOf(":");
                       String make = s.substring(0,n);
                       String model = s.substring(n+1);
                       return new Car(make,model);
                  }
              }
         }
         return null;
     }
}
```

The method getObjectInstance parses the reference's components and tries to construct a reference that describes a Car object. The factory may ignore non-relevant attributes of the reference. For example, there could be an IP address of a remote Car object; this factory could ignore it and just create a new Car instead. If the factory fails to construct a car from the information in the reference, it can return null or throw an exception. The values of a reference object are interpreted by the factory object, so it is possible to have two different factory objects that construct completely different objects based on the same reference. The reference could be valid in both cases. For example, the car factory creates a simple Car object and returns it based on the make and model. However, the same reference could contain other information about the car such as the plant in which it is physically being built as well as the order id. A second factory class could read this extra information out of the reference and create an object that checks on the status of the car at the assembly plant.

The naming package provides quick access to objects provided by naming services. The next section looks at how directory packages can be used to perform more sophisticated queries.

The Directory Package

The directory package javax.naming.directory extends the javax.naming package to provide functionality for accessing directory services in addition to naming services. This package allows applications to do the following:

- Search a directory for objects based on specific attributes or values
- Control and optimize the search results
- Modify attributes of an object

The directory package is an extension to the naming package and leverages the functionality of the naming context operations. The directory package extends this functionality by providing more sophisticated searching and modification facilities that reflect the nature of directory services and tend to be more complex than a simple naming service. However, all of the searching methods described for naming services also apply to directory services.

Search for Objects

In order to search for objects in a directory, first create an object that implements the javax.naming.directory.DirContext interface, such as the class InitialDirContext. Once the context has been initialized, the methods listed in Table 5.6 can be used to execute several types of searches. DirContext extends the Context interface. This means any directory object can also be treated as a naming context.

There are several techniques for searching using the methods of DirContext. The LDAP example configuration and the LDAP service provider are used for the examples in this chapter.

The code snippet that follows Table 5.6 defines a class DirectoryExample that accesses an LDAP directory server. The provider URL references an LDAP server by using the ldap: protocol. The host, MyHost, should be replaced with the name of your LDAP server. The example assumes that there is a context called JNDIExample in your directory server.

Table 5.6 DirContext Searching Methods That Return NamingEnumeration

METHOD	USE
`search(String name, Attributes attrs)` or `search(Name name, Attributes attrs)`	Searches a context for objects that contain a set of attributes.
`search(String name, Attributes attrs, String[] returnAttrs)` or `search(Name name, Attributes attrs, String[] returnAttrs)`	Searches a context for objects that contain a set of attributes and retrieves the attributes specified in String[].
`search(String name, String filter, SearchControls sc)` or `search(Name name, String filter, SearchControls sc)`	Searches in the named context for entries that satisfy the search filter.
`search(String name, String filter, Object[] filterArgs, SearchControls sc)` or `search(Name name, String filter, Object[] filterArgs, SearchControls sc)`	Searches in the named context for entries that satisfy the search filter.

```
import javax.naming.*;
import javax.naming.directory.*;
import java.util.Hashtable;

public class DirectoryExample
{
    public static void main(String[] argc)
    {
        Hashtable env = new Hashtable(11);


        env.put(Context.INITIAL_CONTEXT_FACTORY,
            "com.sun.jndi.ldap.LdapCtxFactory");
        env.put(Context.PROVIDER_URL,
            "ldap://MyHost/o=JNDIExample");
        try
        {
            DirContext dctx = new InitialDirContext(env);
...
```

The DirContext interface defines methods for examining and updating attributes associated with an object in the directory context. The rest of this section describes these search techniques in more detail.

Searching with Attributes

The simplest technique for searching with DirContext is to search for all objects that contain a certain set of attributes. To do this:

1. Set the environment properties as you did for the Naming context.
2. Create a DirContext as demonstrated in the beginning of the "Search for Objects" section.

3. Specify the attributes you are looking for by defining javax.naming.directory .Attribute objects and storing them in a javax.naming.directory.Attributes array.
4. Execute the search by calling the search method of DirContext.
5. Process the results returned in a NamingEnumeration.

The directory package encapsulates an object's values in a javax.naming.directory.Attributes object. The javax.naming.directory.BasicAttributes class provides an implementation of the Attributes interface. Table 5.7 lists the methods defined in the Attributes interface.

NOTE **Don't confuse *Attributes*, an interface for managing collections of attributes, with *Attribute*, an interface for an object that represents a single attribute from a directory service.**

Attributes objects manage collections of objects that implement another interface called Attribute. Objects that implement the Attribute interface map Java objects to

Table 5.7 Attributes Interface Methods

METHOD	USE
`Object clone()`	Returns a copy of Attributes. The new Attributes object contains the same attributes as the original set. However, the attributes themselves are not cloned.
`Attribute get(String id)`	Returns the attribute with the given attribute id from the attribute set.
`NamingEnumeration getAll()`	Returns an enumeration of all attributes in the attribute set.
`NamingEnumeration getIDs()`	Returns an enumeration of the ids of all attributes in the attribute set.
`boolean isCaseIgnored()`	Returns true if the attribute set ignores the case of attribute identifiers when retrieving or adding attributes.
`Attribute put(Attribute attr)`	Adds a new non-null attribute to the attribute set and returns the Attribute that was stored in the Attributes set with the same id. If there was no other object with the id of this Attribute, null is returned.
`Attribute put(String id, Object value)`	Adds a new non-null attribute to the attribute set and sets the id of the attribute to the non-null id parameter value. The method returns the Attribute that was stored in the Attributes set with the same id. If there was no other object with the id of this Attribute, null is returned.
`Attribute remove(String id)`	Removes the attribute with the attribute id from the attribute set and returns this attribute or null if the attribute did not exist in the Attributes set.
`int size()`	Returns the number of attributes in the attribute set.

specific values from a directory service. The class javax.naming.directory.BasicAttribute implements the Attribute interface.

Table 5.8 lists the methods of the Attribute interface.

When the BasicAttributes class needs to create an Attribute, it uses a BasicAttribute. Table 5.9 lists the constructors for BasicAttributes.

For example, here is the code for searching for all people who have an e-mail address and a Web site attribute:

```
...
Hashtable env = new Hashtable(11);
env.put(Context.INITIAL_CONTEXT_FACTORY,
          "com.sun.jndi.ldap.LdapCtxFactory");
env.put(Context.PROVIDER_URL, "ldap://MyHost/o=JNDIExample");

try
{
      DirContext dctx = new InitialDirContext(env);

      Attributes attrs = new BasicAttributes(true);
      attrs.put(new BasicAttribute("email"));
      attrs.put(new BasicAttribute("website"));
```

Table 5.8 Attribute Interface Methods

METHOD	USE
`boolean add(Object value)`	Adds a value to the attribute.
`void clear()`	Deletes all values from this attribute.
`Object clone()`	Copies the attribute and references to its values. The values themselves are not cloned.
`boolean contains(Object value)`	Returns true if the value parameter is a value of this attribute.
`Object get()`	Returns one of this attribute's values. Null may be returned if it is a value of the attribute.
`NamingEnumeration getAll()`	Returns an enumeration of all of the attribute's values.
`DirContext getAttributeDefinition()`	Returns the attribute's schema definition as a DirContext.
`DirContext getAttributeSyntaxDefinition()`	Returns the syntax definition associated with the attribute as a DirContext.
`String getID()`	Returns the non-null id of this attribute.
`boolean remove(Object value)`	Deletes the value object from this attribute.
`int size()`	Returns the number of values in this attribute.

Table 5.9 Basic Attributes Constructors

METHOD	USE
`BasicAttributes()`	Constructs a new instance of BasicAttributes.
`BasicAttributes(boolean ignoreCase)`	Constructs a new instance of BasicAttributes and if ignoresCase is set to true, the cases of each identifier of the attributes added are ignored.
`BasicAttributes(String id, Object value)`	Constructs a new instance of BasicAttributes, with one attribute with the non-null id and the object value specified. If value is null, null is stored as the object value.
`BasicAttributes(String id, Object value, boolean ignoreCase)`	Constructs a new instance of BasicAttributes, with one attribute with the non-null id and the object value specified. If value is null, null is stored as the object value. If ignoresCase is set to true, the cases of each identifier of the attributes added are ignored.

```
        NamingEnumeration result = dctx.search("ou=People", attrs);

        while (result.hasMore())
            System.out.println(result.next());
...
```

In this code, BasicAttribute is created with a constructor that takes a boolean. By passing true into the constructor, the BasicAttributes object that is instantiated ignores the case of attributes it manages. If false was passed in, the BasicAttributes object would be case sensitive. This case sensitivity affects how searching will interpret the contents of the BasicAttributes. After the BasicAttributes object is created, two attributes of type BasicAttribute are added to the BasicAttributes object. After BasicAttributes is created and attributes have been inserted, it is passed to the search method of the context, which searches for all objects that have both a Web site and an e-mail attribute. The result of the search is a NamingEnumeration, which can be processed as it was in the Naming section. The output resembles Figure 5.6.

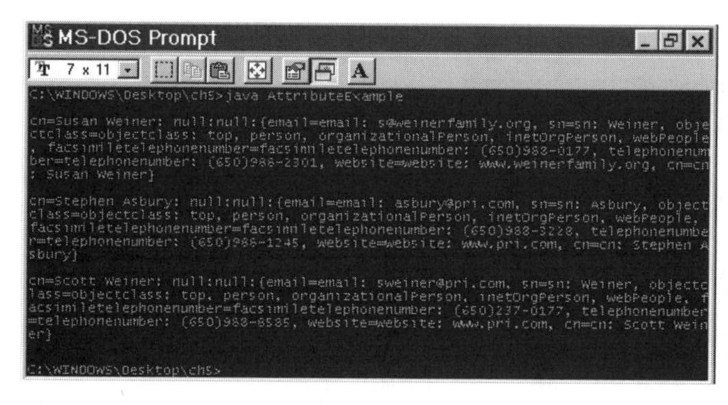

Figure 5.6 Searching with attributes.

By setting values for these searches, you can look for all people who have an e-mail address and the Web site www.pri.com. In the following code you will see that a value of www.pri.com has been added to the construction of the Web site BasicAttribute. The attributes and their values affect the choice of objects that are retrieved as part of the search. An Attributes list can be reused. For example, you could update it to include new values and re-execute the search. In this way you could narrow a search by filling in more and more details, or widen a search by removing attributes from the Attributes collection.

```
...
Hashtable env = new Hashtable(11);
env.put(Context.INITIAL_CONTEXT_FACTORY,
            "com.sun.jndi.ldap.LdapCtxFactory");
env.put(Context.PROVIDER_URL, "ldap://MyHost/o=JNDIExample");
try
{
        DirContext dctx = new InitialDirContext(env);

        Attributes attrs = new BasicAttributes(true);
        attrs.put(new BasicAttribute("email"));
        attrs.put(new BasicAttribute("website","www.pri.com"));

        NamingEnumeration result = dctx.search("ou=People", attrs);

        while (result.hasMore())
             System.out.println(result.next());
...
```

NOTE **Updates to BasicAttributes such as removing an attribute do not affect the corresponding representation in the directory. Updates to the directory can be affected only using modification operations in the DirContext interface.**

The output will resemble Figure 5.7.

A collection of attributes can be used to build a wide or narrow search criteria. Regardless of the directory service you are connected to, a collection of objects that represents matches for the search is returned. However, often you are not interested in getting back

Figure 5.7 Results of fetching with attribute values.

a collection of objects; rather, you would like only certain attributes from the objects. For example, you may want only the telephone numbers for all the customers rather than retrieving all the information you have on the customers. The next section will show you how to do this.

Retrieving Specific Attributes

Another variation of the search method allows us to specify which attributes to fetch from the directory. In other words, rather than retrieving all attributes of all objects returned, we can specify specific attributes to be returned, thus optimizing the search. For instance, if we wanted to retrieve only the name and e-mail of each person in the last example, the code can be modified like this:

```
...
Hashtable env = new Hashtable(11);
env.put(Context.INITIAL_CONTEXT_FACTORY,
        "com.sun.jndi.ldap.LdapCtxFactory");
env.put(Context.PROVIDER_URL, "ldap://MyHost/o=JNDIExample");
try
{
        DirContext dctx = new InitialDirContext(env);

        String[] attrIDs = {"cn", "email"};
        new BasicAttributes(true);
        attrs.put(new BasicAttribute("email"));
        attrs.put(new BasicAttribute("website","www.pri.com"));

        NamingEnumeration result =
            dctx.search("ou=People", attrs, attrIDs );

        while (result.hasMore())
             System.out.println(result.next());
...
```

The output resembles Figure 5.8. Compare the results with Figure 5.7. In Figure 5.8, only the values specified in the attrIDs array were retrieved. In both cases, a set of objects that are stored in a NamingEnumeration were retrieved. The next section discusses how to process these objects.

Figure 5.8 Results of fetching specific attributes.

Processing a Search Result

The result returned from these searches is actually a subclass of Bindings called a search result. Table 5.10 lists the SearchResult methods.

Table 5.10 SearchResult Methods

METHOD	USE
`SearchResult(String name, Object obj, Attributes attrs)`	This constructor creates a search result with the non-null name of the search item relative to the context, the object (which can be null bound to the name), and the list of attributes to return from the search.
`SearchResult(String name, Object obj, Attributes attrs, boolean isRelative)`	This constructor creates a search result with the non-null name of the search item, the object (which can be null bound to the name), and the list of attributes to return from the search. If isRelative is true, the name of the search item is relative to the context of the search. If isRelative is false, name is a complete URL.
`SearchResult(String name, String className, Object obj, Attributes attrs)`	This constructor creates a search result with the non-null name of the search item relative to the context, the name of the class of the object bound to name, the object (which can be null bound to the name), and the list of attributes to return from the search. If className is null, the class name for obj is returned with getClassName(). If obj is null, getClassName() will return null.
`SearchResult(String name, String className, Object obj, Attributes attrs, boolean isRelative)`	This constructor creates a search result with the non-null name of the search item, the name of the class of the object bound to name, the object (which can be null bound to the name), and the list of attributes to return from the search. If isRelative is true, the name of the search item is relative to the context of the search. If isRelative is false, name is a complete URL. If className is null, the class name for obj is returned with getClassName(). If obj is null, getClassName() will return null.
`Attributes getAttributes()`	Returns the attributes of this search result.
`void setAttributes(Attributes attrs)`	Sets the attributes for this search result to attrs.
`String toString()`	Returns a string representation of this binding.

Using a search result, you could you could use the following program to print the results:

```
import java.util.Hashtable;
import javax.naming.*;
import javax.naming.directory.*;

public class AttributeExample
{
    public static void main(String[] argc)
    {
        Hashtable env = new Hashtable(11);
        env.put(Context.INITIAL_CONTEXT_FACTORY,
             "com.sun.jndi.ldap.LdapCtxFactory");

        // Replace MyHost with the host name of your LDAP server.
        env.put(Context.PROVIDER_URL,
            "ldap://MyHost/o=JNDIExample");
        try
        {
            DirContext dctx = new InitialDirContext(env);

            Attributes attrs = new BasicAttributes(true);
            attrs.put(new BasicAttribute("email"));
            attrs.put(new BasicAttribute("website","www.pri.com"));

            NamingEnumeration result =
              dctx.search("ou=People", attrs);

            // Print each search result.
            while (result.hasMore())
            {
                SearchResult sr = (SearchResult)result.next();
                System.out.println("Result = " + sr.getName());
                Attributes srchAttrs = sr.getAttributes();

                NamingEnumeration attributes = srchAttrs.getAll();

                // For each result, print the attributes.
                while(attributes.hasMore())
                {
                    Attribute attr = (Attribute)attributes.next();
                    System.out.println("Attribute: " +
                        attr.getID());
                    NamingEnumeration values = attr.getAll();

                    // Attributes can have multiple values
                    while(values.hasMore())
                    {
                        Object value = values.next();
                        System.out.println("Value = " + value);
                    }
                }
```

```
                }
            }catch(Exception e)
            {
                System.out.println(e);
            }
        }
    }
```

In this code listing, the directory package is imported, and then a context is initialized, as usual. Then the attributes are inserted in a BasicAttributes object and passed into the search method. The search method returns a NamingEnumeration containing a list of search results. Iterate through each search result, obtaining a list of attributes by calling the SearchResult method getAttributes. This method returns another NamingEnumeration containing a list of attributes associated with the current search result. An attribute can have more than one value associated with it, just as a person can have more than one home phone number, so we iterate through these by calling the Attribute method getAll, which returns yet another NamingEnumeration containing a list of values for this attribute. Each of these values is then printed. The output resembles Figure 5.9.

The next section discusses how filters can be used to create even more robust searching criteria by using logical operators and other commands to create specific search criteria.

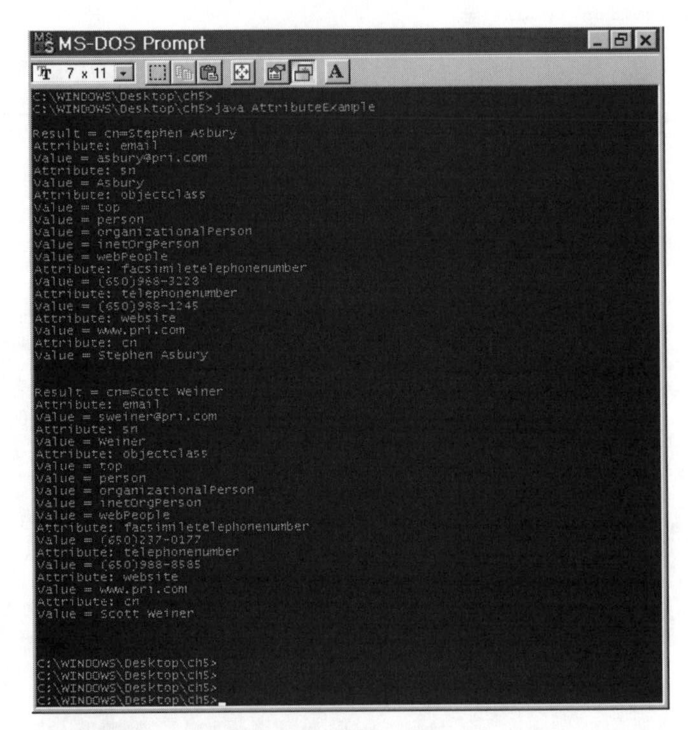

Figure 5.9 Processing SearchResults.

Table 5.11 Search Filter Symbols

SYMBOL	DESCRIPTION
&	Logical and. All items in the list must be true, as in (&(a=1)(b=2)).
|	Logical or. One or more of the items must be true, as in (|(a=1)(b=2)).
!	Not. The negated item must be false, as in (!(3=4)) is true.
=	Checks for equality based on the matching rule of the attribute.
~=	Checks for approximate equality based on the matching rule of the attribute.
>=	Checks that the attribute is greater than the value.
<=	Checks that the attribute is less than the value.
=*	Checks for existence of the attribute.
*	In an equality test; represents a wildcard representing zero or more characters at that position, as in (name=Alb*).
\	Used for escaping *, (, and) inside an attribute value.

Searching with Filters

The search methods of DirContext can take a filter string. The string follows the search expression patterns in RFC 2254. For example, to search for the person with www.pri.com as a Web site and an e-mail address starting with "kerry," you would use "(&(email=kerry*)(website=www.pri.com))".

Each item in the filter contains an attribute identifier and an attribute value or symbols representing the attribute value. Table 5.11 lists the expression symbols. In the example above, (website=www.pri.com) would denote an attribute called website that must have the value www.pri.com. The expression (email=kerry*) means that the attribute email must exist and have a value starting with kerry. It doesn't matter if the full e-mail address is kerry@pri.com, kerry@wiley.com, or some other value. To check if the object has an attribute called phone with any value, use the expression (phone=*). This means that phone attribute must exist, but its value does not matter.

Each set of attribute values must be enclosed in parentheses. Parenthetical attribute/value pairs can be combined using the logical operators in Table 5.11. To combine multiple operators, use parentheses. For example, to create a filter to find all people whose name began with the letter E or who have a phone number, an e-mail address, and a Web site, specify (| (cn=E*)(&(phone=*)(website=*))).

The following code list for a program called FilterExample returns a NamingEnumeration of people with a name beginning with E or having an account with more than $1,005 in it.

```
import javax.naming.*;
import javax.naming.directory.*;
import java.util.Hashtable;
```

```
public class FilterExample
{
    public static void main(String[] argc)
    {
        Hashtable env = new Hashtable(11);

        env.put(Context.INITIAL_CONTEXT_FACTORY,
            "com.sun.jndi.ldap.LdapCtxFactory");
        env.put(Context.PROVIDER_URL,
            "ldap://MyHost/o=JNDIExample");

        try
        {
            DirContext dctx = new InitialDirContext(env);

            String filter = "(&(cn=E*)(account>1005))";

            NamingEnumeration result =
                dctx.search("ou=People", filter, null);

            while (result.hasMore())
            {
                SearchResult sr = (SearchResult)result.next();
                System.out.println("Result = " + sr.getName());
            }
        }catch(NamingException e)
        {
           System.out.println(e);
        }
    }
}
```

This code creates an initial context on our LDAP server, then creates a filter string. The string is passed as a parameter to the search method, which searches the named context (people) relative to the initial context for objects meeting the filter criteria. Then the resulting NamingEnumeration is processed and the results are printed. The output resembles Figure 5.10, which shows that two people fit the filter criteria. Both have names starting with E, and both have an account with a balance greater than $1,005 in the server.

All of the search examples thus far have ignored performance issues because the example LDAP server has very few records. Consider what would happen if a search was performed for all records in the U.S. phone directory. Obviously, limiting the

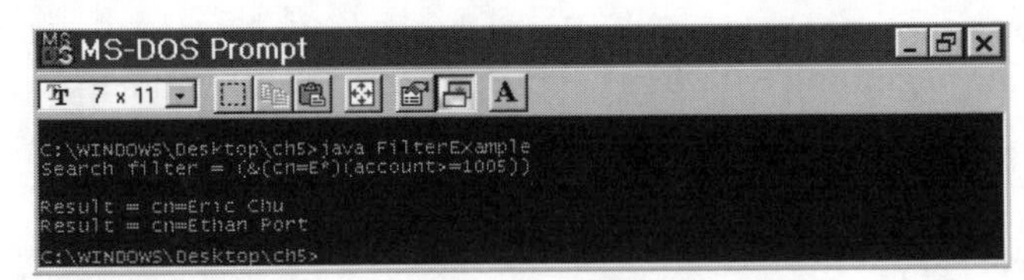

Figure 5.10 Results of using a filter.

search results is important. The next section discusses how to deal with this and other performance issues within JNDI.

Configure the Search with SearchControls

Recall that in the last example, the search method required an additional parameter that was set to null. This parameter is a SearchControls object. SearchControls allows you to fine-tune the performance of your search. The SearchControls methods are listed in Table 5.12.

Table 5.12 SearchControls Methods

METHOD	USE
`SearchControls()`	This constructor creates an instance of SearchControls with defaults set to search one level, with no maximum return limit for search results, with no time limit for a search, that returns all attributes associated with objects that satisfy the search filter, and returns the name and class but not the named object itself. Links are not dereferenced during search.
`SearchControls(int scope, long climit, int tlimit, String[] attrs, boolean retobj, boolean deref)`	This constructor creates an instance of SearchControls with scope set to OBJECT_SCOPE, ONELEVEL_SCOPE, or SUBTREE_SCOPE. The parameter tlimit sets the maximum number of milliseconds to wait before returning if the search is taking awhile. If tlimit is set to 0, the search will wait indefinitely, if necessary. The parameter deref specifies that the search should dereference links during search if deref is set to true. The parameter climit specifies the maximum number of entries to return from the search. If climit is set to 0, return all entries that satisfy the filter. The parameter retobj specifies that the result should return the object bound to the name of the entry if retobj is set to true. The parameter attrs contains the identifiers of the attributes to return. If attrs is null, all attributes are returned. If attrs is not null but contains no identifiers, no attributes will be returned.
`long getCountLimit()`	Returns the maximum number of entries that will be returned as a result of the search.
`boolean getDerefLinkFlag()`	Returns true if links will be dereferenced during the search.
`String[] getReturningAttributes()`	Returns the array of attributes that will be returned as part of the search.

Continues

Table 5.12 SearchControls Methods *(Continued)*

METHOD	USE
`boolean getReturningObjFlag()`	Returns true if object values will be returned as part of the result.
`int getSearchScope()`	Returns the search scope for these search controls. The search scope is OBJECT_SCOPE, ONELEVEL_SCOPE, or SUBTREE_SCOPE.
`int getTimeLimit()`	Returns the maximum time limit in milliseconds that the search controls will wait for results.
`void setCountLimit(long limit)`	Sets the maximum number of entries to be returned as a result of the search.
`void setDerefLinkFlag( boolean on)`	Sets the search controls such that if on is true, the links will be dereferenced during the search.
`void setReturningAttributes( String[] attrs)`	Specifies the attributes that will be returned as part of the search.
`void setReturningObjFlag( boolean on)`	Sets the search controls such that if on is true, the object values will be returned as part of the search results.
`void setSearchScope(int scope)`	Sets the search scope to one OBJECT_SCOPE, ONELEVEL_SCOPE, or SUBTREE_SCOPE.
`void setTimeLimit(int ms)`	Sets the maximum time limit in milliseconds that the search controls will wait for results.

Using the SearchControls, you can limit the number of objects returned from the search.

NOTE **search(name, filter, *null*) is equivalent to search(name, filter, *new SearchControls()*).**

The default SearchControls constructor sets the following values:

- Search one level
- No maximum return limit for search results
- No time limit for search
- Return all attributes associated with objects that satisfy the search filter
- Do not return named object (return only name and class)
- Do not dereference links during search

A SearchControls object is not synchronized, so multiple threads trying to access and modify a single SearchControls instance should lock the object. Table 5.13 lists the values stored when a SearchControls instance is serialized.

The SearchControls can be used to control the attributes returned as well as the objects returned.

Return Selected Attributes Using SearchControls

The search methods of DirContext in Table 5.6 that take a SearchControls parameter do not accept an attribute list. In cases in which you are using SearchControls, you do not need that extra parameter. The SearchControls method setReturningAttributes allows you to specify an array of attribute names. This array specifies which attributes will be returned as a result of the search.

NOTE **If not all of the attributes listed in the returning attributes array are available, the available attributes are returned. The purpose of the setReturningAttributes method is to limit the scope of the results.**

Here is what the code for retrieving a set of attributes using a SearchControls may look like:

```
import javax.naming.*;
import javax.naming.directory.*;
import java.util.Hashtable;

public class SearchControlsExample
{
```

Table 5.13 SearchControls Serialized Values

FIELD	PURPOSE
`String[] attributesToReturn`	Contains the list of attributes to be returned in SearchResult for each matching entry of search. If attributesToReturn returns null, all attributes are to be returned.
`long countLimit`	Contains the maximum number of SearchResults to return.
`boolean derefLink`	Indicates whether JNDI links are dereferenced during search.
`boolean returnObj`	Indicates whether the object is returned as part of the SearchResult.
`int searchScope`	Contains the scope to apply to the search. The scope is one for the following: ONELEVEL_SCOPE, OBJECT_SCOPE, or SUBTREE_SCOPE.
`int timeLimit`	Contains the maximum number of milliseconds to wait before returning from search.

```
    public static void main(String[] argc)
    {
        Hashtable env = new Hashtable(11);

        env.put(Context.INITIAL_CONTEXT_FACTORY,
            "com.sun.jndi.ldap.LdapCtxFactory");
        env.put(Context.PROVIDER_URL,
            "ldap://MyHost/o=JNDIExample");

        try
        {
            DirContext dctx = new InitialDirContext(env);

            String filter = "(&(cn=S*)(account>1005))";

            String[] attrIDs = {"cn", "email"};
            SearchControls sc = new SearchControls();
            sc.setReturningAttributes(attrIDs);

            NamingEnumeration result =
                dctx.search("ou=People", filter, sc);

            while (result.hasMore())
            {
                SearchResult sr = (SearchResult)result.next();
                System.out.println("Result = " + sr.getName());
            }
        }catch(NamingException e)
        {
            System.out.println(e);
        }
    }
}
```

In this example, a SearchControls object is instantiated, and its method setReturningAttributes is passed an array of attribute names. This SearchControls object is passed into the search method and controls the result by limiting the attributes returned to name (cn is an LDAP convention standing for *common name*) and email. This process results in a query similar to passing in an attributes list. The output of the example resembles Figure 5.11.

As you can see, only the attributes specified in SearchControls were retrieved.

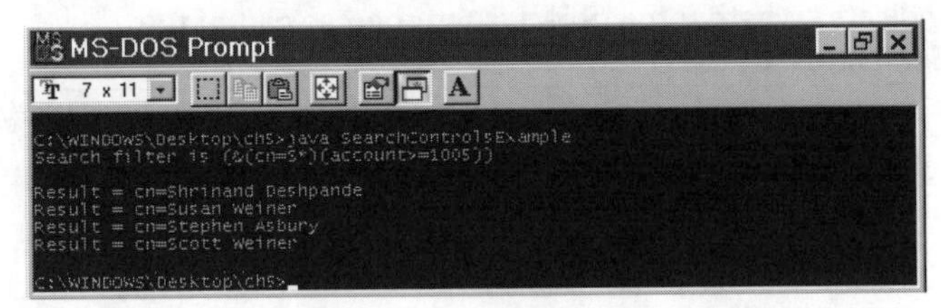

Figure 5.11 Results of fetching specific attributes.

Control the Scope of a Search

By default, using SearchControls when searching a directory sets your search scope to SearchControls.ONELEVEL_SCOPE. Only the currently named context is searched for matches to your filter. Other options include:

- **SearchControls.SUBTREE_SCOPE.** Searches the named context and all sub-contexts.
- **SearchControls.OBJECT_SCOPE.** Searches the named object only to determine if it matches the search filter.

Here is an example of using a SUBTREE_SCOPE:

```
import javax.naming.*;
import javax.naming.directory.*;
import java.util.Hashtable;

public class SearchScopeExample
{
    public static void main(String[] argc)
    {
        Hashtable env = new Hashtable(11);

        env.put(Context.INITIAL_CONTEXT_FACTORY,
            "com.sun.jndi.ldap.LdapCtxFactory");
        env.put(Context.PROVIDER_URL,
            "ldap://MyHost/o=JNDIExample");

        try
        {
            DirContext dctx = new InitialDirContext(env);

            String filter = "(&(cn=S*)(account>1000))";

            String[] attrIDs = {"cn", "email"};
            SearchControls sc = new SearchControls();
            sc.setReturningAttributes(attrIDs);
            sc.setSearchScope(SearchControls.SUBTREE_SCOPE);

            NamingEnumeration result =
                dctx.search("ou=People", filter, sc);

            while (result.hasMore())
            {
                SearchResult sr = (SearchResult)result.next();
                System.out.println("Result = " + sr.getName());
            }
        }catch(NamingException e)
        {
            System.out.println(e);
```

```
            }
        }
    }
```

This code searches the initial context of the named object (People) and any subcontexts beneath it. Figure 5.12 shows how the results differ if the SUBTREE_SCOPE is replaced with OBJECT_SCOPE or ONELEVEL_SCOPE. Use OBJECT_SCOPE to search only the named object, ONELEVEL_SCOPE to search the entire context of the named object, and SUBTREE_SCOPE to search the context and all its subcontexts. Obviously, SUBTREE_SCOPE could be a costly search for a large directory structure.

Search controls are powerful tools for helping you narrow your search and improve performance. However, search controls can do much more, as the next few sections will show.

Traverse Links

Services may support the notion of a link. A *link* is an entry in a context that references another entry. This is similar to a symbolic link in a file system. Your search can be configured to either traverse these links, looking for matches to a search, or it can be configured to ignore the path of the link. To do this, call the SearchControls method setDerefLinkFlag and pass a Boolean. Here is an example:

```
...
SearchControls sc = new SearchControls();
// Traverse links
sc.setDerefLinkFlag(true);
...
```

By setting the dereference link flag to true in this code, a search traverses links in the directory and continues the search. A setting of false would prevent such a traversal and thereby shorten the search.

Retrieve Objects

SearchControls allows you to specify whether you want to retrieve objects that are bound to your directory or just the name of the object and its class. By bringing back only the names of the object and class, you can greatly improve the performance of a

Figure 5.12 SearchControls scopes.

query. To do this, call the SearchControls method setReturningObjFlag and pass a Boolean. Here is an example:

```
...
SearchControls sc = new SearchControls();
// Retrieve the actual object from the directory
sc.setReturningObjFlag(true);
...
```

By setting the return object flag to true in this code, the search returns a set of objects from the directory. This results in a slower search but returns much more data. Setting this flag to false only returns the names of the objects, which is a much faster operation. Set this flag to false if you only want to browse the directory rather than actually fetching and manipulating the objects in it.

Control the Number of Results

At times, you search a directory and your query returns a large number of results. It is often a good idea to control the number of results so your program does not get overwhelmed by gigabytes of data. To do this, call the SearchControls method setCountLimit and pass in the number of results you want. Then your search will not return more than that many results. If there are more results than are returned, the exception SizeLimitExceededException is thrown by the NamingEnumeration. To retrieve all results, set the SearchControl's count limit to 0. Here is an example:

```
...
try
{
    DirContext dctx = new InitialDirContext(env);

    String filter = "(&(cn=E*)(account>1000))";

    SearchControls sc = new SearchControls();
    sc.setCountLimit(5);

    NamingEnumeration result =
         dctx.search("ou=People", filter, sc );

    while (result.hasMore())
         System.out.println(result.next());
} catch(SizeLimitExceededException se)
{

System.out.println("More than five objects returned...");
} catch(NamingException ne)
{
...
```

By setting the count limit to 5 in this code, only the first five results are returned.

Set a Time Limit on Retrieving Results

SearchControls allows you to limit the amount of waiting time for results. This is useful when you don't want your program to block for a long time on searches that are taking awhile due to the performance of the server, the network, and so on. To do this, call the SearchControls method setTimeLimit and pass in the number of milliseconds you are willing to wait. Then the search returns results within that span of time, or the exception TimeLimitExceededException is thrown. Set the time limit to 0 to wait forever. Here is an example:

```
...
try
{
    DirContext dctx = new InitialDirContext(env);

    String filter = "(&(cn=E*)(account>1000))";

    SearchControls sc = new SearchControls();
    // Wait 2 seconds
    sc.setTimeLimit(2000);

    NamingEnumeration result =
          dctx.search("ou=People", filter, sc );

    while (result.hasMore())
        System.out.println(result.next());
} catch(TimeLimitExceededException te)
{

System.out.println("More than two seconds have passed...");
} catch(NamingException ne)
{
...
```

By setting the time limit, you force a search to return in a fixed amount of time. In this code, the setting of 2000 means that if the query cannot return due to a large number of results or a network failure, the search will be canceled after two seconds, which means the user is not subjected to a long wait for a response.

Modify Attributes

Now that values have been retrieved from the directory, let's look at techniques for modifying the values of an object in the directory. The DirContext method modifyAttributes can be used for this purpose. Table 5.14 lists the variations of this method.

The simple form of the modifyAttributes method takes a named object (Name or String), a modification operation (listed below), and a list of attributes to modify (instance of Attributes).

Table 5.14 DirContext modifyAttributes Method Variations

METHOD	USE
`void modifyAttributes(Name name, int mod_op, Attributes attrs)`	Modifies the attributes contained in attrs of the object described by the non-null name. The operation to perform is ADD_ATTRIBUTE, REPLACE_ATTRIBUTE, or REMOVE_ATTRIBUTE. The operations occur in no particular order.
`void modifyAttributes(Name name, ModificationItem[] mods)`	Performs the modifications of the attributes as specified in mods of the object described by the non-null name. The operations occur in the order they are defined in the ModificationItem array.
`void modifyAttributes(String name, int mod_op, Attributes attrs)`	Modifies the attributes contained in attrs of the object described by the non-null name. The operation to perform is ADD_ATTRIBUTE, REPLACE_ATTRIBUTE, or REMOVE_ATTRIBUTE. The operations occur in no particular order.
`void modifyAttributes(String name, ModificationItem[] mods)`	Performs the modifications of the attributes as specified in mods of the object described by the non-null name. The operations occur in the order they are defined in the ModificationItem array.

The modification operation can be one of the following constants:

- DirContext.ADD_ATTRIBUTE
- DirContext.REPLACE_ATTRIBUTE
- DirContext.REMOVE_ATTRIBUTE

For example, given a person named John, suppose that you want to add an e-mail address john@pri.com and an empty website address attribute. The code below uses the modifyAttributes method of DirContext to specify that a set of attributes should be added to the object John in the current context.

```
import javax.naming.*;
import javax.naming.directory.*;
import java.util.Hashtable;

public class Modify1Example
{
    public static void main(String args[])
    {
        Hashtable env = new Hashtable(11);


        env.put(Context.INITIAL_CONTEXT_FACTORY,
```

```
                "com.sun.jndi.ldap.LdapCtxFactory");
        env.put(Context.PROVIDER_URL,
                "ldap://MyHost/o=JNDIExample");
        try
        {
            DirContext dctx = new InitialDirContext(env);
            Attributes attrs = new BasicAttributes(true);
            attrs.put(new BasicAttribute("email","john@pri.com"));
            attrs.put(new BasicAttribute("website"));

            dctx.modifyAttributes("cn=John, ou=People",
                                  DirContext.ADD_ATTRIBUTE,
                                  attrs);
        }catch(Exception e)
        {
            System.out.println(e);
        }
    }
}
```

Using this technique, you can add, modify, and delete attributes. The only problem is that each modify call can perform only a single operation on a set of attributes.

Create a Modification List

The previous modifyAttributes example is useful when you want to perform one atomic operation on one or more attributes. However, it is often more useful to perform several operations at once. For example, let's say a person named Karen moved from the marketing department to the sales department. The program will need to change Karen's attributes to reflect the move. Karen may also require a sales quota attribute with an initial value. Maybe she doesn't have an assistant anymore, so that attribute should be removed. Rather than executing three modifyAttributes calls, you use a ModificationItem list to specify these changes. A ModificationItem consists of one of the operation constants in the preceding example specifying the operation, as well as an Attribute to modify. Modifications are applied in the order in which they appear in the list; either all of the modifications are executed, or none are. The following example performs the position transfer for Karen.

```
import javax.naming.*;
import javax.naming.directory.*;
import java.util.Hashtable;

public class Modify2Example
{
    public static void main(String args[])
    {
        Hashtable env = new Hashtable(11);

        env.put(Context.INITIAL_CONTEXT_FACTORY,
```

```
            "com.sun.jndi.ldap.LdapCtxFactory");
        env.put(Context.PROVIDER_URL,
            "ldap://MyHost/o=JNDIExample");
        try
        {
            DirContext dctx = new InitialDirContext(env);

            ModificationItem[] mods = new ModificationItem[3];
            mods[0] = new ModificationItem(
                DirContext.REPLACE_ATTRIBUTE,
                new BasicAttribute("department", "sales"));
            mods[1] = new ModificationItem(
                DirContext.ADD_ATTRIBUTE,
                new BasicAttribute("quota", "$1,000,000"));
            mods[2] = new ModificationItem(
                DirContext.REMOVE_ATTRIBUTE,
                new BasicAttribute("assistant"));

            dctx.modifyAttributes("cn=Karen, ou=People", mods);
        }catch(Exception e)
        {
            System.out.println(e);
        }
    }
}
```

In this code, a ModificationItem array is created, and all the necessary changes for Karen are added to it. The changes take the form of ModificationItems containing an operation to perform; an attribute to add, remove, or change; and an optional value to which the attribute is set.

Using ModificationItem, you can perform operations that affect the types of attributes contained in the server. This potentially changes the schema of the directory server. The next section shows the features of JNDI that allow you to explore the schema of a directory service.

Schema

For dynamic applications that need to read the structure of a directory, the schema is an important resource. The *schema* describes rules regarding the structure of the namespace and the attributes stored in it. The schema specifies the types of objects that can be added to the directory, the mandatory and optional attributes that are possible, and where the objects can be added in the schema. JNDI supports the notion of schemas expressed as an information tree. Programs can retrieve the schema associated with a directory object if the underlying context provides the appropriate support. The DirContext method getSchema is used to retrieve the root DirContext of the schema tree associated with the directory. The children of the schema root describe the rules that define the structure and attributes of the directory context. These children themselves are each of type DirContext. These contexts have a method getSchemaClassDefinition that contains information about a particular directory in the schema. You can also find out information about an attribute of an object by calling the Attribute methods getAttributeDefinition and getAttributeSyntaxDefinition. These methods are described in Table 5.15.

Using the schema methods of DirContext, you can identify the structure of a directory service and create dynamic queries and updates. For example, you could find out if the directory service supported a certain type of currency, then do your calculations in that currency. Schema access provides you a way to create truly dynamic applications that leverage many directory services with a consistent API.

Exception Handling

The JNDI defines a class hierarchy for exceptions that can be thrown in the course of performing naming and directory operations. The JNDI exceptions are listed in Table 5.16.

The root of this class hierarchy is NamingException. Programs interested in dealing with a particular exception can catch the corresponding subclass of the exception. Otherwise, programs should catch NamingException.

Table 5.15 Schema-Related Methods

METHOD	USE
Schema methods defined in DirContext	
`DirContext getSchema(Name name)`	Returns the schema associated with the named object.
`DirContext getSchema(String name)`	Returns the schema associated with the named object.
`DirContext getSchemaClassDefinition(Name name)`	Returns the schema object class definition for the named object. This object defines how the objects are actually represented in the directory.
`DirContext getSchemaClassDefinition(String name)`	Returns the schema object class definition for the named object. This object defines how the objects are actually represented in the directory.
Schema methods defined in Attribute	
`DirContext getAttributeDefinition()`	Returns the attribute's schema definition.
`DirContext getAttributeSyntaxDefinition()`	Returns the syntax definition associated with the attribute. This is the directory-dependent attribute description rather than the Java description of the attribute. For example, a Java object attribute might have a syntax definition of "money."

Table 5.16 JNDI Exceptions

EXCEPTION	SUPERCLASS	DESCRIPTION
Defined in javax.naming		
AuthenticationException	javax.naming .NamingSecurityException	This exception is thrown when an authentication error occurs while accessing the naming or directory service.
AuthenticationNotSupportedException	javax.naming .NamingSecurityException	This exception is thrown when the particular flavor of authentication requested is not supported.
CannotProceedException	javax.naming.NamingException	This exception is thrown to indicate that the operation reached a point in the name where the operation cannot proceed any further.
CommunicationException	javax.naming.NamingException	This exception is thrown when the client is unable to communicate with the directory or naming service.
ConfigurationException	javax.naming.NamingException	This exception is thrown when there is a configuration problem.
ContextNotEmptyException	javax.naming.NamingException	This exception is thrown when attempting to destroy a context that is not empty.
InsufficientResourcesException	javax.naming.NamingException	This exception is thrown when resources are not available to complete the requested operation.
InterruptedNamingException	javax.naming.NamingException	This exception is thrown when the naming operation being invoked has been interrupted.
InvalidNameException	javax.naming.NamingException	This exception indicates that the name being specified does not conform to the naming syntax of a naming system.

Continues

Table 5.16 JNDI Exceptions *(Continued)*

EXCEPTION	SUPERCLASS	DESCRIPTION
Defined in javax.naming		
LimitExceededException	javax.naming.NamingException	This exception is thrown when a method terminates abnormally due to a user- or system-specified limit.
LinkException	javax.naming.NamingException	This exception is used to describe problems encountered while resolving links.
LinkLoopException	javax.naming.LinkException	This exception is thrown when a loop is detected in attempting to resolve a link, or when an implementation-specific limit on link counts has been reached.
MalformedLinkException	javax.naming.LinkException	This exception is thrown when a malformed link is encountered while resolving or constructing a link.
NameAlreadyBoundException	javax.naming.NamingException	This exception is thrown by methods to indicate that a binding cannot be added because the name is already bound to another object.
NameNotFoundException	javax.naming.NamingException	This exception is thrown when a component of the name cannot be resolved because it is not bound.
NamingException	java.lang.Exception	This is the superclass of all exceptions thrown by operations in the Context and DirContext interfaces.
NamingSecurityException	javax.naming.NamingException	This is the superclass of security-related exceptions thrown by operations in the Context and DirContext interfaces.
NoInitialContextException	javax.naming.NamingException	This exception is thrown when no initial context implementation can be created.

Continues

Table 5.16 *Continued*

EXCEPTION	SUPERCLASS	DESCRIPTION
Defined in javax.naming		
`NoPermissionException`	`javax.naming.NamingSecurityException`	This exception is thrown when attempting to perform an operation for which the client has no permission.
`NotContextException`	`javax.naming.NamingException`	This exception is thrown when a naming operation proceeds to a point at which a context is required to continue the operation, but the resolved object is not a context.
`OperationNotSupportedException`	`javax.naming.NamingException`	This exception is thrown when a context implementation does not support the operation being invoked.
`PartialResultException`	`javax.naming.NamingException`	This exception is thrown to indicate that the result being returned or returned so far is partial and that the operation cannot be completed.
`ReferralException`	`javax.naming.NamingException`	This abstract class is used to represent a referral exception, which is generated in response to a referral such as that returned by LDAP v3 servers.
`ServiceUnavailableException`	`javax.naming.NamingException`	This exception is thrown when attempting to communicate with a directory or naming service and that service is not available.
`SizeLimitExceededException`	`javax.naming.LimitExceededException`	This exception is thrown when a method produces a result that exceeds a size-related limit.
`TimeLimitExceededException`	`javax.naming.LimitExceededException`	This exception is thrown when a method does not terminate within the specified time limit.

Continues

Table 5.16 JNDI Exceptions *(Continued)*

EXCEPTION	SUPERCLASS	DESCRIPTION
Defined in javax.naming.directory		
`AttributeInUseException`	`javax.naming.NamingException`	This exception is thrown when an operation attempts to add an attribute that already exists.
`AttributeModificationException`	`javax.naming.NamingException`	This exception is thrown when an attempt is made to add, remove, modify an attribute, its identifier, or its values that conflicts with the attribute's (schema) definition or the attribute's state.
`InvalidAttributeIdentifierException`	`javax.naming.NamingException`	This exception is thrown when an attempt is made to add or create an attribute with an invalid attribute identifier.
`InvalidAttributesException`	`javax.naming.NamingException`	This exception is thrown when an attempt is made to add or modify an attribute set that has been specified incompletely or incorrectly.
`InvalidAttributeValueException`	`javax.naming.NamingException`	This class is thrown when an attempt is made to add to an attribute a value that conflicts with the attribute's schema definition.
`InvalidSearchControlsException`	`javax.naming.NamingException`	This exception is thrown when the specification of SearchControls for a search operation is invalid.
`InvalidSearchFilterException`	`javax.naming.NamingException`	This exception is thrown when the specification of a search filter is invalid.
`NoSuchAttributeException`	`javax.naming.NamingException`	This exception is thrown when attempting to access an attribute that does not exist.
`SchemaViolationException`	`javax.naming.NamingException`	This exception is thrown when a method in some ways violates the schema.

Summary

JNDI is a powerful tool in your Java arsenal. It provides a seamless interface for accessing all types of information resources. The benefit of a single API for accessing multiple data sources is that you have less to learn and can even change the data source you are accessing by simply changing the values of a few environment variables. Speed of development and maintenance of your code are thus enhanced.

One consideration is performance of using JNDI rather than a native library for accessing your particular directory or naming service. Consider the performance of the JNDI service provider you are using and keep in mind the effects of network traffic and server performance when determining the causes of any performance issues. Even though performance probably won't be a reason not to use JNDI, you may need to consider the limits of the JNDI searching facility. You probably don't need a more sophisticated searching mechanism for a naming and directory service than the ones provided with JNDI, but if you do, this may be a limitation of JNDI that you have to work around.

You need to be aware of the security issues for the environment in which your program will run. For example, if you want to create an applet and allow it to connect to directory server running on another machine, you probably need to sign both your applet and all the JNDI-related jar files that your applet will use. The documentation for your service provider should discuss any specific issues for that provider. Also, read the documentation for your service provider to determine which, if any, of the security-oriented properties can be used and the effects of using them.

Remember that it is up to the service providers to support various capabilities of the JNDI. Make sure you carefully read the documentation that comes with the service provider package to see what features are enabled and what security considerations are handled. For example, the file system provider from Sun supports only naming services. The LDAP provider allows you to serialize objects, but others may not. The RMI provider supports only a flat directory. It also supports the notion of referenceable objects being bound into the RMI registry.

At this point, we have looked at how you can use Java to access enterprise data from a variety of services. The next chapter begins to explore how you can create services of your own, beginning with Web server services in the form of a new application structure called a servlet.

What Are Servlets?

Servlets, Sun's latest contribution for enhancing the capabilities of a Web server, are small Java programs that run on a Web server. The name *servlets* is play on words because servlets are to a Web server as applets are to a Web browser. Servlets replace the need for other server-side programming paradigms with a Java-specific solution. Web servers began as a mechanism for sending static Web documents to a Web browser using a simple protocol, HTTP. Before long, people began looking for ways to extend the capabilities of the Web browser so that more complex forms of elements and objects such as date validation fields and spreadsheet objects could be displayed. At the same time, several technologies emerged for adding program logic on the server.

This chapter shows how typical server-side programming works and compares it to the process of servlet creation and use. This comparison provides you with a basis for understanding how other server-side technologies provide Web client services and at the same time provides an overview of how to use servlets to perform the same tasks in Java. Chapter 7, "Programming Servlets," covers the features and use of servlets in greater detail.

Server-Side Programming Technologies

Many technologies for programming on the server have emerged. The most common technologies include the following:

Common Gateway Interface (CGI). CGI enables developers to create separate applications that communicate with the Web server. The applications (or scripts) generate Web pages or other files dynamically by processing form data and returning documents based on the form values and other criteria.

Plug-ins. Server vendors such as Microsoft and Netscape came out with their own proprietary APIs for extending the application logic of their particular servers. These "plug-in" technologies (ISAPI and NSAPI, respectively) allow the programmer to take advantage of server-specific features for managing the relationship between the Web server and other resources. Plug-ins are custom code extensions that are added directly to the server and run inside the server's memory address space. Plug-ins have the performance advantage of running in the Web server process, but if the plug-in crashes, it also has the potential of crashing the server.

Server-side includes. Many servers support extensions to HTML called server-side includes. Some Web servers have the ability to preprocess HTML before sending it to the Web browser. The Web servers support additional HTML tags that can be dynamically processed by the Web server so that the resulting HTML viewed in the Web browser can be customized by this server-side include. An extension to server-side includes is the concept of server-side scripting. Many servers are now supporting this type of scripting. For example, Microsoft's Web server supports Active Server Pages; Netscape supports Server-Side JavaScript, previously known as LiveWire. These extensions are interpreted by the server.

All of these technologies enable developers to create complete, distributed applications in which the user interface logic is displayed in the Web browser and the business logic is managed in server programs. Enhanced HTML capabilities for developing complete (but rudimentary) user interfaces for the Web browser and the ability to build complex business logic via CGI and other technologies on the Web server clearly changed the way enterprise applications are written for a large number of systems.

Rather than creating a single monolithic application, we define smaller applications that provide a finite number of functions such as validating a credit card or retrieving a product description from a database. These smaller applications work together to perform the functions of a larger enterprise system. Each of these applications can reside on a single server, or they can be distributed throughout the network. This flexibility allows better load balancing, performance tuning, and maintenance of each individual component. For instance, you can upgrade one component such as an application that provides the user with a menu of options without having to change the rest of the application components.

The next section describes how a CGI script can be used to process Web client requests. This discussion forms a basis for comparing CGI and servlets.

Processing Forms with CGI

While each of the server technologies is slightly different in how it performs its tasks, the CGI process illustrates the basic purpose and function of server-side logic. CGI programs can be used to dynamically generate Web pages, as in this simple example using the Perl language:

```
#!/bin/perl

# Send the output mime type to the server to know what output to handle
print "Content-type: text/html\n\n";

print "<HTML>\n";
print "<HEAD><TITLE>Hello World</TITLE></HEAD>\n";
print "<BODY>\n";

print "<H1>Hello World</H1>\n";

print "</BODY></HTML>\n";
exit;
```

Depending on how your Web server is configured, from a Web browser you could type:

```
HTTP://www.myserver.com/cgi-scripts/helloworld.pl
```

to access this program. Typically, CGI programs are used to process HTML forms and then return dynamic HTML; however, CGI can be used to input and output any type of data. Figure 6.1 shows a simple HTML form that is processed with a CGI script.

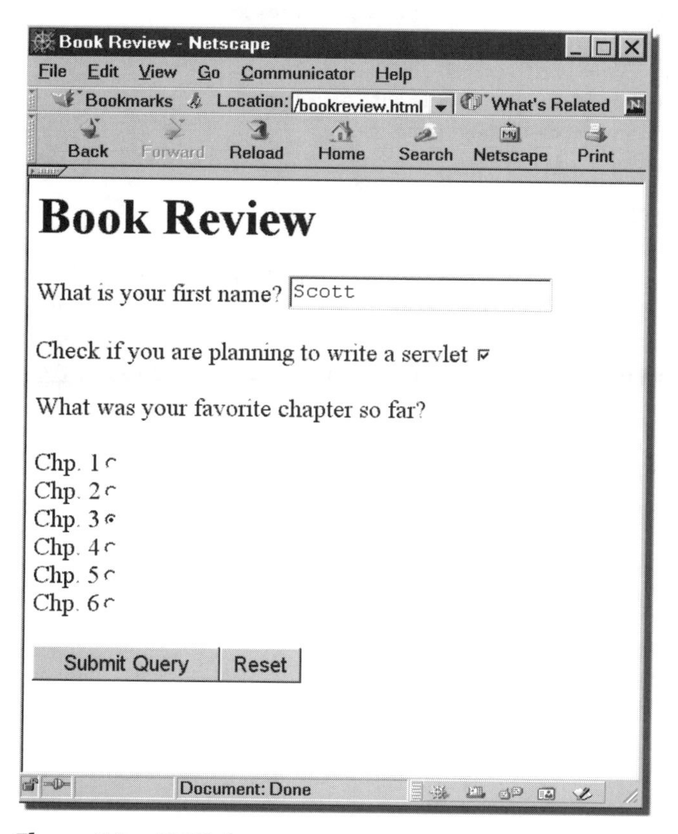

Figure 6.1 HTML form.

After the user enters values in the form, he presses the Submit button. The values are sent to the CGI script as the FORM action. The CGI script processes the values sent to it and then dynamically returns an HTML page thanking the user for the entry.

Here is the HTML for the page:

```
<html>
  <head>
    <title>Book Review</title>
  </head>

  <body>
    <H1>Book Review</H1>
    <form action=HTTP://servername/cgi-bin/bookreview.pl method=POST>
      What is your first name?
      <input type=text name=fname>

      <BR><BR>Check if you are planning to write a servlet
      <input type=checkbox name=writeservlet>

      <BR><BR>What was your favorite chapter so far?<BR>
        <BR>Chp. 1<input type=radio name=favchap value=1>
        <BR>Chp. 2<input type=radio name=favchap value=2>
        <BR>Chp. 3<input type=radio name=favchap value=3>
        <BR>Chp. 4<input type=radio name=favchap value=4>
        <BR>Chp. 5<input type=radio name=favchap value=5>
        <BR>Chp. 6<input type=radio name=favchap value=6>
      <BR><BR><input type=submit><input type=reset>
    </form>
  </body>
</html>
```

Notice that each form element has a unique name and value. When the user presses the Submit button, the form data is packaged up and sent to the CGI program as a request. The CGI program parses the request and processes each of the form element's values. Then the CGI program typically returns another HTML document to the Web browser. Figure 6.2 shows what a response might look like after the preceding form is submitted.

Here is what a CGI program written in Perl might look like:

```
#!/usr/bin/perl

require "cgilib.pl";

print "Content-type: text/html\n\n";

%dataDict = ();

&readData(*data);
&parseData(*data,*dataDict);
```

```
$fName = $dataDict{"fname"};
$chp = $dataDict{"favchap"};
$writeServlet = $dataDict{"writeservlet"};

print "<HTML>";
print "<TITLE>Book Review Response</TITLE>";
print $fName;
print ", thank you for your feedback.<BR>";
print "Your favorite chapter so far is chapter ";
print $chp;
print ".<BR>";
print "<HR>";
print "You are ";

($writeServlet ne "") || print "not ";

print "planning to write a servlet.";

print "</HTML>";
```

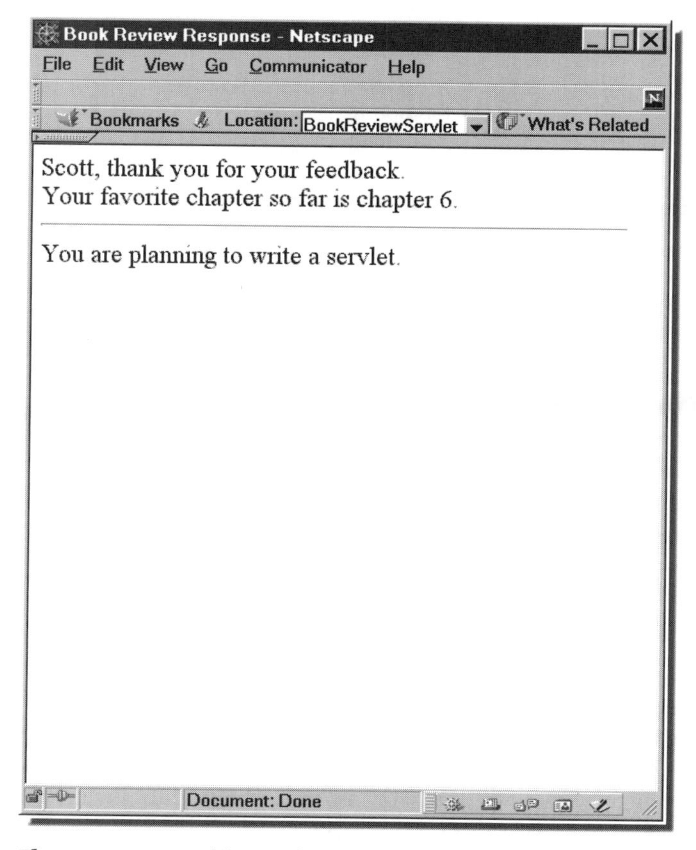

Figure 6.2 Resulting Web page after form is processed.

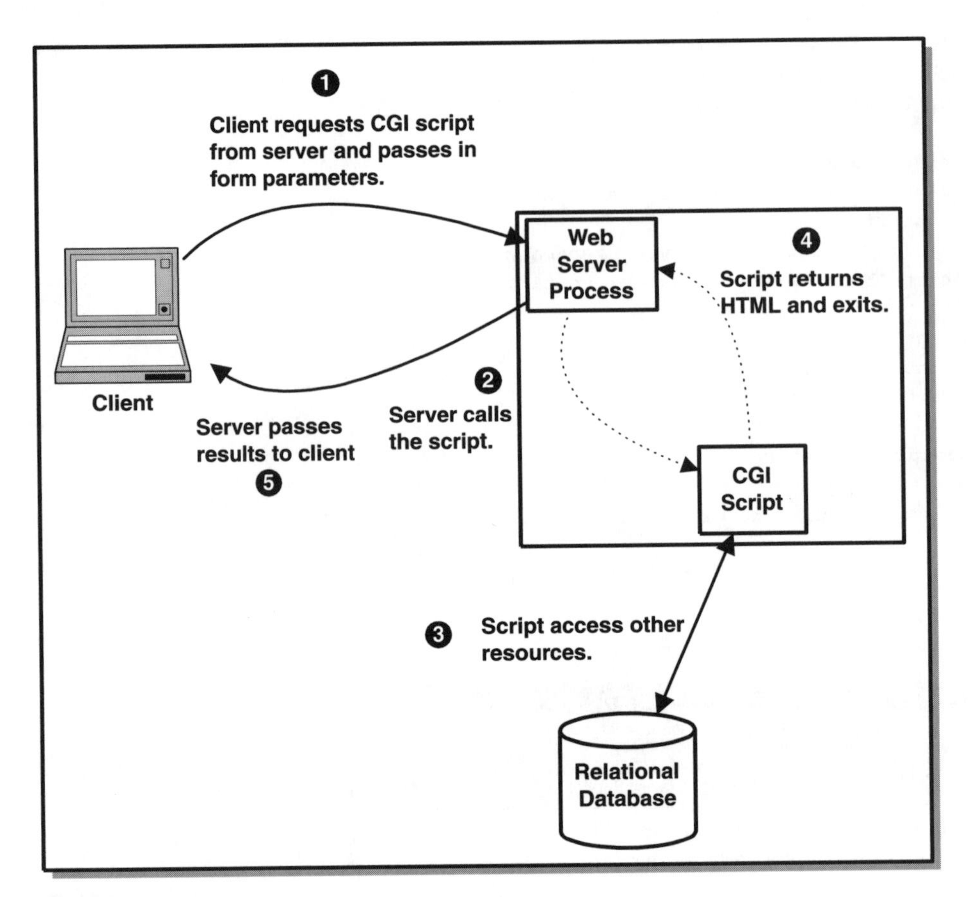

Figure 6.3 Three-tier Web application architecture.

Although the code for these programs may look complex, it is actually quite simple. A Web client sends a set of key-value pairs to the Web server, which forwards the data to the script named in the <FORM> tag. The CGI program processes these values and writes HTML or other information back to the Web server. In the middle of this process, the CGI program may write to a log file or access a database or other server resource. Figure 6.3 illustrates what this three-tier architecture looks like.

Processing Forms with Servlets

When Java came on the scene, applets allowed Web browsers to display even more sophisticated user interfaces in a platform-independent way. Just as applets extend the capabilities of a Web browser, servlets extend the capabilities of Web servers. Servlets can be used as replacements for CGI programs or as plug-ins within JavaSoft's JavaWeb Server and other Web servers supporting the Servlet API.

NOTE The JavaWeb Server packages also come with plug-in support for popular Web servers such as Netscape, Microsoft, and Apache. This means you can write a servlet and have it treated as a vendor-specific plug-in by these Web servers.

Like most Java technologies, servlets are portable and should work on any "servlet-enabled" server. Because the servlet API is a standard, any server that supports servlets should support your servlet. This is a huge advantage over CGI and other server-side technologies. As more and more servers support servlets, the decision of which server you use will not affect the design and implementation decisions you make for building your enterprise application's server logic.

In CGI programming, a server sends a request to a CGI program, which starts up, processes the request, and shuts down. Because the CGI program doesn't remain "open" between requests, resources it uses, such as database connections, must be reestablished between calls. This is a performance bottleneck and often requires more complex programming logic to work around. Unlike CGI programs, servlets are persistent. A database connection created in a servlet can remain open between server requests, greatly enhancing performance.

Both servlets and CGI can be used to write small applications that perform specific tasks. One advantage of CGI is that CGI scripts can be written in almost any language. The disadvantage of CGI is that each time the server needs the services of one of your CGI programs, it must start up a new CGI process. This process has no persistent state unless you write the logic for storing it. For example, if you wanted to keep track of the last credit card processed, you would need to write it to a file or a database of some sort. This means every time a request is made of your CGI program, the Web server must start an instance of your program, then the program must load its state from a file, database, and so on. Also, CGI does not manage the communication between multiple instances of the CGI program, so if multiple clients are accessing your Web server and requesting the CGI, multiple instances of the CGI program must be loaded, taking up memory. These multiple instances will not share state, so you will have to write specific code if you want them to communicate. In other words, CGI programs are represented by multiple single-threaded applications by default. This is one reason that servlets are a good choice for Web server application programming. They do not have these limitations. Servlets are loaded into the server's address space at load time or at the time of the initial request. After the initial request, they respond very quickly. Also, because the servlet can remain resident, it can maintain state between client requests. Figure 6.4 illustrates typical servlet use.

Creating a Servlet

In order to create servlets, use the Java Servlet Development Kit, or JSDK, from Sun. The JSDK consists of two packages: javax.servlet and javax.servlet.HTTP. These packages contain the classes and interfaces needed to create your own servlets. Your Web server might also provide a copy of these packages; if so, you don't have to download this kit. JSDK 2.0 is found on your CD-ROM or it can be downloaded from

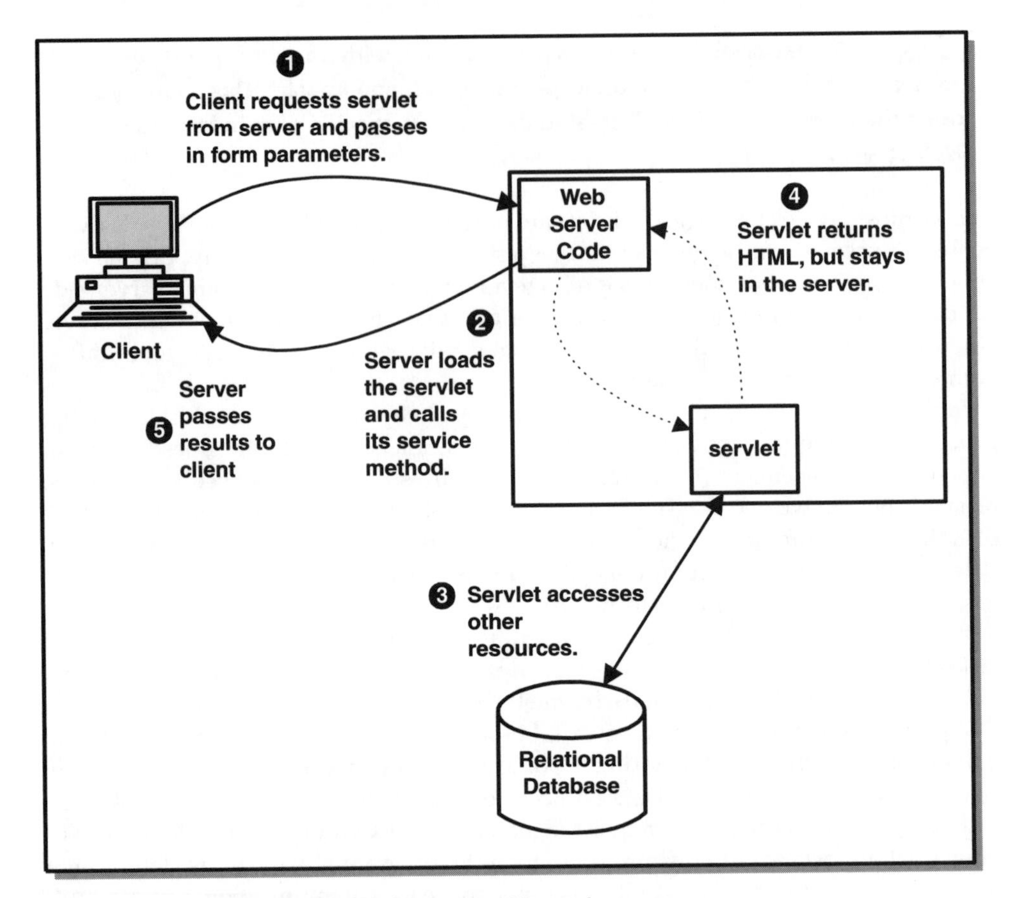

Figure 6.4 Web application architecture with servlets.

http://java.sun.com/products/java-server/servlets/index.html. After installing the JSDK, you can begin creating servlets.

The following discussion provides a brief overview of the major concepts in creating servlets. Chapter 7, "Programming Servlets," covers these concepts in detail and provides a number of demonstrations.

GenericServlet

Remember, when you create an applet, you typically subclass java.applet.Applet. With servlets that aren't specifically used for HTTP processing, you subclass javax.servlet.GenericServlet and override several methods. Typically, you will override init(), which performs any initialization your servlet requires, such as initializing logs, opening database connections, and so on. You will also usually override service(), which is called each time your servlet is invoked. When this method is called, it is passed a javax.servlet.ServletRequest and javax.servlet.ServletResponse object, used to process the client request.

HTTPServlet

If your servlet will be used primarily for processing HTTP requests, subclass javax.servlet.HTTP.HTTPServlet. This abstract subclass of GenericServlet implements a default service() method for processing requests. It calls several other methods that you typically override to handle the request. The most common methods to override include doGet() and doPost(). For example, the method doGet() is called when the form requests are sent in GET, HEAD, or POST format. Each of these request types corresponds to a standard HTTP request mechanism and is passed objects that represent the request and the response.

The two most common request types are GET and POST. A GET request sends information to a servlet using a URL. The results of the GET request should be the contents of the URL. The URL can contain extra data in the form of a query string appended to it with a question mark. For example, the URL www.pri.com/servlets/go?name=stephen passes the key-value pair name=stephen to a servlet. This key-value string is optional, and most of the requests you make with a browser when clicking on links are actually handled with GET requests to the server that do not contain this query string. POST requests send an HTTP body that contains all of the data being sent to the servlet. Normally, POST requests are used as the action for a form, especially when a lot of data is being sent to the servlet or CGI script.

Processing Responses

When one of the processing methods of HTTPServlet is called, the typical steps are to read the values from the request, do any additional processing such as logging or database access, and then write a response to the client.

To write a response to the client, HttpServletResponse has a method getWriter that returns a PrintWriter instance. Use this object to write data to the client. All HTTP responses are expected to include a content type. Because the servlet is handling a specific client request, the servlet should define this type as shown above. The value for this content type is included in the HTTP header returned to the client. Possible content types include text/html, text/plain, image/gif, and any other valid MIME type. Notice that the type is separated into a major and minor type. All text uses the text major type but can either be HTML or plain. Images use the image major type and can use a number of minor types, including gif, jpg, and tiff. The list of acceptable types is constantly growing. New types are often tested using the x- prefix to indicate that they are experimental. You can find more information about the available types by browsing to www.ietf.org/ and looking for a request for comments (RFC) search engine. Then go to RFC 2046. These RFCs can be hard to read, so the other option is to use your browser's preferences dialog to find a list of the types it supports.

In the example that follows, if you don't specify that the data you are sending is HTML, the browser parses HTML tags as regular text and just displays the text. For example, rather than seeing a horizontal rule, you would see <HR> in the browser. To specify the content type for a servlet's response, call the HttpServletResponse method setContentType and pass in an appropriate type. For example, the following line:

```
response.setContentType("text/html");
```

tells the browser we are sending HTML.

Example Servlet

The code that follows defines a basic servlet BookReviewServlet that can be used in place of the CGI program used to display the book review in the section "Processing Forms with CGI." The only change to the HTML file is the <FORM> tag. The new tag looks like this:

```
<form action=http://localhost:8080/servlet/BookReviewServlet method=POST>
```

In the BookReviewServlet code, the servlet performs the same function as the Perl script by processing the form request and sending back an HTML response page. For simplicity, only POST is supported.

```
import java.io.*;
import javax.servlet.*;
import javax.servlet.http.*;

public class BookReviewServlet extends HttpServlet
{
    // Write a response to the client.
    public void doPost(HttpServletRequest req,
                       HttpServletResponse res)
        throws ServletException, IOException
    {
        /*
          Set the "content type" header of the response so that
          the browser knows we are sending HTML, not just raw
          text. If you don't do this, the HTML tags will not
          be interpreted.
          Try commenting out this line to see what happens.
        */
        res.setContentType("text/html");

        //Get the response's PrintWriter to return text to client.
        PrintWriter toClient = res.getWriter();

        // Read form values.
        String fName = req.getParameter("fname");
        String chp = req.getParameter("favchap");
        String writeServlet = req.getParameter("writeservlet");

        // Respond to client with a thank you.
        toClient.println("<HTML>");
        toClient.println("<TITLE>Book Review Response</TITLE>");
```

```
            toClient.print(fName);
            toClient.println(", thank you for your feedback.<BR>");
            toClient.print("Your favorite chapter so far is chapter ");
            toClient.println(chp + ".<BR>");
            toClient.println("<HR>");
            toClient.println("You are ");
            if(writeServlet == null)
                toClient.print("not ");
            toClient.println("planning to write a servlet.");

            toClient.println("</HTML>");


            // Close the writer when response is done.
            toClient.close();
        }
    }
```

Also notice that doService() is a synchronized method. This is because servlets typically run in multithreaded environments. Because there is only one instance of the servlet object created by the Web server, the servlet must be able to service simultaneous requests. Servlets, therefore, need to ensure that they synchronize access to such shared resources as their instance variables, database connections, and file streams.

Running the Servlet

JSDK includes a testing application called servletrunner in the JSDK/bin directory. Put your compiled servlet in the examples directory of the JSDK and then execute servletrunner. If you make any changes to your servlet, restart the servletrunner. To load the servlet from the Web browser, specify the location http://localhost:8080/servlet/ServletName. If servletrunner is on another machine, replace localhost with the server name. Port 8080 is the default port that servletrunner is on.

Once you are comfortable that your servlet works, you can move it to your production Web server. You can also use a Web server such as the Java Web Server for testing purposes. Read the documentation on your server to determine where to put the servlet. For more information concerning adding servlet support to your Web server, read the documentation that comes with the JSDK.

Other Server-Side Features

The Java Web Server provides several mechanisms for creating dynamic content, including server-side includes and servlet chaining. This section provides an overview of these features. If you are going to use the Java Web Server, you may want to check out http://jserv.javasoft.com:80/products/java-server/documentation/webserver1.0.2/index_developer.html for more information on these two features.

Server-Side Includes

Servlets may be invoked by Web servers to preprocess Web pages as server-side includes in Web servers that provide complete servlet support. Server-specific enhancements to the HTML syntax send an indication to the Web server to preprocess. The following code is an example of HTML syntax that sends this message to the server:

```
<SERVLET NAME=ServletName>
<PARAM NAME=param1 VALUE=val1>
<PARAM NAME=param2 VALUE=val2>
This text only displays if the server doesnÌt support Server side
includes for servlets
</SERVLET>
```

The <SERVLET> tag indicates that a servlet ServletName should be loaded and then called with a particular set of parameters. The output of the servlet is included at this point in the HTML file returned to the client. You can think of the <SERVLET> tag as a way of telling the server to "fill in the blank" with values generated by the servlet. You could use this technique to include a table that is dynamically generated by values in a database. Figure 6.5 illustrates the output of the following HTML:

```
<HTML>
Here is your order so far:
<HR>
<SERVLET NAME=ProcessOrderServlet>
    <PARAM NAME=orderid VALUE=123>
</SERVLET>
<HR>
</HTML>
```

The HTML indicates to the Web server that a servlet called ProcessOrderServlet should be called to fill in the HTML that goes between the <HR> tags. The servlet is passed one parameter, the order id, which is used to access the order database, then outputs the result shown in Figure 6.5.

Servlet Chaining

The Java Web Server supports chaining local and remote servlets. The input from the browser is sent to the first servlet in the chain; the output from the last servlet in the chain is sent back as the response to the browser. Each servlet in the chain has the inputs and outputs piped to the servlet before and after it, respectively. You could use this feature to create small servlets that act as data filters or business rules. For instance, a Web page containing an order to process could submit form data to the first servlet, which validates the credit card entered on the form. If it is a valid card, the information is passed on to the order-processing servlet, which checks the inventory database for stock and then forwards the information to the result servlet, which presents the client with the success or failure result of its submission. These chains are configured by using the Administration

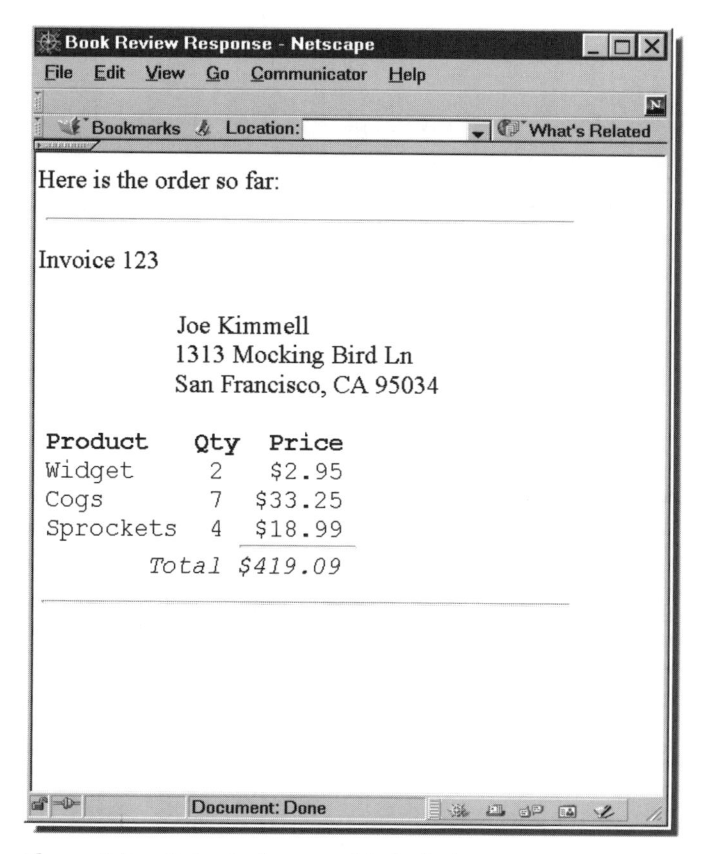

Figure 6.5 Output of server-side include.

tool that is part of the Java Web Server or by configuring an association between a specific MIME type and a list of servlets. This is done in the mimeservlets.properties file residing in the directory <server_root>/properties/server/javawebserver/webpageservice/. For more information on this feature, see the Java Web Server tool kit documentation at http://jserv.javasoft.com:80/products/java-server/toolkit/index.html.

NOTE **Because servlets must be able to support requests from multiple clients, the servlet API supports both single-threaded and multithreaded servlets. The developer still needs to handle synchronizing other resources such as database connections. Chapter 7, "Programming Servlets," covers this in more detail.**

Using servlets as server-side includes allows you to create dynamic Web content. Using servlets in a chain allows you to create small filter services that can parse input from a form and run it through multiple business rules before sending results back to the client. These features are specific to the Java Web Server, but other vendors will be adopting them or something similar as the standards are flushed out.

Summary

Servlets are a natural extension to Java and greatly simplify the task of writing enterprise solutions in Java. The main benefits of servlets are as follows:

- Java servlets enable you to write server-side logic with the same object-oriented power of client-side Java.
- Servlet persistence solves much of the overhead and state-management issues typically encountered with CGI programs.
- Because servlets are written in Java, they can seamlessly take advantage of other Java technologies such as JDBC, JNDI, and others. Chapter 25, "A Four-Tier Online Store," includes an example servlet that accesses an Enterprise JavaBean via JNDI.
- As servlet support is added to more Web servers, servlets will alleviate the need to make design-level decisions about which server to use—an implementation detail that does not affect your server-side logic.

Chapter 7, "Programming Servlets," provides a detailed definition of the process and API required for creating servlets. Chapter 8, "A Servlet-Based Search Engine," walks you through the development of a complete servlet-based search engine that you could use on your own Web site.

Programming Servlets

Servlets represent the extension of applet-style programming onto the Web server. Servlets are usually written by extending an existing class and implementing one or two key methods. However, as servlets have become a common method for implementing server code, they have also become a standard interface between client and server code. This chapter discusses the basic syntax for creating servlets as well as techniques used to design, test, and tune your servlets. As you read through the chapter, you may want to run the examples using the source code on the CD-ROM. In this case, skip to the section "Running and Hosting Servlets" at the end of the chapter for specific information about running the examples. It is important to understand the basics of servlet programming at this point because there are a number of large examples that rely on servlets in later chapters.

This chapter focuses on the mechanics and concepts of programming servlets and contains small examples. Later chapters provide examples of full-fledged servlets. In particular, Chapter 8, "A Servlet-Based Search Engine," provides a large example of a servlet that can be used for searching a Web site.

A Basic Servlet

The first step in defining a servlet is to create an object that implements the javax.servlet.Servlet interface. Once this class is defined, you can implement methods that handle client requests. There are two standard ways to implement the Servlet interface. The first is to subclass javax.servlet.GenericServlet. GenericServlet essentially implements all of the methods of the Servlet interface, as listed in Table 7.1, and provides a few convenience methods. The second way to implement Servlet is to subclass javax.servlet.http.HttpServlet. This implementation of Servlet provides more methods for dealing with servlets interacting with a Web server. Objects can also implement Servlet directly, although this technique is usually used only in cases in which it is necessary for the object to belong to a different inheritance hierarchy.

The Web server associates servlets with URLs. The server may also allow a servlet to be associated with a complete type of URL. For example, Chapter 9, "What Is Server-Side Scripting?" introduces JavaServer Pages. These pages are compiled by a servlet that handles all requests to ".jhtml" files. Essentially, the servlet handles a file request type rather than a particular URL.

When the user accesses a URL represented by a servlet, the Web server first checks to see if it has loaded that servlet. Some Web servers provide an administrative tool for preloading servlets; others wait until the first user request before loading the servlet. Loading the servlet is a two-step process. First, an instance of the servlet's class is created using the default constructor, based on the class name provided when the servlet was configured to a particular URL. Next, the servlet is notified of its loading.

Like applets, servlets are notified of their instance creation and destruction by the servlet host, usually a Web server. In particular, the servlet is sent the message "init" when it is first loaded and "destroy" when it is unloaded from the server. These specific messages are used in place of relying on the constructor to finalize the method, to give the Web server control over when and how it notifies the servlet. In fact, a server could send init and destroy to the same servlet object several times, assuming that it is unloaded before being initialized again.

In the servlet model, only one object is created to service each URL. This object receives the init, service, and destroy messages for that URL. In other words, the init method is called once, regardless of the number of requests, and destroy is called once when the servlet is unloaded. The service method is called on the same servlet object every time any client accesses that URL on the server. See Table 7.1.

The init method takes a ServletConfig object as its argument. For servlets that extend GenericServlet, the configuration object is stored by the servlet for later use in

Table 7.1 Servlet Interface Methods

METHOD	DESCRIPTION
`void destroy()`	Cleans up whatever resources are being held.
`ServletConfig getServletConfig()`	Returns a servlet config object—in particular, the configuration object passed to init.
`String getServletInfo()`	Returns a string containing information about the servlet, such as its author, version, and copyright.
`void init(ServletConfig)`	Initializes the servlet.
`void service(ServletRequest, ServletResponse)`	Called each time a request is made to the servlet.

the GenericServlet's implementation of init. When subclassing GenericServlet and overriding the init method, you should call super.init() in the init method to inherit this behavior. The following code shows the declaration for the init method.

```
public void init(ServletConfig config) throws ServletException
```

Using the provided configuration, init prepares the servlet for work. This initialization might involve creating a network connection, loading a file into memory, or any other potentially lengthy operation. The server guarantees that it will send init once on loading, and it will wait to send any service messages to the servlet until init has returned. This means that init is basically thread safe and will be called only once per servlet load.

If an error occurs during initialization, the servlet throws an exception. The package that contains Servlet also defines the ServletException and UnavailableException classes. UnavailableExceptions are thrown during init if initialization cannot complete. There are two types of unavailable servlets: A servlet can be permanently unavailable, and a servlet can be temporarily unavailable. A permanently unavailable servlet cannot be recovered. A temporarily unavailable servlet can recover after some condition is met. A good example of a permanently unavailable servlet is a servlet configured to use a file that doesn't exist. A temporarily unavailable servlet is one that uses a database that is currently unavailable. The key differentiator is that permanently unavailable servlets require administrative action. Temporarily unavailable servlets may become available later without administrative action, or they may be self-correcting.

Table 7.2 shows the UnavailableException methods that provide information to the servlet host or Web server. The most important method for truly self-correcting servlets is getUnavailableSeconds. Servlets use this method to tell the server how long the servlet needs to correct the current problem. All of these values are set by arguments in the constructor for UnavailableException.

Servlets implement the destroy method to clean up any outstanding resource. For example, a servlet might close a network connection or file that it is holding open. The servlet's host tries to wait on all service requests to be fulfilled before destroy is sent to the servlet.

If the servlet is executing long-running operations, it may be told to destroy before all of the operations are complete. This means that as the developer, if you are using multithreaded servlets, you should plan for destroy to be called during a long-running operation. One possible mechanism for dealing with this situation is to have destroy set a flag and have the servlet check whether the flag is on at the end of each request. If the flag is true and the request is the last one, the servlet will clean up its resources. Put

Table 7.2 UnavailableException Methods

METHOD	DESCRIPTION
`public boolean isPermanent()`	Returns true if the servlet requires administrative intervention before becoming available.
`public Servlet getServlet()`	The servlet in question.
`public int getUnavailableSeconds()`	The number of seconds that the servlet expects to be unavailable.

simply, the servlet might not clean up in the destroy method, but instead in its service method, after checking whether destroy was called.

Keep in mind that most servlets should perform reasonably short operations, in order to provide user responsiveness. In those cases, it is not necessary to plan too extensively around destroy getting called too early. Servlets that do not require open resources, created in init and closed in destroy, may not even need to implement the method.

Handling a Request

Once a servlet is initialized, the key method used to interact with it is:

```
public void service(ServletRequest request,
    ServletResponse response) throws ServletException
```

This service method is made up of a simple interface that takes information about the request and an object that encapsulates the response. Whenever a request arrives at the server for a particular servlet, the server wraps up information about the request, creates a response object to contain information relevant to the response, and calls service. The service method uses a ServletException, a special type of Exception object, to indicate when an exception has occurred.

A simple example of the service method follows in the form of the classic HelloWorld program. The results of accessing this servlet are pictured in Figure 7.1. The bold code shows that the service method is sent a request object containing the details of the client request and a response object used to return values to the client. The method writes "Hello World" to a Web page on the client browser.

```
import java.io.*;
import java.util.*;
import javax.servlet.*;
import javax.servlet.http.*;

public class HelloWorldServlet extends GenericServlet
{
    public void service(ServletRequest request,
                                  ServletResponse response)
                                  throws ServletException,
                                  IOException
    {
        PrintWriter out;

        response.setContentType("text/html");

        out = response.getWriter();

        out.println("<HTML><HEAD><TITLE>");
        out.println("Hello World");
        out.println("</TITLE></HEAD><BODY>");
        out.println("<H1>Hello World</H1>");
```

```
        out.println("</BODY></HTML>");

        out.close();
    }
}
```

Other servlets may have similar versions of service or implementations that are more complex. The important point is that service is the Web server's interface to the servlet. You, as the servlet writer, can do anything you want, as long as Java supports it, inside the service method. This could include using JNDI to look up the e-mail address in an LDAP directory or finding inventory items in a database through JDBC.

SingleThreadModel

The next step in implementing a servlet is to decide if it will support multithreading. This is an important decision for the programmer. If you decide not to support multithreaded access to the servlet, the servlet should implement the SingleThreadModel interface. This interface defines no methods and is instead a typing mechanism. Servlets marked with SingleThreadModel are guaranteed by the server to be accessed

Figure 7.1 Hello World.

only by a single thread. When a servlet implements SingleThreadModel, it is really saying that it doesn't want the service method called from more than one thread.

Several issues go into the decision of servlet multithreading:

1. Does it make sense for the action performed by the servlet to occur twice simultaneously? For example, if the servlet returns data from a cache, it is reasonable that the servlet could respond to multiple queries at the same time. However, to ensure file integrity, you may want a servlet that deletes files to delete only one file at a time.
2. Does the servlet alter information that may not be thread safe? Does it access a file or another object that is not thread safe? Does it use a socket to interact with another application? If so, is access to the socket synchronized? If a resource being accessed by the servlet is not itself thread safe, the servlet should be single threaded to protect that resource.
3. Will there be performance implications if the servlet is marked single threaded? If the requests performed by the servlet in a single-thread model are time consuming, other requests may be delayed too long. In this case, if possible, the servlet should be written to support multiple threads.

Keep in mind that supporting multiple threads is more flexible than marking the servlet as single threaded. Marking it single threaded is certainly easier on the program design, but it is more limiting in your program design. We will discuss multithreaded servlets in detail in the upcoming section, "Multithreaded Servlets."

ServletRequest

Each call to service includes an object that implements the ServletRequest interface. This object stores information about the request made by the client to the servlet. Request information comes in three forms. First, there is information about the client/server environment. Second, there is raw access to the client request. Third, there are processed versions of the client request. The difference between the last two types of information is very easy to describe in the context of a servlet that hosts an HTML form. When the form is submitted, the client sends an encoded string containing the name and value of each form element. The servlet can access this string directly (the second form), or it can access the values of each form element by their names (the third form).

All of the methods for ServletRequest are listed in Table 7.3.

Servlets that are designed to respond to HTML form requests will normally use the getParameterValue and getParameterValues methods to obtain information about the form request. Servlets that expect a string of text to be supplied should use getReader to obtain an appropriate reader; servlets that expect binary input should use getInputStream to access data from the request.

Later in this chapter, in the HttpServletRequest discussion, an example demonstrates how to access form information using the request object. Because HttpServletRequest is a special type of ServletRequest, the majority of the methods used in that example are from Table 7.3.

Table 7.3 ServletRequest Methods

METHOD	DESCRIPTION
`Object getAttribute(String)`	Returns the value of the named attribute of the request or null if the attribute does not exist. Attributes can provide arbitrary, server-specific information, like access to SSL configurations.
`String getCharacterEncoding()`	Returns the character set encoding for the input of this request. This information is used by the method getReader to provide the appropriate reader for the requests input.
`int getContentLength()`	Returns the size of the request entity data or -1 if not known. This method is particularly used when a form POST request is made. Content length will indicate the size, in bytes, of the input sent by the form. For CGI programmers, this is equivalent to the CONTENT_LENGTH environmental variable.
`String getContentType()`	Returns the Internet Media Type of the request entity data or null if not known. For CGI programmers, this is equivalent to the CONTENT_TYPE environmental variable.
`ServletInputStream getInputStream()`	Returns an input stream for reading binary data in the request body. If the servlet is expecting textual data, it should use getReader instead. The reader will account for character encodings; the stream will not.
`String getParameter(String)`	After parsing the input, this method returns a string containing the lone value of the specified parameter or null if the parameter does not exist. If the parameter specified contains multiple values, this method will return the first one.
`Enumeration getParameterNames()`	After parsing the input, this method returns the parameter names for this request as an enumeration of strings or, if there are no parameters or the input stream is empty, as an empty enumeration.
`String[] GetParameterValues( String)`	After parsing the input, this method returns the values of the specified parameter for the request as an array of strings or null if the named parameter does not exist. This method is used to access parameters with multiple values. For example, an HTML list might send back multiple selections.
`String getProtocol()`	Returns the protocol and version of the request as a string of the form <protocol>/<major version>.<minor version>.

Continues

Table 7.3 ServletRequest Methods *(Continued)*

METHOD	DESCRIPTION
`BufferedReader getReader()`	Returns a buffered reader for reading text in the request body. This reader will be initialized with the appropriate character encoding to ensure that the data read is correct.
`String getRealPath(String)`	Applies alias rules to the specified virtual path and returns the corresponding real path or null if the translation cannot be performed for any reason. Passing in the value of / will return the document root for this servlet.
`String getRemoteAddr()`	Returns the IP address of the agent that sent the request. For CGI programmers, this is the REMOTE_ADDR environmental variable.
`String getRemoteHost()`	Returns the fully qualified host name of the agent that sent the request. For CGI programmers, this is the REMOTE_HOST environmental variable.
`String getScheme()`	Returns the scheme of the URL used in this request—for example, "http," "https," or "ftp."
`String getServerName()`	Returns the host name of the server that received the request. For CGI programmers, this is the SEVER_NAME environmental variable.
`int getServerPort()`	Returns the port number on which this request was received. For CGI programmers, this is the SEVER_PORT environmental variable.

Although the remaining methods are self-explanatory, the getAttribute method deserves further discussion. The getAttribute method is provided by the ServletRequest interface to provide server-specific information to the servlet. Not all servers provide the same attributes. As a result, Sun has documented several attributes that its server may provide and named them in a way that ensures the Sun-specific meaning. These attributes are listed in Table 7.4.

Refer to your server's documentation for a complete list of the attributes that are provided to your servlets.

ServletResponse

The server provides the servlet with an object that implements the ServletResponse interface in each call to service. This object provides methods for sending a response to the user in the form of a MIME-typed message. The message can be either text or binary, and like the request, the text provided can be encoded in a number of ways.

The methods provided by ServletResponse are listed in Table 7.5. You will notice immediately that these objects are set up in a way such that more information is provided

Table 7.4 Sun-Defined Attributes

ATTRIBUTE NAME	ATTRIBUTE TYPE	DESCRIPTION
`javax.net.ssl .cipher_suite`	string	The string name of the SSL cipher suite in use if the request was made using SSL.
`javax.net.ssl .peer_certificates`	array of javax.security.cert .X509Certificate objects	The chain of X.509 certificates that authenticates the client. This is available only when SSL is used with client authentication.
`javax.net.ssl .session`	javax.net.ssl.SSLSession	An SSL session object, if the request was made using SSL.

about a generic request than a generic response. This is because it is up to the servlet to define the response, and in most cases, the response will require only a type, a size, and a body. HttpServlets will have access to more response parameters that correspond to the values in an HTTP header. However, because the servlet's service method is passed both objects, it can use the information from the request to compose its response.

Because the content type is used to determine the character encoding for the output writer, set the content type before accessing the writer. Also, in the case of HTTP style servlets, the content type is returned to the client in the header of the HTTP reply, while the output stream and writer return data in the body. This means that you should set the content type first, before using either method to return data to the client. Bottom line: Set the content type before sending any output. Also, use the content length, if possible.

Table 7.5 ServletResponse Methods

METHOD	DESCRIPTION
`String getCharacterEncoding()`	Returns the character set encoding used for this MIME body. Use the setContentType method to change this encoding. This method is used to create the appropriate writer for sending text data to the client.
`ServletOutputStream getOutputStream()`	Returns an output stream for writing binary response data.
`PrintWriter getWriter()`	Returns a print writer for writing formatted text responses.
`void setContentLength(int)`	Sets the content length for this response in bytes. If the servlet knows how much data is going to be written, it should provide this information here.
`void setContentType(String)`	Sets the content type for this response as a standard MIME type. The default is text/plain.

ServletConfig

When a servlet is initialized, it is passed an object that implements the ServletConfig interface. Table 7.6 lists the methods defined in this interface. This object is designed to provide information to the servlet about the server and how the servlet is currently configured. Essentially, the configuration object provides two pieces of information. First, the configuration provides access to configuration parameters defined when the servlet was installed on the server. Second, the configuration object provides access to the servlet's context.

Depending on the server you install, a servlet on the initialization parameters may be defined differently. For example, the Java Web Server provided by Sun uses a configuration applet to set initialization parameters; the JSDK uses a properties file.

ServletContext

The ServletConfig interface provides specific information about the servlet's configuration, but the ServletContext interface defines methods that provide information about the environment in which the servlet itself is running. These methods are listed in Table 7.7. The context is accessed via the configuration object using the method getServletContext.

The context provides access to both the servlet log file and the other servlets on the server. Like the similar feature in AppletContext, access to other servlets may be considered a security risk and therefore not to be implemented on all servers. Refer to your server's documentation for information on what these methods do.

GenericServlet

Perhaps the easiest way to create a servlet is to subclass GenericServlet. GenericServlet implements the Servlet interface and provides a number of convenient methods for accessing information from the servlet configuration. These methods are listed in Table 7.8.

Table 7.6 ServletConfig Methods

METHOD	DESCRIPTION
`String getInitParameter(String)`	Returns a string containing the value of the named initialization parameter of the servlet or null if the parameter does not exist.
`Enumeration getInitParameterNames()`	Returns the names of the servlet's initialization parameters as an enumeration of strings or an empty enumeration if there are no initialization parameters. Use the getInitParameter method to get the value for each named parameter.
`ServletContext getServletContext()`	Returns the servlet's context, as defined by the server.

Table 7.7 ServletContext Methods

METHOD	DESCRIPTION
`Object getAttribute(String)`	Like the request method of the same name, this method provides access to server-specific information.
`String getMimeType(String)`	Returns the MIME type of the specified file or null if not known. This method may or may not be implemented by the server, and servlets should plan for the possible null return value.
`String getRealPath(String)`	Applies alias rules to the specified virtual path and returns the corresponding real path.
`String getServerInfo()`	Returns the name and version of the network service under which the servlet is running.
`Servlet getServlet(String)`	Returns the servlet of the specified name or null if not found.
`Enumeration getServletNames()`	Returns an enumeration of the Servlet object names in this server.
`void log(Exception, String)`	Writes the stacktrace and the given message string to the servlet log file.
`void log(String)`	Writes the given message string to the servlet log file.

Many of these methods are covers for ServletConfig or ServletContext methods. These methods simply forward messages to the appropriate object.

HTTP Servlets

Although GenericServlet provides a good base for writing a servlet, it does not provide convenient access to HTTP-specific information. In particular, generic servlets do not distinguish among the varieties of request types provided by the HTTP specification. HTTP also defines specific headers for requests and has been extended to support concepts like cookies.

Rather than require all servlets to work via the Web protocol HTTP, the servlet libraries allow programmers to choose their servlet implementation. In the previous examples, we used GenericServlet as the parent class. This allowed access to HTTP style requests, but it also allows other forms of requests such as RMI or CORBA. For servlets intended to handle only HTTP requests, the javax.servlet.http.HttpServlet class specializes GenericServlet.

Perhaps the most telling of the methods added by HttpServlet, as listed in Table 7.9, are the ones used to deal with specific request types. For example, doGet is provided

Table 7.8 GenericServlet Methods

METHOD	DESCRIPTION
`public void destroy()`	Logs the destruction in the servlet log file.
`public String getInitParameter(String)`	Returns a string containing the value of the named initialization parameter or null if the requested parameter does exist.
`public Enumeration getInitParameterNames()`	Returns the names of the servlet's initialization parameters as an enumeration of strings or an empty enumeration if there are no initialization parameters.
`public ServletConfig getServletConfig()`	Returns a servletConfig object containing any startup configuration information for this servlet. This object was set in the init method.
`public ServletContext getServletContext()`	Returns a ServletContext object, which contains information about the network service in which the servlet is running. The context is acquired from the configuration.
`public String getServletInfo()`	Returns a string that contains information about the servlet, such as its author, version, and copyright. This method should be overridden appropriately by subclasses. For example, you might return the string "Search Servlet, Stephen & Scott, version 1.0 1998."
`public void init(ServletConfig)`	Initializes the servlet by storing the config object in an instance variable and logs the initialization.
`public void log(String)`	Writes the class name of the servlet and the given message to the servlet log file.
`public void service(ServletRequest, ServletResponse) throws ServletException, IOException`	Implements the service method by doing nothing. This method is intended to be overridden.

Table 7.9 HttpServlet Methods

METHOD	DESCRIPTION
`void doDelete(HttpServletRequest, HttpServletResponse)`	Performs the HTTP DELETE operation; the default implementation reports an HTTP BAD_REQUEST error to the client, indicating that DELETE operations are not supported.
`void doGet(HttpServletRequest,`	Performs the HTTP GET operation; the default implementation reports an HTTP

Table 7.9 *Continued*

METHOD	DESCRIPTION
`HttpServletResponse)`	BAD_REQUEST error to the client, indicating that GET operations are not supported.
`void doOptions(HttpServletRequest, HttpServletResponse)`	Performs the HTTP OPTIONS operation; the default implementation of this method automatically determines the HTTP Options that are supported by checking the Java run time for the methods defined in the servlet's class. If a subclass overrides one of the doXXX methods, that request option will automatically show up in doOptions.
`void doPost(HttpServletRequest, HttpServletResponse)`	Performs the HTTP POST operation; the default implementation reports an HTTP BAD_REQUEST error to the client, indicating that POST operations are not supported.
`void doPut(HttpServletRequest, HttpServletResponse)`	Performs the HTTP PUT operation; the default implementation reports an HTTP BAD_REQUEST error to the client, indicating that PUT operations are not supported.
`void doTrace(HttpServletRequest, HttpServletResponse)`	Performs the HTTP TRACE operation; the default implementation of this method causes a response with a message containing all of the headers sent in the trace request. Servlets will rarely override this method.
`long getLastModified( HttpServletRequest)`	Gets the time the requested entity was last modified. This time is returned in a long integer indicating milliseconds since midnight, January 1, 1970, UTC. The default implementation returns a negative number, indicating that the modification time is unknown. In this case, the modification time should not be used for GET or other cache operations.
`void service(HttpServletRequest, HttpServletResponse)`	Checks the request method and calls the appropriate request handler. For example, POST requests result in a call to doPost. If the method is unknown, an error message is sent to the client.
`void service(ServletRequest, ServletResponse)`	Checks whether this is an HTTP request. If not, an exception is thrown. If this is an HTTP request, the request and response objects are cast appropriately, and the previously defined service method is called.

to handle HTTP GET requests; doPost is provided for HTTP POST requests. The second important specialization provided by HttpServlet is the creation of special request and response objects that provide access to HTTP-specific information.

Notice that many of these methods report errors to the client if a particular request type is not supported. These errors are defined and managed in the HttpServletResponse object, as described in the upcoming section, "HttpServletResponse." To support HTTP style servlets, the javax.servlet.http library also provides the class HttpUtils. This class provides three methods, as listed in Table 7.10, for managing HTTP-specific data.

For the most part, these methods are used by the library and will probably not be accessed directly by servlets.

HttpServletRequest

HTTP requests are represented by HttpServletRequest objects. These objects implement the ServletRequest interface and are created by the server before it calls the servlet's service method. The primary function of a request is to provide data to the servlet. This data comes in several forms, including connection information, request information, and the data sent with the request. For example, a form submitted by the user will be represented to a servlet as an HttpServletRequest object. The request can tell the servlet if this was a POST or GET request; the authentication mechanism, if any, used to identify the client; and the data contained in the form.

For accessing the data sent with the request, use the methods provided by the ServletRequest interface, such as getParameter and getReader. The getReader methods return the raw client input; getParameter processes the input into key-value pairs for easy access. You should not mix these two mechanisms, because getParameter has to process all of the data before it can respond and may make the reader unavailable. ServletRequest also defines some of the standard methods for accessing client information such as the client's IP address. The HttpServletRequest class adds methods to the interface that provide specific HTTP information. These methods are listed in Table 7.11.

Table 7.10 HttpUtils Methods

METHOD	DESCRIPTION
`StringBuffer getRequestURL( HttpServletRequest)`	Using information from the request, this method builds the URL that the client uses to access the servlet.
`Hashtable parsePostData(int, ServletInputStream)`	Parses HTML form data as passed using a POST request, stores it in a hash table, and returns the table. Multivalued element names will have arrays for their value in the hash table.
`Hashtable parseQueryString(String)`	Parses a query string, as provided in a GET request, and builds a hash table of key-value pairs, where the values are arrays of strings. If there is only one value for a key, the array is length 1.

Table 7.11 HttpServletRequest Methods

METHOD	DESCRIPTION
`String getAuthType()`	Gets the authentication scheme of this request. For standard Web server authentication, this may be "basic." In this case, a simple username/password scheme is used.
`Cookie[] getCookies()`	Gets the array of cookies found in this request.
`long getDateHeader(String)`	Gets the value of the requested date HTTP header field of this request. The return value is a long integer indicating milliseconds since midnight, January 1, 1970, UTC. Use this long integer to create a Date object.
`String getHeader(String)`	Gets the value of the requested HTTP header field of this request.
`Enumeration getHeaderNames()`	Gets the HTTP header names for this request.
`int getIntHeader(String)`	Gets the value of the specified integer HTTP header field of this request.
`String getMethod()`	Gets the HTTP method (for example, GET, POST, PUT) with which this request was made.
`String getPathInfo()`	Gets any optional extra path information following the servlet path of this request's URI but immediately preceding its query string. For example, if the servlet called go is accessed by the URL http://server/servlet/go/run/fast, this value will be "/run/fast," the path information after the servlet request.
`String getPathTranslated()`	Gets any optional extra path information following the servlet path of this request's URI but immediately preceding its query string and translates it to a real path.
`String getQueryString()`	Gets any query string that is part of the HTTP request URI. This will be a string that is included in the URL of the request after a question mark. For example, the query string http://server/servlet/go?one has the query string "one."

Continues

Table 7.11 HttpServletRequest Methods *(Continued)*

METHOD	DESCRIPTION
`String getRemoteUser()`	Gets the name of the user making this request. This value will be empty if no authentication scheme is in place.
`String getRequestedSessionId()`	Gets the session id specified with this request.
`String getRequestURI()`	Gets, from the first line of the HTTP request, the part of this request's URI that is to the left of any query string.
`String getServletPath()`	Gets the part of this request's URI that refers to the servlet being invoked.
`HttpSession getSession(boolean)`	Gets the current valid session associated with this request if create is false or, if necessary, creates a new session for the request if create is true.
`boolean isRequestedSessionIdFromCookie()`	Checks whether the session id specified by this request came in as a cookie.
`boolean isRequestedSessionIdFromUrl()`	Checks whether the session id specified by this request came in as part of the URL.
`boolean isRequestedSessionIdValid()`	Checks whether this request is associated with a session that is valid in the current session context.

HttpServletRequest also adds new functionality to the request object for managing session information. Sessions are discussed in detail under the heading "HttpSessions," but for now notice the methods for managing the session id and session object.

As an example of the information provided by the request object, we have created a servlet that displays the headers, parameters, and information from the request back to the client. Notice that depending on your environment, some of these methods may not work successfully. See the section on "Debugging Servlets" for more information on how to find these errors. The results of running this servlet are pictured in Figure 7.2. The input from a form was included, along with the environmental information. All of the code for this example is included in the single-class PrintEnvServlet that extends HttpServlet. The service method is implemented to print information from the request in an HTML page and return the HTML to the client.

```
import java.io.*;
import java.util.*;
import javax.servlet.*;
import javax.servlet.http.*;
```

```
public class PrintEnvServlet extends HttpServlet
{
    public void service(HttpServletRequest request,
                        HttpServletResponse response)
                        throws ServletException, IOException
    {
        PrintWriter    out;
        Enumeration headers;
        String curHeader;
```

The content type for a servlet's response is set using the response object. In this case, we will return HTML, which has the MIME type text/html. Once the content type is set, the servlet prints the beginning of the HTML page.

```
        response.setContentType("text/html");

        out = response.getWriter();

        out.println("<HTML><HEAD><TITLE>");
        out.println("Print Environment");
        out.println("</TITLE></HEAD><BODY>");
```

Next, the servlet uses the HttpUtils class and the request object to recreate the exact URL used by the client to access the servlet. For example, this code constructs a string such as http://zero:8080/servlet/printer.

```
        out.println("<H1>Requested URL</H1>");
        out.println(HttpUtils.getRequestURL(request).toString());
        out.println("<BR>");
```

After printing the request URL, the servlet prints all of the header fields in the request and their associated values.

```
        out.println("<H1>Headers</H1>");
        headers = request.getHeaderNames();

        while(headers.hasMoreElements())
        {
            curHeader = (String) headers.nextElement();

            out.println(curHeader
                        +"="+request.getHeader(curHeader)+"<BR>");
        }
```

HttpServletRequest provides a number of direct methods for accessing information about a request. The following code displays all of these values with their corresponding names. Table 7.11 describes the meaning of each value. Some of these values overlay the headers printed above.

```
        out.println("<BR>");
        out.println("<H1>Request Information</H1>");
```

```
try
{
    out.println("AuthType="+request.getAuthType()+"<BR>");
    out.println("Scheme="+request.getScheme()+"<BR>");
    out.println("Method="+request.getMethod()+"<BR>");

//Crashes on some servers.
//  out.println("Char Encoding="
                +request.getCharacterEncoding()+"<BR>");

    out.println("Request URI="
                +request.getRequestURI()+"<BR>");
    out.println("Request protocol="
                +request.getProtocol()+"<BR>");
    out.println("Servlet path="
                +request.getServletPath()+"<BR>");
    out.println("Path Info="+request.getPathInfo()+"<BR>");
    out.println("Path Translated="
                +request.getPathTranslated()+"<BR>");
    out.println("Query String="
                +request.getQueryString()+"<BR>");
    out.println("Content length="
                +request.getContentLength()+"<BR>");
    out.println("Content type="
                +request.getContentType()+"<BR>");
    out.println("Server name="
                +request.getServerName()+"<BR>");
    out.println("Server port="
                +request.getServerPort()+"<BR>");
    out.println("Remote user="
                +request.getRemoteUser()+"<BR>");
    out.println("Remote address="
                +request.getRemoteAddr()+"<BR>");

//Times out if no DNS.
//    out.println("Remote host="
                +request.getRemoteHost()+"<BR>");
}
catch(Exception exp)
{
    out.println("Exception: "+exp+"<BR>");
}
```

Next, the servlet checks any parameters and prints them. These will be defined by forms or manually by the HTML and browser. Parameters can be single valued or multivalued. This code checks for both and, if the parameter is multivalued, prints a list. Otherwise, a single string is printed.

```
out.println("<BR><H1>Parameter Information</H1>");

Enumeration parameters;
```

```
        String[] values;
        String curParam;
        String value;
        int i,max;

        parameters = request.getParameterNames();

        while(parameters.hasMoreElements())
        {
            curParam = (String) parameters.nextElement();

            values = request.getParameterValues(curParam);
            value = request.getParameter(curParam);

            out.println(curParam+"=<BR><UL>");

            if((values != null)&&(values.length>1))
            {
                max = values.length;

                for(i=0;i<max;i++)
                {
                    out.println("<LI>"+values[i]);
                }
            }
            else if(value != null)
            {
                out.println("<LI>"+value);
            }

            out.println("</UL>");
        }
```

Finally, the HTML page is concluded, and the output stream to the client is closed.

```
        out.println("</BODY></HTML>");

        out.close();
    }
}
```

The HTML page shown activates the servlet. Notice that the form action URL has extra path information passed in order to show, in the servlet and in the output, how this information is passed to the servlet and processed as PathInfo data. A list of options is also provided in order to show how multivalued input is handled.

```
<HTML>
<HEAD>
<TITLE>
Print Env Form
</TITLE>
```

```
</HEAD>
<BODY>
<FORM METHOD=POST
    ACTION="/servlet/printenvservlet/xtrapathinfo">

<INPUT NAME="Field" VALUE="Field Value"><BR>
<SELECT SIZE=2 NAME="List" MULTIPLE>
<OPTION NAME="ListItem1" VALUE="Item One" SELECT>Item One
<OPTION NAME="ListItem2" VALUE="Item Two" SELECT>Item Two
<OPTION NAME="ListItem3" VALUE="Item Three">Item Three
</SELECT><BR>
<INPUT TYPE="Submit" NAME="Submit" VALUE="Go">

</FORM>
</BODY>
</HTML>
```

On the CD-ROM, this file is called PrintEnvTester.html. When used, it results in a page like the one pictured in Figure 7.2.

This section demonstrated how the request object can be used to process client input. The next section demonstrates how the response object can be used to output results to the client.

HttpServletResponse

Like the HttpServletRequest object, HttpServletResponse provides HTTP-specific access to the servlet's response. This information includes the ability to set headers, add cookies, encode URLs, send error codes, and redirect the client to another URL. These methods are listed in Table 7.12.

Four of these methods are used to notify the client using status codes. These methods include both sets of the setStatus and sendError methods. The two methods called setStatus are used if no error occurs, but the servlet will not return a document if, for example, a put was successful or a file is temporarily unavailable. The sendError methods also cause the servlet to not return a document, but in that case, the client is told that an error has occurred. In both cases, a status code and optional messages can be sent to the client in place of any other data.

The available status codes are provided as static variables of HttpServletResponse. Some of the more common ones are listed in Table 7.13. The complete list is available in the javax.servlet documentation.

When a servlet encounters a problem from which it cannot recover, it should use the status codes and error codes in Table 7.13 to indicate the error to the client.

The following example demonstrates how a servlet can return non-HTML data. In this case, the servlet returns the data for an image. The motivation of this example was to have a servlet that rotated through a set of banner ads. The ads are stored in a directory, and when the servlet is initialized, it reads the directory for available images. When a request is made, the servlet returns the next image in the list. The directory of images is indicated to the servlet via an initialization/configuration parameter to maximize flexibility. We implemented the getLastModified method to indicate that the

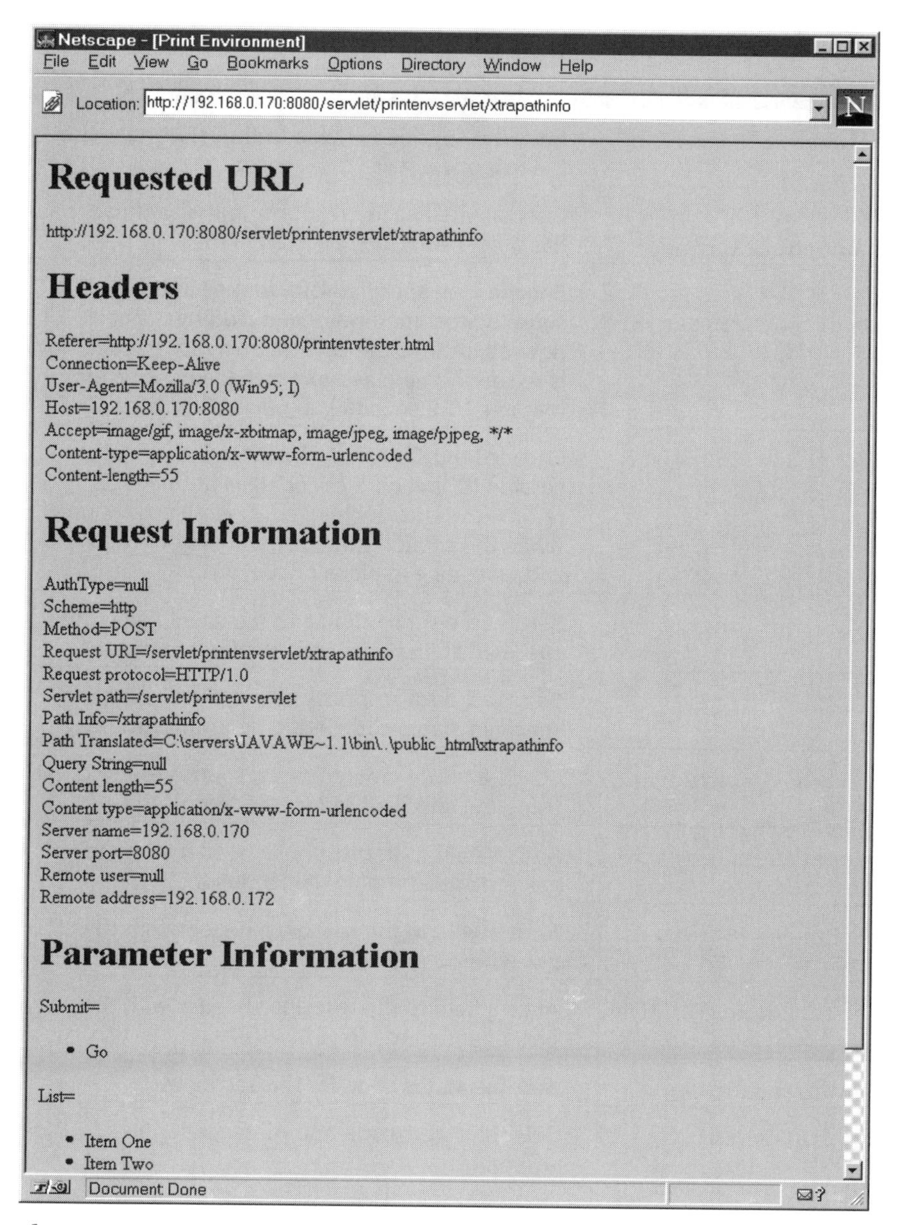

Figure 7.2 PrintEnvServlet results.

resource is always new, always just modified. Because this servlet returns an image, it would normally be used as the SRC value for an IMG tag, but it could be accessed directly. Figure 7.3 shows what it looks like to directly access the ad rotator.

AdRotatorServlet extends HttpServlet and, for simplicity, marks itself single threaded by implementing SingleThreadModel. A Vector instance variable called imageFiles is used to keep a list of images; an integer called curIndex is used to keep

Table 7.12 HttpServletResponse Methods

METHOD	DESCRIPTION
`void addCookie(Cookie)`	Adds the specified cookie to the HTTP header of the response.
`boolean containsHeader(String)`	Checks whether the response message header has a field with the specified name.
`String encodeRedirectUrl(String)`	Encodes the specified URL for use in the sendRedirect method or, if encoding is not needed, returns the URL unchanged. This method is used when the session management system requires URL encoding in place of cookies.
`String encodeUrl(String)`	Encodes the specified URL by including the session ID in it or, if encoding is not needed, returns the URL unchanged. This method is used when the session management system requires URL encoding in place of cookies.
`void sendError(int)`	Sends an error response to the client using the specified status code and a default message.
`void sendError(int, String)`	Sends an error response to the client using the specified status code and a descriptive message.
`void sendRedirect(String)`	Sends a temporary redirect response to the client using the specified redirect location URL.
`void setDateHeader(String, long)`	Adds a field to the response header with the given name and date-valued field.
`void setHeader(String, String)`	Adds a field to the response header with the given name and value.
`void setIntHeader(String, int)`	Adds a field to the response header with the given name and integer value.
`void setStatus(int)`	Sets the status code for this response.
`void setStatus(int, String)`	Sets the status code and message for this response.

track of the current image to display. These two variables are combined so that the servlet returns a different image from the list on each request.

```
import java.io.*;
import java.util.*;
import javax.servlet.*;
import javax.servlet.http.*;

public class AdRotatorServlet extends HttpServlet
implements SingleThreadModel
```

Table 7.13 Common HTTP Status Codes

HTTPSERVLETRESPONSE STATIC VARIABLE	DESCRIPTION OF STATUS CODE
SC_ACCEPTED	Indicates that a request was accepted for processing but was not completed.
SC_FORBIDDEN	Indicates that the server understood the request but refused to fulfill it.
SC_METHOD_NOT_ALLOWED	Indicates that the method specified is not allowed for that URL.
SC_NOT_FOUND	Indicates that the requested resource is not available.
SC_NOT_MODIFIED	Indicates that a conditional GET operation found that the resource was available and not modified.
SC_OK	Indicates that the request succeeded normally.
SC_REQUEST_TIMEOUT	Indicates that the client did not produce a request within the time that the server was prepared to wait.
SC_SERVICE_UNAVAILABLE	Indicates that the HTTP server is temporarily overloaded and unable to handle the request.
SC_UNAUTHORIZED	Indicates that the request requires HTTP authentication.

```
{
    Vector imageFiles;
    int curIndex;
```

The init method loads the available images into the imageFiles Vector based on the imageDir configuration parameter. Only GIF and JPG files are supported for simplicity.

```
    public void init(ServletConfig config) throws ServletException
    {
        String imageDirName;
        File imageDir=null;
        String[] files;
        int i,max;
        File curFile;

        super.init(config);

        imageFiles = new Vector();
```

```
        imageDirName = getInitParameter("imagedir");

        if(imageDirName != null) imageDir = new File(imageDirName);

        if((imageDir!=null) && imageDir.exists()
                            && imageDir.isDirectory())
        {
            files = imageDir.list();

            max = files.length;

            for(i=0;i<max;i++)
            {
                if(files[i].endsWith("jpg")||
                    files[i].endsWith("gif"))
                {
                    curFile = new File(imageDir,files[i]);
                    imageFiles.addElement(curFile);
                }
            }
        }
        else
        {
            log("Cannot find image dir: "+imageDirName);
        }
    }
```

When the servlet receives a GET request, it gets the next image file and outputs the correct content type. Then, using standard Java I/O, the content of the image is sent to the client. If no images are available, the SERVICE_UNAVAILABLE error is sent to the client. The NOT_FOUND error is used if the image file is, for some reason, in the list but not on the disk.

```
    public void doGet(HttpServletRequest    request,
                      HttpServletResponse    response)
                      throws ServletException, IOException
    {
        File curFile;
        int len = imageFiles.size();
        String ctype;
        String fileName;
        FileInputStream fileIn;
        BufferedInputStream bufIn;
        OutputStream out;
        ServletContext ctxt;
        int cur;

        if(len>0)
        {
            curFile = (File) imageFiles.elementAt(curIndex);
            fileName = curFile.getName();
```

```
            ctxt = getServletConfig().getServletContext();
            ctype = ctxt.getMimeType(fileName);

            if(ctype == null)
            {
                if(fileName.endsWith(".jpg"))
                {
                    ctype = "image/jpeg";
                }
                else
                {
                    ctype = "image/gif";
                }
            }

            response.setContentType(ctype);

            try
            {
                fileIn = new FileInputStream(curFile);
                bufIn = new BufferedInputStream(fileIn);

                out = response.getOutputStream();

                while((cur=bufIn.read())!=-1)
                {
                    out.write(cur);
                }

                out.close();
                bufIn.close();
            }
            catch(FileNotFoundException exp)
            {
                response.sendError(
                  HttpServletResponse.SC_NOT_FOUND);
            }
            catch(Exception exp)
            {
               response.sendError(
                   HttpServletResponse.SC_SERVICE_UNAVAILABLE);
            }

            curIndex= (curIndex+1)%len;
        }
        else
        {
            response.sendError(
                  HttpServletResponse.SC_SERVICE_UNAVAILABLE);
        }
    }
```

```
    public long getLastModified()
    {
        return System.currentTimeMillis();
    }
}
```

This example also demonstrates how to use the error codes in the try/catch blocks to indicate a nonrecoverable problem in the servlet. In this case, different status codes are used to indicate that a file is no longer available or an unknown exception occurred.

You could also implement this servlet using redirection. In this case, the servlet would use the method sendRedirect, along with the appropriate URL back to the client. Then the client would make a new request to the server for the specified resource. The servlet could also be extended to associate links with ads.

The opposite version of this ad rotator that sends images is a servlet that supports file uploads. An example of this type of servlet is provided on the CD-ROM in the chapter_07 directory under the fileupload package. This example is a larger exercise in parsing the input to the servlet to determine the start and end for each file, so we have not included it in the text. However, we strongly suggest that you look at this example if you are thinking about supporting file uploading on your server. Many servers provide their own support for uploads, but it can't hurt to know the basics of what they are doing.

HttpSession

One of the more powerful features provided by the HTTP servlet library is the ability to track session information. A session is a single continuous interaction with a particular

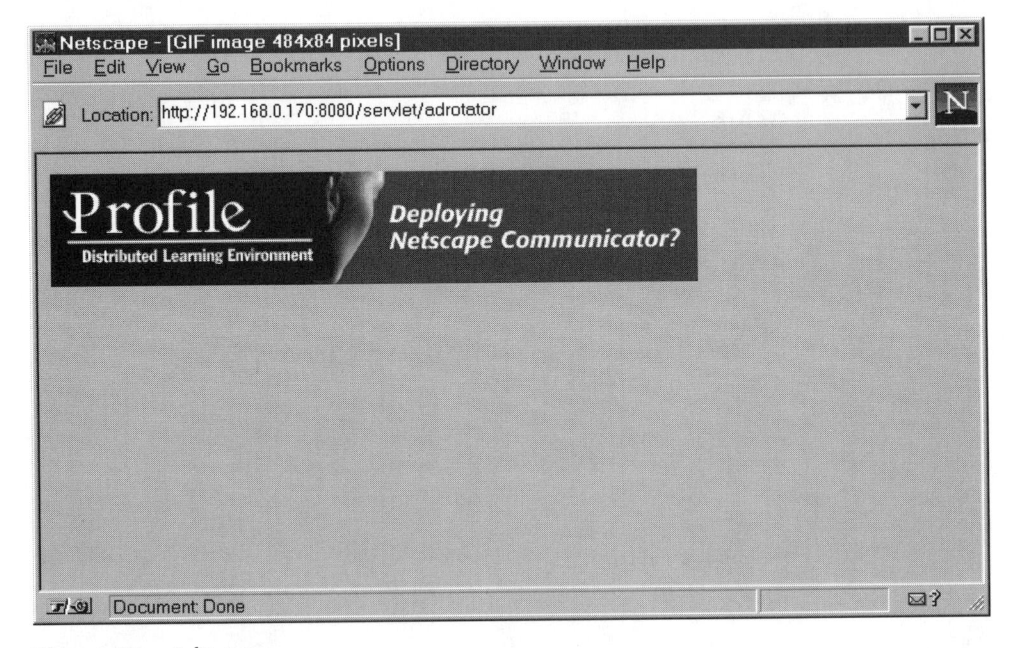

Figure 7.3 AdRotator.

user. The session-tracking mechanism allows an arbitrary collection of objects to be associated with a session. The actual implementation of session tracking is server dependent. One common mechanism is to use an id to track the session and associate a hash table of some sort with this id. The hash table is stored in memory throughout the session.

In some servers with a large number of sessions open, the data may be stored to disk using serialization. When a session begins, the id is created. This id is passed between the client and server to identify the session. Remember that HTTP is a stateless protocol, so the client and server are not always in contact. By sending the id back and forth, the client and server are able to maintain an ongoing session. You as a programmer get access to the session via the HttpSession object and can manipulate or query it using the methods in Table 7.14.

The current HttpSession is acquired from the HttpServletRequest using the method getSession. This method takes a single Boolean argument that indicates whether the session exists and whether it should be created if it does not. By using this flag, you can wait to create a session and simply check if one currently exists. On large Web sites, this is an important technique. To see why, imagine an online store. Thousands of people are shopping, but only those with a shopping cart need a session. Limiting sessions to those people can reduce server resource usage dramatically.

Table 7.14 HttpSession Methods

METHOD	DESCRIPTION
`long getCreationTime()`	Returns the time the session was created, in milliseconds, since midnight, January 1, 1970, UTC.
`String getId()`	Returns the session's id.
`long getLastAccessedTime()`	Returns the last time the client sent a request using this session id, in milliseconds, since midnight, January 1, 1970, UTC.
`HttpSessionContext getSessionContext()`	Returns the session context.
`Object getValue(String)`	Returns the object value based on the string name.
`String[] getValueNames()`	Returns an array of the names of all the objects in the session.
`void invalidate()`	Causes this representation of the session to be invalidated and removed from its context.
`boolean isNew()`	Returns true if the session is new, false otherwise.
`void putValue(String, Object)`	Adds an object to the session with the given name.
`void removeValue(String)`	Removes the value with the specified name from the session.

Once you get the session object, you can use it to access the session data as a set of named values. There are also methods for getting the session's id and information about its creation. All of these are listed in Table 7.14.

When a session is first created, it is considered new. The session remains new until the client "knows" about the session. There are two ways the client learns about the session. First, the session-tracking mechanism tries to use cookies to tell the client about the session id. If the browser supports and accepts the cookie, this mechanism is transparent to the programmer. The other way to tell the client about the session is to send the session id as part of a URL. In this case, the programmer must encode all URLs sent to the client so that they include the session id. Obviously, cookies are easier to program with, but URL encoding is more portable between browsers. However, URL encoding works only if all the servlets and pages that contain URLs on the site encode them appropriately. This is often too much to ask of a large site, and many simply do not support sessions on browsers that do not support cookies. To encode a URL, use the methods encodeUrl and encodeRedirectUrl in the HttpResponse object.

The values in a session are all objects. On the Java Web Server, it is helpful to make these objects serializable so that they can be saved to disk, if necessary. However, any object will do. If you want to store custom objects, you can also implement the HttpSessionBindingListener interface. In this case, the object is notified when it is added or bound to a session and again when it is unbound. HttpSessionBindingListener defines the methods:

```
public void valueBound(HttpSessionBindingEvent event)
public void valueUnbound(HttpSessionBindingEvent event)
```

The server calls these methods when the object is bound and unbound from the session. You might use this notification to update cached information or free resources being held by the object. For example, you might associate objects in a session with Enterprise JavaBeans. When the object is unbound, the relationship can be discontinued.

Normally, it is up to the server configuration to determine when a session is no longer valid. Often this is a question of how much time has passed since the last access, but many servers are configurable. You can also invalidate a session directly by using the invalidate method of HTTPSession.

The following example code shows a simple servlet that keeps a counter for each time the servlet is accessed in the given session. It also prints some of the information provided by the session to the servlet.

The first time this servlet is accessed, it sets the counter to 0 and displays a page like the one in Figure 7.4. Accessing the servlet again displays a page like the one in Figure 7.5.

All the code for this servlet is included in the doGet method. The bold code creates the session and checks whether it is new before constructing the appropriate output. In all cases, a string containing a link back to the servlet is included for the user to press.

```
import java.io.*;
import java.util.*;
import javax.servlet.*;
import javax.servlet.http.*;
```

```
public class SessionInfoServlet extends HttpServlet
{
    public void doGet(HttpServletRequest request,
                      HttpServletResponse response)
    throws ServletException, IOException
    {
        HttpSession session = request.getSession(true);

        response.setContentType("text/html");
        PrintWriter out = response.getWriter();

        out.println("<HTML>");
        out.println("<HEAD>");
        out.println("<TITLE>");
        out.println("Session Info Servlet");
        out.println("</TITLE>");
        out.println("</HEAD>");
        out.println("<BODY>");

        if(session.isNew())
        {
            out.println("<H1>New Session</H1>");
            out.println("The count is set to 0.");

            session.putValue("sessioninfo.count",new Integer(1));
        }
        else
        {
            Integer count;
            int intCount=0;

            count = (Integer)
                    session.getValue("sessioninfo.count");
            if(count != null) intCount = count.intValue()+1;

            out.println("<H1>Session Information</H1>");
            out.println("The count is set to "+intCount+".");
            out.println("<BR>");

            session.putValue("sessioninfo.count"
                             ,new Integer(intCount));

            out.println("Session ID: " + session.getId());
            out.println("<BR>");
            out.println("Creation Time: "
                    + (new Date(session.getCreationTime())));
            out.println("<BR>");
            out.println("Last Accessed Time: "
                    + (new Date(session.getLastAccessedTime())));
            out.println("<BR>");
        }
```

```
            out.println("<A HREF=\"");
            out.println(response.encodeUrl(request.getServletPath()));
            out.println("\">");
            out.println("Press Here");
            out.println("</A>");
            out.println("To reload the page, with url encoding.");
            out.println("</BODY>");
            out.println("</HTML>");
            out.close();
        }
    }
```

If you try this servlet, you will find that reloading the Web page increments the counter and updates the last accessed time. Also, if you leave the servlet alone long enough—about 10 to 30 minutes—the session expires, and the next time you access it, you will get a new counter. This expiration time is usually configurable by the server administrator.

Cookies

Sessions provide a method for storing data about a current user interaction, but they are not intended for storing information permanently. *Cookies,* on the other hand, are key-value pairs that a servlet can associate with a client and that can have an arbitrary expiration time. The drawbacks for cookies are threefold. First, they can only be strings. Second, cookies are stored on the client, so they take up client disk space; as a result most browsers limit their number and size. As a guideline, each server can

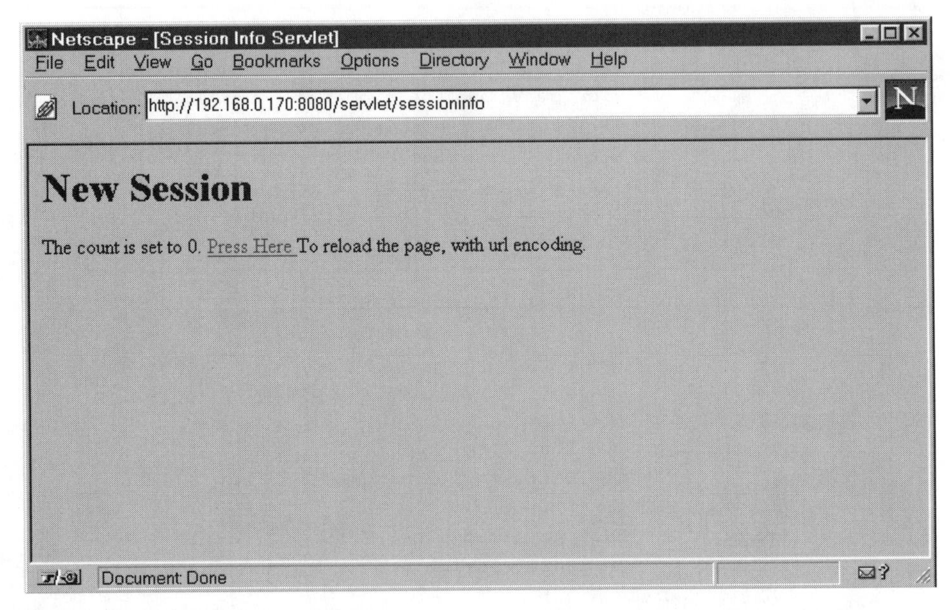

Figure 7.4 First time to servlet.

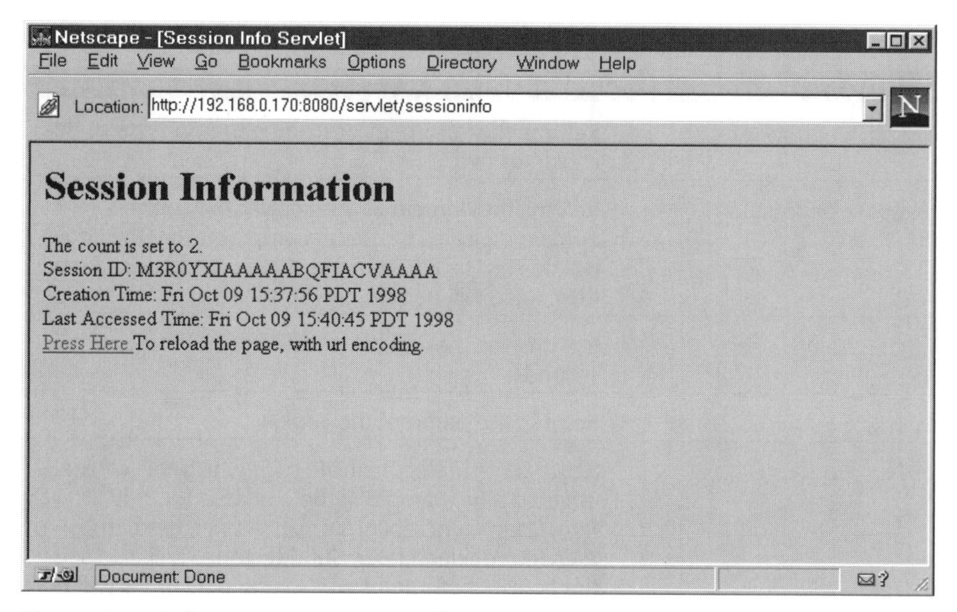

Figure 7.5 Subsequent access to servlet.

assign 20 or so cookies to the client, with a total size of 4K. Finally, cookies have to be sent over the Internet with each request. In HTTP, the cookies are part of the header for a request and reply.

The good thing about cookies is that they are easy to program, are flexible, and can be used to store small pieces of information about a particular program on the client's machine, thus freeing up server resources. Cookies are also associated with a specific server and path, preventing other servers from reading the information they contain. Cookies can be assigned expiration dates, making them persist between sessions. The servlet library uses the class Cookie to represent the cookies provided with an HttpRequest or returned with a response. Table 7.15 shows the methods provided by Cookie.

To determine the cookies for a request, use the HttpServletRequest object's getCookies method. This returns an array of Cookie objects. To associate cookies with the response, use the HttpServletResponse method addCookie. This call should always happen before you send HTML to the client, because the HTML body may force the HTTP header to be sent, and the cookie must be part of the header. If you have cookies from the response that you want to return to the client, add them using addCookie as well.

The following code example implements a basic counter using a cookie. Another cookie is assigned to track the initial time that the first cookie was assigned. This second cookie doesn't change, but it needs to be reassigned to the response to ensure its continued existence. The code for creating and adding the cookies is highlighted to draw attention to it. The surrounding code is used to increment over the list of available cookies and display a page to the user, indicating the results as pictured in Figure 7.6.

```
import java.io.*;
import java.net.*;
```

Table 7.15 Cookie Methods

METHOD	DESCRIPTION
`String getComment()`	Returns the comment describing the purpose of this cookie or null.
`String getDomain()`	Returns the domain of this cookie. The cookie's domain indicates the set of computers that the cookie will be sent to. For example, if the domain is sun.com, the cookie will be sent only to sun.com computers.
`int getMaxAge()`	Returns the maximum specified age of the cookie in seconds.
`String getName()`	Returns the name of the cookie.
`String getPath()`	Returns the prefix of all URLs for which this cookie is targeted. For example, if the cookie is for only http://sun.com/servlet/cookiecounter, the path is /servlet/cookiecounter. Subdirectories will also see the cookie, but parent and sibling directories will not.
`boolean getSecure()`	Returns the value of the secure flag. If the cookie is secure, it will be sent over only secure channels such as https, not over standard http.
`String getValue()`	Returns the value of the cookie.
`void setComment(String)`	Used by the Web browser to indicate its purpose to the user.
`void setDomain(String)`	Sets the cookie's domain.
`void setMaxAge(int)`	Sets the cookie's maximum age in seconds. A negative value tells the cookie that it should persist for only the current session. Zero means that the cookie should be deleted. A positive number indicates the time, in seconds, for which the cookie should persist.
`void setPath(String)`	Sets the cookie's path as described above.
`void setSecure(boolean)`	Turns the secure flag on and off.
`void setValue(String)`	Sets cookie's value.

```
import java.util.*;
import javax.servlet.*;
import javax.servlet.http.*;

public class CookieCounterServlet extends HttpServlet
{
    public void doGet(HttpServletRequest request,
                      HttpServletResponse response)
    throws ServletException, IOException
```

```
{
    response.setContentType("text/html");
    PrintWriter out = response.getWriter();

    //Get list of current cookie values from request object.
    Cookie cookies[] = request.getCookies();
    int i,max=0;
    String countStr=null;
    String createStr = null;
    Cookie curCookie=null;
    Cookie countCookie=null;

    if(cookies != null) max = cookies.length;

    for(i=0;i<max;i++)
    {
        curCookie = cookies[i];

        if("count".equals(curCookie.getName()))
        {
            countStr = curCookie.getValue();
            countCookie = curCookie;
        }
        else if("create".equals(curCookie.getName()))
        {
            createStr =
                URLDecoder.decode(curCookie.getValue());
            //Don't change just re-add
            response.addCookie(curCookie);
        }
        else
        {
            response.addCookie(curCookie);
        }
    }

    //Set the cookie first, since it goes in the header.
    if((countStr == null)||(countCookie == null))
    {
        countStr = "0";
        curCookie = new Cookie("count",countStr);
        response.addCookie(curCookie);

        createStr = (new Date()).toString();
        createStr = URLEncoder.encode(createStr);

        curCookie = new Cookie("create"
                            ,createStr);

        createStr = URLDecoder.decode(createStr);
        response.addCookie(curCookie);
    }
```

```
        else
        {
            int intCount=0;

            intCount = Integer.parseInt(countStr) + 1;
            countStr = String.valueOf(intCount);
            countCookie.setValue(countStr);

            response.addCookie(countCookie);
        }

        out.println("<HTML>");
        out.println("<HEAD>");
        out.println("<TITLE>");
        out.println("Cookie Counter Servlet");
        out.println("</TITLE>");
        out.println("</HEAD>");
        out.println("<BODY>");

        out.println("The count is set to "+countStr+".");
        out.println("<BR>");
        out.println("The creation time was "+createStr+".");
        out.println("</BODY>");
        out.println("</HTML>");
        out.close();
    }
}
```

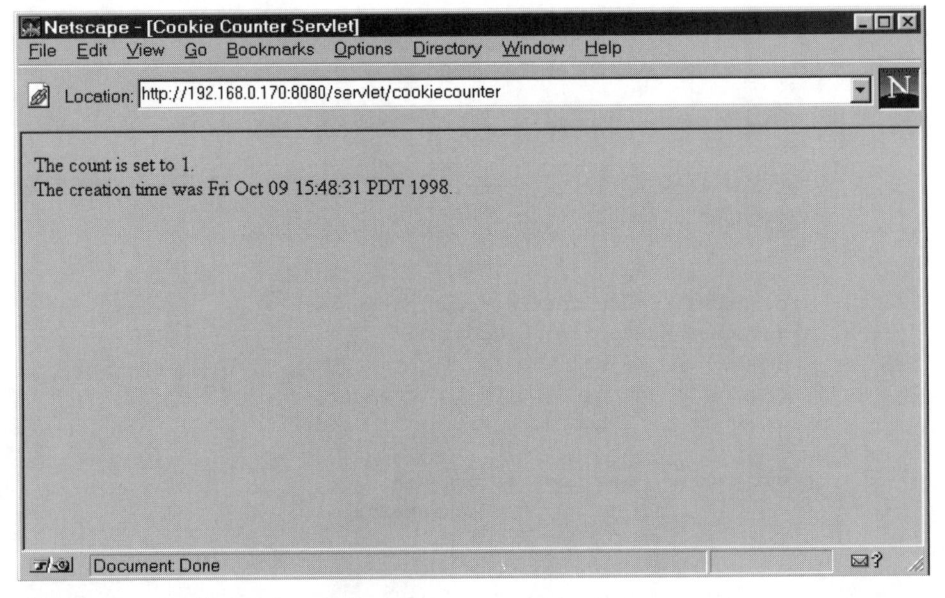

Figure 7.6 Cookie servlet results page.

To ensure that the data sent in the cookie referenced in this code is valid HTTP style data, it is encoded with the URLEncoder class provided in java.net. However, we must write our own URLDecoder to recover the original data string. This class is provided on the CD-ROM.

Because cookies are limited by the client, keep in mind the total use of cookies by your Web server, including session ids, when adding new cookies to the list. One interesting use of cookies—and a way around the size limitations—is to create your own sessions by creating ids and storing them in cookies. Associate the ids with data in a file or in the database. This allows the session to be persistent with the session id on the client and the session information on the server.

Multithreaded Servlets

The section "SingleThreadModel" discussed the decision of whether or not to make a servlet multithreaded. Given the environment that servlets live in, the question remains: Should a servlet be multithreaded, and if it is, how do we write it? Put simply, a multithreaded servlet is one that allows its service method to be called by more than one thread at a time. This means that any data accessed in service must be protected and thread safe. This section covers some of the techniques specific to servlets that support multiple threads.

There are two basic ways to handle thread issues in servlets. One way is to make sure that each request works independently of the others, without sharing data. The other mechanism is to use synchronization to protect shared resources. For servlets that can work autonomously, handling each request with resources that are independent of other requests, write them that way. This is especially easy for servlets that perform an algorithmic task and don't actually return data from another source. These servlets can usually store all of the data they need in local variables, preventing overlap between one thread's execution of the service method and another thread's.

In the case of a servlet that shares resources between requests, the shared resources are often files or database connections. Sometimes you might also share objects in memory. Protecting files and connections can be a complex task because the object representing that resource may not be able to provide true thread-safe access. For example, a file can't protect itself between the time you ask if it exists and the time you test its length. There is always a chance that in this small amount of time, another thread will execute code to delete the file.

As an example of one way to deal with this situation within a servlet, we have created a FileLock object listed in the code below. This object uses standard lock/unlock semantics to protect a file object. Servlets can use these lock objects to protect their access to shared files. Unfortunately, this object is limited to working within a single virtual machine and requires the program to be written with locking in mind. Although several servlets may share the FileLock class and thus the locks for that server, another Web server instance or another program can still create an unsafe situation. The solution to these situations is to minimize the chance of their occurrence by copying files, caching, and so on.

```
import java.io.*;
import java.util.*;

public class FileLock extends Object
{
    private boolean locked;
    private File file;

    private static Hashtable locks;
```

The getLockFor method gets a file lock for a file. It is synchronized so that multiple requests block until the first one is finished.

```
    public static synchronized
        FileLock getLockFor(String path)
    {
        FileLock retVal = null;
        File tmp = new File(path);
        String absPath = tmp.getAbsolutePath();

        try
        {
            if(locks == null)
            {
                locks = new Hashtable();
            }
            else
            {
                retVal = (FileLock) locks.get(absPath);
            }

            if(retVal == null)
            {
                retVal = new FileLock(tmp);
                locks.put(absPath,retVal);
            }
        }
        catch(Exception exp)
        {
            retVal = null;
        }

        return retVal;
    }
```

Each FileLock object knows which File it is associated with and stores this information in the file instance variable.

```
    protected FileLock(File f)
    {
```

```
        file = f;
    }

    public File getFile()
    {
        return file;
    }
```

When a thread attempts to lock the file, it waits until the locked flag is not true or it can assign a time-out and only wait until the time-out occurs. Time-outs result in exceptions.

```
    //Waits to acquire a lock.
    public synchronized void lock()
    {
        while(locked)
        {
            try
            {
                wait();
            }
            catch(Exception exp)
            {
            }
        }

        locked = true;
    }

    //Waits to acquire a lock.
    //timeout in millis
    public synchronized void lock(int timeout)
    throws InterruptedException
    {
        while(locked)
        {
            wait(timeout);
        }

        //If wait throws and exception
        //we don't get here.
        locked = true;
    }
```

Unlocking the FileLock sets the locked flag to false and notifies any waiting threads that the lock is not available.

```
    //Notifies threads waiting for lock.
    public synchronized void unlock()
    {
```

```
            locked = false;
            notifyAll();
        }
    }
```

The following servlet called FileLockingServlet was written to test the file lock and appends messages to a specific file. By using the lock, the servlet is guaranteeing that each message will be written fully before the next message begins. Locks are obtained from the FileLock class, by file path. Each lock should be unique for a specific path. Once the lock is acquired, it can be locked. There are two versions of the lock method: one takes a time-out and the other doesn't. If you use the time-out and the time-out occurs, you will get an exception. Handle this exception appropriately, keeping in mind that the file lock was not acquired if the time-out occurred and the file is not safe to access. When the servlet is done with the file, it unlocks it.

```
import java.io.*;
import java.util.*;
import javax.servlet.*;
import javax.servlet.http.*;

public class FileLockingServlet extends GenericServlet
{
   public void service(ServletRequest    request,
                       ServletResponse    response)
                       throws ServletException, IOException
    {
        PrintWriter    out;
        String message;
        FileOutputStream fileOut;
        PrintWriter log;
        FileLock lock;
        File file;

        response.setContentType("text/html");

        out = response.getWriter();

        out.println("<HTML><HEAD><TITLE>");
        out.println("Log Tester");
        out.println("</TITLE></HEAD><BODY>");

        out.println("<H1>Logged</H1>");

        message = request.getParameter("Message");

        out.println(Thread.currentThread()+"  "+message);

        out.println("</BODY></HTML>");

        /*
```

```
            The servlet gets a file lock for the locktest.txt file.
            This may block if other clients are trying to access the
            same file.
          */
          lock = FileLock.getLockFor("c:\\temp\\locktest.txt");
          lock.lock();

          // Once the file is actually locked, read in the file.
          file = lock.getFile();
          fileOut = new
                      FileOutputStream(file.getAbsolutePath(),true);
          log = new PrintWriter(fileOut,true);
          log.println(Thread.currentThread().hashCode()+" "
                          +message);
          log.close();

          // Done with the file, release it for other clients.
          lock.unlock();

          out.close();
      }
}
```

Another way to deal with the problem of shared resources is to create a cache. If the resources are used only for reading and aren't changed, they can be cached in memory and accessed freely. Reading resources is not a problem with multiple threads; writing is the problem. We have even heard of one example in which a company created a servlet that cached an entire directory of files and handled all requests from this read-only cache. Although this is extreme, the authors of this servlet report no thread issues, and they say that the servlet's performance is great.

Servlets and Applets

Servlets are a powerful mechanism for serving dynamic Web pages. They have begun to fill an important role in Java client/server programming. Many developers are creating applet/servlet pairs that cooperate to form a complete application. Applications are often split for reasons that include improving performance, minimizing network traffic, and centralizing business logic. The decision to use servlets and applets is often one of portability and accessibility. Applets run on most browsers, making them a portable client choice. Servlets run as part of the Web server, making them accessible via HTTP through most corporate firewall configurations. By splitting a program into this type of pair, the programmer is basically guaranteed that anyone can run an application.

Connecting an applet to a servlet is really more of an applet programming problem than a servlet one. The applet can use standard HTTP to communicate with the servlet, so the servlet doesn't need to do anything special. However, for servlets that are designed to talk to an applet, the servlet can optimize its communication by return text or binary data instead of HTML. The following example implements the classic Eliza computer psychologist as an applet/servlet pair. The applet displays a user interface, and the servlet performs all of Eliza's processing. The engine for Eliza is provided in a special package, augmented slightly from the public domain package written by Charles Hayden. (Thanks, Charles!)

As you can see from the servlet code that follows, both GET and POST requests are handled, and the Eliza engine is used to handle the incoming message. Plain text is returned to minimize the applet's job in interpreting it. The DebugLog object, discussed in the section "Debugging Servlets," is also used. This servlet has two init parameters for debugging and one for defining the script file Eliza uses. This script file is provided on the CD-ROM with the other files in the Eliza package and can be edited to respond differently.

```
import java.io.*;
import java.util.*;
import javax.servlet.*;
import javax.servlet.http.*;

import Eliza.*;

public class ElizaServlet extends HttpServlet
implements SingleThreadModel
{
    ElizaMain eliza;
    DebugLog logger;
```

The initialization for this servlet prepares the DebugLog (discussed later) and loads the Eliza engine based on the configured script file.

```
    public void init(ServletConfig conf) throws ServletException
    {
        super.init(conf);

        String logFile,logServer,scriptFile;
        int res;

        logFile = getInitParameter("logfile");
        logServer = getInitParameter("logserver");
        scriptFile = getInitParameter("scriptfile");

        eliza = new ElizaMain();

        if((logFile != null)||(logServer != null))
        {
            logger = DebugLog.getSharedLog();

            synchronized(logger)
            {
                if(!logger.initialized())
                {
                    if(logServer != null)
```

```
                {
                    logger.logTo(logServer);
                }
                else
                {
                    logger.logTo(new File(logFile));
                }
            }
        }
    }

    try
    {
        res = eliza.readScript(scriptFile);
        eliza.setLog(logger);
    }
    catch(Exception exp)
    {
        res = -1;
        logger.log(exp);
    }

    if(res != 0) logger.log("Couldn't create eliza main.");
}
```

When a GET or POST request is received, the servlet calls its internal respondToMessage method to handle the request.

```
public void doGet(HttpServletRequest request,
                  HttpServletResponse response)
{
    String message;

    message = request.getParameter("message");
    respondToMessage(message,response);
   }

public void doPost(HttpServletRequest request,
                   HttpServletResponse response)
{
    String message;

    message = request.getParameter("message");

    respondToMessage(message,response);
}
```

The respondToMessage method checks if a message was entered. If no message was sent then a welcome reply is returned. If a message was sent, Eliza is queried. If Eliza is unavailable, an apology is returned to the user. All responses are simply text messages.

```
    protected void respondToMessage(String message
                                   ,HttpServletResponse response)
    {
        PrintWriter    out=null;
        String reply;

           try
           {
           if(message==null)
            {
                reply = "Please enter a message to Eliza.";
            }
            else if(eliza != null)
            {
                reply = eliza.processInput(message);
            }
            else
            {
                reply = "Sorry, Eliza is not available.";
            }
        }
        catch(Exception exp)
        {
            reply = "I am having trouble hearing, "
                    +"please repeat.";
            logger.log(exp);
        }

        try
        {
            response.setContentType("text/plain");

            out = response.getWriter();

            out.println(reply);
        }
        catch(Exception exp)
        {
        }
        finally
        {
            if(out != null) out.close();
        }
    }

    public void destroy()
    {
        logger.closeLog();
    }
}
```

The applet for Eliza creates a simple user interface and responds to action events from the text field. This applet is pictured in Figure 7.7. It is certainly not pretty, but it provides the necessary code to demonstrate applet servlet messaging. Standard JDK 1.0 event handling is used to maximize portability, although the applet has been tested only on Netscape Navigator 3.0 and 4.0.

The majority of the applet/servlet code is in the action method. In the following code, the applet checks whether the parameters say to use GET or POST to talk to the servlet. If POST is used, the applet creates a URLConnection; otherwise, a URL with a query string is used to connect to the servlet. POST messages require the connection to support output, in this case a URL-encoded key-value pair containing the user's message to Eliza. Notice the one piece of code changing the content type. This is required to get the applet to work in Netscape. Once the message is posted to the servlet, the applet reads the response as plain text and displays it in a label.

```
import java.awt.*;
import java.applet.*;
import java.net.*;
import java.io.*;

public class ElizaApplet extends Applet
{
    Label response;
    TextField request;
    String server;

    public void init()
```

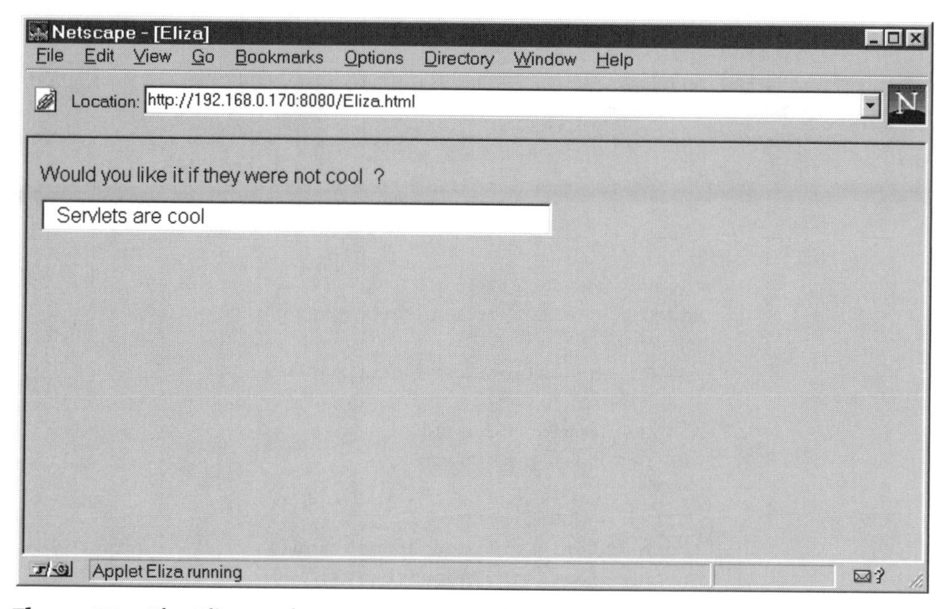

Figure 7.7 The Eliza applet.

```
{
    Font f = new Font("Times-Roman",Font.PLAIN,16);
    Label message;

    response = new Label("Eliza will see you know.");
    response.setFont(f);

    request = new TextField(24);
    request.setFont(f);

    setLayout(new GridLayout(2,1,5,5));

    add(response);
    add(request);

    try
    {
        server = getParameter("server");
    }
    catch(Exception exp)
    {
        server = null;
    }
}

public boolean action(Event evt,
                    Object what)
{
    if(evt.target == request)
    {
        String reply;
        String message;
        DataInputStream reader;
        InputStream in=null;
        URL url;

        try
        {
            message = "message=";
            message += URLEncoder.encode(request.getText());

            if("POST".equals(getParameter("method")))
            {
                URLConnection connection;
                PrintStream printOut;

                url = new URL(server);
                connection = url.openConnection();
                connection.setDoOutput(true);
                connection.setDoInput(true);
```

```
                    connection.setUseCaches(false);

                    //Work around for netscape settings for
                    //post requests.
                    connection.setRequestProperty("Content-Type"
                            , "application/x-www-form-urlencoded");


                    printOut=new
                        PrintStream(connection.getOutputStream());

                    printOut.print(message);
                    printOut.flush();
                    printOut.close();

                    in = connection.getInputStream();
                }
                else
                {
                    url = new URL(server+"?"+message);

                    in = url.openStream();
                }

                reader = new DataInputStream(in);

                reply = reader.readLine();

                reader.close();
                in.close();
            }
            catch(Exception exp)
            {
                reply = "Error, network may be down.";
            }

            response.setText(reply);
            request.selectAll();
        }

        return true;
    }
}
```

Notice that the applet uses regular HTTP requests to talk to the server and simply reads the results in the expected format. In this case, the results are a text string, but the servlet could return an image, file, or other resource—even a serialized object. In other words, although the applet/servlet relationship is affected by the performance of HTTP and intervening firewalls, it is a very flexible mechanism for distributed computing. Even this technique's reliance on HTTP makes it portable across most installations.

Designing Servlets

Perhaps one of the hardest decisions to make when using servlets, or any other Web server application, is how to break the program into logical pieces. In the case of a Web-based program, these logical pieces are often associated with Web pages. When creating a Web application with several Web pages, the first step is to determine what types of pages will be displayed. For example, in an online catalog, there might be pages that list available items and pages that display item details. There may be numerous versions of each type; there are certainly many different items that have details, and those items may be categorized into separate lists.

Given the types of pages you need, ask yourself: Is the data on this type of page dynamic? If it is, the next question is, how dynamic? Does the data change for every request, or just once in a while? For example, the pages at amazon.com are personalized for each registered visitor. This means that the Amazon site has to update the page for each request. On the other hand, an online magazine might add stories daily, but once added, the stories aren't changed for each request. In between these two examples is a Web page that shows data from a database changing hourly. In this case, all users within a given hour see the same page.

For truly dynamic pages, assign a servlet to them. If a page is simply added on a regular basis, just add HTML pages to the site. For pages that change regularly but for which all users see the same version, you have two choices. First, you could use a servlet. This requires the data to be created for each request, or possibly cached in memory. Second, you could have a servlet or another program update the HTML files on disk. This method maximizes the performance of each request and still allows pages to change dynamically.

The bottom line is that you want to use servlets only for pages that change with each request. A great example of this is the search servlet described in Chapter 8, "A Servlet-Based Search Engine." Each search is unique and needs to be handled individually.

Servlets should be assigned by page type and not by individual page. Unless your site has only one page type, you may use numerous servlets to build the site. By specializing the servlets, you minimize the amount or work each one has to do to fulfill a request. Figure 7.8 shows an example of a servlet-based Web application that has been broken up using this philosophy.

The other kind of servlet you might need to write is one that handles the server-side portion of an applet/servlet pair, or a servlet that provides server code to another type of program, such as a Java application. Again, try to minimize the work each servlet does to respond to a request, or at least organize the code to handle the request in a way that makes it easy to maintain. For example, have the service method call other methods based on the client request in the same way that an HttpServlet calls doGet for GET requests and doPost for POST requests. You might even put the code for handling each request type in another class to minimize the size of the servlet code, making it more readable. Testing the servlet and finding errors or performance bottlenecks will also be easier.

There are a number of simple rules you can follow to improve the design and security of your servlets beyond what Java already provides.

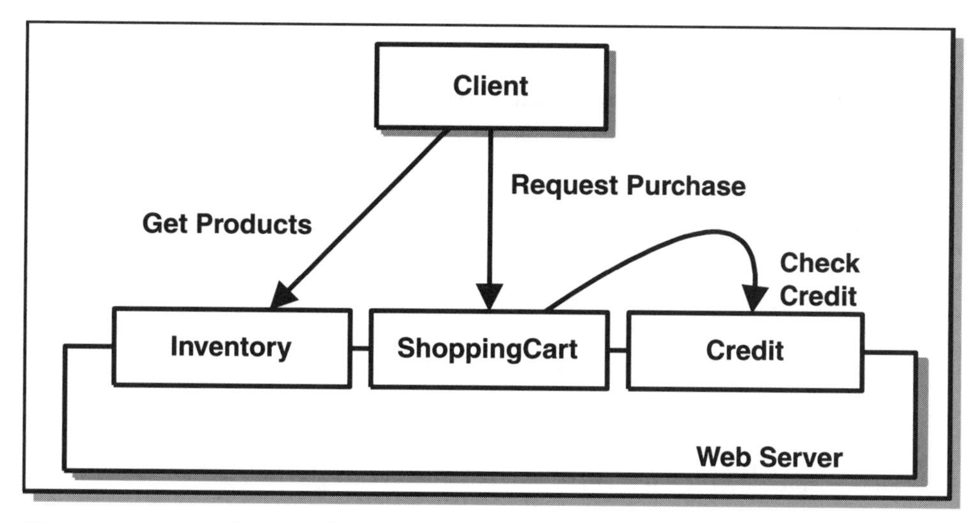

Figure 7.8 Example of servlet application.

1. Double-check any assumptions you make about the user input. Many of the security risks that can occur are the result of faulty assumptions about input. These include the content or the amount of input.
2. Be careful and check that you are not allocating too much memory. In particular, watch out when you are reading data, and don't read an arbitrary amount. Use limits. A hacker could make a POST request with a CONTENT_LENGTH that is outrageously large. This might cause you script problems.
3. Don't assume that the data sent to your script is valid. Check the data first to make sure that it can be used the way you plan to use it. For example, make sure that an int is really an int or use try-catch blocks to handle any exceptions thrown when trying to parse data.
4. Don't assume that all the form elements were filled in. The user may not fill in any or all of the form elements. You might want to check that required elements exist; if they do not, send the user a page that explains the missing fields and provides him or her with a link back to the form.
5. Don't assume that the key-value pairs sent to your script necessarily correspond to actual form elements. A cracker could generate a false request with other fields.
6. Don't return an arbitrary file to the client.
7. Don't assume that path information sent to your script describes a real file. The path sent to a script may not describe a valid file path.
8. Don't assume that path information sent to a script is safe. A cracker could send the path to a file that you don't want him or her to see, such as /etc/passwd. One of the authors once mailed a programmer his password file to prove this point. Always limit access to the file system.
9. Don't assume that a selection is made in a selection list.

10. Make sure your Web server is not running as root. This is a *huge* security risk and could allow an attacker to bring your machine to a grinding halt. Most servers are run as nobody. You might create a user called www and an accompanying group. This allows you to control file permissions more specifically. For instance, all scripts can have group execution and reading permissions without being readable by everyone. You should also test the script as the user who will run it to ensure that that user has the needed file access.
11. Double-check any uses of e-mail from inside a script. Make sure users cannot mail themselves an arbitrary file. They might try to get the password file this way. Also make sure it is okay for users to change e-mail addresses that are hard-coded into your Web pages as arguments to a script.
12. Make sure you don't give a client too much information. Don't return unneeded information about the server.
13. Don't assume that hidden fields are really hidden. Users won't see these in the browser, but they will see them if they view the source. This means that the user can also change them.
14. Don't try to invent your own encryption algorithms. It is common in large scripts to make data persistent by using hidden fields or cookies. This is a useful technique, but these cookies and fields are visible to the user. You might decide that you want to encrypt the fields to hide them from prying eyes. This too is a reasonable solution. However, encryption is a difficult business. Use a proven encryption scheme rather than inventing one yourself. If you do invent your own, make it public and ask for help testing it. We highly suggest the book *Applied Cryptography, Second Edition: Protocols, Algorithms and Source Code in C* by Bruce Schneier (John Wiley & Sons Inc., 1995) as a resource for finding an encryption scheme and learning why writing your own is usually a bad idea. This is a lesson you don't want to learn the hard way.
15. Be careful using native code in servlets. This may be necessary to access some resources, but it also introduces into the Web server the possibility of memory leaks and server-crashing code. When possible, use 100 percent Pure Java servlets to protect both the servlet itself as well as the server from leaks and errors.
16. Double-check all of your service methods that make network connections or perform any operation that could take a long time. Make sure that you use timeouts where possible, and minimize the client's waiting as much as possible.

NOTE **In order to simplify the code, not all of our examples use all of these rules. We often assume that a value is correct before using it. In your production code, do not do this. Instead, follow this book's larger program examples, where we have checked all input before use.**

Hopefully, these guidelines will help you with your servlet designs. This is not a complete list and probably never could be, but it does represent a good starting point for thinking about servlet issues. For other guidelines and tips, keep an eye on www.javaworld.com for articles and other tips that may solve some of your problems before they happen.

Running and Hosting Servlets

There are a growing number of products that support servlets. In writing this book, we have used several providers. First, the Java Servlet Development Kit, or JSDK, provides a command-line program called servletrunner. This program loads servlets and handles servlet requests, but it does not support normal HTML requests, so it doesn't provide the same complete environment as a Web server. Second, the Java Web Server, a product provided by Sun, supports both servlets and JavaServer Pages, as discussed in later chapters. BEA WebLogic Application Server also supports servlets. All of these hosts support initialization arguments that the servlet acquires via the ServletConfig object.

Regardless of the host you pick, you need to know several things before running servlets:

Where do the servlet's class files go? Often the host provides a directory called servlets for these files. The Java Web Server has a directory called servlets; servletrunner uses command-line arguments to indicate the directory all the servlet classes are contained in.

Where do supporting classes go? Most likely, supporting files will go with the servlet, in the CLASSPATH, or in another special directory defined by the host. The Java Web Server provides a directory called classes that is a sibling to the servlets directory. Supporting classes should go in this directory. For servletrunner, the supporting classes should be in either the same directory as the servlet class or in the CLASSPATH used to run servletrunner.

How is the server told about a servlet? In most cases, either a special file or tool is used to tell the server about servlets. The Java Web Server provides an administrative tool that can be used to add servlets to the server, set their names, and assign a class to each name. This name is used in the URL to indicate the servlet using the form http://*server*/servlet/*servletname*. The servletrunner uses a properties file and expects lines of the form:

```
servlet.adrotator.code=AdRotatorServlet
```

This indicates a servlet's name and class. This properties file can be assigned as a command-line argument to servlet runner.

How are initialization parameters set? As with the previous question, either a file or tool is often used to set these parameters. The Java Web Server provides an administrative tool that can be used to add servlets to the server, set their names, and assign a class to each name. This name is used in the URL to indicate the servlet using the form http://*server*/servlet/*servletname*. The servletrunner uses a properties file and expects lines of the form:

```
servlet.adrotator.initArgs=\
                        imagedir=c:\\temp\\chapter_07\\images
```

This code indicates a servlet's arguments. Multiple arguments should be comma delimited, and the \ character can be used to break the arguments across lines. A \ in the argument must be escaped, as shown in the preceding code. This properties file can be assigned as a command-line argument to servlet runner.

The Java Web Server provides excellent support for servlet programming. Even better is the fact that there is every indication that other major server vendors are adopting this technology as well. Expect support and additional functionality to appear in most server products. This means that if you write servlets now, you should see enhanced features and performance in the years to come at very little cost to you.

The servlet development kit is included on the CD-ROM that accompanies this book. Visit java.sun.com for information on downloading a trial version of the Java Web Server or check with your server provider to see if it supports servlets. You might also want to browse to www.livesoftware.com, a company that provides tools for adding servlet support to your existing Web server.

Debugging Servlets

Perhaps one of the hardest aspects of programming servlets is testing them—not testing the features as much as the reliability. Consider that the servlet runs on the Web server and therefore is probably not accessible to a debugger. Certainly, some servlet hosts might provide debug capabilities, but it is not the norm. When an uncaught exception occurs in a servlet, it simply fails to return data. The programmer won't get any information from the client about the error beyond the nagging message, "document contains no data." Also, many developers may write and test their servlets on one Web server and deploy them to another one, making it hard to expect normal debugging facilities. Finally, although servlets do have access to the log file, there are a number of issues with using log statements to debug the program.

The destination for the log is server dependent. Strings sent to the log may be altered and may have other log messages interspersed between them. Log-style debugging is also time consuming in the sense that you will often add logging comments to the code and then remove them for deployment. More important, the log is intended for administratively significant messages, not debugging. Despite these drawbacks, log-style debugging is perhaps the most portable and stable debugging mechanism for servlets.

To make log-style, or printf-style, debugging easier with servlets and other distributed programs, we have created a class listed in the code that follows; this code defines a class named DebugLog. The goal of this class is to provide multiple logging destinations, rather than just supporting the servlet log. In particular, the DebugLog object can be told to send log messages to a file, stream, or even to a log server that has been provided. This server prints messages to System.out or a file. In the case of the log server, you can watch log messages in real time while testing the servlet. Two methods are provided: one to log string messages and the other to log an exception's stack trace. This can be especially useful when an exception occurs.

We also want to minimize the code changes required to move from development to production. The technique we use to accomplish this is a simple one. First, the DebugLog object is not initialized with a specific log destination. If no destination is provided, the logging code will simply ignore all logging messages. This means that you can leave debugging code in your servlets at the cost of a message send and an if statement. In the context of a server, this is a minimal requirement for reducing the maintenance required to remove debugging code.

The code for DebugLog follows. Notice that the main issues are keeping track of the server in a way that allows the server to go down and the logger to reconnect appropriately. In fact, if either the servlet goes away or the server goes down, the other will self-correct.

```
import java.io.*;
import java.net.*;
import LogServer;

public class DebugLog extends Object
{
    private Socket server;
    private String serverName;
    private BufferedReader serverReader;

    private PrintWriter log;

    private static DebugLog sharedLog;

    public static synchronized DebugLog getSharedLog()
    {
        if(sharedLog == null) sharedLog = new DebugLog();
        return sharedLog;
    }

    public DebugLog()
    {
        log = null;
    }

    public synchronized boolean initialized()
    {
        return ((log != null)||(serverName!=null));
    }

    public synchronized void log(String str)
    {
            //exit quick if no log
        if((log != null)||(serverName!=null))
        {
            log(str,true);//retry
        }
    }

    public synchronized void log(Exception exp)
    {
```

```
        if((log != null)||(serverName!=null))
        {
            StringWriter out;
            PrintWriter printOut;
            String logTrace;
            StringReader in;
            BufferedReader bufIn;
            String curLine;

            try
            {
                out = new StringWriter();
                printOut = new PrintWriter(out);

                exp.printStackTrace(printOut);
                printOut.close();

                logTrace = out.toString();

                in = new StringReader(logTrace);
                bufIn = new BufferedReader(in);

                while((curLine = bufIn.readLine()) != null)
                {
                    log(curLine,true);
                }

                bufIn.close();
            }
            catch(Exception ex)
            {
            }
        }
    }

    //protected method that allows the logger to reconnect
    //to a server
    protected synchronized void log(String str,boolean retry)
    {
        boolean error=false;

        if(log != null)//exit quick if no log
        {
            try
            {
                log.println(str);

                if(serverReader != null)
                {
                    //Read the response, but ignore
                    //This should force an exception
```

```
                // if the socket is closed
                serverReader.readLine();
            }
        }
        catch(Exception ex)
        {
            error = true;
            closeLog();
        }
    }
    else
    {
        error = true;
    }

    if((serverName != null) && error)
    {
        if(retry)
        {
            logTo(serverName);
            log(str,false);//only retry one time
        }
        else
        {
            closeLog();
        }
    }
}

public synchronized void logTo(File f)
{
    if(f!=null)
    {
        closeLog();

        try
        {
            FileWriter fileIn = new
               FileWriter(f.getAbsolutePath(),true);
            log = new PrintWriter(fileIn,true);
        }
        catch(Exception exp)
        {
            log = null;
        }
    }
}

public synchronized void logTo(OutputStream stream)
{
    if(stream!=null)
```

```
        {
            closeLog();

            try
            {
                log = new PrintWriter(stream,true);
            }
            catch(Exception exp)
            {
                log = null;
            }
        }
    }

    public synchronized void logTo(String logServer)
    {
        if(logServer!=null)
        {
            closeLog();

            serverName = logServer;

            try
            {
                server = new
                   Socket(logServer,LogServer.DEFAULT_PORT);

                InputStreamReader readIn;
                readIn = new
                  InputStreamReader(server.getInputStream());
                serverReader = new BufferedReader(readIn);

                log = new
                      PrintWriter(server.getOutputStream(),true);
                server.setSoTimeout(2000);//two seconds
            }
            catch(Exception exp)
            {
                log = null;
                server = null;
            }
        }
    }

    public synchronized void closeLog()
    {
        if((log!=null)&&(server!=null))
        {
            try
            {
                log.println(LogServer.DISCONNECT_MSG);
```

```
                }
                catch(Exception exp)
                {
                }
            }

            if(log != null)
            {
                log.flush();
                log.close();
                log = null;
            }

            if(server != null)
            {
                try
                {
                    if(serverReader != null) serverReader.close();
                    server.close();
                    server = null;
                    serverReader = null;
                }
                catch(Exception ex)
                {
                }
            }
        }

        public synchronized void finalize()
        {
            closeLog();
        }
    }

    class DebugLogTester
    {
        public static int MSG_COUNT=100;

        public static void main(String[] args)
        {
            DebugLog logger = DebugLog.getSharedLog();
            int i;

            System.out.println("Created log.");
            logger.logTo("192.168.0.172");
            System.out.println("Set log dest.");

            System.out.println("Logging messages.");

            for(i=0;i<MSG_COUNT;i++)
            {
```

```
                try
                {
                    logger.log("Test "+i);

                    Thread.sleep(100);
                }
                catch(Exception exp)
                {
                    System.out.println("Exception: "+exp);
                }
            }

            System.out.println("Closing log.");
            logger.closeLog();
        }
    }
```

To use the DebugLog class, you can either make an instance or use the shared instance provided by the class method getSharedLog. Once you have a DebugLog, initialize log to a specific destination using one of the logTo methods. Finally, send log messages to forward strings to the log. In the case of a servlet, the log will probably stay alive for the life of the servlet. However, you can close the log using closeLog. This closes connections and files that are open. Throughout the code, auto-flushing is used with our PrintWriters to ensure that the log messages are sent to the underlying streams immediately.

The log server is implemented in a class called LogServer. The code for this class is available on the CD-ROM but, to save space, has not been included here. The LogServer is a single Java class that uses a separate thread to handle connections from DebugLog clients. Each log message sent by the client is either printed to System.out or a file, depending on the command-line arguments. To make it easier to track messages, they are prepended with the IP address of the client that sends them. The CD-ROM also contains the DebugLog.java file. A class called DebugLogTester is included as part of this file for testing purposes.

For servlets that want to share a single DebugLog object, the method initialized is provided to check if another servlet has initialized the log. This method should be used inside a synchronized block with the call to logTo in order to ensure that one servlet doesn't initialize the log between the time that another calls initialized and logTo. The following servlet finds and initializes the log in its init method using configuration parameters for the destination. This servlet, called LoggingServlet, can be used to test the log features. It takes a parameter called message and logs the message. All of the code for interacting with the debug log is in bold in the code that follows. The surrounding code is simply support for the servlet to return Web pages and determine configuration parameters.

```
import java.io.*;
import java.util.*;
import javax.servlet.*;
import javax.servlet.http.*;

public class LoggingServlet extends GenericServlet
```

```
{
    DebugLog logger;

    public void init(ServletConfig conf) throws ServletException
    {
        super.init(conf);

        String logFile,logServer;

        logFile = getInitParameter("logfile");
        logServer = getInitParameter("logserver");

        logger = DebugLog.getSharedLog();

        if((logFile != null)||(logServer != null))
        {
            //Need to protect against access by multiple clients.
            synchronized(logger)
            {
                if(!logger.initialized())
                {
                    if(logServer != null)
                    {
                        logger.logTo(logServer);
                    }
                    else
                    {
                        logger.logTo(new File(logFile));
                    }
                }
            }
        }
    }

    public void service(ServletRequest    request,
                        ServletResponse    response)
                        throws ServletException, IOException
    {
        PrintWriter    out;
        String message;

        response.setContentType("text/html");

        out = response.getWriter();

        out.println("<HTML><HEAD><TITLE>");
        out.println("Log Tester");
        out.println("</TITLE></HEAD><BODY>");

        out.println("<H1>Logged</H1>");
```

```
            message = request.getParameter("Message");

            logger.log(message);

            out.println(message);

            out.println("</BODY></HTML>");

            out.close();
        }

        public void destroy()
        {
            logger.closeLog();
        }
}
```

An HTML page called LoggingTester.html follows. This Web page activates the LoggingServlet. The HTML contains a field for the message and a Submit button.

```
<HTML>
<HEAD>
<TITLE>
Logging Tester
</TITLE>
</HEAD>
<BODY>
<FORM METHOD=POST ACTION="/servlet/logservlet">
Message to log:
<INPUT NAME="Message" VALUE=""><BR><BR>
<INPUT TYPE="Submit" NAME="Submit" VALUE="Log">

</FORM>
</BODY>
</HTML>
```

As tools improve, the Web servers that host servlets may begin to provide better debugging tools. Until that time, log-style debugging is a powerful technique.

WARNING **We have found that servlets often crash if you try to print an invalid or null string to the output writer. Be careful when printing dynamic strings, and take into account the possibility that they may be null.**

Using the DebugLog object allows you to create servlets with the necessary log messages, without having to change a lot of code when you deploy the servlet. In fact, you can even use a configuration argument to specify the logging destination, thus changing no code when deploying. More important, not changing code means that you won't introduce new bugs while deploying.

You may also want to use www.javaworld.com as a jumping-off point to find tools that help servlet debugging. Live Software, mentioned previously, provides one solution, and other companies provide some tools as well. As enterprise Java programming becomes more mainstream, more debugging and testing tools will become available, so keep an eye out for the "latest and greatest."

Performance Tuning

As you deploy your servlet-based applications, you will probably be concerned about performance. As with all performance-tuning activities, the first step in improving servlet performance is to measure it. To aid in testing the performance of servlets, a simple class follows; its instances use multiple threads to make requests to an arbitrary URL. Currently this class, called LoadTester, supports only GET requests, but it could be updated to support a wider range of request types. The purpose of load tester is to create a load on the server and measure the average response time.

Keep in mind that the implementation of LoadTester is a simple one, mainly to serve as an example for the book. But it does provide a good starting point for testing the general response time of your servlets. Given an optional data file, a load tester even sends data to the servlet for processing. In return, the load tester prints timings for the request and average request times to System.out. Given these times, you can begin to tune performance and check your progress. You can even assign a pause between requests to improve realism.

The LoadTester class that follows exercises a servlet or Web server by making consecutive requests. If no data is provided to the tester, it will get the contents of the specified URL. If data is provided, that data is sent to the URL and the reply read. Both methods use GET requests (the default).

```
import java.net.*;
import java.io.*;

/* *
 * Timing for each request is logged to standard out.
 *
 * Usage: LoadTester numTests numThreads pause url optionalDataFile
 *
 * The data file should be in the form:
 * key value
 * key2 value2
 *
 * using spaces for delimeters.
 *
 * If numTests==0 then the tester will continute
 * indefinately. Each thread will make the specified
 * request numTests times.
 *
 * pause is the time between tests in milliseconds.
 *
```

```
 * The results of each test are read and thrown away.
 * Timing is performed from the request to the first byte read,
 * and to the last byte.
 */
public class LoadTester extends Object
{
    private URL url;
    private String data;
    private int numTests;
    private int numThreads;
    private int pause;

    static public void main(String[] argv)
    {
        LoadTester tester=null;
        int threads, tests,pause;

        if(argv.length < 4)
        {
            System.out.println("Usage: LoadTester numTests "
                    +numThreads pause url optionalDataFile");
            System.exit(0);
        }

        try
        {
            tests = Integer.parseInt(argv[0]);
            threads = Integer.parseInt(argv[1]);
            pause = Integer.parseInt(argv[2]);

            tester = new LoadTester(threads,tests,pause,argv[3]);

            if(argv.length == 5)
            {
                tester.setData(argv[4]);
            }

            tester.start();
        }
        catch(Exception exp)
        {
            System.out.println(exp);
            System.exit(0);
        }
    }

    public LoadTester(int nthds,int ntsts,int p,String u)
    throws MalformedURLException
    {
        numTests = ntsts;
```

```
        numThreads = nthds;
        url = new URL(u);
        pause = p;
    }
```

The setData method reads a file of key-value pairs to create the input for a servlet. This file can be used to define the parameters that a user would normally type into a form.

```
    public void setData(String fileName)
    throws Exception
    {
        FileReader fileIn;
        BufferedReader bufIn;
        String curLine;
        String key,value;
        StringBuffer dataBuf = new StringBuffer();
        boolean firstLine = true;
        int index;

        fileIn = new FileReader(fileName);
        bufIn = new BufferedReader(fileIn);

        while((curLine=bufIn.readLine()) != null)
        {
            index = curLine.indexOf(" ");

            if(index<0) break;

            key = curLine.substring(0,index);
            value = curLine.substring(index+1).trim();

            if(!firstLine) dataBuf.append('&');

            dataBuf.append(URLEncoder.encode(key));
            dataBuf.append('=');
            dataBuf.append(URLEncoder.encode(value));

            firstLine = false;
        }

        data = dataBuf.toString();
        bufIn.close();
    }
```

When started, the load tester creates a special thread subclass to do the actual work and starts the thread running.

```
    public void start()
    {
        LoadTesterThread thread;
        URL tmpURL;
```

```
            int i;

            try
            {
                for(i=0;i<numThreads;i++)
                {
                    tmpURL = new URL(url.toExternalForm());
                    thread = new
                         LoadTesterThread(numTests,tmpURL,pause,data);
                    thread.start();
                }
            }
            catch(Exception ex)
            {
                System.out.println("Tester failed...");
            }
        }
}
```

A LoadTesterThread stores information about each test. The run method runs the specified number of tests and prints the results to the console.

```
class LoadTesterThread extends Thread
{
    private URL url;
    private String data;
    private int pause;
    private int numTests;
    private int curTests;
    private int curTotal;
    private int curTotalFinal;

    public LoadTesterThread(int ntsts,URL u,int p,String s)
    {
        numTests = ntsts;
        url = u;
        pause = p;
        data = s;
    }

    public void run()
    {
        if(numTests > 0)
        {
            int i;
            long testStart,testEnd;
            double totalTime;
            double average;

            testStart = System.currentTimeMillis();
```

```
            for(i=0;i<numTests;i++)
            {
                runTest();
                try
                {
                    if(pause != 0)
                    {
                        sleep(pause);
                    }
                }
                catch(Exception ex)
                {
                }
            }

            testEnd = System.currentTimeMillis();

            totalTime = ((double)((testEnd-testStart)-
                             (numTests*pause))/1000);//in seconds

            synchronized(System.out)
            {
                System.out.print(numTests+" performed in ");
                System.out.print(totalTime);
                System.out.print(" seconds ");
                System.out.print(totalTime/numTests);
                System.out.println(" avg.");
            }
        }
        else
        {
            while(true)
            {
                runTest();
            }
        }
    }
```

Each test is executed by connecting to the specified URL, making the request with the provided data, and reading the response. Two times are tracked for reading—the time to start reading and the time to actually read the data—because long responses obviously take longer than short ones.

```
    public void runTest()
    {
        long start,end,realEnd;
        URLConnection connection;
        PrintWriter writer;
        InputStream in;
        int cur;
```

```
try
{
    connection = url.openConnection();
    connection.setDoOutput(true);

    if(data != null)
    {
        connection.setDoInput(true);
        writer = new
        PrintWriter(connection.getOutputStream(),true);

        start = System.currentTimeMillis();

        writer.print(data);

        writer.close();
    }
    else
    {
        start = System.currentTimeMillis();
    }

    in = connection.getInputStream();

    cur=in.read();
    end = System.currentTimeMillis();

    while(cur != -1)
    {
        cur=in.read();
    }

    in.close();

    realEnd = System.currentTimeMillis();

    curTotal += end-start;
    curTotalFinal += realEnd-start;
    curTests++;

    synchronized(System.out)
    {
        System.out.print("Initial ");
        System.out.print(end-start);
        System.out.print(" (");
        System.out.print((double)(curTotal/curTests));
        System.out.print(") ms : Final ");
        System.out.print(realEnd-start);
        System.out.print(" (");
        System.out.print((double)(curTotalFinal/curTests));
        System.out.println(") ms.");
```

```
                }
            }
            catch(Exception exp)
            {
                System.out.println("Test Failed.");
            }
        }
    }
```

Of course, the other method for testing performance is just to use the servlet. In this case, you are testing perceived performance. In reality, perceived performance is more important than actual performance in servlets that respond to user requests. The user will not notice a five-millisecond difference that the computer might. However, when multiple users access the servlet, it will have a different perceived performance than when one programmer tests it. As a result, you may want to combine the load tester with personal testing. Have the load tester imitate a reasonable number of users, then test the servlet by hand, to check perceived performance.

NOTE **Often you can improve perceived performance via user feedback. It is easier to wait 30 seconds watching a moving progress bar than waiting 20 seconds with no feedback. For users, the most important thing to perceive is that work is being done on their behalf.**

In case the total response time of a servlet is considered too long, the first step is to figure out why. Unfortunately, there is no easy way to profile a running servlet, unless the server provides a profiling tool. Live Software also provides a tool for load-testing servlets. You might also find a tools provider for this type of profiling in journals, magazines, or on the Web. Without a tool to discover specific choke points, the next best thing is to evaluate standard performance bottlenecks. In general, this includes items such as:

- Opening network connections—for example, database connections
- Opening and closing files, general I/O
- Allocating memory
- Poorly written algorithms

Of these, the first two can often be solved by pooling resources, or caching. For example, a servlet can share database connections between requests, assuming that there is no security reason not to. In this case, only the init method suffers the performance hit of making a connection. However, sharing connections and keeping them open uses resources. On large Web servers, it is important to consider the effects of holding resources, as much as it is to consider the time it takes to keep reconnecting. It may also be possible to cache the results of database or other queries. In this case, only the first query requires network access, while the others just access data in memory.

Along the same lines, files can be cached in memory. Although this seems like overkill at first, it can increase performance dramatically. However, it does require memory, and the total memory usage of the servlet should be considered before caching lots of files. Regardless of caching, always use buffered readers or streams to read and write files. This can improve performance 5 to 10 times, in some cases.

One of the advantages of servlets over other server plug-in technologies like NSAPI or ISAPI is that they run inside the virtual machine and are subject to garbage collection. This means, in one sense, that you don't have to worry about memory. However, the reality is that creating objects takes time, and a servlet that creates a lot of objects will reflect that time usage in its performance. There are several ways to deal with the allocation issue. First, keep in mind that you should write simple code first. Don't try to avoid memory allocation issues before you even test the program the first time. Second, avoid simple allocations issues by:

1. Using StringBuffers to create large strings rather than appending strings together. This will ensure that only one buffer is used to create the result.
2. Reusing objects when possible rather than creating new ones.
3. Avoid using Sessions unless they are necessary.
4. Avoiding the creation of immutable objects, like Strings, for data that has to change. This is especially true in your own libraries.

Third, set object references to null when you are done with the object to ensure its availability to the garbage collector. Finally, the next generations of virtual machines, including Sun's HotSpot, are designed to reduce the overhead of creating a lot of temporary objects. If you have good code that needs to make a bunch of objects, look into trying a different VM and see if that improves performance sufficiently.

Algorithms represent the foundation of your servlet or any program. In many cases, you will not be using the classic algorithms like sorting or searching, but your servlet will rely on some form of recipe for performing its job. The hard part of tuning your algorithms is the desire to tune them too early. Always use the simplest algorithm first. If testing shows a problem and you can associate the performance problem with the algorithm, it is worth improving.

Extending this discussion to code in general, write simple, solid, maintainable code first. Experience has shown that your performance bottleneck will probably be in less than 10 percent of that code, so don't try to optimize the whole thing. Instead, try to find the key performance issues, then rewrite that code, if necessary, to use fancier and faster techniques.

As always, the fastest code is the code you don't write. Small, targeted servlets can be much faster, once you deal with any network/file issues, than an equivalent large, multipurpose servlet. In the same vein, the fastest servlet is the one you don't have to write. Basically, this means that you should let the Web server do its job whenever possible. In particular, Web servers are great at sending files to the user. Don't write a servlet to do the same thing unless you are adding value to the process. A good example of this would be a site with an online catalog. Let's say the catalog changes once a day. Instead of using servlets to dynamically display the data from the database for each request, you could rebuild the HTML pages once a day, and have the Web server serve the HTML directly from disk. Basically, if the data for a Web page is not customized on every request, try to cache it to disk and let the Web server do its job, rather than programmatically creating HTML each time.

To conclude the discussion on performance, we should at least mention the hardware vendor's motto for performance: more memory, faster CPU, bigger computers, spend money. Basically, you may have good code, but the demand has outstripped the platform you run it on. For Java, this platform extends beyond the hardware into the virtual machine. From an objective point of view, there are a number of things to try, not all of which cost money:

- Compiler options; use optimization when possible
- New compiler
- New virtual machine
- New servlet host (Web server/application server)
- More memory
- Different network cards
- New OS or new network drivers
- New hardware

Certainly you may be constrained to maintain the existing version of any of these items, but keep them in mind when tuning performance.

As always, performance tuning is a hard process and very application specific. The most important rule is always to measure before you tune. If you don't measure, you can spend a lot of time on parts of the code that don't really affect performance one way or the other.

Summary

Servlets represent a powerful mechanism for extending a Web server's functionality and implementing the server portion of a servlet/applet pair or a Web application. As with all client/server programming, there are important performance and design issues to consider:

- Minimize the time required to perform each service request. This often means providing several servlets, one for each request type in an application.
- If possible, support multiple threads. This will allow the most flexibility and, on a multiprocessor computer, may allow you to take advantage of multiple processors. However, you will need to protect shared resources with locks and/or isolation.
- Keep security in mind. Servlets are run on your computer and should not be programmed to execute the client's whims, but your own well-planned actions.
- Measure performance before tuning in a situation that is as realistic as possible. Use tools allowing you to test the servlet under a real-world request load.
- Use the DebugLog or some other tool to implement debugging code early on. Even in writing this book, we relied on the DebugLog to find errors. In most cases, we removed the debugging code to make the example easier to read, but

in the larger examples in later chapters, this code was left in to show how it could be used to find errors.

- Rely on the Web server to do its job. Don't write servlets because you can, write them because you need the dynamic output that they provide.
- Use HTTP servlets when you can. This will provide an easier implementation framework, and the request and response objects will provide more information than the generic equivalents.

The next chapter focuses on a larger servlet-based application. Following chapters cover JavaServer pages. These server pages actually create servlets and rely on all of the information discussed so far. At the end of the book are a number of large examples, some of which use servlets to provide HTTP tunneling. Servlets are a flexible, powerful mechanism for creating server code and will probably fill a key role in your enterprise applications over the next few years.

A Servlet-Based Search Engine

This chapter is the first in the set of larger example programs that are included in this book. This example is a servlet that implements a simple Web page search engine. It demonstrates a number of the concepts we discussed in Chapter 7, "Programming Servlets," such as initialization parameters, path information and parameters from the request, thread synchronization, error codes, and redirection. Searches can be constrained to a maximum number of hits, and navigation links are provided to view the next block of hits if the query results in more than the maximum. Queries can either be plain words or Boolean statements consisting of ands, ors, and nots. The performance for this servlet is adequate for a Web site and can be configured to use custom help pages and support multiple, separately indexed directories. All search results are displayed in a Web page like the one pictured in Figure 8.1. A navigation bar is dynamically generated for moving through large result sets.

The core search engine for this servlet is provided in a package called index, which provides the code needed to index and search HTML files. Indices are represented by HTMLIndex objects in memory and text files on disk. The index objects use hash tables as their internal representation. This makes searches very fast, at the cost of some memory overhead. However, although the size of an index file depends on the number of unique words and files, experience shows that it is approximately one tenth of the size of the pages indexed. Part of this size reduction comes via the use of a skip table that contains words that aren't indexed. This table can be edited, although it requires recompilation of one of the classes in the index package. Although this example servlet does not take advantage of it, the indices also include the number of occurrences for each word. (This book does not go into the details of the index package.) In a later section, this chapter looks at the index manager that handles loading and unloading of indexes. For details on the index itself, refer to the source code on the CD-ROM that accompanies this book.

NOTE In order to run this example, you will need to install it on a Web server that supports servlets. You will also need to configure the initialization parameters described below.

HTMLSearchServlet

The Web interface to the search engine is the class HTMLSearchServlet. This servlet extends HttpServlet and defines an instance variable, logger, to store a DebugLog object (described in Chapter 7, "Programming Servlets"), the helpPage instance variable stores a string containing the URL for a help page, and the instance variable noIndexPage stores

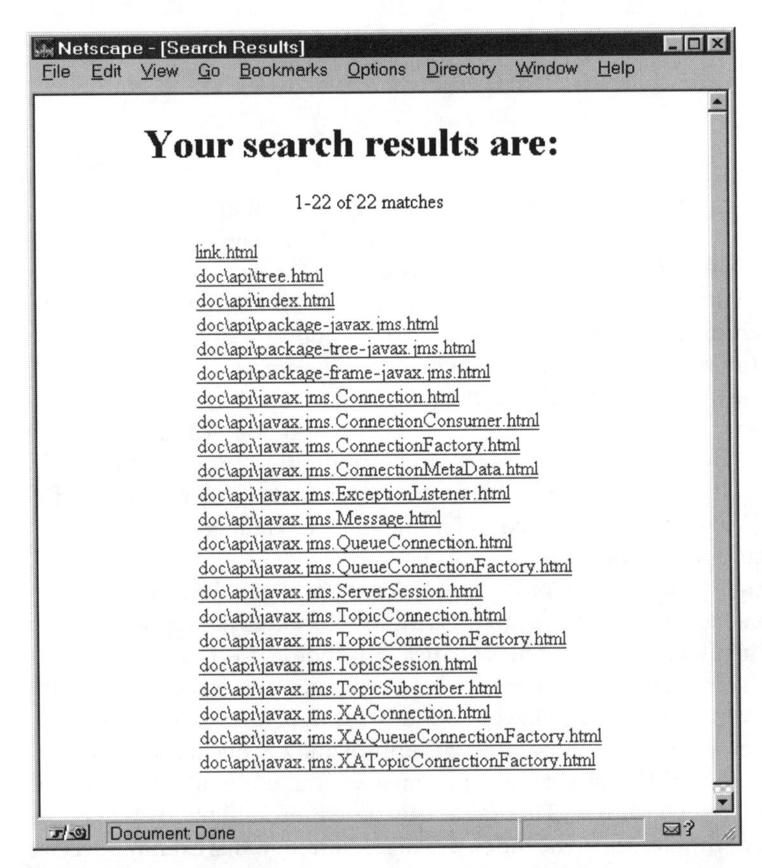

Figure 8.1 Search results.

a string containing the URL for a page to display when the requested search cannot be performed. The static variable DEFAULT_MAX_HITS is defined to indicate the default maximum hits to display at one time. QUERY_FIELD_NAME, MAX_FIELD_NAME, CURRENT_FIELD_NAME SUBMIT_FIELD_NAME, and HELP_NAME are defined to indicate the names of the parameters that the servlet expects from the client. Static variables for these names are used to improve documentation and reduce the number of magic strings in our code.

The following code listing is the beginning of the HTMLSearchServlet class file. It contains the required import statements and the defintion of the static variables used in the class.

```
import java.io.*;
import java.util.*;
import java.net.*;
import javax.servlet.*;
import javax.servlet.http.*;

import index.*;

public class HTMLSearchServlet extends HttpServlet
{
    protected DebugLog logger;
    protected String noIndexPage;
    protected String helpPage;

    protected static final int DEFAULT_MAX_HITS=25;

    public static final String QUERY_FIELD_NAME="query";
    public static final String MAX_FIELD_NAME="maxhits";
    public static final String CURRENT_FIELD_NAME="hitstart";
    public static final String SUBMIT_FIELD_NAME="submit";
    public static final String HELP_NAME="help";
```

The HTMLSearchServlet relies on four parameters: the query parameter, the maxhits parameter, the hit-start parameter, and the submit parameter. The query parameter indicates the user's query. The maxhits parameter is used to change the number of hits to display. If one is not provided, the default is assumed. The hitstart parameter is used internally when a query exceeds the maximum number of hits and the user is scrolling through the blocks of results. If it is not part of a request, the servlet displays the first set of results, without exceeding the maxhits value. The submit parameter is used to determine if the user wants the help page displayed. If the submit parameter is equal to the help name, the help page is displayed; otherwise, the request is interpreted as a query.

The following code segment defines the init method of the HTMLSearchServlet. All of the instance variables are initialized in the init method from configuration parameters listed in Table 8.1.

The debug log is created from a file or server, depending on the available parameters. If no file or server is provided, the log will ignore debug messages. (For more discussion on the debug log, see Chapter 7, "Programming Servlets.") Because the class

Table 8.1 HTMLSearchServlet Configuration Parameters

PARAMETER	DESCRIPTION	DEFAULT
`logfile`	To file to log messages to.	`not set`
`logserver`	The IP address of the DebugLogServer.	`not set`
`helppage`	The URL for the help page to display if the user requests it.	`/SearchHelp.html`
`noindexpage`	The URL for the page to display if no index is available.	`/NoIndex.html`
`updateinterval`	The number of seconds to wait between checking whether files have changed on the disk and the index should be rebuilt.	`not set`

IndexBuilder that creates the indexes for the servlet also uses the shared debug log, if the servlet initializes it, the index builder will print messages to the log as well. An updateInterval can be specified as one of the configuration parameters. If this interval is non-zero, it represents the number of seconds between times that the index manager checks whether the index is up to date with the directory it indexes. If it is not up to date, the index is rebuilt.

```
public void init(ServletConfig config)
throws ServletException
{
    super.init(config);

    String logFile,logServer;

    logger = DebugLog.getSharedLog();

    logFile = getInitParameter("logfile");
    logServer = getInitParameter("logserver");
    helpPage = getInitParameter("helppage");
    noIndexPage = getInitParameter("noindexpage");
    updateIntervalString = getInitParameter("updateinterval");

    if(updateIntervalString != null)
    {
        try
        {
            updateInterval = Long.parseLong(updateIntervalString);
            IndexManager.updateInterval = updateInterval;
        }
        catch(Exception exp)
        {
        }
    }
```

```
        if((logFile != null)||(logServer != null))
        {

            //Index builder uses the same log.

            synchronized(logger)
            {
                if(!logger.initialized())
                {
                    if(logServer != null)
                    {
                        logger.logTo(logServer);
                    }
                    else
                    {
                        logger.logTo(new File(logFile));
                    }
                }
            }
        }
    }
```

The help and no index files are defined relative to the document root for the Web server and are complete URLs for that server. A sample of each file is provided on the CD-ROM. The example help file is called SearchHelp.html. If this file is placed in the Web server's document root, the helppage configuration parameter should be set to /SearchHelp.html. If you type SearchHelp.html without the slash, the server will try to redirect the client to this file as though it were inside the servlet itself, resulting in an error.

The HTMLSearchServlet processes client requests through the doGet method. The code for this method it listed below. The doGet method does two things: First, it checks whether the client wanted to see the help page or wanted to perform a query. Second, the servlet displays the help page or performs the query and returns the results. This decision relies on the way that the search request is submitted. The form submitting the request is expected to name its submit button SUBMIT_FIELD_NAME. If the value of this name is HELP_NAME, the help page is displayed, using redirect. If the help page was not defined in our configuration, the client is sent an error code indicating that help is unavailable.

```
public void doGet(HttpServletRequest request,
                    HttpServletResponse response)
throws IOException
{
    String requestType;

    requestType = request.getParameter(SUBMIT_FIELD_NAME);

    /*
      If the submit field contains the name of the help page,
      then send the client to the help html page.
    */
```

```
        if((requestType != null)
            &&(requestType.equalsIgnoreCase(HELP_NAME)))
        {
            logger.log("Got help request");

            if(helpPage != null)
                response.sendRedirect(helpPage);
            else
         response.sendError(HttpServletResponse.SC_SERVICE_UNAVAILABLE);
        }
        else//null is the same as do query
        {
            handleQuery(request,response);
        }
    }
```

If the submit field retrieved in the doGet method does not contain a request for help, the handleQuery method defined to handle the specifics of the query request is called.

The handleQuery method contains the majority of the HTMLSearchServlet code. The method handleQuery is defined with the same parameters as the doGet method, to make it easy to call. Local variables in the handleQuery method are defined to contain any temporary information that might be necessary. The following code defines the handleQuery method signature and its local variables.

```
    protected void handleQuery(HttpServletRequest request,
                                HttpServletResponse response)
    throws IOException
    {
        HTMLIndex index;                    // The index
        String query;                       // The query to execute
        Vector results;                     // A list of search results
        int i;                              // A local counter
        intmax;                             // Maximum return results
        resultCount=0;                      // Number of query results
        String maxString;                   // Temporary string
        int maxHits = DEFAULT_MAX_HITS;     // Max results displayed
        String curHitStartString;           // Temporary string
        int curHitStart=0;                  // Where to start displaying
        PrintWriter writer;                 // Output writer
        String dir;                         // Directory path
        String fullDir;                     // Full directory path
        String curFileName=null;            // Current file to display
        String myURL;                       // The servlet's URL
```

These local variables are used throughout the handleQuery method.

PathInfo and Query Initialization

Instead of using configuration parameters to indicate the directory to search, the concept of HTTP path information is used. Path information, provided as a file path, appears after the servlet's name in the URL that the client uses to access the servlet. For example, if the search servlet is installed as htmlsearch and you want to search a directory called doc2, you would use the URL:

```
http://servername/servlet/htmlsearch/doc2
```

This tells the servlet to look in /doc2 for the index and documents. Using path information rather than another mechanism such as a configuration parameter is a good choice because the HttpServletRequest already knows how to convert path information into a real file path on the server. The path information itself is assumed relative to the document root by the HttpServletRequest. This means that both the correct URL and file path for the search directory can be acquired easily. The limitation is that the implementation does not handle spaces in file names.

The two values for the search directory are stored in local variables and follow the code listed above:

```
dir = request.getPathInfo();
fullDir = request.getPathTranslated();
```

All other values that we may need are then initialized. The response type is set to tell the client that an HTML document is being returned. The writer for the output to the client is stored along with the various client request parameter values. The variable myURL stores the URL from the request for processing later. Then the maxString and curHitStartString variables are converted to integers and stored in maxHits and curHitStart, respectively. The code for this is listed below:

```
response.setContentType("text/html");

writer = response.getWriter();
query = request.getParameter(QUERY_FIELD_NAME);
maxString = request.getParameter(MAX_FIELD_NAME);
curHitStartString = request.getParameter(CURRENT_FIELD_NAME);

myURL = HttpUtils.getRequestURL(request).toString();

if(maxString != null)
{
    try
    {
        maxHits = Integer.parseInt(maxString);
    }
    catch(Exception exp)
    {
        maxHits = DEFAULT_MAX_HITS;
    }
}

if(curHitStartString != null)
{
```

```
        try
        {
            curHitStart = Integer.parseInt(curHitStartString);
        }
        catch(Exception exp)
        {
            curHitStart = 0;
        }
    }
```

After the necessary parameters have been retrieved from the client request, the method tries to load the index. All of the indices are managed by the IndexManager class discussed later in this section. An index is requested based on the directory it searches, and IndexManager returns either the index object or null if the directory is not indexed. Because indexing takes a while, don't make the user wait for it. However, do make the first user to search a directory wait for the index to be loaded. In other words, the first user to search a directory that is not indexed receives an error message telling them that the index is not available. But that user also triggers the creation of the index. The first person to access a directory with an index will wait for the index to load, before his or her query is processed. Once loaded, IndexManager keeps track of the index and returns it when requested. The indexes are thread safe once loaded, because IndexManager is used to protect them during loading and to allow index sharing, which improves performance. If you try this example from the CD-ROM, notice that the first search can be slow due to the load, but subsequent searches are nearly immediate.

The following code in the handleQuery method logs a status message to the log and then attempts to load the index for the current directory.

```
logger.log("Requesting index for: "+dir);

index = IndexManager.indexForDirectory(fullDir,dir);
```

In this code, IndexManager is given both the relative and absolute paths to the directory so that the index can be found on disk and so that it returns file paths relative to the servers document root, instead of real file paths.

The next section discusses how to check whether the index was returned or whether the manager returned null.

Handling Non-Query Requests

The preceding code attempted to load the index. The following code shows how handleQuery works in case the index is unavailable. If the index is unavailable, an attempt is made to redirect the client to the no-index page indicated by the configuration parameters. If this page is unavailable, an error code is sent to the client, indicating that the service is unavailable.

```
if(index == null)
{
```

```
            logger.log("Index not available for: "+fullDir);

            if(noIndexPage != null)
                response.sendRedirect(noIndexPage);
            else
         response.sendError(HttpServletResponse.SC_SERVICE_UNAVAILABLE);
        }
        else
        {
            ...
```

These error codes are a poor choice for communicating the situation to the user. The error codes should be used as a last resort. Another consideration is that the HTMLIndex class has a main method that will build an index for a directory. This means that you can build the initial directory early instead of waiting for a user request. The builder will also rebuild the index if any files in the directory or subdirectories are newer than the existing index. You might want to update the indices regularly, although the servlet will do this automatically. If the update interval configuration parameter is set, the servlet will check the index after the specified number of seconds pass and update it if necessary.

If the index described is not null, a query is performed. The next section describes the code executed in this case (under the else condition) in the handleQuery method.

Handling Queries

When a query request arrives, the servlet's first step is to ask the index for the files associated with that query. The index parses the query for "and," "or," and "not," searches its hash table, and returns the matching files in a vector called results. The servlet then uses this vector to determine the number of hits.

```
results = index.filesForQuery(query);

if(results != null) resultCount = results.size();

logger.log("Got "+resultCount+" results for query: "+query);
```

Next, write the header for the results page using the writer of the response object. The following code shows how the handleQuery method does this by first writing the header, which wraps the results in a centered table to make them more readable. The results themselves will be displayed as links.

```
writer.println("<HTML>");
writer.println("<HEAD>");
writer.println("<TITLE>");
writer.println("Search Results");
writer.println("</TITLE>");
writer.println("</HEAD>");
writer.println("<BODY TEXT=\"#000000\" BGCOLOR=\"#FFFFFF\""
        +" LINK=\"#0000EE\" VLINK=\"#551A8B\""
```

```
                +" ALINK=\"#FF0000\">");

        writer.println("<CENTER>");
        writer.println("<TABLE>");
        writer.println("<TR>");
        writer.println("<TD>");
```

Once the header is written, figure out whether there were any result hits. If there were no hits, an appropriate message is displayed. If there are hits, determine whether the number of results exceeds the maximum hits to display by comparing the maxHits to the resultCount minus the numeric index of the curHitStart. The variable curHitStart contains the counter for the first element to display. In other words, you could have counted 100 items indexed from 0 to 99, but if you start by displaying the element at index 95, there are only five elements to display. The actual number of hits to display on this page is stored in the local variable max. Before displaying the results, a message is displayed that tells the user how many hits occurred and which ones are displayed on this page.

```
        if(resultCount > 0)
        {
            writer.println("<H1>Your search results are:</H1>");
            max = Math.min(resultCount-curHitStart
                            ,maxHits);

            //inc printout by one to make it 1-25 not 0-25
            writer.println("<CENTER>"+(curHitStart+1)+"-"
                            +(curHitStart+max)
                            +" of "+resultCount
                            +" matches</CENTER>");

            outputHitsNavigator(maxHits,curHitStart,resultCount
                                ,query,myURL,writer);

            writer.println("<BLOCKQUOTE>");

            try
            {

                for(i=0;i<max;i++)
                {
                    curFileName = (String)
                            results.elementAt(curHitStart+i);
                    outputFile(curFileName,dir,writer);
                }
            }
            catch(Exception exp)
            {
                logger.log("Bad file name: "+curFileName);
            }
```

```
            writer.println("</BLOCKQUOTE>");

            outputHitsNavigator(maxHits,curHitStart
                        ,resultCount
                        ,query,myURL,writer);
        }
        else
        {
            writer.println("<H1>No files matched your "
                        +"query.</H1>");
        }
```

After all of the files are displayed, the result page's footer is printed to the client, and the handleQuery method concludes as defined in the code that follows.

```
        writer.println("</TD>");
        writer.println("</TR>");
        writer.println("</TABLE>");
        writer.println("</CENTER>");
        writer.println("</BODY>");
        writer.println("</HTML>");
    }
}
```

Each of the results in the preceding code is displayed using a method called outputFile. This method displays a link for each file, with the link's text equal to the file's name. The code for outputFile is as follows.

```
protected void outputFile(String file,String dir,PrintWriter w)
{
    String fileName = file.substring(dir.length());
    w.print("<A HREF=\"");
    w.print(file.replace('\\','/'));//make sure the URL is valid
    w.print("\">");
    w.print(fileName.replace('\\','/'));
    w.println("</A><BR>");
}
```

Managing a Large Number of Hits

The navigation bar for moving around in large result sets is displayed by the method outputHitsNavigator. This method first determines if a navigation bar is needed by comparing the number of results to be displayed to the maximum number of hits allowed to be displayed. For example, if there are 100 results to a query and maxhits is 20, the first 20 result hits are displayed and a navigation bar is used to allow access to the last 80 hits. If the bar is not required, the method returns without sending any HTML to the client. If a bar is required, the method determines if the Previous and Next buttons are needed. If the display is the first block of the result set, the Previous button is not needed; if it is the last block, the Next button is not needed. The navigation buttons are displayed as gray text when deactivated or links when active. The bar is always centered. The following code defines the outputHitsNavigator method.

```
protected void outputHitsNavigator(int maxHits,int current
                                    ,int curMax,String query
                                    ,String url,PrintWriter w)

{
    boolean needPrev,needNext;
    int prev,next;

    if(curMax>maxHits)
    {
        /*
           Only need a previous button if we are not displaying
           the first set of results
        */
        needPrev = (current != 0);

        /*
           Only need a next button if we are not displaying
           the last set of results
        */

        needNext = ((current+maxHits)<curMax);

        w.println("<CENTER>");
        if(needPrev)
        {
            w.print("<A HREF=\"");
            w.print(url);
            w.print("?");
            w.print(QUERY_FIELD_NAME);
            w.print("=");
            w.print(URLEncoder.encode(query));
            w.print("&");
            w.print(MAX_FIELD_NAME);
            w.print("=");
            w.print(maxHits);
            w.print("&");
            w.print(CURRENT_FIELD_NAME);
            w.print("=");
            prev = (current-maxHits);
            w.print(prev);
            w.println("\">&lt;prev</A> ");
        }
        else
        {
            w.print("<FONT COLOR=\"#777777\">");
            w.print("&lt;prev ");
            w.println("</FONT>");
```

```
            }

            if(needNext)
            {
                w.print("<A HREF=\"");
                w.print(url);
                w.print("?");
                w.print(QUERY_FIELD_NAME);
                w.print("=");
                w.print(URLEncoder.encode(query));
                w.print("&");
                w.print(MAX_FIELD_NAME);
                w.print("=");
                w.print(maxHits);
                w.print("&");
                w.print(CURRENT_FIELD_NAME);
                w.print("=");
                next = (current+maxHits);
                w.print(next);
                w.println("\">next&gt;</A>");
            }
            else
            {
                w.print("<FONT COLOR=\"#777777\">");
                w.print("next&gt;");
                w.println("</FONT>");
            }

            w.println("</CENTER>");
        }
    }
```

The navigation links use query strings to tell the servlet the query, the maximum number of hits to display as defined in the initial request, and the start for the result block to display, if the link is selected. The Next button moves up maxHits items, and the Previous button moves back maxHits. The URL for the servlet itself was determined in handleQuery, and the query is encoded to make this a proper URL. Using the example HTML file SearchTester.html listed at the end of the chapter, this navigation bar will contain HTML such as the following:

```
<CENTER>

<A HREF="http://192.168.0.173:8080/servlet/htmlsearch/
?query=java&maxhits=25&hitstart=0">&lt;prev</A>

<A HREF="http://192.168.0.173:8080/servlet/htmlsearch/
?query=java&maxhits=25&hitstart=50">next&gt;</A>

</CENTER>
```

That completes the HTMLSearchServlet class. The results from a search with this servlet look like Figure 8.2.

Next let's look at the IndexManager to see how to use synchronization to protect the indices.

IndexManager

IndexManager uses a hash table to associate directories and indices. When the servlet or any other object requests an index, IndexManager checks whether the index is already loaded. If the index is available, it is returned. The index is thread safe and uses minimal synchronization because it is basically read-only once it is loaded. The trick is to protect the index during loading and to load only one index per directory.

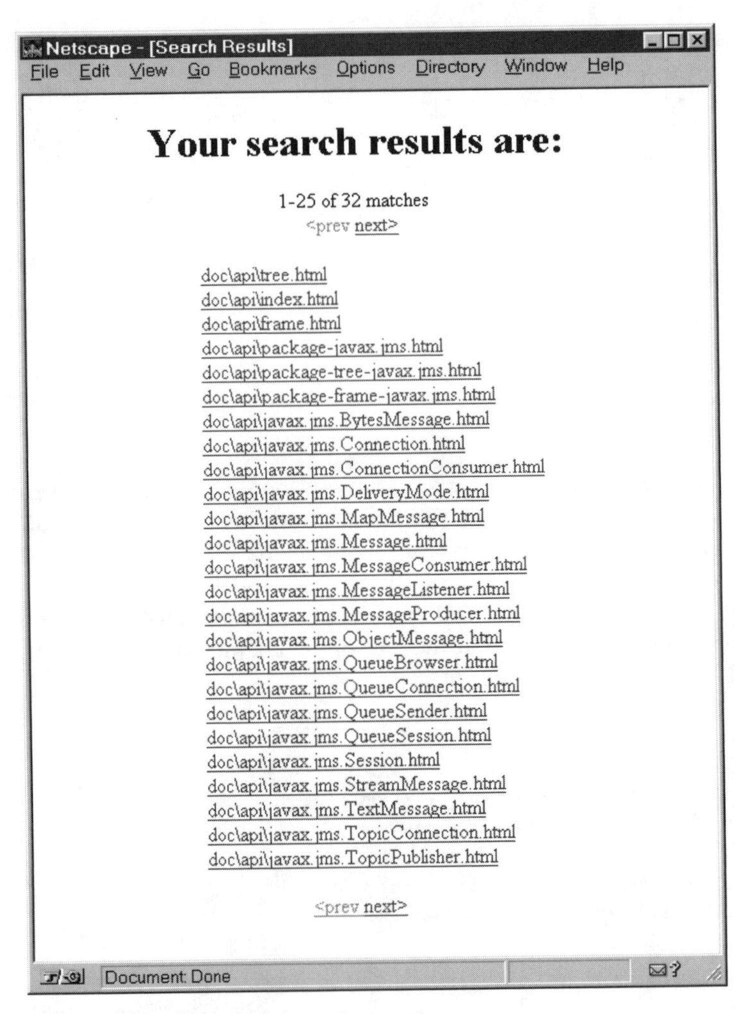

Figure 8.2 HTMLSearchServlet results.

To manage the loading process for each index, IndexManager uses subclasses of thread called IndexLoader. These loaders and the manager itself avoid loading indices multiple times by synchronizing on the manager's hash table whenever a decision is made to load an index. The loader locks the hash table to add a new index to the available pool. When a request comes in for an unloaded index, the manager puts the indexloader in the hash table with the requested directory. If another thread requests that index, the manager knows to return null, without creating a new loader.

An updateInterval is defined to tell the manager when to recheck a directory for changes. The default is to check only the first time the index is loaded. You can set this to any time, in seconds, using the updateinterval configuration parameter on the HTMLSearchServlet. To help manage updates, the manager uses a hash table containing the last index load time. The following code defines IndexManager.java.

```
package index;

import index.*;
import java.util.*;
import java.io.*;

import DebugLog;

public class IndexManager
{
    protected static Hashtable indices;
    protected static Hashtable loadtimes;

    public static long updateInterval = 0;//seconds

    // Cache once and then reuse.
    static
    {
        indices = new Hashtable();
        loadtimes = new Hashtable();
    }

    public static HTMLIndex indexForDirectory(String dir
                                              ,String rel)
    {
        HTMLIndex retVal = null;
        Object test = null;
        IndexLoader loader=null;

        if(dir == null) return null;

        // Support multithreaded access.
        synchronized(indices)
        {
            // Does the directory exist in the hash table?
            test = indices.get(dir);
```

```
if(test == null)
{
    // No, then load it.
    loader = new IndexLoader(dir,rel,indices);

    indices.put(dir,loader);
    // Keep track of how long it took to load.
    loadtimes.put(dir,new Date());
}
else if(test instanceof HTMLIndex)
{
    retVal = (HTMLIndex) test;

    if(updateInterval>0)
    {
        try
        {
            Date now = new Date();
            Dateload;
            long nw,ld;

            load = (Date) loadtimes.get(dir);

            nw = now.getTime();
            ld = load.getTime();

            if(nw > (ld+(updateInterval*1000)))
            {
                if(retVal.indexNeedsRebuilding())
                {
                    //reload
                  loader =
                     new IndexLoader(dir,rel,indices);

                  indices.put(dir,loader);
                  loadtimes.put(dir,new Date());

                    retVal = null;
                }
                else
                {
                    //Update load time.
                    loadtimes.put(dir,new Date());
                }
            }
        }
        catch(Exception exp)
        {
            retVal = (HTMLIndex) test;
            indices.put(dir,retVal);//just in case
            loadtimes.put(dir,new Date());
```

```
                }
            }
        }
          //else it is the index loader working...
    }

    if(loader != null)
    {
        if(loader.needsBuild())
        {
            loader.start();
        }
        else
        {
            loader.load();
              retVal = (HTMLIndex) indices.get(dir);
        }
    }

    return retVal;
  }
}
```

In this code, IndexManager is not as concerned about loading indices as building them. If an index file is available for a directory, it is loaded in the same thread that requested the index. Only directories that do not yet contain an index file cause the manager to spawn a thread to build the index and return null. Notice that the use of synchronization around the loading thread is minimized so that when one thread loads an index, the others can't get it, but they also don't have to wait for it to load before they can access another index or get the null return value.

IndexLoader is defined in the same file as IndexManager. Its job is to load the index and add it to the manager's hash table. The loader tells the index to rebuild, if necessary, if it is run in a background thread, but it will simply load the existing file if the index is up to date. This prevents the index from checking whether it needs to update twice: once when asked by the manager and once when told to load. Here is the code for IndexLoader as defined in IndexManager.java:

```
class IndexLoader extends Thread
{
    protected String dir;
    protected String rel;
    protected Hashtable indices;
    protected HTMLIndex newIndex;
    protected boolean buildIfNec;

    public IndexLoader(String d,String r,Hashtable holder)
    {
        dir = d;
        rel = r;
        indices = holder;
```

```
            buildIfNec = false;

            newIndex = new HTMLIndex(new File(dir));
        }

        public boolean needsBuild()
        {
            return newIndex.indexNeedsRebuilding();
        }

        public void run()
        {
            buildIfNec = true;
            load();
        }

        public void load()
        {
            if(dir == null) return;

            if(rel!=null) newIndex.setRelativePath(rel);

            newIndex.loadIndex(buildIfNec);

            synchronized(indices)
            {
                indices.put(dir,newIndex);
            }
        }
    }
```

Both the manager and loader use the provided relative path to tell the index how to return files. If this relative path is not provided, a file's absolute path is returned from queries. Although this absolute path is not useful to a servlet, you might use it in an application that relies on the index package.

SearchTester.html

To test the servlet, we created an HTML file called SearchTester.html. This file provides a form with two input elements and two submit buttons, as pictured in Figure 8.3.

One input element is a text field for entering the query. The second input element is a pull-down list for choosing the maximum number of hits to display. One submit button initiates a search; the other requests that the help file be displayed. The following code listing is the SearchTester.html file.

```
<HTML>
<HEAD>
<TITLE>
Search Tester
```

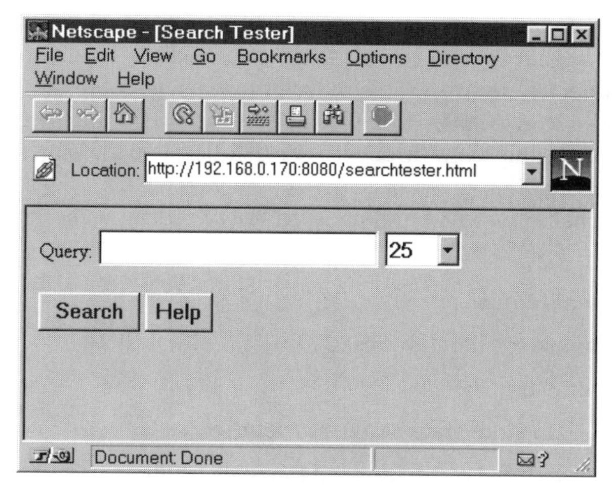

Figure 8.3 SearchTester.html.

```
</TITLE>
</HEAD>
<BODY>
<FORM METHOD=GET
    ACTION="/servlet/htmlsearch/">
Query:
<INPUT NAME="query" VALUE="" SIZE=25>
<SELECT NAME="maxhits" SIZE=1>
<OPTION VALUE="25">25
<OPTION VALUE="50">50
<OPTION VALUE="100">100
</SELECT>
<BR><BR>
<INPUT TYPE="Submit" NAME="submit" VALUE="Search">
<INPUT TYPE="Submit" NAME="submit" VALUE="Help">

</FORM>
</BODY>
</HTML>
```

Notice in the HTML that the form ACTION provides a / for the path information. This causes the search servlet to search the document root of the Web server.

Summary

The Web site searching servlet discussed in this chapter demonstrates a number of important guidelines. First, don't make the user wait too long for a response. In this case, a special page is used to prevent the user from waiting for an index to be built, because this can be a lengthy operation. Second, support multiple threads if possible.

This can take a lot of your design time, but it improves perceived performance in most cases. Finally, let the Web server do what it does best. Instead of displaying the help and no index available pages in code, use redirect. This makes those pages more flexible, because the Web administrator can change them. It also means that they are served directly from disk instead of having to go through a servlet. Because the pages aren't dynamic, this is perfectly reasonable.

This chapter took advantage of the Servlet API and showed how you can leverage this API in several ways:

- Read parameters from the client request.
- Write dynamic HTML in response to client requests.
- Generate a dynamic navigation bar.
- Use the query fields of the URL to store state between client requests.
- Use the path information from HttpServletRequest to parse the query.

As you saw in this chapter, servlet programming requires you to hard code the HTML you want to generate into your Java code, or at best read it from a file. For some purposes, this is fine; however, it makes it hard for Java programmers to work with graphic design and layout people, who are more adept at HTML layout, because they can't directly modify Java code.

The next two chapters look at a technology called server-side scripting and how you can take advantage of this technology in Java to isolate the Java program logic from the HTML, even when you want a dynamic result.

What Is Server-Side Scripting?

Server-side scripting is a technique by which program code is embedded in HTML documents and then parsed by a Web server. This technique enables more flexibility in the layout of HTML documents during Web application development. Sun provides a form of server-side scripting called JavaServer Pages (JSP). JSP features special HTML pages that include embedded Java code. This code is interpreted on the server and the results, instead of the original Web page, are sent to the client. JavaServer Pages are a type of server-side scripting.

This chapter provides an overview of the JSP technology and compares it to similar technologies available on other platforms. Chapter 10, "Creating JavaServer Pages," shows how to take advantage of JSP in your applications.

Web-Based Application Structure

Most Web server vendors have recognized the need to provide more separation between the presentation of the Web page (primarily HTML) and the business logic used to dynamically update the page. For example, consider a company benefits system on the Web. This system allows users to type their Social Security numbers and passwords into a standard HTML form and see their 401k status in a dynamically generated table, shown in Figure 9.1. Based on what you have learned so far, you have a few choices for implementing this system:

CGI. Using CGI, you could write an application that handles an HTML form request. This requires a graphics person to lay out the HTML form, then a programmer to write the CGI script separately. If the layout of the table returned from the CGI script needs to be modified, most of the work will be done to the CGI script rather than the HTML.

Server plugin. Using the API of the specific server, a library of code is created that can be added to the server to handle specific requests. Unlike CGI, which is based on a published standard, this solution would work only with servers for which the plugin was created. Again, if the dynamic HTML returned from the plugin needed improvement, most of the work would be done in your C, Java, Visual Basic, or other programming code, not directly in an HTML document.

Applet. An applet that contains the form could be created. The applet could connect to a server process or directly to the database and return the results. This puts most of the layout burden on the developer and may have significant security considerations such as interaction through a firewall.

Servlet. Instead of CGI or a server plugin, you could use the servlet API discussed in Chapter 7, "Programming Servlets," to dynamically create the Web page. However, as with CGI, changing the HTML for a servlet is a programming process, not really a page design process.

Consider the CGI example. You might create a CGI script that sits on the server and waits for requests from the HTML form. When the Web client sends a request, the CGI

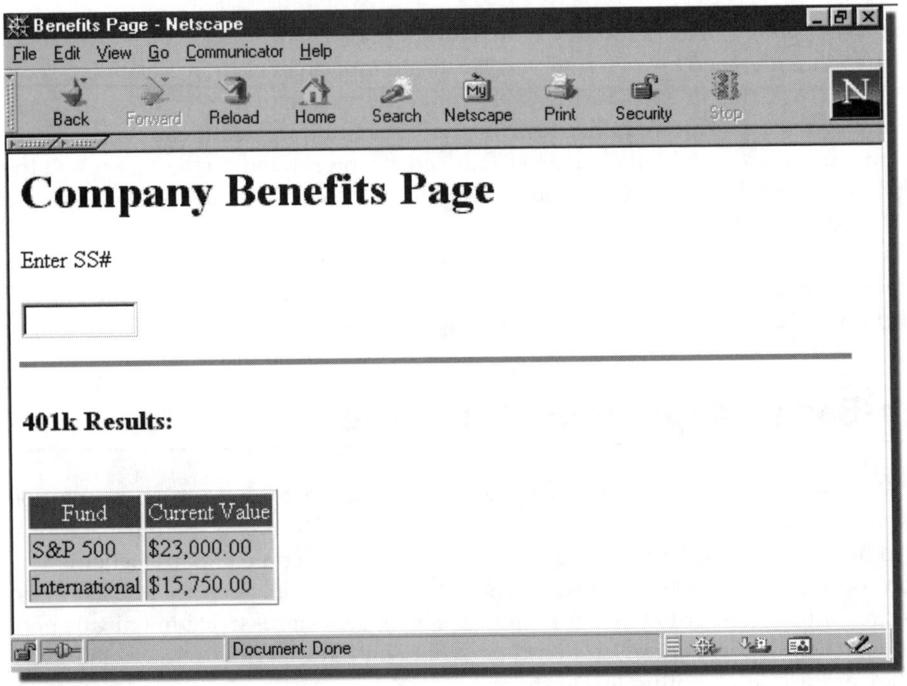

Figure 9.1 Example benefits page.

script can process the form, access the database, and then output HTML back to the client. This would require the creation of a script that generates HTML based on dynamic content. As the developer of the script, you would be responsible for the visual appearance of the data on the page because the HTML would have to be "hard coded" in the CGI script. It's not reasonable to expect a graphic layout person to learn how to write CGI scripts, so what choice do you have? This means that an expensive engineering resource must be utilized to change the font in a table. If this sounds unreasonable to you, you're not alone. This is why server-side scripting was created.

Server-Side Scripting

The idea behind server-side scripting is that rather than embedding the presentation code (HTML, in this case) inside the application (the CGI script, in this case), it would be better if the business logic could simply be referred to from the presentation. In other words, graphics layout experts could put together a complex HTML page that included a table. They would have server-side scripting tools that allowed them to simply specify what values need to be displayed in the table at specific locations in the Web page. These tools would refer to more complex developer-created business rules that actually did the work of processing the form, accessing data sources, logging the transaction, and returning values. The graphics layout experts simply use special tags to identify placeholders for values in their Web page. When this special HTML page is requested, the server executes the business logic created by the developer and inserts the values dynamically in the HTML template created by the graphics layout people. This allows the font, color, alignment, and so on to be changed without the need to have the developer recompile or modify the code. The developer can focus on business processes while the graphics people focus on presenting the results. Figure 9.2 shows the server-side scripting model.

There are several solutions for server-side scripting. The most common are as follows:

- Active Server Pages (ASP) from Microsoft
- Server-side JavaScript (previously referred to as LiveWire) from Netscape Communications
- JavaServer pages from Sun Microsystems

All of these solutions have some common properties:

Access to resources. Usually, these scripting languages provide some mechanism for accessing resources on the server, such as files, databases, and JavaBeans.

Compilation. The special HTML pages are usually compiled so that they are more efficient when called several times by a user. This is a great improvement over a CGI script written in PERL, for example, which must be interpreted every time it is called.

Programming language. Usually, these scripts are written in one specific language because servers generally know how to process only one kind of script based on the file extension. The language could be Java, Visual Basic, JavaScript, and so on.

Special HTML pages. Most of the solutions require an HTML page in which these scripts are embedded. The pages usually have different file extensions such as .js

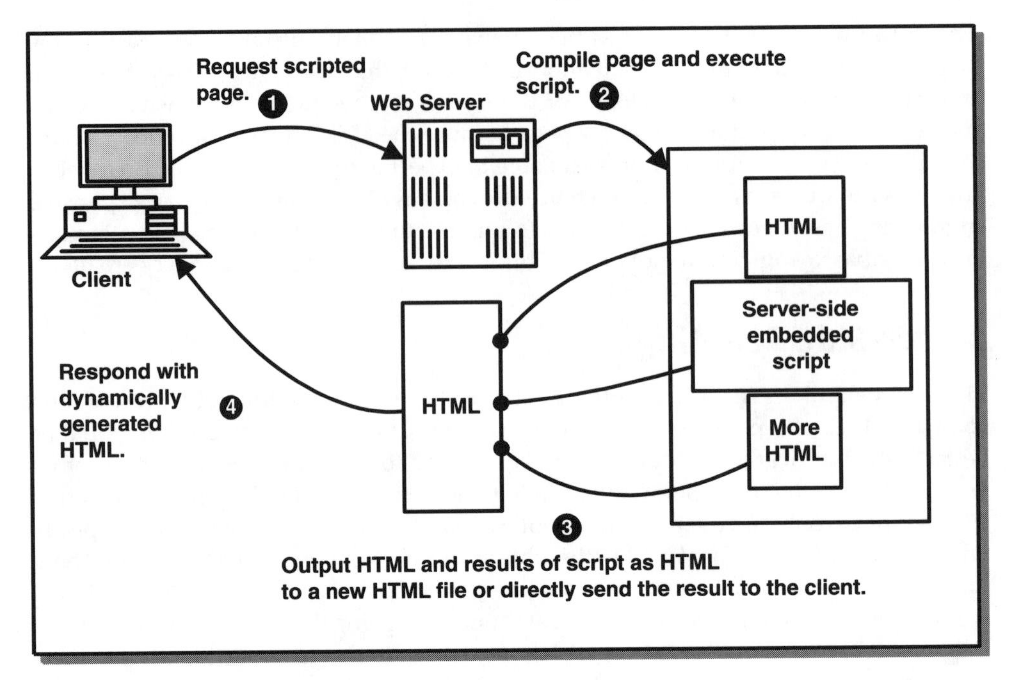

Figure 9.2 A typical server-side scripting model.

or .asp rather than .htm or .html. This is how the server knows that these files require special processing when a client requests them.

Most server-side scripting solutions aim to fill the gap between layout features of HTML and more powerful programming languages required in enterprise applications. Each of the server-side scripting solutions described previously has benefits and weaknesses. This section looks at each with the perspective of what an enterprise developer will want to consider, such as programming language integration and cross-platform development capabilities.

Active Server Pages

Active Server Pages (ASP) is part of Microsoft's Active Platform strategy. It is an additional component added to the Microsoft Web server that can process scripts inside files with the extension .asp. These files can contain various supported scripting languages, but primarily they use a scripting extension to HTML called VBScript. VBScript is based on Visual Basic and has the capability to call out to ActiveX components. This strategy is a Microsoft-centric solution that is implemented in its Internet Information Server (IIS).

Like most server-side scripting solutions, ASP is not intended to replace client-side scripting. Instead, it is designed to provide "glue" between the HTML and client side scripting (like JavaScript) and the business logic that resides on the server.

An ASP application is typically composed of:

- HTML
- Scripting code
- ActiveX components

The following code represents the contents of a file called Hello.asp. The output from executing this Active Server Page is shown in Figure 9.3. The code defines a function called WriteDate, which is executed in the body of the HTML document between special ASP tags <% and %>.

The interesting part of the script is in the body of the actual HTML. The <% tag is used to designate a script. When the client requests the Web page Hello.asp, the server treats the HTML in the file as a template. The server interprets the script and inserts the results of executing the VBScript code into this HTML. Finally, the resulting data is then sent to the client.

```
<%@ LANGUAGE="VBSCRIPT" %>
<SCRIPT RUNAT=SERVER LANGUAGE=VBSCRIPT>
Sub WriteDate()
    Response.Write("<B>The current date is " & Date & "</B><BR>");
End Sub
</SCRIPT>

<HTML>
<HEAD>
<TITLE>ASP Example</TITLE>
</HEAD>
<BODY>
The next line is an ASP script embedded in the HTML: <BR><BR>
<%
    Call WriteDate()
    Response.Write("That was the date.");
%>

</BODY>
</HTML>
```

Because the file name of the code above ends in .asp and assuming the code is placed in the correct directory for your server, the server automatically interprets it as a server-side application. This means that all code designated by the scripting tags will be replaced with the results of executing the code. The <%@ tag designates that this is a script written using VBScript. The <SCRIPT> tag designates that this script is expected to be executed on the server. Further extension to Web clients may allow for client-side processing as well. Everything between the <SCRIPT></SCRIPT > tags is definition for a simple VBScript subroutine.

Here is what the client would see if it were to view the source of the Web page on the client:

```
<HTML>
<HEAD>
```

```
<TITLE>ASP Example</TITLE>
</HEAD>
<BODY>
The next line is an ASP script embedded in the HTML: <BR><BR>
<B>The current date is 8/10/98</B><BR>
That was the date.

</BODY>
</HTML>
```

The major advantage of ASP is that it is well integrated with other Microsoft technologies. It also supports an API for adding other scripting languages such as JScript or PERL. However, ASP works only with Microsoft server solutions and does not directly work with standard Java libraries. This means it has limited value to enterprise Java developers.

Server-Side JavaScript

JavaScript, originally called LiveScript, was developed to make client-side HTML scripting possible. Scripting enables a Web page to do some processing such as field validation on the client, saving the extra trip on the network. As Figure 9.4 shows, early scripters started creating HTML forms and using JavaScript to handle form validation, such as making sure people type their Social Security numbers correctly.

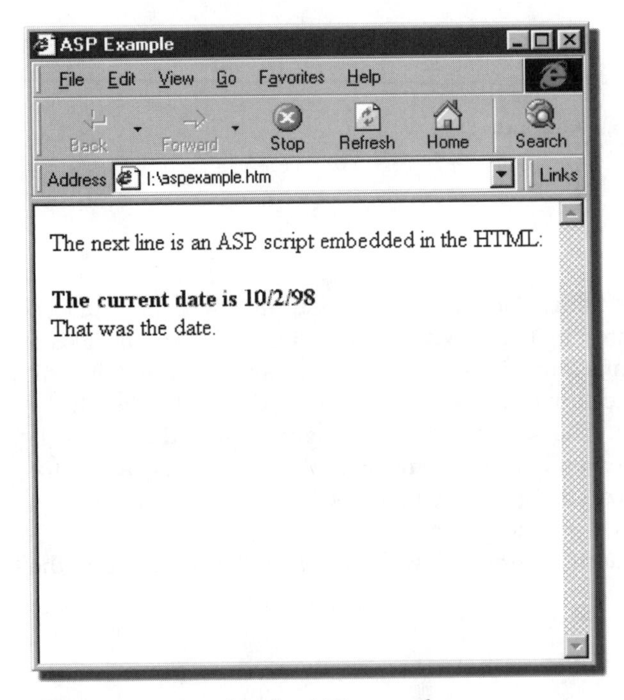

Figure 9.3 Running the ASP example.

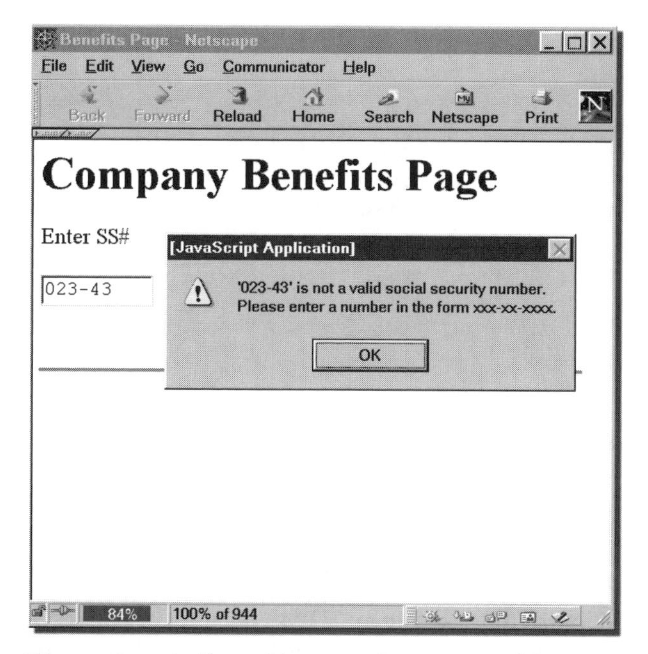

Figure 9.4 A client-side JavaScript processed form.

NOTE **JavaScript actually shares little with Java in terms of its object model or the programming paradigm it uses. However, the syntax is close enough that it is easy for Java programmers to learn and use. Over time, the language evolved. Microsoft released JScript, which is essentially Microsoft's implementation of JavaScript. The industry feared that the language would be splintered, so the European standards group European Computer Manufacturers Association (ECMA) developed ECMAScript, which has become the standard that all derivations of JavaScript support. For more information, see www.ecma.ch/news/E262-II.htm.**

It wasn't long before these scripters wanted to handle what happened to their forms once they were submitted to the server. To help make this possible, Server-Side JavaScript, originally called LiveWire, was developed. LiveWire was one of the first server-side scripting solutions. It enabled JavaScript programmers to process forms, access databases, and create dynamic HTML on the Web server in much the same way ASP does. JavaScript also has the ability to make calls to programming libraries that use the Netscape API. In general, Server-Side JavaScript plays the same role as VBScript does in ASP.

Here is what the HelloWorld program, written for ASP, would look like when written using Server-Side JavaScript:

```
<HTML>
<HEAD>
<TITLE>Server-side JavaScript Example</TITLE>
</HEAD>
```

```
<BODY>
<SERVER>
function writeDate()
{
    var theDate = new Date();
    var theDateString = theDate.toLocaleString();
    write("<B>The current date is " & theDateString & "</B><BR>");
}
</SERVER>

The next line is in Server-Side JavaScript embedded in the HTML:
<BR><BR>
<SERVER>
    writeDate()
    write("That was the date.");
</SERVER>

</BODY>
</HTML>
```

As with ASP, Server-Side JavaScript is embedded in an HTML document. This document is compiled into byte codes, which are interpreted by the Server-Side JavaScript component of a Netscape server. The tags used to delimit a server script are different, and the syntax is that of JavaScript instead of VBScript or some other ASP-supported language. Other than that, ASP and Server-Side JavaScript are comparable in form.

Because the choices for server-side scripting provided by the major Web server vendors are similar, your choice comes down to your preferences based on the languages supported, specific features and performance issues in your particular environment, and your overall product preference. Each of the scripting solutions described so far was designed with specific goals in mind, and each solution requires that you commit to either the Microsoft server platform or Netscape's. The JavaScript language on which Server-Side JavaScript is based was designed specifically for the Web and has little overhead for non-Web-related issues such as UI. VBScript, which is primarily used with ASP and is a modified and stripped-down version of VisualBasic, a more sophisticated and heavyweight language. People debate which of these server-side languages and platforms are better for Web scripting. If you are a Java developer, we suggest you also consider a third option, JavaServer Pages. JavaServer Pages give you more flexibility than ASP or Server-Side JavaScript, and JSP leverages Java as its primary language, which means there is less to learn and better integration with other Java components than either of the other two scripting solutions mentioned here.

JavaServer Pages

A JavaServer Page processes Java code embedded in an HTML document and returns results to the browser. You may have noticed that many of the Java technologies and standards provided by Sun duplicate the functionality of technologies found in other environments. Often, these Java solutions improve on the other technologies, but the ultimate objective is to provide a seamless Java solution for all development needs. JavaServer Pages closely duplicate the functionality of Server-Side JavaScript from Netscape and even more closely resemble Active Server Pages from Microsoft. At the same time, JavaServer Pages leverage all of the advantages of Java programming, including garbage collections and the enterprise technologies discussed in this book.

The first example in this chapter described a simple HR system that may use CGI to process the results of a form. In order to do this with CGI, you need to write a CGI script that reads the request from the browser and then generates a set of HTML tags and dynamic values coming from a data source. This requires that the presentation of the data be embedded in the logic for validating the id/password and accessing the database. This design is hard to support and maintain and makes it difficult for graphic designers and page layout experts to work on these pages. This section and Chapter 10, "Creating JavaServer Pages," look at how you can use JavaServer Pages to easily integrate Java programming logic with HTML layout for presentation of data. You create these scripted pages using a file format similar to HTML, called JHTML.

Using JHTML

Developing enterprise applications that leverage Web technologies requires you to make many design decisions. One of the decisions you need to make is how to most effectively separate the presentation of your application from the business logic. This is an important design consideration for simplifying the support and maintenance of your application. Sun introduced JavaServer Pages to aid in this task.

JavaServer Pages are a relatively new standard. However, JSP is already entering a second generation. The first generation of JavaServer Pages, called JHTML, uses a technique called *page compilation*. The process is as follows:

1. Create an HTML file with Java code embedded between <java> HTML tags.
2. Save the files with the extension .jhtml.
3. In the case of the Java Web Server, when the Web client requests this file, the server sends the file to the PageCompileServlet that is a part of the package com.sun.server.webserver. The Servlet uses this .jhtml file as a template and generates a servlet that outputs the HTML in your file, plus it executes the Java code between the <java></java> tags.
4. From then on, whenever a client requests the .jhtml file, the new servlet is sent the request and responds accordingly.

If you change the .jhtml file, the servlet is recompiled automatically on the next request.

NOTE For the examples in this chapter, the Java Web Server from Sun is used. A trial version of this server is available at http://java.sun.com under the products directory. If you would like to try out these examples, download the trial version and follow the setup instructions after you install it. Put your .jhtml files in the public_html directory under the Java Web Server directory to access them from a browser.

Here is an example .jhtml file:

```
<HTML>
<HEAD>
<TITLE>Sample1 JHTML File</TITLE>
</HEAD>

<BODY>
Hello
<java>
    String name;
    if ((name = request.getParameter("name")) != null)
        out.print(name);
</java>

<!--
    Note that for simplicity, the form calls the same file
    with the value for the name text field filled in.
-->
<FORM METHOD=POST ACTION="sample1.jhtml">
  Enter your name and press submit
  <INPUT TYPE=TEXT NAME=name>
  <BR><BR><INPUT TYPE=SUBMIT>
</FORM>

<java>
    for(int i=1;i<6; i++)
        out.print("<H"+ i +"> Heading " + i );
</java>

</BODY>
</HTML>
```

Figure 9.5 illustrates what this file looks like before and after submitting a name.

The first time that the file sample1.jhtml is requested, the PageCompilation servlet is called by the Java Web Server, and it generates and compiles a servlet called _sample1.java. The resulting _sample1.class file is stored by default in a directory called pagecompilation. The servlet is called from then on whenever a request for the sample1.jhtml file is made. If the .jhtml file is changed, the whole process is repeated. The advantage of this model is that the servlet does not need to be recompiled every time it is requested. Here is what the sample1.java file would look like:

```
package pagecompile;

import java.io.*;
import java.util.*;
import javax.servlet.*;
import javax.servlet.http.*;
import com.sun.server.webserver.pagecompile.filecache.*;
import com.sun.server.webserver.pagecompile.ParamsHttpServletRequest;
```

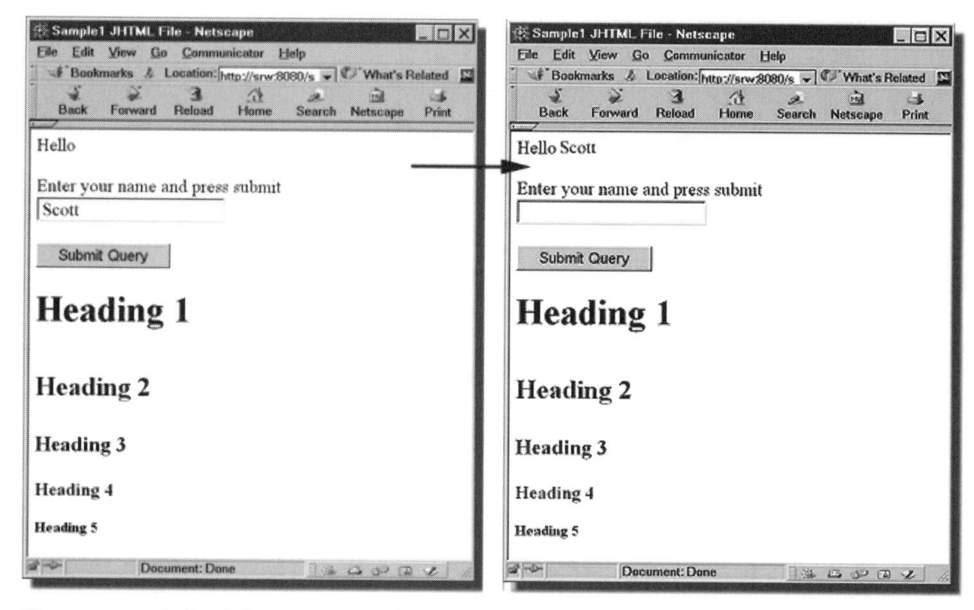

Figure 9.5 Submitting a request for sample1.jhtml.

```
import com.sun.server.webserver.pagecompile.*;

public class _sample1
extends HttpServlet{

//------------------------------
  static {
  }

  //-------------- The service method
  public void service (HttpServletRequest request,
                         HttpServletResponse response)
      throws ServletException, IOException
  {
    ServletOutputStream out = response.getOutputStream ();
    ByteFileData __fileData = null;
    try {
      __fileData = (ByteFileData) ServletUtil.getJHtmlSource(this,
"F:\\JAVA\\JWS\\BIN\\..\\public_html\\sample1.jhtml", null,
904548732000L);
      if (__fileData == null) throw new ServletException("FileChanged");

      /*** lines: 1-8 */
      __fileData.writeBytes (0, 78, out);

    String name;
    if ((name = request.getParameter("name")) != null)
        out.print(name);
```

```
        /*** lines: 12-12 */
        __fileData.writeBytes (183, 143, out);
        out.print(ServletUtil.encodeURL (request, response,
"sample1.jhtml"));
        /*** lines: 12-21 */
        __fileData.writeBytes (339, 107, out);


      for(int i=1;i<6; i++)
          out.print("<H"+ i +"> Heading " + i );
        /*** lines: 25-27 */
        __fileData.writeBytes (531, 18, out);
      }
      finally {
        if (__fileData != null) __fileData.close();
      }
    }
  }
```

As you can see, the code put between <java> tags is inserted into the service method of the servlet. The servlet reads the .jhtml file into the variable __fileData. It then writes all the HTML that is not between <java> tags. Wherever <java> tags are located, it executes the actual Java code.

JHTML is flexible and supports all the power of Java. Examples of other capabilities of JavaServer Pages include:

- Declaring variables
- Conditional HTML
- Inserting values in HTML tags

Chapter 10, "Creating JavaServer Pages" discusses these capabilities in detail as well as providing a number of Java Server Page examples.

JHTML and JSP

While JHTML represents the first generation of JavaServer Pages, the second generation (.jsp files) is already being specified by Sun and its partners. The main design differences between JHTML and JSP are that JSP is designed to provide scripting capabilities on the Web server and potentially on the Web browser as well. Also, JSP is designed to support multiple scripting languages, although currently it supports only Java. The basic syntax, as of version 0.9, for JSP is similar to JHTML. However, the goal for JSP is to integrate it more into the existing community of server-side scripting. As a result, JSP looks a lot like ASP, with the code in Java rather than VBScript or JScript. Hopefully, as these standards merge, it will be possible to use the same basic syntax to indicate where the scripts are and use any of these languages to implement the script. Like JHTML, JSP will probably rely on a servlet to process pages and generate a servlet from them—at least, the 0.9 version of the JSP standard uses this technique, as shown below.

Here is an example of a simple.jsp file that duplicates the first .jhtml example in this chapter:

```
<HTML>
<HEAD>
<TITLE>Sample5 JSP File</TITLE>
</HEAD>

<BODY>
Hello <%= request.getParameter("name") %>

<!-- Note that for simplicity the form calls the same file, with the
value for the name text field filled in. -->
<FORM METHOD=POST ACTION="sample5.jsp">
Enter your name and press submit
<INPUT TYPE=TEXT NAME=name>
<BR><BR><INPUT TYPE=SUBMIT>
</FORM>

<%
    for(int i=1;i<6; i++)
        out.print("<H"+ i +"> Heading " + i + "</h" + i + ">" );
%>
</BODY>
</HTML>
```

The most noticeable difference is that the <java> tag is replaced by <% ... %> and the <%= tag is used for printing Java values. Here is what the servlet generated looks like:

```
package pagecompile;

import java.io.*;
import java.util.*;
import javax.servlet.*;
import javax.servlet.http.*;
import java.beans.Beans;
import com.sun.server.http.pagecompile.ParamsHttpServletRequest;
import com.sun.server.http.pagecompile.ServletUtil;
import com.sun.server.http.pagecompile.filecache.CharFileData;
import com.sun.server.http.pagecompile.NCSAUtil;


public class _sample5_xjsp extends javax.servlet.http.HttpServlet
{
    private static final String sources[] = new String[]
    {
        "F:\\JAVA\\JWS\\BIN\\..\\public_html\\sample5.jsp",
    };

    private static final long lastModified[] =
    {
        904558366000L,
    };
```

```
    public void service(HttpServletRequest request,
                        HttpServletResponse response)
        throws IOException, ServletException
    {
        PrintWriter out = response.getWriter();
        CharFileData data[] = new CharFileData[sources.length];
        try
        {
            for (int i = 0 ; i < data.length ; i++)
                data[i] = ServletUtil.getJHtmlSource(this,
                          sources[i], "8859_1", lastModified[i]);
        } catch (Exception ex)
        {
            ex.printStackTrace();
            throw new ServletException("fileData");
        }
        // com.sun.server.http.pagecompile.jsp.CharArrayChunk
        // F:\JAVA\JWS\BIN\..\public_html\sample5.jsp 1,1-
        // F:\JAVA\JWS\BIN\..\public_html\sample5.jsp 7,7
        data[0].writeChars(0, 74, out);

        // com.sun.server.http.pagecompile.jsp.ScriptletChunk
        // F:\JAVA\JWS\BIN\..\public_html\sample5.jsp 7,7-
        // F:\JAVA\JWS\BIN\..\public_html\sample5.jsp 7,42
        out.print(ServletUtil.toString( request.getParameter("name")
                 ));
        // com.sun.server.http.pagecompile.jsp.CharArrayChunk
        // F:\JAVA\JWS\BIN\..\public_html\sample5.jsp 7,42-
        // F:\JAVA\JWS\BIN\..\public_html\sample5.jsp 16,1
        data[0].writeChars(109, 261, out);
        // com.sun.server.http.pagecompile.jsp.ScriptletChunk
        // F:\JAVA\JWS\BIN\..\public_html\sample5.jsp 16,1-
        // F:\JAVA\JWS\BIN\..\public_html\sample5.jsp 19,3
        for(int i=1;i<6; i++)
            out.print("<H"+ i +"> Heading " + i + "</h" + i + ">" );
       // com.sun.server.http.pagecompile.jsp.CharArrayChunk
       // F:\JAVA\JWS\BIN\..\public_html\sample5.jsp 19,3-
       // F:\JAVA\JWS\BIN\..\public_html\sample5.jsp 21,7
      data[0].writeChars(462, 18, out);
    }
}
```

Notice that this servlet looks very much like the JHTML version. Both of these scripting solutions provide excellent choices for merging Java and HTML.

Summary

Server-side scripting provides a great mechanism for creating dynamic Web pages that contain designed HTML and programming logic. Although ASP and Server-Side

JavaScript both provide the basic functionality required for server-side scripting, JavaServer Pages represent a leap forward by relying on a full-fledged programming language. Of course, the drawback of this technology is that Java is more complete and takes longer to learn than VBScript or JavaScript. But with that time comes more power. Both JHTML and the upcoming JSP standard enable you to create Web pages that leverage the full power of Java. Java programmers can use JavaServer Pages to create dynamic Web pages that access server-side business logic and data sources. One other point to note is that this technology is currently supported only as a server-side scripting technique. This means that all processing is done on the server. The way JSP is designed, it is reasonable that the Web browsers will be enhanced so that some of the processing can be done in the Web browser in the future. JSP marks a milestone in maintainable and extensible Web applications. Chapter 10, "Creating JavaServer Pages," demonstrates the specific techniques used to create JavaServer Pages.

Creating JavaServer Pages

Chapter 9 discussed the purpose of server-side scripting techniques and the benefit of JavaServer Pages. This chapter discusses the syntax for creating JavaServer Pages. Chapter 11, "A JavaServer Page Online Store," explores a larger example of how JavaServer Pages can be used.

Currently, JavaServer Pages are implemented using a technology called *page compilation* in the Java Web Server. These pages are marked with a .jhtml extension to indicate that they combine Java and HTML. Sun is currently in the process of creating a more standard version of JavaServer Pages that uses a .jsp extension. At the time of this writing, the JHTML version of JavaServer Pages is available for commercial use; the JSP version is still being developed. Therefore, the discussions here are focused on JHTML.

NOTE **JHTML and JSP are very similar, and you should have no trouble updating to the new JSP standard when it is finalized.**

All of the examples in this chapter were written and tested using the Java Web Server. To try a copy of this server, access the Sun Web site at java.sun.com/products. You should also check the documentation for your existing Web server or contact the provider to see if it offers support for JavaServer Pages.

How JavaServer Pages Work

The Web server handles a request for JavaServer Pages (JSP) by forwarding the request to a special servlet. This servlet, called the PageCompileServlet, takes requests for JSP and converts them into the appropriate action. If the page is requested for the first time, the appropriate action is to compile the JSP into a servlet and ask the servlet to service the request. Subsequent requests for the page results in a direct request to the servlet generated from the JSP. The PageCompileServlet generates a servlet for each JSP, and that servlet handles all further requests.

To get a handle on what the servlets generated from JavaServer Pages look like, let's take the example of a JSP that doesn't have any Java—in other words, a plain HTML file that has been labeled with the .jhtml extension, indicating to the server that it is a JavaServer Page and should be handled by the PageCompileServlet. Like all of the examples in this book, the following Hello World page is available on the CD-ROM.

```
<HTML>
<HEAD>
<TITLE>
Hello World
</TITLE>
</HEAD>
<BODY>
<H1>Hello World!</H1>
</BODY>
</HTML>
```

When the PageCompileServlet receives the request for this page, it generates the code for a servlet, then compiles the code. The servlet returns an HTML page like the one pictured in Figure 10.1.

In this example, the servlet code looks like this:

```
package pagecompile;

import java.io.*;
import java.util.*;
import javax.servlet.*;
import javax.servlet.http.*;
import com.sun.server.webserver.pagecompile.filecache.*;
import com.sun.server.webserver.pagecompile.ParamsHttpServletRequest;
import com.sun.server.webserver.pagecompile.*;

public class _HelloWorldNoCode extends HttpServlet
{

//-------------------------------
  static { }

  //-------------- The service method
```

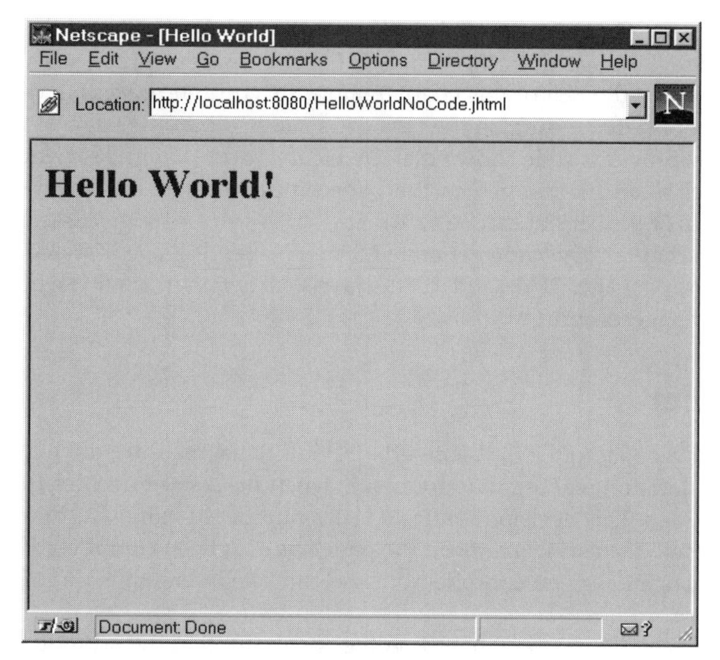

Figure 10.1 A simple JavaServer Page.

```
    public void service (HttpServletRequest request,
                             HttpServletResponse response)
        throws ServletException, IOException
    {
      ServletOutputStream out = response.getOutputStream ();
      ByteFileData __fileData = null;

      try
      {
        __fileData = (ByteFileData) ServletUtil.getJHtmlSource(this,
     "D:\\JAVA\\JWS1.1\\BIN\\..\\public_html\\HelloWorldNoCode.jhtml"
      , null, 902608452000L);

        if (__fileData == null)
          throw new ServletException("FileChanged");

        /*** lines: 1-10 */
        __fileData.writeBytes (0, 96, out);
      }
      finally
      {
        if (__fileData != null) __fileData.close();
      }
    }
  }
```

The servlet for this page simply opens the .jhtml file and outputs the data from the file to the client. In this case, because all of the data is HTML, the output process is a simple one. As the examples in the rest of this chapter show, this output process may be broken into several sections, depending on the Java code inserted into the page.

The boldface type in the previous code shows that the Hello World example servlet extends the HttpServlet class and is defined in the pagecompile package. Both the package and the superclass of the servlet can be modified. These values are discussed in more detail later in this chapter. The code generated for a JavaServer Page is stored in a directory named for the package. By default, on the Java Web Server, this will be in the server directory under pagecompile.

PageCompileServlet

The PageCompile servlet has a simple job. It converts JSP into Java, compiles it, and executes it. The only real decision making that goes on is when the servlet decides to recompile the JavaServer Page. This decision is affected by a number of values, as diagrammed in Figure 10.2. First, the servlet checks if the page has ever been compiled. If not, it is compiled. If the page has been compiled but the compiled version is out of date, the page is recompiled.

The page is recompiled when it changes, based on the constraint that the administrator can configure the servlet to wait for a minimum amount of time before checking whether the recompile needs to occur. In situations in which the page doesn't change often, increasing this minimum time may improve performance slightly because the check will be done less frequently. Recall that the page compiler has to compile the Java code the first time a JSP is accessed. This means that the very first user to access the page may experience a delay that others, accessing the page later, will not encounter. If an error occurs during the compilation process, the PageCompileServlet formats it and returns the error information to the client. This allows the developer to see errors during testing.

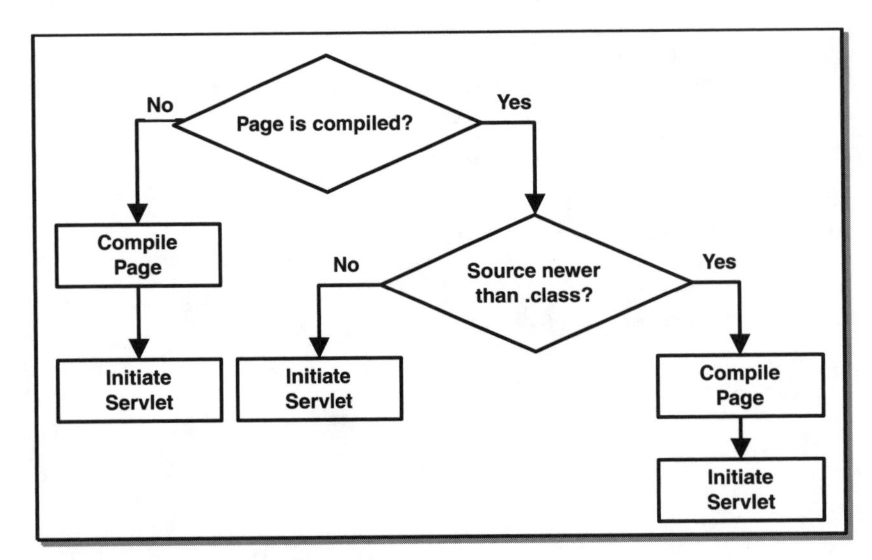

Figure 10.2 A page compiler decision tree.

In addition to allowing the administrator to configure the minimum time to check whether a page changed, the Web server can provide other parameters for configuring the way that JavaServer Pages are treated. The parameters for the PageCompileServlet as implemented for the Java Web Server are listed in Table 10.1. Other Web servers may provide the same or different parameters than the ones listed here.

Refer to the documentation for your Web server to determine what configuration parameters it provides for JavaServer Pages.

When to Use JavaServer Pages

One obvious question is, when should we use JSP in place of servlets? The answer, as usual in this type of decision, is a resounding, "It depends." JSP is a great way to include dynamic information in the context of an HTML page. Unlike a servlet, the JSP doesn't require any changes to code in order to change the HTML output. This means that HTML designers can use well-defined Java code inside their HTML pages without

Table 10.1 PageCompileServlet Configuration Parameters

PROPERTY	DESCRIPTION
`workingDir`	The directory for storing generated .java and .class files. By default, the workingDir is set to *javaServerInstallDir/* pagecompile/.
`defaultEncoding`	Defines the default encoding to use for servlets. Any encoding name that is supported by the java.io package is a valid encoding string value for this property. The default value of null causes PageCompileServlet to treat the file as an array of bytes.
`verbose`	If true, prints a message when compiling a .jhtml file. The default value is false.
`pageCheckSeconds`	The number of seconds to wait before checking a .jhtml file for any changes occurring after initial compilation. The default value of 0 tells the servlet to always check for modifications.
`defaultPageClassName`	The name of the class to use as a base class for pages that do not explicitly specify it. The default value is set to HttpServlet.
`packagePrefix`	The package name to prepend onto the name of the generated class. The default value is set to pagecompile.
`compileCommand`	The command for compiling the JSP servlets. The default value is javac -d *buildDirectory sourceFile.* When executed, the value of the workingDir property is substituted for the string buildDirectory, and the absolute path of the source file is substituted for the string sourceFile.

necessarily knowing how to write a servlet from scratch. Also, because the PageCompileServlet does the compilation automatically, the development process is easier.

On the down side, JSP is intended to represent Web pages. It is not intended for responding to requests from applets, managing redirects, or even providing a mechanism for creating dynamic images. Rather, JSP creates dynamic Web pages, no more, no less. These pages are designed to make servlet writing easier in a situation in which the servlet is generating HTML and most of that HTML is static—or at least the dynamic HTML is in the context of a static page design.

An important point should be included in this discussion: Don't make every HTML page a JSP. This technology is designed for dynamically changing pages, pages that look different for every or almost every request. Normal HTML should still be defined in HTML files and returned directly by the Web server.

Basic Java in a JSP

The first example of a JSP didn't include Java embedded in the HTML in order to show you the most basic servlet generation. The next example includes Java in our JSP by using the <java> and </java> tags. These tags can contain the attributes defined in Table 10.2. For the purpose of this example, use the <java> tag without attributes or with the single attribute type=code. Because <java type=code> is the same as <java>, the type=code attribute will often be left out for clarity. This form of the java tag tells the PageCompileServlet to include code from the JHTML file into the servlet generated for it.

The Java code inside the <java> tags will be included in the server page's servlet as is. For example, if a simple update to our Hello World page is performed as follows:

```
<HTML>
<HEAD>
<TITLE>
Hello World
```

Table 10.2 Java Tag Attributes

ATTRIBUTE	PURPOSE
<java type=code></java>	Performs the same function as <java></java>.
<java type=import></java>	Defines the name of a class to import.
<java type=extends></java>	Defines the name of a class from which to extend the servlet.
<java type=print></java>	Defines an expression in Java to send to the output stream.
<java type=implements></java>	Defines a list of interfaces the servlet must implement.
<java type=class></java>	Describes member variables and defining methods of the page class directly.

```
</TITLE>
</HEAD>
<BODY>
<java>
    out.println("<H1>Hello Java World!</H1>");
</java>
</BODY>
</HTML>
```

and we have the PageCompileServlet compile our new dynamic JSP into a servlet, the result is code like this:

```
package pagecompile;

import java.io.*;
import java.util.*;
import javax.servlet.*;
import javax.servlet.http.*;
import com.sun.server.webserver.pagecompile.filecache.*;
import com.sun.server.webserver.pagecompile.ParamsHttpServletRequest;
import com.sun.server.webserver.pagecompile.*;

public class _HelloWorld
extends HttpServlet{

//------------------------------
  static {}

  //------------- The service method
  public void service (HttpServletRequest request,
                       HttpServletResponse response)
      throws ServletException, IOException
  {
    ServletOutputStream out = response.getOutputStream ();
    ByteFileData __fileData = null;

    try
    {
      __fileData = (ByteFileData) ServletUtil.getJHtmlSource(this,
      "D:\\JAVA\\JWS1.1\\BIN\\..\\public_html\\HelloWorld.jhtml"
      , null, 902608528000L);

      if (__fileData == null)
        throw new ServletException("FileChanged");

      /*** lines: 1-8 */
      __fileData.writeBytes (0, 58, out);

      out.println("<H1>Hello Java World!</H1>");

      /*** lines: 10-12 */
      __fileData.writeBytes (116, 17, out);
```

```
        }
        finally
        {
          if (__fileData != null) __fileData.close();
        }
      }
    }
```

Notice that the regular HTML is still output directly from the file to the client, while the Java code is executed in place. This takes advantage of an aspect of the generated code in the server page. This is the automatic definition of the variable out, to represent the stream back to the client. This allows the JSP writer to return output easily, without dealing with the response object.

Scoping

The straight <java> tags indicate code that will be included verbatim in the generated service method. This means that variable definitions are scoped according to the code that surrounds them in the JSP, but they can exist beyond a single set of <java> tags. As an example of how scoping works, three JSPs have been created here. The first page contains two sets of <java> tags. The first set defines a variable name and prints it. The second set reassigns the name and prints it, showing what happens when you try to redeclare a variable. The third page shows what the servlet looks like when you define two Java code blocks. Here is the code for the first Web page.

```
<HTML>
<HEAD>
<TITLE>
Try Reassign
</TITLE>
</HEAD>
<BODY>
<H2>Java Block One</H2>
<java>
    String name = "Mister Zero";
    out.println(name);
</java>
<H2>Java Block Two</H2>
<java>
    name = "Master Blaster";
    out.println(name);
</java>
</BODY>
</HTML>
```

Notice the assignments in the boldfaced code in this HTML. The second set of tags doesn't need to redefine the variable, because it is already defined in the first set. The servlet code that follows was generated from this JSP. The reassignment code is in boldface type.

```
package pagecompile;

import java.io.*;
import java.util.*;
import javax.servlet.*;
import javax.servlet.http.*;
import com.sun.server.webserver.pagecompile.filecache.*;
import com.sun.server.webserver.pagecompile.ParamsHttpServletRequest;
import com.sun.server.webserver.pagecompile.*;

public class _tryreassign
extends HttpServlet{

//-------------------------------
  static {
  }

  //-------------- The service method
  public void service (HttpServletRequest request,
                        HttpServletResponse response)
      throws ServletException, IOException
  {
    ServletOutputStream out = response.getOutputStream ();
    ByteFileData __fileData = null;

    try
    {
      __fileData = (ByteFileData) ServletUtil.getJHtmlSource(this,
      "D:\\JAVA\\JWS1.1\\BIN\\..\\public_html\\tryreassign.jhtml"
      , null, 902610758000L);

      if (__fileData == null)
       throw new ServletException("FileChanged");

      /*** lines: 1-9 */
      __fileData.writeBytes (0, 83, out);

      String name = "Mister Zero";
      out.println(name);

      /*** lines: 12-14 */
      __fileData.writeBytes (147, 25, out);

      name = "Master Blaster";
      out.println(name);

      /*** lines: 17-19 */
      __fileData.writeBytes (232, 17, out);
    }
    finally
    {
```

```
            if (__fileData != null) __fileData.close();
        }
    }
}
```

The separate <java> blocks are combined into the single service method with only a single line of code between them writing out the HTML that separated the </java> and <java> tags that end and begin the two blocks.

This means that the HTML code in the following page will not work, because it tries to redefine a variable in a scope that already defines it.

```
<HTML>
<HEAD>
<TITLE>
Try Redeclare
</TITLE>
</HEAD>
<BODY>
<H2>Java Block One</H2>
<java>
    String name = "Mister Zero";
    out.println(name);
</java>
<H2>Java Block Two</H2>
<java>
    String name = "Master Blaster";
    out.println(name);
</java>
</BODY>
</HTML>
```

This page will not compile because of the redefinition of the name variable. Instead, the client is sent a message indicating the error, as pictured in Figure 10.3.

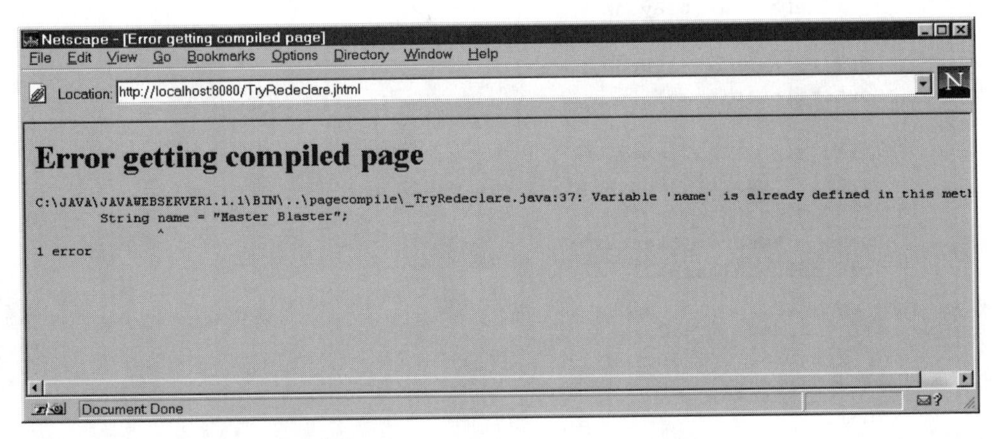

Figure 10.3 Attempt to redefine error page.

If you want the <java> blocks to have separate scopes in the resulting servlet code, use curly brackets to delimit them, as in the following file:

```
<HTML>
<HEAD>
<TITLE>
Two Code Blocks
</TITLE>
</HEAD>
<BODY>
<H2>Java Block One</H2>
<java>
{
    String name = "Mister Zero";
    out.println(name);
}
</java>
<H2>Java Block Two</H2>
<java>
{
    String name = "Master Blaster";
    out.println(name);
}
</java>
</BODY>
</HTML>
```

This file results in the code:

```
package pagecompile;

import java.io.*;
import java.util.*;
import javax.servlet.*;
import javax.servlet.http.*;
import com.sun.server.webserver.pagecompile.filecache.*;
import com.sun.server.webserver.pagecompile.ParamsHttpServletRequest;
import com.sun.server.webserver.pagecompile.*;

public class _twocodeblocks extends HttpServlet
{

//-------------------------------
  static {}

  //-------------- The service method
  public void service (HttpServletRequest request,
                       HttpServletResponse response)
      throws ServletException, IOException
  {
```

```
      ServletOutputStream out = response.getOutputStream ();
      ByteFileData __fileData = null;

      try
      {
        __fileData = (ByteFileData) ServletUtil.getJHtmlSource(this,
        "D:\\JAVA\\JWS1.1\\BIN\\..\\public_html\\twocodeblocks.jhtml"
        , null, 902611208000L);

        if (__fileData == null)
          throw new ServletException("FileChanged");

        /*** lines: 1-9 */
        __fileData.writeBytes (0, 86, out);

        {
          String name = "Mister Zero";
          out.println(name);
        }

       /*** lines: 14-16 */
        __fileData.writeBytes (154, 25, out);

        {
          String name = "Master Blaster";
          out.println(name);
        }

        /*** lines: 21-23 */
        __fileData.writeBytes (250, 17, out);
      }
      finally
      {
        if (__fileData != null) __fileData.close();
      }
    }
  }
```

which creates separate blocks for each variable and compiles appropriately.

Conditionals and Looping

Keeping in mind the simple inclusion mechanism used to create the Java code for a JSP, loops and conditionals can be created as well. In this case, the code block for the if portion of a conditional can begin in one <java> block and conclude in another. By combining these <java> tags and curly brackets indicating Java blocks, conditional HTML can be created, as in the following example. This example sets a variable called test and displays the string "True" if test is true, or it displays "False" if test is false.

```
<HTML>
<HEAD>
<TITLE>
Conditional HTML
</TITLE>
</HEAD>
<BODY>
<H2>Setting Value to False</H2>
<java>
    boolean test = false;
</java>
<H2>The value is:
<java>
if(test)
{
</java>
True
<java>
}
else
{
</java>
False
<java>
}
</java>
</H2>
</BODY>
</HTML>
```

Note the multiple <java>-</java> blocks surrounding the if-else statement and the HTML it displays. When compiled, this JSP defined results in the following Java servlet code.

```
package pagecompile;

import java.io.*;
import java.util.*;
import javax.servlet.*;
import javax.servlet.http.*;
import com.sun.server.webserver.pagecompile.filecache.*;
import com.sun.server.webserver.pagecompile.ParamsHttpServletRequest;
import com.sun.server.webserver.pagecompile.*;

public class _Conditional extends HttpServlet
{

//------------------------------
  static {}

  //------------- The service method
```

```
    public void service (HttpServletRequest request,
                            HttpServletResponse response)
        throws ServletException, IOException
    {
      ServletOutputStream out = response.getOutputStream ();
      ByteFileData __fileData = null;

      try
      {
        __fileData = (ByteFileData) ServletUtil.getJHtmlSource(this,
        "D:\\JAVA\\JWS1.1\\BIN\\..\\public_html\\Conditional.jhtml"
        , null, 902612394000L);

        if (__fileData == null)
          throw new ServletException("FileChanged");

        /*** lines: 1-9 */
        __fileData.writeBytes (0, 95, out);

        boolean test = false;

        /*** lines: 11-13 */
        __fileData.writeBytes (132, 19, out);

        if(test)
        {
          /*** lines: 16-18 */
          __fileData.writeBytes (176, 6, out);
        }
        else
        {
          /*** lines: 22-24 */
          __fileData.writeBytes (205, 7, out);
        }

        /*** lines: 26-29 */
        __fileData.writeBytes (228, 23, out);
      }
      finally
      {
        if (__fileData != null) __fileData.close();
      }
    }
}
```

The if-else block has been turned into an if-else statement in the servlet. The HTML outside the <java> tags is sent to the client conditionally, based on the if-else statement.

The same technique can be used to create a loop over a piece of HTML, as demonstrated in the following code. This JSP loops through an array of names and prints them using the implicit variable out. In this example, out is the servlet's output stream or PrintWriter as appropriate. The out variable and the other resources available in a JSP are discussed in detail in the next section.

```
<HTML>
<HEAD>
<TITLE>
Looping HTML
</TITLE>
</HEAD>
<BODY>
<java>
    String names[]={"Tommy"
                    ,"Kristan"
                    ,"Cheryl"
                    ,"Stephen"};

    int i,max;

    max = names.length;

    for(i=0;i<max;i++)
    {
</java>
I see <java>out.println(names[i]);</java>.<BR>
<java>
    }
</java>
</BODY>
</HTML>
```

The result of this code is shown in Figure 10.4.

Using loops and conditionals that operate on regular HTML is a powerful technique that allows HTML designers to fill in the contents of a dynamic page while still relying

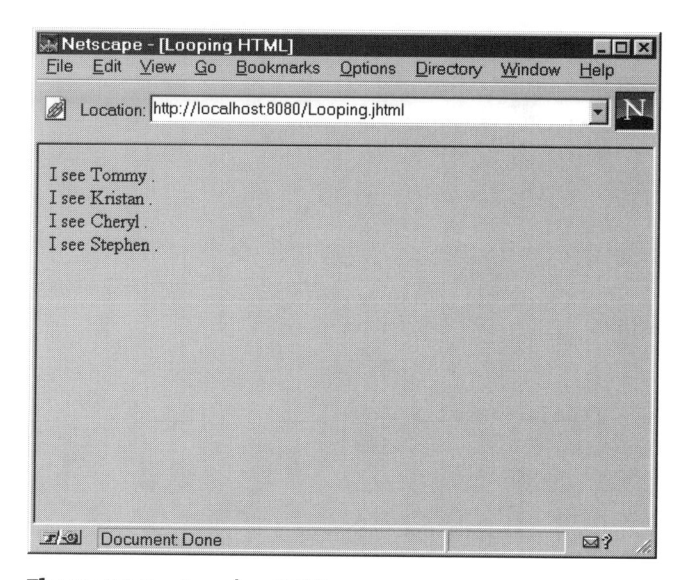

Figure 10.4 Looping HTML.

on Java code to perform complex business and application logic. For example, in the case of a database query, the programmer can use Java code to fetch data and loop over the query results, relying on HTML from the designer to display each result. In this same query example, the programmer can branch based on the number of results, and the designer can provide different pages to the client based on whether data exists.

Accessing Servlet Information

By default, the expected encoding for JSP is regular ASCII HTML. In this case, HTML is returned to the client as bytes that match their character equivalents. As discussed previously, the PageCompileServlet automatically creates a stream for accessing the pipe to the client and calls it out. If you want to use another character-encoding scheme, specify it in the initialization parameters for the PageCompileServlet. For custom encodings, the variable out will be a PrintWriter object rather than a ServletOutputStream. In most cases, this shouldn't affect your calls to print or println, but it is an important fact for programmers who use non-ASCII character encodings in their pages.

Besides out, the JSP has access to two variables, as defined in the generated service method. These values are request, an HttpServletRequest object, and response, an HttpServletResponse object. Both values can be referred to by name between the <java> and </java> tags. The following example uses the request object to print information about the client. This example is based on the PrintEnvServlet in Chapter 7, "Programming Servlets."

```
<HTML>
<HEAD>
<TITLE>
Print Environment
</TITLE>
</HEAD>
<BODY>
<H1>Requested URL</H1>

<java>
out.println(HttpUtils.getRequestURL(request).toString());
</java>

<BR>
<H1>Headers</H1>

<java>
        Enumeration headers;
        String curHeader;

        headers = request.getHeaderNames();

        while(headers.hasMoreElements())
        {
            curHeader = (String) headers.nextElement();
```

```
            out.println(curHeader+"="
                        +request.getHeader(curHeader)+"<BR>");
        }
</java>

<BR>
<H1>Request Information</H1>

<java>
        try
        {
            out.println("AuthType="+request.getAuthType()+"<BR>");
            out.println("Scheme="+request.getScheme()+"<BR>");
            out.println("Method="+request.getMethod()+"<BR>");

        //Crashes on some servers.
        //  out.println("Char Encoding="
        //              +request.getCharacterEncoding()+"<BR>");

            out.println("Request URI="
              +request.getRequestURI()+"<BR>");
            out.println("Request protocol="
              +request.getProtocol()+"<BR>");
            out.println("Servlet path="
              +request.getServletPath()+"<BR>");
            out.println("Path Info="+request.getPathInfo()+"<BR>");
            out.println("Path Translated="
              +request.getPathTranslated()+"<BR>");
            out.println("Query String="
              +request.getQueryString()+"<BR>");
            out.println("Content length="
              +request.getContentLength()+"<BR>");
            out.println("Content type="
              +request.getContentType()+"<BR>");
            out.println("Server name="
              +request.getServerName()+"<BR>");
            out.println("Server port="
              +request.getServerPort()+"<BR>");
            out.println("Remote user="
              +request.getRemoteUser()+"<BR>");
            out.println("Remote address="
              +request.getRemoteAddr()+"<BR>");

        //Times out if no DNS.
        //    out.println("Remote host="
        //          +request.getRemoteHost()+"<BR>");
        }
        catch(Exception exp)
        {
            out.println("Exception: "+exp+"<BR>");
        }
```

```
</java>

<BR>
<H1>Parameter Information</H1>

<java>
        Enumeration parameters;
        String[] values;
        String curParam;
        String value;
        int i,max;

        parameters = request.getParameterNames();

        while(parameters.hasMoreElements())
        {
            curParam = (String) parameters.nextElement();

            values = request.getParameterValues(curParam);
            value = request.getParameter(curParam);

            out.println(curParam+"=<BR><UL>");

            if((values != null)&&(values.length>1))
            {
                max = values.length;

                for(i=0;i<max;i++)
                {
                    out.println("<LI>"+values[i]);
                }
            }
            else if(value != null)
            {
                out.println("<LI>"+value);
            }

            out.println("</UL>");
        }
</java>

</BODY>
</HTML>
```

When compiled and accessed, this page displays the results shown in Figure 10.5.

Like the equivalent servlet, the preceding JSP has access to the client's query string and request information. In the preceding example, the JSP is actually accessed using the URL:

```
http://localhost:8080/printenv.jhtml?yes=no&ray=sun&ray=beam
```

which includes a query string for testing.

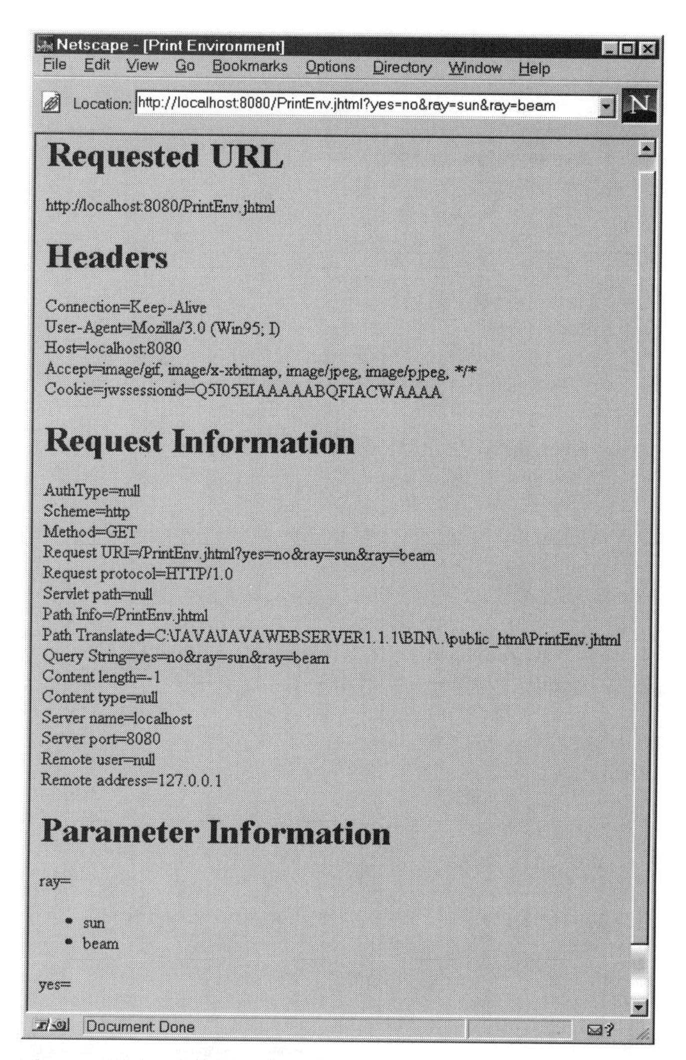

Figure 10.5 PrintEnv.jhtml.

Access to the user request indirectly provides access to the user's session state. As discussed in Chapter 7, this session state represents a single contiguous set of interactions between the client and the Web server. The session is represented by an HttpSession object that provides methods for storing values associated with the session.

The following example uses the session to store a counter. Conditional HTML is used to display a different message the first time the user accesses the page than when they return to it.

```
<HTML>
<HEAD>
<TITLE>
Session Info
</TITLE>
```

```
</HEAD>
<BODY>
<java>

       HttpSession session = request.getSession(true);

    if(session.isNew())
    {
</java>

<H1>New Session</H1>
The count is set to 0.

<java>
        session.putValue("sessioninfo.count",new Integer(0));
    }
    else
    {
        Integer count;
        int intCount=0;

        count = (Integer) session.getValue("sessioninfo.count");
        if(count != null) intCount = count.intValue()+1;
</java>

<H1>Session Information</H1>

<java>
        out.println("The count is set to "+intCount+".<BR>");

        session.putValue("sessioninfo.count",new Integer(intCount));

        out.println("Session ID: " + session.getId());
        out.println("<BR>");
        out.println("Creation Time: "
                        + (new Date(session.getCreationTime())));
        out.println("<BR>");
        out.println("Last Accessed Time: "
                  + (new Date(session.getLastAccessedTime())));
        out.println("<BR>");
    }

</java>

<A HREF="`request.getRequestURI()`">
Press Here</A> to reload the page, with url encoding.

</BODY>
</HTML>
```

A running version of this example is pictured in Figure 10.6.

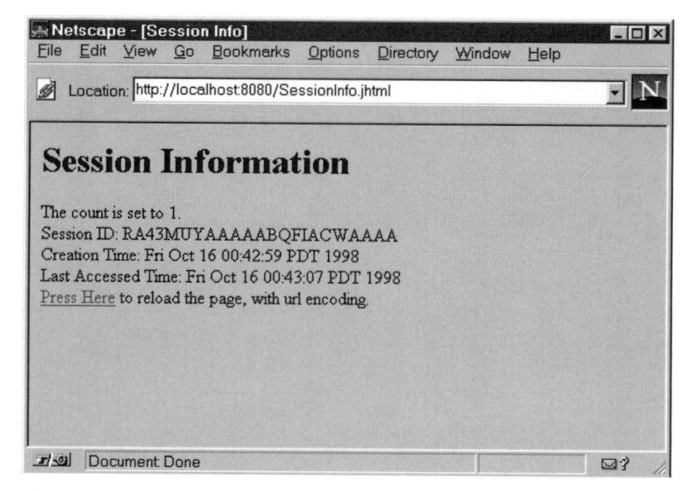

Figure 10.6 SessionInfo.jhtml.

In the previous code, reloading the page updates the counter as well as the information about the session modification time displayed in the JSP.

Using Backquotes

To preserve the strict distinction between <java> blocks and HTML, you are not allowed to embed <java> blocks inside another HTML tag. For example, the code:

```
<font size=<java>out.print(i)</java>>Hello</font>
```

is incorrect. Instead, you can use backquote characters (`) to indicate a value that you want to print to the client. This value can be any object or primitive type. If it is a primitive type, it is converted to a string using the wrapper classes. If it is an object, the toString method is used. In case a null value is provided, the empty string is inserted where the backquotes appear.

NOTE **Outside of a tag, the backquotes act as normal backquotes and are not interpreted by the PageCompileServlet.**

The following example shows how you might use these quotes to change font size in a looping construct. Notice how the Java block sets up a for loop but doesn't close it. This is followed by HTML code that will be generated as part of the loop. A second Java block closes the for loop.

```
<HTML>
<HEAD>
<TITLE>
Backquotes in Tags
</TITLE>
```

```
</HEAD>
<BODY>
<java>
    int i,max;

    max = 8;

    for(i=1;i<max;i++)
    {
</java>

<font size=`i`>`Hello World`</font><BR>
<java>
    }
</java>
</BODY>
</HTML>
```

When accessed, this page looks like the one in Figure 10.7.

Notice that the backquotes around the Hello World string remain intact because they are not inside an HTML tag.

Printing Values

For situations outside of HTML tags for which you want to print the value of a Java construct, you can use the <java type=print> and </java> tags to indicate a Java expression that you want to have sent to the client. This is a shortcut for using out.print. The contents of the two tags can be any Java value, basically any object or primitive, that could be sent to the String.valueof method. As with backquotes, the objects are toString'ed and the primitives are converted by the wrapper classes.

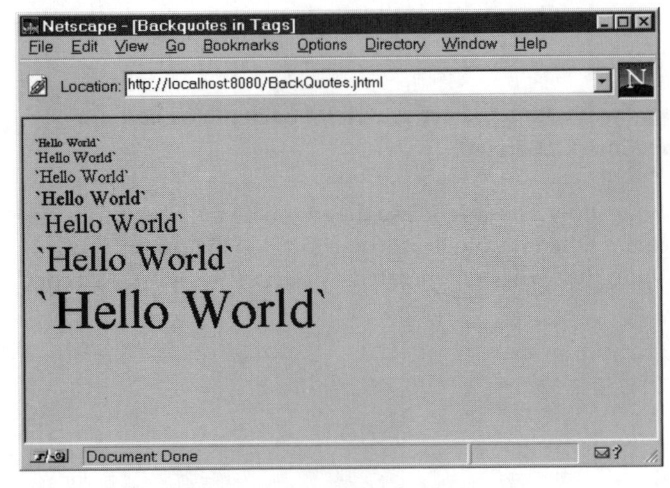

Figure 10.7 Using backquotes in the font tag.

The following example modifies the previous one to use the <java type=print> and </java> tags to print the value font size as part of the HTML.

```
<HTML>
<HEAD>
<TITLE>
Printing Values
</TITLE>
</HEAD>
<BODY>
<java>
    int i,max;

    max = 8;

    for(i=1;i<max;i++)
    {
</java>

<font size=`i`>
Font Size = <java type=print>i</java>
</font>
<BR>

<java>
    }
</java>
</BODY>
</HTML>
```

When displayed, this code looks like the page in Figure 10.8.

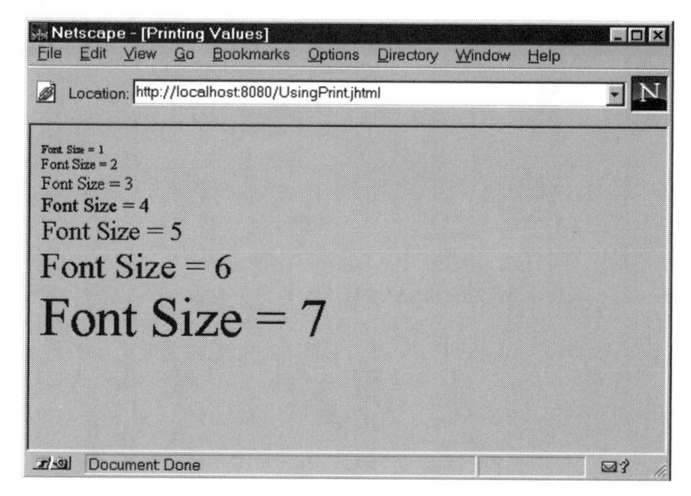

Figure 10.8 Using print.

As you can see in the JSP above, the print attribute provides the same functionality outside an HTML tag as the backquote does inside a tag.

Changing a Page's Servlet Class Definition

JSP can configure the output of the PageCompileServlet by using special <java> tags. There are three variations of the <java> tag for changing the code that the PageCompileServlet generates. First, you can specify new import statements so that you can include custom Java code, or non-default packages. Second, you can specify the servlet's superclass, although the class you specify must subclass HttpServlet. Third, you can specify code that is not part of the service method. All of these variations on the standard tag are implemented as types.

The first type is import. Use tags of the form:

```
<java type=import>java.net.*</java>
```

to import other packages or classes into the JSP servlet. By default, the servlet packages, as well as java.io and java.util, are imported in your generated servlet. The PageCompileServlet also imports several packages that provide special classes for the generated code. A good example of using this tag is to import java.sql into a page that uses JDBC to access a database.

The second type of <java> tag that changes the class definition is extends. Use the tag:

```
<java type=extends>SuperclassName</java>
```

to specify a new superclass for the servlet. The superclass for your servlet must be in the Web server's class path. For example, on the Java Web Server, you can place the superclass in the classes directory under the JWS root directory or compile it into the pagecompile package (or whatever package you configure the PageCompileServlet to use).

The following example creates a JSP that defines a simple servlet called CountingServlet. CountingServlet keeps track of a current value in the instance variable count. This servlet extends HttpServlet This class will be referred to from a JSP, showing that a JSP can extend custom servlet classes.

```
import java.io.*;
import java.util.*;
import javax.servlet.*;
import javax.servlet.http.*;

public class CountingServlet extends HttpServlet
{
    protected int count;

    public CountingServlet()
    {
        count = 0;
    }
}
```

In the subclass, this value can be accessed and incremented directly from the JSP, as demonstrated in the boldface code of the following page.

```
<HTML>
<HEAD>
<TITLE>
Using Extends
</TITLE>
</HEAD>
<BODY>
<java type=import>CountingServlet</java>
<java type=extends>CountingServlet</java>

<H2>
The Current Count is <java type=print>(count++)</java>.
</H2>

</BODY>
</HTML>
```

Be sure to import the class you are extending. Because the code generated from the JSP is in a package, this import statement is required to get to classes not in the page-compiler's package.

Using extends can make your Web sites easier to maintain by grouping reusable code into a servlet for extending. This way, each JSP can reuse rather than reimplement code for the site. For example, your site could use a servlet superclass that provides data validation or formatting functions to the JSP. You might even implement the superclass to implement some form of resource pooling. This pooling would depend on the Web server's willingness to share a class between servlets.

NOTE **If you change the code for the parent class of a JSP and recompile it, you may need to restart the Web server to see the changes.**

The final type of <java> tag for altering the generated code uses the type class. This tag takes the form:

```
<java type=class>java code</java>
```

The information in this block is treated as part of the servlet's class definition. It is not included in the service method, but it is included in the class. This type of <java> block can be used to define methods and instance variables.

As an example of what you can do with the type=class tag, we implemented a JavaServer Page that uses the Eliza package discussed in Chapter 7. This page defines the servlet's init method to initialize Eliza, our virtual psychologist, which is then stored in an instance variable. Requests made to the page result in an initial greeting (if no request is made) or a response to the previous input. Requests always display a form for talking to Eliza. The form uses backquotes and the HttpServletRequest to get the correct URL for the JSP. Normal <java> tags are used to display the necessary HTML, and an import tag is used to import the Eliza package.

```
<HTML>
<HEAD>
<TITLE>
Eliza JSP
</TITLE>
</HEAD>
<BODY>

<java type=import>Eliza.*</java>

<java type=class>

    ElizaMain eliza;

    public void init(ServletConfig conf) throws ServletException
    {
        super.init(conf);

        String scriptFile=
            "D:\\java\\jws1.1\\classes\\Eliza\\script";

        eliza = new ElizaMain();

        try
        {
            eliza.readScript(scriptFile);
        }
        catch(Exception exp)
        {
            eliza = null;
        }
    }

    protected String replyToMessage(String message)
    {
        String reply;

            try
            {
            if(message==null)
             {
                 reply = "Please enter a message to Eliza.";
             }
             else if(eliza != null)
             {
                 reply = eliza.processInput(message);
             }
             else
             {
                 reply = "Sorry, Eliza is not available.";
             }
```

```
        }
        catch(Exception exp)
        {
            reply = "I am having trouble hearing, "
                    +"please repeat.";
        }

        return reply;
    }

</java>

<java>

String message;
message = request.getParameter("message");

if(message == null)
{
</java>
Enter a message for Eliza.
<java>
}
else
{
    out.println(replyToMessage(message));
}
</java>

<FORM ACTION=`HttpUtils.getRequestURL(request)` METHOD="GET">
<INPUT TYPE="text" NAME="message" SIZE=36>
<INPUT TYPE="submit" VALUE="Send">
</FORM>
</BODY>
</HTML>
```

When accessed, this page should look like the one in Figure 10.9.

The Eliza package is available on the CD-ROM and should be included in the server's class path.

Accessing Other Servlets

As well as defining all the code that they need, JavaServer Pages can access other servlets. This access is provided via the servlet tag. The servlet tag uses the following syntax:

```
<servlet name=ServletName
code=ServletCode
codebase=ServletCodeBase
```

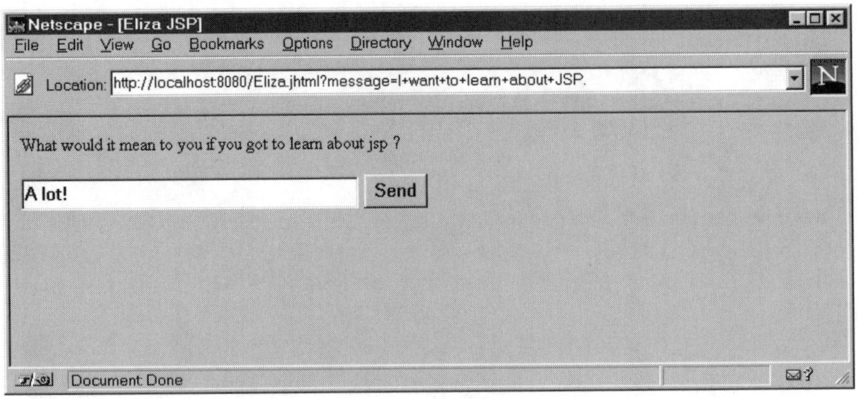

Figure 10.9 Eliza JavaServer Page.

```
initParam1=initArg1 initParam2=initArg2>

<param name=param1 value=val1>
<param name=param2 value=val2>
.
.
.
</servlet>
```

The attributes initParam1 and initParam2 are the actual names of initialization parameters for the servlet. These initialization parameters are used to load the servlet into the Web server. You can provide as many of these values as necessary to initialize the servlet. The param tags are used to pass parameters to the servlet in the same way an HTML form defines parameters. The name you provide is the name that the server uses to identify the servlet, and the code value is the name of the servlet's class. The code base can provide a directory for the servlet code. The code base is optional and is the server's class path by default.

When the page compiler sees the servlet tag, it is translated into a request to an instance of this servlet via the service method. For example, the following page accesses a servlet called AdLinkRotatorServlet and provides a number of initialization parameters.

```
<HTML>
<HEAD>
<TITLE>
Accessing a Servlet
</TITLE>
</HEAD>
<BODY>
<H2>A servlet is used to place an ad underneath this line.</H2>
<HR>
<servlet name="AdLinkRotator"
```

```
    code="AdLinkRotatorServlet"
    imagedir="c:\\servers\\javawebserver1.1\\public_html\\ads"
    imageroot="/ads">
</servlet>
</BODY>
</HTML>
```

The AdLinkRotator servlet sends an IMG tag to the client. The servlet does not assign a response type or encoding, nor does it create a full HTML page to return. This is the responsibility of the JSP, not the helper servlet. The AdLinkRotator servlet, listed in the following code, is based on the one in Chapter 7 but has been updated for use as a helper rather than for use by direct access. It reads a directory for available ads, based on the configuration, and rotates through these ads for each request.

```
import java.io.*;
import java.util.*;
import javax.servlet.*;
import javax.servlet.http.*;

public class AdLinkRotatorServlet extends GenericServlet
implements SingleThreadModel
{
    Vector imageFiles;
    int curIndex;
    String imageURL;

    public void init(ServletConfig config) throws ServletException
    {
        String imageDirName;
        File imageDir=null;
        String[] files;
        int i,max;
        File curFile;

        super.init(config);

        imageFiles = new Vector();

        imageDirName = getInitParameter("imagedir");
        imageURL = getInitParameter("imageroot");

        if(imageDirName != null)
                imageDir = new File(imageDirName);

        if((imageDir!=null)
              && imageDir.exists() && imageDir.isDirectory())
        {
            files = imageDir.list();

            max = files.length;
```

```
                for(i=0;i<max;i++)
                {
                    curFile = new File(imageDir,files[i]);
                    imageFiles.addElement(curFile);
                }
            }
            else
            {
                log("Cannot find image dir: "+imageDirName);
            }
        }

        public void service(ServletRequest request,
                            ServletResponse response)
                            throws IOException,ServletException
        {
            File curFile;
            String fileName;
            ServletOutputStream out=null;

            out = response.getOutputStream();

            int len = imageFiles.size();
            if(len>0)
            {
                curFile = (File) imageFiles.elementAt(curIndex);
                fileName = curFile.getName();

                out.print("<IMG SRC=");
                out.print(imageURL);
                out.print("/");
                out.print(fileName);
                out.println(">");

                curIndex= (curIndex+1)%len;
            }
            else
            {
                out.println("No Ads Today!");
            }
        }
    }
```

Perhaps the most important point about this example is that the servlet defines a service method, as expected. The servlet tag in the JSP initiates contact through this method rather than a special one. If possible, the page will try to reuse an existing instance of the servlet. Depending on the Web server, this may or may not work, because it is based on the servlet context. If an existing servlet cannot be found, a new one is created and used instead.

Handling Interrupts

Users will often interrupt large pages using the Stop button on their browser. In this case, the servlet that is handling the user request receives an IOException message. You can handle this exception in your JSP as well. In general, when the user requests that the page terminate, the servlet's best response is to clean up any resources that were created for the client, such as network connections.

The following example demonstrates how you can use try-catch to handle the users' termination of a request. It is also important in this type of page to include regular calls to flush, to make sure that the server is not buffering the reply. If you do buffer the reply, clients may not see any response, before or after they press the Stop button. This is a simple example that displays a series of numbers "sleeping" between each number.

```
<java>
try
{
</java>

<HTML>
<HEAD>
<TITLE>
Handling Stop
</TITLE>
</HEAD>
<BODY>
<java>

    int i,max;

    max = 1000;

    for(i=0;i<max;i++)
    {
</java>
Number <java>out.println(i);</java>.<BR>
<java>

        out.flush();

        //sleep a second to slow the loop down
        try
        {
            Thread.sleep(1000);
        }
        catch(InterruptedException ex)
        {
        }
    }
</java>
```

```
</BODY>
</HTML>

<java>
}
catch(IOException exp)
{

}
</java>
```

The entire page is wrapped in a try-catch to ensure that as soon HTML begins to return, we are ready to handle the user termination. Thread.sleep is also used to make the counting take longer; in this case, it is necessary to catch InterruptedException for the sleep statement, but IOExceptions are let through to the outer try-catch block. When users access this page, they see a growing list of numbers and an error message when the transfer is interrupted. An example of this page being interrupted is shown in Figure 10.10.

Using this technique, regular Java exception handling can provide a mechanism for handling Web client interrupts. JSP provides a great blend of HTML layout options with the enterprise-class programming technologies of Java.

A Preview of the New JSP Standard

Although the JSP standard is not completed, we were able to get a preview release to discuss here. This discussion is by no means complete, but it should provide a good starting point if you decide to update your JHTML files to JSP.

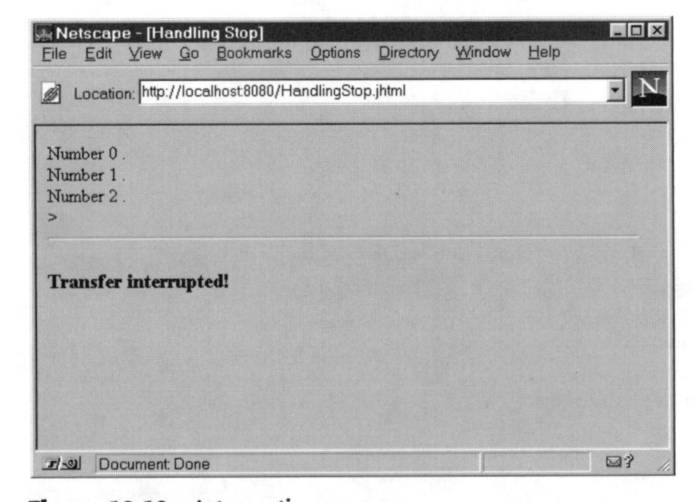

Figure 10.10 Interrupting a page.

NOTE This section is based on preview code and should not be used as the basis for production implementations.

The most notable difference between the upcoming standard and JHTML is a change in file extension from .jhtml to .jsp. The second most noticeable difference is the change in the tags. JSP uses a format similar to Active Server Pages by creating tags of the form <% ... %>. This specific tag is used in place of the <java type=code> and </java> tags. For example, you can write:

```
<%
int i=1;
%>
```

instead of

```
<java>
int i=1;
</java>
```

There are also special forms of the JSP tag, as there were attributes for the <java> tag. The first form of the JSP tag is the configuration form. These configuration tags can contain attributes that take the form <%@ {variable = " < value >"}+ %>. The variables include:

language. Defines the scripting language used in the file. Java is the only value that *language* can accept at this time. For example:

```
<%@ language = "java" %>
```

import. Defines the list of packages that will be imported by the servlet. For example:

```
<%@ import = "java.io.*, java.util.*, java.rmi.* %>
```

A JSP can also use the tag <%= ... %> to print Java expressions. This is similar to the <java type=print> tag for JHTML. The <% %> tag is valid inside another tag, so you don't need to use the backquotes. For example:

```
<A HREF="/unzip/<%= curEntry.getName() %>>
```

is a valid tag for a JSP.

The following example JSP takes a query string that includes the name of a Zip archive in the Web server's root document directory or a subdirectory. This page opens the file and displays a table containing information about each entry. The names of the entries are links to a servlet, provided on the CD-ROM, that extract an entry from the Zip archive and return it to the client. Access to the archive is managed with the java.util.zip package, and a NumberFormat object is used to format the sizes for files that may be large. When run, this page looks like the one in Figure 10.11.

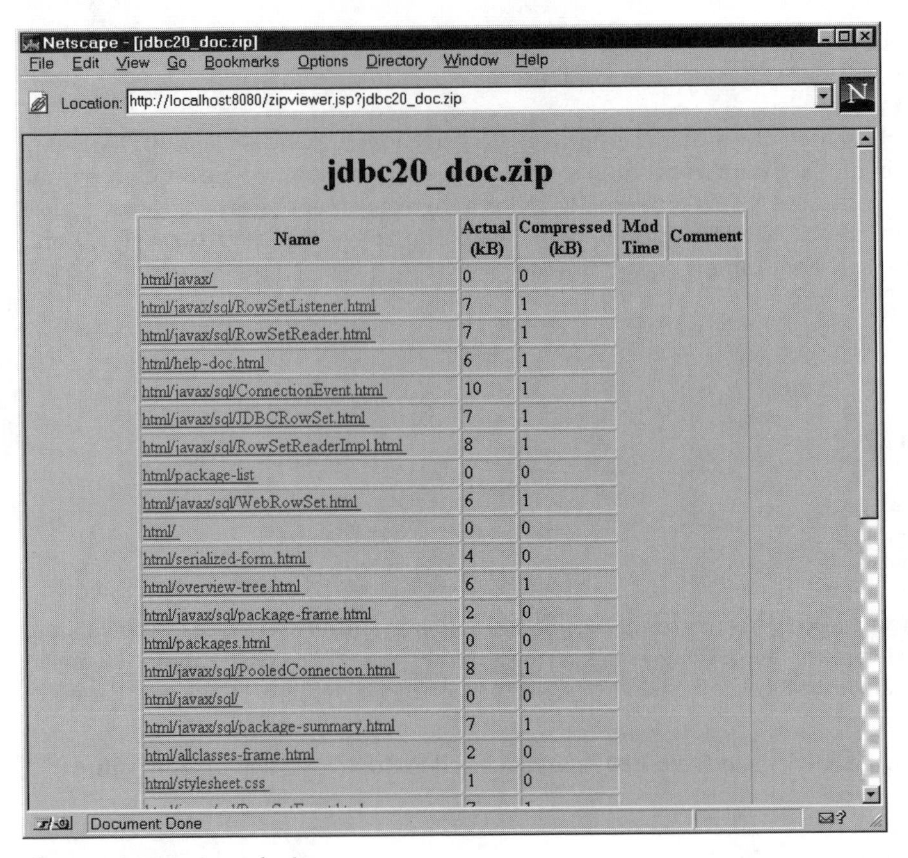

jdbc20_doc.zip

Name	Actual (kB)	Compressed (kB)	Mod Time	Comment
html/javax/	0	0		
html/javax/sql/RowSetListener.html	7	1		
html/javax/sql/RowSetReader.html	7	1		
html/help-doc.html	6	1		
html/javax/sql/ConnectionEvent.html	10	1		
html/javax/sql/JDBCRowSet.html	7	1		
html/javax/sql/RowSetReaderImpl.html	8	1		
html/package-list	0	0		
html/javax/sql/WebRowSet.html	6	1		
html/	0	0		
html/serialized-form.html	4	0		
html/overview-tree.html	6	1		
html/javax/sql/package-frame.html	2	0		
html/packages.html	0	0		
html/javax/sql/PooledConnection.html	8	1		
html/javax/sql/	0	0		
html/javax/sql/package-summary.html	7	1		
html/allclasses-frame.html	2	0		
html/stylesheet.css	1	0		

Figure 10.11 zipreader.jsp.

The Java code in this example is in boldface type; the HTML is left plain.

```
<%@ import = "java.util.zip.*,java.util.*,java.text.*" %>

<%
      String zipFileName;
      String fullZipFileName;
      ZipFile zipFile;
      Enumeration entries;
      NumberFormat formatter;

      zipFileName = request.getQueryString();
      fullZipFileName = getServletContext().getRealPath(zipFileName);
      formatter = NumberFormat.getNumberInstance();

      try
      {
            zipFile = new ZipFile(fullZipFileName);
            entries = zipFile.entries();
      }
```

```
        catch(Exception exp)
        {
                zipFile = null;
                entries = null;
        }

%>

<HTML>
<HEAD>
<TITLE>
<%= zipFileName %>
</TITLE>
</HEAD>
<BODY>

<CENTER>
<TABLE WIDTH=500>

<%
        if((zipFile == null)||(entries==null))
        {
%>

<H2>No Zip file specified.</H2>

<%
        }
        else if(!entries.hasMoreElements())
        {
%>

<H2>That Zip file contains no elements.</H2>

<%
        }
        else
        {
                ZipEntry curEntry;
%>

<H1><%= zipFileName %></H1>

<CENTER>
<TABLE WIDTH=450 BORDER=1 CELLSPACING=2>
<TR>
<TH>Name</TH>
<TH>Actual (kB)</TH>
<TH>Compressed (kB)</TH>
<TH>Mod Time</TH>
<TH>Comment</TH>
```

```
</TR>

<%
            while(entries.hasMoreElements())
            {
                    curEntry = (ZipEntry) entries.nextElement();
%>

<TR>
<TD>
<A HREF="/unzip/<%= curEntry.getName() %>?zipFile=<%= zipFileName %>">
<%= curEntry.getName() %>
</A>
</TD>
<TD><%= formatter.format(curEntry.getSize()/1024) %></TD>
<TD><%= formatter.format(curEntry.getCompressedSize()/1024) %></TD>
<TD><%= curEntry.getComment() %></TD>
</TR>

<%
            }
%>
</TABLE>
</CENTER>
<%
    }
%>
</TABLE>
</CENTER>

</BODY>
<HTML>
```

The UnZipServlet used in this example must be installed on the Web server under the name unzip for this page to work. You should also set up a servlet alias that forwards all requests that start with the path /unzip to the unzip servlet. To understand why the alias was used, let's consider the case where you extract an HTML file from the Zip archive. This HTML page may have links to other files in the archive. The browser treats these relative links correctly and passes them to the server using the alias as a directory. This means that if you extract an HTML page from the archive and click on a relative link to another page in the archive, the link is valid and the new page returned. Also, all of the images on a page that come from the archive are also valid. We strongly suggest trying this example or the JHTML equivalent. It is a great tool and a powerful addition to any Web site that wants to store information in archived format.

The new JSP standard will also provide strong support for including and accessing JavaBeans within a JSP. By using bean's a JSP can leverage existing components and classes. This syntax and others will be defined in the product's final release. Please refer to java.sun.com/products/jsp for the latest information on JavaServer Pages.

Summary

JavaServer Pages are a great middle ground between pure Java servlets and static HTML pages. They create an excellent combination of the two by using a simple tag mechanism for inserting Java code into an HTML page. Perhaps the most important thing to remember about JSPs is that the code inside the standard <java> and </java> tags will appear verbatim inside a generated servlet's service method. Variable declarations, loops, and everything will be included. The HTML for a page is displayed using byte/character oriented input/output (i/o) and appears in the service method as i/o calls.

Server pages are designed for use in situations where the developer wants to leverage existing HTML created by a page designer rather than hard coding it into a servlet. However, JavaServer Pages are not meant to be used as static pages. They are for use only when dynamic data is required. As with servlets, you should use Java code only to create a response for the client if it is needed.

WARNING **Some versions of the Java Web Server contain a bug that allows clients to get a JSP as is. This means that they see the Java source code rather than results from the generated servlet. Be careful about including information in the Java code that you don't want the user to access. Because the .jhtml file is on the server, this bug or as yet undiscovered ones could be used to access any information you include.**

The next chapter examines a complete JSP application that implements a small online store. The example shows you what a complete implementation could look like.

A JavaServer Page Online Store

One large and growing sector of Web applications is the online store—a Web site for electronic commerce, also called *e-commerce*. This chapter sets up a simple online store created with JavaServer Pages. This example also uses the AdLinkRotatorServlet example from Chapter 7, "Programming Servlets," and Chapter 10, "Creating JavaServer Pages." This example should not be considered a complete commercial product, but instead the beginning of one. Some of the decisions made when creating this example were for educational reasons. For example, the HTML pages describing products are based on images and HTML pages that were easily available. Some pages have added features that are not provided on others, so the discussion focuses on a particular concept. That said, this is a nice, simple online store, with the restriction: You can't really buy anything.

This chapter is organized into three parts. The first part looks at how the site is organized and what the requirements are. The second part looks at the two main JSP used to create the site. The final part looks at the shopping cart servlet created for the site. As with all of the examples in this book, the HTML and code for this example are available on the CD-ROM.

How the Store Works

The online store needs to be dynamic and have the ability to easily add items for sale. At the same time, it would be useful to categorize the items so that the customer doesn't have to look through long lists. Finally, the store should provide a shopping cart for keeping track of the customer's selected items.

To make this example work, an index.jhtml or home page is created for the site, which dynamically displays a list of categories based on the directories contained in the site's main directory on the Web server. For example, on the CD-ROM is a directory containing the main page and two subdirectories, one called Books and the other called Courses. The main page displays two links, one to Books/index.jhtml and one to Courses/index.jhtml.

Another category is planned for inside each JSP. This category page performs a similar function as the main page by dynamically listing the files in the directory. When a category index page is accessed, it looks at the available HTML pages in its directory and creates them as a list of links. Each of these pages should represent a single product for sale in that category. This organization is illustrated in Figure 11.1.

The pages for each product on the site are simple HTML pages rather than servlets. This improves performance; the site might have thousands of products, and you don't want to have thousands of servlets sitting in memory. Instead, JSPs are used only for the main page and categories.

The shopping cart is a servlet instead of a JSP because it will output a variety of messages based on the user's actions. (The example in Chapter 25, "A Four-Tier Online Store," extends this servlet to access an Enterprise JavaBean.) The servlet outputs a fair

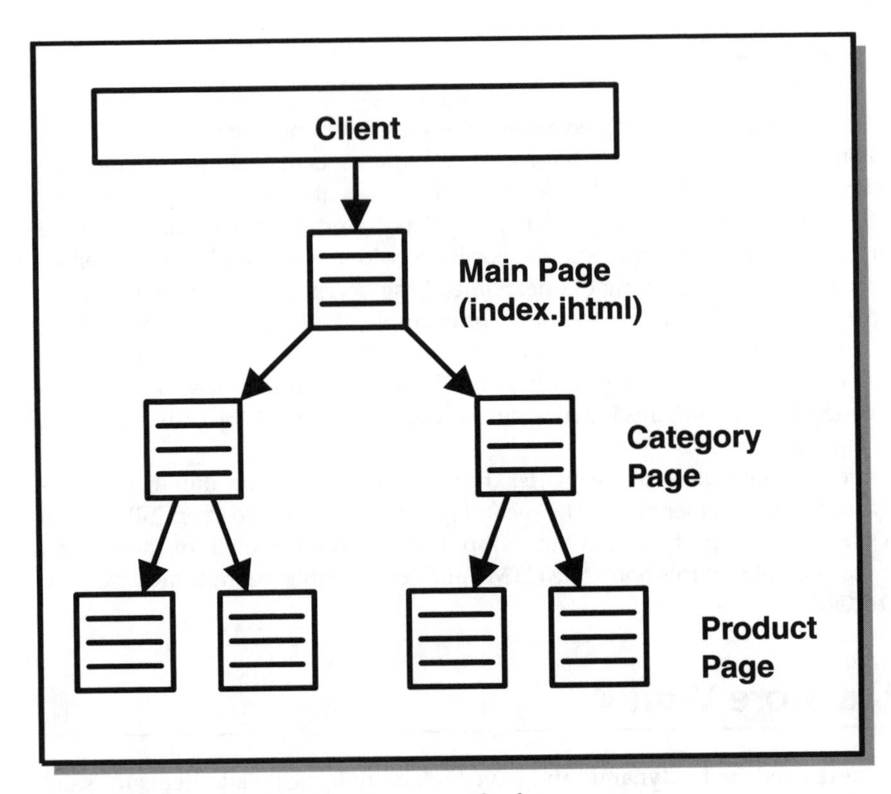

Figure 11.1 Example online store organization.

amount of HTML and could certainly be changed to a JSP instead. The shopping cart uses parameters to tell it what you want to do, including adding and removing items as well as simply displaying the cart. A mechanism for e-commerce is not implemented in this example, because this capability can be very site dependent and is outside the scope of the current discussion. On a real site, you might access a database, create an e-mail invoice, or use some other mechanism for placing the order.

The Main Page

The goal of the main page is to display a list of the available categories, as pictured in Figure 11.2. The categories are determined by looking at the subdirectories in the main pages directory. Figure 11.2 shows how these directories are organized on the CD-ROM.

The first step in creating the main page is to define some instance variables and a method for loading the list of categories. For simplicity, this example stores the categories in a vector, where each element in the vector is the string name for the category and corresponding directory. To load the vector, a method called initCategories is called that takes a directory path and loads the categories for that path. The JSP creates the path from the request URL using the HTTPRequest object's getRealPath method. Because the initCategories method is outside the generated servlet's service method, the definition for it is placed between <java> tags with a type=class.

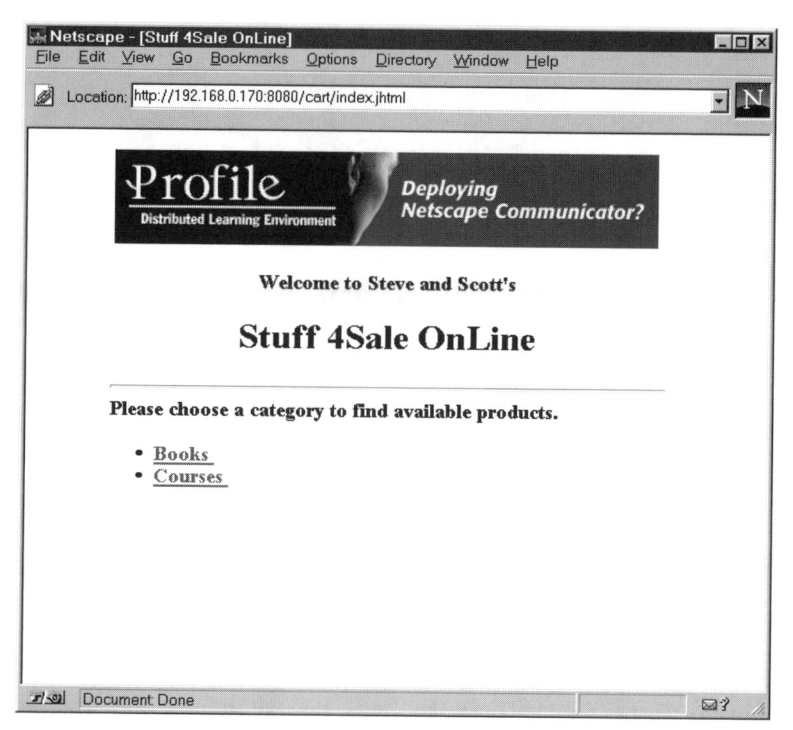

Figure 11.2 The main page.

```
<java type=class>
    Vector categories;
    String docRoot;

    public void initCategories(String rt)
    {
        File rootDir=null;
        String[] files;
        int i,max;
        File curFile;

        docRoot = rt;

        categories = new Vector();

        try
        {
            rootDir = new File(docRoot);

            if(!rootDir.isDirectory())
                rootDir = new File(rootDir.getParent());

            if((rootDir!=null) && rootDir.exists())
            {
                files = rootDir.list();

                max = files.length;

                for(i=0;i<max;i++)
                {
                    curFile = new File(rootDir,files[i]);

                    if(curFile.exists()
                            && curFile.isDirectory())
                    {
                        categories.addElement(files[i]);
                    }
                }
            }
        }
        catch(Exception exp)
        {
            categories.removeAllElements();
        }
    }
</java>
```

The next step is to define the HTML for the page header and the point where the categories should be output. Notice in the HTML code that follows, the servlet AdLinkRotatorServlet is reused, as defined in Chapter 10. This servlet dynamically rotates through advertisements displayed on this Web page. The image directory is hard coded to the directory where the ads are located. You should change this to reflect the directory in which your ads are stored on your Web server. Otherwise, this is straight HTML.

```
<HTML>
<HEAD>
<TITLE>
Stuff 4Sale OnLine
</TITLE>
</HEAD>
<BODY TEXT="#000000" BGCOLOR="#FFFFFF" LINK="#FF0000" VLINK="#800080">
<CENTER>
<TABLE WIDTH=500 BORDER=0>
<TR>
<TD>

<CENTER>
<servlet name="AdLinkRotator"
    code="AdLinkRotatorServlet"
    imagedir="d:\\java\\jws1.1\\public_html\\ads"
    imageroot="/ads">
</servlet>
<BR>
<H3>Welcome to Steve and Scott's<H3>
<H1>Stuff 4Sale OnLine</H1>
<HR>
</CENTER>

Please choose a category to find available products.
<UL>
```

The last line of this HTML starts an unordered list. This list displays each of the categories and closes in the HTML page's footer.

The next step is to make sure the category list is initialized with the correct directories. Use the requestURI to get the directory that the main page is in. Then, using the initCategories method, load the categories. Notice that this is done only once. In case the directories change, a reload time can be set in the category index page described later in this chapter.

```
<java>
    int i,max;
    String uri = request.getRequestURI();
    int ind;

    if(categories == null)
    {
        initCategories(request.getRealPath(uri));
    }
```

```
max = categories.size();

//Clean off the file name from the requestURI

ind = uri.lastIndexOf("/");

if(ind != (uri.length()-1))
{
    uri = uri.substring(0,ind);
}
```

The code is placed in a default <java> tag because it is executed when the page is requested. The <java> tag isn't closed yet because a looping HTML construct needs to be used to output the category names. Notice, however, that the URI was altered to make sure that a URI exists for the directory containing the main page, not the page itself. The URI is used to create a link for each category page; it contains the name of the main page, index.jhtml. The last lines of the preceding code remove that file name, leaving any other path information intact. The lastIndexOf is used to find the / character in the URL. This ensures support for the store "living" in a subdirectory of the Web site's document root.

Next, display a link to each category. The main page assumes that each category directory contains a page called index.jhtml. This page is created in the next section, "Category Pages." The following code listing iterates through the list of elements and dynamically generates the list of links. Notice how the <java> tag closes after defining the for loop, then a second <java> tag is used to add the end brace for the loop.

```
for(i=0;i<max;i++)
    {
</java>
    <LI>
    <A HREF="`uri+"/"+categories.elementAt(i)+"/index.jhtml"`">
    <java type=print>categories.elementAt(i)</java>
    </A>
    <BR>
<java>
    }
</java>
```

Backquotes are used to create the list item and link for each category.

Finally, the code that follows is used to close the list and end the Web page.

```
</UL>
</TD>
</TR>
</TABLE>
</CENTER>
</BODY>
</HTML>
```

This page shows the simplest mechanism for creating a dynamic list of categories using the file system. The next section looks at the category index pages. These are similar, but they add some complexity to this file system-based model.

Category Pages

Each category's directory should contain an index.jhtml file. To minimize the amount of work required to create a new category, create a single JSP that can be placed in all of the category directories and customize itself appropriately. This means that you don't have to write a new page for each category, just copy this one into the appropriate directory. To make this generic page work, take the category name from the directory, in the same way as the main store page. The category page also loads the list of products using the file system. Each HTML file in the category directory is assumed to represent a product. The final category page for the courses directory on the CD-ROM is pictured in Figure 11.3.

The category page adds two features to the model presented by the main page. First, the category page servlets will check whether they need to update the list of products based on adding new files, modifying files, or removing files. Second, each product file is also read to find its title, which is used as the name of the product. This makes the page look a lot nicer than just displaying HTML file names.

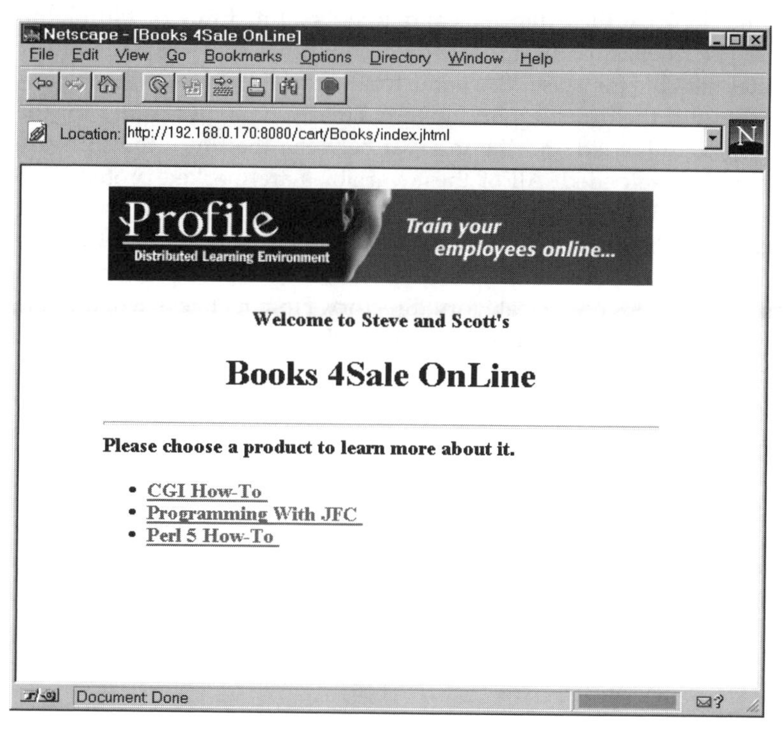

Figure 11.3 Books category page.

Because the servlet is used to display category information, it is named CategoryPageServlet. The code for this class is listed as follows. This servlet extends HttpServlet so that it acts as the parent class for the JSP. A lot of instance variables are defined to support the dynamic product list, automatic updating, and using titles as product names.

```
import java.io.*;
import java.util.*;
import javax.servlet.*;
import javax.servlet.http.*;
import WebPageFileFilter;

public class CategoryPageServlet extends HttpServlet
{
    protected Vector products;
    protected Vector titles;
    protected String docRoot;
    protected WebPageFileFilter filter;
    protected String category;
    protected long lastInitTime;
    protected long updateInterval;
```

In the preceding code, the products and titles variables hold the file names and titles of the product files. This example uses a small custom class called WebPageFileFilter, available on the CD-ROM, to ignore all non-HTML files when the directory is searched for products. This filter looks at file extensions and accepts .htm, .html, or .shtml, but no other extensions. The filter is easily updated to accept other types. Create a filter and store it in the filter variable for reuse. The name for the category is stored in the category instance variable and the directory in docRoot. Finally, define variables for the last time the products were loaded and the interval between the times the software checks if the list should be reloaded. All of these variables are marked protected to make them accessible to the JSP that extends this servlet.

The first method that CategoryPageServlet defines is called needsInit and can be used by the JSP to determine if the page needs to reload the list of products. This method performs several checks on the category directory. First, it checks whether the list was ever initialized; if not, then it returns true. Next, the method checks whether a sufficient amount of time has passed since the last initialization to check for modified, new, or removed files. If the correct time has passed, another method called checkInitForDir is called to test that directory. The current number of products is used as a metric to determine whether files were added or removed. By default, the update time is 0, meaning that this method will always look for file modifications. In the index.jhtml file, this value is updated to 60 seconds, although you may want to make it an hour or more to improve performance. Here is the code for the needsInit method:

```
    public boolean needsInit(String rt)
    {
        File dir;
        boolean retVal = false;
        long now = System.currentTimeMillis();
```

```
        if((lastInitTime==0)
            ||(products == null))
        {
            retVal = true;
        }
        else if((now-lastInitTime)>(updateInterval*1000))
        {
            dir = new File(rt);

            try
            {
                retVal = checkInitForDir(dir,products.size());
            }
            catch(Exception exp)
            {
                retVal = true;
            }
        }

        return retVal;
    }
```

The method checkInitForDir, defined next, looks for files that are modified and compares the number of HTML files with the expected number.

```
    protected boolean checkInitForDir(File dir,int expected)
    {
        String[] list;
        File curFile;
        int i,max;
        boolean retVal = false;

        list = dir.list(filter);

        max = list.length;

        //Return true if different number of files.
        if(max != expected) return true;

        for(i=0;i<max;i++)
        {
            curFile = new File(dir,list[i]);

            if(curFile.lastModified()>lastInitTime)
            {
                retVal = true;
                break;
            }
        }

        return retVal;
    }
```

The initProducts method loads the product list. The code for this method follows. This method is a bit different from the equivalent one in the stores main page because it may be called more than once. In order to have a reasonable object-oriented design, objects were reused where possible rather than recreating them. This method looks at the current directory, using the WebPageFileFilter, and adds product file names to the products vector. The titles for files are determined using another method called titleForFile and placed in the titles vector.

```
public void initProducts(String rt)
    {
        File rootDir=null;
        String[] files;
        int i,max;
        File curFile;

        docRoot = rt;

        if(products == null)
            filter = new WebPageFileFilter();

        if(products == null)
            products = new Vector();
        else
            products.removeAllElements();

        if(titles == null)
            titles = new Vector();
        else
            titles.removeAllElements();

        try
        {
            rootDir = new File(docRoot);

            if(!rootDir.isDirectory())
                rootDir = new File(rootDir.getParent());

            if((rootDir!=null) && rootDir.exists())
            {
                category = rootDir.getName();

                files = rootDir.list(filter);

                max = files.length;

                for(i=0;i<max;i++)
                {
                    products.addElement(files[i]);

                    curFile = new File(rootDir,files[i]);
```

```
                    titles.addElement(titleForFile(curFile));
                }
            }
        }
        catch(Exception exp)
        {
            products.removeAllElements();
        }

        lastInitTime = System.currentTimeMillis();
    }
```

The titleForFile method that follows opens an HTML file and looks for the <title> and </title> tags. The string between these tags is returned and the file closed.

```
protected String titleForFile(File file)
    {
        FileReader fileIn;
        LineNumberReader lineIn;
        String retVal = null;
        char cur;
        StringBuffer curString = new StringBuffer();
        StringBuffer titleString = new StringBuffer();
        boolean inTag=false;
        boolean gotTitle=false;

        if(file==null) return "";

        try
        {
            fileIn = new FileReader(file);
            lineIn = new LineNumberReader(fileIn);

            cur = (char)lineIn.read();

            while(cur != -1)
            {
                if(cur == '<')
                {
                    inTag = true;
                    curString.setLength(0);
                }
                else if(cur == '>')
                {
              if(curString.toString().equalsIgnoreCase("title"))
                    {
                        gotTitle = true;
                    }
                    else
                if(curString.toString().equalsIgnoreCase("/title"))
                    {
```

```
                    retVal = titleString.toString();
                    break;
                }

                inTag = false;
                curString.setLength(0);
            }
            else if(gotTitle && !inTag)
            {
                titleString.append(cur);
            }
            else
            {
                curString.append(cur);
            }

            cur = (char) lineIn.read();
        }

        lineIn.close();
        fileIn.close();
    }
    catch(Exception exp)
    {
        retVal = null;
    }

    if("".equals(retVal) || (retVal == null))
         retVal = file.getName();

    return retVal;
}
```

That concludes the CategoryPageServlet definition. Next, let's look at the index.jhtml page for each category directory. The category index page in each category lists the items available in that specific category. This page is very similar to the main store page, with the primary exception that it extends a servlet. Here is the JSP for the index page that extends CategoryPageServlet and can be customized based on the product category.

```
<java type=import>CategoryPageServlet</java>
<java type=extends>CategoryPageServlet</java>

<java>
    String uri = request.getRequestURI();
    String realPath=request.getRealPath(uri);
    int ind;

    /**
     * Seconds between checks for updating available
     * products. Default is 0.
```

```
      */
     updateInterval = 60;

     if(needsInit(realPath))
     {
         initProducts(realPath);
     }

     //Clean off the file name from the requestURI

     ind = uri.lastIndexOf("/");

     if(ind != (uri.length()-1))
     {
         uri = uri.substring(0,ind);
     }
</java>

<HTML>
<HEAD>
<TITLE>
<java type=print>category</java> 4Sale OnLine
</TITLE>
</HEAD>
<BODY TEXT="#000000" BGCOLOR="#FFFFFF" LINK="#FF0000" VLINK="#800080">
<CENTER>
<TABLE WIDTH=500 BORDER=0>
<TR>
<TD>
<CENTER>
<servlet name="AdLinkRotator"
    code="AdLinkRotatorServlet"
    imagedir="d:\\java\\jws1.1\\public_html\\ads"
    imageroot="/ads">
</servlet>
<BR>
<H3>Welcome to Steve and Scott's<H3>
<H1><java type=print>category</java> 4Sale OnLine</H1>
<HR>
</CENTER>

Please choose a product to learn more about it.
<UL>
<java>
    int i,max;
    max = products.size();

    for(i=0;i<max;i++)
    {
</java>
    <LI>
```

```
        <A HREF="`uri+"/"+products.elementAt(i)`">
        <java type=print>titles.elementAt(i)</java>
        </A>
        <BR>
    <java>
        }
    </java>
    </UL>
    </TD>
    </TR>
    </TABLE>
    </CENTER>
    </BODY>
    </HTML>
```

This page also uses the needsInit method to decide whether the products need to be initialized and sets the update interval to 60 seconds. You can alter this to any number of seconds. A higher number will have the page check less often for changes to the products. Because each check takes time, pick the highest reasonable time. You can add and remove files from the example directory and see that they aren't removed from the page for one minute from the last update.

The Shopping Cart

The servlet created to act as the shopping cart performs two functions. First, it provides a mechanism for adding and removing items from the cart. Second, it displays the current contents of the cart, as pictured in Figure 11.4. The actual shopping cart is a hash table in the session object. This hash table stores ShoppingCartItem objects that are created when the user adds them to the cart. By relying on the session, the store can support multiple users and let the Web server's session tracking code do a lot of the work.

Each item in the shopping cart is represented by a ShoppingCartItem object and has a description, price, and quantity. So that it's easier to display a logically organized cart to the user, a quantity field is used instead of adding multiple items of the same type. This holder class also provides a convenient method for determining the total price for all of the items of a particular type.

```
public class ShoppingCartItem
{
    public String desc;
    public float price;
    public int quantity;

    public ShoppingCartItem(String s,float p,int q)
    {
        desc = s;
        price = p;
        quantity = q;
    }
```

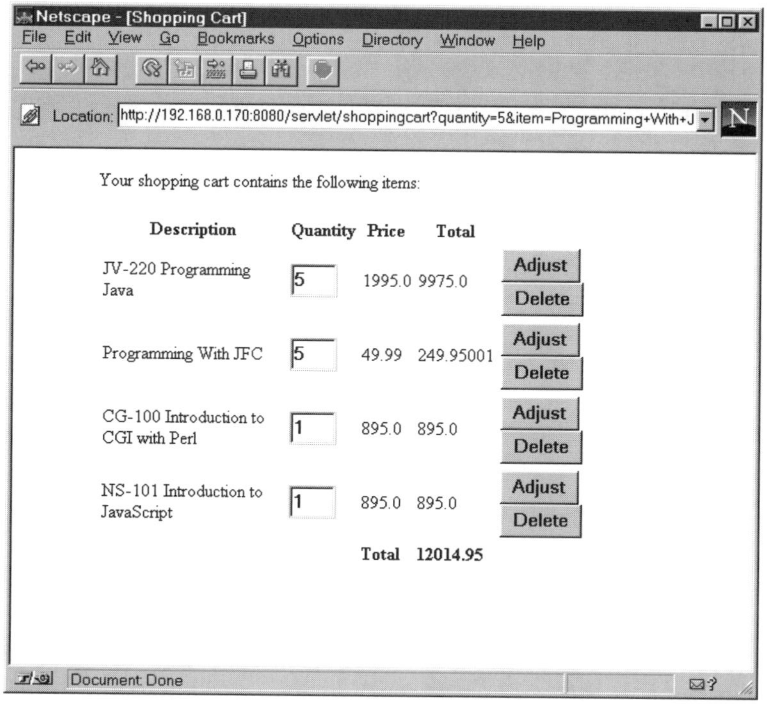

Figure 11.4 A full cart.

```
    public float getTotal()
    {
        return quantity*price;
    }
}
```

The servlet that implements the shopping cart supports four primitive actions. First, it displays the cart. Second, it adds items to the cart. Third, it removes items from the cart. Fourth, the servlet adjusts the quantity of a specific item. In the case of adding, removing, or adjusting, the quantity value of the appropriate shopping cart item is changed. If the item being added is new, a new shopping cart item is created. If the quantity of an item goes to zero, the item is completely removed.

After each request, the shopping cart servlet displays the current cart. This Web page, pictured in Figure 11.5, provides a text field for altering the number of items of a particular type in the cart or deleting items from the cart. Keep in mind that this servlet was created for educational purposes, and a real shopping cart would probably provide a more stylish interface.

The shopping cart servlet is implemented as a subclass of HttpServlet called ShoppingCartServlet. The code for this servlet is provided below. Most of the work is managed in the doGet method, with a separate method for drawing the entry for each item in the cart. A table is used to organize the items and display a total at the bottom of the list. A form is used to provide actions for each item, where the target of the form is the

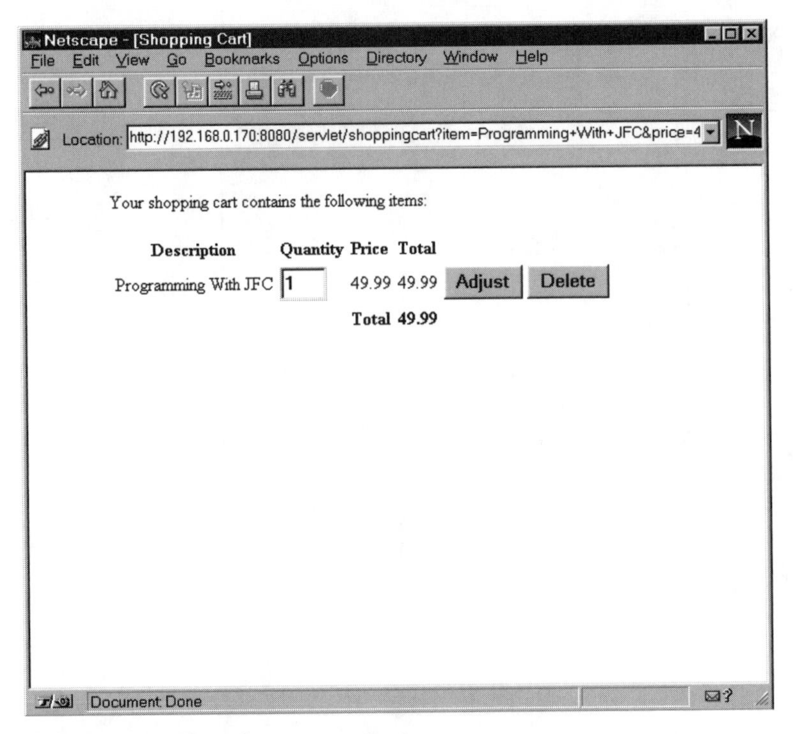

Figure 11.5 Shopping cart contents.

servlet itself. This servlet supports four inputs: an action that can add, adjust, delete, or view; an item that is a text description of the item; a unit price; and a quantity, the number to affect.

```
import java.io.*;
import java.util.*;
import javax.servlet.*;
import javax.servlet.http.*;

/**
 * This servlet supports four input parameters:
 * action: either add, adjust, delete, or view
 * item: a text description of the item
 * price: the items unit price
 * quantity: the number to affect
 *
 * When accessed, the servlet displays the current contents of the cart.
 */
public class ShoppingCartServlet extends HttpServlet
{
```

All of the servlet's behavior is implemented in doGet. The first action in this method is to declare variables, access the servlet's URL from the request object, get the user's session, and get the PrintWriter for output.

```
    public void doGet(HttpServletRequest request, HttpServletResponse
response)
    throws ServletException, IOException
    {
        HttpSession session = request.getSession(true);
        PrintWriter out;
        Hashtable items;
        Enumeration itemKeys;
        String action;
        int quantity=0;
        float price=0;
        float total=0;
        String desc=null;
        ShoppingCartItem item;
        String errorMessage = null;
        String requestURL =

HttpUtils.getRequestURL(request).toString();


        response.setContentType("text/html");
        out = response.getWriter();
```

If this is a new session, the servlet adds a hash table that will contain the current shopper's items in it. If the session is not new, it should already have this hash table.

```
        if(session.isNew())
        {
            session.putValue("shoppingcart.items",new Hashtable());
        }

        items = (Hashtable) session.getValue("shoppingcart.items");
```

Next, the servlet checks to see which action was requested and initializes the possible values for the current order. These values include a description of the item to be purchased, the requested quantity, and the price. In some cases, these values will not be set; for example, they may not have a value if the user is trying to view his or her cart.

```
        action = request.getParameter("action");

        try
        {
            desc = request.getParameter("item");
            price =
            (new Float(request.getParameter("price"))).floatValue();
            quantity =
             Integer.parseInt(request.getParameter("quantity"));
        }
        catch(Exception exp)
        {
            //reset and don't do anything
            desc = null;
        }
```

A series of if-else statements is used to handle the various actions. The first action to handle is adding items to the cart. In this case, the servlet checks to see whether the user is adding more of an existing item or adding a new item. Each item is represented by an instance of ShoppingCartItem that has a quantity associated with it. Adding more existing items to a cart simply adjusts the value of this quantity variable. Truly new items result in the creation of a new ShoppingCartItem. This new item is added to the items hash table being stored in the user's session.

```
if("add".equalsIgnoreCase(action))
{
    if(desc != null)
    {
        item = (ShoppingCartItem) items.get(desc);

        if(item == null)
        {
            item =
              new ShoppingCartItem(desc,price,quantity);
            items.put(desc,item);
        }
        else
        {
            item.price = price;
            item.quantity += quantity;
        }
    }
    else
    {
        errorMessage = "Unable to add item(s).";
    }
}
```

The adjust action tells the servlet to change the quantity of an existing item. In this case, an error occurs if the shopper attempts to adjust a nonexistent item.

```
else if("adjust".equalsIgnoreCase(action))
{
    if(desc != null)
    {
        item = (ShoppingCartItem) items.get(desc);

        if(item != null)
        {
            item.quantity = quantity;
        }
        else
        {
            errorMessage =
                "Item(s) was not contained in the cart.";
        }
```

```
        }
        else
        {
            errorMessage = "Unable to adjust item(s).";
        }
    }
```

There are three possible actions on a delete request. If the quantity of items being deleted is more than the existing quantity, the item is totally removed from the cart. If the quantity to remove is less than the existing quantity, the existing quantity is adjusted. If the shopper attempts to delete a nonexistent item, an error will occur.

```
    else if("delete".equalsIgnoreCase(action))
    {
        if(desc != null)
        {
            item = (ShoppingCartItem) items.get(desc);

            if(item != null)
            {
                if(item.quantity > quantity)
                {
                    item.quantity -= quantity;
                }
                else
                {
                    items.remove(desc);
                }
            }
            else
            {
                errorMessage =
                   "Item(s) was not contained in the cart.";
            }
        }
        else
        {
            errorMessage = "Unable to remove item(s).";
        }
    }
    //else just view
```

At the bottom of doGet, the servlet sends a Web page back to the client. If there was an error message, it is returned; otherwise, the current list of items is sent back to the user. Because each item requires some processing, the internal method outputItem is called to create the HTML for each item in the cart. All of the output is formatted into an HTML table with a running total of the shopper's current purchases.

```
    out.println("<HTML>");
    out.println("<HEAD>");
```

```
out.println("<TITLE>");
out.println("Shopping Cart");
out.println("</TITLE>");
out.println("</HEAD>");
out.println("<BODY TEXT=\"#000000\" BGCOLOR=\"#FFFFFF\"");
out.println(" LINK=\"#FF0000\" VLINK=\"#800080\">");
out.println("<CENTER>");
out.println("<TABLE WIDTH=500 BORDER=0>");
out.println("<TR>");
out.println("<TD>");

if(errorMessage == null)
{
    out.println("Your shopping cart contains"
                +" the following items:<BR>");
    out.println("<TABLE>");
    out.println("<TR>");
    out.println("<TH>Description</TH>");
    out.println("<TH>Quantity</TH>");
    out.println("<TH>Price</TH>");
    out.println("<TH>Total</TH>");
    out.println("<TH></TH>");
    out.println("</TR>");
    itemKeys = items.keys();

    while(itemKeys.hasMoreElements())
    {
        item =
       (ShoppingCartItem) items.get(itemKeys.nextElement());

        outputItem(item,out,requestURL);

        total += item.getTotal();
    }

    out.println("<TR>");
    out.println("<TD></TD>");
    out.println("<TD></TD>");
    out.println("<TD><B>Total</B></TD>");
    out.print("<TD><B>");
    out.print(total);
    out.println("</B></TD>");
    out.println("<TD></TD>");
    out.println("</TR>");

    out.println("</TABLE>");
}
else
{
    out.println(errorMessage);
}
```

```
        out.println("</TD>");
        out.println("</TR>");
        out.println("</TABLE>");
        out.println("</CENTER>");
        out.println("</BODY>");
        out.println("</HTML>");
        out.close();
    }
```

The outputItem method creates a form for each item that provided a text field for changing the quantity and buttons for initiating an adjustment or deletion. Data that is read-only to the shopper, like the item description, is included as hidden items in the form so that it will be returned to the servlet. This method is called with the URL for the servlet as the act argument to define the action of this form.

```
    protected void outputItem(ShoppingCartItem item
                              ,PrintWriter out,String act)
    {
        out.print("<FORM ACTION=\"");
        out.print(act);
        out.println("\" METHOD=\"GET\">");
        out.println("<TR>");
        out.print("<TD>");
        out.print(item.desc);
        out.println("</TD>");
        out.print("<TD><INPUT TYPE=\"TEXT\""
                 +" NAME=\"quantity\" VALUE=\"");
        out.print(item.quantity);
        out.println("\" SIZE=3></TD>");
        out.print("<TD>");
        out.print(item.price);
        out.println("</TD>");
        out.print("<TD>");
        out.print(item.getTotal());
        out.println("</TD>");

        //Output the change form buttons and hidden fields.
        out.println("<TD>");

        out.print("<INPUT TYPE=\"HIDDEN\" NAME=\"item\" VALUE=\"");
        out.print(item.desc);
        out.println("\">");
        out.print("<INPUT TYPE=\"HIDDEN\" NAME=\"price\" VALUE=\"");
        out.print(item.price);
        out.println("\">");

        out.println("<INPUT TYPE=\"SUBMIT\""
                   +" NAME=\"action\" VALUE=\"Adjust\">");
        out.println("<INPUT TYPE=\"SUBMIT\""
                   +" NAME=\"action\" VALUE=\"Delete\">");
```

```
            out.println("</TD>");

            out.println("</TR>");

            out.println("</FORM>");
        }
    }
```

This servlet also displays an error message if there is a problem with the request. You can see in the code that the forms used for each item include hidden fields that contain the information needed to create complete requests to the servlet.

Using the Shopping Cart

The other pages discussed thus far that access the shopping cart are the product pages. The product page pictured in Figure 11.6 displays information about a single book about JFC that is available at the store. This page shows how a form containing hidden fields can be used to access the cart and add an item to it.

The code that follows defines the Web page. The first boldfaced code defines a form that adds an item to the cart when the Submit button is pressed by sending the form data to the shopping cart servlet with the hidden form element named item containing the value of the book title to add. The second boldfaced form requests that the servlet

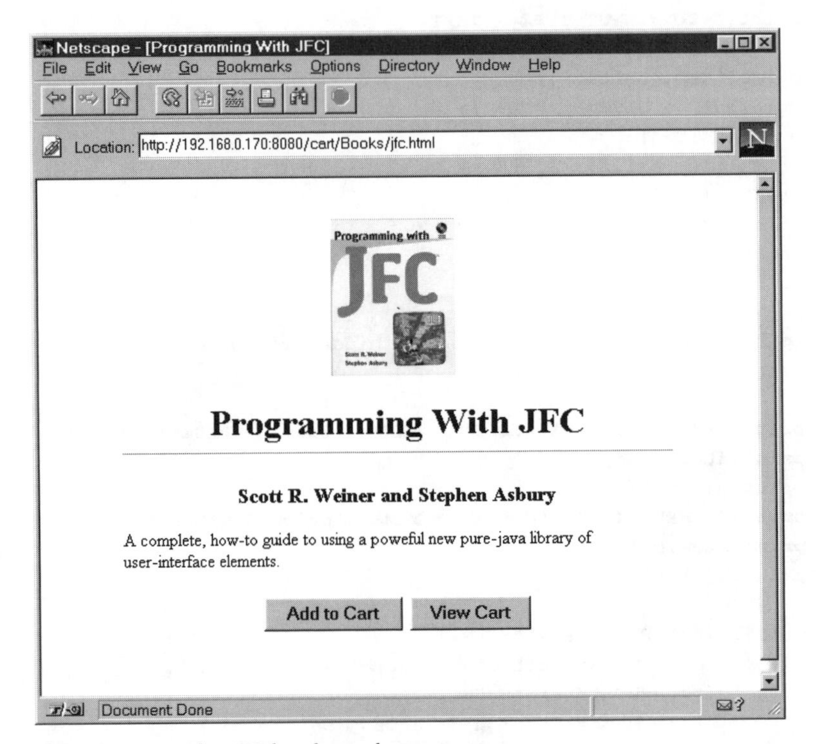

Figure 11.6 The JFC book product page.

display the current cart contents when the form is submitted to the same shopping cart servlet. It performs this secondary action of displaying the cart because the hidden form field named action contains a value of view.

```
<HTML>
<HEAD>
   <TITLE>Programming With JFC</TITLE>
</HEAD>
<BODY TEXT="#000000" BGCOLOR="#FFFFFF" LINK="#FF0000" VLINK="#800080">
 
<CENTER><TABLE BORDER=0 WIDTH="500" >
<TR>
<TD>
<CENTER><IMG SRC="jfc.gif" NOSAVE HEIGHT=140 WIDTH=112> </CENTER>

<CENTER>
<H1>
Programming With JFC<BR>

<HR SIZE=1 NOSHADE WIDTH="100%">
</H1></CENTER>

<CENTER>
<H3>
Scott R. Weiner and Stephen Asbury</H3></CENTER>
A complete, how-to guide to using a powerful new pure-Java library of
user-interface
elements.


<BR><BR>
<CENTER>
<TABLE WIDTH="50%">
<TR>
<TD>
<H2>
<FORM ACTION="/servlet/shoppingcart">
<INPUT TYPE="HIDDEN" NAME="item"
    VALUE="Programming With JFC">
<INPUT TYPE="HIDDEN" NAME="price" VALUE="49.99">
<INPUT TYPE="HIDDEN" NAME="quantity" VALUE="1">
<INPUT TYPE="HIDDEN" NAME="action" VALUE="add">
<INPUT TYPE="SUBMIT" VALUE="Add to Cart">
</FORM>
</H2>
</TD>
<TD>
<H2>
<FORM ACTION="/servlet/shoppingcart">
<INPUT TYPE="HIDDEN" NAME="action" VALUE="view">
<INPUT TYPE="SUBMIT" VALUE="View Cart">
```

```
</FORM>
</H2>
</TD>
</TR>
</TABLE>
</CENTER>
</TD>
</TR>
</TABLE></CENTER>
 
</BODY>
</HTML>
```

Using the hidden fields of the forms, allow a single servlet to provide multiple actions for an HTML page or a set of HTML pages. To save space in a real store application, you may opt to use product ids rather than the full name of the product, which in this case is a book title. We used a book title to keep the example simple.

Summary

This online store example has provided some ideas of how to use JavaServer pages and combine them with other Web resources to create a complete Web site application. In particular, keep in mind that straight HTML has been used whenever possible. Doing so improves maintenance and performance. In the same vein, inheritance is used when possible to minimize duplicate code in our JSP. Overall, perhaps the most important lesson is to remember that JavaServer Pages are a powerful tool for combining servlets and HTML. This means that due to their hybrid nature, they have some maintenance issues, such as sharing between programmers and designers, but they can also be used to create well-formatted, easily designed, dynamic Web pages.

Setting up an online store requires that you handle the presentation that allows a way for users to select from product categories, to select items to purchase, and to review and revise their choices. Ultimately, an online store provides a mechanism for purchasing items. The example in Chapter 25, "A Four-Tier Online Store," extends this version of an online store to use Enterprise JavaBeans to perform the purchasing functionality.

Keep in mind that a number of transactional and security issues associated with electronic commerce are beyond the scope of this example. In particular, a real commercial site needs to be sure to prevent invalid purchases. This store takes the price as it is input; a smart shopper could get a really good deal in this situation. The example in Chapter 25 fixes this problem by double-checking prices against an internal database. Even then, issues such as secure connections with SSL and protecting the server from hackers must be considered, despite their lack of coverage here.

In order to create a complete enterprise application that leverages servlets and JSP, you will want to access remote services. Previous chapters have looked at how you can access databases and other data services. The next few chapters look at how you can access remote Java applications using a technique called distributed objects.

Overview of Distributed Objects

The next two chapters deal with distributed object solutions using a Java technology called Remote Method Invocation (RMI). This chapter provides you with a brief overview of widely accepted distributed object technologies. This overview is intended to provide you with the background necessary to understand the benefits and use of RMI. If you already have grounding in distributed objects, this chapter is a useful refresher. If you don't feel you need a refresher, you might want to skip ahead to Chapter 13, "Introduction to Java RMI."

Distributed Computing

Developing enterprise applications often requires integrating multiple processes and the applications handling them. These applications may be running on separate computers. In order to achieve communication between applications, a scheme for sending messages from one process to another must be developed.

Distributed computing refers to computer applications in which the application code, the data it works on, and the actual computations performed are spread across multiple computers. The goal is to distribute the heavy computing and network load that users put on an enterprise application by leveraging the processing power of multiple computers.

One of the benefits for creating a distributed application is that the design of one component can be used by several others. As the example in Figure 12.1 illustrates, you

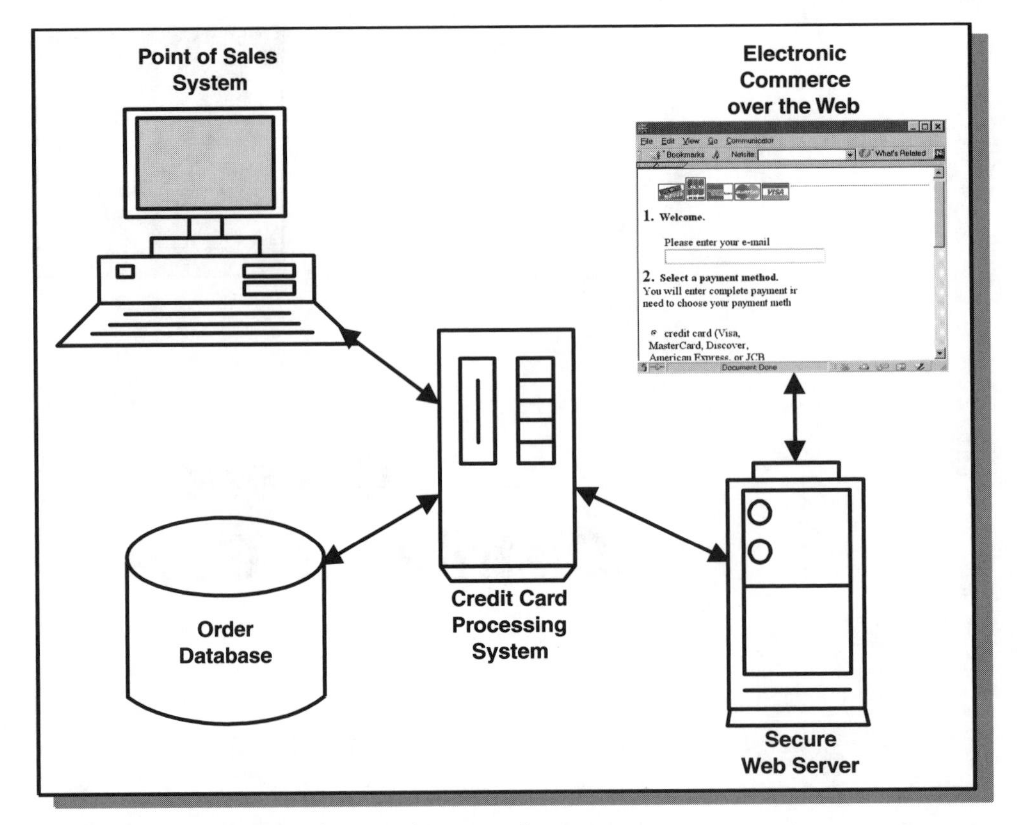

Figure 12.1 A distributed computing example.

could create a credit card verification subsystem that is simultaneously used by a point-of-sales system in a retail store as well as an electronic commerce Web site.

Rather than building the credit card verification component into every application that uses it, we would typically establish a distributed messaging protocol that allows messages to be sent from one application to another. In this way, the credit card application can be considered as just another network service that can be accessed and utilized by several applications.

Examples of messaging schemes that applications have used include:

Sockets. The method of standard TCP sockets for communication between two processes requires the developer to write an extensive amount of communication code because sockets do not define high-level data structures, such as the notion of a credit card object. In addition, socket programming requires that you handle data loss and marshaling of the information being sent.

Remote procedure calls (RPC). This higher-level mechanism handles some of the communication issues but still doesn't provide high-level data structures, only a simple function calling mechanism. RPC is simply a library of function calls (typically implemented with a C interface) that handles the actual communication between two applications. You still have to handle most of the data type issues yourself. This means that your credit card object would have to be broken down into its raw elements such as credit card number, date, name, and so on. The elements would have to be reconstructed on the other side of the connection for processing.

Programmers have used many schemes, but most of these older strategies make the developer think too much about solving the network communication issues as opposed to solving critical business problems. This is an issue because it means that changing the behavior of the service provider or one of its clients can mean a drastic amount of coding to handle network communication issues such as network failure, data formats, and so on. This is a *plumbing* problem, and highly paid enterprise developers should be focused on more critical business process issues. As object-oriented programming grew in popularity, it became obvious that the inherent mapping between object modeling and business processes would be a natural fit. It wasn't long before object designers began to look for a way to send these object encapsulations of business processes over the network. This was the beginning of distributed objects.

Distributed Objects

A *distributed object* mechanism allows objects implemented on one computer to send messages to objects running in another memory address space, typically across the network. In other words, if a standard mechanism could be developed so that an object developed in, say, Java could transparently send messages to an object on another computer as easily as it sends messages to an object in the same application, objects could truly bridge the gap between business processes and software development in a distributed application environment.

The number of hurdles in accomplishing this task is enormous. For instance, the designer of such a distributed object system would have to handle issues such as:

Heterogeneous platforms. In a distributed object environment, it is reasonable to expect that the various software components and network services you want to access are running on different hardware platforms under various operating systems. The transmission mechanism for these distributed objects has to manage data format issues such as byte ordering.

Location. In a distributed object environment, there must be some scheme for locating the object that will provide you the service. For example, how does the point-of-sales application locate the credit card verification object and the specific machine on which it is located?

Memory management. Sending a message to an object that is actually in another address space adds several new issues to the object paradigm. For example, if you wanted to request a customer name from a *remote* object, how does the string representing the name get passed back to you? By reference? By value? It can't truly be by reference, because references to a foreign address space have no meaning in your application. Figure 12.2 illustrates this concept. If the name is sent by value, what happens if the value changes? The original string won't be updated, only the copy will be, so how would you have the original string updated? In addition, if you have a reference to a remote object, how does the remote object application

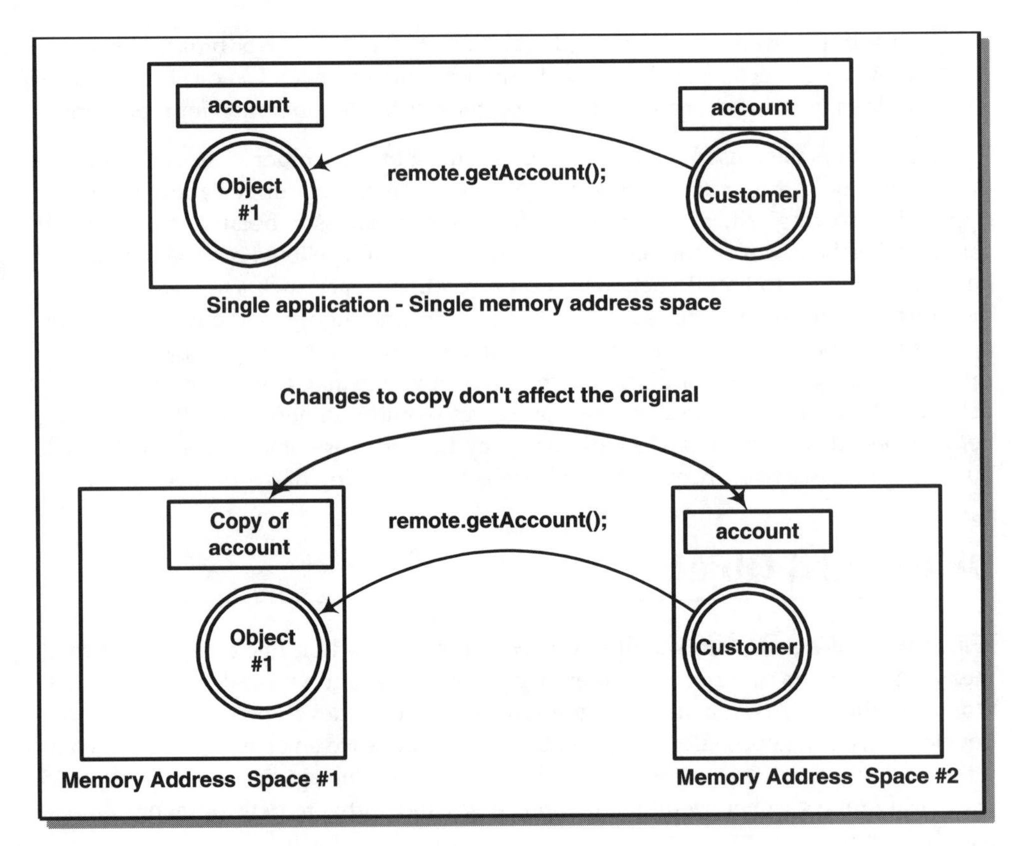

Figure 12.2 Accessing a remote object.

"know" when it can delete or garbage-collect the object? The distributed object scheme would have to handle these issues and several others.

Multiple languages. Unfortunately, no one computer language meets all application needs. This means that it is reasonable that distributed object services and their client applications could be written in different programming languages and therefore have completely different language concepts. For example, how does a Java application send messages to a C++ object when the C++ language supports multiple inheritance and the Java language doesn't, or vice versa? The distributed object scheme should be able to perform language mappings. This way, a message sent from an application written in C++ could be interpreted and executed by a Java object running on another computer or in another address space on the same computer.

Network communication. Object messages would have to be sent in such a way that the client application did not have to deal with the networking issues required to communicate with the object service it was connecting to. This means a mechanism is required to handle network protocols and network failure. For instance, when you send a message inside an application, you always expect the message to be received. In a distributed object scheme, due to hardware or software difficulties along the way, it is quite possible that the message will never reach its destination. Although it is impossible for any networking technology to completely hide the inherent issues in distributed computing, the more the technology can handle without programmer knowledge, the better.

Persistence. Communicating with objects over a network also brings up the question of how to maintain a reference to the remote object so that later sessions with your client application are possible. Some global referencing scheme may be necessary.

Standardization. Even if solutions to all these problems and the dozens of other issues that have emerged are found, the most pressing one is that of standards. If the distributed object scheme is not widely accepted, it has little value. After all, what difference does it make if we have a way of connecting applications and services together with a seamless object layer if third-party applications and vendors don't support the mechanism? How useful is it to create a distributed object layer that no one supports? For a distributed object solution to truly benefit the industry, it must have the support of advocates and a standards body.

Creating a distributed object solution that is robust and well received by the industry is critical for its success. There are several features than any distributed object architecture should address. Here is a general description of these features.

Creating a Solution

A successful distributed object scheme, at a minimum, will:

- Support heterogeneous platforms
- Allow discovery of an object
- Handle memory management issues
- Support communication among multiple programming languages
- Transparently handle network communication
- Provide a mechanism for storing references to remote objects
- Gain industry support

If you were to solve these problems yourself, you would come up with a solution similar to the most popular schemes today. These solutions include:

- A mechanism for handling the communication issues between objects over standard protocols such as TCP/IP
- A scheme for locating remote objects
- A mechanism for marshaling and unmarshaling the object data over the network
- A scheme for providing an interface for a remote object in the local address space
- A reference scheme for keeping track of valid references to an object

In essence, to the programmer, distributed object application code should look just like a non-distributed application's code. Consider the following incomplete Java code sample.

```
HelloObject h = new HelloObject();
h.sayHelloTo("John");
```

In the distributed version, imagine a HelloObject is created and instantiated on a remote machine. This object is then registered with some type of naming service so that the object could be located later by clients. The distributed version might look something like this fictitious scheme:

```
HelloInterface h = new HelloFactory("myserver", "objectname");
h.sayHelloTo("John");
```

The differences are subtle. First, the object returned is defined as an interface rather than an actual object. This way, the remote object implementation can change without affecting the code. Second, a mechanism is needed for locating the machine on which the remote object is located. A reasonable way to do this is to create a subclass of our distributed object mechanism class that takes as parameters the machine name and the registered name for the object. The distributed object mechanism is a class that performs the necessary communication to connect with the remote server, locate the named object, and instantiate a stand-in, or proxy, for the remote object in your client's address space. This proxy implements the HelloInterface; however, each method called is converted into a distributed message using some underlying protocol. In other words, when you call sayHelloTo(), the parameter "john" is sent to the remote object for processing. The mechanism for sending this data is hidden from the programmer, allowing for a transparent operation.

Although the various distributed object schemes available today vary, they all solve the problems listed above.

Current Solutions

Today, there are many distributed object solutions. Each addresses some or all of the issues mentioned previously, and more. An enterprise Java developer should be aware of three schemes:

- Common Object Request Broker Architecture (CORBA) developed by the Object Management Group (OMG).
- Distributed Component Object Model (DCOM) developed by Microsoft.
- Remote Method Invocation (RMI) developed by Sun.

Let's take a look at each of these in more detail.

OMG and CORBA

OMG was formed in 1989 by a group of vendors for the purpose of creating a standard architecture for networked distributed objects. The architecture that resulted is the Common Object Request Broker Architecture (CORBA). Both the International Standards Organization and X/Open have sanctioned CORBA as the standard architecture for distributed objects.

NOTE **For more information on OMG, you may want to check out their Web site at www.omg.org.**

Figure 12.3 illustrates the basic CORBA architecture.

CORBA is a specification and architecture for creating, distributing, and managing distributed program objects in a network. CORBA relies on an Object Request Broker (ORB) to enable a client object to make a server request without having to know where in a network the server object or component is located and exactly what its interfaces are. In brokering a client request, an ORB may provide services such as:

- **Concurrency control service.** Allows an ORB to manage locks to data for which transactions or threads may compete.
- **Licensing service.** Allows use of a component to be measured for purposes of compensation.
- **Life-cycle services.** Defines how to create, copy, move, and delete a component.
- **Naming service.** Allows a component to find another component by name and supports existing naming systems or directories, including DCE, X.500, and Sun's NIS.
- **Persistence service.** Provides the ability to store data in object databases, relational databases, and plain files.
- **Properties service.** Lets a component contain a self-description that other components can use.

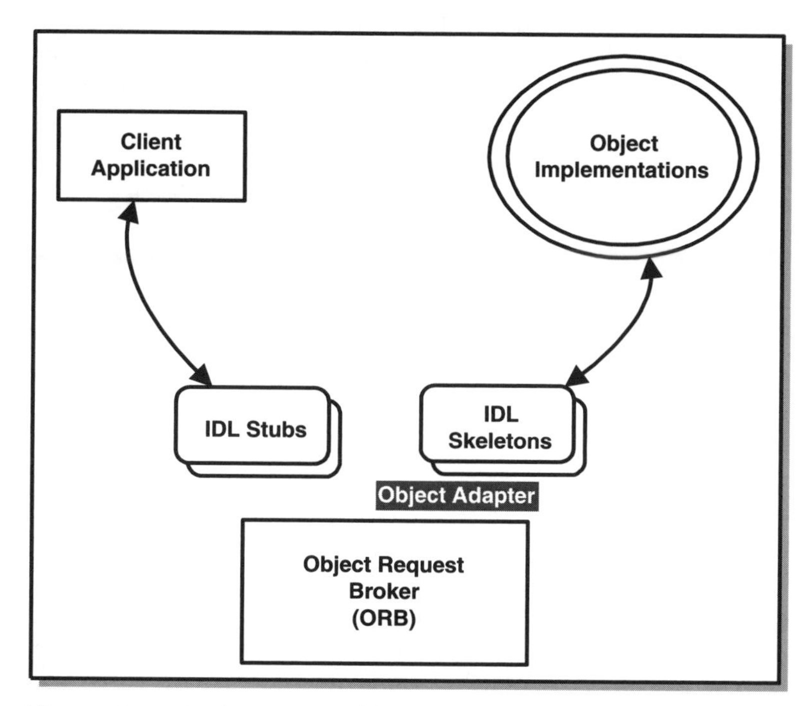

Figure 12.3 Basic CORBA architecture.

- **Query service.** Allows a component to query a database. This service is based on the SQL3 specification and the Object Database Management Group's (ODMG's) Object Query Language (OQL).
- **Relationship service.** Creates and tracks dynamic associations between objects (references).
- **Transaction service.** Ensures that when a transaction is completed, changes are committed or, if not, that database changes are restored to their pretransaction state.
- **Security service.** Provide a mechanism to control access to the remote object.

To make requests or return replies between the ORBs, programs use the General Inter-ORB Protocol (GIOP) and, for the Internet, its Internet Inter-ORB Protocol (IIOP), as shown in Figure 12.4. IIOP is an object-oriented protocol that makes it possible for distributed programs written in different programming languages to communicate over the Internet. IIOP maps GIOP requests and replies to the Internet's Transmission Control Protocol (TCP) layer in each computer. The programmer's API layer hides this detail, however.

IIOP use is becoming so popular that vendors that haven't fully implemented CORBA products are supporting IIOP. This means that your CORBA-compliant, or at least IIOP-compliant, objects should be able to communicate with these products easily.

Because of the wide acceptance of CORBA and, more important, IIOP, you can write an application that is able to interact with third-party objects and services. This means that you can purchase key technologies such as directory services and integrate them into your enterprise with little change in your own code or the way in which you design your applications.

A number of products have begun to use CORBA, and it appears to be the strategic architecture for distributed objects. The OMG currently claims to have over 700 member companies supporting, influencing, and using its architecture. Developing multitier

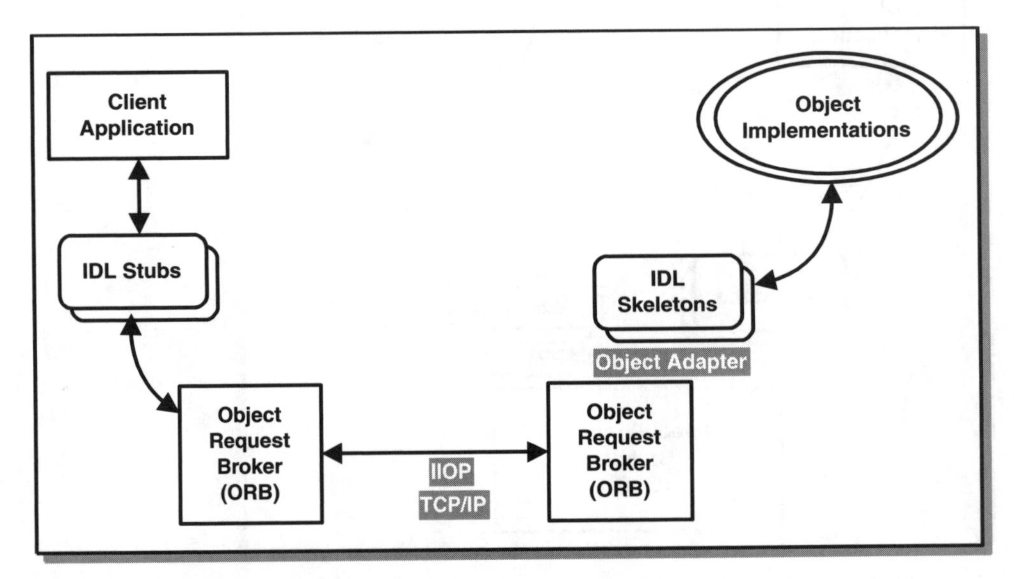

Figure 12.4 ORBs and IIOP.

applications using CORBA holds great promise because this technology supports interoperability across languages and platforms, as well as enhancing maintainability and adaptability of the application. CORBA has gained popularity, but Microsoft has not embraced it due to the fact that it has its own distributed object architecture, the Distributed Component Object Model (DCOM).

DCOM and COM

DCOM is Microsoft's approach to a networkwide environment for object communication and services. DCOM is a set of program interfaces based on Microsoft concepts in which objects in a client program request services from objects running inside server applications on other computers in the network. The model extends the Microsoft Component Object Model (COM), which provides a set of interfaces allowing applications to communicate on a single computer running a Windows 95 or NT operating system.

COM is aimed at providing capabilities similar to those defined in CORBA but for applications on a single computer. The COM model is found in higher-level Microsoft technologies such as Object Linking and Embedding (OLE). OLE allows application to be built from smaller components. For example, an Excel spreadsheet could be embedded in a Microsoft Word document. COM provides support for handling the low-level communication between the applications; however, it wasn't intended for extensive network use.

COM does support some network capabilities, but it requires the developer to write RPC error-handling code, so COM is not a seamless solution for object developers. The idea is to think of your application as a small component providing a service, such as spell checking. By using a common interface such as COM, developers could "put together" an application by combining COM-compliant application objects called *components*. The capabilities COM provides include:

- A binary standard for function calling between components
- A provision for strongly typed groupings of functions into interfaces
- A mechanism for finding object services
- A life-cycle mechanism that implements reference counting so you know when to destroy the object
- A mechanism for naming unique objects

For example, a word processor application could load a spell-checker component using COM by simply referring to it by a predefined name.

DCOM is an improved version of COM for the network. It allows the developer to send messages to components over the network as seamlessly as COM provides services on a single machine. The developer is completely insulated from the network issues. DCOM uses standard protocols such as TCP/IP and comes as part of NT 4.0 and Windows 98. It is also provided as a free upgrade for Windows 95. DCOM should be available on major UNIX platforms soon.

NOTE **For more information on DCOM, check out the Microsoft Web site at www.microsoft.com/com/ or the book *COM and DCOM: Microsoft's Vision for Distributed Objects,* by Roger Sessions (John Wiley & Sons, 1998).**

Several companies are working on standards to improve interoperability between CORBA and COM/DCOM. The OMG has developed a mapping between CORBA and COM/DCOM that is supported by several products. In addition, Microsoft is working on interoperability, which means that applications could leverage both types of object services on a network.

RMI

As enterprise Java developers, both of these models have one specific flaw. They are not Java-centric solutions. What this means is that although you could integrate them with either CORBA or DCOM, you would have to write some code in other languages, using non-Java libraries. This leads to more complex and less maintainable code.

In the case of CORBA, you would need to create language mappings to an intermediate format called the Interface Definition Language (IDL). IDL is part of a language-neutral strategy provided by CORBA. Every language has a mapping to and from IDL. These IDL interfaces represent a method-calling API that can be used to access your object from other languages, such as C++. This mapping limits the capabilities of the distributed capabilities you have to that IDL. Although IDL was designed to be as comprehensive as possible, it certainly is not a Java solution, and therefore it requires you to familiarize yourself with another computer language.

In the case of DCOM, you can send messages only to Microsoft platforms. Because one of the benefits of Java is its cross-platform nature, this is a hard limitation. On top of that, you will need to call out to Microsoft DCOM libraries because today there is no transparent solution for Java to DCOM as, although the BEA WebLogic server does provide a wrapper mechanism for accessing COM objects with RMI. This means you will probably need to write at least some code in another language such as C if you want to use DCOM. This code is cumbersome and harder to maintain than pure Java. It also defeats the purpose of a distributed object solution, which is to create a seamless process.

If you want a seamless, powerful solution that is Java-centric, RMI is your best bet today. Developed by Sun, RMI is a Java solution for distributed objects. The model illustrated in Figure 12.5 has been influenced by other vendors and is widely becoming accepted as a standard way for remote Java applications to communicate. Versions of RMI that support IIOP will be coming soon as well. Once this happens, true interoperability between objects using RMI and objects using CORBA will be possible. In addition, any application that supports IIOP will be accessible to RMI objects.

The goals for RMI include:

- Capability to use multiple transports such as IIOP
- Distributed garbage collection for active objects
- Ease of use
- Integrate the distributed object model into the Java language in a natural way while retaining most of the Java language's object semantics
- Make apparent the differences between the distributed object model and local Java object model
- Make writing reliable distributed applications as simple as possible while maintaining the Java security and safety features

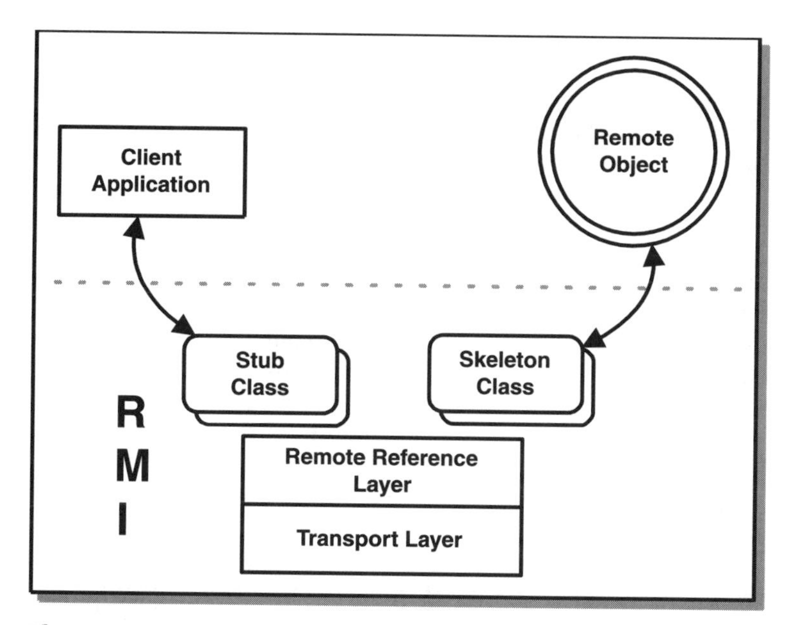

Figure 12.5 RMI model.

- Support for non-persistent, persistent, and lazy activated objects—that is, objects that are instantiated when first called
- Support seamless remote invocation on objects in different virtual machines

RMI's distributed object scheme is comprised of the following:

- An interface (called a stub) that represents your remote object in your local address space:

```
public interface CreditCardVerifyer extends java.rmi.Remote
```

- A set of classes that you can subclass to create your remote object:

```
public class CreditCardVerifyerImpl
        extends UnicastRemoteObject
        implements CreditCardVerifyer
```

- A server called rmiregistry that tracks registered objects by name. To register your object, you would call the bind method of java.rmi.Naming. This method binds the instantiated object into rmiregistry with the associated name:

```
CreditCardVerifyerImpl ccv = new CreditCardVerifyerImpl();
java.rmi.Naming.bind("rmi://myserver.com/creditcard", obj);
```

To access a remote object, call the lookup () method of a class called java.rmi.Naming. In this method, specify the URL for the object you want to access. For example:

```
CreditCardVerifyer ccv = new CreditCardVerifyerImpl();
String url = "rmi://myserver.com/creditcard";
// bind url to remote object
java.rmi.Naming.bind(url, ccv);
        ...
// lookup account
ccv = (CreditCardVerifyer)java.rmi.Naming.lookup(url);
```

As shown in Figure 12.5, RMI consists of three layers. One layer is the stub/skeleton layer, which acts as a stand-in used for communicating with the remote object. Another is the remote reference layer, which handles the strategy for connecting to the remote object, including point-to-point connection, object replication, reconnection strategies if the object becomes unavailable, and so on. The final layer is the transport layer, which initializes a connection with the remote object's address space and manages remote object tracking.

Summary

Distributed object programming is a valuable tool for enterprise developers. The scheme you use depends on the tools and applications with which you plan to communicate. If you are planning to connect with legacy systems, CORBA should be considered because it is supported by the greatest number of vendors. If you need a Microsoft-centric solution, DCOM seems like an obvious choice. In general, if you are planning to implement a new system in Java, you should consider RMI the most logical choice. It takes advantage of features of Java such as the object model, security, and garbage collection. With the addition of multiple transport support, such as IIOP, you can integrate with systems that implement CORBA as well. RMI seems like the best of both worlds for the Java programmer.

The next chapter explores the entire RMI API and builds a small, distributed example. Chapter 14, "A Network File-Locking Server," provides a more extensive example of using RMI.

Introduction to Java RMI

Java Remote Method Invocation (RMI) became a core part of the JDK in version 1.1 and continues to supply the main distributed object interface for Java programmers. RMI is a mechanism that enables an object on one Java virtual machine to invoke methods on an object on another Java virtual machine. The relationship between the two objects is defined by an interface that extends the remote interface. On the client machine, a proxy called a *stub* is used to send messages from the local machine to the remote object. This stub implements all the methods of the remote interface of the remote object. The stub's implementation forwards the messages, including parameters, to the remote object.

This chapter discusses how to program with RMI. The discussion is based on both the JDK 1.1 and Java 2 implementations of RMI. Java 2 has streamlined RMI in some ways, so much of this discussion is based on 1.1 concepts, with changes in Java 2 noted. However, all of the tables of methods are based on Java 2 for completeness, with deprecated methods noted. Because the final version of Java 2 was not available at the time this book is written, this discussion is based on 1.2 beta 4 early access 2, which was the last beta before the final release.

NOTE **The message sender in these discussions is called the *client*; the receiver is called the *server*. These terms should not be confused with client/server computing. In RMI, it is possible for the same object or program to act as both a client and a server.**

What Is RMI?

RMI defines a set of classes that manage communication between two programs. On the client side, an object called the *stub* represents an object on the server. Messages to the stub are packaged up and sent across the network to the server. On the server, the RMI libraries unpackage the message and forward it to the appropriate object. In JDK 1.1, a helper object called the *skeleton* manages this unpacking. In Java 2, the RMI libraries themselves handle it. The relationship between the client and server is pictured in Figure 13.1.

The process of packaging up the message and parameters is called *marshalling*. When the messages arrive at the remote server, the message and parameters are unmarshalled and the real object method is invoked. The method's return value is marshalled and returned to the client, where it is unmarshalled and returned to the original caller. The effect of this process is that issuing remote calls is nearly transparent to the developer of the client application.

RMI is used for creating communication channels between Java application objects. For communication between Java and other languages through CORBA, it is recommended that you use another Java facility known as Java IDL. Java IDL provides a mapping between Java and CORBA's Interface Definition Language (IDL). CORBA programs use IDL as a programming language-neutral mechanism for defining the interface between client and server applications.

NOTE **More information about Java IDL can be found at http://java.sun.com/products/jdk/1.2/docs/guide/idl/index.html.**

Unlike CORBA, in which an intermediate IDL is used, all of the remote object interfaces used in RMI are defined in Java. Currently, Java RMI uses a combination of Java serialization and the Java Remote Method Protocol (JRMP) to turn simple method invocations into remote method invocations. Along with Java RMI, JRMP continues to be supported and enhanced as the native protocol for Java RMI. However, other protocols such as IIOP will also be supported in future versions of RMI. This means that

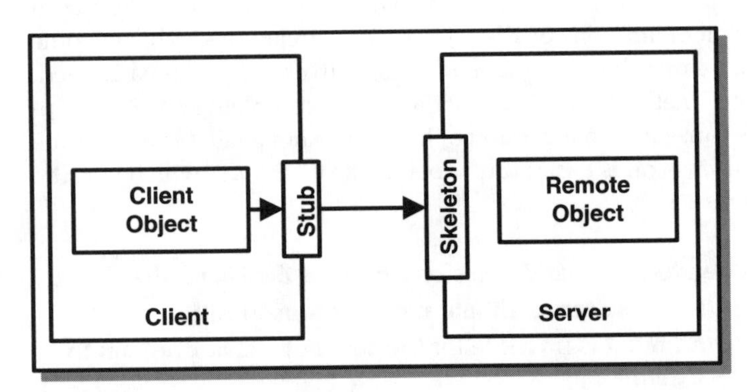

Figure 13.1 RMI architecture.

by writing Java RMI application today, you can communicate with other Java RMI applications or with CORBA applications tomorrow.

RMI consists of five packages and three utilities. Table 13.1 lists the purpose of each. It may seem that RMI is large, but for most cases, you need to use only a few methods and interfaces from each package to successfully implement a distributed object solution with RMI. The next few sections introduce the classes and interfaces in these packages, then provide several examples to show how RMI is used to create distributed programs. In Chapter 14, "A Network File-Locking Server," a larger RMI example is discussed.

RMI on the Client

RMI is designed so that the client application programmer needs to know little about the network protocol, the marshalling and unmarshalling of data, and the actual implementation of the remote object. The client needs only a description of the remote methods that can be invoked on the remote object and the class file for the remote object stub that provides the actual communication with the remote object. The description takes the form of an interface that the remote object implements. The stub implements the interface by forwarding messages from the client to the remote object.

Creating an RMI client is a two-step process. First, the client needs to connect to the server. Second, the client must handle networking-related exceptions. Connecting to the server is accomplished using the RMI registry, as discussed in this chapter in the "Connecting the Client and Server" section or with JNDI. In either case, the client ends up with an instance of the stub class to which it can send messages.

Table 13.1 RMI Components

COMPONENT	PURPOSE
`java.rmi`	Organizes client-side RMI classes, interfaces, and exceptions.
`java.rmi.server`	Organizes server-side RMI classes, interfaces, and exceptions.
`java.rmi.registry`	Organizes classes for managing the RMI naming services.
`java.rmi.dgc`	Organizes classes used to manage distributed garbage collection.
`java.rmi.activation`	Organizes the classes used to implement activate-on-demand RMI services.
`rmic`	A compiler that generates the stubs and skeletons used by RMI to implement distributed communication.
`rmiregistry`	A utility server that provides a naming service for RMI. This service associates names with objects.
`rmid`	A utility server that supports the RMI activation framework.

RMI obviously requires network connectivity. In Java, connections to the network are controlled by a SecurityManager. This manager also restricts class loading and access to other resources. Non-applet Java code that plans to use RMI must set the systemwide security manager to a class that supports RMI. The java.rmi.RMISecurityManager is the default choice for this operation. To set the security manager, use the following line of code:

```
System.setSecurityManager(new RMISecurityManager());
```

Java 2 introduces a new policy-based security system. By default, application-specific code is not allowed to access resources without specific permission. This permission is provided by either editing the default JDK properties or providing a policy file. Here is a simple policy used for the examples in this chapter:

```
grant
{
    permission java.net.SocketPermission "*:1024-65535"
                                    , "connect,accept";
    permission java.lang.RuntimePermission
                                    "setSecurityManager";
    permission java.lang.RuntimePermission
                                    "createSecurityManager";
};
```

This policy file allows the programs to create and set the RMI security manager as well as connect to and accept connections on all of the ports from 1024 to 65535. The policy-based security provided in Java 2 is very powerful but will require some relearning on the part of application programmers who are not accustomed to security restraints.

To activate the custom security policy, you need to set the system property called java.security.policy. The value of this property is used to load an additional security policy file into the system, appending it to the existing policies.

This property can be set as a flag to the java interpreter. For example:

```
java -Djava.security.policy=server.policy server.Server
```

runs java on the server.Server class with the policy file named server.policy.

NOTE **For more information on security with Java 2, check out http://java.sun.com/products/jdk/1.2/docs/guide/security.**

Once connected, the client can send messages to the server. However, remote messaging can generate network-specific exceptions. For example, the network could go down or the server machine could be unplugged, resulting in an error on the client's side. In some sense, the possibility of these non-local exceptions is the only difference between using an RMI object and using a local one. However, don't underestimate the difference network programming can make in your projects; it can be significant.

A list of the exceptions that a client may have to deal with when using a remote object is provided in Table 13.2. In addition to these RMI-specific exceptions, the client may also have to deal with custom exceptions thrown by the server.

Table 13.2 RMI Client Exceptions

EXCEPTION CLASS	MEANING
`java.rmi.AccessException`	Indicates that a message was sent that the caller does not have permission to execute.
`java.rmi.ConnectException`	The requested connection was refused.
`java.rmi.ConnectIOException`	An I/O exception was thrown while making the network connection.
`java.rmi.MarshalException`	An I/O exception occurred while sending a message that was related to packaging up the message. This exception may occur even if the message got through.
`java.rmi.NoSuchObjectException`	The server object is no longer available, making the stub invalid.
`java.rmi.NotBoundException`	The client attempted to access a server object that was not registered.
`java.rmi.RemoteException`	Common superclass for RMI exceptions.
`java.rmi.RMISecurityException`	Deprecated exception class previously used for security exceptions during RMI. Unused in Java 2.
`java.rmi.ServerError`	Indicates that a message sent by the client caused the server to throw an error.
`java.rmi.ServerException`	Indicates that a message sent by the client caused the server to throw an exception.
`java.rmi.ServerRuntimeException`	Deprecated class indicating that a message sent by the client caused the server to throw an exception. Unused in Java 2.
`java.rmi.StubNotFoundException`	The class file for a stub could not be found.
`java.rmi.UnexpectedException`	Wraps an exception thrown by the server that is not one of the exception types declared in the remote interface.
`java.net.UnknownHostException`	The client is unable to find the requested host.
`java.rmi.UnmarshalException`	An exception occurred while either the server was unmarshalling the parameters for a message or the client was unmarshalling the return value.

Most of the exceptions from Table 13.2 extend the RemoteException class. Clients that want to distinguish remote- from application-specific exceptions can use these classes in a try-catch block to handle all RMI-related issues. RemoteException objects have an instance variable called detail that may contain another throwable object indicating the actual problem. For example, the ServerError exception will contain the error that occurred.

RMI on the Server

Creating an RMI server is a three-step process. First, you must implement the remote interface. Second, the server may need to configure the RMI libraries. Finally, you must register the server and make it accessible to clients.

Implementing the remote interface requires that you create an object that extends the class java.rmi.server.RemoteObject. RemoteObject overrides many of the java.lang.Object methods to make them network aware. These methods include hashCode, toString, and equals. The stub received by the client will also extend RemoteObject appropriately.

NOTE **Java 2 may loosen the requirement that the interface between client and server extends Remote. Methods should also be able to declare that they throw the superclasses of RemoteException instead of having to throw RemoteExceptions. This would include Exception and IOException. All methods in the remote interface, whether it extends Remote or not, must declare that they can throw one of these three exception types.**

Currently, the RMI implementation suggests that your initial server extend a subclass of RemoteObject. Two subclasses are provided for this purpose: UnicastRemoteObject and Activatable. Both of these classes are direct subclasses of RemoteServer, which extends RemoteObject.

NOTE **Some implementations of RMI may require that the server object implement UnicastRemoteObject. Read the latest documentation to determine if this restriction applies to your application.**

RemoteServer defines three static methods that all RMI server objects may find useful. First, the RemoteServer can return the host name of the client using this method:

```
public static String getClientHost()
                         throws ServerNotActiveException
```

This method throws a ServerNotActiveException when called from a method not associated with a client request. Otherwise, the RemoteServer class uses information about the current thread to determine the client and its host name. The RemoteServer class also manages a stream that can be used for logging messages. The methods for managing this stream are as follows:

```
public static void setLog(OutputStream out)
public static PrintStream getLog()
```

Setting the log to null turns off any automatic logging.

UnicastRemoteObject is the primary superclass for RMI server objects. Objects can also extend Activatable to indicate that they want to participate in the activation framework as discussed in the section "Remote Object Activation." UnicastRemoteObject defines the basic semantics of being a server object and handling network accessibility. Constructors are provided as part of UnicastRemoteObject to control the networking code used by the RMI packages to support a server object. The default constructor uses an anonymous port and the default sockets factories to create network connections. Two other constructors, listed here, allow the programmer to configure these values:

```
protected UnicastRemoteObject(int port)
                       throws RemoteException;

protected UnicastRemoteObject(int port,
                              RMIClientSocketFactory csf,
                              RMIServerSocketFactory ssf)
                       throws RemoteException;
```

All three constructors are marked protected so that only a subclass can call them. You cannot instantiate a UnicastRemoteObject directly. When the UnicastRemoteObject is created, it opens a network connection for receiving messages. This connection is managed by the RMI library code. The process by which an object is associated with a network connection is called *exporting*. Programs can export objects manually, without subclassing UnicastRemoteObject. The simplest method for exporting an object is as follows:

```
public static RemoteStub exportObject(Remote obj)
                             throws RemoteException
```

Other methods are provided to allow the caller to configure the port and socket factories for the object's network connections. Any method that is expected to receive remote messages should be exported either directly or as part of the constructor it inherits from UnicastRemoteObject.

Like the client, the server should use the RMISecurityManager; in Java 2, this may require a policy file. Also like the client, the server will have some RMI-specific exceptions to deal with. These are listed in Table 13.3.

RMI has the ability load classes over the network. If you try to communicate with an object for which you do not have the class in your virtual machine, RMI automatically loads the class, provided you have set up the correct system properties. A list of the server-related properties for RMI is included in Table 13.4. These properties can be set either inside a program or using the command line.

Perhaps the most important of these properties is the server code base. This value must be set if your program wants to send an object to a client when the object's class is not in the client's CLASSPATH. Keep in mind that this value must be set if any of the

Table 13.3 RMI Server Exceptions

EXCEPTION CLASS	MEANING
`java.rmi.server .ExportException`	An attempt to export an object failed.
`java.rmi.server .ServerCloneException`	An exception occurred trying to clone a UnicastRemoteObject.
`java.rmi.server .ServerNotActiveException`	The server tried to call getClientHost when not in a remote method.
`java.rmi.server .SkeletonMismatchException`	Deprecated Exception, no longer used in Java 2. Indicates that a message was sent to the server that was not part of the remote interface, possibly caused by failing to run rmic to update the stub and skeleton files.
`java.rmi.server .SkeletonNotFoundException`	Deprecated Exception, no longer used in Java 2. Indicates that the skeleton-class files for the server cannot be found.
`java.rmi.server .SocketSecurityException`	The server does not have permission to create a server socket.

classes are not in the CLASSPATH. If the client and server are on the same computer, the code base can be a file URL. However, if the client and server are on different computers, a Web server is necessary to provide a host for the class files, and the URL should target this Web server.

The last part of the RMI relationship is the connection between the client and server.

Table 13.4 Server System Properties

PROPERTY	DESCRIPTION
`java.rmi.server.codebase`	A URL indicating the code base from which classes should be loaded for network clients.
`java.rmi.server.disableHttp`	If true, RMI will not use HTTP to try to tunnel through firewalls. The default is false, indicating that HTTP is used to wrap RMI calls.
`java.rmi.server.hostname`	Sets the server's fully qualified host name, if the name is unavailable via DNS. This value is not set by default.
`java.rmi.dgc.leaseValue`	The time in milliseconds until the server notices that the client is no longer connected. The default is 10 minutes.
`java.rmi.server.logCalls`	If true, the RMI library will log information about calls. The default is false.

Connecting the Client and Server

All distributed object systems must be able to locate remote objects on the network and provide mechanisms for communicating between objects. These mechanisms are used to create the initial connection between two programs based on the well-known locating service.

RMI provides a service called the rmiregistry that keeps track of objects by name. An application connects to the registry on a known port and requests access to an object based on the unique name with which it was registered. Once this connection is made, the client object can invoke methods of the remote object as though it were located in the same virtual machine as the client. Think of the registry as a telephone operator that can connect you to a specific person based on a known value—their telephone number. Everyone knows how to locate the operator, so everyone can access other objects.

Use the java.rmi.Naming class to locate a registry and bind or lookup objects in it. The Naming class uses a string URL of the format //host:port/name to indicate the host and port for the object's rmiregistry process and the name of the object itself. For example, the URL //192.168.0.172:8099/blaster will locate the object named blaster on the machine 192.168.0.172 at port 8099. If no port is provided, the default port for the rmiregistry service is used.

NOTE Don't confuse the java.rmi.Naming class with the JNDI Naming package. Although they do provide similar services, the RMI Naming class specifically locates objects in an RMI registry. Sun provides a JNDI provider that accesses the RMI registry if you prefer to use it instead of the Naming class.

The methods defined in Naming are similar to the methods in a JNDI context. However, all of the methods for Naming are static and don't require the creation of any objects to access them. A complete list of methods for java.rmi.Naming is provided in Table 13.5. Essentially, objects can be bound to the registry with a name or found in the registry by name.

All of the exceptions listed in Table 13.5 are either MalformedURLExceptions, indicating that the URL is incorrect, or described in Tables 13.2 or 13.3.

Programs will often use the rebind method in Naming to insure that if the name is in use, it is replaced. This could be dangerous if several programs used the same name, but it can help during the development phase by allowing the server to be run over and over without trouble.

Servers don't have to rely on the rmiregistry service to make themselves available to Naming lookups. Instead, a server can create a private registry. This will allow the server to run autonomously, without requiring that the rmiregistry process be run concurrently to manage lookup requests.

To create a private registry, use the class rmi.registry.LocateRegistry. This class provides two methods, listed here, for creating a private registry.

```
public static Registry createRegistry(int port)
                                    throws RemoteException;

public static Registry createRegistry(int port,
```

```
                          RMIClientSocketFactory csf,
                          RMIServerSocketFactory ssf)
                        throws RemoteException
```

The objects returned from these methods implement the Registry interface. Registry provides the same methods as Naming and defines the static variable REGISTRY_PORT that indicates the default port used for a private registry.

LocateRegistry also provides methods for finding a registry based on a port and host name. These methods are used by the Naming class to locate the rmiregistry service's registry object. They can also be used to locate a private registry. However, clients need to access the registry using the LocateRegistry object only if the server is expecting the client to use a custom Socket class.

When a client looks up a server, it receives a stub that implements the server's remote interface. Messages sent to this stub can take three kinds of arguments. Primitive types, like int, are sent as data across the connection. Objects that implement Serializable are serialized and sent along with the message, thus creating a copy on either end. Objects that implement Remote initiate the creation of an RMI relationship between the receiver and the sender. Thus passing remote objects across the wire can create more RMI relationships. However, for an object to be available for RMI, it must be exported using the UnicastRemoteObject classes exportObject methods or using the Activation frameworks.

Remember that if two programs have a bidirectional conversation in which both are sending and receiving messages, they are both clients and servers. This situation usually occurs when one program registers in the registry and the other finds it before sending itself as an argument to a message. The registry is the bootstrap used to create

Table 13.5 java.rmi.Naming Methods

METHOD	DESCRIPTION
`public static Remote lookup(String name) Throws NotBoundException, MalformedURLException, RemoteException`	Look up a remote object by URL and return it or throw an exception if a problem occurs.
`public static void bind(String name, Remote obj) Throws AlreadyBoundException, MalformedURLException, RemoteException`	Bind an object to a specific URL or throw an exception if a problem occurs.
`public static voidunbind(String name) Throws RemoteException, NotBoundException, MalformedURLException`	Unbind an object from a specific URL or throw an exception if a problem occurs.
`public static void rebind(String name, Remote obj) throws RemoteException, MalformedURLException`	Replace the object currently bound to a URL with a new one.
`public static String[] list(String name) Throws RemoteException, MalformedURLException`	Retrieve a list of the URLs from the registry specified by the URL in the argument.

the initial connection. Passing remote objects across the connection is the mechanism for adding bidirectionality to the relationship.

Creating an RMI Application

The general steps for creating a client/server application using Java RMI are as follows:

1. Create and compile a remote object interface that extends java.rmi.Remote.
2. Implement a server application that contains a remote object class that implements your interface.
3. Compile the server application and run rmic to generate the necessary stub classes.
4. Install the class files in a known location, such as your Web server's classes directory. Actually, RMI doesn't require the use of a Web server, but this is the preferred mechanism for sharing classes between applications on different machines.
5. Run rmiregistry on the server machine so that it can manage remote objects.
6. Run the server application and have it install an instance of the remote object with a unique name in the registry.
7. Implement a client application that connects to the server and looks up the remote object by name in a remote object registry.
8. Compile the client application.
9. Run the client.

The next few sections show the implementation of several client/server applications.

A Simple Client/Server Application

This section walks you through the steps to build a simple client/server application that uses RMI to perform the communication.

The application is implemented in three packages. The client package contains the definition of a client application that allows you to type in string messages on a console, then send the messages to the server. The server package contains the definition of the server implementation that can receive messages from multiple clients, then print them on its console. The message package contains the interface that describes the remote messages the server can receive. The message package is shared by both client and server. Figure 13.2 shows the final directory structure.

Creating the Remote Interface

The first step in building the application is to define the methods or services the remote object will provide to its clients. To do this, create an interface that extends java.rmi.Remote. The Remote interface declares no methods, but it serves to identify

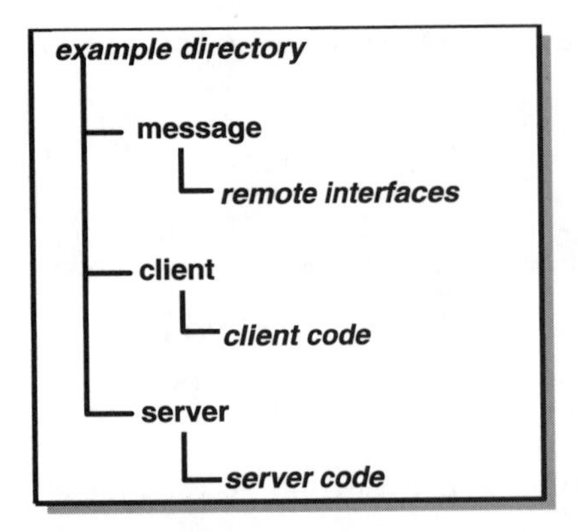

Figure 13.2 Directory structure.

interfaces whose methods may be invoked from a non-local virtual machine. Every remote object must directly or indirectly implement this interface. Only methods specified in an interface that extends java.rmi.Remote are available remotely.

Here is the code for the MessageServer interface that is located in the package called message. Every method declared in the interface should throw RemoteException to indicate that it represents a network message. The String SERVER_NAME is the default name that is used to register the server in the registry. It is declared in this class so that the server that implements this interface can register using the name and the client using this interface can find the server using the default name. The interface defines a single remote method called send, which takes two parameters. The parameter name is an identifier of the client so that the server can print the client name. The second parameter is a message that the client wants to display on the server.

```
package message;

import java.rmi.Remote;
import java.rmi.RemoteException;

public interface MessageServer extends Remote
{
    static String SERVER_NAME = "Message_Server";

    void send(String name, String message)
        throws RemoteException;
}
```

To compile this interface, access a command line, change the current directory appropriately, and type:

```
javac message/MessageServer.java
```

The class file created will need to be available to the client and server. One way to make the interface available is to put it in a Jar file and add it to the client's and server's

CLASSPATHs. If the client is an applet, install it in the same directory as the applet or download it using the browser.

Implementing the Server

Once the interface is defined, you can create a server called Server.java that implements the MessageServer interface. The code for this discussion is broken down by method. First, let's look at the class declaration. The class is declared in the server package. It includes the required rmi packages and the message package. The Server listed in the code that follows extends the most common RemoteObject subclass, UnicastRemoteObject.

```
package server;

import java.rmi.*;
import java.rmi.server.*;
import java.rmi.registry.*;
import message.*;

public class Server extends UnicastRemoteObject
                            implements MessageServer
{
```

The constructor for the remote object must throw RemoteException. This is because it is a subclass of UnicastRemoteObject, which could throw this exception if the remote object could not be created for some reason, such as a stub not being available. The UnicastRemoteObject also registers the server instance with the RMI system upon construction. In the following code example, the constructor of Server simply calls the superclass constructor to perform the necessary network configuration.

```
    public Server() throws RemoteException
    {
        super();
    }
```

The send method listed here is the implementation of the remote message described in the MessageServer interface. All messages that can be accessed remotely must throw RemoteException. The send method simply prints out the name of the calling client and its message on the server console. This server could be accessed by multiple clients, and their output would be interspersed on the console. RMI handles the connection for each remote client. It also manages the use of resources such as sockets so that resources can be reused when they are released or shared by multiple clients on the same machine, and so on.

```
    public void send(String name, String message)
        throws RemoteException
    {
        System.out.println(name + ": " + s);
    }
```

The remote object could be installed in a registry through a separate server application or, as in this case, the remote object might define a static main method that installs an instance of the class in the registry. The first step is to install a security manager. This example runs as an application, so java.rmi.RMISecurityManager is used. RMISecurityManager provides an example security manager for use by RMI applications that use downloaded code. RMI's class loader will not download any classes from remote locations if no security manager has been set. If the client is an applet, it is not necessary to install a security manager; the browser's security manager will suffice.

Once the security manager is installed, an instance of the Server class is created and bound in the RMI registry. Once the server is bound in the registry, it can be called by remote clients. This code defines the main method:

```
    public static void main(String[] args)
    {
         System.setSecurityManager(
                new RMISecurityManager());

        try
        {
            // Create an instance of the server.
            MessageServer srv = new Server();

            // Bind server to local registry on default port.
            Naming.rebind(MessageServer.SERVER_NAME, srv);

            System.out.println("Server bound and started");
        } catch (Exception e)
        {
            System.err.println("Server exception: " +
               e.getMessage());
            e.printStackTrace();
        }
    }
}
```

Compiling and Installing the Server

To compile the server, run javac and rmic. In this example, it is assumed you are in the root directory of the project and that "." is in your CLASSPATH for convenience. Then, on Windows, compile the server and create the stubs as shown here:

```
javac server\Server.java
rmic -d . server.Server
```

The rmic utility generates Server_Stub.class and Server_Skel.class in the server directory. The stub and skel implement the marshalling code for the client and server. These files need to be accessible from the client and server, so either include them in the

CLASSPATH or make them network accessible by placing them in a public directory on your Web server.

NOTE **Skeleton files are not required for RMI in Java 2. To control rmic under Java 2, use the -vcompat flag to create files that work with both JDK 1.1 and Java 2, or use the flags -v1.1 to create 1.1 files and -v1.2 to create Java 2 files.**

Once the Server is ready, run it by first starting the RMI registry and then running the server. To start the registry on Windows, type:

```
start rmiregistry
```

rmiregistry is located in the java\bin directory by default.

Under JDK 1.1, start the server from the project root directory by typing:

```
start java server.Server
```

To start the server under Java 2, type:

```
start java -Djava.security.manager
    -Djava.security.policy=server.policy server.Server
```

-Djava.security.manager tells the program to use only the security policy server.policy provided in the example directory.

Now that the server is started, build the client application.

Implementing the Client

The client application is defined in the package called client. This object has a main method that installs a security manager, finds the registry on the local host, and requests the remote object server. The registry sends the client a Server_stub that implements the MessageServer interface. Using this stub, the client can send messages in the messageServer interface to the stub and they will be forwarded to the server. At this point, the only difference between invoking methods of local objects and remote objects is that the remote object may throw a RemoteException if there is a network failure, so you must catch and handle these. The application loops. Each time through the loop, it waits for the user to input messages on the console. When the user presses Return, the messages are sent to the server, which prints the messages on the server console. The program ends when the user types "exit." The code for the client follows.

```
package client;

import java.io.*;
import java.rmi.*;
import java.rmi.server.*;
import message.*;

public class Client
```

```
{
    static String name;          // name of this client
    static MessageServer server; //Connection to the server

    public static void main(String args[])
    {
        // Require the user to type a name to identify client.
        if(args.length<1)
        {
            System.out.println("Usage: java client.Client
                ClientName");
            System.exit(-1);
        }

        //Get the client name from the command line.
        name = args[0];

        System.setSecurityManager(
                new RMISecurityManager());

        try
        {
            // Find the object on the registry.
            server = (MessageServer)Naming.lookup(
                MessageServer.SERVER_NAME);

            // Process input from user until 'exit' is typed.
            boolean notDone = true;
            String message = null;
            BufferedReader br = new BufferedReader(
                new InputStreamReader(System.in));

            System.out.println("Type 'exit' to end.");

            while(notDone)
            {
                System.out.print("Enter message:");
                message = br.readLine();
                if(message.startsWith("exit"))
                    notDone=false;
                else
                    // Send the message to the remote object.
                    server.send(name,message);
            }
        } catch (Exception e)
        {
            System.err.println("Client exception: " +
                e.getMessage());
            e.printStackTrace();
            System.exit(-1);
        }
```

```
        }
    }
```

If the stub class or other necessary files are not accessible in the client's CLASSPATH, they will be loaded from the remote server, provided that the proper java.rmi.server.codebase property is set. A typical example is accessing the remote objects through a Web server. In this case, the files would have to be in known locations on the Web server, such as the classes directory. Of course, the location is server dependent.

Compiling and Running the Client

To compile and run the example, change directories to the root of the project and execute these commands:

```
javac client\*.java
start java
    -Djava.security.policy=server.policy client.Client Client1
start java
    -Djava.security.policy=server.policy client.Client Client2
```

This code executes two clients to demonstrate that multiple clients can be supported. In this example, the names of the clients are Client1 and Client 2, but they can be named anything you want. In this example, a String was passed to the server. All objects used with remote objects should implement either the java.io.Serializable or java.rmi.Remote interface so they can be marshalled correctly. In the next example, objects are passed to the server so that the client can send messages to the server and the server can send messages to each client.

Example with Bidirectional Messaging

This example extends the messaging application by adding the ability for clients to register themselves with the server so the server can call back to each client. A rudimentary user interface is also added to allow the user to type messages and see messages being typed from other clients. The idea is that the client registers with the server, the server stores the client object in a hash table, and when a client sends a message to the server, it forwards the message to each client in the hash table. This creates a simple networked chat program. To implement this application, each object in the previous example is modified and a new interface called MessageReceiver is introduced. MessageReceiver is implemented by the client program and called by the server.

Implementing MessageReceiver

The MessageReceiver interface declares the methods of the client that may be called by the server. The interface is defined in the message package because it is needed by both the client and the server. The MessageReceiver interface that follows declares one remote method called print, which takes a string as a parameter.

```
package message;

import java.rmi.*;

public interface MessageReceiver extends Remote
{
    void print(String s) throws RemoteException;
}
```

Remember that each method in a remote interface must declare throws RemoteException. In the MessageServer, an additional message is added that can be sent to a MessageServer.

Updating MessageServer

The MessageServer interface for this example is extended to include two static variables, called SUCCESS and FAILURE, that indicate the success or failure of a client registering with a MessageServer. A method called register has also been added. The register method takes two parameters, a unique name for the message server client and a client object that implements the MessageReceiver interface. The updated code is indicated in boldface type:

```
package message;

import java.rmi.Remote;
import java.rmi.RemoteException;

public interface MessageServer extends Remote
{
    static String SERVER_NAME = "Message_Server";
    static int FAILURE = -1;
    static int SUCCESS = 0;

    void send(String name, String s) throws RemoteException;

    int register(String name, MessageReceiver m)
     throws RemoteException;
}
```

Now that both the interfaces have been updated, they can be compiled and stored in a jar. To do this, change directories to the root of this project and type the following:

```
javac mes341sage\*.java
```

The class files created should be accessible by the client and server.

Updating the Server

Now that the interfaces are updated, modify the server to implement the new method. In order to do this, add a hash table to contain the list of clients that will be registering, then implement the register method. Modify the send method so that rather than printing the messages sent to the server on the console, each registered client is told to print the message. New code is indicated with boldface type in the following listing:

```
package server;

import java.util.Enumeration;
import java.util.Hashtable;
import java.rmi.*;
import java.rmi.server.*;
import java.rmi.registry.*;
import message.*;

public class Server extends UnicastRemoteObject
                            implements MessageServer
{
    // Add a hashtable to track registered clients.
    static Hashtable receivers = new Hashtable(5);
```

There are no changes to the constructor.

```
    public Server() throws RemoteException

    {
        super();
    }
```

The send method has been modified to send the massage to all registered clients.

```
    public void send(String name, String s)
        throws RemoteException
    {
        // Iterate through the registered clients.
        for (Enumeration e = receivers.elements() ;
            e.hasMoreElements() ;)
        {
            MessageReceiver m =
               (MessageReceiver)e.nextElement();
            // All messageReceivers implement print.
            m.print(name + ": " + s);
        }
    }
```

The register method adds the client to the hash table and returns a success code to the client. This way the client knows if it was successfully added. The register method fails if the client name is already taken or if null is passed in for either parameter.

```
    public int register(String name, MessageReceiver m)
    {
        int retval = MessageServer.FAILURE;

        // Don't register a null client.
```

```
        if((name !=null) && (m != null))
        {
            // Only add a client with a unique name.
            if(receivers.get(name) == null)
            {
                // Add client to hash table.
                receivers.put(name,m);

                System.out.println("Added " + name);
                retval = MessageServer.SUCCESS;
            }else
            {
                System.out.println(
                    "Could not add client because " + name +
                    " already exists on server.");
            }
        }

        return retval;
    }
```

In the main method, notice that the java.rmi.Naming rebind method has been replaced with a call to the registry rebind method. The java.rmi.registry.LocateRegistry method createRegistry is used to create a private RMI registry. The createRegistry method returns an object that implements the Registry interface. Registry extends Remote. The Registry variable REGISTRY_PORT defines a known port id used for registries. By creating a registry directly, the server becomes a stand-alone application that does not require starting the rmiregistry application.

```
    public static void main(String[] args)
    {
        System.setSecurityManager(
               new RMISecurityManager());

        try
        {
            MessageServer srv = new Server();

            // Bootstrap registry
            Registry reg =  LocateRegistry.createRegistry(
                 Registry.REGISTRY_PORT);

            reg.rebind(MessageServer.SERVER_NAME, srv);

            System.out.println("Server bound and started");
        } catch (Exception e)
        {
            System.err.println("Server exception: " +
                e.getMessage());
```

```
                e.printStackTrace();
            }
        }
    }
```

Once the server has been modified, compile it and generate stubs using the following command under Windows in the project's root directory:

```
javac server\*.java
rmic -d . server.Server
```

Run the server by typing:

```
start java
    -Djava.security.policy=server.policy server.Server
```

Again, you don't need to start the rmiregistry utility, because the server creates its own registry. Now let's modify the client to work with this server.

Updating the Client

Client.java is modified the most often of all the program components. This is due to the fact that a user interface has been included to make the application easier to use. The RMI code for this example is minor compared to the user interface code, as we would hope. This shows how little impact RMI should have on your application when you choose to make it support RMI. Figure 13.3 shows what the new UI looks like.

The main difference between this example and the previous one is that Client is now a subclass of Frame so that a UI can be displayed without introducing more object classes. Client also implements MessageReceiver so that it can behave as a remote object. To handle user input, the client implements both ActionListener and WindowListener. The boldface type in the code that follows indicates the changes to the class:

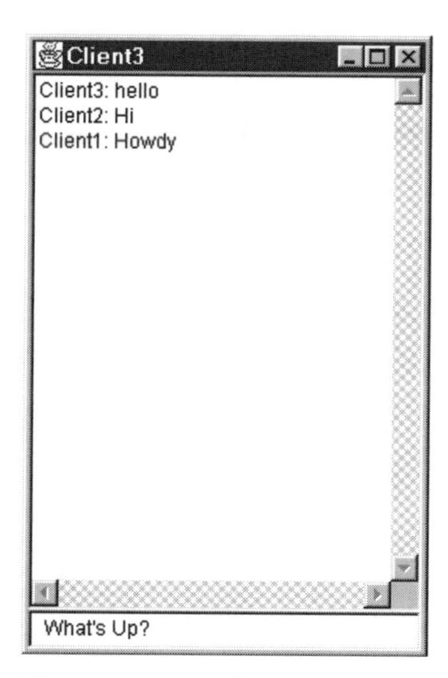

Figure 13.3 Client UI.

```
package client;

import java.awt.*;
import java.awt.event.*;
import java.rmi.*;
import java.rmi.server.*;
import message.*;

public class Client extends Frame implements MessageReceiver,
ActionListener, WindowListener
{
    TextField tf; // Message text field
    TextArea ta; // Message server output text area
    static String name; // name of this client
    static MessageServer server; //Connection ot the server
```

A constructor was added so that an instance of the class can be initialized. The constructor throws RemoteException so that it can participate as a remote object. The constructor creates the UI elements and installs this object as an action and window listener. Finally, the UnicastRemoteObject static method exportObject is called to enable this object to accept remote calls from the server on an anonymous port. If you do not do this step, the client will not receive remote messages. It would, however, be able to send messages to remote objects.

```
public Client() throws RemoteException
{
    setTitle(name);

    setLayout(new BorderLayout());

    tf = new TextField(30);
    tf.addActionListener(this);
    add("South",tf);

    ta = new TextArea(20,20);
    add("Center",ta);

    addWindowListener(new WindowCloser());

    UnicastRemoteObject.exportObject(this);
}
```

The actionPerformed method that follows reads the value of the text field when the user presses Enter and sends this value to the server. The server then forwards this message to all registered clients.

```
public  void actionPerformed(ActionEvent ae)
{
    try
    {
        server.send(name,tf.getText());
```

```
        } catch (Exception e)
        {
            System.err.println("Client exception: " +
                e.getMessage());
            e.printStackTrace();
        }
        tf.setText("");
        tf.selectAll();
    }
```

The print method listed here is implemented as part of the MessageReceiver interface. This method is called by the server when a message from any client is sent to the server. The method simply appends the string passed in to the text area in the user interface.

```
    public void print(String s)
    {
        ta.append(s + "\n");
    }
```

The only change to the main method is that it instantiates a Client object and displays its frame so that the user can type in messages and see messages broadcast from the server. It also calls the MessageServer method register that takes a unique name and an instance of a MessageReceiver as a parameter. The register method will fail if a client with the same name is already registered or if either parameter is null.

```
public static void main(String args[])
    {
        if(args.length<1)
        {
            System.out.println(
                "Usage: java client.Client ClientName");
            System.exit(-1);
        }

        name = args[0];

        if (System.getSecurityManager() == null)
        {
            System.setSecurityManager(
                new RMISecurityManager());
        }

        try
        {
            Client cf = new Client();
            cf.pack();
            cf.show();
            server = (MessageServer)Naming.lookup(
                MessageServer.SERVER_NAME);
```

```
                int s = server.register(args[0],cf);
                if(s == MessageServer.FAILURE)
                    throw new Exception(
                        "Couldn't connect to server");
            } catch (Exception e)
            {
                System.err.println("Client exception: " +
                    e.getMessage());
                e.printStackTrace();
                System.exit(-1);
            }
        }
    }
```

A helper class called WindowCloser is listed here. This class is defined in Client.java and handles closing the Client when the user clicks on the window's close box.

```
class WindowCloser extends WindowAdapter
{
    public void windowClosing(WindowEvent e)
    {
        Window win = e.getWindow();
        win.setVisible(false);
        System.exit(0);
    }
}
```

To compile and run the client, type the following:

```
javac client\*.java
rmic -d . client.Client
start java
    -Djava.security.policy=server.policy client.Client Client1
```

Because this class now acts as a remote object, you must call rmic to generate the Client_Stub.class and Client_Skel.class. These classes must be accessible for the client and network accessible for the server. Another option is to copy the stubs to the server so that a copy resides at both ends. In both of these examples, notice that the server application had to be running in order for the clients to connect. This is not always optimal, because the process could be resource intensive if no clients are connecting and several remote object servers are running.

Class Loading

Table 13.4 listed the properties that a server might use to configure itself. One of these properties, java.rmi.server.codebase, is used to define the location for class files that the client may need to access. This value should be a URL and normally points to a Web server from which clients can get class files. However, it can also be a file URL if the server and client share a file system.

NOTE **If you want to use the code base, make sure that the registry is run from a directory that doesn't have direct access to the server-class files to ensure that the class loading all occurs from the specified code base.**

The following example demonstrates how the server can set the java.rmi.server .codebase variable using the system properties. The server returns an object when the getNextObject method is called. The objects to return are stored in an array and include several objects that are part of the server package. The code base for this server is set using a command-line argument, so that it can be run with or without a Web server. The compile.bat file in the example directory was designed for our installation and copies the server files to a Web server's document root before running the server with this code base. You could remove all references to the server and insert a file URL instead.

```
package server;

import java.util.*;
import java.rmi.*;
import java.rmi.server.*;
import java.rmi.registry.*;
import objects.*;

public class Server extends UnicastRemoteObject
                            implements ObjectServer
{
    Object[] objects;
    int curIndex;

    public Server() throws RemoteException
    {
        super();

        objects = new Object[7];

        //All of these are serializable.
        objects[0] = new String("Hello");
        objects[1] = new Vector();
        objects[2] = new Hashtable();
        objects[3] = new Object[0];
        objects[4] = new ClassOne();
        objects[5] = new ClassTwo();
        objects[6] = new ClassThree();
    }

    public Object getNextObject() throws RemoteException
    {
        Object retVal = objects[curIndex];

        curIndex = (curIndex+1)%objects.length;
```

```
        return retVal;
    }

    public static void main(String[] args)
    {
        System.setSecurityManager(new RMISecurityManager());

        if(args.length<1)
        {
            System.out.println("usage: java Server codebase");
            System.exit(-1);
        }

        try
        {
            Properties sysProps;

            //Update the code base property.
            sysProps = System.getProperties();
            sysProps.put("java.rmi.server.codebase" ,args[0]);
            System.setProperties(sysProps);

            ObjectServer srv = new Server();

            Naming.rebind(ObjectServer.SERVER_NAME, srv);

            System.out.println("Server bound and "
                                                +"started");
        }
        catch(Exception e)
        {
            System.err.println("Server exception: "
                                    +  e.getMessage());
            e.printStackTrace();
        }
    }
}
```

The Java 2 security policy file was updated for this example to allow the server complete freedom. This file, which follows, contains the single permission called AllPermission. Although valid and useful for testing and examples, this permission should be used with extreme care because it bypasses all of the security checks provided by the new Java 2 security API.

```
grant
{
    permission java.security.AllPermission;
};
```

The client for this example simply accesses the server and requests 10 objects. The code is similar to the previous examples and is not included here. The ObjectServer interface is also not included, but both are available on the CD-ROM. The important part of this example is to realize what happens when it is run.

The client is run from its own directory and does not have access to the server's CLASSPATH. As a result, when the client first connects to the server, it needs to find the stub file somewhere other than in its CLASSPATH variable. RMI requests encode the code base in them so that when the server registers with the rmiregistry, the code base URL is included in the binding. When the client wants the stub file, it is given the URL and loads the class file from there. All of this requires that the client has access to the URL and is using a security manager that allows it to load a class that is not in its CLASSPATH.

Some of the objects returned to the client from the server are instances of classes that the client can load from its CLASSPATH, such as String and Vector. Others, such as ClassOne, require the client to access the code base again. All of this loading is transparent to the client programmer, assuming that the server properly registered the code base and, if a Web server is required, makes the files available there.

One good way to test your server is to run the rmiregistry without the server files in its CLASSPATH. This causes the registry to use the code base to get to the stub files in the same way as a client. If the server does not have the code base set up properly, it fails to bind to the registry as a result.

Garbage Collection

One common feature that an enterprise server requires is the ability to receive notifications when the client exits or becomes disconnected. To handle this situation, the remote object can implement the java.rmi.server.Unreferenced interface. This interface defines a single method called unreferenced that is sent to the server when no more clients hold references to it. The java.rmi.dgc package defines the interfaces and classes to implement the distributed garbage collection algorithm used to determine when this unreferencing happens.

As a programmer, you have several ways to configure your program to take advantage of the unreferenced notification. By default, you will receive this message when no clients have tried to access the remote object for 10 minutes, when all of the stub files are finalized, or a combination of these two possibilities. You can configure the client time-out by setting the java.rmi.dgc.leaseValue property to the number of milliseconds that the server should wait if there is no response from a client.

Finally, you can program your clients to initiate the finalize methods on their stub files to ensure that the notification happens as quickly as possible.

NOTE **The objects that you bind to the registry will not receive unreferenced as long as they are in the registry, because it holds a reference to them.**

The following excerpt shows how the server implements unreferenced and can update the time-out property. This code is based on the previous messaging examples, but an object, called ServerServer, is created that hands out MessageServers. This ServerServer is registered in the rmiregistry, but MessageServers is not. As a result, MessageServers is unreferenced, but ServerServer is not.

```
package server;

//Imports remoted to save space.

public class ServerServer extends UnicastRemoteObject
 implements MessageServerServer, Unreferenced
{
    public ServerServer() throws RemoteException
    {
        super();
    }

    public void unreferenced()
    {
        System.out.println("ServerServer unreferenced"
                                +", exiting...");
        System.exit(0);
    }

    public MessageServer getMessageServer()
        throws RemoteException
    {
        return new Server();
    }

    public static void main(String[] args)
    {
        System.setSecurityManager(new RMISecurityManager());

        try
        {
            MessageServerServer srv = new ServerServer();
            Properties sysProps;

            //Update the code base property.
            sysProps = System.getProperties();
            sysProps.put("java.rmi.dgc.leaseValue"
                            ,new Integer(60*1000));
            System.setProperties(sysProps);


            Naming.rebind(MessageServerServer.SERVER_NAME
                                                    , srv);

        System.out.println("Server bound and started");
        }
        catch (Exception e)
        {
            System.err.println("Server exception: "
                                +  e.getMessage());
            e.printStackTrace();
```

```
        }
    }
}
```

This code is taken from a complete file on the CD-ROM in the chapter_13/garbage_collect example directory. The client for this example, listed in part here, tries to ensure that the stubs are finalized by setting the reference to null and calling System.runFinalization and System.gc.

```
MessageServerServer ss;
MessageServer server;

ss = (MessageServerServer)
Naming.lookup(MessageServerServer.SERVER_NAME);

int i,max = 20;

for(i=0;i<max;i++)
{
    System.out.println("Sending: "+i);
    server = ss.getMessageServer();
    server.send(name,"message: "+i);
    server = null;

    System.gc();
    System.runFinalization();
}
```

Again, this is an excerpt from a complete file on the CD-ROM. In general, you will probably want all of your RMI applications to use unreferenced to clean up resources.

NOTE **Some implementations of RMI may take a long time to call unreferenced due to the easygoing nature of the garbage collector. This is considered a bug and should be fixed in future releases.**

The next sections look at how RMI can be integrated with HTTP for tunneling through firewalls.

RMI and Firewalls

A *firewall* is a program or machine that prevents certain network connections. RMI is designed to work with firewalls. By default, RMI wants to make a direct connection from the client to the server. Unless the firewall is configured to permit arbitrary connections, making it a pretty bad firewall, it won't allow default RMI to work.

However, there is hope. Firewalls are normally used to protect an intranet from the Internet. At the same time, users inside the firewall often need to make some connections outside the firewall. In particular, users often want to browse the Web using

HTTP. To support this activity, most firewalls are configured to allow HTTP requests. RMI has been written to support use of HTTP to communicate between the client and server, thus allowing it to "tunnel" through the firewall.

There are two sides to the firewall discussion. First, there is the RMI program on the inside of a firewall trying to get out. In this case, the firewall probably uses what is called a *proxy server* to forward requests from the inside to the outside. Users make requests to the proxy server, and it forwards the requests out. To use RMI in this situation, set the http.proxyHost System property to the IP address of the proxy server. If the proxy server supports connections to any port (a potential security risk), you are good to go. The RMI library sends HTTP POST requests to a port on the proxy, expecting them to be forwarded to that port on the actual server. If the proxy doesn't allow connections on any port, you can configure a CGI script provided with the JDK called java-rmi.cgi to forward standard HTTP requests for you. Handling the proxy is automatic for the RMI libraries, so the only configuration on your part is to make sure that the CGI script is installed at the following URL:

```
http://hostname:80/cgi-bin/java-rmi.cgi
```

where hostname is the proxy server. Note that the server must accept the connection at port 80 for this to work.

Unfortunately, forwarding with both ports and CGI scripts does not allow unsolicited calls into the RMI object, and the CGI script can be a bit of a security issue because it forwards all requests to any port.

On the other side of the firewall discussion are programs outside the firewall that want to send messages in. You can use several mechanisms to accomplish this goal. First, you can set up a specific port for your RMI server and configure the firewall to allow connections on that port. Second, you can use a generic proxy that will forward TCP/IP packets through the firewall to the RMI server. Finally, you can use RMI to create a custom proxy server that controls connectivity into the intranet, yet allows arbitrary connections from the outside. This is a very configurable solution but can be a lot of work.

NOTE **By default, RMI programs try to use HTTP to communicate, just in case a proxy or firewall is in use. To disable all use of HTTP, set the System property called java.rmi.server.disableHttp to false.**

All of these mechanisms can require some work on your part. Please refer to the RMI home page at java.sun.com/products/rmi for up-to-the-minute information on RMI and firewalls.

Remote Object Activation

A UnicastRemoteObject allows you to create an instance of a remote object that can be accessed from a server program. The server program has to be accessible at all times to allow client connection. This can be a great performance hit if you have many remote object servers supporting various business processes. Java 2 introduces the notion of remote object activation.

Activation is managed by a small program called rmid that runs on the server. When a client requests a service, rmid starts the remote object, and communication proceeds normally. This way, you can have many services that take up processing time only when the service is actually requested. In order for this process to work, you must configure rmid so that it knows where to find your server program and the remote objects. Then, rmid handles the rest.

NOTE **Activation as a whole is a complex topic and beyond the scope of this book. Instead of trying to cover it completely, we have included a short discussion with an example. Please refer to the documentation in Java 2 for more complete information on the RMI activation framework as implemented in the java.rmi.activation package.**

An activatable server object can be created by subclassing java.rmi.activation.Activatable or by exporting a Remote object using the static method of Activatable.exportObject. The following code example illustrates the steps for modifying our first messaging example so that it becomes an activatable remote object server. The process involves moving an existing remote object implementation that extends UnicastRemoteObject to a class that extends java.rmi.activation.Activatable. Then it is necessary to create a program that will install the activation information about our remote object. After compiling these objects, both the rmiregistry and rmid must be run with the appropriate configurations. Next, run the setup program that installs the configuration information with rmid. After that, the client can call the remote object as usual, but the remote object will not actually run until the client makes a request.

Modifying Server

The first step is to modify the Server class so that it becomes an activatable object. Begin by importing the activation package and changing the class so that it extends Activatable instead of UnicastRemoteObject.

```
package server;

import java.rmi.*;
import java.rmi.server.*;
import java.rmi.registry.*;
import message.*;

//Add support for activation.
import java.rmi.activation.*;


/*
  Object must extend java.rmi.activation.Activatable instead of
  java.rmi.server.UnicastRemoteObject.
```

```
*/
public class Server extends Activatable
        implements MessageServer
{
```

Next, remove the empty constructor required for the subclass of UnicastRemoteObject and replace it with a constructor that takes two parameters: an ActivationID and a MarshalledObject. The ActivationID, which will be passed in by the activation system, represents a remote reference to the object's activator and a unique identifier for the object.

A MarshalledObject facilitates passing objects in RMI calls that are not automatically deserialized by the remote peer. The object contains a byte stream with the serialized representation of an object given to its constructor. The contained object is serialized and deserialized, with the same serialization semantics used for marshalling and unmarshalling parameters and return values of RMI calls. When the serialized form is created, classes are configured with a URL from which the class may be loaded, and any remote object referenced in the MarshalledObject is represented by a serialized instance of its stub. MarshalledObjects are not necessary and thus not used for this example.

The following code defines the new constructor, which calls its superclass constructor, passing in the id for this object and zero so that the object will be exported on an anonymous port.

```
public Server(ActivationID id, MarshalledObject data)
     throws RemoteException
{
     // Register the object with the activation system,
     // then export it on an anonymous port.
     super(id, 0);
}
```

No changes need to be made to the remote message sent, as the code that follows shows. This means that making an object activatable does not affect your core business logic.

```
public void send(String name, String s)
     throws RemoteException
{
     System.out.println(name + ": " + s);
}
```

Because the server object will now be created and run by the activation system, there is no need to bootstrap the process, so the main method from previous examples has been deleted.

Creating ConfigureServer

The next step in the process is to create a setup program that actually installs your remote object class in the activation system. Define a class called ConfigureServer in the server package. This class has one method that installs the server in the activation system.

Unlike the RMI server class that must stay alive as long as the implementation needs to be made available, the activatable class needs to be instantiated only when called. The ConfigureServer class passes information about the activatable class to the rmid process by registering an instance of the activatable class's stub class and a name with the rmiregistry. The information about the object is stored in an ActivationDesc (activation descriptor) object.

An ActivationDesc object contains the information necessary to activate an object, including the object's group identifier, class name, code location of the class, and optional object-specific initialization data in the form of a MarshalledObject. A descriptor registered with the activation system can be used to recreate/activate the object specified by the descriptor. The MarshalledObject in the object's descriptor is passed as the second argument to the remote object's constructor for object to use during reinitialization/activation. In this example, this is not included, because it is assumed that no default initialization data is needed.

For completeness, this example shows how the server can create an activation group to identify it. This group is associated with a Java virtual machine (VM). When objects in a group are activated, they run in this VM. Objects in other groups are assigned their own VM.

```
package server;

import java.util.*;

import java.rmi.*;
import java.rmi.activation.*;

import message.*;

public class ConfigureServer
{
    public static void main(String[] args) throws Exception
    {

        System.setSecurityManager(new RMISecurityManager());

        MessageServer srv;
        String servname = "server.Server";

        String location = "file:///temp/";

        MarshalledObject data = null;

        Properties props = new Properties();

        props.put("java.security.policy",
            "/temp/server.policy");
```

```
        ActivationGroupDesc.CommandEnvironment ace = null;

        ActivationGroupID id =
            ActivationGroup.getSystem().registerGroup(
                    new ActivationGroupDesc(props, ace));

        ActivationDesc desc = new ActivationDesc(id
                                ,servname, location, data);

        srv = (MessageServer)Activatable.register(desc);
        System.out.println("Registered and got Server_Stub");

        Naming.rebind(MessageServer.SERVER_NAME, srv);
        System.out.println("Exported MessageServer");

        System.exit(0);
    }
}
```

Notice that the configuration program essentially puts the activatable object in rmid using the Activatable class's register method. This returns a stub that is registered with the rmiregistry. Clients access the stub, triggering the activation of the real object. Once the ConfigureServer code is complete, you can compile and run by changing the directory to the project root and issuing the following commands in Windows:

```
javac server\*.java
rmic -d . server.Server
copy server c:\temp\server
copy server.policy \temp

start rmiregistry -J-Djava.security.policy=/temp/server.policy

start rmid

java -Djava.security.policy=server.policy -
Djava.rmi.server.codebase=file:///temp/ server.ConfigureServer
```

Notice that when starting the configuration application, you must specify a CODEBASE that can take the form of a valid file or HTTP URL. The slash at the end of the URL is mandatory. Without the slash you will get a java.lang.ClassNotFoundException, as you would if your class could not be found for some other reason. In this example, the server files are copied to temp for convenience.

To run the client, execute the following:

```
start java -Djava.security.manager
    -Djava.security.policy=server.policy client.Client Client1
```

The results should be similar to the first example. The difference is that the server is not actually running (activated) until the client makes a request by sending it a message.

Summary

The goals for RMI are to support seamless remote invocation on objects in different virtual machines as well as callbacks from servers and applets. The semantics of RMI are well integrated with the Java programming language, so you need very little knowledge of network communication to invoke remote objects. Because RMI is divided into several layers, you could replace the default transport of TCP with some other protocol.

RMI is both flexible and easy for the Java programmer to use. With the addition of activation in Java 2, RMI is also able to be responsive to client requests without taking up system resources. Clearly, for Java object communication, RMI is a good choice for creating enterprise solutions. However, if you intend to invoke methods of non-Java objects through CORBA, you may want to consider Java IDL or using an IIOP transport. Information on these topics can be found at the Sun Web site.

One last tidbit: When creating your RMI programs, you can use the built-in logging feature to help with debugging. Use the flag -Djava.rmi.server.logCalls=true when running a program to see a list of the calls that arrive to the RMI object.

The next chapter looks at a practical use of Java RMI: a file-locking server that provides multiuser access to networked files through Java.

A Network File-Locking Server

To demonstrate how RMI can be used in the real world, a remote file-locking utility is created in this chapter. The file-locking utility enables you to lock resources on a remote machine.

Our motivation is three-fold. First, file locking involves some interesting issues when used in an environment in which files are shared between computers, such as on a network file server. Second, this example can be broken into two pieces: local file locking for files shared by another application running on the same computer as your application and global file locking for remote files shared by applications on multiple computers, allowing for the addition of new ideas to the example as the discussion proceeds. These two versions of the same idea are also best implemented with differing levels of RMI, making them good, complementary examples.

Finally, file locking is an important mechanism for enterprise computing. Enterprise JavaBeans, servlets, and other network programming tools support multithreaded programs and can often be scaled to multiple computers. These computers and programs may share the same files, and file locking is necessary to protect shared files from corruption. Providing both a local and remote implementation of file locking gives you a starting point for protecting important data in your enterprise applications.

NOTE **Keep in mind that these and all examples in this book are designed for educational purposes. We hope to provide robust code that acts as a starting point for your own applications, but we have not implemented every corner case and test.**

In both the local and global implementations for file locking, temporary files are used to represent the lock on a file. This temporary file is visible to the user, so if there is a problem with a stale lock, it can be deleted manually. Using a temporary file is also useful in the global-locking situation in which different machines may get to the same file via different paths. Regardless of the path, the lock appears in the same directory as the file being locked, so either client can see it.

Both implementations are advisory locking schemes. This means that if a program doesn't use them, it can still execute corrupting actions on a file. In other words, for this locking to work, you as the programmer have to use it; any program that doesn't breaks the entire locking scheme. Although it would be nice to create a mandatory locking scheme, this is not possible at the application level without complete control of the file I/O libraries.

Both RMI and locking come at some cost. Once set up, the RMI connections in these examples don't require much network bandwidth, but the locking may take time as threads are synchronized and the server handles multiple requests. As a result, the best way to protect files, as with any data, is to not share them. If you do share files, these examples provide a good framework for protecting them.

Local Shared Locks

First, let's look at an RMI-based server for managing file locks on the local system. This server, called the *network lock server*, or NLS, provides access to objects that manage the lock for a single file path. This lock is represented by a SharedFileLock object and is unique for the machine. When a client wants to lock a file on his system, he contacts the lock server and asks for a lock based on an absolute path. The lock is returned as a remote object and can be used to lock and unlock the file. The server also provides a method for testing whether a file currently has a shared lock on it. This relationship between the client and server is pictured in Figure 14.1.

The same server is used for the global lock implementation, but it relies on a different client mechanism. The actual interaction between the client and server for the shared locks is defined in two interfaces, NetworkLockServer and FileLock. Let's look at each of these in detail.

FileLock Interface

The file lock interface is pretty simple. It defines three methods: one to test if the file is locked, one to lock it, and one to unlock it.

```
import java.rmi.*;

public interface FileLock extends Remote
{
    public boolean isLocked()
        throws RemoteException;

    public void lock()
```

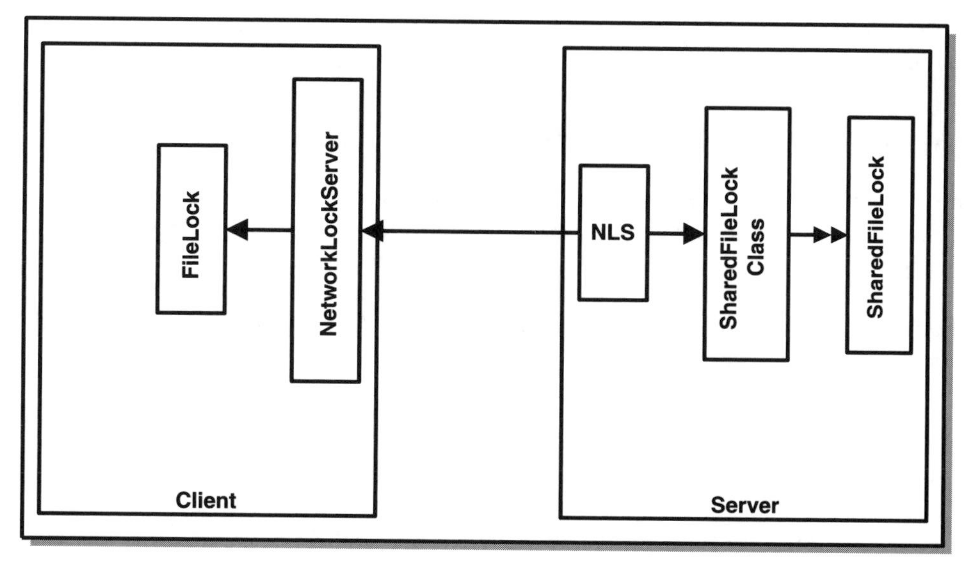

Figure 14.1 Shared lock architecture.

```
            throws RemoteException,FileLockingException;

        public void unlock()
            throws RemoteException,FileLockingException;
    }
```

Because this is an interface for an RMI object, it extends Remote. The methods also throw RemoteExceptions for the same reason.

FileLockingException

Both the lock and unlock methods in FileLock can throw a custom exception type called FileLockingException. This happens when a problem occurs in the underlying locking machinery. This exception class is very simple and is provided only for data typing. The following code defines the FileLockingException class that extends the Exception class.

```
public class FileLockingException
 extends Exception
{
    public FileLockingException(String msg)
    {
        super(msg);
    }

    public FileLockingException()
    {
    }
}
```

When an exception occurs in the locking machinery, FileLocking exceptions are used to distinguish them from normal RMI or run-time exceptions.

NetworkLockServer Interface

The NetworkLockServer interface provides two sets of methods. One set is used for the local, shared locks discussed in this example, and the other set is used for the global locking discussed in the next section. The following code declares the NetworkLock-Server interface. The interface provides methods for getting a lock on a file, checking whether a file is locked already, and unlocking a file. As always, all remote methods must throw RemoteException.

```
import java.rmi.*;

public interface NetworkLockServer extends Remote
{
    // Default registry name for bound to the server
    public static String NLS_NAME="server.nls";

    public FileLock getSharedLockFor(String absPath)
        throws RemoteException;

    public boolean isFileLocked(String absPath)
        throws RemoteException;

    public void lock()
        throws RemoteException;

    public void unlock()
        throws RemoteException;
}
```

In particular, the lock and unlock methods are used by global locks and will not be used by the shared lock implementation. NetworkLockServer defines the name that the server registers, as in the RMI registry. This static variable helps prevent typing errors in client applications. In general, try to use static variables for all "magic" strings in your applications. This reduces the danger of typing errors and improves readability, in most cases.

NLS: The Lock Server

The NetworkLockServer interface is implemented in a class called NLS. The following code defines the NLS class that extends UnicastRemoteObject and provides implementations for all of the remote methods. Most of the work in handling shared file-lock requests is actually handled by the SharedFileLock class, which keeps a list of unique locks for each path. These locks are used to test whether a file is locked when the server is asked.

```
import java.io.*;
import java.util.*;
import java.security.*;
import java.rmi.*;
import java.rmi.server.*;

public class NLS extends UnicastRemoteObject
implements NetworkLockServer
{
    private boolean locked;

    public NLS() throws RemoteException
    {
    }

    public FileLock
     getSharedLockFor(String path)
    {
        return SharedFileLock.getLockFor(path);
    }

    public boolean isFileLocked(String absPath)
        throws RemoteException
    {
        FileLock lock;

        lock = getSharedLockFor(absPath);

        return lock.isLocked();
    }
```

The lock method ensures that multiple requests to lock this file will not collide. The first request locks the file, and all others must wait until the file lock is released.

```
    public synchronized void lock()
    {
        while(locked)
        {
            try
            {
                wait();
            }
            catch(Exception exp)
            {
            }
        }

        locked = true;
    }
```

The lock is released, and the next request to lock the file can now be processed. The method notifyAll wakes up all threads that are waiting on this object based on the wait method called in the lock method described previously.

```
public synchronized void unlock()
{
    locked = false;
    notifyAll();
}
```

The main method is the bootstrap for the NLS. It installs the standard RMI security manager, creates an NLS instance, and binds it in the registry specified in the URL passed into main as args[0].

```
public static void main(String args[])
{
    // Create and install a security manager.
    SecurityManager mng;
    NLS nls;

    try
    {
        System.out.println("Setting Security Manager.");
        mng = new RMISecurityManager();
        System.setSecurityManager(mng);
        System.out.println("Set Security Manager.");

        System.out.println("Creating server.");
        nls = new NLS();
        System.out.println("Created server.");

        System.out.println("Starting to bind server.");

        if(args.length>0)
            Naming.rebind("//"+args[0]+"/"
                    +NetworkLockServer.NLS_NAME, nls);
        else
        {
            System.out.println("No Server Specified.");
            System.exit(0);
        }

        System.out.println("NLS bound in registry");
    }
    catch (Exception e)
    {
        System.out.println("Network Lock Server: "
                            + e.getMessage());
        e.printStackTrace();
        System.exit(0);
    }
```

```
        }
    }
```

NLS provides a main method that sets up the correct SecurityManager, creates an NLS object, and registers and binds it. Notice that command-line arguments are used to specify the server for the RMI registry.

SharedFileLock: The FileLock Implementation

The SharedFileLock class is the most complex in this example. It is the one that implements the FileLock interface. The following code defines the SharedFileLock class by importing the necessary packages and declaring the class as extending UnicastRemoteObject and implementing the FileLock interface.

```
import java.io.*;
import java.util.*;
import java.rmi.*;
import java.rmi.server.*;

public class SharedFileLock
 extends UnicastRemoteObject implements FileLock
{
```

Next, two instance variables are defined to store a file object that represents the file that the lock is locking and the lock file that embodies the lock itself.

```
    private File file;
    private File lockFile;
```

Then a static hash table called locks is used to map paths onto file locks, so that a unique lock can be used for each path, rather than having multiple locks per file.

```
    private static Hashtable locks = new Hashtable();
```

In order for this unique lock mechanism to work, the class provides a method for getting a lock based on a path. This method, getLockFor, creates a lock, if necessary, and stores it in the lock's hash table under its absolute path.

```
    public synchronized static SharedFileLock
     getLockFor(String path)
    {
        SharedFileLock retVal = null;
        File tmp = new File(path);
        String absPath = tmp.getAbsolutePath();

        try
        {
            retVal = (SharedFileLock) locks.get(absPath);
```

```
            if(retVal == null)
            {
                retVal = new SharedFileLock(tmp);
                locks.put(absPath,retVal);
            }
        }
        catch(Exception exp)
        {
            retVal = null;
        }

        return retVal;
    }
```

In order to force programs to use the getLockFor method, the constructor for SharedFileLock is defined as protected. This constructor accepts a File object representing the file to lock and creates another file object using the primary file's path of the File object to represent the lock file. A lock file with a name of the form *.filename*.lck is used, where *filename* is the actual name of the file. On some UNIX systems, this file will be hidden and may also be hidden in Windows, depending on the user's settings.

```
    protected SharedFileLock(File f)
    throws RemoteException
    {
        String parent,name;
        String lckPath;

        file = f;

        parent = file.getParent();
        name = file.getName();

        lckPath = parent+File.separator+"."+name+".lck";

        lockFile = new File(lckPath);
    }
```

To check if the lock is active, we test if the lock file exists, using the following isLocked method.

```
    public synchronized boolean isLocked()
    {
        return lockFile.exists();
    }
```

To lock the file, first wait until it is not locked, then create the lock file. Because this wait can take an inordinate amount of time in the case of a file locked for editing, the isLocked methods are provided to allow programs to check whether they want to attempt the lock. A wait statement is used inside a while loop to reduce CPU usage. When a client requests that a SharedFileLock lock, the request first waits for the object's lock, then checks to see whether the file is already locked. If the file is locked, the client's requesting thread waits for notification. This notification is provided in the unlock method, discussed below.

The lock method relies on the RMI libraries' promise to handle different clients in separate threads. Otherwise, we would have a deadlock if the lock fails.

```
//Waits to acquire a lock.
public synchronized void lock()
    throws FileLockingException
{
    while(isLocked())
    {
        try
        {
            wait();
        }
        catch(Exception exp)
        {
        }
    }

    reallyLock();
}
```

For clarity, the actual locking code is isolated in the method reallyLock, which follows. This method creates the lock file by opening and closing it. If a problem occurs, a FileLockingException is thrown. This exception will ultimately be passed to the client.

```
private synchronized void reallyLock()
    throws FileLockingException
{
    FileOutputStream fileOut;

    //Create the lock file on disk.
    try
    {
        fileOut = new FileOutputStream(lockFile);
        fileOut.close();
    }
    catch(Exception exp)
    {
        throw new FileLockingException("File error.");
    }
}
```

To unlock the SharedFileLock, delete the lock file and notify any waiting threads. This allows the threads stuck in the lock method to check for the lock's availability. The first one to check gets the lock, and the others resume waiting. The following code defines the unlock method that deletes the lock file and notifies other threads waiting on this file.

```
    public synchronized void unlock()
        throws FileLockingException
    {
        lockFile.delete();
        notifyAll();
    }
}
```

All three locking methods defined in the previous example are synchronized to make sure that one thread doesn't delete the file while another is checking its existence, or some other inappropriate scenario. This locking is an important part of this program and is the reason that the shared locks must be unique. If synchronized methods were not used, two threads may create the lock file, one immediately after the other, as pictured in Figure 14.2.

With synchronized methods, only one thread can create the lock file at a time, as pictured in Figure 14.3, assuming that there is only one SharedFileLock for that file. This is where the unique locks come in.

Because only one object represents the file and the lock method is synchronized, at any one time only one thread can lock the file, thus creating the file lock.

A Test Program

A program called SharedLockTester for testing these shared file locks follows and is also available on the CD-ROM. This test program looks up the network lock server using a hard-coded address, requests the lock for a file specified on the command line, and locks the file. The lock is held for 30 seconds and then released. Holding the lock provides time for another copy of the test program to run and have to wait for the lock. The isFileLocked method is used to test whether the file is locked before attempting to lock it. In this case, an attempt to get the lock is made anyway, but in a real program you would probably notify the user that the file is unavailable rather than waiting for the lock indefinitely.

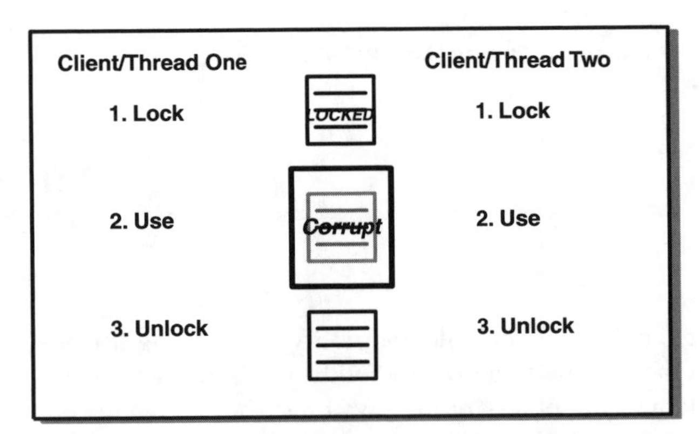

Figure 14.2 Locks can fail without synchronization.

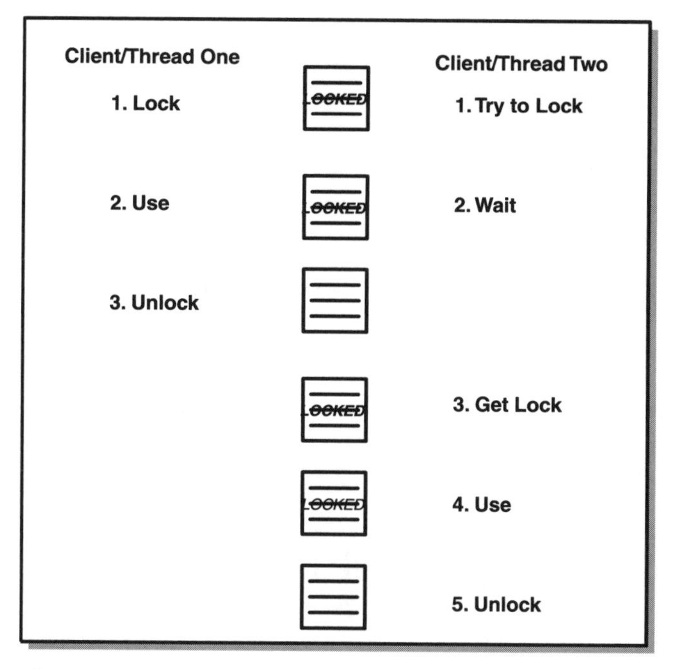

Figure 14.3 Locking with synchronization.

```
import java.io.*;
import java.util.*;
import java.rmi.*;

public class SharedLockTester
{
    public static void main(String args[])
    {

        SecurityManager mng;

        if(args.length < 1)
        {
            System.out.println("usage SharedLockTester file");
            System.exit(0);
        }

        try
        {
            NetworkLockServer server;
            FileLock lock;
            String lookup;

            System.out.println("Setting Security Manager.");

            // Create and install a security manager.
```

```
            mng = new RMISecurityManager();
            System.setSecurityManager(mng);

            /*
              The server network address is hard coded for
              the example.  You should change the IP address
              192.168.0.172 to the network address of the
              machine where you RMI registry is located.
            */
            lookup = "//192.168.0.172/"+NetworkLockServer.NLS_NAME;

            System.out.println("Looking up server.");

            server = (NetworkLockServer) Naming.lookup(lookup);

            System.out.println("Got Server.");

            System.out.println("Checking for lock.");

            if(server.isFileLocked(args[0]))
                System.out.println("The file is locked.");
            else
                System.out.println("The file is not locked.");

            System.out.println("Creating lock object.");

            lock = server.getSharedLockFor(args[0]);

            System.out.println("Got lock object.");

            System.out.println("Trying to acquire lock.");
            lock.lock();
            System.out.println("Got lock");

            //Hold the lock for 30 seconds.
            Thread.sleep(30000);

            System.out.println("Unlocking.");
            lock.unlock();
            System.out.println("Unlocked.");
        }
        catch (Exception e)
        {
            System.out.println("SharedLockTester Error: "
                                + e.getMessage());
            e.printStackTrace();
        }
    }
}
```

Now let's look at the global locking scheme.

Global Locks

The global locking mechanism requires a bit different architecture from that of the shared locks. The reason for this difference is the fact that different machines can refer to the same file by different paths. For example, in Windows, a directory may be mapped from your C drive to my G drive. This means that the file you call c:\temp\test we might call g:\test.

The shared locking scheme required that each file path have a unique lock object. This works because all of the programs on the same computer use the same absolute path for each file, and all paths are translated to an absolute path before using them. But now we can't rely on this uniqueness, because the route to the file may differ based on how the file is accessed on each computer. We can, however, rely on the lock files being seen, because they are located in the same directory as the file that is locking. The trick is to find a way to make sure that two clients don't touch this lock file at the same time or in too close succession. To do this, include a simple locking scheme in the NetworkLockServer.

The LockServer

The lock server provides one method for locking and another for unlocking. Both of these rely on the Boolean instance variable called locked, and both are synchronized. Clients that want to affect a lock file must first lock the network lock server. This is a bit more heavy handed than the shared scheme in which client's using different files had little interaction. Here, a client locking one file may have to wait for a client locking another file to unlock the server. However, this does ensure that no two clients are touching lock files at the same time or in a corrupt manner.

The code for lock and unlock is very similar to the methods with the same name in the SharedFileLock object, because they perform the same function. The same wait-notifyAll technique is used to reduce CPU usage for threads waiting on the lock. Here is the code for the lock method, implemented as part of the global lock server:

```
public synchronized void lock()
{
    while(locked)
    {
        try
        {
            wait();
        }
        catch(Exception exp)
        {
        }
    }

    locked = true;
}

public synchronized void unlock()
```

```
    {
        locked = false;
        notifyAll();
    }
```

The process of locking the server and creating lock files is encapsulated into the class GlobalFileLock.

GlobalFileLock

GlobalFileLock is not a remote class. It is a local class that accesses the NetworkLock-Server via RMI. This is a different technique in that RMI is encapsulated behind a library class rather than providing library objects via RMI.

The GlobalFileLock class that follows extends Object and implements the FileLock interface. Instance variables store File objects representing the file to lock and the lock file. A static hash table is used to provide unique global locks within a program, thus reducing memory usage, and the NetworkLockServer's remote stub.

```
import java.io.*;
import java.util.*;
import java.rmi.*;

public class GlobalFileLock
 implements FileLock
{
    private File file;
    private File lockFile;

    private static NetworkLockServer server;
    private static Hashtable locks = new Hashtable();
```

The GlobalFileLock class provides the setLockServer method to clients so that they can specify to the server host that the lock server is on. Remember that the lock server is used to ensure that lock files are not corrupted, so all of the programs that share a particular file should use the same lock server. All servers use the same name to register.

```
    public synchronized static void setLockServer(String host)
    {
        String lookup;
        SecurityManager mng = new RMISecurityManager();

        try
        {
            System.setSecurityManager(mng);

            lookup = "rmi://"+host+"/"+NetworkLockServer.NLS_NAME;

            server = (NetworkLockServer) Naming.lookup(lookup);
        }
```

```
        catch(Exception exp)
        {
            server = null;
        }
    }
```

For convenience, the SecurityManager is set when the connection is made to the server. You may want to change this setting if you are setting the SecurityManager somewhere else in the program. The getLockServer method is used to get the lock server object stub from the class. This method creates an object for the local host if the server has not already been provided.

```
    protected static NetworkLockServer getLockServer()
    {
        if(server == null) setLockServer("localhost");
        return server;
    }
```

To improve performance and reduce memory usage, a unique lock is provided for each path. The getLockFor method that follows implements this behavior. These locks are available only for a single program, so the absolute paths are unique. The unique locks are not shared with clients on other machines that may use different paths. However, they do afford us the ability to rely on synchronization of the lock object as well as locking the server.

```
    public synchronized static GlobalFileLock
     getLockFor(String path)
    {
        GlobalFileLock retVal = null;
        File tmp = new File(path);
        String absPath = tmp.getAbsolutePath();

        try
        {
            retVal = (GlobalFileLock) locks.get(absPath);

            if(retVal == null)
            {
                retVal = new GlobalFileLock(tmp);
                locks.put(absPath,retVal);
            }
        }
        catch(Exception exp)
        {
            retVal = null;
        }

        return retVal;
    }
```

Again, to make sure that clients don't create their own GlobalFileLocks, the constructor is marked protected. This constructor is basically identical to the SharedFileLock's constructor, as you can see in the GlobalFileLock constructor that follows.

```
protected GlobalFileLock(File f)
throws RemoteException
{
    String parent,name;
    String lckPath;

    file = f;

    parent = file.getParent();
    name = file.getName();

    lckPath = parent+File.separator+"."+name+".lck";

    lockFile = new File(lckPath);
}
```

Like the shared lock, the lockFile's existence is used to check whether the file is locked.

```
public synchronized boolean isLocked()
{
    return lockFile.exists();
}
```

Requests to lock a file result in a call to the lock method. This method will check for a lock server; if one does not exist, then an exception is thrown.

```
//Waits to acquire a lock.
public synchronized void lock()
    throws FileLockingException
{
    NetworkLockServer serv = getLockServer();

    if(serv == null)
        throw new FileLockingException("No Server Available");

    // reallyLock, defined later, verifies lock has been placed.
    if(!reallyLock(serv))
    {
        throw new FileLockingException("Lock Unavailable");
    }
}
```

If there is a server, try to lock it by calling the server's lock method. Once the server is locked, double-check that the lock file is not already in place by calling isLocked. This check is required for global locks because a client might have locked the file between the time we checked for the lock file and the time the server was locked. Again, all changes to the lock file occur within the confines of a locked NetworkLock-Server. If the file is locked, an exception is thrown. This is different from the shared lock that waits for the lock to be available. Here, we try and fail quickly. If a program wants to wait, it can sleep and try again, shown by the test program in the following section. The code for the reallyLock method that follows implements this behavior.

```
private synchronized boolean reallyLock(NetworkLockServer serv)
    throws FileLockingException
{
    boolean retVal = false;
    FileOutputStream fileOut;

    //Create the lock file on disk.
    try
    {
        serv.lock();

        if(!isLocked())
        {
            fileOut = new FileOutputStream(lockFile);
            fileOut.close();
            retVal = true;
        }
        //else return false

        serv.unlock();
    }
    catch(Exception exp)
    {
        throw new FileLockingException("File error.");
    }

    return retVal;
}
```

To unlock a file, call the unlock method. The unlock method gets the lock server, locks it, removes the lock file, and unlocks the server. If no server is available or the locking fails, an exception is thrown.

```
//Notifies threads waiting for lock.
public synchronized void unlock()
    throws FileLockingException
{
    NetworkLockServer serv = getLockServer();

    if(serv == null)
        throw new FileLockingException("No Server Available");

    try
```

```
            {
                serv.lock();
                lockFile.delete();
                serv.unlock();
            }
            catch(Exception exp)
            {
                throw new FileLockingException("File error.");
            }
        }
    }
```

As you can see, these global locks are different from the shared ones because you cannot assume in a global locking system that the absolute file paths are sufficient keys for identifying the file. Even though there is a difference between the lock schemes, they rely on the same principles. Use files to represent locks, and use synchronization to ensure that only one client changes the lock file at a time.

A Test Program

A program to test the GlobalFileLock class follows; it is also available on the CD-ROM. This program uses command-line arguments to determine the lock server and file path. This program continues to try to acquire the lock every five seconds until it succeeds. In a real program, you might ask the user what to do if the lock fails.

```
import java.io.*;
import java.util.*;
import java.rmi.*;

/*
  Example use:
  java GlobalLockTester \dir\myfile myLockServerHost
*/
public class GlobalLockTester
{
    public static void main(String args[])
    {
        if(args.length < 1)
        {
            System.out.println("usage GlobalLockTester"
                                    +" file [lockserver]");
            System.exit(0);
        }

        try
        {
            FileLock lock;

            System.out.println("Setting LockServer.");
```

```
            if(args.length>1)
                GlobalFileLock.setLockServer(args[1]);

            System.out.println("Creating lock object.");

            lock = GlobalFileLock.getLockFor(args[0]);

            System.out.println("Got lock object.");

            while(true)
            {
                try
                {
                    System.out.println("Trying to acquire lock.");
                    lock.lock();
                    System.out.println("Got lock");

                    //Hold the lock for 30 seconds.
                    Thread.sleep(30000);
                    break;
                }
                catch(FileLockingException ex)
                {
                    System.out.println("Lock is unavailable.");
                    System.out.println("Sleeping 5 seconds.");

                    try
                    {
                        Thread.sleep(5000);
                    }
                    catch(InterruptedException exp)
                    {
                    }
                }
            }

            System.out.println("Unlocking.");
            lock.unlock();
            System.out.println("Unlocked.");
        }
        catch (Exception e)
        {
            System.out.println("GlobalLockTester Error: "
                                    + e.getMessage());
            e.printStackTrace();
        }
    }
}
```

This test program is best demonstrated in the situation in which two machines share a file with different paths for accessing the file.

Summary

The first thing to note about these two examples is that *they don't mix*. If you use SharedFileLocks, don't use GlobalFileLocks for the same files, because the two mechanisms have different protection schemes.

The second thing to notice is that network programming has a lot of issues that non-distributed programming does not. In this case, we had to deal with different file paths and the possibility of multiple programs accessing resources, as well as multiple threads sharing resources. In a non-distributed program, you can use synchronization to protect shared resources; distributed programs require some form of rendezvous point, such as a file or server. In some cases, an operating system provides this rendezvous point in the form of a system call. For example, many systems support a call such as flock that will lock a file. However, this mechanism is OS dependent and will not work in a network situation. Some network file systems, like NFS, provide their own locking schemes. Our design is loosely based on some of these network schemes.

Using RMI in this example made the network communication issues for the application virtually transparent. This is why RMI is such an important technology for enterprise developers; it helps simplify a common requirement: object communication over the network. The next few chapters begin to explore Enterprise JavaBeans. This API provides an architecture for a server-based component model for building robust, extensible enterprise applications.

What Are Enterprise JavaBeans?

Enterprise JavaBeans (EJB) is a specification for components that live on a server. The goal of the EJB specification is to define a standard way of creating components that participates in distributed object-oriented applications. In the same way that JavaBeans define a standard interface for application components, EJB defines a standard for server components. Using enterprise beans, Java developers will be able to build distributed programs more quickly by plugging together targeted, well-defined pieces. Figure 15.1 diagrams a possible application of this technology.

The motivating factor behind Enterprise JavaBeans is to make it easier to create network-enabled applications. This requires the application to have an easy way to define its various components. JavaBeans is the standard used to define client-side components, and Enterprise JavaBeans is the standard for defining server-side components. Of course, some large, multitier applications may actually use JavaBeans and EJBs in the same application because this application might be a server for one tier and a client for another. A great example of this is the new set of JavaBeans announced for JDBC 2.0. These include a data source object for accessing the database. An EJB might use this JavaBean to access its supporting database. One tier is the client, another the EJB, and a third the database.

In creating this standard, Sun and its partners strove to make server computing easier. Making things easy is often a hard goal, especially in server computing, in which transaction processing, database access, and resource management are all amplified by the number of clients accessing an application. However, the EJB specification does a great job of hiding these complexities from the program. In particular, EJB programmers

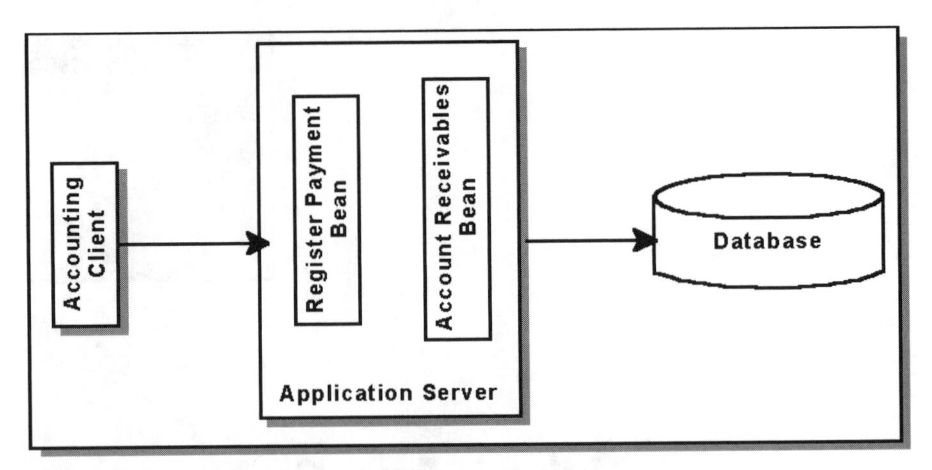

Figure 15.1 An example EJB application.

don't have to worry about multithreading, transactions, or many of the other features in advanced servers, such as connection pooling. As well as making programming easier, Enterprise JavaBeans have the following goals:

- Clearly define the way that applications are partitioned: client versus EJB versus server and so on.
- Create a model that improves scalability and performance. Enterprise JavaBeans live on servers; they can communicate with other services like JBDC and with other enterprise beans. A network of enterprise beans can be used to create a highly scaled, optimized distributed application. By organizing the applications into tiers, a designer can gain the benefit of scalability and localization to increase the total number of clients supported.
- Increase reliability by moving important code to a well-defined container. This container can protect a bean from interactions with other server entities, as well as protecting the server from the bean. Exceptions are also used to define a clear error-handling interface for EJB programming.
- Centralize resources to increase manageability.
- Promote reuse via well-defined, portable components.
- Support multiple types of clients, from Java applets to legacy systems, smart cards, and personal digital assistants (PDAs) to supercomputers.

An Enterprise JavaBean, like the ones created in the next chapter, is really just a Java object. Like an applet, the EJB doesn't define a complete application, only a specific part of the application. The applet is hosted by a browser, but an EJB is hosted by a server that uses a program entity called a *container* to define the bean's interactions with the outside world. This container creates a safe environment for the bean and provides services to it. A great example of the container providing services to a bean is resource pooling. Take the example in which you are using JDBC to access a database. JDBC represents database connections with Connection objects. These connections take up resources on the client and, often, on the server. As a result, many programmers like to use as few connections as possible.

In a large application, connections are often shared via pools. The pool will contain several connections, and an object will borrow a connection from the pool when it needs one. Of course, this technique is used mainly in situations in which multiple objects are doing work in separate threads. If there is only one thread in an application, there is less motivation to share resources, because there can be only one thread open at a time. So, in the multithreaded case, a pool is used to allow several objects to share a connection. This sharing is based on two principles. First, it is assumed that there are enough connections to provide reasonable response; second, the objects do not require connections all the time.

For example, if three clients are accessing three server objects, but only about half of the client operations require database access, that means that two connections can be used to provide the clients with acceptable performance. This scenario, pictured in Figure 15.2, is similar to the concept of modem pooling used by Internet service providers. These providers don't buy a modem for every customer. Instead, they bet that not all of the customers would call at the same time. The real science of this type of pooling is figuring out exactly how many resources are enough to provide sufficiently good performance to the user. In general, this decision should be based on experience testing an application with a variety of resource settings.

One way that the server supports these services is by hiding the bean behind the container, as pictured in Figure 15.3. Clients do not actually talk directly to bean objects, even through RMI. Instead, beans talk to stubs and skeletons, or some other proxy, generated by the container. This proxy includes the code that manages pools, resources, transactions, and the bean's very existence. As a developer, you must understand that the bean is separated from the client by the container while at the same time realizing that in 90 percent of the cases, you can ignore this situation. For clients, this separation is transparent and should not affect their programming style.

At the same time that the EJB specification hides complexity, it also provides hooks for advanced programmers to get under some of the covers represented by the con-

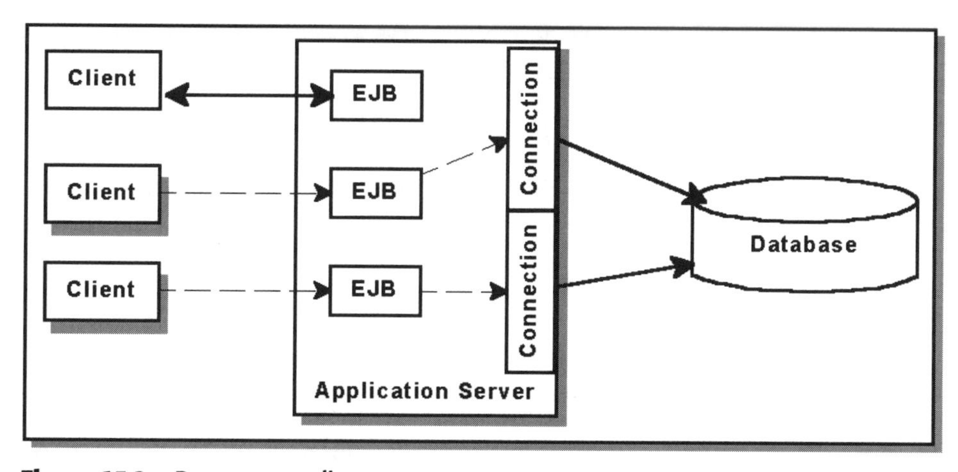

Figure 15.2 Resource pooling.

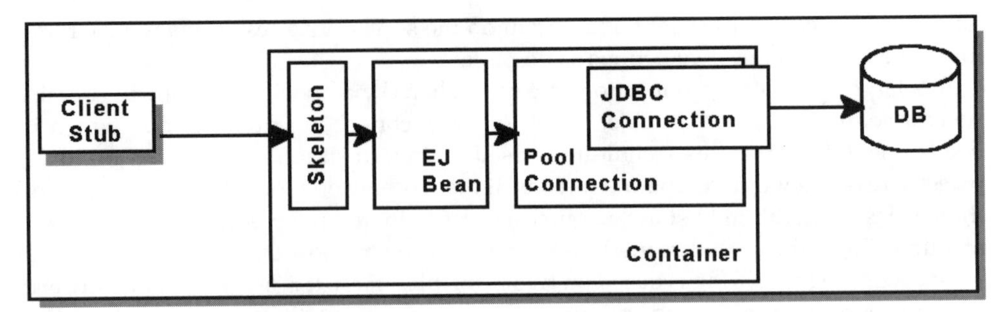

Figure 15.3 Container-protected EJB.

tainer and directly access low-level services. For example, most EJB programmers don't need to think about transaction processing with their applications. However, developers can manage their own transactions if they choose to.

The container defined by the EJB specification performs another key benefit. It defines the services that EJB programmers can expect to have available to them. This includes database access, transaction management, the bean's life cycle, and JNDI. By demanding these services be available through the standard interfaces, EJB promotes the concept of reusable, write-once, run-anywhere server components. Ideally, an EJB can be deployed on any server that supports the specification, without being recompiled.

Although EJBs are defined as Java objects, the specification does not intend them to be limited to Java applications. In other words, a C++ or Visual Basic programmer might access Enterprise JavaBeans on the server to perform work for those other programs. This interaction might happen through a custom protocol supported by the bean's container or through CORBA, as discussed later in this chapter. Regardless of the mechanism, EJBs are intended to provide a standard component architecture for server objects, not a Java-only technology for pure Java applications. This distinction is especially important in applications that access legacy data.

Roles

The EJB specification defines a number of roles in the EJB application development and deployment process. In many cases, one person or company will perform multiple roles, but here they are separated to clarify who does what and where the lines are drawn when using this technology.

Developers

The first role in creating EJB applications is the EJB programmer. This is the person who creates the Enterprise JavaBeans. He or she will be a Java developer who understands the specification and creates Jar files containing Enterprise JavaBean code. Part of this person's job is to define two key Java interfaces for an EJB. The first interface, called the Home interface, defines how programs can create EJBs on the server. For example, are their arguments used to create an object, or do you possibly find existing objects without creating them directly?

The second interface that an EJB developer defines is the bean's direct interface. This interface extends the java.rmi.Remote interface, making it represent a set of distributed object messages. Although the interface is defined using RMI, it may ultimately be accessed with CORBA or another technology. The EJB specification doesn't say how the interface is accessed, only that it is defined this way. The main purpose of the bean's remote interface is to succinctly state the messages that a client can send to a bean.

Assemblers

Programmers who use Enterprise JavaBeans are called *assemblers*. In the simplest case, these programmers use JNDI to access the home interface for a bean, then use this interface to gain access to the beans themselves before sending messages to them. As the EJB specification gains industry support, tools vendors are beginning to support visual tools for assembly or including Enterprise JavaBeans in an application. The compiled results of the assembler's work can range from other EJBs to JavaBeans to applets to applications. Basically, any form of Java project might take advantage of EJBs for server programming.

Deployers

Enterprise JavaBeans are hosted on a server within a specific container. This container has a number of settings that configure the bean and its surrounding environment. A *deployer* is the person who defines what the bean's environment looks like and actualizes this environment by deploying the bean to a specific server host. One example of a deployer's job is to define any resource pools used by a bean or transaction scopes associated with a bean's methods.

Chapter 17, "Deploying Enterprise JavaBeans," provides a short discussion of deploying beans but should not be considered a complete text. Each server provides different tools for deploying Enterprise JavaBeans, and you should refer to the documentation for your server to determine what steps the deployer takes and what options he or she has available to them.

Beans are deployed to a server and bound to a JNDI context for access by the client. By using the standard JNDI to access enterprise beans, the EJB specification minimizes the learning curve and maximizes the naming options for enterprise bean systems.

Server Providers

The company or organization that provides a server for hosting enterprise beans is expected to implement as much of the EJB specification as it requires. However, the provider may also implement other features that differentiate it from its competition. This specification is considered a minimum. Providers can create other libraries that augment their products or tools that make them easier to use.

One of the great things about Enterprise JavaBeans is that many types of servers can support them. For example, an application server can host EJBs as part of the server portion of a distributed application. An application server is expected to provide a fast, secure, robust environment for the beans, but it doesn't need to provide a lot of bells and whistles. Rather, it is a middle tier in a larger application, intended to provide processor power and networking connections. The application server provider's main job is to make writing that middle tier as easy as possible, and that's where Enterprise JavaBeans fit in.

Several database vendors have also announced support for Enterprise JavaBeans. In this case, the beans will likely have very direct access to the data in a database. Rather than use the database as a processing hub for standard requests, the EJB developer will use an EJB-enabled database to implement smart data management. The bean can search data locally before responding to requests from the client. In a high-performance situation like the one pictured in Figure 15.4, an application might do preprocessing on an application server, send specific requests to a database EJB for data optimization, and return the results to the user after post-processing them on the application server again. Essentially, enterprise beans become super-smart, object-oriented stored procedures on the database.

Operating systems vendors may even use the EJB specification as a way to host services for users on that machine.

Container Providers

An integral part of the beans specification is the container. This container is considered the real service provider; the server is just a host for the container. In reality, the EJB server provider will almost always be the container provider. This is because the container needs to deal with the server for threading information, resource management, and numerous other facilities that will be hard to define in a way that makes separating the server and container reasonable. However, that is one goal of future versions of

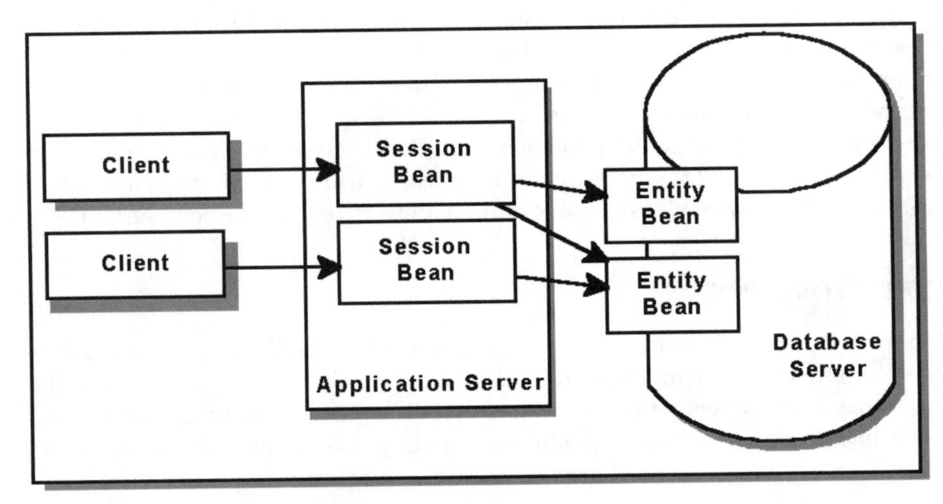

Figure 15.4 Enterprise beans on several tiers.

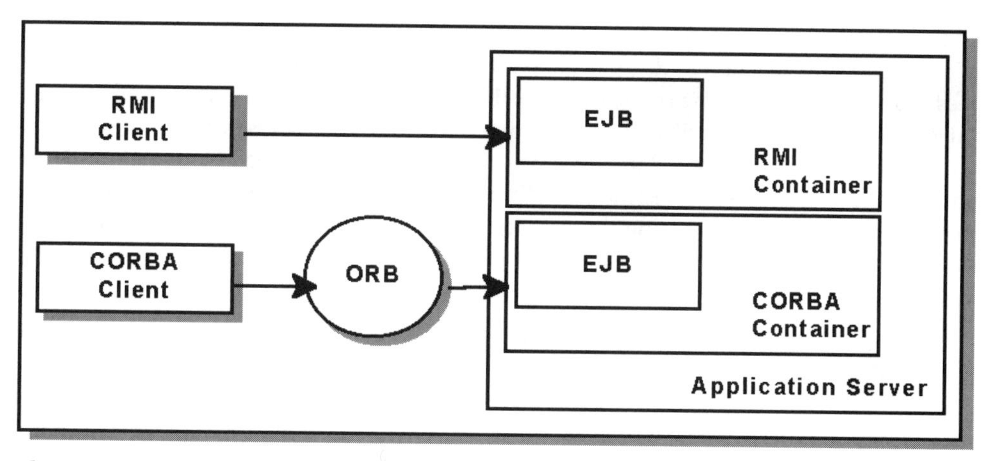

Figure 15.5 Multiple container types.

the EJB specification and may eventually become standard. Until then, the container providers will probably be the server providers, and most server providers will provide a single type of container. Some may provide multiple containers that define services in different ways. For example, Sun might provide one container that uses CORBA and another that uses straight RMI to communicate, as pictured in Figure 15.5.

Other constraints on the container might be the databases it can access or the transaction-processing services that it can use. Although the existence of these services is required by the specification, their implementation is not. Some services may be available through varying incompatible mechanisms, and it is the container's job to translate the EJBs' requests to their specific format. It will be the deployer's job to determine which container, or server, to use to support the other applications in a distributed system.

Administrators

Because EJBs represent network resources, they may need to be administered. The administrator will be tasked with keeping track of resource usage, making sure that the JNDI contexts are properly initialized, and any other tasks that guarantee the EJB's continued availability.

When to Use EJBs

Enterprise JavaBeans fall into two broad categories: session beans and entity beans. *Session beans* provide application services. A session bean is used when the server should provide a particular service to the client, such as adding two numbers or performing a database query. *Entity beans* are data objects. An entity bean represents a part of an application, such as a customer name or checking account. Developing enterprise beans involves choosing which type of bean to use. Under the EJB 1.0 specification, EJB hosts are not required to support entity beans, although some do already.

Session beans fall into two subcategories: stateless and stateful. *Stateless session beans* are really just a collection of disassociated methods. When a client interacts with a stateless bean, he may send one message to one bean and the next message to another bean, all without noticing the switch. By definition, a stateless bean has no state. *Stateful session beans* do have state. When a client creates or finds a stateful session bean, he implicitly starts a session that uses the same bean throughout. When the client finishes using the bean, he removes it, thus ending the session. While the session is open, the stateful bean may use its instance variables to store information about the ongoing interaction.

Session beans share the following characteristics:

Session beans represent application functionality. Beans do take up server resources, deployment time, and administrative resources. Don't create a different bean for every single method in an application. Use beans that group like functionalities together, such as using an ATM bean that supports withdrawals and deposits instead of a withdrawal bean and a deposit bean. That said, don't go too far in the other direction, creating beans with hundreds of methods. In many cases, 5 to 15 methods is just right. If the bean is really specific to a particular problem, you might provide fewer; it is rare that more is a good idea. In cases in which beans provide a lot of functionality, rely on frameworks and libraries underneath them to create an effective object-oriented model. Think of the bean as the interface to your model in the same way a graphical user interface sits on top of a client application.

Each bean interacts only with one client at a time. The server may use pools of beans to minimize the total number of beans created, but a bean will not be used for two clients at the same time. Stateless beans may, however, be used for several clients on a message-by-message basis. For example, client one might send executeA to a bean, then client two might send executeA before client one sends executeB. This is okay for stateless beans because they don't assume any shared data across message calls. A server can even load-balance requests to a stateless bean between multiple computers transparently to the client.

Session beans can be aware of transactions. These transactions can be propagated to the resources that an EJB accesses, such as database connections and other EJBs.

Sessions beans do not represent persistent data but can access it. If the server crashes, all of the session beans are recreated from scratch, as needed. They are not backed up. The partial exception to this rule is that stateful session beans should be serializable because the server may need to offload them to disk if the client is not currently sending messages to them, the server load is high, and the client session is still open. For example, if the client went to lunch early, the server could be busy and want to free up resources. In this case, the server will notify the bean that it is storing it temporarily. The bean will be notified again when it is reloaded to service a client message.

Session beans can be thought of as short-lived. Although a server may keep the same bean in a pool for many months, the client interaction really defines a bean's lifetime.

Entity beans also fall into two subcategories. *Container-managed entity beans* rely on their container to make them persistent. Writing container-managed beans allows the programmer to ignore persistence and the deployer to define and change persistence, without conflicts between them. *Bean-managed entity beans* are responsible for managing their own persistence. Although the bean may use JDBC to manage its state, this is up to the developer. Think of these beans as representing a row in a database. The server automatically keeps the row and object in sync. These beans are especially useful when the EJB host is a database. In this situation, the bean has direct access to its data, and the server can create beans as needed for each row in a table. At the same time, clients interact with objects, joyfully naïve to the database activities occurring on their behalf.

Some specific characteristics of entity beans:

Entity beans are transactional. Changes to their persistent state occur inside a transaction scope, unless the deployer specifically turns this off.

Entity beans can be accessed by multiple users at the same time. For example, a bean representing a customer account may be accessed by a sales person and the credit department simultaneously.

Entity beans are persistent. A bean representing an American Express customer might indicate the person has been a member since 1990 or earlier. These beans should survive server crashes transparently to the client.

Both types of beans "understand" the concept of transactions. These transactions are distributed, not local, so the client that accesses a bean can start a transaction that propagates to the JDBC connections created by the bean. Distributed transaction support is a feature of the container, and should be provided transparently to the bean developer. Chapter 23, "Using Transactions with Enterprise JavaBeans" discusses how the developer can interact with transactions and how the deployer can define the transactional behavior for a bean.

Deciding when to use Enterprise JavaBeans is really a part of the design process. Designing a distributed enterprise application requires you to break the problem into pieces that will be deployed on various computers. If you plan to install an entire application on one computer—the client—EJBs aren't really necessary. Where they become important is at the back end of a two-plus-tier application.

When defining these multitier applications, session beans should be used to offload processing from the client. The desire to move processing from the client can take a number of forms:

Improved performance. Bigger computers are often used to improve performance for a simulation or complex data analysis.

Centralized business process definition. An enterprise bean can encapsulate a business rule. Chapter 18, "Enterprise JavaBean Business Rules Engine," contains an example of how a bean can be used to authorize a check request or perform some other business decision.

Protected application implementation. Developers may want to protect some of their code by placing it on the server. This is especially true in Java, in which code can be easily decompiled if it is not obfuscated. Developers may want to hide key intellectual property from the user to protect it.

Centralized security. EJBs allow the administrator to define access to them. This access and its implementation are centralized, protecting attacks that spoof the implementation in some way.

Legacy connectivity. Many enterprise applications need to communicate with existing applications. EJBs can be used to encapsulate this connectivity so that if the legacy system is replaced, the client does not need to be updated. Also, only the EJB needs to have the software necessary to communicate with the legacy code; the clients do not.

Entity beans are really used to represent parts of an application. In situations in which an application accesses a database that supports EJB, the entity beans can be used to abstract the specifics of the database model. For example, a Customer object can be designed to provide access to its accounts. Accounts will also have a list of associated customers. For the Java programmer, it is much easier to interact with these two types of objects and their relationships as enumerations than to understand the database tables used to implement the many-to-many relationship. The entity bean, or even a session bean, also hides the database implementation from the client program. The database can change without the client being redesigned or reinstalled—an overall maintenance win.

EJB and CORBA

The EJB specification does not dictate the protocol used to communicate with a bean. One particular mechanism that the specification expects to be supported by many servers is CORBA. This support can be obtained either by running RMI over IIOP or by straight CORBA support in the EJB server, as pictured in Figure 15.6.

In order for this relationship to work, the specification states that the remote and home interfaces for EJBs can be mapped to IDL using the standard Java-to-IDL mapping. The transaction services defined in the Java Transaction frameworks are specifically designed

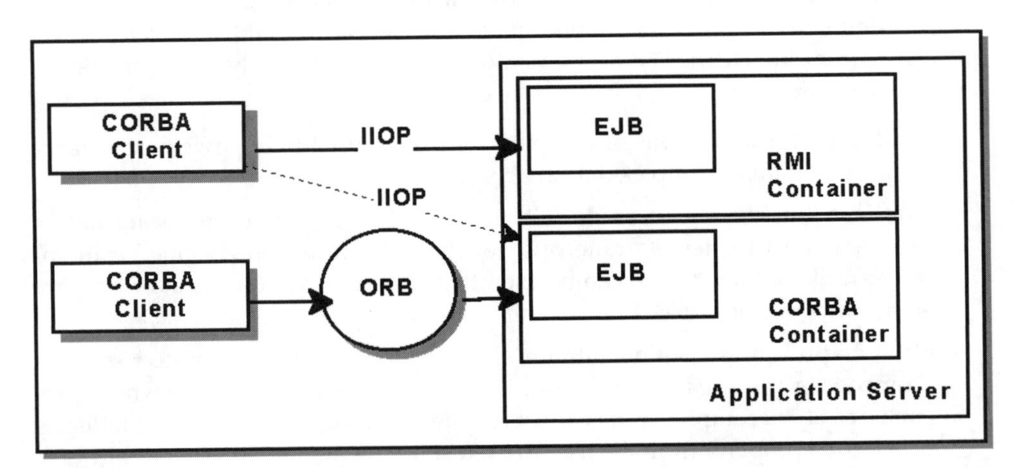

Figure 15.6 Server support for CORBA.

to work with CORBA. Finally, enterprise beans do have support for a security identity that can be associated with security properties for CORBA or any other provider.

Using CORBA in Java is a big topic and the subject of several books. Therefore, we did not try to shortchange it here. Instead, we highly suggest *Client/Server Programming with Java and CORBA, Second Edition* by Bob Orfali and Dan Harkey (John Wiley & Sons Inc., 1998). Our other motivation for keeping this discussion minimal was based on the complexity of examples using RMI and a desire not to add to that complexity. If you try to run the examples from this book, especially the larger ones, you will see that they require a lot of setup and administration. This is a by-product of the subject matter and the desire to create real-world examples. We decided that CORBA would add an unnecessary layer of complexity on top of the already potentially confusing situation.

Future Enhancements

Sun and its partners are already working on the next version of EJB as we write this book. Stay tuned to java.sun.com for updates. Also check with your server provider to see what its plans are. Keep in mind that the specification will lead the implementation by several months for most vendors. In general, EJB 2.0 should provide more features, refine the existing ones, fix any hiccups or bugs, and improve the services and portability that enterprise beans provide.

Summary

Enterprise JavaBeans are a powerful tool for designing, implementing, deploying, and managing enterprise level applications. The specification and technology have garnered rave reviews and are being adopted by numerous server vendors, from database vendors to application server vendors and transaction monitor vendors. The next chapter describes how to start programming with Enterprise JavaBeans. Other chapters in this book, including Chapters 18, "Enterprise JavaBean Business Rules Engine," and Chapter 25, "A Four-Tier Online Store," include larger examples that depend on enterprise beans for server processing and data management. Combined with servlets for supporting HTTP-style clients and JMS, Enterprise JavaBeans are perhaps the most important technology to consider when designing your applications over the next few years. By building on JNDI, JDBC, JTA, and other supporting technologies, Enterprise JavaBeans are a strong force in today's enterprise development environment.

Programming Enterprise JavaBeans

One of the main topics addressed in this book is how to create Enterprise JavaBeans. Chapter 15, "What Are Enterprise JavaBeans?" provided an introduction to this powerful standard for server programming. This chapter begins to discuss the concepts and techniques used to build Enterprise JavaBeans, often called EJBs.

However, because EJBs are an enterprise-level standard, live on a server, and support a number of services, the discussion is broken into four pieces. This chapter focuses on the programming techniques used to build a bean and the supporting objects. Chapter 17, "Deploying Enterprise JavaBeans," discusses the server-dependent process of deploying a bean to a server. That chapter discusses the BEA WebLogic application server in detail; a demo of the BEA WebLogic server is provided on the CD-ROM. Chapter 18, "Enterprise JavaBean Business Rules Engine," provides the first large example of an EJB application set. Chapter 23, "Using Transactions with Enterprise JavaBeans,"discusses the use of the new Java transactions services and their interaction with EJBs. These concepts are mentioned in this chapter but are discussed in more detail there. Chapter 25, "A Four-Tier Online Store," provides a larger example that combines Enterprise JavaBeans with servlets and several other technologies discussed in this book.

Many concepts and technologies support Enterprise JavaBeans. This chapter starts off with a long discussion of EJBs and their environment, followed by a number of specific types of EJBs and examples of each. Keep in mind that Enterprise Java Beans are used extensively in the remaining examples, so the concepts and techniques introduced here will be reused in a number of places later in this book.

WARNING You should read Chapter 17, "Deploying Enterprise JavaBeans," before trying to run the examples from this chapter off the CD-ROM.

An Enterprise JavaBean's Environment

Let's begin our discussion of programming EJBs by looking at the environment in which they live. An EJB can live in a variety of locales, including application servers and databases. However, the Enterprise JavaBean specification, as defined by Sun and its partners, is designed to create a portable, predictable environment for beans to live in. This environment is defined as a set of services and classes that the bean expects to be available to it. All of the beans' environment is set up to be 100-percent Pure Java to make sure that an EJB can be written in Java and run on all hosts.

This does not, however, mean that all EJB hosts are implemented in the same manner. Some hosts are implemented in Pure Java; others are written in C, C++, and other languages. On top of the obvious difference in programming language, EJB hosts can use a variety of techniques and technologies to provide their services. For example, IBM might use CICS to implement transactions, while BEA might use TopHat/Tuxedo. One application server might keep all of the EJBs in a single address space, while another creates processes for each bean. These implementation details are not an issue for the programmer as much as the analyst/manager who determines which host to purchase. In other words, programming Enterprise JavaBeans doesn't depend on the final deployment platform. In fact, it is reasonable that a company would write a set of EJBs for a specific problem space and sell them to different companies with different EJB hosts.

These statements are not intended to downplay the importance of choosing an EJB host. Choosing the right EJB host is a key business decision based on legacy applications, future goals, budget considerations, and other issues. However, many of these issues are driven by your current deployment environment and are too numerous to address here. Rather, this book focuses on the fundamental concept of an EJB as a Pure Java solution to enterprise development and leaves the specifics of your deployment situation to the expert: you. The beauty of the EJB specification is that it was designed for just such a separation of development and deployment decisions.

Expected Services

An Enterprise JavaBean's host is expected to provide a number of services:

State and life-cycle management. The bean's host will cooperate with the bean to manage its current state and define a life cycle for the bean.

Security. The host should provide some form of security for the bean.

Persistence. The host may need to provide a persistence mechanism for the bean's state.

Communication. The host provides the underlying communication mechanism for the bean.

Transactions. The host should implement the transaction services expected by a bean.

Let's take a look at each of these in more detail.

State and Life-Cycle Management

A bean's life cycle depends on several factors. First, beans can be used for session-oriented interactions. These beans are called *session beans* and their life cycle is based on a client session. In fact, two kinds of session beans are defined in the EJB specification. *Stateful session beans* maintain state with a particular client. *Stateless session beans* maintain state across a single interaction or method.

Second, beans can be used to represent particular entities, such as customers or accounts. These beans are called *entity beans* and can either manage their own data or rely on the host to manage their data. Not all servers in the 1.0 specification of EJB are required to implement or support entity beans. The BEA WebLogic server used in the examples in this book supports entity beans, as will all servers that meet the 2.0 specification when it is released. The specific life cycle for each type of bean is discussed in the "Creating an Enterprise JavaBean" section of this chapter.

All types of beans, except stateless session beans, maintain some kind of state. The host is expected to cooperate with the bean to maintain this state and provide information about the beans' environment and context.

Security

Security for enterprise beans is based on the JDK 1.1 security concept of an *identity*. An identity, represented by a java.security.Identity object, defines a particular person or role. The EJB's host is expected to associate an identity with the bean. This identity limits access to the bean. Normally, the bean will not need to know about its identity unless it wants to compare its identity to a specific role in order to perform a particular action. For example, a bean might allow managers to perform an action that other employees cannot. A key aspect of the EJB specification is that although the bean does have an associated identity, the determination of this identity is up to the server. It is not the bean's job to identify the client. Rather, the bean should specify its expected security configuration when it is deployed.

Java 2 updates this security model to use the concept of a Principal rather than an Identity. Expect future versions of the EJB specification to remove the Identity class appropriately.

Persistence

Both stateful session beans and entity beans require some form of persistence for their internal data. Usually, a stateful session bean relies on the host to serialize it, if necessary, for persistence, while entity beans represent data in a more permanent store, such as a database. In this case, the entity bean can either manage its own relationship with the database or rely on the host to store its data. All three of these cases are discussed further in later sections of this chapter. Perhaps the most important concept to remember at this point is that each host may provide persistence services differently. The specification says what the bean has to do, but the host can use the information provided by the bean in a number of ways.

Communication

Enterprise JavaBeans are designed to live on a server of some type and are accessed by other servers and clients. This implies some form of network communication. However, the specification does not require that a specific communication mechanism or protocol be used. In a Pure Java situation, in which the client is a Java program and the host is a Java program, it is likely that the client and server will use RMI to communicate. This communication can happen over the RMI protocol called Java Remote Method Protocol (JRMP), or it could happen over the Internet Inter-Orb Protocol, IIOP, when RMI over IIOP is supported. A host might also provide other interfaces. For example, a host could provide an OLE interface to enterprise beans, or it could provide a custom client API that uses a special protocol. The bean writer should not be affected by this implementation detail; rather, the decision of which host to choose is affected by the expected client support.

In reality, there is some effect on an EJB from the communication protocol. This effect is due to the different mechanism that each protocol supports. Currently, RMI supports more types of interactions, or at least different ones, than IIOP does. However, Sun and other companies are working to close this gap. In cases in which you are using IIOP or another non-RMI protocol, you may have to use some coding conventions to constrain your EJB to work within the communication infrastructure.

Transactions

All enterprise beans understand the fundamental concept of a transaction. Although the configuration and deployment specifics for EJBs are discussed in Chapter 17, it is important to note here that beans implicitly execute within a transaction depending on its configuration. In the simplest case, the bean developer doesn't have to do anything to take advantage of transactions, even distributed transactions across several applications. In order for these transactions to work, the EJB host implements the Java Transaction Service and links this implementation to any of the EJBs' JDBC code. In other words, the host takes control of the transaction management for a bean's JDBC connection to hide that complexity from the bean writer. Of course, you can configure a bean to completely manage its own transactions, as well as combine bean and host transaction management. For the remainder of this chapter, the default values for transaction management are used, as provided by the EJB host. In Chapter 23, the various options available to bean developers for managing transactions are discussed in more detail.

In addition to these five services, the host provider will also be expected to provide some form of deployment tools, as described in Chapter 17. These tools can range from a command-line utility for installing a bean into a server to a graphical tool that provides controls for setting all of the beans' attributes. The deployment tools and their associated features will greatly affect your choice of bean host. Hosts may also provide services beyond the standard bean specification.

Possible Services

An EJB host can provide two key services that are not part of the specification. First, the host can provide some form of pooling. This could include connection pooling and thread pooling. Second, the host can provide some form of caching. In addition to these two common extended services, a host can provide other services such as timed events and support for hosting servlets or other distributed objects.

Pooling

Pooling is the process of sharing a finite set of resources and is often employed to minimize resource usage. For example, thread pooling is usually implemented to provide a set number of threads inside the host. As requests come in to the server, they are handled by an available thread. If no thread is available, the request waits for the next available thread to handle it. By controlling the number of threads, the host can have more control over the execution state in the server.

The second kind of pooling common to EJB hosts is database *connection pooling*. In this case, several EJBs might share the same connection. As with threads, only one bean can use the connection at a time. But by pooling, the host can reduce the time needed to connect to the database and at the same time control the number of database resources being used. Because the EJB host will often control a connection for transaction purposes anyway, adding connection pooling can be transparent to the programmer. Often, connection pooling will be handled in the deployment and configuration process.

Depending on the EJB host, these pools could be shared by a particular kind of EJB or across all of the beans on a particular computer.

Caching

Caching is the process of storing information from a request for use by subsequent requests. Web browsers often cache Web pages that the user views, making it unnecessary to download the page for subsequent viewings. Caching is used to trade memory for time. A host can cache the results of database queries, for example, to minimize the time it takes to make subsequent queries. As with all caches, this technique works best with data that doesn't change often. However, given an application that operates on a large, fairly stable data set, caching can improve performance drastically.

Other Services

Another easy service for the host to provide is some form of timed events. For example, an EJB might be able to register for notification on a given interval. This would allow the bean to perform regular maintenance, like updating log files or indices.

EJB hosts may also provide hosting services for servlets and general RMI objects. This is mainly a side effect of the host provider's main goal, which is to provide a stable enterprise-programming platform that appeals to the widest range of programmers and users.

As the Enterprise JavaBeans standard works its way into a variety of hosts, providers will certainly create other services to woo customers. Be sure to look into these main services as well as others, but don't take them for granted. They may differ from host to host.

Container

Because a variety of application types can act as the host for a deployed enterprise bean, Sun decided to standardize the vocabulary for discussing the host's responsibility. The term *container* is used to refer to the environment in which an Enterprise JavaBean runs. This container can take on a number of forms based on the host. In fact, the same host might use a variety of container types to support different services. For example, the same host might provide a CORBA-based container that uses CORBA protocols and services as well as an RMI-based container that uses Java technology to provide its services.

In all cases, it is the host provider's responsibility to implement and document the container or containers they provide. The container used by a bean will probably be decided at deployment time, and the bean exists inside its container, oblivious to the implementation details that the container represents. There has been some discussion of users writing their own containers, but this is unlikely in the current specification because the host, container, and deployment tools will need to work very closely together.

One of the tasks that the container and deployment tool collaborate on is to provide any code or libraries necessary for the client to access the Enterprise JavaBean. Recall that with RMI, it was the server programmer's job to create the stub and skeleton files used to access a remote object. In an EJB situation, the deployment tool creates these files, if it uses RMI, or any other files required by the communication protocol. For example, a CORBA-based host/container should create the IDL files required by the client to access the enterprise bean.

For the bean programmer, containers represent the construct in which a bean lives. A bean lives inside its own container. The type of container associated with the bean is based on its class and is determined by the deployment process. The container is the actual entity that provides the services discussed in the previous section. For example, it is the container that manages the bean's life cycle. However, although this is the container's responsibility and the word *container* implies that it somehow holds the enterprise bean, it is up to the container writer to actually define its implementation. The container could include a separate virtual machine, a Java object, or a thread inside an existing process. Certainly, the container will include access to the appropriate libraries, like JDBC, JTS, RMI, and so on. It is up to the container/host provider to decide the container's actual implementation. This is one of the areas that you should investigate when deciding on a EJB host provider.

In all cases, the container is transparent to the client. The client will interact with the bean's EJBHome and EJBObject, as pictured in Figure 16.1, but will not need to know how the container created these objects.

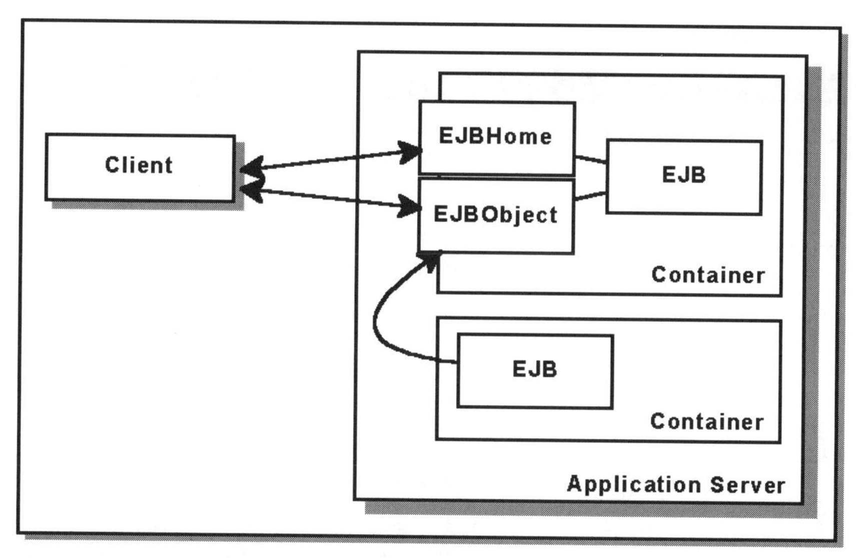

Figure 16.1 EJB architecture.

Bean Context

A bean's container provides an object called the EJB context to the bean for retrieving information from the container. This context object implements the javax.ejb.EJBContext interface, which defines a number of methods for accessing information. These methods are listed in Table 16.1. Most of these methods will seem cryptic at this point because they represent access to information that has not been used in this chapter. However, they are introduced here to give you a basic grasp of the division of work in the EJB specification.

The one method that should be clear from the beginning is the getEnvironment method. This method returns a Properties object that provides key-value pairs defined in the bean's deployment/configuration. For example, you might use these environment properties to define the database, user name, and password for your bean.

Depending on the type of bean, session, or entity, the context provided is an extended version of EJBContext. In the case of a session bean, the context implements SessionContext, which provides the method:

```
public EJBObject getEJBObject() throws IllegalStateException
```

You can use this method to access the EJBObject or distributed front end to your bean. One useful example of accessing this object is to pass your bean's id into a method or return it from a method.

Entity beans are provided a context that implements javax.ejb.EntityContext. This interface includes the getEJBObject method as well as the method:

```
public Object getPrimaryKey() throws IllegalStateException
```

Keeping in mind that entity beans represent actual data being stored somewhere, this method returns the primary key used to represent the entity bean. This primary key is

Table 16.1 EJBContext Methods

METHOD	DESCRIPTION
`public EJBHome getEJBHome()`	Returns the EJBHome object associated with this bean.
`public Properties getEnvironment()`	Returns the environment variables associated with this bean during deployment.
`public Identity getCallerIdentity()`	Returns the Identity object associated with the bean based on the user's login or other security action.
`public boolean isCallerInRole(Identity role)`	Checks whether the bean's identity is a member of a specified role. For example, is the bean being used by a Manager?
`public UserTransaction getUserTransaction() throws IllegalStateException`	Accesses the bean's transactions management infrastructure. This is discussed more in Chapter 23, "Using Transactions with Enterprise JavaBeans," after the Java transaction APIs are introduced.
`public void setRollbackOnly()`	Tells the context that this bean cannot commit its actions to any permanent store, possibly due to an unrecoverable error.
`public boolean getRollbackOnly()`	Returns true if the context will support only rollbacks. Beans might use this method to make sure that the action they are about to perform will be able to commit or determine whether it is superfluous.

managed by the EJB host, so the bean may want to access it for use in methods or as a return value.

Given this environment, context, and container that the EJB host provides, let's look at the steps to create an Enterprise JavaBean.

Creating an Enterprise JavaBean

Creating an enterprise JavaBean is a several-step process. This process is affected by the fact that EJBs are usually accessed over the network. This means that you will need to provide a small, concise interface to the bean's services. The process is also affected by the fact that the EJB specification takes into account multiple EJB host types. Finally, the EJB specification tries to make it easy for the bean developer to focus on the business logic that must be implemented rather than the infrastructure that the developer needs to rely on. In order for it to meet all of these goals, the specification uses several design patterns that separate the actual bean object from the client.

Let's take a minute to review the basic structure of a deployed bean application, as pictured in Figure 16.1. First, the client for an EJB may or may not exist in the same application as the EJB. Second, the client gains access to the EJB through an object that implements an interface called EJBHome. This object acts as a factory for the EJBs, creating them for the client and removing them when the client is done. Third, the client gains access to the EJB through a remote interface. This interface is implemented by an object that the EJB host constructs in the deployment process. Finally, the interface, or proxy, forwards messages to the EJB as appropriate. The object implementing the home interface will also work with the bean to initialize it.

It is the container's responsibility to provide the EJBHome and EJBObject for an enterprise bean. To motivate this architecture, let's look at two of the services that the EJB host might provide. First, the host might want to support pooling for the enterprise beans. For example, if the client doesn't need to interact with the same bean for every request, the server could keep a pool of beans available to all clients, reducing the total resources used. This pooling is accomplished by the home, which creates only the necessary number of beans and the proxy that gets a bean from the pool as needed. The other service that this architecture supports is the basic persistence mechanisms. The home can provide a simple interface to a bean that has to be loaded from the database or some other persistent store. All of this persistence can be implemented in the home and container, insulating the bean programmer from it. In other words, this architecture allows the bean host to implement services transparently to the EJB programmer.

Speaking of the programmer, what is his or her job? It comes down to the following steps:

1. Define the remote interface.
2. Define the home interface.
3. Define the enterprise bean.
4. Create any additional classes you need.
5. Define necessary deployment information.
6. Compile the bean.
7. Package the bean for deployment.
8. Deploy the bean.

Let's take a look at each of these in detail, keeping in mind that deployment is discussed at more length in Chapter 17.

Define the Remote Interface

This is perhaps the easiest step for the programmer, although it is a lot of work for the application designer. The remote interface is a standard Java interface that extends Remote and EJBObject. Remote is defined in java.rmi and doesn't define any methods. It is the typing mechanism used to tell the system that the object that implements our remote interface is really a potential remote object. EJBObject, on the other hand, is defined in the javax.ejb package. The methods defined in EJBObject and listed in Table 16.2 are ultimately implemented by the proxy object created by the EJB host during deployment. These methods are one layer in the host's code that implements the EJB specification. Throughout this discussion and in other enterprise JavaBean documents, the proxy object that implements the remote interface is often referred to as the EJBObject.

For example, the getHandle method returns a handle to the bean. This handle must be defined by the EJB host's deployment tools. Each handle uniquely identifies a bean, so the host might use some form of unique id or hash as part of the handle object. The handle's only method is getEJBObject, which returns the remote interface to the object specified by the handle. The implementation for these handles is really up to the host provider and is intended to be transparent to you, the bean programmer.

Your job is to define your remote interface with the methods that you need to provide to clients. For example, in the stateless example on the CD-ROM, the following one-method interface is defined as the StatelessId bean's remote interface:

```
package stateless;

import javax.ejb.*;
import java.rmi.RemoteException;
import java.rmi.Remote;

public interface StatelessId extends EJBObject, Remote
{
    public int getId() throws RemoteException;
}
```

Table 16.2 EJBObject Methods

METHOD	DESCRIPTION
`public EJBHome getEJBHome() throws RemoteException`	Returns the home object for the bean that this proxy represents.
`public Object getPrimaryKey() throws RemoteException`	Returns the primary key for this proxy's bean. This method is primarily used for entity beans
`public void remove() throws RemoteException, RemoveException`	Removes the associated bean from the server. This method may act differently in a pooling situation, but the client should think of it as destroying the bean.
`public Handle getHandle() throws RemoteException`	Returns a handle to the bean; this handle provides access back to this object and can be serialized by the client.
`public boolean isIdentical(EJBObject obj) throws RemoteException`	Tests equality between two EJBObjects. This equality is based on primary keys and handles and may say that two independent bean objects are identical.

Notice that only one application-specific method, called getId, exists and that it can throw RemoteExceptions. All of the methods in your remote interface should also be declared to throw RemoteExceptions. The EJBObject interface also uses the Remove-Exception type to indicate a special problem or situation. You can also define custom exceptions to use in your RemoteInterface.

NOTE **The possibility of RemoteExceptions is the primary lack of transparency behind Enterprise JavaBeans and all distributed computing in Java. Although this generic exception type does narrow and group the dangers of network computing into one concept, it is also unused in programs that don't rely on distributed programming techniques. In other words, you can't forget that EJBs are not part of your program because they can, and sometimes will, throw RemoteExceptions.**

The easy part of this step is writing the interface. The hard part is creating a design for your distributed applications. This can be a political and tedious process, but once you have the design, you can map it onto a Java interface, and the remote interface is then done.

Define the Home Interface

Creating the home interface for your EJB is both simple and tricky. From one perspective, all you need to do is implement an interface that extends the EJBHome interface. This interface defines three methods, as listed in Table 16.3.

However, none of these methods actually defines how to create a bean or get access to one. In order to maximize flexibility, Sun decided to use a coding convention to specify factory methods for enterprise beans. This coding convention says that the home interface for a bean should do the following:

- Provide methods named create with application-specific arguments.
- Use the remote interface as a return type for all create methods.
- Declare that each create method can throw CreateExceptions and RemoteExceptions.
- Use only argument types that are allowed by the RMI standard.

Table 16.3 EJBHome Methods

METHOD	DESCRIPTION
`public void remove(Handle handle) throws RemoteException, RemoveException`	Removes a bean from the server based on its handle.
`public void remove(Object primaryKey) throws RemoteException, RemoveException`	Removes a bean from the server based on its primary key.
`public EJBMetaData getEJBMetaData() throws RemoteException`	Returns metadata for a bean type.

Given these guidelines, you can define any number of create methods that are used by the server to instantiate enterprise beans. The create methods that you define are the ones used by clients to generate and access enterprise beans on the server. This means that you will want to think about what the client expects when deciding on the create methods to define.

In the stateless id example from above, the following home interface is defined:

```
package stateless;

import javax.ejb.*;
import java.rmi.RemoteException;
import stateless.*;

public interface StatelessIdHome extends EJBHome
{
    StatelessId create() throws CreateException, RemoteException;
}
```

In this case, only one method was needed; it didn't require any arguments. You might create other methods that take arguments such as primary keys, names, file locations, database log in information, and any other data necessary for your EJB to be created appropriately for your applications. The example below, from the CD-ROM, provides two methods for creating beans:

```
package nextprime;

import javax.ejb.*;
import java.rmi.RemoteException;
import nextprime.*;

public interface NextPrimeHome extends EJBHome
{
    NextPrime create() throws CreateException, RemoteException;
    NextPrime create(long start) throws CreateException,
RemoteException;
}
```

As demonstrated later in this chapter, you may also define a set of find methods in the home interface. These find methods are like the create methods in that they are defined by convention rather than by implementing methods from an interface. Their purpose is to make entity beans searchable. For example, a home interface for checking-account beans might provide a find method that accepts a checking-account number and returns the associated bean.

Define the Enterprise Bean

The first step in defining an enterprise bean is to define its typing information. The typing information is defined by the superclass and implemented interfaces. The EJB specification doesn't require beans to have any particular superclass. Most of the beans in the examples in this book simply extend Object. However, all enterprise JavaBeans must implement the javax.ejb.EnterpriseBean interface. This interface is used for typing and doesn't provide any methods.

Beans must also implement one of two interfaces, EntityBean or SessionBean. These interfaces actually extend EnterpriseBean, so you need to declare only that your class implements SessionBean or EntityBean; the reset is automatic. Remember that session beans are used to perform actions for a client. For example, a session bean might represent an ATM session for a bank customer. Entity beans are used to represent data of some sort. Using the same example, an entity bean might represent the customer's checking account. The details of these two interfaces are discussed in a moment. Each require the bean class to implement a number of methods.

The second step in defining the enterprise bean is to define methods that correspond to the home interface's create methods. For each create method in the home interface, the EJB must have a method named ejbCreate that contains the same arguments as the create method from the home interface. The create method should also declare any exceptions that the ejbCreate method declares. However, the ejbCreate method doesn't need to declare that it can throw remote exceptions. The return type for this ejbCreate method depends on the type of bean. For session beans, it is void; for entity beans, it is usually an object that represents the primary key.

One interesting feature of the EJB architecture is that these create methods are not really constructors, as are those that would be defined for most objects. Enterprise beans are constructed using the default constructor via the newInstance method in their class. This allows the EJB host to create a bean from a class name, without having to be recompiled to support the new bean type. However, it also means that these create methods are more like initialization methods performed by the beans themselves rather than constructors that represent special Java constructs.

The final step is to implement the methods defined in the remote interface and any other methods that the bean requires. This is the meat of the programming task, and the entire specification is designed to focus your time on this step. Although this step has been minimized in this discussion, implementing your business logic will probably represent a vastly larger task than the mechanics of meeting the EJB specification as described here.

The stateless id example actually doesn't do much. It is discussed more later, but it is used as a test tool here. Each bean gets a unique id, which the client can request from the bean. The complete code for the bean is as follows:

```
package stateless;

import javax.ejb.*;
import java.io.Serializable;
import java.util.*;

import stateless.*;

public class StatelessIdBean implements SessionBean
{
```

```
    protected SessionContext context;
    protected int id;

    protected static int nextId=0;

    public static int nextId()
    {
        return (nextId++);
    }

    public void ejbActivate()
    {
       // id = nextId();
    }

    public void ejbRemove()
    {
    }

    public void ejbPassivate()
    {
    }

    public void setSessionContext(SessionContext ctx)
    {
        context = ctx;
    }

    public void ejbCreate()
    {
        id = nextId();
    }

    public int getId()
    {
        try
        {
            Thread.sleep(1000);
        }
        catch(Exception exp)
        {
        }
        return id;
    }
}
```

In this case, because the business logic is almost nonexistent, the bean code outweighs it. You probably can guess how that could change in a real application that includes tens, hundreds, or even thousands of lines of application-specific code.

WARNING **This bean demonstrates one of the programming rules for EJBs, or at least anti-demonstrates it. Beans cannot be rely on static variables, because it is possible that each client gets a separate virtual machine. Therefore, your beans should not use this technique for storing ids; they should use entity beans or a database instead.**

In general, EJB developers should use the following programming rules:

1. Beans should not create threads or terminate running threads.
2. Beans should not use mutable static variables. All static variables for EJBs should be marked as final for safety.
3. Beans should not use thread synchronization primitives, because they may interfere with the host's thread management.
4. Unless a bean specifically indicates that it will manage transactions, the bean should not perform any transaction management.
5. Beans are assigned a security identity and should not attempt to change it.
6. Beans that rely on the container for transaction management should not manage JDBC transactions; the container will perform this operation for them.

Programming enterprise beans is designed to be easier than programming a complete server by hand. The EJB host is expected to provide many services; as a result, it is necessary to write beans more simply than some server programmers may be accustomed to. For example, the threading issues for beans is primarily handled by the server, so the bean programmer can ignore these issues, even though in a totally handwritten program, the programmer would need to take threads into consideration. The bottom line is that beans should be written with their hosts' services in mind; the programmer should not try to overimplement services that the host is already providing.

Create Any Additional Classes You Need

Often, your bean will access other beans or other code. This step is included for completeness in this discussion, but there really isn't anything to creating these classes that isn't part of writing any Java application. The one thing to keep in mind is that because enterprise beans are accessed on the network, they are subject to performance measures and stability requirements beyond most client applications. As a result, don't scrimp on the time you spend testing your supporting libraries—they are a key part of the total application.

Define Necessary Deployment Information

Beans can have a number of configuration parameters set at deployment time. Most EJB hosts will provide a tool that allows you to define this information in an easy way. The final result of collecting this information will be a serialized object that the EJB host will load. This is discussed in more detail in Chapter 17.

Compile the Bean

Compiling the bean itself is the same as compiling any other Java code. Just be sure that you have access to the javax.ejb and javax.ejb.deployment packages as well as any other packages you use in the class path on the machine on which you compile the code.

Package the Bean for Deployment

The deployment information and a manifest file are packaged into a jar file for most EJB hosts. You may also package the bean itself into a jar file, although this depends on the host and its deployment tools. Chapter 17 discusses this step in detail. You may also want to read the documentation for your EJB host to determine its specific needs.

The jar file in which the bean is deployed should contain all of the classes necessary to run the bean, including any supporting classes. Certainly, if you use the same libraries in multiple beans, the host may provide a mechanism for sharing classes.

Deploy the Bean

Deploying a bean relies on tools specific to your host. In this step, the host creates the proxies for your remote interface and home interface. The tools also read the deployment information and possibly perform some configuration based on that information. The result of this step is a version of the bean and supporting material that the EJB host can load. Depending on the host, you may also have to tell the host to load the bean. For example, on BEA WebLogic's application server, deployment creates class files and a jar file containing the deployment information. You add a pointer to the deployment jar file in a properties file, and the server loads it.

Given these general steps for creating an enterprise bean, let's look at the specific cases of creating a session bean and then an entity bean.

Creating a Session Bean

As previously mentioned, session beans are used to perform operations, whereas entity beans are used to represent data or entities. Session beans fall into two categories: stateful and stateless. Stateful beans exist in a one-to-one relationship with the client. When a client creates a stateful session bean, it gets a bean that it can use without worrying about another bean taking its place, as long as the connection with the server is kept open or a handle to the bean is maintained. Stateless beans are more of a shared resource. The client can create stateless beans, but the server is not required to create the bean immediately, nor is it required to create a stateless bean for each client. Instead, stateless beans are shared as needed and determined by the EJB host.

All of the requests to a session bean are organized into a single serial train of messages. This means that a session bean will not get two methods at the same time, nor should it get a message while it is performing a method. As a result of this message serialization, code cannot loop back to a session bean. For example, an account manager bean can call an account bean, but that account bean should not send a message to the manager as a result. At least, it should not send a message through the EJBObject. Keep in mind this key distinction. The EJB is usually accessed via the EJBObject that acts as a proxy. This access is serialized. Your library code could certainly directly access the bean, but because the EJB host is providing a number of services via the EJBObject, use it to access enterprise beans whenever possible, even if the beans are in the same application space.

In addition to the messages sent to a session bean from the client, the host notifies the session bean of various life-cycle information. This life cycle is summarized in Figure 16.2. This chapter uses a simple case in which the bean uses default transactions. Chapter 23 discusses how session beans can also receive notification of changes to their transaction state as well as the following messages. The actual timing for these events is different for stateful and stateless beans; each are discussed in detail below.

The creation of a session bean is broken into three steps. First, session beans are created using their classes newInstance method. This results in the default constructor being called.

Second, the bean is sent the message setSessionContext that tells it about its context. The argument to this method is a SessionContext object that implements the BeanContext interface discussed at the beginning of the chapter.

Third, the bean is sent one of its ejbCreate methods based on the client's request.

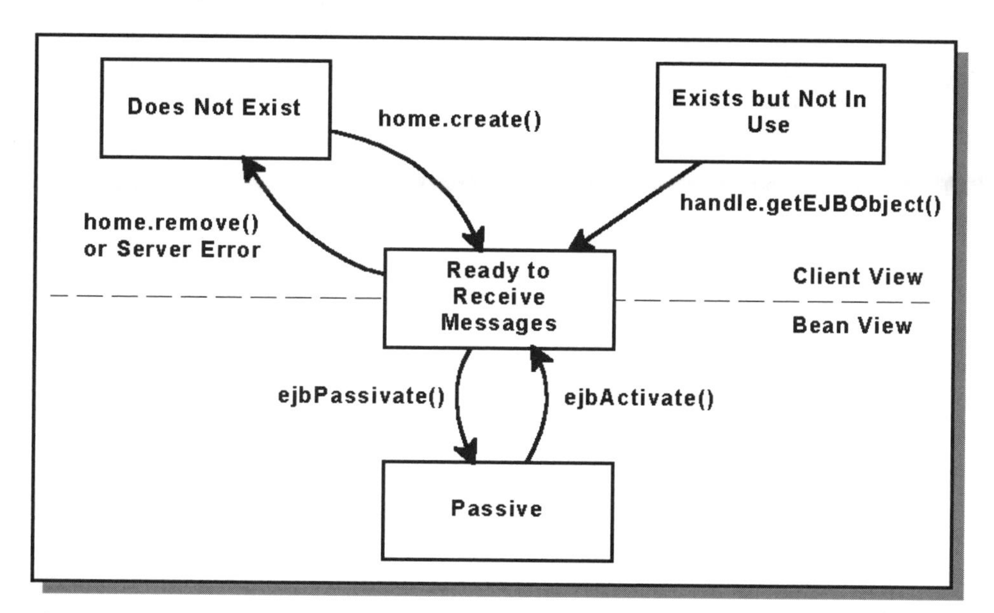

Figure 16.2 Session bean life cycle.

Table 16.4 SessionBean Methods

METHOD	DESCRIPTION
`public void setSessionContext(SessionContext ctx) throws RemoteException`	Used by the container to tell the bean about its context.
`public void ejbRemove() throws RemoteException`	Notification to the bean that it is being removed from the host.
`public void ejbActivate() throws RemoteException`	Notification to the bean that it is being taken out of storage for use by a client.
`public void ejbPassivate() throws RemoteException`	Notification to the bean that it is going into storage.

At this point, the bean is ready for client messages. If the client initiates a removal of the bean from the host, the message ejbRemove is sent to the bean. Clients should remove beans when they are done with them.

The only two other messages that the host will send are ejbActivate and ejbPassivate. These are used by the host to notify a stateful session bean that it doesn't seem to be in use, but has not been removed, so it will be put into a temporary holding area. Often, this holding area is a serialized file, but it doesn't have to be. The bean can, and should, use these notifications to clean up any nonserializable resources such as files and database connections. Because a stateless bean doesn't have any state to serialize, it will not be passivated or activated and will therefore not receive these two messages.

All of the notification messages are part of the SessionBean interface that all session beans are required to implement. These methods are listed in Table 16.4.

Let's take a look at a couple of session beans, provided on the CD-ROM. The next chapter discusses the steps required to compile and deploy these beans. If you are on Windows NT, a script that builds and deploys them on the BEA WebLogic server is provided.

An Example Stateless Session Bean

The first bean that a stateless session bean calls IsPrimeBean. This bean performs the task of checking a number to determine if it is prime or not. Remember that a prime number is only divisible by itself and 1. A really simple algorithm is used to test numbers. This algorithm is by no means the fastest, but it gets the job done. On our test computer (a 200MHz Pentium running NT), the results from this algorithm were basically instantaneous, so it should be okay for your testing as well.

Remember the steps to write a bean. First, define the remote interface. In this case, two methods are defined: one for testing integers and one for testing longs.

```
package isprime;

import javax.ejb.*;
import java.rmi.RemoteException;
import java.rmi.Remote;
```

```
public interface IsPrime extends EJBObject, Remote
{
    public boolean isPrime(long num) throws RemoteException;
    public boolean isPrime(int num) throws RemoteException;
}
```

Next, define a home interface. Because this is a stateless bean, the client should always use a create method with no arguments so the home interface is only one method. Notice that the return type is IsPrime, the remote interface. This is an important rule for all of your home interfaces.

```
package isprime;

import javax.ejb.*;
import java.rmi.RemoteException;
import isprime.*;

public interface IsPrimeHome extends EJBHome
{
    IsPrime create() throws CreateException, RemoteException;
}
```

Finally, define the session bean itself. As with most simple examples, it wasn't necessary to implement the SessionBean methods with any real code. They were implemented because the interface was implemented, but nothing is done in them. Larger examples will use these methods to perform the appropriate activation semantics.

```
package isprime;

import javax.ejb.*;
import java.io.Serializable;
import java.util.*;

import isprime.*;

public class IsPrimeBean implements SessionBean
{
    protected SessionContext context;

    public void ejbActivate()
    {
    }

    public void ejbRemove()
    {
    }

    public void ejbPassivate()
    {
    }
```

```
    public void setSessionContext(SessionContext ctx)
    {
        context = ctx;
    }

    public void ejbCreate()
    {
    }

    public boolean isPrime(long num)
    {
        long test;
        long max;
        boolean retVal = true;

        if((num==0)||(num==1)) return false;

        num = Math.abs(num);

        max = num/2 + 1;

        for(test=2;test<max;test++)
        {
            if(num%test == 0)
            {
                retVal = false;
                break;
            }
        }

        return retVal;
    }

    public boolean isPrime(int num)
    {
        return isPrime((long)num);
    }
}
```

An Example Stateful Session Bean

Along the same lines as this IsPrime bean, the second example bean returns a series of prime numbers. In this case, the bean has a starting point and calculates primes from that point on. This means that the bean has to have state between each method and is therefore a stateful session bean.

Again, start by defining the remote interface. In this case, the remote interface has methods for getting the next prime based on the last prime as well as getting the next prime after a specified number.

```
package nextprime;

import javax.ejb.*;
import java.rmi.RemoteException;
import java.rmi.Remote;

public interface NextPrime extends EJBObject, Remote
{
    public long nextPrime() throws RemoteException;
    public long nextPrimeAfter(long num) throws RemoteException;
}
```

Next, define two create methods. The first takes no arguments, and the second takes a long as an argument. Use the semantics that if this long is not a prime number, the bean will throw a CreateException. This way the client can create only beans that start with a prime number.

```
package nextprime;

import javax.ejb.*;
import java.rmi.RemoteException;
import nextprime.*;

public interface NextPrimeHome extends EJBHome
{
    NextPrime create() throws CreateException, RemoteException;
    NextPrime create(long start) throws CreateException
                                        , RemoteException;
}
```

Finally, implement the bean. Again, the bean is required to implement all of the SessionBean methods and didn't really need to do anything in all of them. Notice that the create method uses a custom exception. You could also use this exception in the nextPrime method, in which case the client would see the custom class if it caught it.

```
package nextprime;

import javax.ejb.*;
import java.io.Serializable;
import java.util.*;

import nextprime.*;

public class NextPrimeBean implements SessionBean
{
    transient protected SessionContext context;
    protected long current;

    public void ejbActivate()
    {
```

```
    }

    public void ejbRemove()
    {
    }

    public void ejbPassivate()
    {
    }

    public void setSessionContext(SessionContext ctx)
    {
        context = ctx;
    }

    public void ejbCreate()
    {
        current = 1;
    }

    public void ejbCreate(long start) throws NotPrimeException
    {
        if(!isPrime(start))
        {
            //Only except primes
            throw new NotPrimeException(start);
        }
        else
        {
            current = start;
        }
    }

    public long nextPrime()
    {
        current = nextPrimeAfter(current);
        return current;
    }

    public long nextPrimeAfter(long num)
    {
        while(!isPrime(++num)){}

        return num;
    }

    public boolean isPrime(long num)
    {
        long test;
        long max;
        boolean retVal = true;
```

```
        if((num==0)||(num==1)) return false;

        num = Math.abs(num);

        max = num/2 + 1;

        for(test=2;test<max;test++)
        {
            if(num%test == 0)
            {
                retVal = false;
                break;
            }
        }

        return retVal;
    }
}
```

Both of these examples kept track of the SessionContext when given it. This is not necessary, but it is a reasonable habit to get into because the context may be used in more complex beans.

Using a Session Bean

Because Enterprise JavaBeans are network objects, it is most likely that you will gain access to them through JNDI, as discussed in Chapter 4, "What Is JNDI?" and Chapter 5, "Using JNDI." The service provider that is used to access the bean really depends on the EJB host. For example, a host that uses RMI for communication might use the RMI registry to make EJBs available, while a host that uses CORBA might opt for the CORBA naming services. The examples in this book use WebLogic's JNDI context to gain access to the beans.

Access to a bean is in the form of the bean's home interface. A client will get the bean's home from JNDI, for example, and ask the home to create a session object. If the request is for a stateful bean, a bean will probably be created, and if not, one will be activated. In either case, an EJBObject referring to the real bean will be returned to the client. If the request is for a stateless bean, the host will note the request and create an EJBObject to return to the client, but it will probably wait for a real request before creating the bean or selecting one from the pool.

Once the client has the EJBObject, it can begin to send application-specific messages to the EJB.

The following complete example, a client for the IsPrimeBean, demonstrates how to create the initial JNDI context, access the home, create the EJBObject, and send messages to it.

```
import javax.ejb.*;
import javax.naming.*;
import java.rmi.*;
```

```
import java.util.*;
import java.io.*;

import isprime.*;

public class IsPrimeClient
{
    public static void main(String[] args)
    {
        Context ctx=null;

        try
        {
            ctx = getInitialContext(args);
            InputStreamReader readIn;
            BufferedReader bufIn;
            String testStr;
            long test;

            IsPrimeHome home =
               (IsPrimeHome) ctx.lookup("isprime.IsPrimeHome");
            IsPrime checker = home.create();

            readIn = new InputStreamReader(System.in);
            bufIn = new BufferedReader(readIn);

            do
            {
                System.out.print("Please enter a number");
                System.out.println(" or \'q\' to quit.");

                testStr = bufIn.readLine();

                try
                {
                    test = Long.parseLong(testStr);

                    if(checker.isPrime(test))
                    {
                        System.out.print(test);
                        System.out.println(" is prime.");
                    }
                    else
                    {
                        System.out.print(test);
                        System.out.println(" is not prime.");
                    }
                }
                catch(NumberFormatException exp)
                {
                    //ignore it
```

```
                }
            }
            while(!testStr.equals("q"));

            home.remove(checker.getHandle());
        }
        catch (Exception e)
        {
            System.out.println("Error.");
            e.printStackTrace();
        }
        finally
        {
            try
            {
                ctx.close();
            }
            catch(Exception exp)
            {
            }
        }
    }

    static public Context getInitialContext(String[] args)
    throws Exception
    {
        Properties p = new Properties();
        String url = "t3://localhost:7001";
        String user=null;
        String password=null;

        if ((args != null) && (args.length > 1))
        {
            for (int i = 0; i < args.length; i++)
            {
                if (args[i].equals("-url"))
                    url = args[++i];
                else if (args[i].equals("-user"))
                    user = args[++i];
                else if (args[i].equals("-password"))
                    password = args[++i];
            }
        }

        p.put(Context.INITIAL_CONTEXT_FACTORY,
                "weblogic.jndi.T3InitialContextFactory");

        p.put(Context.PROVIDER_URL, url);

        if (user != null)
        {
```

```
                p.put(Context.SECURITY_PRINCIPAL, user);

                if (password == null) password = "";

                p.put(Context.SECURITY_CREDENTIALS, password);
            }

            return new InitialContext(p);
        }
    }
```

The majority of the code in this example is used to read the command-line arguments to build the initial context and to read the command line for input from the user. The actual work of accessing the EJB is only a few lines of code, making Enterprise JavaBeans a powerful and elegant solution for enterprise computing.

This example also shows how the bean is removed from the host by getting its handle and instructing the home object to remove the bean from the server based on that handle. In the case of a stateless bean, this may have no effect on the actual bean object. The server may just keep the bean in a pool for later use by other clients or it may remove the bean. What happens depends on the host's implementation.

The client for the NextPrimeBean is similar to the IsPrimeClient. It is shown here for completeness. In the rest of this book, complete client code is not shown; the complete solutions are available on the CD-ROM but are not repeated in the text. In this case, the method includes code for getting two other command-line flags, so it is actually valuable to examine in this discussion. The important point for this client compared with the other one is that the NextPrimeBean is stateful, so the client can take advantage of the fact that the EJB remembers the last prime number between calls to nextPrime.

```
package nextprime;

import javax.ejb.*;
import javax.naming.*;
import java.rmi.*;
import java.util.*;
import java.io.*;

import nextprime.*;

public class NextPrimeClient
{
    static long start = 0;
    static int max = 10;

    public static void main(String[] args)
    {
        Context ctx=null;

        try
        {
            ctx = getInitialContext(args);
```

```
            long next;
            int i;

            NextPrimeHome home = (NextPrimeHome)
                ctx.lookup("nextprime.NextPrimeHome");
            NextPrime creator;

            if(start != 0) creator = home.create(start);
            else creator = home.create();

            System.out.println("The first "+max+" primes are:");

            for(i=0;i<max;i++)
            {
                System.out.println(creator.nextPrime());
            }

            home.remove(creator.getHandle());
        }
        catch (CreateException e)
        {
            System.out.println("Error "+e);
        }
        catch (Exception e)
        {
            System.out.println("Error.");
            e.printStackTrace();
        }
        finally
        {
            try
            {
                ctx.close();
            }
            catch(Exception exp)
            {
            }
        }
    }

    static public Context getInitialContext(String[] args) throws
Exception
    {
        Properties p = new Properties();
        String url = "t3://localhost:7001";
        String user=null;
        String password=null;

        if ((args != null) && (args.length > 1))
        {
            for (int i = 0; i < args.length; i++)
```

```
            {
                if (args[i].equals("-url"))
                    url = args[++i];
                else if (args[i].equals("-user"))
                    user = args[++i];
                else if (args[i].equals("-password"))
                    password = args[++i];
                else if (args[i].equals("-start"))
                    start = Long.parseLong(args[++i]);
                else if (args[i].equals("-max"))
                    max = Integer.parseInt(args[++i]);
            }
        }

        p.put(Context.INITIAL_CONTEXT_FACTORY,
                "weblogic.jndi.T3InitialContextFactory");

        p.put(Context.PROVIDER_URL, url);

        if (user != null)
        {
            p.put(Context.SECURITY_PRINCIPAL, user);

            if (password == null) password = "";

            p.put(Context.SECURITY_CREDENTIALS, password);
        }

        return new InitialContext(p);
    }
}
```

Both of these examples use finally blocks to clean up the context from the server. This is a safety precaution and a reasonable habit for your enterprise applications.

Clients for enterprise beans don't have to be applications. They can be servlets, as in the example from Chapter 25, other enterprise beans, or any Java program that has access to the beans server. The following example bean implements the same functionality as the preceding NextPrime bean, except this one uses an IsPrime bean to test numbers rather than implementing that code internally. Some of the code for this example is commented out to save space; the important code that links the two beans appears in boldface.

```
package partnerprime;

//imports removed to save space

public class PartnerPrimeBean implements SessionBean
{
    transient protected SessionContext context;
```

```
protected long current;
protected IsPrime isprime;

//Unused Session Bean methods removed to save space

public void setSessionContext(SessionContext ctx)
{
    Context jndi;
    IsPrimeHome home;

    context = ctx;

    try
    {
        jndi = getInitialContext();
        home = (IsPrimeHome) jndi.lookup("isprime.IsPrimeHome");

        isprime = home.create();
    }
    catch(Exception exp)
    {
        isprime = null;
    }
}

public void ejbCreate()
{
    current = 1;
}

public void ejbCreate(long start) throws NotPrimeException
{
    if(!isPrime(start))
    {
        //Only except primes
        throw new NotPrimeException(start);
    }
    else
    {
        current = start;
    }
}

public long nextPrime()
{
    current = nextPrimeAfter(current);
    return current;
}

public long nextPrimeAfter(long num)
```

```
{
    while((isprime != null) && !isPrime(++num)){}

    return num;
}

public boolean isPrime(long num)
{
    boolean retVal = false;

    try
    {
        if(isprime != null) retVal = isprime.isPrime(num);
    }
    catch(Exception exp)
    {
        retVal = false;
    }

    return retVal;
}

public Context getInitialContext() throws Exception
{
    Properties p = new Properties();
    String url = "t3://localhost:7001";
    String user=null;
    String password=null;
    Properties environ;

    if(context != null)
    {
        environ = context.getEnvironment();
        url = environ.getProperty("jndiurl");
        user = environ.getProperty("jndiuser");
        password = environ.getProperty("jndipassword");
    }

    p.put(Context.INITIAL_CONTEXT_FACTORY,
            "weblogic.jndi.T3InitialContextFactory");

    p.put(Context.PROVIDER_URL, url);

    if (user != null)
    {
        p.put(Context.SECURITY_PRINCIPAL, user);

        if (password == null) password = "";

        p.put(Context.SECURITY_CREDENTIALS, password);
    }
```

```
            return new InitialContext(p);
        }
    }
```

Notice that the bean uses its environment to create an initial JNDI context for finding the EJBHome of the IsPrime bean.

Other Session Bean Examples

Leveraging the DebugLog object from Chapter 7, "Programming Servlets," the following example creates a pair of session beans, one stateless and one stateful, that log messages when they receive their life-cycle notifications. A single client that uses both beans is included in this example to activate the beans' life cycles. This is an interesting experiment because it shows the different treatment for each type of bean.

The code for the two beans is analogous, so let's just look at the stateless version. First, the remote interface:

```
package statelesssessionprint;

import javax.ejb.*;
import java.rmi.RemoteException;
import java.rmi.Remote;

public interface StatelessSessionPrint extends EJBObject, Remote
{
    public void log(String str) throws RemoteException;
}
```

When the bean receives the log message, it forwards it to the debug log object.

The home interface uses the simplest create method:

```
package statelesssessionprint;

import javax.ejb.*;
import java.rmi.RemoteException;
import sessionprint.*;

public interface StatelessSessionPrintHome extends EJBHome
{
    StatelessSessionPrint create()
        throws CreateException, RemoteException;
}
```

The actual bean code shows two things. First, notice that each life-cycle message has an associated string printed to the log. Second, the environment properties are used to get the name of the log file or log server. The complete contents of the environment are logged when the context is set. The value of this environment is determined during deployment. In this case, one computer is set up as a log server, and the other computer logs to that server. You could change the deployment information to log to a file or localhost instead.

```
package statelesssessionprint;

import javax.ejb.*;
import java.io.*;
import java.util.*;

import sessionprint.*;

public class StatelessSessionPrintBean implements SessionBean
{
    protected SessionContext context;
    protected DebugLog logger;

    public void ejbActivate()
    {
        logger.log("Stateless- Activating");
    }

    public void ejbRemove()
    {
        logger.log("Stateless- Removing");
    }

    public void ejbPassivate()
    {
        logger.log("Stateless- Passivating");
    }

    public void setSessionContext(SessionContext ctx)
    {
        String logFile=null,logServer=null;
        Properties environ;

        context = ctx;
        environ = context.getEnvironment();

        logger = new DebugLog();

        if(environ != null)
        {
            logFile = environ.getProperty("logfile");
            logServer = environ.getProperty("logserver");
        }

        if(logServer != null)
        {
            logger.logTo(logServer);
```

```
            }
            else if(logFile != null)
            {
                logger.logTo(new File(logFile));
            }

            logger.log("Stateless- Set Context");

            if(environ != null)
            {
                Enumeration names = environ.propertyNames();
                String key,value;

                while(names.hasMoreElements())
                {
                    key = (String)names.nextElement();
                    value = environ.getProperty(key);

                    logger.log("Stateless- "+key+"="+value);
                }
            }
        }

        public void ejbCreate()
        {
            logger.log("Stateless- Creating");
        }

        public void log(String str)
        {
            logger.log("Stateless- "+str);
        }
    }
```

The client for the two beans—this one and the StatefulSessionPrintBean on the CD-ROM—creates one instance of each bean and allows the user to log messages to both beans. The results of running this client, as viewed by the log server, should look something like those pictured in Figure 16.3. If viewed in real time, the connection messages for the stateful bean are printed when the client is launched. The connection messages for the stateless bean are printed when the first message is sent, indicating that the server waits until the stateless bean is needed to create it.

Keep in mind that different EJB hosts may treat stateless beans differently, so this is just one possible example. However, it does show the interesting possibility that a stateless bean is not created until its first real message.

All the code for SessionPrintClient is included in a single main method. This method accesses, then creates, one each of the session printing beans before accepting user input. Each string entered by the user is sent to both beans. When the user enters the string q, the beans are removed and the program exits.

Figure 16.3 SessionPrint LogServer output.

```
package sessionprintclient;

import javax.ejb.*;
import javax.naming.*;
import java.rmi.*;
import java.util.*;
import java.io.*;

import statelesssessionprint.*;
import statefulsessionprint.*;

public class SessionPrintClient
{
    public static void main(String[] args)
    {
        Context ctx=null;
        InputStreamReader readIn;
        BufferedReader bufIn;
        String str;

        try
        {
            ctx = getInitialContext(args);

            StatelessSessionPrintHome lesshome =
            (StatelessSessionPrintHome)
                            ctx.lookup("statelesssessionprint"
```

```
                                +".StatelessSessionPrintHome");
            StatelessSessionPrint lesslogger = lesshome.create();

            StatefulSessionPrintHome fulhome =
            (StatefulSessionPrintHome)
                            ctx.lookup("statefulsessionprint"
                                +".StatefulSessionPrintHome");
            StatefulSessionPrint fullogger = fulhome.create();

            readIn = new InputStreamReader(System.in);
            bufIn = new BufferedReader(readIn);

            do
            {
                System.out.print("Please enter a phrase to log");
                System.out.println(" or \'q\' to quit.");

                str = bufIn.readLine();

                lesslogger.log(str);
                fullogger.log(str);
            }
            while(!str.equals("q"));

            lesshome.remove(lesslogger.getHandle());
            fulhome.remove(fullogger.getHandle());
        }
        catch (Exception e)
        {
            System.out.println("Error.");
            e.printStackTrace();
        }
        finally
        {
            try
            {
                ctx.close();
            }
            catch(Exception exp)
            {
            }
        }
    }

    static public Context getInitialContext(String[] args) throws
Exception
    {
        //Removed to save space
    }
}
```

To save space, the getInitialContext method for this client doesn't appear here. It is available on the CD-ROM and is equivalent to the implementation from the IsPrime-Client and others earlier in the chapter.

A stateful version of the session id bean that was discussed previously is also included on the CD-ROM. This pair of beans is useful for investigating the difference between statefulness and statelessness. If you run several clients for each bean, you will see that the stateful beans' clients always "talk" to the same bean, while the stateless beans' clients often "wander" between various beans in the pool.

Programming Rules for Session Beans

Based on the specification, the following rules indicate the guidelines you should follow when creating session beans:

1. Session beans must implement the javax.ejb.SessionBean interface.
2. Session beans must not be abstract.
3. Session beans must implement all of the necessary ejbCreate methods described in their home interfaces. These methods must be public, and the return type must be void.
4. Session beans must implement their remote interfaces, including any Exception throws declarations. These methods must be public.
5. The home interface for a session bean must define a create method that takes RMI-safe arguments and uses the remote interface for their return type. Stateless beans should only have a create method with no arguments. Stateful beans must have at least one create method. All create methods can throw CreateException and RemoteException.
6. The home interface must extend EJBHome.
7. Remote methods must be declared to throw RemoteException.
8. The remote interface must extend EJBObject.
9. Clients should remove beans when they are done with them.

Certainly, you should also follow standard programming conventions, but these guidelines summarize some of the specific issues surrounding session beans.

Container Responsibilities

The container for a session bean has a number of responsibilities:

- The container provider should also provide tools to create the classes that implement the remote and home interfaces. These classes should forward methods appropriately, that is, create messages to the home object, which should initiate ejbCreate messages to the bean.

- The code generated by the container should allow only one client to talk to a session bean at a time.
- A serializable handle must be provided.

In general, these requirements are met by the EJB host's deployment tools, although they may be part of another tool as well.

Pros and Cons

So why are there two kinds of session beans? Certainly, as seen from the example, there is a need for stateful beans, but why does the specification define stateless beans? To answer this question, let's look at the pros and cons of each type of session bean.

Stateful beans will save state for a client. This allows the client to create a relationship with the bean and expect the bean to remember changes made by earlier messages. However, because stateful beans save information, they must be created for each client, which takes up system resources. Stateless beans don't use a lot of resources because they are associated with a client only on a message basis. This means that a client may talk to several different beans throughout its relationship with the server and cannot rely on a particular method to know what has happened previously. These pros and cons are summarized in Table 16.5.

Next, let's create some entity beans.

Creating an Entity Bean

Entity beans are part of the EJB 1.0 specification, but they are not required for 1.0 hosts. According to Sun, entity beans will be required in the 2.0 specification. The BEA WebLogic server was chosen for the examples because it already implements entity beans, allowing us to show working examples here.

An entity bean represents an actual business entity. For example, an entity might represent a client's shopping cart or a check request. Regardless of their purpose, all

Table 16.5 Pros/Cons of Session Bean Types

	PROS	CONS
Stateful	Clients can rely on a single point of contact on the server. The server manages persistence for long-running sessions.	The server has to create one bean per client.
Stateless	The server can optimize resources by minimizing the number of beans and sharing them. The server doesn't have to worry about persistence.	Clients may see several beans in one session. The client's remove message may not result in a bean really being removed (which is potentially confusing).

entity beans share a common property: They are persistent. When we say they are persistent, we mean that the data represented by the bean will persist, even if the bean is not currently in the server's memory.

Persistence can be implemented in numerous ways. For example, you can use a relational database or object serialization. However, you are not limited to just these two examples.

To maximize flexibility, the EJB specification defines two types of persistent beans: those that manage their own data and those that rely on the container to manage their data. Because entity beans are not required for 1.0 hosts, you may find some providers that support only one type of persistence. Ultimately, everyone should provide both.

Container persistence is an interesting concept. Basically, you tell the container how to map your objects onto a persistent store. This store depends on the EJB host. For example, BEA WebLogic supports JDBC mappings as well as object serialization. BEA WebLogic has also said that it will soon support custom container-managed persistence. A database vendor that supports enterprise beans might provide optimized mapping to the database for container-managed entity beans.

NOTE **Beans that use one type of persistence may not be able to make use of other persistence mechanisms. In particular, the current version of BEA WebLogic's server does not allow beans using file-based container managed persistence to access JDBC databases, because of the different transaction semantics between these storage devices. Future releases should ease this limitation. Be sure to read the documentation on your specific host to determine its support for container-managed beans.**

Beans that manage their persistence themselves rely on the container to notify them that it is time to save or time to reload data. At that point, the bean must get the data or store it. For example, the bean might execute JDBC commands or serialize its data to a file. The key difference is that the bean manages the specifics of the process, not the container.

All entity beans, regardless of their persistence mechanism, are required to implement the EntityBean interface. The EntityBean interface is similar to the SessionBean interface but adds a few new methods and semantics. All of these methods are listed in Table 16.6.

From these methods, it becomes clear that the main difference between entity and session beans is that the entity bean manages data that must be synchronized with an underlying store and that the bean is perhaps longer lasting, so it needs to be notified when it is no longer in use. Because an entity bean may be in memory for an extended period of time, the load and save methods may be called more than once on the same bean. This could represent triggers going off in a database, telling the container to update the bean because the underlying data has changed.

Another difference that isn't clear from these methods is that entity beans are intended to uniquely, or almost uniquely, represent a specific item. This means that if multiple clients are accessing the same checking account, they will probably be accessing the same checking-account entity bean. In other words, the bean may be accessed from multiple clients. However, the EJB host should allow you to force the bean to be accessed by one client at a time during deployment.

Table 16.6 EntityBean Methods

METHOD	DESCRIPTION
`public void setEntityContext(EntityContext ctx) throws RemoteException`	Used by the container to tell the bean about its context.
`public void unsetEntityContext() throws RemoteException`	Tells the bean that it is no longer part of this context; this is the last message sent to the bean before the container forgets about it and it is garbage collected.
`public void ejbRemove() throws RemoteException`	Notification to the bean that it is being removed from the host.
`public void ejbLoad() throws RemoteException`	Tells the bean to synchronize with its data store by loading the store data into the bean. (Not used by container-managed beans.)
`public void ejbStore() throws RemoteException`	Tells the bean to synchronize with its data store by loading the bean data into the store. (Not used by container-managed beans.)
`public void ejbActivate() throws RemoteException`	Notification to the bean that it is being associated with an EJBObject for use by a client.
`public void ejbPassivate() throws RemoteException`	Notification to the bean that it will no longer be associated with an EJBObject.

In order to approach uniqueness for entity beans and thereby save space on the server, it is necessary to do two things. First, beans must be identifiable. Second, beans must be findable. To make entity beans identifiable, they have a primary key. To make them findable, the EJB specification adds a pattern, like the create methods, that creates find methods.

The primary key for an entity bean is represented by an object. For container-managed beans, this should be (and may be required to be) a class that defines an instance variable that holds the primary key. The bean should also have an instance variable with the same name that holds the primary key. When an entity bean is created, a primary key is also created and associated with it. This key can be used to determine whether two beans are identical. The primary key should also be serializable. In the next example, the following class is used to represent the primary key:

```
package containercart;

public class CartPK implements java.io.Serializable
{
  public String cartName;
}
```

Depending on your EJB host, you may be able to use non-custom classes for primary keys. Some hosts may require the use of a custom primary key class. In practice, you should always create a custom primary key class just in case it is required by the host.

Given a primary key object, a client can find the associated bean by using the entities home's findByPrimaryKey method. This is a new method that is not available to session beans. It searches the server's memory and checks the persistent store for the associated entity bean. The argument to findByPrimaryKey is the primary key object. All entity beans' home interfaces are required to define this method. For container-managed beans, the container may automatically generate the code. For bean-managed persistence, you will need to implement ejbFindByPrimaryKey in the bean class.

You can also define other find methods in your home interface. These correspond to ejbFind methods in the entity bean. For example, if you define a method findByName in the home interface, the bean should define ejbFindByName with the same arguments. Finding is like performing a select on the database, except that the data store doesn't have to be an SQL database. Every find method should return a primary key or an enumeration of primary keys.

This possibility of being found gives entity beans a different life cycle from session beans. Figure 16.4 shows what an entity bean's life cycle looks like and how it differs from the life cycle of a session bean.

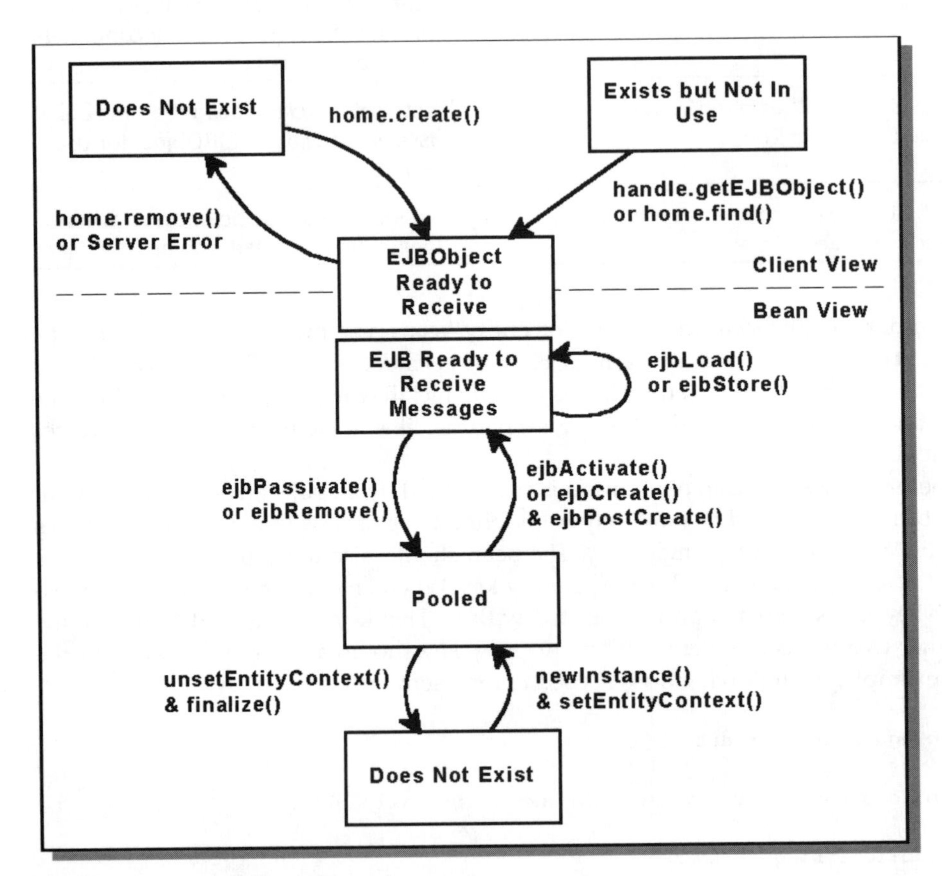

Figure 16.4 Entity bean life cycle.

One of the hardest concepts to come to grips with from this model is that you essentially ask a bean to find itself. For example, the EJB host might create an account bean and ask it to find account #111. The bean would then either turn into the bean for account #111 or, through a FindException, tell the server that the requested primary key is unavailable.

Entity beans can also have create methods. In this case, the bean can provide multiple ejbCreate methods with various arguments. In the case of a bean stored in the database, a create is like an insert. Unlike session beans, an entity bean's home interface doesn't have to have these create methods. If no create methods are provided, no new entities can be created. The entity bean's version of create is also different from the session bean's in that it should return a primary key for the bean. The session bean just returns void from the same method.

After an entity bean is sent ejbCreate, it is sent the method ejbPostCreate with the same arguments. This means that the bean must implement two methods for every create method defined in the home interface. This post-create method is provided because of the underlying store. When a bean gets create, it returns a primary key, but it doesn't have access to the EJBObject that represents it. PostCreate has access to the EJBObject, so the entity bean can send a reference to itself as part of a message.

Removing an entity bean removes it from the underlying store.

Example of Container Persistence

Let's take a look at a bean that uses container-managed persistence. This example uses a simple shopping cart. This bean stores a list of items in a cart. The client can add items or get a list of available items. Our primary key is a name stored in a CartPK object. The definition for CartPK follows.

```
package containercart;


public class CartPK implements java.io.Serializable
{
  public String cartName;
}
```

The remote interface to the cart contains two methods. An array is used to return the current items in the cart. The Vector classes Enumeration will not serialize, so that technique could not be used. An array is the best alternative for providing a read-only version of the list.

```
package containercart;

import javax.ejb.*;
import java.rmi.RemoteException;
import java.rmi.Remote;
import java.util.*;

public interface ShoppingCart extends EJBObject, Remote
```

```
{
    public void addItem(String item) throws RemoteException;
    public Object[] getItems() throws RemoteException;
}
```

The home interface is different from the ones for session beans because of the find method. The create method in the home interface returns the same thing that it would for a session bean, but this is not the case for the corresponding ejbCreate method in the bean class. Where session beans return null from create methods, entity beans must return their primary key objects.

```
package containercart;

import javax.ejb.*;
import java.rmi.RemoteException;
import containercart.*;

public interface ShoppingCartHome extends EJBHome
{
    ShoppingCart create(String name) throws CreateException,
                                            RemoteException;

    ShoppingCart findByPrimaryKey(CartPK key)
         throws RemoteException,FinderException;
}
```

This entity bean demonstrates several interesting concepts. First, the create method initializes the bean and creates a primary key for it. Second, a method called isModified indicates when the bean has changed. This method is used by the WebLogic container to check whether a bean really needs to be saved before saving it. Third, the bean doesn't have a find method because the container is providing it. When a bean that manages its own persistence is created, the find method should be implemented as part of the bean. An example of a find method implementation is included in the next example.

Because the container is managing the persistence, the fields in this bean are marked as public to give the container access to them.

```
package containercart;

import javax.ejb.*;
import java.io.Serializable;
import java.util.*;

import containercart.*;

public class ShoppingCartBean implements EntityBean
{
    transient protected EntityContext context;
    transient boolean isModified;
```

```
public Vector items;
public String cartName;

public void ejbActivate()
{
}

public void ejbRemove()
{
}

public void ejbPassivate()
{
}

public void ejbLoad()
{
    //container managed
}

public void ejbStore()
{
    //container managed
}

public void setEntityContext(EntityContext ctx)
{
    context = ctx;
}

public void unsetEntityContext()
{
    context = null;
}

public CartPK ejbCreate(String nm)
{
    CartPK pk = new CartPK();
    pk.cartName = nm;

    cartName = nm;
    return pk;
}

public void ejbPostCreate(String nm)
{
}

public boolean isModified()
{
```

```
        return isModified;
    }

    public void addItem(String item)
    {
        if(items == null)
            items = new Vector();

        isModified = true;
        items.addElement(item);
    }

    public Object[] getItems()
    {
        if(items == null)
            items = new Vector();

        Object[] retVal = new Object[items.size()];
        items.copyInto(retVal);

        return retVal;
    }
}
```

Next, let's look at the same bean, but with bean-managed persistence.

Example of Bean-Managed Persistence

The shopping cart bean is implemented using bean-managed persistence by serializing the list of items to a file named after the cart. This makes the find process as simple as looking for a file with the specified name. If the file is not found, a FindException is thrown. Loading the bean requires reading the items list from file, and saving is accomplished by writing it to file. Because everything is file based, the response to a remove request is to remove the file.

```
package beancart;

import javax.ejb.*;
import java.io.*;
import java.util.*;
import java.rmi.*;

import beancart.*;

public class ShoppingCartBean implements EntityBean
{
    transient protected EntityContext context;
    transient boolean isModified;
    public Vector items;
```

```
    public String cartName;

    public void ejbActivate()
    {
    }
```

The remove method checks whether the given cart name is associated with a file and, if so, the file is removed.

```
    public void ejbRemove() throws RemoteException
    {
        try
        {
            File file = fileForCartName(cartName);

            if((file != null)&&(cartName != null))
            {
                if(file.exists())
                {
                    file.delete();
                }
            }
        }
        catch(Exception exp)
        {
            items = null;
            throw new RemoteException("File doesn't exist.");
        }
    }

    public void ejbPassivate()
    {
    }
```

The bean is loaded by finding the appropriate file and, if it exists, reading the items Vector from the file. If the file is not available, a new Vector is created.

```
    public void ejbLoad() throws RemoteException
    {
        try
        {
            File file = fileForCartName(cartName);

            if((file != null)&&(cartName != null))
            {
                if(file.exists())
                {
                    FileInputStream fileIn;
                    ObjectInputStream objIn;

                    fileIn = new FileInputStream(file);
```

```
                    objIn = new ObjectInputStream(fileIn);

                    try
                    {
                        items = (Vector) objIn.readObject();
                    }
                    finally
                    {
                        objIn.close();
                    }
                }
                else if(items == null)
                {
                    items = new Vector();
                }
            }
        }
        catch(Exception exp)
        {
            items = null;
            throw new RemoteException("Unable to load.");
        }
    }
```

The bean is stored only if it is modified to improve performance. Storing is a process of getting the correct file name and serializing the item's Vector to the file.

```
    public void ejbStore() throws RemoteException
    {
        if(!isModified()) return;

        try
        {
            File file = fileForCartName(cartName);

            if((file != null)&&(cartName != null))
            {
                if(file.exists())
                {
                    FileOutputStream fileOut;
                    ObjectOutputStream objOut;

                    fileOut = new FileOutputStream(file);
                    objOut = new ObjectOutputStream(fileOut);

                    try
                    {
                        objOut.writeObject(items);
                    }
                    finally
```

```
                    {
                        objOut.close();
                    }
                }
            }
        }
        catch(Exception exp)
        {
            throw new RemoteException("Unable to store.");
        }
    }
```

For simplicity, the bean keeps track of its context in case it needs to use it in another method.

```
    public void setEntityContext(EntityContext ctx)
    {
        context = ctx;
    }

    public void unsetEntityContext()
    {
        context = null;
    }
```

All entity beans should return an instance of their primary keys from their create methods. The cart bean both returns this key and initializes its instance variables when created.

```
    public CartPK ejbCreate(String nm) throws CreateException
    {
        CartPK pk = new CartPK();
        pk.cartName = nm;

        items = new Vector();
        cartName = nm;
        return pk;
    }

    public void ejbPostCreate(String nm)
    {
    }
```

To find a bean by primary key, the cart first checks the key's cartName and associates it with a file. If the file is unavailable, the bean throws a FinderException to indicate that the request failed. If the file exists, the bean initializes its instance variables to the specified cart name and waits to have the load method called to initialize the contents.

```
    public CartPK ejbFindByPrimaryKey(CartPK pk)
        throws FinderException
    {
```

```
        File file = null;
        String ctName = null;
        CartPK retVal = null;

        if(pk != null) ctName = pk.cartName;

        if(ctName != null) file = fileForCartName(ctName);

        if((file != null)
            &&(ctName != null)
            &&(file.exists()))
        {
            retVal = pk;
            cartName = ctName;
        }
        else
        {
            throw new FinderException("Couldn't locate bean.");
        }

        return retVal;
    }
```

The isModified method is used to check whether the bean's data has changed.

```
    public boolean isModified()
    {
        return isModified;
    }
```

This bean provides methods for adding items to the cart and getting the items in the cart:

```
    public void addItem(String item)
    {
        isModified = true;
        items.addElement(item);
    }

    public Object[] getItems()
    {
        Object[] retVal = new Object[items.size()];
        items.copyInto(retVal);

        return retVal;
    }
```

The following example hard codes the location for cart files. All carts are stored in a file in the temp directory based on their cart name.

```
    protected File fileForCartName(String nm)
    {
        return new File("c:\\temp\\"+nm+".ser");
    }
}
```

This shopping cart bean has a pretty simple implementation for findByPrimaryKey. In general, the implementation for this method should perform the following steps:

1. Try to locate a bean with the specified key.
2. If the bean exists, return the primary key for it.
3. If the bean does not exist, throw a FinderException.

When a database is used for persistence, the first step is accomplished by querying the database. Other persistence mechanisms require their own techniques for testing whether a bean exists by primary key.

Using an Entity Bean

Clients should think of entity beans as persistent objects on the server. Depending on the available create and find methods, you may treat these persistent objects differently, but you should not treat them like session beans that you create and remove all the time.

The client created to test this shopping cart bean allows the user to enter a name for the cart and then add items. When the user quits the program, the list of items is printed. Again, the getInitialContext method has been left out because it is the same as the ones used in previous examples.

```
package containercart;

import javax.ejb.*;
import javax.naming.*;
import java.rmi.*;
import java.util.*;
import java.io.*;

import containercart.*;

public class ShoppingCartClient
{
    public static void main(String[] args)
    {
        Context ctx=null;

        try
        {
            ctx = getInitialContext(args);

            InputStreamReader readIn;
```

```
BufferedReader bufIn;
String testStr;
Object[] items;
ShoppingCartHome home = (ShoppingCartHome)
     ctx.lookup("containercart.ShoppingCartHome");
ShoppingCart cart=null;
CartPK pk;

readIn = new InputStreamReader(System.in);
bufIn = new BufferedReader(readIn);

System.out.print("Please enter a name");
System.out.println(" or \'q\' to quit.");

testStr = bufIn.readLine();

if(!testStr.equals("q"))
{
    pk = new CartPK();
    pk.cartName = testStr;

    try
    {
        cart = home.findByPrimaryKey(pk);
    }
    catch(Exception exp)
    {
        cart = home.create(testStr);
    }
}

while(cart != null)
{
    System.out.print("Please enter an item");
    System.out.println(" or \'q\' to quit.");

    testStr = bufIn.readLine();

    if(testStr.equals("q")) break;

    cart.addItem(testStr);
}

if(cart != null)
{
    items = cart.getItems();

    System.out.println("The items in the cart are:");

    int i,max;
    max = items.length;
```

```
                    for(i=0;i<max;i++)
                    {
                        System.out.println(items[i]);
                    }
                }
            }
            catch (Exception e)
            {
                System.out.println("Error.");
                e.printStackTrace();
            }
            finally
            {
                try
                {
                    ctx.close();
                }
                catch(Exception exp)
                {
                }
            }
        }

        static public Context getInitialContext(String[] args)
          throws Exception
        {
            ...
        }
    }
```

One interesting technique used in this example is that a bean is created if it is not found. Therefore, the first try is to find a bean with the given name, and if that fails, create a new one.

Entity Bean Programming Rules

Based on the specification, the following rules indicate the guidelines you should follow when creating session beans:

1. Entity beans must implement the javax.ejb.EntityBean interface.
2. Entity beans must not be abstract.
3. Entity beans must define a custom primary key class.
4. The entity bean should have an instance variable for the primary key with the same name as the variable in the primary key class that stores the same key.
5. Container-managed fields should be public.
6. Entity beans must implement all of the necessary ejbCreate methods described in their home interfaces. These methods must be public, and the return type

must be the primary key type. However, an entity bean does not have to have any create methods.

7. Entity beans must implement all of the necessary ejbPostCreate methods described in their home interfaces. These methods must be public, and the return type must be void. However, an entity bean does not have to have any create methods.
8. Entity beans must implement all of the necessary ejbFind methods described in their home interfaces. These methods must be public, and the return type must be the primary key. However, an entity bean might be able to rely on the container for these methods.
9. Entity beans must implement their remote interfaces, including any Exception throws declarations. These methods must be public.
10. The home interface for an entity bean must define create methods that take RMI-safe arguments and use the remote interface for their return type.
11. The home interface must define findByPrimaryKey and can define other find methods. These methods must start with find and can throw FinderExceptions.
12. All find methods must return a primary key or an enumeration of primary keys.
13. The home interface must extend EJBHome.
14. Remote methods must be declared to throw RemoteException.
15. The remote interface must extend EJBObject.

Again, this is not a complete list of every convention in Java programming. It is a list of the guidelines based on the EJB specification and represents a standard set of rules to use in addition to your normal Java programming conventions.

Container Responsibilities

The container for a session bean has a number of responsibilities::

- The container provider should also provide tools to create the classes that implement the remote and home interfaces. These classes should forward methods appropriately, that is, create messages to the home object that should initiate ejbCreate messages to the bean. These methods should also manage any container-managed fields.
- A serializable handle must be provided.

In general, these requirements are met by the EJB host's deployment tools, although they may be part of another tool as well.

Pros and Cons

Why are there two kinds of entity beans? To answer this question, let's look at the pros and cons of each type of entity bean. Container-managed persistence is easier to code, because you don't have to code anything. However, the EJB host imposes limits on

Table 16.7 Pros/Cons of Bean- and Container-Managed Entity Beans

	PROS	CONS
Bean managed	Bean can optimize resource usage. Arbitrary find methods.	May have to port bean if you change platforms. Requires more code.
Container managed	Less code in the bean. Container may allow you to change the persistence without recompiling. Can change containers without recompiling.	Less control over persistence. May not support all find methods.

container management, so you may not be able to do everything that you need to do with this mechanism. Bean-managed persistence requires that the programmer implement persistence code. This code may have to be ported between hosts, but the bean can be much more flexible than a container-managed bean can be. These issues are summarized in Table 16.7.

Metadata, Handles, and Exceptions

One of the mechanisms provided in the EJB specification for tools vendors is the ability to get some metadata from beans. This EJBMetaData actually comes from the bean's home and includes the home interface class, the remote interface class, the primary key, and whether or not the bean is a session bean.

The following example prints the metadata from the IsPrime example:

```
package metaclient;

import javax.ejb.*;
import javax.naming.*;
import java.rmi.*;
import java.util.*;
import java.io.*;

import isprime.*;

public class MetaClient
{
    public static void main(String[] args)
    {
        Context ctx=null;

        try
        {
```

```
            ctx = getInitialContext(args);

            IsPrimeHome home = (IsPrimeHome)
                        ctx.lookup("isprime.IsPrimeHome");
            IsPrime bean = home.create();
            EJBMetaData data = home.getEJBMetaData();

            System.out.println("HomeInterfaceClass: "
                    +data.getHomeInterfaceClass().getName());

            System.out.println("RemoteInterfaceClass: "
                    +data.getRemoteInterfaceClass().getName());

            System.out.println("Session Bean: "
                            +(data.isSession()?"true":"false"));

            if(bean.getPrimaryKey() != null)
            {
                System.out.println("PrimaryKeyClass: "
                        +data.getPrimaryKeyClass().getName());
            }

            home.remove(bean.getHandle());
        }
        catch (Exception e)
        {
            System.out.println("Error.");
            e.printStackTrace();
        }
        finally
        {
            try
            {
                ctx.close();
            }
            catch(Exception exp)
            {
            }
        }
    }

    static public Context getInitialContext(String[] args)
     throws Exception
    {
        //commented out to save space, see the CD-ROM
    }
}
```

Basically, beans are simple objects and don't have a lot of associated metadata. However, this information can be useful to tools that need to determine information about a bean at run time. In particular, this metadata provides access to the bean's home and remote interface class names that might be needed for testing or development tools.

Table 16.8 EJB Exception Classes

CLASS	USAGE
`CreateException`	Indicates a failure during a create method. All create methods must declare that they can throw this type of exception.
`DuplicateKeyException`	The requested object cannot be created, because an object with the same key already exists.
`EJBException`	Generic exception that can be used to wrap other exceptions. For example, you could create an EJBException from a NullPointerException.
`FinderException`	An object with the requested information could not be found. All find methods must declare that they can throw this type of exception.
`ObjectNotFoundException`	Used by find methods that return a single EJB to indicate that the object could not be found. This is a subclass of FinderException.
`RemoveException`	The request to remove a bean failed.

As you may have noticed, the Enterprise JavaBeans specification defines a number of exception classes. These are summarized in Table 16.8.

Many of these exceptions are targeted at specific bean life-cycle messages, such as the CreateException and the create methods. Beans can also use custom exceptions to notify callers of a problem. These custom exceptions should be serializable so that they can be transported to the client.

Both session and entity beans support the concept of handles. A handle is an object that implements the javax.ejb.Handle interface. This handle is a serializable object that contains the information necessary to contact the bean. Another client for the container-managed cart discussed earlier, called HandlingCartClient, is provided on the CD-ROM. This client demonstrates how a bean's handle can be serialized to disk, then unserialized and used to recontact an enterprise bean. These handles might be used by client applications that need to save their relationship with an EJB to disk.

The relevant code from the HandlingCartClient example to save a bean to disk is as follows:

```
try
{
     fileOut = new FileOutputStream(testFile);
     objOut = new ObjectOutputStream(fileOut);

     handle = cart.getHandle();

     objOut.writeObject(handle);

     objOut.close();
}
```

```
catch(Exception exp)
{
      exp.printStackTrace();
      cart = null;
}
```

To restore the bean connection, the following code is used:

```
try
{
      fileIn = new FileInputStream(testFile);
      objIn = new ObjectInputStream(fileIn);

      handle = (Handle) objIn.readObject();

      objIn.close();

      cart = (ShoppingCart) handle.getEJBObject();
      System.out.println("Created cart from handle: "
                                                  +cart);
}
catch(Exception exp)
{
      cart = null;
      exp.printStackTrace();
}
```

Unfortunately, there is a problem with serializing the handles provided with our version of the BEA WebLogic server, so this example is not completely tested. However, the specification does state that handles are serializable and can be used for this purpose, and we expect future versions of Tengah to support this technique.

Security and Enterprise JavaBeans

The security for enterprise beans is managed primarily by the container. The bean gets access to its security information through the context. The extent of this information is the identity or role of the caller. In this respect, EJB security is not a complex issue.

However, there is a lot going on "under the covers." First, the bean has a number of security options set during deployment. These include the ability to define roles and individuals associated with the bean. Second, the bean can use one of three security modes: run as the client, run as a system object, or run as a specified identity. This specified identity depends on the client and the type of bean. Stateful session beans are assigned an identity at creation and maintain it throughout the session. All other beans must keep the same identity within a transaction. Beans may also be able to specify if they want to control identity at a method level or at the level of the entire bean. In other words, a bean might allow managers to execute the update method and allow employees to execute everything else.

Although the bean developer/deployer can set up the security parameters, it is the EJB host that tracks the current identity for a bean.

Summary

Enterprise JavaBeans represent a powerful new standard for enterprise computing. Enterprise beans fall into four categories and should be used appropriately:

- *Stateless session beans* are used to implement stateless operations. For example, a stateless bean might be used to perform a query, implement a business rule, or perform a numerical calculation.
- *Stateful session beans* store information throughout a session. These beans should be used when the client wants to interact with a single bean throughout the session. For example, an ATM bean might track the current users' accounts while they perform various operations such as balance inquiries and deposits.
- *Entity beans with container-managed persistence* represent application objects that rely on the server to store them. These beans should be used whenever possible, keeping in mind the limitations placed on the bean by the container's management configuration techniques and features.
- *Entity beans with bean-managed persistence* represent a flexible mechanism for representing persistent application objects. Bean-managed entities should be used when the container cannot provide the search capabilities, cannot be optimized appropriately, or doesn't support the desired persistent store.

All bean developers should follow a number of programming guidelines, according to the specification:

- Beans should not create threads or terminate running threads, because doing so may interrupt the EJB host.
- Beans should not use mutable, static variables. All static variables for EJBs should be marked as final for safety. Beans may be accessed in a separate VM for each client, so these static variables don't really get shared anyway. Note that some of the examples in this text break this rule for simplicity, and this is definitely an example of do as we say, not as we do—heed our warnings! The larger examples at the end of the book form a more "correct" representation of these rules because they represent more real-world applications of the Java enterprise technologies.
- Beans should not use thread synchronization primitives, because they may interfere with the host's thread management.
- Unless a bean specifically indicates that it will manage transactions, the bean should not perform any transaction management.
- Beans are assigned a security Identity and should not attempt to change it.
- Beans that rely on the container for transaction management should not manage JDBC transactions; the container will perform this operation for them.

All enterprise beans must be hosted. This host will be expected to provide services, but your decision of which host to buy may also be driven by the legacy application that you want to access. For example, if you want to use entity beans to represent COBOL data, you may have to choose a different host than if you want to use entity beans in a relational database. Once you make the host decision, you should be able to create portable, robust beans that will run on that server or another one if you choose to update it.

Deploying Enterprise JavaBeans

One of the hard parts about learning to use Enterprise JavaBeans is the fact that you have to deploy them for testing. Deployment takes time, is server dependent, and may require you to shut down your test server each time you change the bean. This is a bit more complex than using an applet or application, which you can just run. The actual steps for deploying an Enterprise JavaBean will depend on the EJB host to which you are deploying. However, there are some basic steps that all hosts require and some guidelines for what the deployment process should accomplish.

NOTE **Once you familiarize yourself with these basic steps, you should review the documentation for your server to determine how to deploy the beans in your environment.**

The EJB specification says that all beans are deployed with a descriptor that tells the host how to treat the bean. This descriptor is an object that provides an API for learning about the programmer's intentions. Programmers package this descriptor into a jar file, then tell the host about the jar file. Again, the actual steps may vary, and some hosts may provide sophisticated tools for managing the deployment process.

Table 17.1 Deployment Descriptor Attributes

ATTRIBUTE	DESCRIPTION
Access Control Entries	Security entries that indicate which users can access the bean or a particular method of the bean. You can, for example, provide a bean that everyone can access but that only managers can tell to perform a particular method.
Bean Home Name	The name that the bean will be registered under in JNDI.
Control Descriptors	Control attributes for transactions; these are discussed in detail in the text.
Enterprise Bean Class Name	The name of the Enterprise JavaBean's Class.
Environment Properties	Key-value pairs that are passed to the bean via the EJBContext's getEnvironment method.
Home Interface Name	The name of the Home interface.
Is Reentrant	This attribute applies only to entity beans and is used to define whether or not a transaction can reaccess a bean or whether a new transaction is required for each access.
Remote Interface Name	The name of the bean's remote interface.

The DeploymentDescriptor

The main information about deployment is represented by an instance of javax.ejb.deployment.DeploymentDescriptor. This class defines a set of accessor methods for setting and getting information about the bean being deployed. Rather than list the methods, Table 17.1 provides descriptions of each of the deployment descriptor attributes. In most cases, you will be setting these attributes with a tool or in a file.

All of the examples on the CD-ROM include a file that contains the deployment descriptor information for the example beans. Also included is a build script for Windows NT that uses BEA WebLogic tools to generate the descriptor object from one of these files and serialize it to disk.

For example, the isPrime bean example has the following descriptor file. Remember that this file is BEA WebLogic specific and that other hosts may use other formats or tools. BEA WebLogic does provide a tool for creating these files as well.

```
(SessionDescriptor

  beanHomeName                    isprime.IsPrimeHome

  enterpriseBeanClassName         isprime.IsPrimeBean

  homeInterfaceClassName          isprime.IsPrimeHome

  remoteInterfaceClassName        isprime.IsPrime
```

```
isReentrant                     false

stateManagementType             STATELESS_SESSION

sessionTimeout                  10; seconds

; end session EJBean-specific properties

(accessControlEntries

); end accessControlEntries

(controlDescriptors
  (DEFAULT
     isolationLevel             TRANSACTION_SERIALIZABLE
     transactionAttribute       TX_REQUIRED
     runAsMode                  CLIENT_IDENTITY
  ); end isolationLevel

); end controlDescriptors

(environmentProperties
  ; Application-specific environment properties

  ; end Application-specific environment properties

  maxBeansInFreePool            100

  maxBeansInCache               100

  idleTimeoutSeconds            60
); end environmentProperties

); end EntityDescriptor or SessionDescriptor
```

Some of the properties in this file will be discussed in a moment, but notice that the file basically defines each attribute in the descriptor. To turn this file into a descriptor object, run the BEA WebLogic tool called weblogic.ejb.utils.DDCreator, which reads the file and generates a serialized object file. You can also use BEA WebLogic's DeploymentTool, pictured in Figure 17.1, which uses wizards to set each of these values and create the serialized object.

Some of these properties, such as the number of beans to keep in the cache, are BEA WebLogic specific. Other hosts may provide their own special settings as part of the bean's standard environment properties.

Session- and Entity-Specific Descriptors

Both session and entity beans actually use a subclass of DeploymentDescriptor for their deployment information. Session beans use an instance of SessionDescriptor, which adds a few attributes to the generic set.

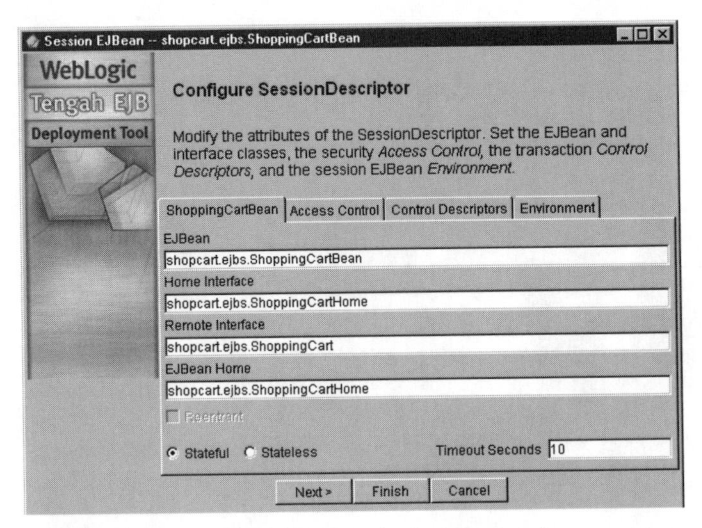

Figure 17.1 The WebLogic EJB deployment tool.

First, session beans have a time-out. The time-out indicates how long the session should be held open by the server, even if the client and server have not communicated. For example, if the time-out is 10 minutes, and the person using the client goes to lunch, the session will end in the person's absence. This value can be important when the session bean is performing sensitive operations and you don't want to leave the session open for extended periods of time.

The second session-specific descriptor is its management type. This value is either stateless or stateful, indicating the session beans type. Entity beans use an instance of EntityDescriptor, which adds a few attributes to the generic set. First, entity beans must indicate which of their fields, if any, are container-managed. By indicating a field in this list, the bean is stating that it will not manage persistence of that field and expects the container to do so. Second, the entity bean must define a primary key class name. This is the name for the class of object used to identify the entity beans in the server. Normally, this is a custom class, as discussed in Chapter 16, "Programming Enterprise JavaBeans."

Control Descriptors

A separate set of descriptors is provided for managing transaction control on a bean. These descriptors are discussed further in Chapter 23, "Using Transactions with Enterprise JavaBeans," but are provided here for completeness in terms of the current discussion. Each of the control descriptors can be assigned to a specific method, or a default can be defined that applies to all of the methods without their own descriptor. All of the examples in Chapter 16 use a single default set of control descriptors for all methods.

The first control descriptor is the transaction attribute. This determines how the bean interacts with transactions around it. For example, if a bean that uses transactions calls a method in another bean, do they share the transaction, is a new one created, or is the transaction ignored by the second bean? The second descriptor is the isolation level. This level determines what types of overlap are possibly between transactions. For example, allowing one transaction to access data uncommitted by another transaction is a specific isolation level. All of the possible values for the transaction attribute and isolation level are discussed in Chapter 23.

The last two control descriptors indicate the security associated with a bean. The first descriptor is called Run As Mode. The run mode of a bean can tell the server to run the bean with the identity of the client, CLIENT_IDENTITY, the identity of the server, SYSTEM_IDENTITY, or a specified identity, SPECIFIED_IDENTITY. If the identity is supposed to be specified, the Run As Identity control descriptor is used to indicate the specific java.security.Identity.

There is one limitation on the security control descriptors. For stateful session beans, the identity of the create method will propagate to the other methods, so they shouldn't have a conflicting descriptor. For stateless session beans and entity beans, the identity can be applied on a per-method basis.

The Deployment Process

Once the deployment descriptor is created for a bean, it is placed into a jar file. This jar file contains the serialized descriptor and a manifest file that lists the descriptor and indicates that it is for an Enterprise JavaBean. The format for this manifest file is a series of sections of the form:

```
Name: the name of the serialized bean file
Enterprise-Bean: True, if this file represents an EJB
```

For example, the isPrime example from the CD-ROM has the following manifest file:

```
Name: ejava/chapter_16/isprime/deployment/IsPrimeBeanDD.ser
Enterprise-Bean: True
```

This jar file should also contain the class files for the EJB and its interfaces, although BEA WebLogic's server will allow you to simply copy the classes to BEA WebLogic's classes directory.

Once the enterprise bean's jar file is created, the next step is to create the container and associated code. Each host provides a tool for this purpose. This deployment tool performs a number of operations, including creating the stub and skeleton files for your EJBHome and EJB. The tool must create the container-specific classes that implement the EJB and EJBHome interfaces before the stubs are created.

In many ways, this deployment tool represents the "magic" of Enterprise JavaBeans. It is responsible for creating all of the special code that accounts for your host's underlying network protocol and container implementation. This tool also ensures that the bean will be provided its environment variables at run time via its context. One way to think of the results of the deployment tool is as a jar file containing the bean's container. Really, the container is a combination of code in the server and the stubs and skeletons generated by this deployment tool.

Once you create the container, the next step is to deploy the bean. Some hosts may provide a tool for this, or it may be part of another tool. BEA WebLogic requires that you add an entry to the weblogic.properties file that indicates the name of the jar file containing the deployment information for the EJB. Other servers may provide a command-line tool or user interface for deploying the bean. Refer to your server's documentation for the exact details for this step.

The CD-ROM Examples

For the examples on the CD-ROM, an NT build script based on one provided by BEA WebLogic is included. This script creates the descriptor from the descriptor file, creates the jar file, and runs the deployment/container tool. The script is also designed to copy files to the directory where you installed BEA WebLogic. Open the build.bat file and make sure that the WEBLOGICHOME variable is defined correctly if you want to use these scripts.

To run the build script simply type:

```
build
```

and the name of the example on the command line. For example, to build the isPrime example, change directory in a shell to the chapter_16 directory and type:

```
> build isprime
```

This copies the files appropriately. When the script is finished, edit the weblogic.properties file found in the root directory of your BEA WebLogic installation to include the isprime.jar file. Search for the word "deploy" in this file to find the correct line. By default, it is commented out and contains the jar files for all of the examples.

Summary

Because the steps for each EJB host vary, we strongly suggest that the first step you take before deploying any enterprise beans is to look at the documentation for your host, even if you are using the BEA WebLogic application server discussed here. Despite their different processes, hosts should follow the same basic steps:

1. Create a deployment descriptor.
2. Store a serialized version of the descriptor in a jar file with a manifest that indicates that it is associated with an Enterprise JavaBean.
3. Run the host's deployment/container creation tool.
4. Tell the host to make the bean available to clients.

Whether or not a graphical tool is provided for each step, there will be some mechanism for accomplishing it and moving to the next step in this process.

NOTE **You should review the documentation for your server before attempting to deploy any of the examples in this book.**

The next chapter discusses a larger example that uses Enterprise JavaBeans to implement a business rule. This example, like the ones from Chapter 16, "Programming Enterprise JavaBeans," can be deployed to the demonstration BEA WebLogic server provided on the CD-ROM.

CHAPTER

18

Enterprise JavaBean Business Rules Engine

This chapter focuses on one of the more powerful applications of Enterprise JavaBeans (EJB): implementing business rules. EJBs are a great platform for implementing business processes and rules because EJBs can be shared by numerous client applications. One example of such an application, discussed later in this chapter, is a check request application that an employee could use to request payment for a business expense. The rules for allowing or not allowing the payment are encapsulated into an EJB. This allows the company to alter the check request rules in a central location and also separates the rules from the client application that handles the request and/or database engine that might store the request. This check request rules architecture is pictured in Figure 18.1.

Because business rules—especially check request rules that depend on projects, budgets, and other factors—can change, a generic rules engine is implemented for this example. This generic engine provides a simple scripting language for defining rules in terms of Rule objects. The library also supports Action objects that perform business processes such as requesting a check or ordering replacement inventory. By placing the definition of the rules in a separate script file, it is possible to edit the rules without altering the code. This means that an enterprise application can use the rules, change the rules, and change process without having to be taken down or redeployed. The syntax for the rules scripts is tag-based and is similar to both XML and HTML.

This chapter is broken into two sections. The rules engine is discussed first, including the simple parser that is provided to read rules files, and two example rules. (There are other rules on the CD-ROM.) After discussing the engine, this chapter explores the

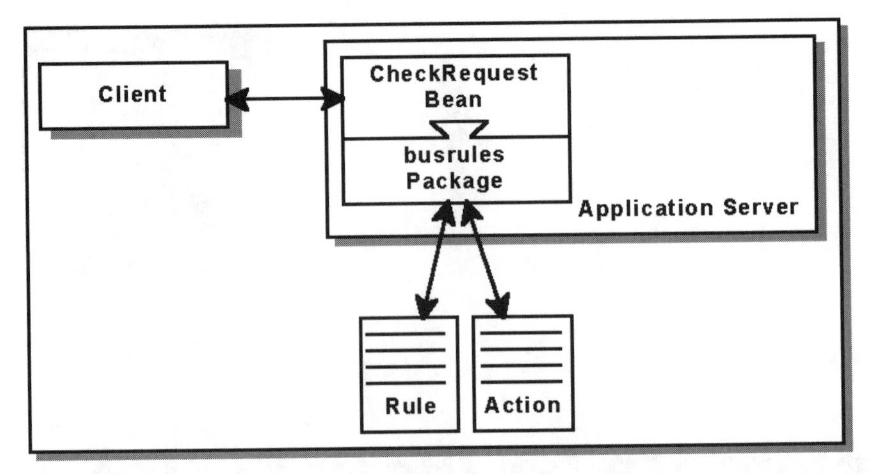

Figure 18.1 Architecture for check request rules example.

check request example, which uses a custom rule and custom action as well as existing rules and actions.

The Rules Engine

The rules engine, as implemented in the busrules package, defines two types of objects; rules and actions. Rules are objects that check the validity of data in a hash table. For example, a login rule might take a hash table with a user name and password in it and return true if the user name and password are valid. Actions are objects that act on the data in a hash table. For example, a connect action might take the data in a hash table as connection information for a database and use it to create a database connection. Essentially, rules represent business decisions, and actions represent business processes.

All of the rules used by this engine implement the Rules interface defined below.

```
package busrules;

import busrules.*;
import java.util.Hashtable;

public interface Rule
{
    public boolean isValidFor(Hashtable data);
    public double validityFor(Hashtable data);
}
```

Rule defines two methods: one for Boolean validity and one for a sliding validity. The concept of partial validity is provided to check whether the majority of rules in a group are true and to execute an action if the majority are true, but it does not require complete validity. For example, your company might require that more than 50 percent of its stockholders ratify a large purchase. You would use Rules objects to represent each stockholder's vote, possibly based on an e-mail response. A rules group could average the results of these rules to determine if the purchase can move forward. You might even add a rule that both this voting rule and a minimum number of voters rule must be true to execute the purchase. You can combine and extend this simple concept of a rule to cover a wide range of decision-making situations.

Processes in the rules engine are represented by objects that implement the Action interface. This interface only defines a single method called executeOn.

```
package busrules;

import busrules.*;
import java.util.Hashtable;

public interface Action
{
    public void executeOn(Hashtable data);
}
```

The executeOn method should perform an operation such as accessing a database or altering data in the hash table. The busrules package includes a kind of action called a *task* that invokes a set of actions in the order in which they were added to the task in the script file. There is also a decision tree that holds pairs of rules and actions. The first pair in the tree with a valid rule has its action executed when the tree is executed. This tree object shows the potential complex processes that can be modeled with this simple rule-action combination.

Hash tables are used in this example as the generic data transport for all actions and rules because they can easily store any type of object, including key-value pairs. In a sense, the hash table is a generic object with arbitrarily named attributes. Specific rules will expect specific values to be available in the hash tables passed to them. These expected values should be documented in the Rule's source code and javadoc file.

An Example Rule

Let's take a look at an example rule. This one, called AlwaysRule, looks at a single value in the hash table and is valid if that value is true. If the value is any other string or is not a string at all, the rule will return false.

```
public class AlwaysRule implements Rule
{
    protected String key;

    public boolean isValidFor(Hashtable data)
    {
        Boolean tf = Boolean.FALSE;
        String value = null;
```

```
        try
        {
            if(key != null)
                value = (String) data.get(key);
            if(value != null)
                tf = Boolean.valueOf(value);
        }
        catch(Exception exp)
        {
            tf = Boolean.FALSE;
        }

        return tf.booleanValue();
    }

    public double validityFor(Hashtable data)
    {
        return (isValidFor(data)) ? 1.0 : 0.0;
    }

    public void setKey(String s)
    {
        key = s;
    }
}
```

Because the AlwaysRule is only true or false, its validity is either 0.0 or 1.0. The key code in this example rule is the fact that it implements the Rule interface and the accessor method that is provided to change the key used to determine the rules value from the hash table.

An Example Action

A simple example action is the PrintLnAction provided with the busrules package. This action also has a programmer-defined key. The value in the hash table at this key is printed to System.out whenever the action is executed.

```
public class PrintLnAction implements Action
{
    protected String key;

    public void setKey(String s)
    {
        key = s;
    }

    public void executeOn(Hashtable data)
    {
        System.out.println(data.get(key));
    }
}
```

This action was created as a debugging tool because it acts like a logging statement in the context of a rules script.

Another action included in the busrules package is a task. A task stores a list of actions. The Task class provides methods for adding actions to its list, inserting actions in the list, or removing actions from the list. The executeOn method iterates over the list of actions, executing each one with the same data that the task provided. In some cases, this data may get changed by an action so that the next one in the task can use the new data to perform its work. For example, a task might include actions to get data from a database operates on the data and updates the database. The actions in this set communicate by adding data to the hash table passed into their executeOn method.

```
public class Task implements Action
{
    Vector actions;

    public Task()
    {
        actions = new Vector();
    }

    public void addItem(Action newItem)
    {
        actions.addElement(newItem);
    }

    public void insertItem(Action newItem)
    {
        actions.insertElementAt(newItem,0);
    }

    public void removeItem(Action delItem)
    {
        actions.removeElement(delItem);
    }

    public void executeOn(Hashtable data)
    {
        int i,max;
        Action curAction;

        max = actions.size();

        for(i=0;i<max;i++)
        {
            curAction = (Action) actions.elementAt(i);
            curAction.executeOn(data);
        }
    }

    public void removeAllItems()
    {
```

```
            actions.removeAllElements();
        }
    }
```

As you can see, the Task class provides methods for managing the list of actions. In larger scripts, tasks can be used to create more complex processes.

The Parser

Given rules and actions, both the ones provided and custom ones, a programmer can create a script that defines how to plug rules together. Actually, you could just write Java code to build complex rules and complex actions. However, one of our goals is to provide a mechanism for changing business rules without having to recompile the enterprise bean or RMI object that acts as an interface for the rule. A simple scripting file is used to make this separation between the definition of a rule and the interface that uses it. Also provided is a class called RulesParser that can read the script files and convert them into Java objects.

To use this scripting tool kit, follow these five steps:

1. Create the script file. This file will define either a single rule or a single action. This single rule/action can be built from other rules and actions.
2. Implement any custom rules and actions and the parsing code required to handle them.
3. Create a Java object to act as an interface to the rule and/or action.
4. Implement the Java object to invoke the rules parser. The parser will read the script file and create the Rule or Action object that the script defines.
5. Use the rule or action created by the parser.

These steps rely on a key concept; the rule or action defined in the script file is directly created from Java objects that implement the Rule or Action interfaces. In other words, the rules file is a shortcut for implementing the Java code that would, for example, create a Task object and add several actions to it. In other words, nothing is done in the script file that couldn't be done in Java, but the separation allows the Java code to remain in use while the rules change.

Step two refers to the creation of parsing code. This code is discussed in a moment. It is based on the generic parsing engine that is provided with the busrules package. This generic engine is implemented in the class RulesParser. The RulesParser provides four methods for parsing a script:

```
public Action parseAction(String script, Enumeration handlers)
        throws ParsingException;
public Action parseAction(Reader script, Enumeration handlers)
        throws ParsingException;

public Rule parseRule(String script, Enumeration handlers)
        throws ParsingException;
```

```
public Rule parseRule(Reader script, Enumeration handlers)
        throws ParsingException;
```

The first two methods parse a script and return an Action object. The second two parse a script and return a Rule object. For each type of script, a method is provided that supports using a Reader or String to define the script. The second argument to all of these methods is an enumeration of TagHandlers. These are the custom code that you can write to support custom rules and actions in your scripts. All of the methods will throw a ParsingException if the script is bad.

The complete code for RulesParser is provided on the CD-ROM, along with the class called TagParser that performs the actual parsing. The RulesParser is really a front end to a TagParser. This tag parser looks at HTML-like input and calls TagHandler objects for each tag it encounters. Let's look at an example script to see how the script defines these tags for the parser to evaluate.

An Example Script

This script defines a DecisionTree. A *tree* is an action that contains rule-action pairs. When the tree is executed, it executes the first action for which the rule is valid.

```
<TREE>

<PAIR>
<COMPARISONRULE OPERATOR="11" CONSTANT="true" KEY="false">
<PRINTLNACTION KEY="message_one">
</PAIR>

<PAIR>
<ALWAYSRULE KEY="true">
<PRINTLNACTION KEY="message_two">
</PAIR>

</TREE>
```

This tree has two rule-action pairs. The first uses the ComparisonRule to test if the value at the key "false" is not equal to, using string equality, the constant value "true." This ComparisonRule object supports a number of comparison operators, including numeric and string comparisons. When the rule is tested, it compares the value at its key with the constant value provided to it using the assigned operator. The second pair in this tree tests whether the value of the key "true" is true. Both rules are associated with PrintLnActions that print a message indicating their success.

This example shows the tagged nature of the scripting language. In this case, the TREE tags bracket the entire definition for the main action, a decision tree. The PAIR tags bracket each rule-action pair, and the individual rules and actions are defined using singleton tags that use attributes to define their properties. For example, the ALWAYSRULE tag indicates an AlwaysRule object, and the KEY attribute defines its key instance variable. In a moment you will see how a RulesParser object converts these tags into Rule and Action objects. Keep in mind that this tag-based language was chosen because it is familiar. You could define any type of scripting language to define rules and actions.

Using the Example Script

To test the example script, we created a simple Java program that creates a hash table, loads it with data, loads the action from the script file, and executes it on the sample data. The following program also shows how the parser is created and accessed. The parser is implemented to allow use of only a shared instance. The constructor for RulesParser is protected so that it cannot be instantiated.

```
package busrules;

import busrules.*;
import java.util.*;
import java.io.*;

public class RulesParserTest extends Object
{
    public static void main(String args[])
    {
        FileReader fileIn;
        RulesParser parser;
        Action act;
        Hashtable data;

        if(args.length > 0)
        {
            try
            {
                parser = RulesParser.sharedRulesParser();
                fileIn = new FileReader(args[0]);

                System.out.println("Preparing Data");

                data = new Hashtable();

                data.put("message_one"
                ,"The value of false is not equal to true.");

                data.put("message_two"
                        ,"The value of true is true.");

                data.put("true","true");
                data.put("false","false");

                System.out.println("Parsing");

                act = parser.parseAction(fileIn,null);
```

```
                    System.out.println("Got Action: "+act);

                    //parser closes the stream

                    System.out.println("Executing");
                    act.executeOn(data);
                    System.out.println("Completed");
                }
                catch(ParsingException exp)
                {
                    System.out.println("Script exception "
                                                +"occurred.");
                    exp.printStackTrace();
                }
                catch(IOException exp)
                {
                    System.out.println("IO exception occurred.");
                    exp.printStackTrace();
                }
                catch(Exception exp)
                {
                    System.out.println("Miscellaneous exception"
                                        +" occurred.");
                    exp.printStackTrace();
                }
            }
            else
            {
                System.out.println("Usage: java RulesParserTest"
                                        +" filename");
            }
        }
    }
```

Once the parser and data are created, the parser is told to parse the script file and return the action defined in it. This will return null if no action is defined, or it will throw a ParsingException if the script file is bad. The parsing operation returns an Action object that is executed on the data. The script file in this example is specified on the command line.

In a larger program, you might parse the script file once and use the action or rule it contains repeatedly on different data sets as needed.

Handling a Tag

When the parser is told to parse a script, it uses a TagParser object to read the script. This tag parser uses a callback-style interface to notify the RulesParser when tags are encountered. More important, regardless of the tags, the parser will parse any tag-based file. In order for the parsing to result in any callbacks, the parser has to be told about two things. First, the parser needs to know which tags are pairs, like <HTML>

and </HTML>. All other tags are assumed to be singletons, like <BR>. Second, the parser needs handlers to tell when a tag is encountered. The interface used to notify an object of a tag is defined by the TagHandler interface.

```
public interface TagHandler
{
    public String handleTag(String tag,String data
                            ,String etag,Hashtable atts)
        throws ParsingException;

    public void registerWith(TagParser parser);
}
```

This interface defines two methods. The handleTag method is passed a tag, its end tag, the data between the start and end tag, and any attributes from the start tag. For tags that don't have an end tag, the etag and data parameters are null. The registerWith method should tell what tag it handles and register any end tags that it expects. If the parser is given an end tag, it waits to call handleTag until the end tag is encountered. The data parameter of handleTag contains all of the data between the start and end tag, with the caveat that any subtags may have been handled by another tag handler. In this case, the return value of handleTag for the subtag is inserted in the data passed to the supertag in place of the tags themselves.

For example, the RulesParser acts as a TagHandler for the rules and actions provided in the busrules package. Whenever it handles a rules tag, it replaces the tag with the empty string. If, for example, you run the parser on the script:

```
<TREE>

<PAIR>
<COMPARISONRULE OPERATOR="11" CONSTANT="true" KEY="false">
<PRINTLNACTION KEY="message_one">
</PAIR>

<PAIR>
<ALWAYSRULE KEY="true">
<PRINTLNACTION KEY="message_two">
</PAIR>

</TREE>
```

Handle tag is first called for the COMPARISONRULE tag, then the PRINTLNACTION tag is handled. Next the </PAIR> tag triggers the PAIR tag handler, which is passed an empty data string because the handler for COMPARISONRULE and PRINTLNACTION returned an empty string. This parsing continues until the </TREE> tag triggers the TREE tag handler. Again, the RulesParser handles all of these tags itself. Our check request example demonstrates how custom tag handlers are implemented.

To register with the TagParser, use the methods:

```
public void registerTagHandler(String tag,TagHandler handler);
public void registerEndTag(String tag,String etag);
```

Looking at the complete code for the RulesParser that follows, you see how it registers itself with a TagParser for all of the tags in the busrules package. Furthermore, see how the RulesParser handles tags by pushing the objects they represent onto a stack. So, in the example script, the COMPARISONRULE is pushed onto the rule stack, then the PRINTLNACTION is pushed onto the action stack. When the pair is encountered, it pops the rule and action, creates a Pair object, and pushes the pair onto the pair stack. The next pair is handled the same way. The tree tag causes a DecisionTree object to be created and all of the pairs to be added to it in order.

The RulesParser uses three stacks to manage the rules, actions, and pairs encountered. These are all defined as instance variables.

```
package busrules;

import busrules.*;
import java.util.*;
import java.io.*;

public class RulesParser
implements TagHandler
{
    protected Stack rules;
    protected Stack actions;
    protected Stack pairs;
```

Programs should use the shared rules parser to ensure that all of the tag handlers have access to the same rules, actions, and pairs.

```
    protected static RulesParser shared;

    public static RulesParser sharedRulesParser()
    {
        if(shared == null)
            shared = new RulesParser();

        return shared;
    }

    protected RulesParser()
    {
        rules = new Stack();
        actions = new Stack();
        pairs = new Stack();
    }
```

The RulesParser provides methods to parse a script as a Reader or a string and return either a rule or an action. All of the parse methods accept a list of handlers to register.

```
    public Action parseAction(String script, Enumeration handlers)
        throws ParsingException
    {
```

```
        TagParser parser;

        parser = new TagParser();
        registerHandlers(parser,handlers);
        parser.parse(new StringReader(script));

        return popAction();
    }

    public Action parseAction(Reader r, Enumeration handlers)
        throws ParsingException
    {
        TagParser parser;

        parser = new TagParser();
        registerHandlers(parser,handlers);
        parser.parse(r);

        return popAction();
    }

    public Rule parseRule(String script, Enumeration handlers)
        throws ParsingException
    {
        TagParser parser;

        parser = new TagParser();
        registerHandlers(parser,handlers);
        parser.parse(new StringReader(script));

        return popRule();
    }

    public Rule parseRule(Reader r, Enumeration handlers)
        throws ParsingException
    {
        TagParser parser;

        parser = new TagParser();
        registerHandlers(parser,handlers);
        parser.parse(r);

        return popRule();
    }
```

Handlers are registered with the parser before the actual parsing is performed. Each handler is responsible for telling the parser the tags it handles and any end tags it uses. The RulesParser uses the handler's registerWith method to trigger this registration.

```
    protected void registerHandlers(TagParser parser
                                    ,Enumeration handlers)
```

```
{
    TagHandler cur;

    /*
     * Register ourself first, so others can override.
     */
    registerWith(parser);

    if(handlers == null) return;

    while(handlers.hasMoreElements())
    {
        cur = (TagHandler) handlers.nextElement();

        cur.registerWith(parser);
    }
}
```

As a convenience, the RulesParser provides a method to manipulate the rules, actions, and pairs stacks.

```
public void pushRule(Rule r)
{
    rules.push(r);
}

public Rule popRule()
{
    Rule retVal = null;

    try
    {
        retVal = (Rule) rules.pop();
    }
    catch(EmptyStackException exp)
    {
        retVal = null;
    }

    return retVal;
}

public void pushAction(Action a)
{
    actions.push(a);
}

public Action popAction()
{
    Action retVal = null;
```

```
        try
        {
            retVal = (Action) actions.pop();
        }
        catch(EmptyStackException exp)
        {
            retVal = null;
        }

        return retVal;
    }

    public void pushPair(Pair p)
    {
        pairs.push(p);
    }

    public Pair popPair()
    {
        Pair retVal = null;

        try
        {
            retVal = (Pair) pairs.pop();
        }
        catch(EmptyStackException exp)
        {
            retVal = null;
        }

        return retVal;
    }
```

The shared RuleParser object is the tag handler for all of the rules and actions included in the busrules package. As a result, its handleTag method is quite lengthy because it has to check for a number of possible tags. Custom handlers will probably only check for the one or two tags that they handle.

```
    /******* Tag Handler Methods **********/

    public String handleTag(String tag,String data
                            ,String etag,Hashtable atts)
    throws ParsingException
    {
        if(tag.startsWith("<PAIR"))
        {
            Pair newPair = new Pair();

            newPair.setRule(popRule());
            newPair.setAction(popAction());
```

```
        pushPair(newPair);
    }
    else if(tag.startsWith("<BOOLEANRULE"))
    {
        BooleanRule r = new BooleanRule();
        String type;

        type = (String) atts.get("TYPE");

        if(type != null)
        {
            r.setType(type);

            if(!"not".equals(type))
            {
                r.setRule2(popRule());
            }

            r.setRule1(popRule());

            pushRule(r);
        }
    }
    else if(tag.startsWith("<ALWAYSRULE"))
    {
        AlwaysRule r = new AlwaysRule();
        String key;

        key = (String) atts.get("KEY");

        if(key != null)
        {
            r.setKey(key);

            pushRule(r);
        }
    }
    else if(tag.startsWith("<COMPARISONRULE"))
    {
        ComparisonRule r = new ComparisonRule();
        String op,comp,val;

        op = (String) atts.get("OPERATOR");
        comp = (String) atts.get("CONSTANT");
        val = (String) atts.get("KEY");

        if((op != null)
            &&(comp != null)
            &&(val != null))
        {
            try
```

```
                {
                    r.setOperator(Integer.parseInt(op));
                    r.setConstant(comp);
                    r.setValueKey(val);

                    pushRule(r);
                }
                catch(NumberFormatException exp)
                {
                    throw
                        new ParsingException("Operator should "
                                            +"be int.");
                }
            }
        }
        else if(tag.startsWith("<RULES"))
        {
            RuleGroup grp = new RuleGroup();
            Rule cur;
            String type;

            type = (String) atts.get("TYPE");

            if(type != null)
            {
                grp.setType(type);
            }

            while((cur = popRule())!= null)
            {
                grp.insertItem(cur);
            }

            pushRule(grp);
        }
        else if(tag.startsWith("<TASK"))
        {
            Task grp = new Task();
            Action cur;

            while((cur = popAction())!= null)
            {
                grp.insertItem(cur);
            }

            pushAction(grp);
        }
        else if(tag.startsWith("<QUALIFIEDACTION"))
        {
            QualifiedAction act = new QualifiedAction();
```

```
            act.setRule(popRule());
            act.setAction(popAction());

            pushAction(act);
        }
        else if(tag.startsWith("<PRINTLNACTION"))
        {
            PrintLnAction r = new PrintLnAction();
            String key;

            key = (String) atts.get("KEY");

            if(key != null)
            {
                r.setKey(key);

                pushAction(r);
            }
        }
        else if(tag.startsWith("<TREE"))
        {
            DecisionTree tree = new DecisionTree();
            Pair cur;

            while((cur = popPair())!= null)
            {
                tree.insertPair(cur);
            }

            pushAction(tree);
        }

        return "";
    }
```

The shared RulesParser registers all of the rules and actions from the busrules example, along with their end tags. The method registerTagHandler is used to register handlers; the method registerEndTag associates tags and their associated end tags.

```
    public void registerWith(TagParser parser)
    {
        parser.registerTagHandler("TREE",this);
        parser.registerTagHandler("PAIR",this);
        parser.registerTagHandler("QUALIFIEDACTION",this);
        parser.registerTagHandler("TASK",this);
        parser.registerTagHandler("PRINTLNACTION",this);
        parser.registerTagHandler("ALWAYSRULE",this);
        parser.registerTagHandler("BOOLEANRULE",this);
        parser.registerTagHandler("COMPARISONRULE",this);
        parser.registerTagHandler("RULES",this);
```

```
            parser.registerEndTag("RULES","</RULES>");
            parser.registerEndTag("TASK","</TASK>");
            parser.registerEndTag("QUALIFIEDACTION"
                                  ,"</QUALIFIEDACTION>");
            parser.registerEndTag("PAIR","</PAIR>");
            parser.registerEndTag("TREE","</TREE>");
            parser.registerEndTag("BOOLEANRULE","</BOOLEANRULE>");
        }
    }
```

Notice that the main drawback of the simple parser is that the RuleGroup, Task, and DecisionTree are very greedy. They will pop everything off the stack. This means that you can't put two RuleGroups into a RuleGroup, using the existing parser. In addition, see from the code how the parseRule and parseAction methods simply return the last object on the stack. If no object is available, null is returned or an exception is thrown.

Check Request Example

Given this generic rules engine, let's look at the specific example of a check request application. First, define an EJB that provides an interface for applications wanting to make check requests. However, we don't want everyone to be able to request a check, so we'll use a rule script to determine if a request is valid. We'll also use an action script to implement the request mechanism.

CheckRequest: The Interface

The interface for the CheckRequest bean defines a single method for making a check request.

```
package checkreq;

import javax.ejb.*;
import java.rmi.RemoteException;
import java.rmi.Remote;

public interface CheckRequest
 extends EJBObject, Remote
{
    public boolean requestCheck(String payee
                              ,String project
                              ,double amount
                              ,String desc)
    throws RemoteException;
}
```

Notice that clients only provide the necessary information to make a request; they don't interact with the script file or the rules implementation.

CheckRequestHome: The Home Interface

Because a check request is a basic stateless operation, a stateless session bean is used to implement it. This allows a very simple home interface.

```
public interface CheckRequestHome extends EJBHome
{
    CheckRequest create()
        throws CreateException, RemoteException;
}
```

The CheckRequestHome simple creates a CheckRequest bean and returns it. The standard exceptions are declared to account for a problem during creation or an RMI exception.

CheckRequest: The Bean

The bean itself is more complex. Let's look at the bean in three sections. First, there are the import statements and some basic methods required by the SessionBean interface. Also defined is an instance variable to hold the SessionContext for use in all of the methods. Notice that the java.security package is included in order to use the Identity provided by the SessionContext to identify the client. The actual client login is managed by the JNDI interface, as shown in the client code.

```
import javax.ejb.*;
import java.security.*;
import java.io.Serializable;
import java.util.*;
import java.io.*;

import checkreq.*;
import busrules.*;

public class CheckRequestBean implements SessionBean
{
    protected SessionContext context;

    public void ejbActivate()
    {
    }

    public void ejbRemove()
    {
    }

    public void ejbPassivate()
    {
    }
```

```
public void setSessionContext(SessionContext ctx)
{
    context = ctx;
}

public void ejbCreate()
{
}
```

Next, implement a convenience method called buildRule to build the rule used to determine whether a request is valid. This method uses an environmental variable to determine the script file from which to load the rule. This environmental variable is defined at deployment time. On the CD-ROM, these variables are included as part of the DeploymentDescriptor.txt file used to build a deployment descriptor for the WebLogic server.

The buildRule method also registers a custom tag handler called IdentityRuleHandler with the RulesParser. This handler and the custom rule it generates are discussed in the "IdentityRuleHandler: A Custom Handler" section.

```
protected Rule buildRule()
{
    Properties env;
    Rule retVal = null;
    String scriptFile;
    FileReader fileIn;
    RulesParser parser;
    Vector handlers;

    try
    {
        env = context.getEnvironment();
        parser = RulesParser.sharedRulesParser();

        scriptFile = env.getProperty("rulesScriptFile");

        fileIn = new FileReader(scriptFile);

        handlers = new Vector();
        handlers.addElement(new IdentityRuleHandler());

        retVal = parser.parseRule(fileIn
                        ,handlers.elements());
    }
    catch(Exception exp)
    {
        retVal = null;
    }

    return retVal;
}
```

In the same way we created a method for building the rule for validating a request, the method buildAction is used to create an action for handling the request. This method also uses an environmental variable to determine the script file and registers a custom tag handler.

Although these custom handlers have been hard-coded here, you could also read them from a file, making the entire parsing process highly dynamic.

```
protected Action buildAction()
{
    Properties env;
    Action retVal = null;
    String scriptFile;
    FileReader fileIn;
    RulesParser parser;
    Vector handlers;

    try
    {
        env = context.getEnvironment();
        parser = RulesParser.sharedRulesParser();

        scriptFile = env.getProperty("actionScriptFile");

        fileIn = new FileReader(scriptFile);

        handlers = new Vector();
        handlers.addElement(new LogRequestHandler());

        retVal = parser.parseAction(fileIn
                                  ,handlers.elements());
    }
    catch(Exception exp)
    {
        retVal = null;
    }

    return retVal;
}
```

Finally, implement the requestCheck method. This method builds a hash table with the provided data. The keys used in the hash table should be documented so that anyone writing a script for the rule or action will know what data is provided and its meaning. This method also includes the Identity of the client in the hash table. The rule and action are loaded from the file with each request, and if the rule is valid, the action is executed. If the rule is not valid, the Boolean false is returned from the method, indicating that the request failed.

```
public boolean requestCheck(String payee
                           ,String project
                           ,double amount
```

```
                                    ,String desc)
    {
        Rule rule = buildRule();
        Action action = buildAction();
        boolean valid = false;
        Hashtable data;

        data = new Hashtable();

        data.put("payee",payee);
        data.put("project",project);
        data.put("amount",String.valueOf(amount));
        data.put("desc",desc);
        data.put("identity",context.getCallerIdentity());

        if(rule != null) valid = rule.isValidFor(data);

        if(valid && (action != null))
        {
            action.executeOn(data);
        }

        return valid;
    }
}
```

We choose to load the scripts for every request in this example to make it easier for you to change the script and rerun the example. In a larger program, you might provide a trigger method that tells the bean to reread the script or use the modification time to test when to reread the script.

IdentityRule: A Custom Rule

The custom rule for this example checks the name of the client's identity against its specified name. You might reimplement this rule to use a specific security provider if that is appropriate for your installation.

```
package checkreq;

import javax.ejb.*;
import java.security.*;
import java.util.*;

import busrules.*;

/**
 * If an identity is provided, then the
 * "identity" key in the data is used.
 *
```

```
 * <IDENTITYRULE IDENTITY="">
 */
public class IdentityRule implements Rule
{
    protected String identity;

    public boolean isValidFor(Hashtable data)
    {
        boolean retVal = false;

        try
        {
            if(identity != null)
            {
                Identity id;

                id = (Identity) data.get("identity");

                retVal = id.getName().equals(identity);
            }
        }
        catch(Exception exp)
        {
            retVal = false;
        }

        return retVal;
    }

    public double validityFor(Hashtable data)
    {
        return (isValidFor(data)) ? 1.0 : 0.0;
    }

    public void setIdentity(String s)
    {
        identity = s;
    }
}
```

This is a fairly simple rule. In a larger application, you might create rules that access database data or even look up a user in an LDAP directory to determine the user's permissions.

IdentityRuleHandler: A Custom Handler

The handler for the IdentityRule uses the RulesParser's stacks to handle the Identity tags. First, the handler registers for all occurrences of the IDENTITY tag. This registration is implemented in registerWith but is called by RulesParser. When an IDENTITY tag is encountered, the handler creates an IdentityRule object and uses the tag attributes to determine the name to associate with the rule. Once the rule is initialized, it is pushed onto the RulesParser's rules stack.

```
package checkreq;

import busrules.*;
import checkreq.*;

import java.util.*;
import java.security.*;

public class IdentityRuleHandler
implements TagHandler
{
    /******* Tag Handler Methods **********/

    public String handleTag(String tag,String data
                            ,String etag,Hashtable atts)
    throws ParsingException
    {
        IdentityRule r = new IdentityRule();
        String id,role;

        id = (String) atts.get("IDENTITY");

        if(id != null)
        {
            r.setIdentity(id);

            RulesParser.sharedRulesParser().pushRule(r);
        }

        return "";
    }

    public void registerWith(TagParser parser)
    {
        parser.registerTagHandler("IDENTITYRULE",this);
    }
}
```

In general, custom tag handlers will handle one or two tags. The handle tag method will create the appropriate object, initialize it from the information in the tag attributes and data between the start and end tags, and push it onto the appropriate RulesParser stack. In this way, an action's tag handler pushes the new action on the action stack, and a rules handler pushes rules onto the rules stack.

LogRequestAction: A Custom Action

The custom action implemented for this example simply prints the check request information to the console. In a real application, you might log this request to the database or a financial application for processing. To make printing the request easier, we implement a custom action called LogRequestAction that prints the data for a check request to the console.

```
package checkreq;

import java.util.*;
import busrules.*;
import checkreq.*;

/**
 * Logs payee, amount and desc.
 * from the hashtable
 * to the console.
 *
 * <LogRequestAction>
 */
public class LogRequestAction implements Action
{
    public void executeOn(Hashtable data)
    {
        System.out.print("Pay to the order of: ");
        System.out.println(data.get("payee"));
        System.out.println("$"+data.get("amount"));
        System.out.println(data.get("desc"));
    }
}
```

The handler for this action is available on the CD-ROM and is implemented in a manner very similar to the IdentityRuleHandler.

An Example Rule Script

Using the IdentityRule and others provided in the busrules package, the following test Rule Script is provided on the CD-ROM for testing this example.

```
Only need one rule to be true.

<RULES TYPE="or">
<IDENTITYRULE IDENTITY="stephen">
<BOOLEANRULE TYPE="and">
<IDENTITYRULE IDENTITY="scott">
<COMPARISONRULE OPERATOR="10" CONSTANT="secret" KEY="project">
</BOOLEANRULE>
</RULES>
```

This script defines a rules group that contains two rules. The first rule says that Stephen can request any check. The second says that Scott can request any check for the secret project, but no other project. This script includes a comment at the top to show how the parser will ignore normal text outside of tags or text ignored by a tag handler.

An Example Action Script

The action script created for this example is only one line and causes a LogRequestAction to be created.

```
<LOGREQUESTACTION>
```

Certainly more complex actions for this request can be created.

An Example Client

The client created to test the check request bean is a simple command-line program. The program uses command-line arguments to assign the URL for the JNDI context, the user, and the password. This user and password must be defined by the EJB provider to make them valid to the enterprise bean. In this case, the users Stephen and Scott are defined for the BEA WebLogic server, with the passwords stephena and scottscott, respectively. If the client is run in the installation with any other user or password, including no user name, the check requests always fail because the rule will be invalid.

```
package checkreq;

import javax.ejb.*;
import javax.naming.*;
import java.rmi.*;
import java.util.*;
import java.io.*;

import checkreq.*;

public class CheckRequestClient
{
    public static void main(String[] args)
    {
        Context ctx=null;

        try
        {
            ctx = getInitialContext(args);
            InputStreamReader readIn;
            BufferedReader bufIn;
            String payee;
            String project;
            String amtStr;
            double amount;
            String desc;
            boolean success;
```

```
            CheckRequestHome home = (CheckRequestHome)
                    ctx.lookup("checkreq.CheckRequestHome");
            CheckRequest request = home.create();

            readIn = new InputStreamReader(System.in);
            bufIn = new BufferedReader(readIn);

            System.out.println("Please enter the payee.");

            payee = bufIn.readLine().trim();

            System.out.println("Please enter the project.");

            project = bufIn.readLine().trim();

            System.out.println("Please enter a description.");

            desc = bufIn.readLine().trim();

            System.out.println("Please enter the amount.");

            amtStr = bufIn.readLine().trim();

            try
            {
                amount = Double.valueOf(amtStr).doubleValue();

                success = request.requestCheck(payee,project
                                        ,amount,desc);

                if(success)
                    System.out.println("Your request was"
                                    +" processed.");
                else
                    System.out.println("Insuffecient permission"
                                        + " for request.");
            }
            catch(NumberFormatException exp)
            {
                System.out.println("That is an invalid amount.");
            }

            home.remove(request.getHandle());
        }
        catch (Exception e)
        {
            System.out.println("Error.");
            e.printStackTrace();
        }
        finally
        {
```

```
            try
            {
                ctx.close();
            }
            catch(Exception exp)
            {
            }
        }
    }

    static public Context getInitialContext(String[] args)
          throws Exception
    {
        Properties p = new Properties();
        String url = "t3://localhost:7001";
        String user=null;
        String password=null;

        if ((args != null) && (args.length > 1))
        {
            for (int i = 0; i < args.length; i++)
            {
                if (args[i].equals("-url"))
                    url = args[++i];
                else if (args[i].equals("-user"))
                    user = args[++i];
                else if (args[i].equals("-password"))
                    password = args[++i];
            }
        }

        p.put(Context.INITIAL_CONTEXT_FACTORY,
                "weblogic.jndi.T3InitialContextFactory");

        p.put(Context.PROVIDER_URL, url);

        if (user != null)
        {
            p.put(Context.SECURITY_PRINCIPAL, user);

            if (password == null) password = "";

            p.put(Context.SECURITY_CREDENTIALS, password);
        }

        return new InitialContext(p);
    }
}
```

If you run this client from the CD-ROM with the enterprise bean and the test script files installed on the server, stephen is validated for all requests and scott is validated for requests for the secret project. Try adding other rules that restrict the limit of a check's amount or make sure that the payee is not the writer.

Summary

Combining Enterprise JavaBeans with scripting is a powerful tool for enterprise applications. Enterprise beans create a separation between client code and core logic. They also rely on powerful features of the EJB host, such as connection pooling and transactional scoping, as discussed in Chapter 16, "Programming Enterprise JavaBeans," and demonstrated in the larger example in Chapter 25, "A Four-Tier Online Store." These host-provided services make programming with Enterprise JavaBeans easier than standard client/server applications. By integrating scripting, we created a bean that is easy to write and deploy and can still be updated as needed. This allows us to implement business rules easily and change them as needed. In the example, new people can easily be added to the request rules as they are given check-signing authority or removed as they lose authority. This chapter demonstrates that enterprise beans provide the foundation for a simple but powerful approach to multitier enterprise computing.

The next chapter begins to discuss one of the other services that an application server can provide: messaging. Messaging is another form of interprogram communication that Java programs can use to share information and notifications.

What Are Messaging and the Java Messaging Service?

Messaging is a mechanism for programs to communicate with each other. In one sense, messaging is like RMI or even sockets, in that all three allow programs to communicate with each other. However, messaging is based on a fundamental entity called a *message*. A message represents the content of a single communication between two or more programs. Programs that use messaging send and receive messages. In this respect, messaging is more like using TCP/IP packets or even UDP datagrams than it is like sockets. In effect, messaging is the process of communicating between programs by creating, sending, and receiving messages.

Normally, messaging support is provided via a library, server, or some other middleware. The term *message-oriented-middleware*, or MOM, is often used to refer to an infrastructure that supports messaging. MOM defines what a message looks like to the program, how a program sends a message, and how a program receives a message. The Java Messaging Service (JMS) provides a standard Java-based interface to the messaging services of a MOM or some other provider.

There are two basic designs for a messaging provider. The first, pictured in Figure 19.1, uses messages to communicate between applications but still connects the two applications that are communicating.

The second design, pictured in Figure 19.2, uses a server to support messaging. In this case, clients connect to a server that distributes messages for them. Clients that want to receive messages register with the server for notification. This design is more like the post office, where a central entity manages message delivery.

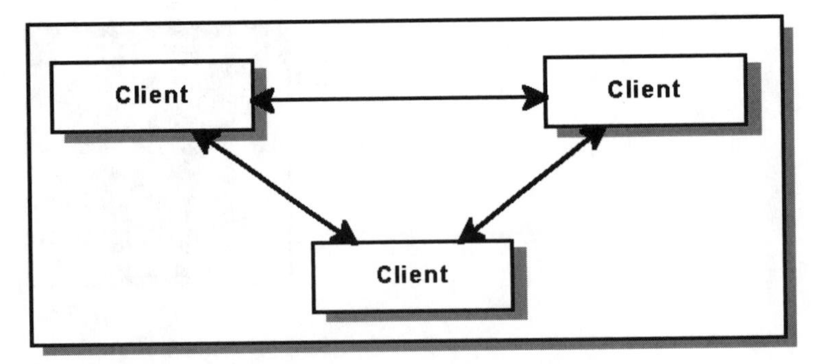

Figure 19.1 Client-based messaging.

The advantage of the server approach is that services such as load balancing, message persistence, and security can be administered and upgraded in a single location. This brings up an important point: Messaging providers can include a variety of services on top of the basic ability to send and receive messages. When considering a provider, ask the following questions:

What happens to a message if the intended receiver is not available? Many providers either store messages for later delivery or if specified, ignore these messages.

What happens when the server goes down? Obviously, messages won't go anywhere, but how does the client figure this out?

Do all clients receive all messages? Providers normally define the concept of a message destination. Clients that want to receive messages indicate the destination to which they are listening.

Can any client send messages to any other client? Providers can provide mechanisms for limiting the targets for a client's message. Often, the target for a message is called a *destination* because it could represent one or more other programs. The messaging provider can provide limitations on the destinations to which a client can send or at least require clients to choose a destination to limit the receivers for a message.

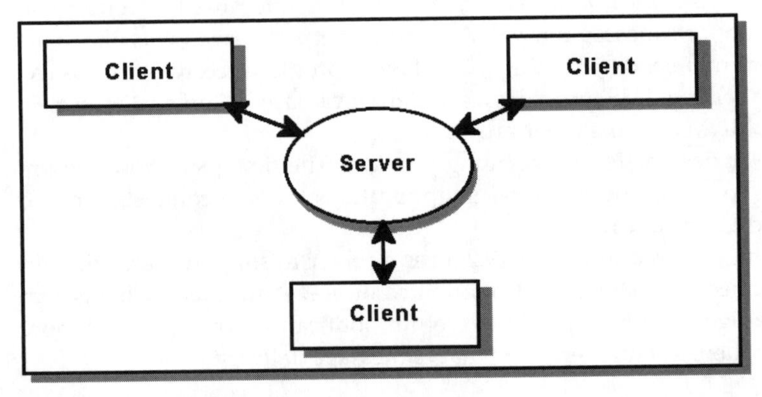

Figure 19.2 Server-based messaging.

What can a message include? On top of the basic design for a messaging system, there is the definition of the messages themselves. Depending on a provider's goals, it might support binary messages, text messages, messages that have key-value pairs, or even messages that support objects as the message body. The limitations on message content are often driven by the systems that a provider supports and the performance constraints that the provider places on their products. For example, sending arbitrary objects can be a performance nightmare because it involves an arbitrary format and size. On the other hand, saying that all messages are 10-character strings allows the provider to optimize their software for these messages. In general, the actual choices available to a messaging programmer lie somewhere toward the arbitrary side of these two extremes, with a performance cost associated with message size and complexity.

Hopefully, these questions help you determine your requirements and the provider that can fulfill them.

At this point, you may be asking yourself, So what? What do I get for using these messages? The answer is, It depends. For some applications, RMI, HTTP, or sockets are the right solution. For example, if you just want to talk to your Oracle database, you probably don't need to add the messaging abstraction in the middle of that relationship. The time when messaging is useful is when you want to separate the destination or networking from the client's code. For example, a messaging service might ensure the arrival of the insert statements that you want to make for that database. If the database is unavailable now—because, for example, you are using a laptop on an airplane—the service will deliver the insert messages later. The messaging service decouples the sender and receiver, allowing them to work together without being designed to specifically and only work with each other. This decoupling has advantages in a number of areas, which are discussed later in the chapter. First, we need to address a few core concepts of messaging.

Messaging Domains

The simple concept of messaging can be further specialized into several domains. These domains are used to define which client receives a message. The most common of domains are:

- Point-to-point
- Publish-subscribe
- Request-reply

Each of these domains defines different models for the programs that are communicating. Not all MOM providers provide all of these models.

Point-to-Point Messaging

Point-to-point messaging is designed to allow one client to send messages to another client. This may or may not be a one-way relationship. In other words, a client to the messaging system might only send messages, only receive messages, or send and receive messages. Another client can also send and/or receive messages. So, in the simplest case, a client sends messages to another client. In the more complete case, both clients send and receive messages to each other.

There are two basic models for point-to-point messaging. The simplest is to have a client directly send a message to another client. This is similar to RMI and may be equivalent, depending on the messaging provider's implementation. For example, a messaging interface might hide some of the mechanics of sending a message, such as making sure the network is available or saving messages to a database to make sure that they are sent.

The more common point-to-point model is based on the concept of a queue, as pictured in Figure 19.3. Senders put messages into a queue. The receiver takes messages out of the queue. Often, this queue is stored on the messaging server and may even be stored in a relational database for reliable persistence. The Java Messaging Service uses the queue approach to point-to-point messaging, although it doesn't prohibit the implementation from using direct messaging.

The defining factor in point-to-point messaging is that there is a single receiver for the messages. For example, an HR system might send messages to the financial system indicating a required change in the company financials. These messages are intended only for the financials system; other applications in the enterprise should not receive them.

Publish-Subscribe Messaging

Publish-subscribe messaging is designed for situations in which multiple programs should receive the same messages. JMS defines publish-subscribe around the concept of a topic. Publishers send messages to a topic, and subscribers receive all of the messages sent to that topic. This model is especially useful in situations in which a group of programs want to notify each other of a particular occurrence. For example, the HR system could publish a message indicating a new hire to a topic called newHire. All of the applications that want to receive a notification when a new person is hired would subscribe to the newHire topic. Through this subscription, the financial applications could use the notification to update the payroll database, and the facilities system could generate a new phone number.

The defining factor in this model is that there may be multiple senders and receivers. It is not necessary that the programs act as both, only that the systems support both. An example of publish-subscribe messaging is pictured in Figure 19.4.

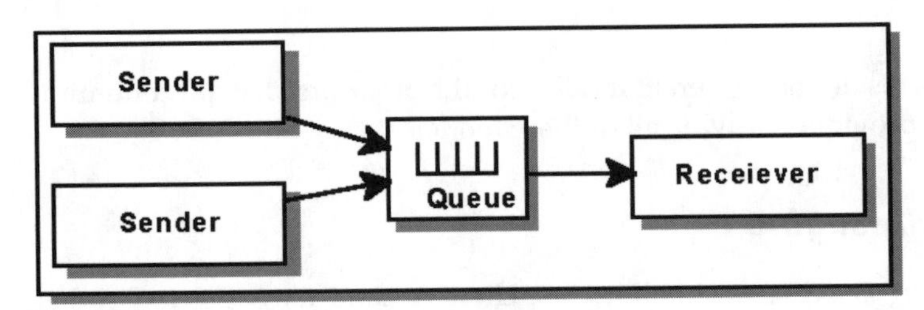

Figure 19.3 Queue-based messaging.

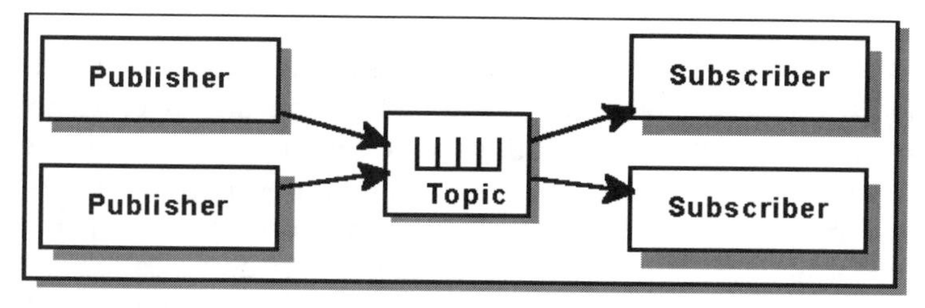

Figure 19.4 Publish-subscribe messaging.

Request-Reply Messaging

Request-reply messaging is the standard object-messaging format. In this case, a program sends a message and expects to receive a message in return. Often, this messaging domain is defined as a subset of one of the other two. For example, a point-to-point system can support, publish, and subscribe by making both points sender and receiver. In our HR example, the HR system might send a message to the facilities system's queue requesting a new phone number and receive a message containing the new number.

JMS doesn't specifically support request-reply messaging, although it does allow it in the context of the other methods via the use of a "reply to" field in a message. In JMS, you can reply to a message by checking for the replyTo field and sending a message to the queue or topic that it contains.

Applications of Messaging

Messaging has gained popularity over the past few years because of its flexibility and the advantages it provides in a variety of applications, such as distributed programming, business integration, and notification.

By definition, messaging is a form of distributed programming. However, messaging adds the level of abstraction generated by the concept of a message. Unlike distributed programming systems such as RMI or CORBA, messaging encapsulates the message being sent into its own publicly defined entity. Programs can change the message type in most messaging systems, making them very flexible. This abstraction also makes it possible to use messaging to link systems. For example, a C programmer could send and receive messages using function calls, while a Java programmer sends and receives messages using method calls. The messages can travel between these two programs without either client knowing the implementation language of the other. In fact, the implementation of one program could change and the other wouldn't need to know unless the message definition changed with it.

Messaging can also save network resources. Server-based messaging systems will usually require only a single network connection from the client to the server. This connection is used for all of the messages sent by the client, even if the messages are going to different destinations. The client can also use the same connection to receive messages from the server. This means that a set of four clients need only four network connections to communicate, instead of the six connections required to support direct client-to-client communication.

Distributed programming is often used to implement the notification systems used as examples in this book. This is one of the main applications of messaging. With persistent messaging, in which the server stores messages for clients that are not currently available, applications can be sure that their notifications are received, even if the receiver is currently unavailable. For example, a company might post important messages using publish-subscribe techniques. When a sales person returns from a trip and connects her computer to the network, any pending messages will be downloaded and the user notified. Although programmers could implement this persistence by hand, the messaging system can handle it for them, encapsulating the work behind a robust, well-tested interface.

Perhaps the hottest application of messaging is business integration. *Business integration* is defined by one system talking to another system. Realizing that these systems may be created with very different technologies, messaging is a powerful translator. The HR system could be a PeopleSoft system, while the financial system could be an Oracle one. A programmer could create adapters that tie these systems together through messaging. When a change occurs in PeopleSoft, the adapter would send a message to the financial adapter, which in turn would update Oracle. If the financial system changes to SAP, then the adapter changes, but the other systems remain the same. The messages become the interface definition for distributed computing.

Java Messaging Service

The Java Messaging Service (JMS) is a Java messaging specification designed by a group of MOM providers and Sun. JMS defines a set of Java interfaces. JMS providers implement these interfaces for the programmer by layering the JMS interface on top of their messaging services. JMS defines both Queues and Topics, but it doesn't require the provider to implement both.

The primary goal for JMS was to provide an interface to messaging that was complete enough to make it useful but not a conglomeration of all of the features provided by existing messaging products. Instead, it tries to maximize portability with as many features as possible. Ideally, the providers that implement JMS will do so in 100-percent pure Java to maximize portability, but this is not a requirement of the specification.

The primary features for JMS are as follows:

- JMS defines the concept of a destination as the target for a message. This destination can be a Queue or a Topic. Queues are used for point-to-point messaging; Topics are used for publish-subscribe messaging.
- JMS defines the concept of connection factories that create the connections to a JMS provider.
- Point-to-point and publish-subscribe messaging are implemented and defined by separate interfaces so that a provider doesn't have to support both.
- All of the provider's code is defined by interfaces in JMS, freeing the implementation from subclassing limitations.
- JMS supports distributed transactions.

Each of these features is discussed in more detail in Chapter 20, "Programming with the Java Messaging Service." A number of companies provide MOM, many of which have signed up to provide a JMS interface to their products. To get a list of the current JMS partners, go to http://java.sun.com/products/jms.

Summary

Messaging is a great addition to the other programming techniques described in this book. Although it is not the be-all and end-all of distributed programming, messaging does provide many advantages in situations in which the programmer wants to decouple the implementation of the distributed programming from the interface to it. JMS applications can potentially switch JMS providers transparently. This freedom to change is limited only by the provider's ability to implement the specification, not the programmer's code. Of course, the messaging abstraction comes at a price. Messages are bigger than their contents, often containing a header that provides system-specific delivery information. Messages often go through the server, making them slower than direct connections. However, in many situations, these costs are far outweighed by the benefits of portable, persistent messaging.

Chapter 20 introduces the syntax for JMS and discusses the provider used in the examples. Chapter 21, "A JMS-Based Alarm System," is a larger JMS example; Chapter 26, "MiniJMS: A Java Messaging Service Provider," includes a sample JMS provider that implements JMS using JDBC, JNDI, and RMI.

Programming with the Java Messaging Service

As you discovered in Chapter 19, "What Are Messaging and the Java Messaging Service?" messaging can be a powerful technique for building enterprise applications. In particular, the persistence and easy use of messaging makes it an interesting part of your programming tool kit. This chapter discusses the techniques and concepts used to program with the Java Messaging Service (JMS).

JMS is actually two interface definitions. The first interface defines the relationship between a client and the messaging service. The second interface defines the relationship between JMS and an application server that hosts it. This chapter focuses on the client side of the JMS specification and discusses the application server interfaces only minimally.

JMS relies on a number of the other interfaces in the Enterprise Java suite. In particular, JNDI and JTA are both part of the JMS specification. Although this chapter does not focus on these relationships, you need to understand the basic principles behind JNDI to completely understand the examples. Please refer to Chapter 5, "Using JNDI," for detailed information on JNDI.

JMS, like JDBC, is an interface-based API. This means that you can't use JMS without a JMS provider that implements the JMS interfaces. The provider implements the services discussed in this chapter using whatever underlying mechanism it chooses. For example, Active Software might implement JMS using its broker technology, while IBM might rely on MQ-series for the underlying messaging transportation. A JMS provider that we created and called MiniJMS is used for all of the examples in this book and included on the CD-ROM.

MiniJMS: The Example Provider

MiniJMS is an almost complete implementation of the JMS specification. The implementation of MiniJMS uses RMI, JNDI, and JDBC, tying together a number of the concepts discussed in this book. In fact, it is such a good example of how these technologies can be combined that Chapter 26, "MiniJMS: A Java Messaging Service Provider," includes a discussion of the MiniJMS implementation.

MiniJMS implements the majority of the JMS API, but it is not intended for commercial use. It does not currently support distributed use, in the sense that the JNDI service provider, the file system context, doesn't support networked operation. This implementation also doesn't support the message selectors discussed in this chapter and is not designed to plug into an application server or to be used with distributed transactions.

Despite these limitations, MiniJMS does provide an example of a JMS provider that uses server-based message management. It provides persistent messaging, saving messages to a JDBC database and the file system. Also, MiniJMS provides an easy testing ground for understanding and testing JMS applications. On top of this, MiniJMS implements both of the messaging models defined by JMS, even though this is not required by the specification.

In order to use MiniJMS, install the JMS libraries on your computer; you'll find them on the CD-ROM in a package called javax.jms. You will also need the JNDI libraries discussed in Chapter 5, and the file system JNDI service provider. All of these libraries can be obtained from the CD-ROM or the JavaSoft Web site at www.javasoft.com. All of these libraries must appear in your class path.

Running the Examples

In addition to the JMS and JNDI packages, add the minijms.jar file to your class path. This file contains the class and properties files for MiniJMS and is available on the CD-ROM in the Chapter_20 directory.

NOTE The examples in this chapter were tested on JDK 1.1.6 with Swing 1.0.3. If you do not have these versions, be sure that you have a newer version, such as Java 2. Note, however, that Java 2 does change the package names for Swing, so you may need to update the examples for use with this version. If possible, based on the production schedule for this book and Sun's release schedule, a set of the examples for Java 2 and JDK 1.1.n are provided on the CD-ROM. If you are unfamiliar with Swing, we highly suggest our book *Programming with JFC* (John Wiley & Sons, 1997).

The user interface code in this example is secondary to the JMS code and can be skimmed over.

To run the examples from this chapter, follow these steps:

1. Create an ODBC data source called MiniJMS. Use the Microsoft Access database file, provided on the CD-ROM, which contains the data for this database; or use

the MiniJMSserver.BuildDB script to create a database using a different database vendor. See Chapter 26 for more details on BuildDB.

2. Create a directory called c:/temp/jndistore for use by the JNDI file system context. If you don't want to use this directory or you are not using a Windows-based machine, edit the server properties file as discussed in Chapter 26.
3. Start the RMI registry.
4. Start the MiniJMS server. This server is called minijmsserver.MiniJMS and takes a single command-line argument containing the IP address of the local host. This address is used to find the RMI registry. For example, you might enter:

```
> java -nojit minijmsserver.MiniJMS 192.168.0.172
```

Notice that the just-in-time compiler isn't used, because a bug in some versions of the JDK causes errors when using RMI. You may not need to take this precaution with your installation. Now that the server is running, you can run the examples from this chapter and Chapter 21, "A JMS-Based Alarm System."

JMS Fundamentals

JMS divides messaging into two categories: point-to-point and publish-subscribe messaging, as discussed in Chapter 19, "What Are Messaging and the Java Messaging Service?" Both of these mechanisms build on the same fundamental ideas. This first section of the chapter discusses these fundamental concepts and the interfaces that represent them. The next two sections introduce the specific interfaces for the two messaging protocols and provide examples for each.

Perhaps the most fundamental concept in JMS is that of a message. As mentioned in Chapter 19, a message is an object that encapsulates a real-world message to be distributed or received, using JMS. These messages travel between destinations defined in JMS by the Destination interface. A JMS provider's job is to get the message from the sender to the destination and on to any receivers that have registered to receive messages for that destination.

Destinations

Destinations define a provider-independent representation of a message delivery point. The Destination interface doesn't define any methods. Rather, it is any object that the provider chooses to use that defines the location to which messages are delivered. JMS defines two destination subtypes: Queues and Topics. These define the concept of a persistent queue and a shared, subscriber-based topic, respectively. The most important aspect of a destination is that its implementation is defined by the JMS provider. This means that the provider can use whatever mechanism it chooses to implement the Destination interface, while clients can use the Destination objects without seeing the implementation details.

The messages that you send to a destination can be persistent, meaning that they will be sent to a client, even if the client is currently unavailable. They can also be guaranteed via persistence, meaning that the JMS libraries will not say a message is sent until it is stored using a transacted resource such as a database. This persistence ensures message delivery in an enterprise-level situation.

Because JMS is expected to work in a network environment, not within a single application, destinations may represent a network address or a named location in a central server. In any case, the client that wants to send a message to the destination needs to create a connection to the JMS provider's services. This connection is created using a connection factory.

The Connection Factory

In the same way that JDBC provides a DriverManager for hiding the specifics of a JDBC driver author from the programmer, JNDI uses the ConnectionFactory interface to hide the specifics of connecting to a JMS provider from the programmer. ConnectionFactory is an interface without methods. However, two subtypes called QueueConnectionFactory and TopicConnectionFactory, discussed later in this chapter, do provide methods for their respective messaging models. These connection factories are tasked with the job of creating provider-specific connections to the JMS service provider. For example, the MiniJMS connection factories know the RMI URL for the MiniJMS server. This URL is used to create connections to the RMI server as requested by the programmer.

JMS and JNDI: Administered Objects

In order for Destinations and connection factories to maintain their implementation anonymity, their class must be hidden from the user. In JDBC, this class hiding is provided via driver registration and URLs. JMS takes provider hiding a step further using JNDI to create administered objects. An administered object is an object that the program retrieves from a JNDI context. In JMS, both destinations and connection factories are administered objects. The messaging administrator uses tools provided by the JMS provider to create destinations and connection factories before adding them to a JMS context. Programmers simply look these objects up in the context, unaware of their implementation. Although the examples in this chapter use the MiniJMS provider, they can easily be updated to use another provider by simply changing the JNDI initial context information.

MiniJMSUtils

To consolidate the creation of the initial JNDI context and make it easy to configure, the provided examples do two things. First, they use properties files to define their context information. Second, a class called MiniJMSUtils creates a context from a properties file. MiniJMS also installs the RMI security manager, saving the examples that step in the code.

The code for MiniJMSUtils, which follows, is basically a recipe for loading a properties file, reading it, and using the properties to create an initial context for JNDI lookups. The properties file is specified by a file name. The file must be in the class path to be found.

```
package minijms;

import minijms.*;
import minijmsserver.*;
import javax.jms.*;
import javax.naming.*;
import java.io.*;
import java.rmi.*;
import java.util.*;

public class MiniJMSUtils
{
    public static Properties properties;
    public static Context context;

    public static void init(String propsFile)
        throws Exception
    {
        // Create and install a security manager.
        SecurityManager mng;
        InputStream propsIn;
        Properties sysProps;

        mng = new RMISecurityManager();
        System.setSecurityManager(mng);

        //Update the system props for class loading.
        //fails for an applet but that's okay.
        try
        {
            sysProps = System.getProperties();
            sysProps.put("java.rmi.server.codebase"
                    ,"file:/"
                    + sysProps.getProperty("user.dir")
                    +"/");
            System.setProperties(sysProps);
        }
        catch(Exception ignore)
        {
        }

        //Load the properties file.
        propsIn
         = ClassLoader.getSystemResourceAsStream(propsFile);
        properties = new Properties();
        properties.load(propsIn);
```

```
            Properties p = new Properties();

            String user=properties.getProperty("java.naming.user");
            String password
                   =properties.getProperty("java.naming.password");
            InitialContext retVal = null;

            p.put(Context.INITIAL_CONTEXT_FACTORY
              ,properties.getProperty("java.naming.factory.initial"));

            p.put(Context.PROVIDER_URL
                , properties.getProperty("java.naming.provider.url"));

            if (user != null)
            {
                p.put(Context.SECURITY_PRINCIPAL, user);

                if (password == null) password = "";

                p.put(Context.SECURITY_CREDENTIALS, password);
            }

            context = new InitialContext(p);
        }
    }
```

The properties and context static variables are public and provide easy access to a program. The following examples all initialize the MiniJMSUtils class and use its variables to get to the JNDI context. This context is then used to access destinations by name or connection factories by name. Although this utility is included in the MiniJMS package, it doesn't rely on any MiniJMS code beyond the import statements and can be used with other JMS providers or JNDI providers.

Connections

Once a program has a connection factory, it can use the connection factory to create a connection. This connection represents a single channel to the JMS provider. In many cases, this channel is a network connection of some sort to the provider's server daemon. For MiniJMS, the connection forms an RMI relationship between the client and the MiniJMS program.

Depending on the messaging style you choose, you will create connections from the factory differently. In both cases, connections are represented by an object that implements the Connection interface. This interface has two subtypes, QueueConnection and TopicConnection, that represent the two messaging models. Connection itself defines methods that are standard to all JMS connections. These methods are described in Table 20.1.

The first thing you may notice about these methods is that they all can throw JMSExceptions. This is true of every method in the JMS API. A JMSException represents an exception created during the service provider's execution of a method. This error may be caused by networking issues, invalid arguments, or many other reasons.

Table 20.1 Connection Methods

METHOD	DESCRIPTION
`public String getClientID() throws JMSException`	Returns the identifier for this client. This identifier is provider dependent and will normally be set by the factory when the connection is made.
`public void setClientID(String clientId) throws JMSException`	Sets the client identifier. The argument should be a valid provider-specific string.
`public ConnectionMetaData getMetaData() throws JMSException`	Returns an object containing information about the connection and its JMS provider.
`public void setExceptionListener( ExceptionListener listener) throws JMSException`	Sets the exception listener for this connection. This listener is notified of major exceptions that occur in the connections, such as a server disconnect.
`public void start() throws JMSException`	Starts message delivery on the connection.
`public void stop() throws JMSException`	Stops all message delivery on the connection.
`public void close() throws JMSException`	Closes the connection freeing any resources that it maintained.

The Connection interface also defines a close method. This is true of many of the JMS objects. Because JMS is expected to provide network-based messaging, each of the provider's objects might represent network or server resources. When done, close all objects that provide a method for doing so.

The connections exception listener is an object that implements the single method:

```
public void onException(JMSException exception)
```

The connection notifies the listener of major exceptions. However, this is a provider-specific feature, and JMS doesn't dictate when or even if this listener is used.

Both messaging models have a connection factory that takes a user name and password when creating a connection. This identification can be used by the connection to identify the client or user to the JMS server. This identification is optional, and it is up to the provider how an unidentified client is treated.

Connections represent the channel to the JMS provider. To control this channel, the connection objects have a start and stop method. Stop halts all message traffic on the connection, and start resumes the traffic. These methods are useful if you want to initialize your program before receiving messages and don't want the connection to remain in its default running state while you initialize your code.

A JMS Connection can return a ConnectionMetaData object that contains information about the connection's JMS provider. In particular, the ConnectionMetaData interface defines methods for accessing the provider version and name, as well as the JMS version that the provider supports.

Sessions

One of a connection's main jobs, creating sessions, is hidden by the default API. Each of the subconnection types, QueueConnection and TopicConnection, provides methods for creating sessions that support their specific messaging model. As defined by the JMS specification, a session is "a single-threaded context for producing and consuming messages." In other words, a session is the object that provides access to the connection for code that wants to send and receive messages. More important, the session does this in a single-threaded model by serializing message sending and delivery.

For example, if client A sends four messages, client B's session will deliver these four messages one after the other, not at the same time. Even if two programs send a third program messages simultaneously, the session will ensure that the receivers will be notified of one message at a time. Although notification is synchronized, it may occur in a different thread from the one that created the session if the program uses message listeners to receive notification. These listeners are discussed in the "MessageListeners" section and are similar to event listeners in AWT and Swing.

Sessions can also provide a transaction context for messaging. This context stores messages for delivery until they are committed, at which point the messages are sent as a block. An example of how you might use transactions with messages is shown in Figure 20.1. In this example, several sessions are created and sent to the session, but they are not really sent to the server until the transaction is committed. Sessions can also be rolled back, allowing the client to prepare a group of messages to send, then "change its mind" and cancel all of the sends in a single block.

Transactions are optional with messaging and, if turned off, messages are delivered when they are sent.

Sessions without transactions rely on the concept of acknowledgment to indicate when a message is received. When a JMS client acknowledges receipt of a message, that message will not be sent to the client again. In this respect, committing a transacted session is the same as acknowledging all of the messages received in the transaction scope. Because acknowledgment is like a mini-transaction, it too has several options. These are listed and described in Table 20.2. Each of these values is defined as a static variable in the Message interface.

Sessions provide a set of methods for creating message objects. These methods are used by the client to create messages for sending. By providing methods in the session for creating messages, the JMS specification hides the classes used to implement these messages from the programmer. These methods and the others defined in the Session interface are described in Table 20.3. The various types of messages created are discussed later in this chapter.

As with a connection, a session should be closed when a program is done using it.

MessageListeners

Sessions allow the programmer to assign to them an object called a *message listener*. This listener receives notification of any messages received by this session. However,

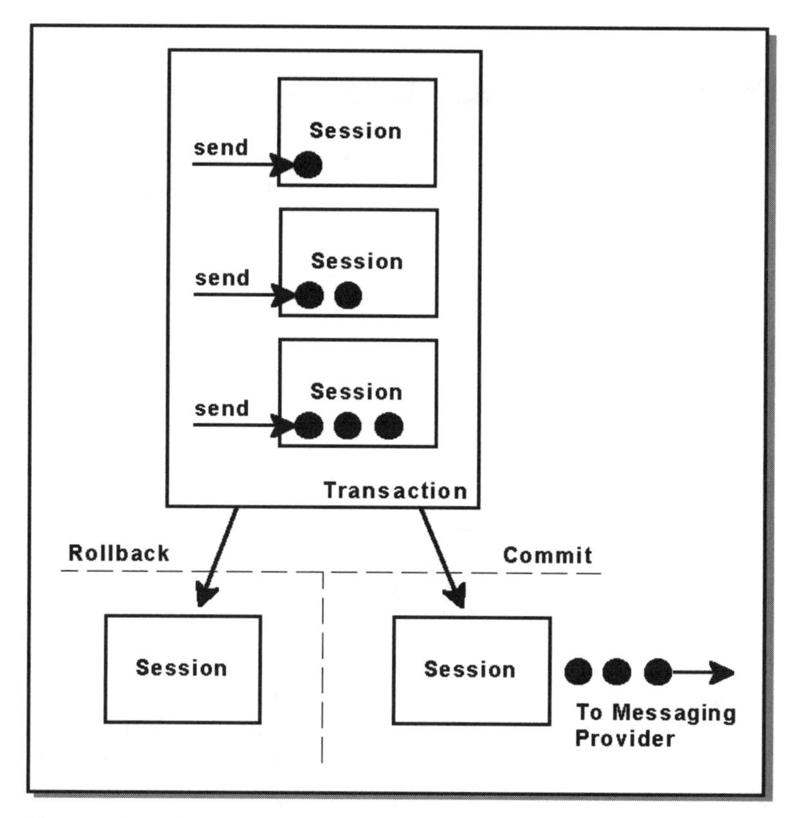

Figure 20.1 Transacted messages.

this facility is really part of the Application Server interface and is not intended for normal client use, because it prohibits all other forms of message delivery.

That said, the MessageListener interface is also used by other objects to provide an asynchronous message delivery mechanism. A message listener defines a single method:

```
public void onMessage(Message message)
```

Table 20.2 Acknowledgment Options

OPTION	DESCRIPTION
AUTO_ACKNOWLEDGE	Each message is automatically acknowledged when it is delivered.
CLIENT_ACKNOWLEDGE	Clients must acknowledge each message programmatically.
DUPS_OK_ACKNOWLEDGE	Messages are acknowledged lazily, and a message may be delivered twice if the connection is broken unexpectedly.

Table 20.3 Session Methods

METHOD	DESCRIPTION
`public BytesMessage createBytesMessage() throws JMSException`	Creates a message that represents a collection of bytes. This type of message is often used to "talk" to systems using non-JMS messaging code.
`public MapMessage createMapMessage() throws JMSException`	Creates a message that stores key-value pairs.
`public Message createMessage() throws JMSException`	Creates a default message that contains no body information.
`public ObjectMessage createObjectMessage() throws JMSException`	Creates a message containing a single, serializable object.
`public ObjectMessage createObjectMessage(Serializable object) throws JMSException`	Creates a message containing a single, serializable object and specifies the object.
`public StreamMessage createStreamMessage() throws JMSException`	Creates a message that contains a stream of self-defining data. Like the BytesMessage, this type of message is often used to interact with non-JMS clients.
`public TextMessage createTextMessage() throws JMSException`	Creates a message containing a string.
`public TextMessage createTextMessage(StringBuffer stringBuffer) throws JMSException`	Creates a message containing a string and defines the string.
`public boolean getTransacted() throws JMSException`	Returns true if the session is transacted; returns false if the session is not using transactions.
`public void commit() throws JMSException`	If the session is transacted, commit sends any waiting messages and acknowledges receipt of any received messages.
`public void rollback() throws JMSException`	If the session is transacted, rollback removes any messages that were sent from being sent and will cause messages that were received to be redelivered.
`public void close() throws JMSException`	Closes the session, freeing any resources that it used.
`public void recover() throws JMSException`	Tells the session to redeliver unacknowledged messages, after marking them as such. New messages will continue to be delivered normally.

Table 20.3 *Continued*

METHOD	DESCRIPTION
`public MessageListener getMessageListener() throws JMSException`	Returns the session's message listener, if one is assigned.
`public void setMessageListener( MessageListener listener) throws JMSException`	Assigns a message listener to the session.

When appropriate, the listener is sent this message with a real JMS message as the argument. The JMS specification makes two statements about these listeners. First, they will not have onMessage called by two threads at the same time. Second, onMessage should not throw any exceptions. Message listeners are discussed more in a moment.

Message Producers

In order to send a message, a client must ask the session to create a message producer for it. This message producer is an object that implements the MessageProducer interface. In fact, a client will create one of two subtypes of MessageProducer: TopicPublisher or QueueSender. Both of these provide specific methods for sending messages using their particular messaging styles. Both also provide the methods that they inherit from MessageProducer. These methods, described in Table 20.4, provide access to a set of default values for the message producer.

Table 20.4 Message Producer Methods

METHOD	DESCRIPTION
`public void setDisableMessageID(boolean value) throws JMSException`	A JMS provider is expected to assign unique ids to each method. If the client doesn't need these ids, it can use this method to tell the provider that they are not required. This can save some resources; however, the provider may create them anyway for internal use.
`public boolean getDisableMessageID() throws JMSException`	Returns whether or not message ids are disabled.
`public void setDisableMessageTimestamp(boolean value) throws JMSException`	Like the message id, the provider is expected to time-stamp messages before they go through the messaging system. Because this

Continues

Table 20.4 Message Producer Methods *(Continued)*

METHOD	DESCRIPTION
	increases message size, clients can hint that they want to disable this feature. However, like the message id, the provider may ignore this flag.
`public boolean getDisableMessageTimestamp() throws JMSException`	Returns whether or not time stamps are disabled.
`public void setDeliveryMode(int deliveryMode) throws JMSException`	Sets the default delivery mode for this producer. Messages will be sent with this mode unless otherwise specified. Possible values are javax.jms.DeliveryMode.PERSISTENT and javax.jms.DeliveryMode .NON_PERSISTENT. The default is persistent.
`public int getDeliveryMode() throws JMSException`	Returns the producer's default delivery mode.
`public void setPriority(int deliveryMode) throws JMSException`	Sets the default priority for a producer. Messages will be sent with this priority unless otherwise specified. The default is 4 on a scale from 0 to 9.
`public int getPriority() throws JMSException`	Returns the producer's default priority.
`public void setTimeToLive(int timeToLive) throws JMSException`	Sets the default time, in milliseconds, that the JMS provider should keep the message available. A value of 0 indicates that the message should not expire. This value is added to the time that a message is sent to determine its actual expiration date. The default is 0.
`public int getTimeToLive() throws JMSException`	Returns the default time-to-live that the producer will use when sending messages.
`public void close() throws JMSException`	Closes the producer and frees any resources.

In essence, the producer is storing default values to use when sending messages. These values are stored in the message itself, as discussed in the following section on message attributes. As with all of the objects in the JMS framework, you should close a producer when you finish using it in order to free any supporting resources.

Message Consumers

Message consumers are created by the session for clients that want to receive messages. Message consumers are attached to a Destination and are designed to retrieve messages sent to their destinations. These consumers must implement the MessageConsumer interface and, as in the producer case, actually implement a subtype of MessageConsumer. This subtype will be either QueueReceiver or TopicSubscriber. Unlike the MessageProducer interface, the majority of the interesting methods for a consumer are in the MessageConsumer interface itself. The subtypes provide only specific information about the destination that is being listened to.

Clients have two options for retrieving messages from a consumer. First, the client can use one of the receive messages listed in Table 20.5. This is a synchronous mechanism that allows the client to keep message delivery in the thread of its choosing. Second, clients can register a message listener with the consumer. This listener will be notified of messages asynchronously but should always receive the onMessage message in the same thread. So, although the onMessage method will probably be called in a different thread from the one that initially created the consumer, it will not be called

Table 20.5 Message Consumer Methods

METHOD	DESCRIPTION
`public String getMessageSelector() throws JMSException`	Returns the consumer's message selector if one is assigned. Selectors are discussed in more detail in the "Message Selectors" section.
`public MessageListener getMessageListener() throws JMSException`	Returns the consumer's message listener.
`public void setMessageListener(MessageListener listener) throws JMSException`	Assigns the consumer's message listener. A consumer can have only one listener at a time.
`public Message receive() throws JMSException`	Returns the next message for the consumer; this method will block and wait until a message arrives.
`public Message receive(long timeOut) throws JMSException`	Returns the next message for the consumer; this method will block and wait until a message arrives or the time-out is reached. If the method times out, null is returned. The time-out is specified in milliseconds.
`public Message receiveNoWait() throws JMSException`	Returns the next message for the consumer or null if one is not available. This method does not block.
`public void close() throws JMSException`	Closes the consumer and frees resources.

from a variety of threads and will not be called by more than one thread at a time. As discussed previously, the onMessage method should not throw any exceptions, because the JMS specification indicates that this method is safe for the provider to call.

NOTE **Unlike the session's message listener, which is not really intended for client use, message consumer message listeners are a core part of the client API and should be used freely.**

Depending on your application design, choose to either receive messages or listen for them. Receiving messages is synchronous, so use that option when you want to wait for a message to arrive or want to control the thread in which messages arrive. Listeners are notified in a thread managed by the session. Use the listeners option when you want asynchronous notification of a message. Do not mix these two mechanisms, because a session is not expected to hold messages for receiving if they have already been sent to a listener. Also, if two consumers are created using the same session and the same destinations, they will not both receive messages. Instead, the session will randomly distribute the messages between the consumers. In general, you should create only one consumer to deal with a particular destination.

Messages

All of this discussion and design would be moot without the fundamental concept of a message. Messages represent the key abstraction in JMS; they are items to be sent or received. Depending on the JMS provider, message implementations can be blandly generic or highly optimized for a specific delivery system. Regardless of messages' implementation, JMS specifies that all messages be represented by objects that implement the Message interface.

The Message interface separates a JMS message into three pieces:

- **Header.** This is the JMS-specific information included with a message. For example, the expiration date, priority, and delivery mode are attributes of a message.
- **Properties.** Optional, often provider-specific, message attributes. These properties can be of any primitive type, a string, or an object. For example, the MiniJMS provider uses a property to keep track of the database id assigned to messages by the persistent store.
- **Body.** This is the content of the message. The type of content provided depends on the message type, as discussed in the next section on message subclasses.

The JMS message header fields are described in Table 20.6. These headers can be defined at different times, and their assignment times are also listed in the same table. A message object provides methods for accessing all of these headers using the standard naming convention. For example, the method setJMSDestination is used to set the JMSDestination header field.

A message can also have arbitrary properties assigned to it in addition to these header values. These properties might be provider specific and may even be required by the provider. They can also be used by the client to configure the message or indicate

Table 20.6 Message Headers

HEADER	DESCRIPTION	ASSIGNMENT
`JMSDestination`	The Destination object to which the message will be, or was, sent.	Assigned as part of the send method.
`JMSDeliveryMode`	The delivery mode for this message. Possible values are DeliveryMode.PERSISTENT and DeliveryMode.NON_PERSISTENT.	Assigned as part of the send method.
`JMSExpiration`	The expiration time for this message. A value of 0 implies no expiration and is the default.	Assigned as part of the send method.
`JMSPriority`	The priority for a message. The value can range from 0 (the lowest priority) to 9 (the highest priority).	Assigned as part of the send method.
`JMSMessageID`	The unique id, within the messaging system, for the message. May not be set if the producer is told to skip assignment.	Assigned as part of the send method.
`JMSTimestamp`	The time at which the message was sent. May not be set if the producer is told to skip assignment.	Assigned as part of the send method.
`JMSCorrelationID`	Used by the client to link messages; can be a message id, a string, or a byte array. This value is for client use and can be assigned to indicate related messages.	May be set by the client.
`JMSReplyTo`	A specific Destination to which the client expects responses to this message.	May be set by the client.
`JMSType`	Used by some providers to indicate the message definition to use for this message. This value can be highly provider dependent, and clients should use the provider documentation to determine if it is required.	May, sometimes must, be set by the client.
`JMSRedeliverd`	Indicates whether the message was delivered previously and not acknowledged.	Set by the JMS provider during redelivery.

its body contents for the receiver. In general, properties may require more resources than the message body and should be used sparingly.

Properties can be of a variety of types, and methods are provided to get and set properties by name for each type listed in Table 20.7. For example:

```
public int getIntProperty(String name) throws JMSException
```

returns an integer property, and

```
public void setStringProperty(String name, String value)
                                        throws JMSException
```

assigns a string property. Table 20.7 also shows the conversions that a message should support when assigning properties. The Xs indicate that a property written with the type in the first column of the row can be read with the type at the top of the column containing the X. So, strings can be used for all types, and floats can be read as floats or doubles.

Properties can also be set as objects using setObjectProperty and getObjectProperty. In this case, the primitive types such as Integer can be used to assign an integer property. This property can be accessed as either an int or an Integer object once assigned.

Clients can test whether a property exists using the method:

```
public boolean propertyExists(String name) throws JMSException
```

To iterate over the entire list of properties, use the method:

```
public Enumeration getPropertyNames() throws JMSException
```

to get the available property names, as strings, and use these names to access the properties. You can even remove all of the properties from a message using the method:

```
public void clearProperties() throws JMSException
```

This technique should not be used if the provider is expecting certain properties to exist.

Table 20.7 Message Property Types

	BOOLEAN	BYTE	SHORT	INT	LONG	FLOAT	DOUBLE	STRING
boolean	X							X
byte		X	X	X	X			X
short			X	X	X			X
int				X	X			X
long					X			X
float						X	X	X
double							X	X
String	X	X	X	X	X	X	X	X

The JMS specification states that the JMSX prefix can be used on properties defined in the specification itself. These properties are listed in Table 20.8, along with the entity that assigns them.

JMSX properties are not required, except that the provider support JMSXGroupID and JMSXGroupSeq. Note: MiniJMS does provide no special support for these properties, but it doesn't prohibit client use of them, either.

The prefix JMS_ is reserved for properties that the provider defines. All other properties are considered application specific by the provider's code.

The body of a message is determined by its class. Regardless of the class, a message body can be cleared using the Message interface's method:

```
public void clearBody() throws JMSException
```

This will remove the contents of the message.

The last method defined in the Message interface is called acknowledge:

```
public void acknowledge() throws JMSException
```

When a message is told to acknowledge, it notifies the JMS provider that the message is received. This means that the message will not be re-sent to the session that delivered

Table 20.8 JMSX Properties from JMS 1.0

PROPERTY	DESCRIPTION	ASSIGNER
`JMSXUserID`	An identifier for the user sending the message.	Provider on send.
`JMSXAppID`	An identifier for the application sending the message.	Provider on send.
`JMSXDeliveryCount`	The number of delivery attempts, starting with 1.	Provider on receipt of message.
`JMSXGroupID`	An identifier for a client-defined message group.	Client.
`JMSXGroupSeq`	The sequence number for a message in a group.	Client.
`JMSXProducerTXID`	The transaction identifier for the producer.	Provider on send.
`JMSXConsumerTXID`	The transaction identifier for the consumer.	Provider on receipt of message.
`JMSXRcvTimestamp`	The time the message was delivered.	Provider on receipt of message.
`JMSXState`	Used for maintaining information about the persistent state of a message, the possible values are 1-waiting, 2-ready, 3-expired, 4-retained. These may or may not be available to the client, depending on the provider.	Provider.

it. Depending on the acknowledgment mode assigned to the session, calling this method may be ignored because the message may have been automatically acknowledged or it may be part of a transaction that doesn't want to have it acknowledged yet.

Message Subclasses

The Message interface does not define any body for the message. Instead, the JMS specification defines five subtypes of Message. These subtypes support various message body types. Although a provider is expected to support all of the types, it may have optimized one type over the others based on its underlying implementation. See the documentation for your provider to find out these specifics. The available subtypes are:

- **StreamMessage.** A message that uses a stream representation for its body. The stream holds a self-describing sequence of Java objects and primitive values.
- **MapMessage.** A message that stores key-value pairs.
- **TextMessage.** A message that provides a single string for its message body.
- **ObjectMessage.** A message that provides a single serialized object as its message body. The type of this object is arbitrary.
- **BytesMessage.** A message that represents a stream of bytes. This type is used primarily for accessing legacy messaging systems and applications. As a result, some providers may prohibit the user of properties with a BytesMessage.

NOTE **MiniJMS does not fully support the Stream and Bytes message types.**

Like the message properties, the messages that take multiple values—StreamMessage and MapMessage—can convert between some value types. These conversions are listed in Table 20.9. As before, items written with the type in column one can be read as the type in the columns with an X.

Both the Stream and Bytes messages provide methods for accessing these values sequentially. For example, the method getInt() is used to read the value in the message body as an int. Because these two message types are read sequentially, they also provide the method:

```
public void reset() throws JMSException
```

to send the cursor back to the beginning of the body.

The MapMessage type provides methods for accessing values by key. For example, the method:

```
public int getInt(String name) throws JMSException
```

is used to access an integer value. Similar methods are provided for writing:

```
public void setChar(java.lang.String name, char value)
throws MessageNotWriteableException, JMSException
```

Table 20.9 Message Body Type Conversions

	BOOLEAN	BYTE	SHORT	INT	LONG	FLOAT	DOUBLE	STRING	BYTE[]
boolean	X							X	
byte		X	X	X	X			X	
short			X	X	X			X	
int				X	X			X	
long					X			X	
float						X	X	X	
double							X	X	
String	X	X	X	X	X	X	X	X	
byte[]									X

Many of the methods for changing a Message's body can throw a MessageNotWritableException or a MessageNotReadableException if the message has been placed in a read-only or write-only state by the JMS provider.

The TextMessage interface defines the methods:

```
public void setText(String string) throws JMSException
```

and

```
public String getText() throws JMSException
```

for assigning the body. In the same manner, the ObjectMessage defines the methods:

```
public void setObject(Serializable object) throws JMSException
```

and

```
public Serializable getObject() throws JMSException
```

for accessing its body.

As you can see, there are a variety of message types and ways to assign their contents. Check the JMS documentation for each type to learn the specifics for that type and the messages it provides.

Message Selectors

In an enterprise environment, many messages may often be created for a particular destination. Some clients may not require notification of all messages. In fact, clients may want to restrict delivery of some messages to improve performance and reduce network traffic. To support message filtering, JMS defines the concept of a message selector. This selector can be used by a consumer to prevent delivery of certain messages. For example, an administrator might ignore log messages that have a "green" state and view only messages in a "yellow" or "red" state.

A message selector is essentially an SQL92 with a clause that references the header or property fields in a message. The selector cannot reference the contents of the message. To make reading selectors easier, all of the predefined literals and key words are in all uppercase.

Selectors can contain four types of information:

- **Literals**. Strings, numbers, TRUE, or FALSE. These are constant values used in comparisons and other expressions. Strings should appear in single quotes.
- **Identifiers.** Names of properties or header fields.
- **Whitespace.** Spaces, tabs, form feeds, or line terminators.
- **Expressions.** Comparisons, arithmetic operations, and groupings of these operations.

Expressions use operators to combine literals and identifiers. These expressions can be grouped using parentheses and combined using the key words AND, OR, and NOT. The supported comparison operators for numbers are:

```
=, >, >=, <, <=, <> (not equal)
```

For example, you might write:

```
JMSPriority >= 5
```

to test if the priority for a message is greater than or equal to 5. You can also use arithmetic operations, including:

```
+,-
```

the unary operators for saying a value is positive or negative, and the operators

```
+,-,*,/
```

for adding, subtracting, multiplying, and dividing. If you want to test whether a number is in a given range, you can use the BETWEEN and NOT BETWEEN key words. These are the same as combining other operators but may be interpreted more quickly. For example:

```
price BETWEEN 10 and 100
```

and

```
price >= 10 AND price <= 100
```

are equivalent.

Strings can be compared using = or <> and with the LIKE operator. For example, you might say:

```
JMSType == 'carrier'
```

LIKE takes a pattern and compares it to an identifier. This pattern is made up of characters, numbers, and the _ or % characters, indicating wildcards. The _ character indicates a single wild character. The % wildcard indicates a sequence of characters, including the empty sequence. For example, you might use:

```
phone LIKE '12%3'
```

to match 123 or 124453, but not 1234, because it ends in 4, not 3. You can also negate the LIKE operator by saying NOTLIKE. To include the _ or % character in a LIKE comparison, use the ESCAPE keyword to define an escape character. For example:

```
name LIKE 'JMS\_%' ESCAPE '\'
```

will test the name for strings like JMS_one but fail for JMStwo. To test whether a string is one of a group of possibilities, use the IN key word. IN takes an array of strings and compares the provided value with the array. For example:

```
name IN ('stephen','scott')
```

matches stephen or scott and no other value. You can negate the IN operator by using NOT IN.

Selectors can also use the key words IS NOT NULL or IS NULL to check the existence of an identifier. For example:

```
JMSType IS NOT NULL
```

will be true if the message has its JMSType header field set.

Regardless of the selector, all comparisons must be made between like types, numbers to numbers, strings to strings, or Booleans to Booleans.

NOTE **MiniJMS provides no support for message selectors.**

Although selectors are used to identify and filter messages, they are not part of the message and are assigned when a client creates a MessageConsumer to receive messages.

Basic Steps for Programming JMS

Given these concepts and interfaces, the basic steps for creating a JMS program are as follows:

1. Retrieve a ConnectionFactory from JNDI.
2. Retrieve the Destinations of interest from JNDI.
3. Use the ConnectionFactory to create a Connection to the JMS provider, probably to the server.
4. Use the Connection to create a Session.
5. Use the Session and Destination objects to create MessageConsumers, MessageProducers, or both.
6. Assign any MessageListeners.
7. Send messages with the producer, receive messages with the consumer.

The next two sections discuss how these steps are implemented for the two messaging styles: point-to-point and publish-subscribe messaging.

Point-to-Point Messaging

Point-to-point messaging, as defined by JMS, uses the concept of a queue to represent a destination. A queue is a sequence of messages that may or may not be persistent, depending on their delivery mode. Queues are created by an administrator and registered with a JNDI context. Clients can send messages to or receive messages from a queue. However, the implied relationship between client and queue is that a single client will receive messages from a single queue, and possibly multiple clients will send messages to the queue. As discussed in the next section, the publish-subscribe model is intended for situations in which multiple clients share the same queue.

Queues are represented by objects that implement the Queue interface. This interface defines a single method:

```
public String getQueueName() throws JMSException
```

that returns the name of the queue. The provider is also expected to override the toString method and return a "pretty" version of the name. Queue is a subinterface of Destination, so a Queue is a full-fledged destination for sending and receiving messages.

The server serializes messages sent to a queue into a single sequence. This ensures that the client checking the queue will receive each message only once and that the messages will be received in the order in which they were sent. The JMS provider is expected to keep messages for a queue available as long as it is running. Persistent messages should be maintained even if the server is shut down and restarted.

Queue Connection Factory

Clients that want to use Queues and the point-to-point messaging model need to retrieve a queue connection factory from JNDI. This factory implements the QueueConnectionFactory interface, which extends the ConnectionFactory interface described previously. The QueueConnectionFactory provides two methods for creating connections:

```
public QueueConnection createQueueConnection() throws JMSException
public QueueConnection createQueueConnection(String userName
                                            , String password)
                                              throws JMSException
```

Both of these methods return an object that implements the QueueConnection interface. The first method uses the default user identification; the second takes a user name and password. These values may or may not be used by the JMS provider.

MiniJMS registers a QueueConnectionFactory in JNDI using the name QueueConnectionFactory, so given a context, you can look it up using code such as:

```
factory = (QueueConnectionFactory)
            context.lookup("QueueConnectionFactory");
```

This code simply looks up an object in the JNDI context and casts it appropriately.

Queue Connections

The QueueConnection is a special kind of Connection designed for point-to-point messaging and inherits the methods from that interface, as listed in Table 20.1. QueueConnection also defines two new methods. The first:

```
public QueueSession createQueueSession(boolean transacted,
                                       int acknowledgeMode)
                                       throws JMSException
```

is used to create a session for your point-to-point messaging. This method takes a Boolean that indicates whether the returned session will use transactions and an integer that indicates the acknowledgment mode.

The second method defined in QueueConnection is:

```
public ConnectionConsumer createConnectionConsumer(Queue queue
                                , String messageSelector
                                , ServerSessionPool sessionPool
                                , int maxMessages)
                                throws JMSException
```

for use in an application server. It is not really part of the client API.

Queue Sessions

The session created by a QueueConnection implements the QueueSession interface. This interface extends the Session interface described previously and adds methods specific to point-to-point messages.

The first thing that a QueueSession can do is create a special type of MessageProducer called a QueueSender. Use the method:

```
public QueueSender createSender(Queue queue) throws JMSException
```

to create this object for a specific queue.

The session can also create special MessageConsumers called QueueReceivers for a queue. There are two methods for creating consumers; both take a Queue and one takes a message selector.

```
public QueueReceiver createReceiver(Queue queue) throws JMSException
public QueueReceiver createReceiver(Queue queue
                                    ,String messageSelector)
                                     throws JMSException
```

A QueueSession can also create an object called a QueueBrowser for inspecting the contents of a queue:

```
public QueueBrowser createBrowser(Queue queue) throws JMSException
public QueueBrowser createBrowser(Queue queue
                                 ,String messageSelector)
                                 throws JMSException
```

JMS does not require the browser to provide an up-to-the-minute picture of the queue.

NOTE **Not all providers will support queue browsers, because they may represent unreasonable resource usage. MiniJMS does not support them.**

The queue browser implements four methods, described in Table 20.10, for accessing its information. These methods are used to get the queue and selector associated with the browser, get an enumeration for the messages in the queue, and close the browser.

The primary method of interest is probably the getEnumeration method, which returns an Enumeration that steps through the messages in the browser's queue.

Finally, the QueueSession can be used to create Queues. The method:

```
public Queue createQueue(String queueName) throws JMSException
```

creates a real queue. This method may not be supported by all providers. Instead, providers may and should provide administration tools for defining queues. The name of a queue can be provider specific, so using create queue is not a portable coding convention.

The QueueSession can also create temporary queues using the method:

```
public TemporaryQueue createTemporaryQueue() throws JMSException
```

Temporary queues are deleted automatically when the client stops using them. You can also use the TemporaryQueue's delete method to force deletion of the queue. Often, temporary queues are created to act as the reply-to destination for messages. The name of a temporary queue is defined by the provider's code, so this method is portable across JMS providers.

The Queue Sender

In order to send messages to a Queue, you use the QueueSession to create a QueueSender. This object defines four methods for sending a message to a queue. These methods are described in Table 20.11.

The sender also provides the method getQueue to access its default queue.

The following example shows how a QueueSender is used in an application. QueueSenderTest defines a JFC application. The application displays a window, pictured in

Table 20.10 QueueBrowser Methods

METHOD	DESCRIPTION
`public Queue getQueue() throws JMSException`	Returns the Queue associated with this browser.
`public String getMessageSelector() throws JMSException`	Returns the browser's assigned message selector.
`public Enumeration getEnumeration() throws JMSException`	Returns an Enumeration for the queue's messages.
`public void close() throws JMSException`	Closes the browser and frees resources.

Table 20.11 QueueSender Methods

METHOD	DESCRIPTION
`public void send(Message msg) throws JMSException`	Sends a message to the sender's queue with the default mode, priority, and timeToLive.
`public void send(Message msg, int deliveryMode, int priority, long timeToLive) throws JMSException`	Sends a message to the sender's queue with the specified mode, priority, and timeToLive.
`public void send(Queue queue, Message message) throws JMSException`	Sends a message to the specified queue with the default mode, priority, and timeToLive.
`public void send(Queue queue, Message message, int deliveryMode, int priority, long timeToLive) throws JMSException`	Sends a message to the specified queue with the specified mode, priority, and timeToLive.

Figure 20.2, that contains fields for assigning the queue to send to and the message to send. Once the user assigns a queue, he or she can send messages to it by typing in the Send field and pressing Enter or the Send button.

NOTE **Many of the examples in this chapter use the same basic style as this one, in the sense that they are JFC programs. As a result, all of the code for each example is not shown every time. The entire code is shown for this first example only. Refer to the CD-ROM for the complete code on further examples.**

This is the first example in the chapter, so be sure to reread the section on running these examples at the beginning of the chapter before you try to run this one or any of the others.

The first part of the QueueSenderTest class definition imports the appropriate packages and defines the class name. Variables for all of the JMS objects that will be created are also defined, as are the text fields that are used to interact with the user. To improve maintenance, constant strings are used for the action commands on the text fields and buttons.

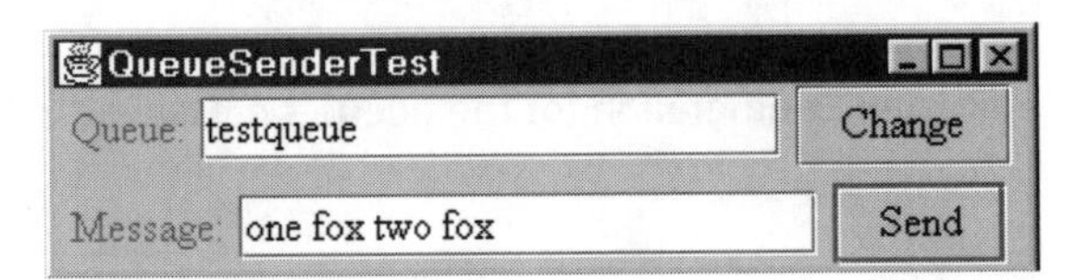

Figure 20.2 QueueSenderTest.

```
import javax.jms.*;
import javax.naming.*;
import minijms.*;

import com.sun.java.swing.*;
import java.awt.*;
import java.awt.event.*;

public class QueueSenderTest extends JPanel
 implements ActionListener
{
    JTextField sendField;
    JTextField queueField;

    javax.jms.QueueSession session;
    javax.jms.QueueSender sender;
    javax.jms.QueueConnection conn;
    javax.jms.QueueConnectionFactory factory;

    public static final String send_action="send";
    public static final String queue_action="queue";
```

Next, define the constructor for the QueueSenderTest object. A user name that will act as the name used to create the connection is provided. MiniJMS uses this name to identify various clients, but it may be ignored by some providers. The first part of the constructor defines variables.

```
    public QueueSenderTest(String user)
    {
        JLabel label;
        JButton button;
        JPanel tmp;
        Context context;
        Font f = new Font("Serif",Font.PLAIN,16);

        setFont(f);
```

Then create the JMS objects for sending messages. At this point, only objects that don't require a destination to be specified are created. Once the user specifies a queue name, the remaining objects are created. Note the use of MiniJMSUtils, discussed earlier, to create the JNDI context using a properties file in the example directory.

```
        try
        {
            MiniJMSUtils.init("queuesender.properties");
            context = MiniJMSUtils.context;

            factory
             = (QueueConnectionFactory)
               context.lookup("QueueConnectionFactory");
```

```
        conn
         = factory.createQueueConnection(user,null);

        session =
        conn.createQueueSession(false,Session.AUTO_ACKNOWLEDGE);

        if(session == null) throw new Exception();
    }
    catch(Exception exp)
    {
        exp.printStackTrace();
        System.exit(0);
    }
```

The remainder of the constructor creates the user interface.

```
    setLayout(new GridLayout(2,1,6,6));

    queueField = new JTextField(20);
    queueField.addActionListener(this);
    queueField.setActionCommand(queue_action);

    label = new JLabel("Queue:");

    button = new JButton("Change");
    button.addActionListener(this);
    button.setActionCommand(queue_action);

    tmp = new JPanel();
    tmp.setLayout(new FlowLayout(FlowLayout.LEFT,6,0));

    label.setFont(f);
    queueField.setFont(f);
    button.setFont(f);

    tmp.add(label);
    tmp.add(queueField);
    tmp.add(button);

    add(tmp);

    sendField = new JTextField(20);
    sendField.addActionListener(this);
    sendField.setActionCommand(send_action);

    label = new JLabel("Message:");

    button = new JButton("Send");
    button.addActionListener(this);
    button.setActionCommand(send_action);
```

```
        tmp = new JPanel();
        tmp.setLayout(new FlowLayout(FlowLayout.LEFT,6,0));

        label.setFont(f);
        sendField.setFont(f);
        button.setFont(f);

        tmp.add(label);
        tmp.add(sendField);
        tmp.add(button);

        add(tmp);
    }
```

Whenever the user changes the current queue, the setQueue method is called. This method makes sure that if we have a sender already, it is closed. Then the queue is looked up, by name, in the JNDI context. Remember that Queues are administered objects, so if a Queue doesn't exist, this operation will fail and cannot proceed. If the Queue is available, a sender is created for it.

```
    public void setQueue(String name)
    {
        Queue queue=null;

        try
        {
            if(sender!=null) sender.close();

            queue
             = (Queue) MiniJMSUtils.context.lookup(name);

            sender = session.createSender(queue);

            if((queue == null)
                ||(sender==null)) throw new Exception();
        }
        catch(Exception exp)
        {
            exp.printStackTrace();
            System.exit(0);
        }
    }
```

When the user presses the Send button, it triggers the sendMessage method to be called with the contents of the send text field. This method uses the session to create a new TextMessage and sets the message's contents to the text field's contents. Then the sender is used to send the message. If an error occurs, a warning is displayed to the user.

```
    public void sendMessage(String text)
    {
```

```
        TextMessage msg;

        try
        {
                msg = session.createTextMessage();
                msg.setText(text);
                sender.send(msg);
        }
        catch(Exception exp)
        {
            JOptionPane.showMessageDialog(this
                                    ,exp.toString()
                                    ,"Send Error"
                                    ,JOptionPane.ERROR_MESSAGE);
        }
    }
```

The actionPerformed method is defined to handle user interactions and calls the setQueue and sendMessage methods appropriately.

```
    public void actionPerformed(ActionEvent evt)
    {
        String cmd = evt.getActionCommand();

        if(send_action.equals(cmd))
        {
            sendMessage(sendField.getText());
        }
        else if(queue_action.equals(cmd))
        {
            setQueue(queueField.getText());
        }
    }
```

QueueSenderTest defines a close method that cleans up the JMS resources. This method will be called when the user closes the window for this application.

```
    public void close()
    {
        try
        {
            sender.close();
            session.close();
            conn.close();
        }
        catch(Exception exp)
        {
            exp.printStackTrace();
        }
    }
```

The main method creates a QueueSenderTest, using command-line arguments or a default for the user name. The user interface is displayed, and a window listener is assigned to the window to handle the close box. This listener calls the QueueSenderTest object's close method when the window is closed.

```
    public static void main(String s[])
    {
        JFrame frame;
        QueueSenderTest panel;
        String user="QueueSenderTest";

        if(s.length>0) user = s[0];

        frame = new JFrame(user);

        panel = new QueueSenderTest(user);

        //So we can catch errors in a log file
        System.setErr(System.out);

        frame.setDefaultCloseOperation(JFrame.DO_NOTHING_ON_CLOSE);
        frame.setForeground(Color.black);
        frame.setBackground(Color.lightGray);
        frame.getContentPane().add(panel,"Center");

        frame.pack();
        frame.setVisible(true);
        frame.addWindowListener(new WindowCloser(panel));
    }
}
```

WindowCloser is a convenience class provided to handle the window's close box and tell the QueueSenderTest to close its JMS resources. All of the JFC-based examples in this chapter have an object similar to this one to handle the window close.

```
class WindowCloser extends WindowAdapter
{
    QueueSenderTest test;

    public WindowCloser(QueueSenderTest test)
    {
        this.test = test;
    }

    public void windowClosing(WindowEvent e)
    {

        Window win = e.getWindow();
        test.close();
        win.setVisible(false);
        System.exit(0);
    }
}
```

If you run this example along with the MiniJMS server, you will be able to send messages to a queue. Currently, MiniJMS defines two default queues, named testqueue and errorqueue. Use these queues for testing.

Two other examples of QueueSenders are included on the CD-ROM; both are very similar to QueueSenderTest. The first, called VolQueueSenderTest, is identical except for the sendMessage method. This method uses a different send method and marks the message as nonpersistent. The complete code for VolQueueSenderTest is available on the CD-ROM, but the sendMessage method follows:

```
public void sendMessage(String text)
{
    TextMessage msg;

    try
    {
            msg = session.createTextMessage();
            msg.setText(text);
            sender.send(msg
                        ,DeliveryMode.NON_PERSISTENT
                        ,Message.DEFAULT_PRIORITY
                        ,Message.DEFAULT_TIME_TO_LIVE);
    }
    catch(Exception exp)
    {
        JOptionPane.showMessageDialog(this
                                ,exp.toString()
                                ,"Send Error"
                                ,JOptionPane.ERROR_MESSAGE);
    }
}
```

The third example of a QueueSender extends the QueueSenderTest idea to include the use of a transacted Session. This required the addition of several buttons to the user interface, as pictured in Figure 20.3. To support transactions, the QueueSession is created using a true for the transacted argument in the QueueConnections createQueueSession method:

```
try
{
    MiniJMSUtils.init("transqueuesender.properties");
    context = MiniJMSUtils.context;

    factory
   = (QueueConnectionFactory)
      context.lookup("QueueConnectionFactory");

    conn
     = factory.createQueueConnection(user,null);

    //Create a transacted session
```

```
        session
         = conn.createQueueSession(true,Session.AUTO_ACKNOWLEDGE);

        if(session == null) throw new Exception();
    }
    catch(Exception exp)
    {
        exp.printStackTrace();
        System.exit(0);
    }
```

The TransactedQueueSenderTest's actionPerformed method supports the new buttons.

```
public void actionPerformed(ActionEvent evt)
{
    String cmd = evt.getActionCommand();

    if(send_action.equals(cmd))
    {
        sendMessage(sendField.getText());
    }
    else if(queue_action.equals(cmd))
    {
        setQueue(queueField.getText());
    }
    else if(commit_action.equals(cmd))
    {
        try
        {
            session.commit();
        }
        catch(Exception exp)
        {
            System.out.println(exp);
        }
    }
    else if(rollback_action.equals(cmd))
    {
        try
        {
            session.rollback();
        }
        catch(Exception exp)
        {
            System.out.println(exp);
        }
    }
}
```

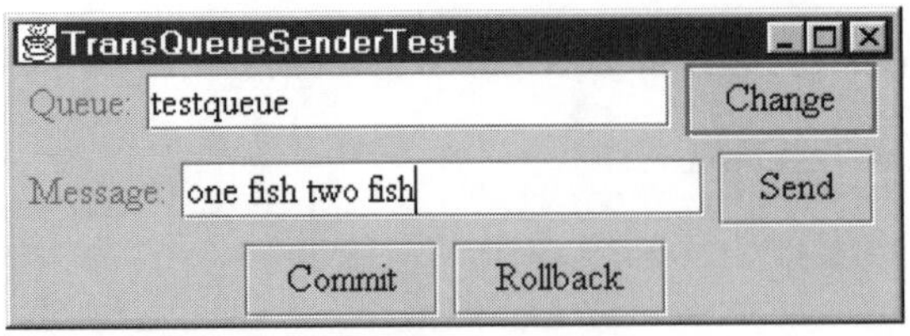

Figure 20.3 Transacted queue sender.

Again, this is not the entire code for this example. If you want to see all of the code, refer to the CD-ROM. If you run this example, you will see that the messages sent by the user are not actually placed in the queue until the Commit button is pressed. If Rollback is pressed, any messages that were sent and not committed are removed from the system.

Of course, to test these examples and see any results, you need a program that receives the messages. This requires the creation of a QueueReceiver.

The Queue Receiver

A QueueReceiver is a MessageConsumer with the added method getQueue for returning its associated queue. Otherwise, programmers interact with a QueueReceiver the same way that they would any other MessageConsumer, using receive messages or a MessageListener.

The following example shows how a QueueReceiver is used with a MessageListener. This example uses Swing/JFC to create a list of received messages. The user is also able to set the queue to which the application is listening. This interface is pictured in Figure 20.4.

The code for this example is similar to the QueueSender examples but contains sufficient differences to warrant inclusion of the majority of its methods. The import statements and the definition of WindowCloser have been left out of the text but are available on the CD-ROM with the complete example.

As with the QueueSender example, the QueueReceiverTest defines instance variables for the relevant JMS entities, including the QueueReceiver object.

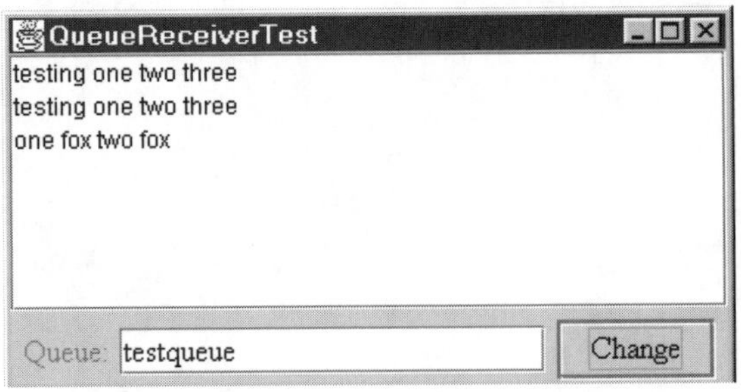

Figure 20.4 QueueReceiverTest.

```
public class QueueReceiverTest extends JPanel
 implements ActionListener,MessageListener
{
    JTextField queueField;
    JList messageList;
    DefaultListModel messages;

    javax.jms.QueueSession session;
    javax.jms.QueueReceiver receiver;
    javax.jms.QueueConnection conn;
    javax.jms.QueueConnectionFactory factory;

    public static final String queue_action="queue";
```

The constructor for this object performs the same JMS initialization as the sender. It also creates the text field used to assign the queue and a list for displaying the messages received.

```
    public QueueReceiverTest(String user)
    {
        JLabel label;
        JButton button;
        JPanel tmp;
        Context context;
        Font f = new Font("Serif",Font.PLAIN,16);

        setFont(f);

        try
        {
            MiniJMSUtils.init("queuereceiver.properties");
            context = MiniJMSUtils.context;

            factory
             = (QueueConnectionFactory)
                context.lookup("QueueConnectionFactory");

            conn
             = factory.createQueueConnection(user,null);

            session
            = conn.createQueueSession(false
              ,Session.AUTO_ACKNOWLEDGE);

            if(session == null) throw new Exception();
        }
        catch(Exception exp)
        {
            exp.printStackTrace();
            System.exit(0);
        }
```

```
        setLayout(new BorderLayout(6,6));

        messages = new DefaultListModel();

        messageList = new JList();
        messageList.setModel(messages);

        add(new JScrollPane(messageList),"Center");

        queueField = new JTextField(20);
        queueField.addActionListener(this);
        queueField.setActionCommand(queue_action);

        label = new JLabel("Queue:");

        button = new JButton("Change");
        button.addActionListener(this);
        button.setActionCommand(queue_action);

        tmp = new JPanel();
        tmp.setLayout(new FlowLayout(FlowLayout.LEFT,6,0));

        label.setFont(f);
        queueField.setFont(f);
        button.setFont(f);

        tmp.add(label);
        tmp.add(queueField);
        tmp.add(button);

        add(tmp,"South");
    }
```

The setQueue method makes sure that any open receivers are closed. If this step isn't taken, the application can receive notification for messages in multiple queues. Once the existing receiver is closed, the requested Queue is looked up in the JNDI context. If found, the Queue is used to create a QueueReceiver. The program then registers a MessageListener with the QueueReceiver. This listener receives messages sent to the queue as notifications via the onMessage method.

```
    public void setQueue(String name)
    {
        Queue queue=null;

        try
        {
            messages.removeAllElements();

            if(receiver != null) receiver.close();

            queue
```

```
                = (Queue) MiniJMSUtils.context.lookup(name);

            receiver = session.createReceiver(queue);

            if((queue == null)
                ||(receiver==null)) throw new Exception();

            receiver.setMessageListener(this);
        }
        catch(Exception exp)
        {
            exp.printStackTrace();
            System.exit(0);
        }
    }
```

The onMessage method is called whenever a message arrives for the receiver's queue. In this case, the string value of the message is displayed in the list on the user interface.

```
    public void onMessage(Message msg)
    {
        try
        {
            messages.addElement(msg.toString());
        }
        catch(Exception exp)
        {
            JOptionPane.showMessageDialog(this
                                        ,exp.toString()
                                        ,"Receive Error"
                                        ,JOptionPane.ERROR_MESSAGE);
        }
    }
```

The actionPerformed method handles user interaction with the queue text field.

```
    public void actionPerformed(ActionEvent evt)
    {
        String cmd = evt.getActionCommand();

        if(queue_action.equals(cmd))
        {
            setQueue(queueField.getText());
        }
    }
```

When the window for this application is closed, the WindowCloser helper object calls the QueueReceiverTest's close method. This method closes the JMS entities that it created.

```
    public void close()
    {
```

```
        try
        {
            receiver.close();
            session.close();
            conn.close();
        }
        catch(Exception exp)
        {
            exp.printStackTrace();
        }
    }
```

The main method creates a QueueReceiverTest, using command-line arguments or a default for the user name. The user interface is displayed, and a window listener is assigned to the window to handle the close box. This listener calls the close method discussed previously.

```
    public static void main(String s[])
    {
        JFrame frame;
        QueueReceiverTest panel;
        String user="QueueReceiverTest";

        if(s.length>0) user = s[0];

        frame = new JFrame(user);

        panel = new QueueReceiverTest(user);

        //So we can catch errors in a log file
        System.setErr(System.out);

        frame.setDefaultCloseOperation(JFrame.DO_NOTHING_ON_CLOSE);
        frame.setForeground(Color.black);
        frame.setBackground(Color.lightGray);
        frame.getContentPane().add(panel,"Center");

        frame.pack();
        frame.setVisible(true);
        frame.addWindowListener(new WindowCloser(panel));
    }
}
```

As with the QueueSenderTest example, this code provides a transacted version of the QueueReceiverTest example that uses a transacted session. This example, called TransQueueReceiverTest and pictured in Figure 20.5, provides buttons for the user to commit, roll back, or recover the session. When a receiver's session is committed, it acknowledges the entire message received to date. If it is rolled back, these messages will be redelivered. Recover tells the session to stop delivery, mark messages that weren't acknowledged as redelivered, and start delivery again. Both rollback and recover may result in duplicate messages, but only recover treats the messages as redelivered.

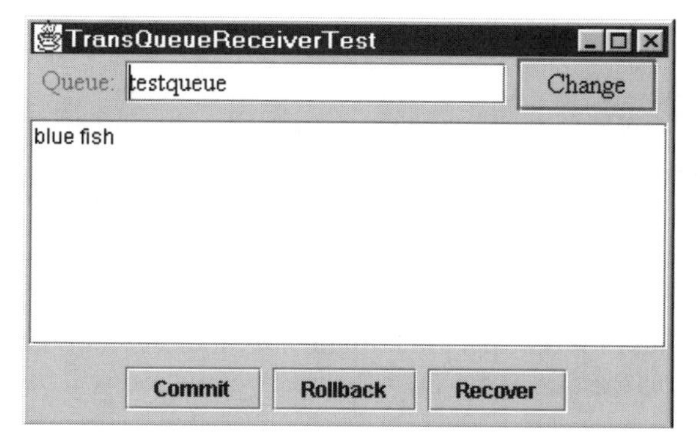

Figure 20.5 Transacted queue receiver example.

Using Receive

The other mechanism for receiving messages from a Queue is to use the receive method. The following example demonstrates this technique in a command-line program. Like the previous examples, the object used to implement this one stores JMS entities in instance variables and uses its constructor to create these objects.

```
//Import statements removed to save space

public class QueueWatcher
 implements Runnable
{
    javax.jms.QueueSession session;
    javax.jms.QueueReceiver receiver;
    javax.jms.QueueConnection conn;
    javax.jms.QueueConnectionFactory factory;

    public QueueWatcher(String user)
    {
        Context context;

        try
        {
            MiniJMSUtils.init("queuewatcher.properties");
            context = MiniJMSUtils.context;

            factory
             = (QueueConnectionFactory)
                context.lookup("QueueConnectionFactory");

            conn
             = factory.createQueueConnection(user,null);

            session
             = conn.createQueueSession(false
                    ,Session.AUTO_ACKNOWLEDGE);
```

```
            if(session == null) throw new Exception();
        }
        catch(Exception exp)
        {
            exp.printStackTrace();
            System.exit(0);
        }
    }
```

The setQueue method creates a receiver for the specified queue after looking it up in JNDI. No MessageListener is assigned to the queue, because the receive method will be used to retrieve messages.

```
    public void setQueue(String name)
    {
        Queue queue=null;

        try
        {
            if(receiver != null) receiver.close();

            queue
             = (Queue) MiniJMSUtils.context.lookup(name);

            receiver = session.createReceiver(queue);

            if((queue == null)
                ||(receiver==null)) throw new Exception();
        }
        catch(Exception exp)
        {
            exp.printStackTrace();
            System.exit(0);
        }
    }
```

This program watches for messages in a separate thread from the main thread. The run method uses a while loop to repeatedly call the QueueReceiver's receive method. A time-out is provided, and if that time-out is exceeded, a message is printed to the console. If a message is received, the message itself is printed to the console. In this example, the time-out is set to 3 seconds, or 3,000 milliseconds.

```
    public void run()
    {
        Message msg;
        long interval=3000;

        while(true)
        {
            try
```

```
            {
                msg = receiver.receive(interval);

                if(msg != null)
                    System.out.println("Message: "+msg);
                else
                    System.out.println("No message in "
                                        +interval+"msec");
            }
            catch(Exception exp)
            {
                System.out.println(exp);
            }
        }
    }
```

The close method cleans up any JMS resources.

```
    public void close()
    {
        try
        {
            receiver.close();
            session.close();
            conn.close();
        }
        catch(Exception exp)
        {
            exp.printStackTrace();
        }
    }
```

The main method creates a QueueWatcher object, assigns its name and Queue, then starts a new thread to watch for messages.

```
    public static void main(String s[])
    {
        QueueWatcher watcher;
        String user="QueueWatcher";
        Thread kicker;

        if(s.length<=0)
            System.out.println("usage: QueueWatcher queueName");

        //So we can catch errors in a log file
        System.setErr(System.out);

        watcher = new QueueWatcher(user);
        watcher.setQueue(s[0]);
        kicker = new Thread(watcher);
        kicker.start();
    }
}
```

As you can see, receive allows the watcher to retrieve messages in the thread of its choosing. In this case, the watcher spawns a thread to listen for messages, but it could have used the main thread just as easily. Message listeners, on the other hand, receive onMessage from the session in a thread managed by the session. The session guarantees that only one thread at a time sends onMessage, but that thread is not under program control.

Using ReplyTo

One of the header fields in a Message is the JMSReplyTo field. This field can be used to send a private queue along with a message. Receivers can use this private queue to respond to the sender, without going through an administered queue. Instead, temporary queues are normally used for reply-to messages.

The following example contains two applications. The first, ReplyToTest, creates a temporary queue and uses it as the JMSReplyTo field for the messages it sends. The other program, Echo, is a command-line program that sends a reply, when possible, for the messages it receives.

ReplyToTest is a combination of the QueueSenderTest and the QueueReceiverTest examples. It provides a field for sending messages and a list of messages received in the temporary reply queue. Because this code is similar to previous examples, the full code is not shown here. The entire example is available on the CD-ROM.

The constructor for the ReplyToTest creates the JMS session and the user interface. Notice that a temporary queue is created for reply-to messages. A receiver is created for the queue, and the ReplyToTest object registers as a MessageListener for the temporary queue.

```
//import statements removed for space
public class ReplyToTest extends JPanel
 implements ActionListener,MessageListener
{
    ... Instance variables for UI ...

    javax.jms.QueueSession session;
    javax.jms.QueueReceiver receiver;
    javax.jms.QueueSender sender;
    javax.jms.QueueConnection conn;
    javax.jms.QueueConnectionFactory factory;

    public static final String queue_action="queue";
    public static final String send_action="send";

    public ReplyToTest (String user)
    {
        ... Local variables for UI ...

        Context context;

        try
```

```
    {
        MiniJMSUtils.init("replyto.properties");

        context = MiniJMSUtils.context;

        factory
         = (QueueConnectionFactory)
              context.lookup("QueueConnectionFactory");

        conn
         = factory.createQueueConnection(user,null);

        session
         = conn.createQueueSession(false
               ,Session.AUTO_ACKNOWLEDGE);

              tempQ = session.createTemporaryQueue();

        receiver = session.createReceiver(tempQ);

        if(receiver == null) throw new Exception();

        receiver.setMessageListener(this);
    }
    catch(Exception exp)
    {
        exp.printStackTrace();
        System.exit(0);
    }

    ... Create the UI ...
}
```

The setQueue method creates a sender for the administered queue with the specified name. Remember that MiniJMS provides the default queues: testqueue and errorqueue.

```
public void setQueue(String name)
{
    Queue queue=null;

    try
    {
        messages.removeAllElements();

        if(sender != null) sender.close();

        queue
         = (Queue) MiniJMSUtils.context.lookup(name);
```

```
            sender = session.createSender(queue);

            if((queue == null)
                ||(sender==null)) throw new Exception();
        }
        catch(Exception exp)
        {
            exp.printStackTrace();
            System.exit(0);
        }
    }
```

The sendMessage method is called when the user sends a message. This method creates a TextMessage, sets its contents, and sets the JMSReplyTo field before sending it.

```
    public void sendMessage(String text)
    {
        TextMessage msg;

        try
        {
                msg = session.createTextMessage();
                msg.setText(text);
                msg.setJMSReplyTo(tempQ);
                sender.send(msg);
        }
        catch(Exception exp)
        {
            JOptionPane.showMessageDialog(this
                                        ,exp.toString()
                                        ,"Receive Error"
                                        ,JOptionPane.ERROR_MESSAGE);
        }
    }
```

The onMessage method is called when a message arrives in the temporary queue, indicating a reply to a message.

```
    public void onMessage(Message msg)
    {
        try
        {
            messages.addElement(msg.toString());
        }
        catch(Exception exp)
        {
            JOptionPane.showMessageDialog(this
                                        ,exp.toString()
                                        ,"Send Error"
                                        ,JOptionPane.ERROR_MESSAGE);
        }
```

```
    }

    ... Event Handling Code ...
```

The close method closes the JMS entities and deletes the temporary queue.

```
    public void close()
    {
        try
        {
                tempQ.delete();
                sender.close();
            receiver.close();
            session.close();
            conn.close();
        }
        catch(Exception exp)
        {
            exp.printStackTrace();
        }
    }

    public static void main(String s[])
    {
        ... Create the UI and display it ...
    }
}
```

The Echo program is similar to the QueueWatcher example. The main difference is in the run method. This method sends messages to the reply-to field of the messages that it receives. In order to send these messages, the Echo object creates a QueueSender from its session.

```
    public void setQueue(String name)
    {
        Queue queue=null;

        try
        {
            queue
             = (Queue) MiniJMSUtils.context.lookup(name);

            receiver = session.createReceiver(queue);
            sender = session.createSender(queue);

            if((queue == null)
                ||(receiver==null)
                ||(sender==null)) throw new Exception();
        }
        catch(Exception exp)
        {
```

```
            exp.printStackTrace();
            System.exit(0);
        }
    }

    public void run()
    {
        Message msg;
        long interval=3000;
        Queue replyTo;
        TextMessage newMsg=null;

        while(true)
        {
            try
            {
                msg = receiver.receive(interval);
                    newMsg = null;

                if(msg != null)
                {
                        replyTo = (Queue) msg.getJMSReplyTo();

                        if(replyTo != null)
                        {
                                newMsg = session.createTextMessage();
                                newMsg.setText("Reply: "+msg);

                                sender.send(replyTo,newMsg);
                        }

                    System.out.println("Message: "+msg);
                    if(newMsg!=null) System.out.println(newMsg);
                }
                else
                    System.out.println("No message in "
                                        +interval+"msec");
            }
            catch(Exception exp)
            {
                System.out.println(exp);
            }
        }
    }
```

The complete code for this example is available on the CD-ROM.

The QueueRequester Utility Class

JMS provides a class called QueueRequester that encapsulates the code used to send a message and receive a reply. This requester object creates a temporary queue and handles the message-receiving code. To use the requestor, you create it with a Queue and a QueueSession. Then you use the method:

```
public Message request(Message message) throws JMSException
```

to send messages and wait for the reply.

The QueueRequestorTest example on the CD-ROM shows a requester in action. The following to methods from this example show how the requester is used. The remaining code is similar to the ReplyToTest example and creates the same user interface.

```
public void setQueue(String name)
{
    Queue queue=null;

    try
    {
        messages.removeAllElements();

        if(requestor != null) requestor.close();

        //requestor closes the session
        session
         = conn.createQueueSession(false
              ,Session.AUTO_ACKNOWLEDGE);

        queue
         = (Queue) MiniJMSUtils.context.lookup(name);

        requestor = new QueueRequestor(session,queue);

        if((queue == null)
            ||(requestor==null)) throw new Exception();
    }
    catch(Exception exp)
    {
        exp.printStackTrace();
        System.exit(0);
    }
}

public void sendMessage(String text)
{
    TextMessage msg;

    try
    {
            msg = session.createTextMessage();
            msg.setText(text);

            msg = (TextMessage) requestor.request(msg);
```

```
                    messages.addElement(msg.toString());
            }
            catch(Exception exp)
            {
                JOptionPane.showMessageDialog(this
                                                ,exp.toString()
                                                ,"Send Error"
                                                ,JOptionPane.ERROR_MESSAGE);
            }
        }
```

Notice that the requester is used synchronously. If no reply occurs, the user will be unable to use the program. In the ReplyToTest example, the user is not waiting for replies before proceeding. The semantics of this send-reply relationship will depend on your application.

Publish-Subscribe Messaging with Topics

JMS defines the publish-subscribe messaging model to support situations in which multiple clients want to receive the same set of messages. Publish-subscribe messaging, as defined by JMS, uses the concept of a topic to represent a destination. A *topic* is a sequence of messages that may or may not be persistent, depending on their delivery mode. Topics are created by an administrator and registered with a JNDI context. Clients can send messages to a topic or receive messages from a topic. Unlike Queues, topics are expected to have multiple subscribers listening for messages.

Topics are represented by objects that implement the Topic interface. This interface defines a single method:

```
public String getTopicName() throws JMSException
```

that returns the name of the topic. The provider is also expected to override the toString method and return a "pretty" version of the name. Topic is a subinterface of Destination, so a Topic is a full-fledged destination for sending and receiving messages.

The server will serialize messages sent to a topic into a single sequence. This ensures that the client checking the queue will receive each message only once, and that the messages will be received in the order in which they were sent. The JMS provider is expected to keep messages for a topic available as long as the provider is running. Persistent messages should be maintained even if the server is shut down and restarted. Unlike Queues, the receivers for a topic may or may not be durable. In other words, a queue receiver expects to get messages that are sent while it is not running, but a topic subscriber can choose to ignore these missed messages.

NOTE Due to the similarities between using Queues and Topics, all of the examples from the discussion on point-to-point messaging are not repeated here. If you are planning to use publish-subscribe messaging, it will be useful to also look over the point-to-point examples for more complete coverage.

Topic Connection Factory

Clients that want to use topics and the publish-subscribe messaging model need to retrieve a topic-oriented connection factory from JNDI. This factory implements the TopicConnectionFactory interface, which extends the ConnectionFactory interface described previously. The TopicConnectionFactory provides two methods for creating connections:

```
public TopicConnection createTopicConnection() throws JMSException
public TopicConnection createTopicConnection(String userName
                                            , String password)
                                              throws JMSException
```

Both of these methods return an object that implements the TopicConnection interface. The first method uses the default user identification; the second takes a user name and password. These values may or may not be used by the JMS provider.

MiniJMS registers a TopicConnectionFactory in JNDI using the name TopicConnectionFactory, so given a context, you can look it up using code such as:

```
factory = (TopicConnectionFactory)
            context.lookup("TopicConnectionFactory ");
```

This code simply looks up an object in the JNDI context and casts it appropriately.

Topic Connections

The TopicConnection is a special kind of Connection designed for publish-subscribe messaging and inherits the methods from that interface, as listed in Table 20.1. TopicConnection also defines three new methods. The first:

```
public TopicSession createTopicSession(boolean transacted,
                                       int acknowledgeMode)
                                       throws JMSException
```

is used to create a session for your publish-subscribe messaging. This method takes a Boolean that indicates whether the returned session will use transactions and an integer that indicates the acknowledgment mode.

The second and third methods defined in TopicConnection are:

```
public ConnectionConsumer createConnectionConsumer(Topic topic
                                       , String messageSelector
                                       , ServerSessionPool sessionPool
                                       , int maxMessages)
                                      throws JMSException
public ConnectionConsumer
        createDurableConnectionConsumer(Topic topic
                                       , String messageSelector
                                       , ServerSessionPool sessionPool
```

```
                                        , int maxMessages)
                                        throws JMSException
```

These methods are for use in an application server and are not really part of the client API.

Topic Sessions

The session created by a TopicConnection implements the TopicSession interface. This interface extends the Session interface described above and adds methods specific to publish-subscribe messages.

The first thing that a TopicSession can do is create a special type of MessageProducer called a TopicPublisher. Use the method:

```
public TopicPublisher createPublisher(Topic topic)
                                      throws JMSException
```

to create this object for a specific topic.

The session can also create special MessageConsumers called TopicSubscribers for a queue. There are four methods for creating consumers. The first two methods create normal subscribers:

```
public TopicSubscriber createSubscriber(Topic topic)
                                        throws JMSException

public TopicSubscriber createSubscriber(Topic topic
                                        , String messageSelector
                                        , boolean noLocal)
                                        throws JMSException
```

The second two create durable subscribers:

```
public TopicSubscriber createDurableSubscriber(Topic topic
                                        , String name)
                                        throws JMSException

public TopicSubscriber createDurableSubscriber(Topic topic
                                        , String name
                                        , String messageSelector
                                        , boolean noLocal)
                                        throws JMSException
```

The noLocal flag in these methods indicates whether a subscriber wants to receive messages sent by the client that created the subscription. The main difference between creating durable subscribers and plain subscribers is that durable subscribers have a name. This name is used to store messages for the subscriber when it is unavailable for message delivery. In usage, the main difference is that a durable subscriber will receive messages that were sent to it while it was not running, and a nondurable subscriber will not.

Because a durable subscriber implies persistence, they require a mechanism for removing them from the JMS system. This mechanism is the TopicSession method:

```
public void unsubscribe(java.lang.String name) throws JMSException
```

which takes the name of the durable subscription and unsubscribes it.

Finally, the TopicSession can be used to create Topics. The method:

```
public Topic createTopic(String topicName) throws JMSException
```

creates a real topic. This method may not be supported by all providers. Instead, providers may and should provide administration tools for defining queues. The name of a topic can be provider specific, so using create topic is not a portable coding convention.

The TopicSession can also create temporary topics using the method:

```
public TemporaryTopic createTemporaryTopic() throws JMSException
```

Temporary topics are deleted automatically when the client stops using them. You can also use TemporaryTopic's delete method to force deletion of the topic. Often, temporary topics are created to act as the reply-to destination for messages. The name of a temporary topic is defined by the provider's code, so this method is portable across JMS providers.

The Topic Publisher

The TopicPublisher provides four methods for sending messages to a topic. These methods are listed in Table 20.12.

The publisher also provides the method getTopic to access its default topic.

The following example program displays a user interface, pictured in Figure 20.6, that allows the user to select a topic and send messages to it. This example is similar to

Table 20.12 TopicPublisher Methods

METHOD	DESCRIPTION
`public void publish(Message message) throws JMSException`	Publish a method to the publisher's default topic with the default priority, timeToLive, and mode.
`public void publish(Message message, int deliveryMode, int priority, long timeToLive) throws JMSException`	Publish a method to the publisher's default topic with the specified priority, timeToLive, and mode.
`public void publish(Topic topic, Message message) throws JMSException`	Publish a method to the specified topic with the default priority, timeToLive, and mode.
`public void publish(Topic topic, Message message, int deliveryMode, int priority, long timeToLive) throws JMSException`	Publish a method to the specified topic with the specified priority, timeToLive, and mode.

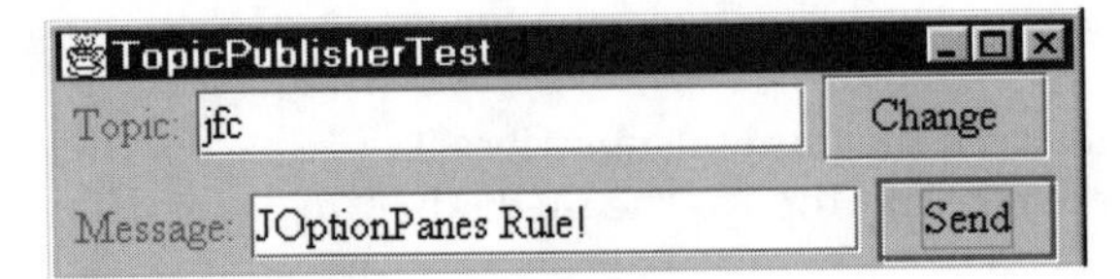

Figure 20.6 Topic publisher test.

the QueueSenderTest described earlier. TopicPublisherTest is a JPanel that handles user events by creating messages for a specified topic.

```
import javax.jms.*;
import javax.naming.*;
import minijms.*;

import com.sun.java.swing.*;
import java.awt.*;
import java.awt.event.*;

public class TopicPublisherTest extends JPanel
 implements ActionListener
{
    JTextField sendField;
    JTextField topicField;

    javax.jms.TopicSession session;
    javax.jms.TopicPublisher sender;
    javax.jms.TopicConnection conn;
    javax.jms.TopicConnectionFactory factory;

    public static final String send_action="send";
    public static final String topic_action="topic";
```

The constructor for TopicPublisherTest creates the user interface and the initial object for accessing JMS. The MiniJMSUtils class, described in "MiniJMSUtils" at the beginning of the chapter, is used to create the JNDI context for this program.

```
    public TopicPublisherTest(String user)
    {
        JLabel label;
        JButton button;
        JPanel tmp;
        Context context;
        Font f = new Font("Serif",Font.PLAIN,16);

        setFont(f);

        try
        {
            MiniJMSUtils.init("topicpublisher.properties");
```

```
        context = MiniJMSUtils.context;

        factory
         = (TopicConnectionFactory)
            context.lookup("TopicConnectionFactory");

        conn
         = factory.createTopicConnection(user,null);

        session
         = conn.createTopicSession(false
                ,Session.AUTO_ACKNOWLEDGE);

        if(session == null) throw new Exception();
    }
    catch(Exception exp)
    {
        exp.printStackTrace();
        System.exit(0);
    }

    setLayout(new GridLayout(2,1,6,6));

    topicField = new JTextField(20);
    topicField.addActionListener(this);
    topicField.setActionCommand(topic_action);

    label = new JLabel("Topic:");

    button = new JButton("Change");
    button.addActionListener(this);
    button.setActionCommand(topic_action);

    tmp = new JPanel();
    tmp.setLayout(new FlowLayout(FlowLayout.LEFT,6,0));

    label.setFont(f);
    topicField.setFont(f);
    button.setFont(f);

    tmp.add(label);
    tmp.add(topicField);
    tmp.add(button);

    add(tmp);

    sendField = new JTextField(20);
    sendField.addActionListener(this);
    sendField.setActionCommand(send_action);

    label = new JLabel("Message:");
```

```
        button = new JButton("Send");
        button.addActionListener(this);
        button.setActionCommand(send_action);

        tmp = new JPanel();
        tmp.setLayout(new FlowLayout(FlowLayout.LEFT,6,0));

        label.setFont(f);
        sendField.setFont(f);
        button.setFont(f);

        tmp.add(label);
        tmp.add(sendField);
        tmp.add(button);

        add(tmp);
    }
```

The setTopic method is called when the user changes the program's target topic. Once the topic is looked up in JNDI, a new publisher is created for it. The old publisher, if it exists, is closed to minimize resource usage.

```
    public void setTopic(String name)
    {
        Topic topic=null;

        try
        {
            if(sender!=null) sender.close();

            topic
             = (Topic) MiniJMSUtils.context.lookup(name);

            sender = session.createPublisher(topic);

            if((topic == null)
                ||(sender==null)) throw new Exception();
        }
        catch(Exception exp)
        {
            exp.printStackTrace();
            System.exit(0);
        }
    }
```

The sendMessage method takes a string, assigns it to a TextMessage, and publishes the message.

```
    public void sendMessage(String text)
    {
        TextMessage msg;
```

```
        try
        {
                msg = session.createTextMessage();
                msg.setText(text);
                sender.publish(msg);
        }
        catch(Exception exp)
        {
            JOptionPane.showMessageDialog(this
                                ,exp.toString()
                                ,"Send Error"
                                ,JOptionPane.ERROR_MESSAGE);
        }
    }
```

The actionPerformed method handles user interaction with the buttons and text fields. It calls setTopic and sendMessage appropriately.

```
    public void actionPerformed(ActionEvent evt)
    {
        String cmd = evt.getActionCommand();

        if(send_action.equals(cmd))
        {
            sendMessage(sendField.getText());
        }
        else if(topic_action.equals(cmd))
        {
            setTopic(topicField.getText());
        }
    }
```

Close is called when the window closes and cleans up the JMS objects that were created.

```
    public void close()
    {
        try
        {
            sender.close();
            session.close();
            conn.close();
        }
        catch(Exception exp)
        {
            exp.printStackTrace();
        }
    }
```

The main method creates a TopicPublisherTest and displays it.

```
    public static void main(String s[])
    {
        JFrame frame;
        TopicPublisherTest panel;
        String user="TopicPublisherTest";

        if(s.length>0) user = s[0];

        frame = new JFrame(user);

        panel = new TopicPublisherTest(user);

        //So we can catch errors in a log file
        System.setErr(System.out);

        frame.setDefaultCloseOperation(JFrame.DO_NOTHING_ON_CLOSE);
        frame.setForeground(Color.black);
        frame.setBackground(Color.lightGray);
        frame.getContentPane().add(panel,"Center");

        frame.pack();
        frame.setVisible(true);
        frame.addWindowListener(new WindowCloser(panel));
    }
}
```

WindowCloser is a convenience class that handles the window close box.

```
class WindowCloser extends WindowAdapter
{
    TopicPublisherTest test;

    public WindowCloser(TopicPublisherTest test)
    {
        this.test = test;
    }

    public void windowClosing(WindowEvent e)
    {

        Window win = e.getWindow();
        test.close();
        win.setVisible(false);
        System.exit(0);
    }
}
```

As you can see, a TopicPublisher is very similar to a QueueSender; the only real changes are the underlying model and the vocabulary. The next section discusses how a program can receive messages for a topic. Although similar to receiving messages from a queue, receiving topic subscribers has the added option of being nonpersistent.

The Topic Subscriber

TopicSubscriber adds two methods to the MessageConsumer interface. These are:

```
public boolean getNoLocal() throws JMSException
public Topic getTopic() throws JMSException
```

The noLocal flag indicates whether or not the subscriber should receive messages from its own client. The getTopic method simply returns the subscriber's associated topic.

The CD-ROM contains an example, called TopicSubscriber test, that is nearly identical to the QueueReceiverTest. The main difference is that TopicSubscriber uses Topic-based API rather than Queue-based API.

Another example on the CD-ROM, called DurableSubscriberTest, creates a durable subscriber rather than a transient one. If you run both the SubscriberTest and Durable-Subscriber test examples, you will notice only one real difference between them. If the durable subscriber is exited before several messages are sent, and then it is restarted, it will receive the messages that it missed. The normal subscriber in this situation will simply miss the messages with no notification that they even occurred.

The TopicRequester Utility Class

JMS provides a class called TopicRequester that encapsulates the code used to send a message and receive a reply. This requester object creates a temporary topic and handles the message-receiving code. To use the requestor, create it with a Topic and a TopicSession. Then use the method:

```
public Message request(Message message) throws JMSException
```

to send messages and wait for the reply.

Distributed Transactions and JMS Providers

JMS supports the use of distributed transactions via the JTA interfaces. These distributed transactions, as discussed in Chapter 22, "Transactions, JTA, and JTS," allow multiple programs to share the same transaction scope. Distributed transactions can be complex and resource intensive. In order to allow programs to choose between JMS with distributed transactions and without, the classes for supporting transactions are separate from the nontransacted versions. These classes, listed in Table 20.13, all have an XA prefix for their name and duplicate the classes used for normal JMS.

Keep in mind that the distributed transactions are related to the Sessions transactions but are not required to support Session transactions. The XASession object provides a method called:

```
public javax.transaction.xa.XAResource getXAResource()
```

Table 20.13 JMS XA Classes

JMS ROOT	POINT-TO-POINT MESSAGING	PUBLISH-SUBSCRIBE MESSAGING
`XAConnection-Factory`	`XAQueueConnection-Factory`	`XATopicConnection-Factory`
`XAConnection`	`XAQueueConnection`	`XATopicConnection`
`XASession`	`XAQueueSession`	`XATopicSession`

that returns the XAResource defined in JTA for transaction management. The XAQueueSession and XATopicSession extend XASession and provide methods for accessing the actual QueueSession and TopicSession, respectively.

NOTE **MiniJMS does not support the XA version of the JMS classes.**

As mentioned throughout this chapter, portions of the JMS specification are not designed for client use. Rather, these interfaces and methods are designed for use by application servers that host a JMS provider. These classes include the ConnectionConsumer that a Connection can create as well as the ServerSession and ServerSessionPool interfaces. Because this chapter is not intended for JMS provider implementers, these interfaces were not covered in detail. However, Chapter 26 does implement the client interfaces without this Application Server support. We made this separation in our implementation because we did not intend for a server to host our provider. In fact, the specification implies that a server must host the JMS provider, and we wanted to show that this is not the case.

Summary

The Java Messaging Service, JMS, defines an API for sending messages between applications. JMS messages can be persistent and guaranteed, ensuring their delivery or at least ensuring that they are delivered if the libraries say they will be. JMS is organized into two types of messaging and their associated APIs. Point-to-point messaging uses queues to handle the transfer of messages from potentially multiple clients to a single receiver. Publish-subscribe messaging allows many clients to communicate and share messages on a named set of topics. To use JMS, you must first acquire an implementation of the specification from a JMS provider. This implementation provides the classes that implement the interfaces discussed in this chapter.

The messages the JMS defines are all represented by objects that have headers for configuration, properties for application, and provider-specific information and a body for content. To send a message:

1. Retrieve a ConnectionFactory from JNDI.
2. Retrieve the Destinations of interest from JNDI.

3. Use the ConnectionFactory to create a Connection to the JMS provider, probably to the server.
4. Use the Connection to create a Session.
5. Use the Session and Destination objects to create MessageConsumers, Message-Producers, or both.
6. Assign any MessageListeners.
7. Send messages with the producer, receive messages with the consumer.

Given the simplicity of sending messages and the power of a persistent delivery mechanism, JMS and the providers that implement it are a powerful addition to the enterprise Java programmer's tool kit. The next chapter combines the techniques discussed in this chapter to create a set of three programs that communicate via messaging to create a single application.

A JMS-Based Alarm System

One of the primary applications of messaging is *notification*. Many of the IS departments using messaging today are using it to tie together different systems. Often, the goal is to notify one system when a value in another system changes. For example, the human resources system might notify the financial system when a new employee is hired. Because one of the easiest examples of notification in the real world is an alarm clock, the alarm clock is used as a symbol in this chapter and extended to the computer using the Java Messaging Service.

In our example, a server program manages a list of registered alarms. These alarms associate a name, a time, and a message with each other. The server saves pending alarms in a file when it is not running and in memory when it is running. When an alarm "goes off," the alarm server notifies other applications using a message published to a JMS Topic.

Alarms are configured by an application called AlarmConfig. This program displays an interface, shown in Figure 21.1, that allows the user to specify the name, time, and message for an alarm. The currently registered alarms are displayed in a list, and the user can update or delete alarms.

Because the alarm server is a command-line utility, it doesn't have an easy way to shut down. In contrast, the AlarmConfig application provides a button for shutting down the server.

The last application in this example is called AlarmDaemon. This application displays a simple window, pictured in Figure 21.2, that displays a button for quitting the

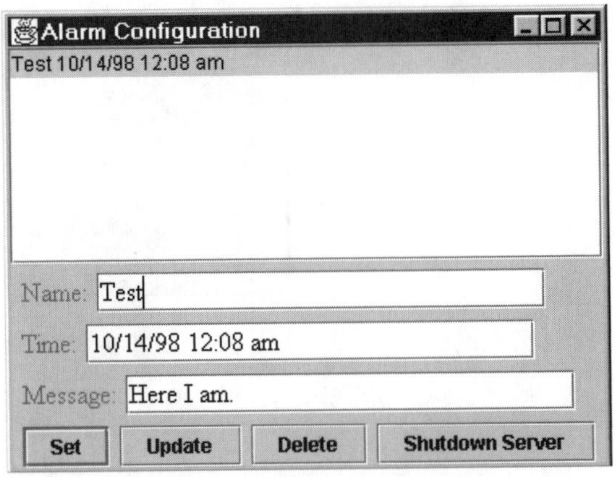

Figure 21.1 AlarmConfig interface.

Figure 21.2 AlarmDaemon interface.

application. The alarm daemon listens to the server's alarm Topic and displays an alert to the user when an alarm "goes off." An example of this alert is pictured in Figure 21.3.

Two JMS destinations are used in this example. The names of these destinations are stored in the AlarmServer class as static variables. The first destination is called ADMIN_QUEUE. This is a JMS Queue used by the AlarmConfig program to communicate with the AlarmServer. A queue is used here because only one server should be receiving administrative messages. Messages in the admin queue are expected to be JMS MapMessages. The contents of the message are named by the keys in the message. AlarmServer defines two keys: ACTION and ALARM. The value of the ACTION key should be a string containing one of the four operations listed in Table 21.1. These operations indicate the administrative action that the server is supposed to take. The value of the ALARM key is an Alarm object.

Notice how you can use a message's contents to define a message type. A JMS application is really a set of programs communicating with messages. The format

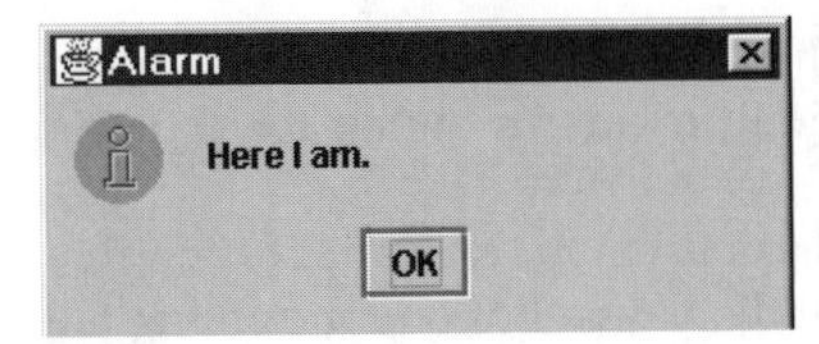

Figure 21.3 Alarm alert panel.

Table 21.1 Alarm Server Actions

ACTION NAME	DESCRIPTION
SHUTDOWN	Tells the server to save existing alarms to file and shut down.
SET	Sets a new alarm.
DELETE	Deletes an existing alarm by name, time, and description.
GET_ALARMS	Requests a list of existing alarms from the server; these are published to the ALARM_TOPIC destination.

and content of these messages is one of the primary design elements in the development process.

The second destination for our alarm system is called ALARM_TOPIC. ALARM_TOPIC is a JMS Topic used by the server to publish notifications when an alarm goes off. The messages on this destination are ObjectMessages containing one of two types of objects: either an Alarm or a Vector. Simple alarm notifications contain an Alarm object, discussed in the "Alarm" section. The server also sends out messages containing a Vector of alarms for use by the configuration program.

The design of this application was motivated by the educational requirement of showing off JMS. As a result, the underlying architecture may be considered heavier than necessary. In the context of a book, this heaviness is an advantage in that the simple Alarm example demonstrates the techniques used in much larger-enterprise scenarios. See Chapter 20, "Programming with the Java Messaging Service," for information on MiniJMS, the JMS provider used throughout this book. Chapter 20 also describes the steps required to run this example and the other JMS examples in the book.

All of the examples in this book use the same properties file, shown below, to define their JNDI information. This properties file also defines the file to which alarms are saved when the server is shut down.

```
java.naming.factory.initial=\
            com.sun.jndi.fscontext.RefFSContextFactory
java.naming.provider.url=file:///temp/jndistore

alarmfile=c:\\temp\\alarms.ser
```

As with the other JMS example, the Alarm application uses the file system JNDI context. The default directory for saving alarms is c:\temp\alarms.ser, but you can change this; \ is an escape character in this format, so use \\ in DOS-style file paths.

Alarm

In this example, alarms are represented by Alarm objects. Alarm is basically a data entity-style class. It stores a name, time, and message in strings. The objects are serializable so that they can be saved to disk or passed as part of messages. The only interesting code for this class is the implementation of hashCode and equals. These methods are overridden to ensure that two alarms having the same name try to hash differently and that two Alarm objects can be equal without being the same object.

All of the objects specifically for this example are contained in the alarm package:

```
package alarm;

import java.io.*;

public class Alarm
 implements Serializable
{
    protected String name;
    protected String time;
    protected String msg;

    public Alarm(String nm)
    {
        name = nm;
    }

    public String toString()
    {
        return name+" "+time;
    }

    public int hashCode()
    {
        return (time+name+msg).hashCode();
    }

    public boolean equals(Object o)
    {
        boolean retVal = false;

        if((o!=null)&&(o instanceof Alarm)
            &&(name!=null)&&(msg!=null)
            &&time!=null)
        {
            Alarm a = (Alarm) o;

            retVal =
                (name.equals(a.getName())
                 && time.equals(a.getTime())
                 && msg.equals(a.getMessage()));
        }

        return retVal;
    }

    public String getName()
    {
```

```
            return name;
        }

        public void setName(String s)
        {
            name = s;
        }

        public String getTime()
        {
            return time;
        }

        public void setTime(String s)
        {
            time = s;
        }

        public String getMessage()
        {
            return msg;
        }

        public void setMessage(String s)
        {
            msg = s;
        }
    }
```

The time for an alarm is saved as a string that will be parsed by the server using a java.text.DateFormat object. This flexibility helps the user define alarm settings. The limitation of this technique is that the DateFormat doesn't permit all date/time formats. A more commercial-level implementation of the configuration application than the one included here would hide these implementation details from the user. For the purpose of testing, you should use strings of the form:

```
mm/dd/yy hh:mm am|pm
```

for assigning alarm times. For example, to set an alarm for 1:00 in the afternoon on October 3, 1999, use:

```
10/3/99 1:00 pm
```

Of course, any string that is usable with DateFormat will work.

Alarm Server

The server for this example is implemented in a single class called AlarmServer. This class defines all of the special strings for messages within the system, including the names of the two destinations used for messaging. The server objects also keep track of their various JMS entities, such as connections and sessions, as well as the current alarms.

The AlarmServer is a Runnable object that checks for messages to the ADMIN_QUEUE in a background thread. The actual alarm timing is managed by a class called PTimer. PTimer is based on the PersonalJava PTimer class and uses PTimer-Spec objects to represent alarm or timer requests. The PTimer uses a background thread to wait for a specified amount of time. When the time passes, a PTimerWentOff-Listener associated with the relevant timer spec is notified.

The server associates a timer spec with each alarm. Two hash tables maintain these relationships. One, called timers, stores the timer specs as keys and the alarms as values. This is used to find an alarm when a timer fires. Another table, called alarm2timer, is used to find a spec for an alarm if it is deleted.

Finally, the server keeps a DateFormat object handy for converting an alarm's time string to a java.util.Date object. The definitions for these constants and instance variables are as follows:

```
package alarm;

//imports removed to save space

public class AlarmServer
 implements PTimerWentOffListener, Runnable
{
    public final static String ADMIN_QUEUE
                            ="alarm_admin_queue";
    public final static String ALARM_TOPIC
                            ="alarm_alarm_topic";

    public final static String ACTION="action";
    public final static String SHUTDOWN="down";
    public final static String SET="set";
    public final static String DELETE="delete";
    public final static String GET_ALARMS="get";

    public final static String ALARM="alarm";

    Queue adminQueue;//the queue for receiving admin messages
    QueueReceiver adminReceiver;
    QueueSender qsender;
    QueueSession session;
    QueueConnection conn;

    Topic alarmTopic;//the topic for sending alarm messages
    TopicPublisher alarmPublisher;
    TopicSession tsession;
    TopicConnection tconn;

    Hashtable timers;//holds the timer specs for each alarm
    Hashtable alarm2timer;//maps the alarms to their timer
    DateFormat dateFormat;//converts string to Date
```

The AlarmServer constructor takes a single string argument that is used when registering with the JMS system. The default value for this name is assigned in the main method for the AlarmServer class.

The constructor creates the two hash tables and the DateFormat object before initializing the messaging components it will use. The MiniJMSUtils class, discussed in Chapter 20, is used to load a properties file and generate an initial JNDI context from it. Once this context and the properties file are loaded, the server loads any persistent alarms from file. The loadAlarms method is discussed below.

Finally, the server initializes a receiver for the ADMIN_QUEUE and a publisher for the ALARM_TOPIC. These destinations are created, if they do not exist already in the JMS system.

NOTE We are relying on MiniJMS to allow the creation of destinations by a client application. Another JMS provider may require you to use administrative tools to create these destinations. You may also have to change the names of the destinations to conform to a provider-specific format.

All of the JMS and JNDI code is contained in a try-catch block to handle exceptions. In case of an error, the server exits because it cannot do any work without the proper JMS connections. The code for the AlarmServer constructor looks like this:

```
public AlarmServer(String user)
{
    Context context;
    TopicConnectionFactory tfactory;
    QueueConnectionFactory factory;

    dateFormat = new SimpleDateFormat();
    timers = new Hashtable();
    alarm2timer = new Hashtable();
    try
    {
        MiniJMSUtils.init("alarm/alarm.properties");
        context = MiniJMSUtils.context;

        loadAlarms();

        factory
         = (QueueConnectionFactory)
              context.lookup("QueueConnectionFactory");

        conn
         = factory.createQueueConnection(user,null);

        session
         = conn.createQueueSession(false
                                   ,Session.AUTO_ACKNOWLEDGE);
```

```
        //Create the queues, or
        //handle failure if they exist
        try
        {
            adminQueue =session.createQueue(ADMIN_QUEUE);
        }
        catch(Exception exp)
        {
        }

        adminQueue  = (Queue)
         MiniJMSUtils.context.lookup(ADMIN_QUEUE);

        adminReceiver = session.createReceiver(adminQueue);

        qsender = session.createSender(adminQueue);
        qsender.setDeliveryMode(DeliveryMode.NON_PERSISTENT);

        //Create the topic related objects

        tfactory
         = (TopicConnectionFactory)
             context.lookup("TopicConnectionFactory");

        tconn
         = tfactory.createTopicConnection(user,null);

        tsession
         = tconn.createTopicSession(false
                                   ,Session.AUTO_ACKNOWLEDGE);
        try
        {
            alarmTopic = tsession.createTopic(ALARM_TOPIC);
        }
        catch(Exception exp)
        {
        }

        alarmTopic  = (Topic)
         MiniJMSUtils.context.lookup(ALARM_TOPIC);

        alarmPublisher = tsession.createPublisher(alarmTopic);
    alarmPublisher.setDeliveryMode(DeliveryMode.NON_PERSISTENT);
    }
    catch(Exception exp)
    {
        exp.printStackTrace();
        System.exit(0);
    }
}
```

The server stores outstanding alarms in a file when it is shut down. For example, if you set an alarm for New Year's Day in June and started and stopped the server in the meantime, this alarm would be written to disk and read from disk each time. However, once an alarm fires, it is removed from the list of pending alarms and will not be saved.

The method loadAlarms, included below, loads a vector from disk and reads the Alarm objects contained in this vector. Each alarm is associated with a PTimerSpec and placed in the two hash tables. The PTimerSpec is scheduled with the PTimer so it will notify the server if it is fired.

```
protected void loadAlarms()
{
    FileInputStream fileIn;//Stream for reading
    BufferedInputStream bufIn;//Stream for reading
    ObjectInputStream objIn;//Stream for reading
    String fileName;//File to read
    Vector readFrom;//Vector read from file
    Alarm alarm;//temp variable
    int i,max;//temp variable
    long now= System.currentTimeMillis();
    long alarmTime;//temp variable
    PTimer timer = PTimer.getTimer();//shared PTimer
    PTimerSpec spec;//temp variable

    try
    {
        fileName
            = MiniJMSUtils.properties.getProperty("alarmfile");
        fileIn = new FileInputStream(fileName);
        bufIn = new BufferedInputStream(fileIn);
        objIn = new ObjectInputStream(bufIn);

        readFrom = (Vector) objIn.readObject();

        objIn.close();

        max = readFrom.size();

        for(i=0;i<max;i++)
        {
            alarm = (Alarm) readFrom.elementAt(i);
            alarmTime
             = dateFormat.parse(alarm.getTime()).getTime();

             if(alarmTime > now)
             {
                spec = new PTimerSpec();
                spec.setAbsoluteTime(alarmTime);
                spec.addPTimerWentOffListener(this);

                timers.put(spec,alarm);
```

```
                    alarm2timer.put(alarm,spec);

                    timer.schedule(spec);
                }
            }
        }
        catch(Exception exp)
        {
            exp.printStackTrace();
        }
    }
```

The saveAlarms method reverses the loadAlarms process by creating a vector of Alarm objects and serializing it to disk. In this case, no changes are made to the existing alarms or their PTimerSpecs.

```
    protected void saveAlarms()
    {
        FileOutputStream fileOut;
        BufferedOutputStream bufOut;
        ObjectOutputStream objOut;
        String fileName;
        Vector toWrite = new Vector();
        Enumeration cursor;

        try
        {
            cursor = alarm2timer.keys();

            while(cursor.hasMoreElements())
            {
                toWrite.addElement(cursor.nextElement());
            }

            fileName
                = MiniJMSUtils.properties.getProperty("alarmfile");
            fileOut = new FileOutputStream(fileName);
            bufOut = new BufferedOutputStream(fileOut);
            objOut = new ObjectOutputStream(bufOut);

            objOut.writeObject(toWrite);

            objOut.close();
        }
        catch(Exception exp)
        {
            exp.printStackTrace();
        }
    }
```

The main method for AlarmServer creates an AlarmServer object, associates a thread with it, and starts the thread running. This background thread checks for messages on the ADMIN_QUEUE. When a message arrives, the server casts it to a MapMessage. If this fails, the server goes back to checking for messages after printing a stack trace. If the cast succeeds, the server checks the value of the ACTION key. This value is used to call an internal message in AlarmServer to handle the request. For example, the SET action triggers a call to handleSet. The implementation for the AlarmServer's run method is as follows:

```
public void run()
{
    Message msg=null;

    while(true)
    {
        try
        {
            MapMessage map;
            String action;

            msg = adminReceiver.receive();

            map = (MapMessage) msg;
            action = map.getString(ACTION);

            if(SET.equals(action))
            {
                handleSet(map);
            }
            else if(DELETE.equals(action))
            {
                handleDelete(map);
            }
            else if(GET_ALARMS.equals(action))
            {
                handleGet(map);
            }
            else if(SHUTDOWN.equals(action))
            {
                handleShutdown(map);
            }
        }
        catch(Exception exp)
        {
            exp.printStackTrace();
        }
    }
}
```

A request to set an alarm requires that the ALARM key in the MapMessage contains an Alarm object. If this is not the case, an exception is thrown, exiting the handleSet method and catching in the run method.

If an alarm is provided, the alarm's time is parsed and a new PTimerSpec is created using the alarm's time. This spec and the alarm are added to the timers and alarm2timer hash tables, and the spec is scheduled. The AlarmServer sets itself up as a PTimerWentOffListener for all of the timer specs in the system to receive notification of an alarm.

Whenever an alarm is added or deleted, the server uses the handleGet method shown below to publish a message containing the new, complete list of alarms. This message is used by the AlarmConfig program to keep its list up to date.

```
protected void handleSet(MapMessage msg)
    throws Exception
{
    Alarm alarm = (Alarm) msg.getObject(ALARM);
    String name;
    long alarmTime;
    PTimer timer = PTimer.getTimer();
    PTimerSpec spec = new PTimerSpec();

    name = alarm.getName();

    alarmTime = dateFormat.parse(alarm.getTime()).getTime();

    spec.setAbsoluteTime(alarmTime);
    spec.addPTimerWentOffListener(this);

    synchronized(timers)
    {
        timers.put(spec,alarm);
        alarm2timer.put(alarm,spec);
    }

    timer.schedule(spec);

    handleGet(null);
}
```

When a delete request is received, the server removes the timer spec and Alarm object from its hash tables and deschedules the PTimerSpec. This tells the PTimer to stop watching for that spec to fire. Finally, the handleGet method is used to notify listeners of the change.

```
protected void handleDelete(MapMessage msg)
    throws Exception
{
    Alarm alarm = (Alarm) msg.getObject(ALARM);
    String name;
    PTimer timer = PTimer.getTimer();
```

```
        PTimerSpec spec;

        synchronized(timers)
        {
            spec = (PTimerSpec) alarm2timer.get(alarm);

            timer.deschedule(spec);

            alarm2timer.remove(alarm);
            timers.remove(spec);
        }

        handleGet(null);

    }
```

Either due to a specific request or because an alarm was added or deleted, all calls to handleGet perform the same action. First, a vector containing the current alarms is created. This vector is inserted into an ObjectMessage, and the ObjectMessage is published to the ALARM_TOPIC.

```
    protected void handleGet(MapMessage msg)
        throws Exception
    {
        Enumeration cursor;
        Vector toReturn = new Vector();
        ObjectMessage reply =
            (ObjectMessage) tsession.createObjectMessage();

        synchronized(timers)
        {
            cursor = alarm2timer.keys();

            while(cursor.hasMoreElements())
            {
                toReturn.addElement(cursor.nextElement());
            }
        }

        reply.setObject(toReturn);

        alarmPublisher.publish(reply);
    }
```

When the server is told to shut down, it saves its alarms to disk, closes the JMS resources, and exits.

```
    protected void handleShutdown(MapMessage msg)
        throws Exception
    {
        saveAlarms();
        close();
        System.exit(0);
    }
```

When the PTimer sees that a PTimerSpec should fire, it sends the listeners for that timer the timerWentOff message. The server receives this message for all of its PTimer-Specs. When a timer fires, the server creates an ObjectMessage containing the associated alarm, removes the alarm and spec from its hash tables, and publishes the new message containing the alarm to the ALARM_TOPIC.

```
public void timerWentOff(PTimerWentOffEvent e)
{
    try
    {
        PTimerSpec spec = e.getTimerSpec();
        Alarm alarm;
        ObjectMessage msg
          = tsession.createObjectMessage();

        synchronized(timers)
        {
            alarm = (Alarm) timers.get(spec);

            timers.remove(spec);
            alarm2timer.remove(alarm);
        }

        msg.setObject(alarm);

        alarmPublisher.publish(msg);
    }
    catch(Exception exp)
    {
        exp.printStackTrace();
    }
}
```

For convenience, the server defines the close method to close all of its JMS resources inside a try-catch block. This method is called when the server is told to shut down.

```
public void close()
{
    try
    {
        adminReceiver.close();
        qsender.close();
        session.close();
        conn.close();

        alarmPublisher.close();
        tsession.close();
        tconn.close();
    }
    catch(Exception exp)
```

```
        {
            exp.printStackTrace();
        }
    }
```

The AlarmServer's main method creates an AlarmServer object and starts a thread that uses the server as its Runnable. This is a simple main method that relies on the server object to implement the real server code.

```
    public static void main(String s[])
    {
        AlarmServer watcher;
        String user="AlarmServer";
        Thread kicker;

        //So we can catch errors in a log file
        System.setErr(System.out);

        watcher = new AlarmServer(user);

        kicker = new Thread(watcher);
        kicker.start();
    }
}
```

The implementation for the AlarmServer is heavily dependent on the ptimer package to implement the real timing for alarms. The ptimer package is based on the PTimer class from the PersonalJava class. The complete code for this package is provided on the CD-ROM and is not discussed here. However, the PTimer class itself does demonstrate an interesting technique in threads programming that is worth discussing in detail.

PTimer

PTimer maintains a list of PTimerSpec objects. These objects have a time associated with them. Specs can be absolute or regular. The alarm example uses only absolute time. However, there can be regular alarms, which occur *in* a specified amount of time rather than *at* a specified time. Regular timer specs can also repeat. For example, you could create a spec that repeats every 10 seconds or even every 10 days.

PTimer uses a background thread to check whether a timer spec should fire and, if so, tells the timer spec to notify its listeners. The interesting code in this class is in the run method. There are several trade-offs when creating a class like this. First, you would like to support very fine-grain timing for games and simulations. On the other hand, you want to support alarm-style timer specs that might be days or even months away. Second, you don't want to have the timer thread take up a lot of unnecessary processor time.

The solution used by this implementation of PTimer is to define three special times. The first, called RESOLUTION, defines the smallest time that the timer will try to distinguish; the default is 10 milliseconds. The second special time is called CUTOFF. Use this time to make sure that the medium-size timer specs are fairly accurate without taking too many resources and defaults to 500 milliseconds. Use the SAFETY time to keep long timer specs accurate and save resources. This value defaults to 100 milliseconds. All three special times are used in the run method discussed in a moment.

Normally, programs will use a shared copy of PTimer that is provided as the return value of the static method getTimer. By using one PTimer object, only one thread is used for all timer specs.

The following code begins the definition of the PTimer class and includes the instance variable, static variables, and constructor definitions:

```
package ptimer;
import ptimer.*;
import java.util.*;

public class PTimer implements Runnable
{
    private static PTimer shared;

    private boolean running;
    private Vector specs;
    private Thread kicker;

    //For debugging, keeps the number of
     //times the timer checked specs
    //to fire.
    public int count;

    private static int RESOLUTION=10;
    private static int CUTOFF=50*10;
    private static int SAFETY=10*10;

    public PTimer()
    {
        specs = new Vector(5);
        running = false;
    }

    public static PTimer getTimer()
    {
        if(shared == null) shared = new PTimer();

        return shared;
    }
```

When PTimer is running, it always synchronizes on itself to make sure that the list of PTimerSpecs is safe from thread conflicts. The first thing that the run method does is start a loop. At the top of this loop, PTimer checks whether there are any PTimerSpecs. If not, the timer calls wait, with no time-out. The timer thread will be notified by another method when timers are scheduled.

```
public void run()
{
    long curTime;
    int i, max;
    PTimerSpec curItem;
    long testTime;
    long minWaitTime;

    synchronized(this)
    {
        running = true;
    }

    while(kicker != null)
    {
        synchronized(this)
        {
            max = specs.size();

            if(max == 0)
            {
                try
                {
                    wait();
                    max= specs.size();
                }
                catch(InterruptedException exp)
                {
                    max=0;
                }
            }
```

When the thread is notified, it gets the current time, then checks with each timer to see whether it should fire. The timer performs this calculation internally and returns the actual time until it should fire. If the value is negative, the timer should fire now; otherwise, the PTimer keeps track of the minimum time until a timer should fire. For example, let's say that there are three timer specs, one for 1:00, one for every 10 minutes, and one for 2:00. If it is currently 1:00, the 1:00 will fire and the 10 minute will fire, but the 2:00 will not. The minimum wait time is 10 minutes because the repeating timer will fire again then.

The timer reads this list backward to allow timer specs to be removed from the list without altering the loop. Specs are removed from the list using the deschedule method.

```
            curTime =  System.currentTimeMillis();
            minWaitTime = curTime;

            count++;

            for(i=(max-1);i>=0;i--)
```

```
{
    curItem = (PTimerSpec) specs.elementAt(i);

    testTime = curItem.timeToFire(curTime);

    if(testTime<=0)
    {
        curItem.notifyListeners(this);
        if(!curItem.isRepeat()
                    || curItem.isAbsolute())
                            deschedule(curItem);
        else testTime = curItem.getTime();
    }

    if(testTime<minWaitTime)
    {
        minWaitTime = testTime;
    }
}
```

Finally, if there were timers, PTimer decides how long to wait until the next check for a timer firing. If the minimum wait time is less than the CUTOFF, 500 milliseconds, the timer thread waits only RESOLUTION (10 milliseconds) before checking again. This ensures that timers for short amounts of time are fairly accurate. If all of the specs will not fire for more than CUTOFF time, the timer thread waits for the minimum time minus the SAFETY, 100 milliseconds. This causes the thread to wake up a little early and start waiting for only 10 milliseconds at a time until it is really time to fire. The long timer specs don't take resources until right before they fire, and they are still very accurate.

Because the schedule method notifies this thread if a new timer spec is added, the PTimer handles the case of a long timer being added, and thus a long wait initiated, followed by a short timer being added. In this case, the long wait is interrupted by the schedule method's notify, and the timer rechecks the correct wait time, adjusting it as necessary. The following code concludes the PTimer's run method and shows this "smart" call to the wait method.

```
if(max != 0)
{
    try
    {
        if(minWaitTime > CUTOFF)
        {
            wait(minWaitTime - SAFETY);
        }
        else
        {
            wait(RESOLUTION);
        }
    }
    catch(InterruptedException exp)
```

```
                        {
                        }
                    }
                }
            }
        }
```

The schedule method, which follows, adds PTimerSpecs to PTimer's list and notifies any waiting threads. If this is the first spec added, PTimer's thread is started. The timer waits until the last minute to start a thread to make sure that a thread is not created if nothing is scheduled. The deschedule method merely removes all occurrences of a timer spec from the list.

```
    public synchronized void schedule(PTimerSpec t)
    {
        PTimerSpec curItem;

        if(t.isAbsolute()
           && (t.timeToFire(System.currentTimeMillis())<0))
        {
            t.notifyListeners(this);
            return;
        }

        t.initTime();

        specs.addElement(t);

        if(kicker == null)
        {
            kicker = new Thread(this);
            kicker.start();
        }

        notifyAll();
    }

    public synchronized void deschedule(PTimerSpec t)
    {
        while(specs.removeElement(t))
        {
        }
    }
}
```

PTimer is a flexible class of performing timed operations. The main advantages of it are that it is fairly accurate, approaching 2*RESOLUTION, and it minimizes resource usage. Of course, the main disadvantage is that listeners are notified in a background thread. This could be remedied by using Swing to integrate the notification into the event thread.

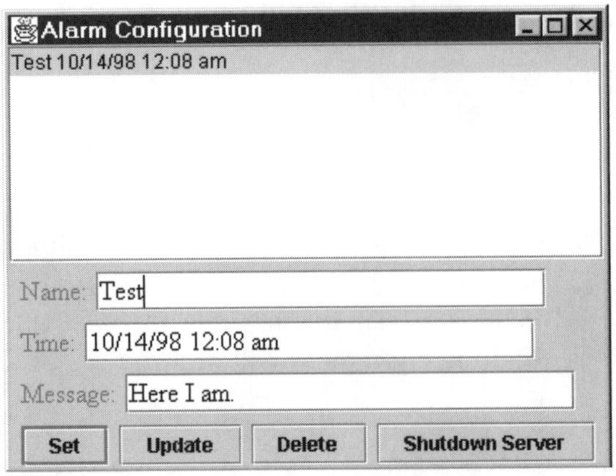

Figure 21.4 AlarmConfig user interface.

AlarmConfig

The AlarmConfig application is implemented in a single class called AlarmConfig and a small helper class for handling the window close messages. This class is very similar to the examples in Chapter 20, so the complete code is not included here (it is available on the CD-ROM, however.) Instead, the implementation for onMessage and the code for telling the server to shut down are included. When run, the AlarmConfig application displays an interface like the one pictured in Figure 21.4.

When created, an AlarmConfig object registers as a subscriber to the ALARM_TOPIC and assigns itself as a MessageListener for this TOPIC. It also registers as a sender for the ADMIN_QUEUE storing the QueueSender instance in the variable sender.

The onMessage method shown here demonstrates how the AlarmConfig application handles the two types of messages on the ALARM_TOPIC. First, if the message contains an Alarm object, the AlarmConfig updates the list of available alarms by deleting the relevant Alarm. If the message contains a vector, the complete list is replaced with the new list of current alarms.

```
public void onMessage(Message msg)
{
    try
    {
        ObjectMessage map = (ObjectMessage)msg;
        Object test = map.getObject();

        if(test instanceof Alarm)
        {
            Alarm alarm = (Alarm) test;
            alarmsModel.removeElement(alarm);
        }
        else if(test instanceof Vector)
```

```
            {
                Vector curAlarms = (Vector) test;

                if(curAlarms != null)
                {
                    int i,max;

                    alarmsModel.removeAllElements();

                    max = curAlarms.size();

                    for(i=0;i<max;i++)
                    {
                        alarmsModel.addElement(curAlarms.elementAt(i));
                    }

                    if(max > 0)
                    {
                        alarms.setSelectedIndex(0);
                        nameField.selectAll();
                        nameField.requestFocus();
                    }

                    repaint();
                }
            }
        }
        catch(Exception exp)
        {
            exp.printStackTrace();
        }
    }
```

Pressing the "Shutdown server" button results in a call to doShutdown. This method creates a MapMessage for the ADMIN_QUEUE and sets the ACTION to SHUTDOWN before sending it. The AlarmConfig application also shuts itself down, because it can't do anything without the server.

```
    protected void doShutdown()
    {
        try
        {
            MapMessage map = session.createMapMessage();

            map.setString(AlarmServer.ACTION,AlarmServer.SHUTDOWN);

            sender.send(map);

            close();

            setVisible(false);
```

```
            System.exit(0);
        }
        catch(Exception exp)
        {
            exp.printStackTrace();
            JOptionPane.showMessageDialog(this
                                    ,"Can't shutdown server."
                                    ,"Error"
                                    ,JOptionPane.ERROR_MESSAGE);
        }
    }
```

If you try this example, you can use the window close box to close the AlarmConfig application without shutting down the server. Restarting the AlarmConfig program causes it to initialize its list from the server, displaying the alarms that didn't fire between the time the program was exited and the time it was restarted.

AlarmDaemon

The AlarmDaemon application, like the AlarmConfig, creates a basic user interface, pictured in Figure 21.5.

The AlarmDaemon has only one button for initiating a shutdown. Otherwise, the daemon simply registers as a MessageListener for the ALARM_TOPIC and displays JOptionPanes when an alarm occurs. The daemon also beeps to warn the user of an alarm. The onMessage method ignores any messages that don't contain an Alarm object by throwing an exception and catching it, as shown below.

```
public void onMessage(Message msg)
    {
        try
        {
            ObjectMessage map = (ObjectMessage)msg;
            Alarm alarm = (Alarm) map.getObject();
            long interval=300;
            int beeps=5;
```

Figure 21.5 AlarmDaemon interface.

```
            int i;
            Toolkit kit = Toolkit.getDefaultToolkit();

            if(alarm != null)
            {
                for(i=0;i<beeps;i++)
                {
                    kit.beep();
                    Thread.sleep(interval);
                }

                JOptionPane.showMessageDialog(null
                                    ,alarm.getMessage()
                                    ,"Alarm"
                                    ,JOptionPane.INFORMATION_MESSAGE);

                kit.beep();
            }
        }
        catch(Exception exp)
        {
        }
    }
```

One addition to this class might be a way to add a filter to the alarms displayed so that not all alarms are displayed. It is also worth noting that the JOptionPane is a model, so the daemon will not receive any more alarm messages until the current one is acknowledged by the user. Another implementation might provide an audio-only alarm or keep a list of alarms that have fired.

This is perhaps one of the simplest clients for listening to alarms. You could create other applications that use the same alarm server, possibly by adding alarms to the server programmatically instead of using the AlarmConfig program. One example of this type of application would be a program that reindexes a Web site or runs reports on a regular basis. By separating the alarm functionality into a separate program that keeps a persistent list, you can rely on alarms without having to reimplement the code each time.

Summary

The AlarmServer is a great example of how messaging can be used to create a standard interface to a network service. Multiple applications can use the AlarmServer by subscribing to the ALARM_TOPIC and sending to the ADMIN_QUEUE. The clients don't have to know how the server is implemented, nor even what mechanism is being used to communicate with it beyond JMS. Using messaging allows the application to use services generically, publishing requests and receiving responses.

This example also demonstrates how the messages you send are an integral part of the application itself. If we decided to use text messages instead of ObjectMessages, it would change the complete design, the client applications, and the server. Message definition must happen early in the design process and should be flexible enough to support changes that you plan to make. For example, you might use MapMessages because they support arbitrary contents for ObjectMessages for the same reason. However, keep in mind that the JMS provider you choose may provide differing levels of support and performance for the various messaging types.

Messaging is a powerful addition to the enterprise toolkit that already contains servlets, JDBC, and Enterprise JavaBeans. Hopefully, this example gives you a few ideas of how you can use messaging to connect systems in a generic way, allowing the individual applications to change as long as the messages stay the same. JMS and messaging are object encapsulation at the application level.

The next chapter introduces the concept of transactions; it is followed by a discussion of transactions and Enterprise JavaBeans.

Transactions, JTA, and JTS

A *transaction* is a single unit of work. Transactions define a boundary around a set of operations. For example, most commercial databases use transactions to group changes to data. These database transactions ensure that if a purchase is recorded, the accompanying customer balance is adjusted accordingly. Failure to perform either operation will cause both to fail.

NOTE **If you are familiar with transactions, you will probably want to skip the next discussion and go directly to the section, "Transactions in Java."**

Transactions are associated with a set of resources and operations. Database transactions, for example, are associated with the database's data and the operations that can interact with it. Transactions enact three basic operations, pictured in Figure 22.1. First, a transaction can be started. Starting a transaction marks the current state of a system. Committing a transaction updates the system to include all of the changes made since the transaction was started. Rolling back a transaction cancels all of the operations performed since the transaction began, returning the system to its initial state.

In a sense, that is all there is to transactions. As a programmer, you will use them to bracket code that should be executed or that will fail as single unit. The term *atomic* is used to indicate this unified nature of transactions. In this context, the word *atomic* means that the transaction can only succeed completely or fail completely. It cannot partially succeed.

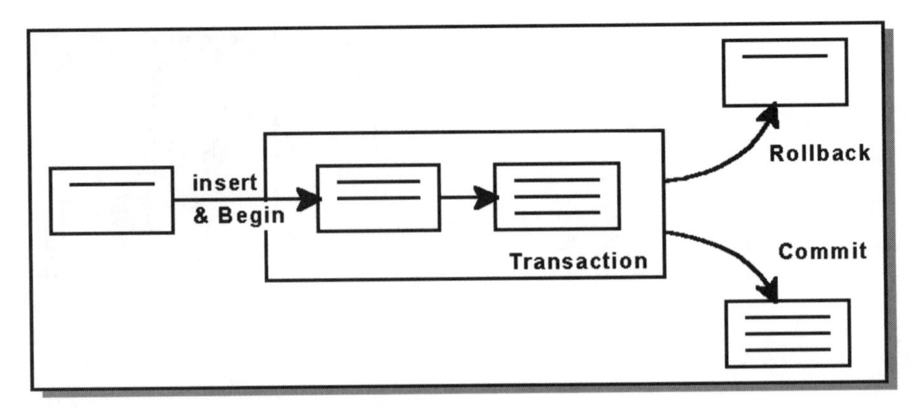

Figure 22.1 Transaction operations.

Logically, it is necessary to associate transactions with some form of locking. For example, if one client tries to update a counter from 4 to 5, then rolls back the change, the counter should be at 4. If the counter is not locked throughout the transaction's scope, another client could update the counter to 5, resulting in either the second change being lost or the first rollback being ineffective. The locks associated with transactions are very similar to the locks used to protect data in multithreaded programs.

Transaction locks can often be grouped into one of several categories. Locks can be *optimistic*, as pictured in Figure 22.2—meaning that the transaction doesn't really lock the data, but hopes that the underlying data is unchanged during its operations.

If there is a change to the underlying data, the commit or rollback operation fails. Optimistic locks are common in situations in which data is not shared very much and reduces the resource usage associated with locking. Figure 22.3 shows an example of how an optimistic lock can fail. In this example, one transaction gets data from the store, updates it, and inserts the data into the store. Another transaction performs the same three operations. But because the operations overlap in time, the update at step 5 will be overridden by the update in step 6, without the transaction that performs the update knowing that the data has changed since it first copied it.

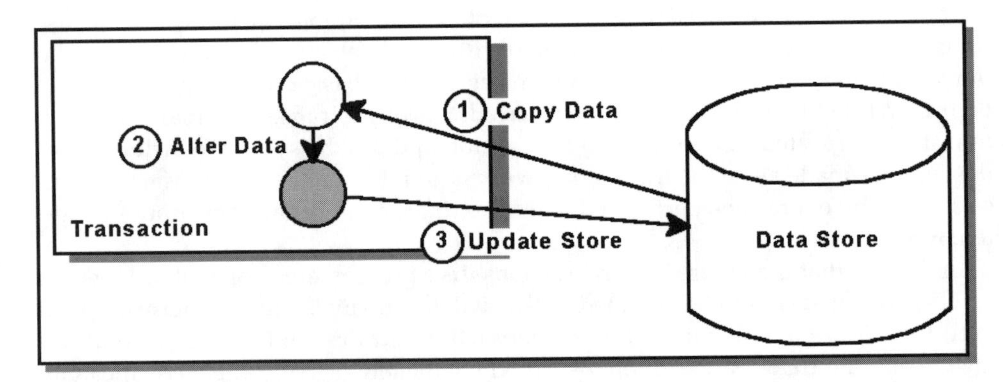

Figure 22.2 Optimistic locking.

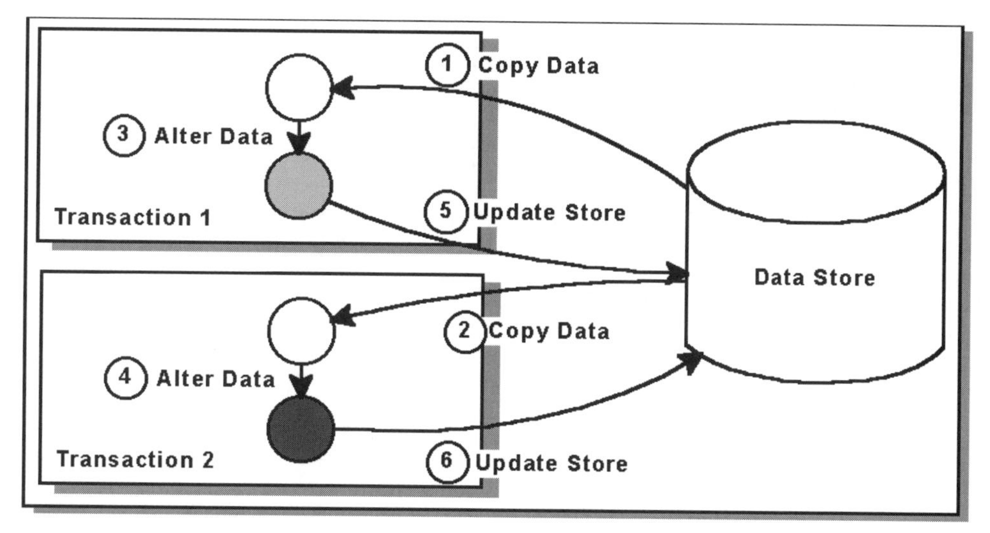

Figure 22.3 Failed optimistic lock.

Pessimistic locks protect their data throughout the transaction scope. This ensures that the commit or rollback will not be affected by other clients or transaction scopes. However, pessimistic locks are the most resource intensive and can, in some instances, make it hard for transactions to share data optimally.

Java programs do not really deal with the locking associated with transactions. You will, however, need to recognize that these locks may underlay the operations that you take. This means that like thread programming, transaction programming can produce deadlocks when a transaction tries to acquire a resource held by another transaction. One example of a deadlock, pictured in Figure 22.4, occurs when the first transaction locks resource 1 before trying to lock resource 2 while the second transaction locks resource 2 and then tries to lock resource 1. As a result, transaction 1 is waiting on transaction 2, and transaction 2 is waiting on transaction 1, so neither can proceed.

Threads are, in fact, a great analogy for transactions. In most cases, transactions are used when multiple clients are accessing a resource. However, transactions can also be used by several threads in a single-client program. In this analogy, transactions group operations the same way that threads group operations.

Database transactions are a great example of a single resource's use of transactions to protect itself and its data. As enterprise-level computing resources have grown and become more complex, there has been a demand for transactions that can span several databases or other resources. These transactions are called *distributed transactions* because their scope can span multiple resources on numerous computers.

Distributed transactions are a very complex topic. Many issues arise when trying to ensure that the operations executed inside a transaction are protected sufficiently for all of the resources affected. For example, in the simple case of two databases being linked, the transaction needs to be sure that during a commit, both databases commit successfully or both are rolled back, or the commit will simply fail. The atomic nature of transactions demands that network traffic, server failure, or some other problem doesn't unlink the two databases in a way that allows changes to one resource inside

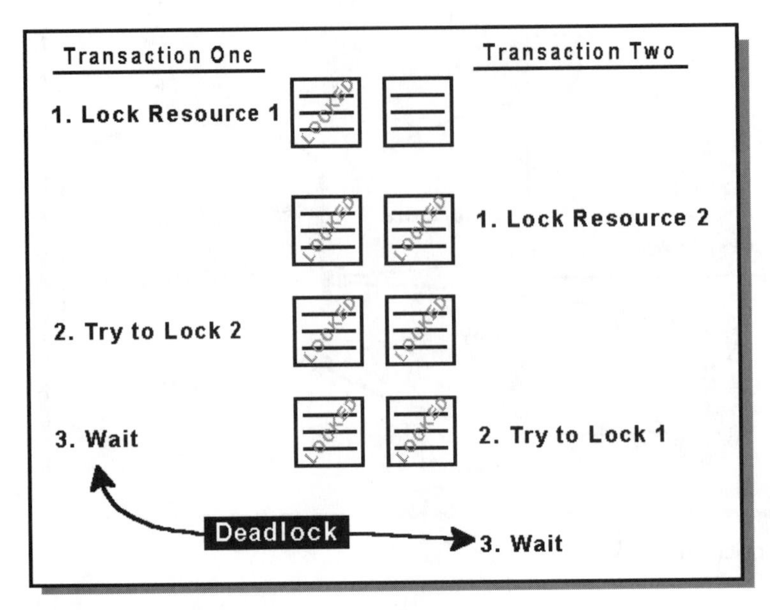

Figure 22.4 Deadlocked transactions.

the distributed transaction to occur without the changes to the other resource. Figure 22.5 displays a simple example of a distributed transaction in which two clients are updating two databases in the same transaction scope.

As a result of the resources and network traffic required to implement distributed transactions, they should be used only when absolutely necessary. In the previous example, with two databases being updated in one transaction, it may be possible to implement the database updates in an EJB that uses standard transactions to ensure that multiple databases are committed as one. In this case, the bean's container uses a simple form of distributed transactions that can exist inside a single application. As

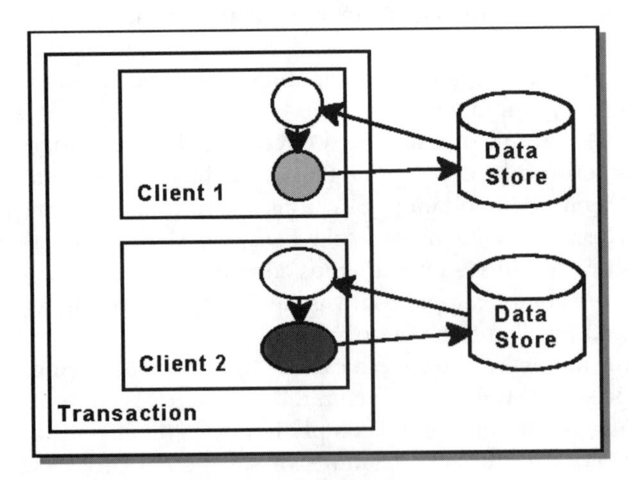

Figure 22.5 Distributed transactions.

discussed in Chapter 23, "Using Transactions with Enterprise JavaBeans," the bean doesn't have to worry about the grouping of transactions because it is managed by the bean's container. Of course, EJB programmers can get under the covers and manage their transactions manually.

Transactions in Java

Chapter 3, "Basic JDBC Programming," discussed how Java programs take advantage of transactions in a database. Java Message Server implementations can also support transactions. Enterprise bean programmers will have access to transactions using an object called the UserTransaction. This object is part of the javax.transaction package defined by the Java Transaction API (JTA). JTA is a specification of UserTransaction and an object called the XAResource associated with them. (UserTransaction is discussed in more detail in Chapter 23.) JTA is an interface for programmers creating resources that should rely on the distributed transaction architecture defined with XAResources representing transactional contexts.

In other words, JTA is for programmers writing things like JDBC drivers that need to link their transactions with other resources such as enterprise beans, JMS messages, or other JDBC connections. This XAResource object, along with the rest of JTA, is a Java mapping of the industry-standard X/Open XA interface that defines how transactions are identified and propagated.

Underneath JTA is another lower-level interface called the Java Transaction Service, or JTS. JTS is an interface defined for programmers implementing applications such as transaction monitors that take the JTA interface out of a single program and onto a network. Figure 22.6 diagrams this relationship between the various entities in an application and the interface associated with or accessed by each.

The details of both JTA and JTS are beyond the scope of this book. They are also hidden from Java programmers by the higher-level interfaces such as JMS, JDBC, and EJB. As a result, Java programmers can easily rely on transactions with only a minimal amount of code.

One way that Java programmers leverage transactions is in conjunction with exceptions. When a programmer is going to perform a set of grouped operations, he begins a transaction at the top of the try-catch block. At the bottom of the block, the transaction

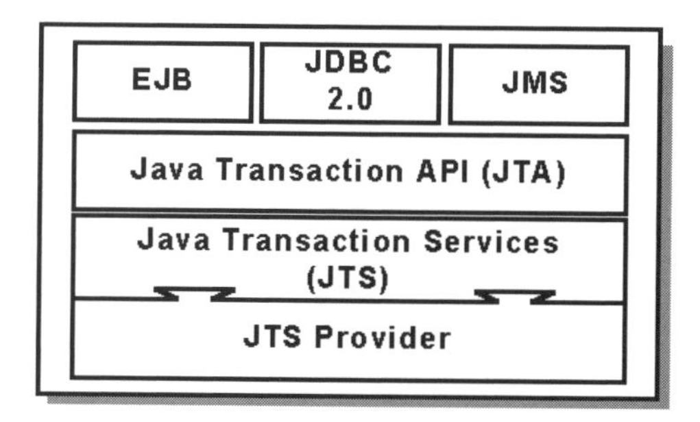

Figure 22.6 Java transaction APIs.

can be committed because no exception occurred. Inside the catch block, the transaction is rolled back. The pseudocode that follows shows how this interaction is commonly implemented:

```
try
{
    trans.begin();

    . . Do work . .

    trans.commit();
}
catch(Exception exp)
{
    trans.rollback();
}
```

Regardless of the code used to interact with transactions, the enterprise Java interfaces are beginning to integrate transactions as a core part of their definitions. For example, an enterprise bean will be able to propagate a transaction to several JDBC connections, other beans, and even a JMS session. Future resources may also build on the JTA interface to seamlessly include them in your enterprise applications.

Summary

Transactions take reliable programming to the next level. By grouping operations together, transactions can be used to ensure that a group of requests succeeds or fails as a single unit. Although common in databases, transactions are working their way into other operations. The next chapter shows how Enterprise JavaBeans can be associated with transactions and how these transactions can be managed programmatically. For these beans, the resources they access can be protected inside a single transactional context.

Using Transactions with Enterprise JavaBeans

Java Transaction Service (JTS) and Java Transaction API (JTA) define a complete transactional framework for enterprise applications, but they are really designed for use by transaction processor writers and resource authors. For example, a JDBC driver vendor might use the interfaces in JTA to include distributed transactions in its JDBC driver. At the level of an Enterprise JavaBean (EJB) author, there is really just one object with which to deal. This object, called UserTransaction, implements the javax.transaction.UserTransaction interface. Aside from this interface and the associated exceptions, EJB programmers rely on their EJB host and container for all transaction management.

Despite the simple interface provided to EJB programmers, when deploying beans that rely on transactions, a number of issues arise. First, a set of options are available to beans in their deployment descriptors. These options define how isolated a bean's transactions are and how the bean interacts with transactions.

Transaction Options

Most EJBs will not have to do anything to be transaction enabled. Instead, the developer assigns a transaction option to the bean at deployment time. The transaction option indicates how the bean or its individual methods should be treated during a transacted operation. Only when the bean programmer wants to take charge of the transaction does the programmer need to implement any code. This simplification of transaction management is another reason that EJBs are a powerful tool for enterprise programming.

A bean's transactional behavior is defined relative to the object that is messaging it. This caller is called the *client*. This client code could be a client application or even another EJB. The purpose of the transaction option is to decide in what transaction context the bean's method should execute. For example, does the bean expect the client to manage the transaction for it, or does the bean perform in the same manner with or without a transaction? In cases in which the bean uses a transaction, it will try to pass that transaction's scope to the resources that it uses. For example, if a transacted bean uses a database connection, both the bean and the connection will share their transaction scope, committing or rolling back as one. If this same bean relies on the client to provide a transaction, the client obtains the transaction, then passes it to the bean, which uses it on the database. You can see how, in a complex application, a transaction could be used to manage a very tricky network of message calls.

Each method in a bean's remote interface can be assigned one of the six transaction options described in Table 23.1. These options range from complete ignorance toward transactions, TX_NOT_SUPPORTED, to demanding a transaction, TX_MANDATORY, to programmer controlled transactions, TX_BEAN_MANAGED.

Beans also have a default transaction option assigned to them for all of the methods that don't specifically define one of these options.

The only restriction between the default- and method-level options is that if one method is TX_BEAN_MANAGED, all of the methods must be TX_BEAN_MANAGED. Otherwise, the options can be mixed freely, although you should check the documentation for your EJB host to be sure.

NOTE **Early implementations of EJB do not support the TX_SUPPORTS correctly, so that option should not be used until EJB 1.1 or greater is released.**

Table 23.1 Transaction Options

OPTION	DESCRIPTION
`TX_NOT_SUPPORTED`	The bean doesn't use transactions, and any active transactions are suspended during the method call.
`TX_SUPPORTS`	If the client has a transaction scope, the bean uses it; otherwise, none is used.
`TX_REQUIRED`	The bean requires a transaction scope; if one is not provided, it is created.
`TX_REQUIRES_NEW`	The bean requires that the container create a new transaction for it.
`TX_MANDATORY`	The bean requires the client to have a transaction scope.
`TX_BEAN_MANAGED`	The bean will manage its scope, creating one if necessary.

Isolation Levels

On top of the transaction options, beans and their methods can have an isolation level associated with them. Isolation levels indicate how strong the transactions restrict the shared reading of data. For example, an isolation level can indicate whether a bean can read the data added to the database by another bean that hasn't committed its transaction yet. In the safest isolation level, called TRANSACTION_SERIALIZABLE, a transaction locks the data it is changing until it commits. Until the commit happens, no other transaction can see the changes. In the loosest isolation level, called TRANSACTION_READ_UNCOMMITED, changes made by a transaction are immediately available, even though they may become invalid if the transaction rolls back. These two levels bracket two other, less obvious, isolation levels.

The third isolation level, called TRANSACTION_REPEATABLE_READ, prohibits what are called dirty and non-repeatable reads but allows so-called phantom reads to occur. A *dirty read* occurs when one transaction reads data that is not committed by another transaction. A *non-repeatable read* occurs when one transaction scope tries to read data from a row that another transaction has changed since the last read. For example, if T1 and T2 are transacting, a non-repeatable read occurs when T1 reads the row, T2 changes the row, and T1 rereads the row and gets different data. The TRANSACTION_REPEATABLE_READ isolation level will not allow either of these types of "weird" reads to occur. However, it does allow phantom reads. A *phantom read* occurs when one transaction rereads a row that satisfies a where clause after another transaction has added a row that satisfies the clause. For example, T1 reads and selects all authors named "joe," T2 inserts "joe green," T1 rereads and gets the new "phantom" row for "joe green."

The final isolation level is called TRANSACTION _READ_COMMITED. This level prevents dirty reads but allows both non-repeatable and phantom reads to occur.

The isolation levels for EJBs are modeled on the JDBC isolation levels. In fact, when a bean makes JDBC calls, it expects the JDBC driver to be set to the correct isolation level defined by the bean. It is up to the container to make sure that the bean's database connections adhere to this rule. Remember that in many cases, the bean's host is providing database connections from a pool. When a method requests one of these connections, it should update the connection's isolation level appropriately.

TRANSACTION_SERIALIZABLE is the safest level to use, because it prevents any strange reads. However, it is also the most costly in terms of locking data, because the transaction must lock all of the data it may change until it is committed. This means that the data is not available to other transactions and those transactions must wait for the data to become available before accessing it.

Be very careful when using the other levels, but you may choose to use them if performance or application considerations warrant. For example, applications that are mainly viewing data should not be greatly affected by phantom reads, because they will only add to the data viewed, without showing false data. Non-repeatable reads are also not as bad for viewing applications, because they simply update the viewer's version of the data. However, you would not want applications that expect data to remain unchanged, such as a commerce program that performs reads to determine account balances, to perform calculations on data and have it changed before updating the row.

To see when each level might be acceptable, let's look at four examples; one for each isolation level. First, a banking program that needs to access a customer's account balances and update them to reflect a money transfer would probably use TRANSACTION_SERIALIZABLE to protect both tables during the operation. A program that processes data by performing a read and follows that read with another read based on the first—a basic employee/manager relationship, for example—could use TRANSACTION_REPEATABLE_READ to ensure that an employee's manager id doesn't change between the first search for the employee's information that includes the manager's id and the subsequent search for the manager's information.

A program that groups data can use TRANSACTION _READ_COMMITED to make sure that all the data it reads is valid while allowing changes to data. Consider the case of a program that performs a read on a list of customers to determine how many there are. The program might reread the data to get the final values of each customer, but you wouldn't mind getting altered data because the latest data would be used anyway. In this example, phantom reads might be ignored and saved for the next time the process is run.

Finally, programs that are appending data to a table can use the TRANSACTION_READ_UNCOMMITED isolation level because they aren't really performing read operations. Keep in mind that these isolation levels are applied mainly when a transaction performs multiple reads on the same data. When transactions perform single, atomic read operations, there is little concern for phantom or non-repeatable reads.

One restriction on a bean's isolation levels: You cannot mix two isolation levels in a single transaction. For example, if a client and a bean share a transaction, the bean cannot require a different isolation level than the client. This is something to be considered at design time, when you define the relationship between your beans and clients.

Bean-Managed Transactions

EJBs that use bean-managed transactions, TX_BEAN_MANAGED, access their transaction scope using a UserTransaction object. UserTransaction defines a number of constants and methods. The methods for UserTransaction are listed in Table 23.2, along with descriptions of their purposes. The constants defined in UserTransaction are used to indicate the status of a transaction and are discussed in the "Transaction Status" section.

Beans obtain their transaction from the EJBContext using this method:

```
public UserTransaction getUserTransaction()
  throws IllegalStateException
```

For example, if a bean stored its context in an instance variable called context, it would access the UserTransaction using the following code:

```
UserTransaction trans = context.getUserTransaction();
```

Once acquired, the transaction can be controlled using the methods in Table 23.2. In particular, you might begin a transaction to initiate it. Then, if an operation completes successfully, commit the transaction. If an operation fails, roll back the transaction.

Table 23.2 User Transaction Methods

METHOD	DESCRIPTION
`public void begin() throws IllegalStateException`	Begins the transaction.
`public void commit() throws TransactionRolledbackException, HeuristicMixedException, HeuristicRollbackException, SecurityException, IllegalStateException`	Commits the transaction and all of the changes that made it its scope.
`public void rollback() throws IllegalStateException,`	Rolls back the transaction, undoing any changes.
`SecurityException public void setRollbackOnly() throws IllegalStateException`	Tells the transaction that it can only be rollback. This method is used when an error occurs that should prevent the transaction from committing.
`public int getStatus()`	Returns the transaction's status.
`public void setTransactionTimeout(int seconds)`	Modify the transaction's time-out value.

Exceptions

As you can see from Table 23.2, a transaction can throw a variety of exceptions. The main exceptions are listed in Table 23.3. These are defined in the javax.transaction package.

Heuristic decisions occur mostly in unusual circumstances, such as network failures, that prevent normal processing. When a transaction makes a heuristic decision,

Table 23.3 Transaction Exceptions

EXCEPTION	MEANING
`SecurityException`	A security violation has occurred.
`IllegalStateException`	The current thread is not associated with the transaction.
`TransactionRolledbackException`	The transaction was marked for rollback only or was rolled back.
`HeuristicMixedException`	Some changes were committed and others rolled back based on a heuristic decision.
`HeuristicRollbackException`	All changes were rolled back based on a heuristic decision.

there is a risk that the decision will differ from the actual outcome of the operation, potentially resulting in loss of data integrity. For example, the transaction might lose touch with the database and assume that a rollback occurred when the attempted commit succeeded. This would leave the transaction in an incorrect state.

Transaction Maintenance

The container for a stateful session bean tries to maintain the same transaction context across the entire session. This transaction maintenance is governed by the following rules:

- If the client request is not associated with a transaction and the instance is not associated with a transaction, the container invokes the instance with no transaction context.
- If the client is associated with a transaction and the instance is not associated with a transaction, the container suspends the client's transaction association and invokes the method with no transaction context.
- If the client request is not associated with a transaction and the instance is already associated with a transaction, the container invokes the instance with the transaction that is associated with the instance.
- If the client is associated with a transaction and the instance is already associated with a transaction, the container suspends the client's transaction association and invokes the method with the transaction context that is associated with the instance.

In cases in which the client has its transaction scope suspended for the EJBs method, the transaction is resumed when the method returns. Stateless beans and entity beans do not share a transaction across messages from the client. However, they could make several transacted calls to other resources using the transaction assigned to them.

Because stateful beans exist for more than one method, they may want to receive notifications from their containers when transaction operations are used on them. In this case, the bean can implement the SessionSynchronization interface. This interface includes these three methods:

```
public void afterBegin() throws RemoteException;
public void beforeCompletion() throws RemoteException;
public void afterCompletion() throws RemoteException;
```

These methods are called to tell the bean that a transaction was begun, that it is going to completed, and that it has completed. Completion for a transaction is either commit or roll back. If a bean wants to ensure that the transaction operating on it rolls back, it can throw an exception in beforeCompletion or call setRollbackOnly on its context.

All bean-managed transactions should be committed or rolled back before the bean completes its interaction with the client. For a stateful session bean, this means the transaction should be completed before the session ends. For all other beans, the transaction should end before the method called by the client returns.

Transaction Status

A transaction's status can be obtained using the getStatus method. This method returns a value defined in a UserTransaction static variable. The possible status values are listed in the documentation and include flags for whether or not the transaction has begun, is rolled back, or has been committed. This status might be used in advanced situations to determine what the bean should do based on a change in status. Possibly the status will change when the bean calls another resource, such as another EJB. In most cases, you as a programmer should not need to access this information.

An Example for Testing Transactions

As both an example of how to use transactions and a test program, we have created a set of EJBs that are to be deployed with a variety of transaction options. The first bean manages its own transactions and calls two other beans that use different options for each method. When the secondary beans are called, they try to insert data into a database. This relationship is shown in Figure 23.1. Each secondary bean is provided a different database URL so that two separate databases are accessed.

The client for this example, pictured in Figure 23.2, allows the user to enter a message. This message is sent to the primary bean using one of three methods. The first method uses no transactions, the second commits its transaction, and the third rolls back its transaction. Each method calls one of the secondary bean's methods based on the selected radio button in the client. Once the primary method returns, the client asks

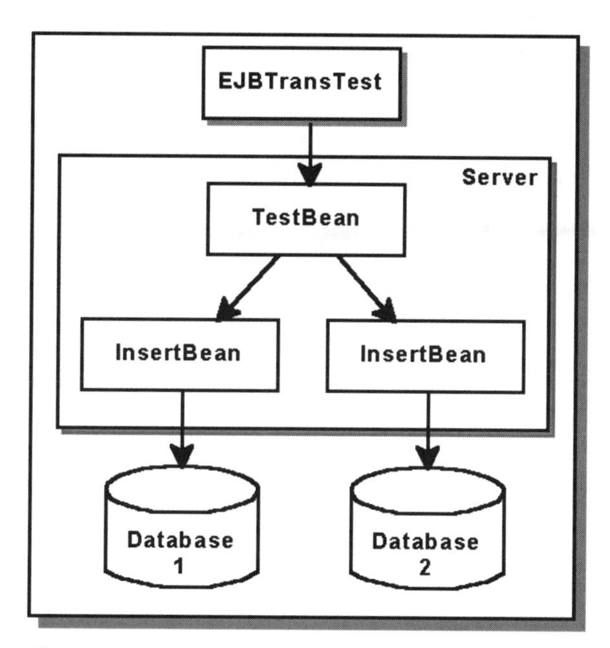

Figure 23.1 Parent and child beans.

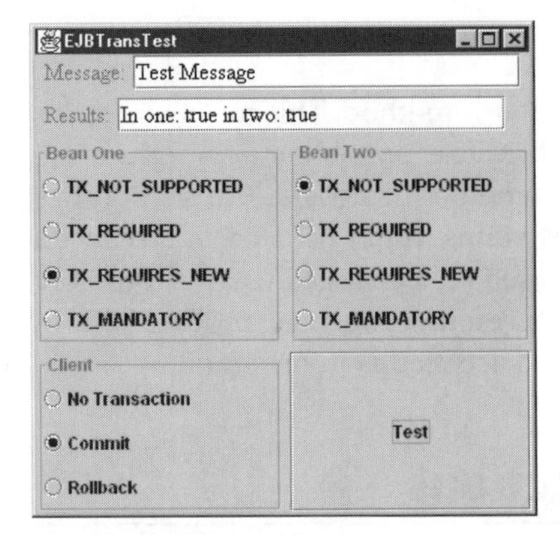

Figure 23.2 EJBTransTest.

the bean to check whether the data was inserted in the database. A resulting string indicates success or failure for beans one and two.

The databases for this example can be built using the provided BuildDB script. This program simply creates a single table called MESSAGES with a single column named MESSAGE. Microsoft Access database files that contain this table are provided on the CD-ROM. The CD-ROM also includes an NT build script that compiles the examples and runs the WebLogic deployment tools on them. Edit this script for your installation or use the tools for your EJB host.

The majority of the code for this example is involved in creating the insert bean that adds data to a database and the client that is mainly user interface code. To save space, these classes are not included here. The class that does have several new techniques is the Enterprise JavaBean implementation called TestBeanBean. This is the primary bean in our example description.

TestBeanBean

TestBeanBean performs three interesting operations. First, it manages its own transactions. Second, it uses JBDC to access the database. Third, it uses JNDI to access the HOME for the InsertBean that we are using as the secondary bean in this example. Once the InsertBean is created, the TestBean sends messages to it, demonstrating how two EJBs can communicate.

The TestBeanBean implementation stores relevant data in instance variables. This data is obtained from the environment provided by the EJBContext. The following code is taken from the TestBeanBean .java file and lists the bean's instance variables, required SessionBean methods, and the implementation for setSessionContext.

```
package testbean;

//imports removed to save space

public class TestBeanBean implements SessionBean
{
```

```
transient protected SessionContext context;
transient protected javax.naming.Context jndi;
public String url1 = null;//url for database 1
public String url2 = null; //url for database 2
public String user=null; //database user name
public String password=null; //database password
public String driver=null; //database driver
public String insertHome=null; //JNDI lookup name

public void ejbActivate()
{
}

public void ejbRemove()
{
}

public void ejbPassivate()
{
}

public void setSessionContext(SessionContext ctx)
{
    context = ctx;
    Properties env = context.getEnvironment();

    user = env.getProperty("user");
    password = env.getProperty("password");
    url1 = env.getProperty("url1");
    url2 = env.getProperty("url2");
    driver = env.getProperty("driver");
    insertHome = env.getProperty("inserthome");

    try
    {
        jndi = getInitialContext(env);
    }
    catch(Exception exp)
    {
        jndi = null;
    }
}
```

The getInitialContext method shown here is used to create the JNDI context based on properties in the environment. Example values are defined in the DeploymentDescriptor.txt file provided on the CD-ROM. In particular, the following environmental properties are defined:

driver: weblogic.jdbc.jts.Driver

url1: jdbc:weblogic:jts:db1

url2: jdbc:weblogic:jts:db2

inserthome: insertbean.InsertBeanHome

These properties assume that the BEA WebLogic server is being used and that it is configured with two database connection pools, one called db1 and the other db2. The JDBC driver used by the TestBean is the BEA WebLogic transaction and connection pool aware driver, and the insert beans are registered with the name insertbean.InsertBeanHome, as indicated in the descriptor.

```
protected Context getInitialContext(Properties env)
 throws Exception
{
    Properties p = new Properties();
    String url = null;
    String user=null;
    String password=null;

    url = env.getProperty("jndi_url");
    user = env.getProperty("jndi_user");
    password = env.getProperty("jndi_password");

    p.put(Context.INITIAL_CONTEXT_FACTORY,
            "weblogic.jndi.T3InitialContextFactory");

    if(url != null)
        p.put(Context.PROVIDER_URL, url);
    else
        p.put(Context.PROVIDER_URL, "t3://localhost:7001");

    if (user != null)
    {
        p.put(Context.SECURITY_PRINCIPAL, user);

        if (password == null) password = "";

        p.put(Context.SECURITY_CREDENTIALS, password);
    }

    return new InitialContext(p);
}
```

The test bean doesn't do anything when sent the create method. All of the real initialization happens when the context is assigned, as shown in this code:

```
public void ejbCreate()
{
}
```

What follows is the first testing method called by the client. This method doesn't begin a transaction before calling the internal test method. This internal method, included in the three methods accessed by the client, performs the actual connection with the other beans.

```
public void testNoTrans(int mode1
                                 ,int mode2
                                 ,String msg)
  throws Exception
{
    UserTransaction trans = context.getUserTransaction();

    try
    {
        test(mode1,mode2,msg);
    }
    catch(Exception exp)
    {
    }
}
```

The next two methods also call test, but both do so inside a transaction scope. The first method commits the transaction and the second rolls it back.

```
public void testCommitNewTrans(int mode1
                                 ,int mode2
                                 ,String msg)
  throws Exception
{
    UserTransaction trans = context.getUserTransaction();

    trans.begin();

    try
    {
        test(mode1,mode2,msg);
    }
    catch(Exception exp)
    {
    }
    finally
    {
        trans.commit();
    }
}

public void testRollbackNewTrans(int mode1
                                 ,int mode2
                                 ,String msg)
  throws Exception
{
    UserTransaction trans = context.getUserTransaction();
```

```
            trans.begin();

            try
            {
                test(mode1,mode2,msg);
            }
            catch(Exception exp)
            {
            }
            finally
            {
                trans.rollback();
            }
        }
```

The test method, which follows, uses the modes provided by the client that tell it what messages to send to the secondary beans. Test is called by one of the previous three methods. The String message is used as the data to insert in the database.

First, the test looks up the EJB home for the secondary beans. Then it creates the beans and messages them. The arguments to the messages are the string to insert in the database and the URL for the database to contact.

```
        public void test(int mode1,int mode2,String msg)
         throws Exception
        {
            InsertBean bean1,bean2;
            InsertBeanHome otherHome;

            otherHome = (InsertBeanHome) jndi.lookup(insertHome);

            bean1 = otherHome.create();

            try
            {

                //Try to insert with the first bean.
                switch(mode1)
                {
                    case TestBean.NONE:

                        bean1.insertNoTrans(msg,url1);
                        break;

                    case TestBean.REQUIRE:

                        bean1.insertRequireTrans(msg,url1);
                        break;

                    case TestBean.NEW:

                        bean1.insertNewTrans(msg,url1);
```

```
                break;

            case TestBean.MANDATE:

                bean1.insertMandateTrans(msg,url1);
                break;
        }
    }
    catch(Exception ignore)
    {
    }
    finally
    {
        try
        {
            bean1.remove();
        }
        catch(Exception exp)
        {
        }
    }

    bean2 = otherHome.create();

    try
    {
        //Try to insert with the second bean.
        switch(mode2)
        {
            case TestBean.NONE:

                bean2.insertNoTrans(msg,url2);
                break;

            case TestBean.REQUIRE:

                bean2.insertRequireTrans(msg,url2);
                break;

            case TestBean.NEW:

                bean2.insertNewTrans(msg,url2);
                break;

            case TestBean.MANDATE:

                bean2.insertMandateTrans(msg,url2);
                break;
        }
    }
    catch(Exception ignore)
```

```
        {
        }
        finally
        {
            try
            {
                bean2.remove();
            }
            catch(Exception exp)
            {
            }
        }
    }
```

After testing the bean, the client uses the result method to see what happened. This method checks each database for the message that was supposed to be inserted. The return value from result indicates if the message is in database one, two, neither, or both.

```
    public String result(String msg)
        throws Exception
    {
        String retVal = "";
        java.sql.Connection conn=null;
        java.sql.Statement statement=null;
        java.sql.ResultSet rs=null;
        boolean inOne=false;
        boolean inTwo=false;
        UserTransaction trans = context.getUserTransaction();

        trans.begin();
        try
        {
            Class.forName(driver);

            conn = DriverManager.getConnection(url1
                                        ,user,password);

            statement = conn.createStatement();
            rs = statement.executeQuery("select * from messages"
                                  +" where message="
                                  +"\'"+msg+"\'");

            if(rs.next()) inOne = true;
        }
        catch(Exception exp)
        {
            retVal = exp.toString();
        }
        finally
        {
            try
            {
```

```
                if(rs!=null) rs.close();
                if(statement != null) statement.close();
                if(conn!=null) conn.close();
            }
            catch(Exception exp)
            {
            }
        }
        trans.commit();

        trans.begin();
        try
        {
            conn = DriverManager.getConnection(url2
                                            ,user,password);

            statement = conn.createStatement();
            rs = statement.executeQuery("select * from messages"
                                    +" where message="
                                    +"\'"+msg+"\'");

            if(rs.next()) inTwo = true;
        }
        catch(Exception exp)
        {
            retVal = exp.toString();
        }
        finally
        {
            try
            {
                if(rs!=null) rs.close();
                if(statement != null) statement.close();
                if(conn!=null) conn.close();
            }
            catch(Exception exp)
            {
            }
        }
        trans.commit();

        retVal += "In one: "+inOne+" in two: "+inTwo;

        return retVal;
    }
```

Before running the test, the client calls prepare, listed here, on the test bean to empty the two databases:

```
    public void prepare()
        throws Exception
    {
```

```
java.sql.Connection conn=null;
java.sql.Statement statement=null;
UserTransaction trans = context.getUserTransaction();

trans.begin();
try
{
    Class.forName(driver);

    conn = DriverManager.getConnection(url1
                                        ,user,password);

    statement = conn.createStatement();
    statement.executeUpdate("delete * from messages");
}
catch(Exception exp)
{
}
finally
{
    try
    {
        if(statement != null) statement.close();
        if(conn!=null) conn.close();
    }
    catch(Exception exp)
    {
    }
}
trans.commit();

trans.begin();
try
{
    Class.forName(driver);

    conn = DriverManager.getConnection(url2
                                        ,user,password);

    statement = conn.createStatement();
    statement.executeUpdate("delete * from messages");
}
catch(Exception exp)
{
}
finally
{
    try
    {
        if(statement != null) statement.close();
        if(conn!=null) conn.close();
```

```
                }
                catch(Exception exp)
                {
                }
            }
            trans.commit();
        }
    }
```

This example shows how EJBs can communicate with each other and how transaction scopes can be transferred to other resources, including beans and JDBC connections.

Reentrant Beans

In general, beans are protected from multiple clients accessing them simultaneously by their container. The container will either create a bean for each client or lock a bean for use by a single client to protect it from concurrent access. This makes life easier for the bean writer, because you don't have to worry about two clients sending messages to the bean at the same time.

However, when beans send messages to each other, one bean could send a message to a second bean that sends a message back to the first bean. This situation is called *reentrance*, because the first bean's code is being reentered. The EJB specification says that beans can be either reentrant or not as configured in their deployment descriptor. All of the examples in this book have been non-reentrant by including the following line:

```
isReentrant         false
```

in their descriptor file. When a bean is non-reentrant, any attempt to access the bean using the same transaction context that it is already using will result in a RemoteException. If the bean is reentrant, it would be possible for it to receive concurrent requests with the same transaction scope.

The specification and documentation strongly suggest that you avoid reentrant beans whenever possible. If you do use them because your design requires callbacks from the bean's resources to the bean, keep the following issues in mind. The container may not be able to tell a new client request from a reentrant request. This means that the container cannot protect a bean from concurrent client access, and two clients could potentially cause the bean to perform an invalid operation by accessing it simultaneously. It also means that you have to program the bean so that the same transaction scope can call a method more than once without causing a problem.

Summary

The Enterprise JavaBean specification was designed to hide the specifics of distributed transactions from the bean programmer. At the same time, the programmer can use bean-managed transactions and the UserTransaction object to control the transaction scope manually. This combination makes EJB transactions easy to use. First, the EJB container manages all of the transaction scoping and processing among a bean, its client, and the resources it uses. For example, even if the bean manages its transaction, the container will tie this transaction to any JDBC connections used, and the bean will not need to directly manage those.

The next chapter reviews the technologies discussed so far and introduces two large examples that demonstrate multiple technologies from this book in a single enterprise application.

Architecture Review

The first 23 chapters of this book introduced, compared, and provided examples for a number of the Java enterprise technologies. This chapter summarizes these technologies and discusses their intended use. A set of general guidelines and other things to consider are also discussed. Chapters 25, "A Four-Tier Online Store," and 26, "Mini-JMS: A Java Messaging Service Provider," demonstrate all of the technologies discussed in this book in the context of two large applications.

The Technologies

The enterprise technologies can be broken into three categories: programming models, supporting libraries, and networking models. JNDI and JDBC are really libraries, or frameworks, for accessing information. Servlets, JavaServer Pages, and Enterprise JavaBeans all define an application type. These join applets and applications in the continuum of Java program models. RMI and JMS are both models for network computing. Both can be used with the available program types to create distributed applications. For example, a servlet could use RMI to contact an Enterprise JavaBean that uses JMS to contact a Java application. As your applications grow to support the entire enterprise, you will likely find more and more complex combinations of these technologies. Hopefully, the following summaries and guidelines will help you decide when and where to use each technology.

JDBC. The Java Database Connectivity libraries are used to connect a Java program to a data source. The initial version of JDBC was targeted at relational databases, but JDBC 2.0 extends this model to other types of data sources. Of all of the technologies discussed, it is perhaps easiest to determine whether JDBC should be used. To access a database, you will probably want to use JDBC. Be very careful to consider the long-term implications of the other options available, such as portability across multiple data sources.

JNDI. The Java Naming and Directory interface, like JDBC, is really an enabling technology more than a library for use all by itself. Many of the technologies discussed in this book rely on JNDI to provide access to objects such as enterprise beans and JMS destinations. With the advent of corporate directory services, JNDI will also find a place as a core connectivity library between Java programs and these directories.

Servlets. Servlets extend Web servers. In an enterprise environment, servlets can be used to solve a number of problems. First, servlets replace CGI in providing server-side processing for HTTP requests. Second, servlets can extend dynamic Web pages using server-side includes or JavaServer Pages. Third, servlets can be used to form a gateway between Web clients and other services, such as databases, Enterprise JavaBeans, and JMS. Finally, servlet interfaces can be used as a generic interface for services. For example, programmers might use the service method as an interface for generic RMI objects or even enterprise beans.

Making the decision to use a servlet over another Java technology is usually based on the deployment environment more than anything else. If you want to support clients using Web browsers to access your program's functionality, a servlet will likely be involved somewhere. On the other hand, if the clients are Java applications on an intranet, it is likely that they would contact the server directly. Between these two cases are the Java clients that are separated from the server by a firewall. In this case, servlets can preprocess requests for the server, or RMI can be tunneled through the firewall. RMI tunneling requires some configuration on the server but simplifies the client/server relationship, while servlets act as a filter point that supports both browser-based and custom clients.

JavaServer Pages. JavaServer Pages are used to create dynamic Web pages using Java as a scripting language. JSPs are primarily used in situations in which a Web page changes with each request. Ultimately, JSPs compile to servlets, so the real decision for using a JavaServer Page is whether to use it instead of a servlet, or some other server-side scripting solution. In this first comparison—JSP versus servlet—the decision to use a JSP should be based on two criteria. First, are there a lot of similar pages being returned, and if so, can they share the JSP? If not, a servlet may use fewer server resources. Second, does the displayed Web page require editing by a page designer? If so, JSPs are much easier for the designer and programmer to collaborate on than HTML compiled into a straight servlet.

The second comparison between JSP and other technologies such as Active Server Pages and server-side JavaScript is also decided by several criteria. Certainly, you can use JSPs only if your Web server supports them. Otherwise, the server may support one of the other technologies. Second, the people scripting the pages need to know enough Java to do their job. This can actually be an advantage, because the programmers writing Java applications and applets can support the Java in a JSP, although they may not know Visual Basic or JavaScript to support those technologies. Finally, each of these technologies provides slightly different features; one or two of these features may make the decision for you. In this last case, the important thing to remember is that Java and JSPs are probably the most flexible choices of the server-side page scripting technologies and will often provide better long-term support for the features you require.

RMI and distributed objects. Like JDBC, RMI is an enabling technology. Many applications and libraries use RMI to form their network connections. Other applications may rely on raw sockets or HTTP connections to interact with servlets and the Web Server. The goal of RMI is to provide a transparent link between two Java applications. Of course, this link can never be completely transparent, because of the issues inherent with network programming, especially that crazy guy with an ax that keeps cutting ethernet cables. All networking solutions involve some issues. RMI tries to encapsulate possible errors into RemoteException objects that can be handled with standard Java exception handling.

As mentioned in Chapter 1, "An Introduction to Java Enterprise Development," Java IDL and other Java/CORBA technologies are not included in this book. This omission was based on the amount of material that would need to be discussed and not intended to disparage CORBA in any way. In fact, we believe that CORBA and Java IDL are likely to form the foundation for many enterprise applications. Many programmers will probably use RMI over IIOP as well. At the time of this writing, RMI over IIOP was not sufficiently implemented to include in our discussion. However, from your perspective, it should not be very different from general RMI. Sun is working with the Object Management Group to make CORBA, IIOP, and Java work together as closely and transparently as possible.

Enterprise JavaBeans. Enterprise JavaBeans are designed to become the standard building blocks for corporate server applications. Whenever your application is implemented on a server, definitely consider using an EJB host server, such as WebLogic, and Enterprise JavaBeans. This combination allows you to rely on heavily tested services from the server provider and focus your resources on application-specific programming. The component design of Enterprise JavaBeans makes them a great way to encapsulate business rules and processes. They can also form the foundation of a library that provides standard services that your enterprise applications require, such as data processing or report generation.

In a very real sense, Enterprise JavaBeans are simply a way to do work. Deciding whether or not to use them is really a decision of whether or not you want to purchase an EJB host, if you do not already have one. Certainly, smaller deployments may not warrant the expense or overhead of an EJB installation. In this case, consider using straight RMI or CORBA to access the server. In mixed installations, you could possibly provide RMI wrappers for Enterprise JavaBeans on small boxes, such as laptops, and save the EJB hosts for larger deployments, such as the corporate network. This design allows you to reuse the Enterprise JavaBeans at both levels.

Java Messaging Service. The Java Messaging Service is designed to act as a front end to messaging providers. In many cases, these providers use some form of server to implement messaging and may provide transaction management and

Enterprise JavaBeans hosting as well. Messaging as a technology is a great way to objectify the communication between applications. Messaging providers ensure the integrity of this communication and even support delayed communications, storing a message until a receiver is available. The other big advantage of messaging, when a server is involved, is that a client can maintain a single connection to the server that provides access to dozens, hundreds, or even thousands of other programs. This resource optimization alone makes messaging a powerful distributed computing technique.

Given that messaging is a powerful tool, the question is, why use it, or why use anything else? The answer is not simple, but there are a few things that make it easier to consider. First, messaging decouples the communicating programs. This is great when you may want to change the program at either end of the communication or if you want to allow multicast-style communication in which one client talks to multiple listeners. The down side to decoupling is that there is a performance cost. For example, accessing a database with messages is not likely to be as efficient as a direct connection and would be efficient only if the messages were highly optimized, network traffic low, and the database library implementation poor. Messaging is really a great example of trading flexibility for performance and resources. In some ways, as in the case of network connections, you can save resources. In others, as in the case of the number of network hops to access a program, you increase resource usage. When deciding between messaging and direct connections, weigh the resource usage and performance as a primary guide against the flexibility that you can gain.

Example Designs

The last two chapters of this book describe two large examples. Each example is in excess of 2,500 lines of code and combines several of the technologies described in this book. By including these examples, our intention was to provide a kind of closure to this seminar-style discussion of multiple technologies by bringing the separate examples and concepts together into a larger, unified whole.

The first large example is an online store that provides a Web front end using servlets and JavaServer Pages. The back end is managed by servlets and an Enterprise JavaBean that stores data with JDBC. The second example is the implementation for our JMS provider called MiniJMS. This JMS provider uses RMI to communicate between the client and server, JBDC to store messages, and JNDI for publishing destinations and factories. The basic design of each example is discussed here, with explanations. The implementations for these examples are discussed in Chapters 25 and 26, respectively.

The Online Store

The primary goal for the online store example is to demonstrate an application that provides a Web front end and implements some form of business logic in the back end. We chose an online store because it is a familiar concept and lends itself to this primary goal. In our case, our decision regarding what technology to use was driven by two goals: first, to demonstrate the technologies in this book, and second, to demonstrate them in a reasonable way. In other words, we didn't choose servlets because we had to, we chose them because in a good way they do the job we want done.

The first requirement for the online store is that it has a Web-based interface. This immediately indicated the use of HTML and probably JHTML or servlets. Leveraging on the design from Chapter 11, "A JavaServer Page Online Store," we decided to use JavaServer Pages to display a list of categories for the products available at the store and to display the products in each category. The initial page for this example, pictured in Figure 24.1, was updated to include access to the search servlet from Chapter 8, "A Servlet-Based Search Engine." The decision to use a servlet for searching was an easy one, because we wanted to manage a lot of code for indexing and still provide a Web interface. We could also have used a JSP for searching the front end without a great deal of changes to the code or design. This is one example where we chose a servlet more to distinguish between algorithms and user interface than anything else.

The front page for this store also displays an advertisement. We implemented the code to produce these ads in a servlet so that it could be included in the JSP using a server-side include. The servlet in this example reads a file containing link and image information and uses that information to place linked images on Web pages. The relationship between the servlets and JSPs that make up the front page are shown in Figure 24.2.

Users of the online store can fill up a virtual shopping cart that is managed by a servlet. The choice to use a servlet for this purpose was driven by our desire to demonstrate a

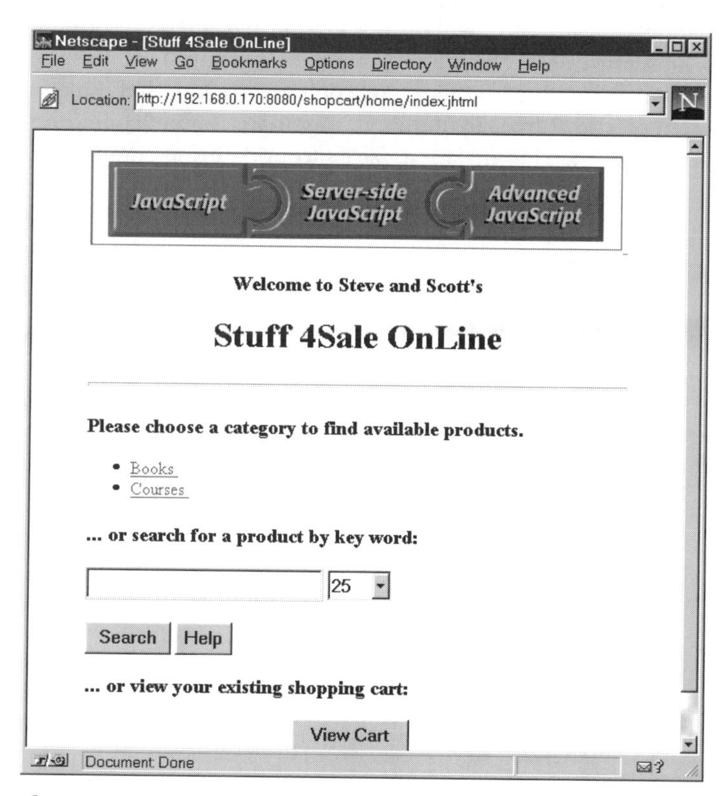

Figure 24.1 Online store front page.

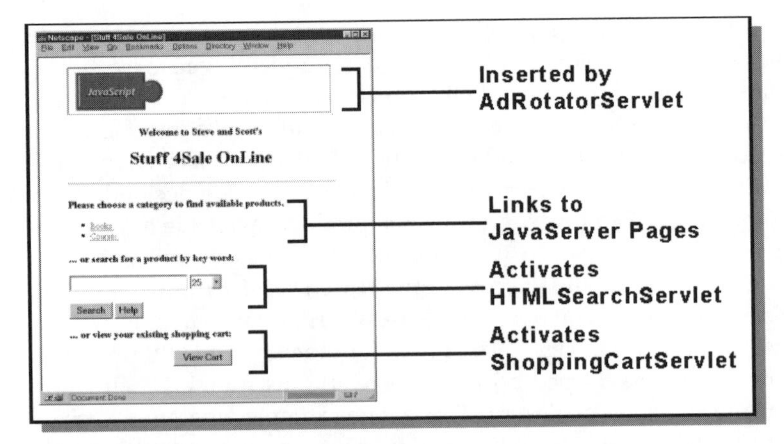

Figure 24.2 Front page components.

larger servlet that displays several types of pages. In this case, the cart can display the cart, an error page, a confirmation page, and a receipt. Another design would have been to use separate servlets, or even JavaServer Pages, for these various interface elements. However, the servlet is also responsible for talking to an Enterprise JavaBean that manages the commercial aspect of the site. By using a single servlet, the JNDI code, and the connection to the bean, home can be kept open between requests.

Figure 24.3 shows the relationship between the shopping cart servlet and the shopping cart enterprise bean. The bean maintains a connection to a database using JDBC to store purchases and customer information. Although the servlet could have connected directly to the database, we decided to offload the credit and inventory management code from the servlet to an Enterprise JavaBean. This makes it easier to update the commercial

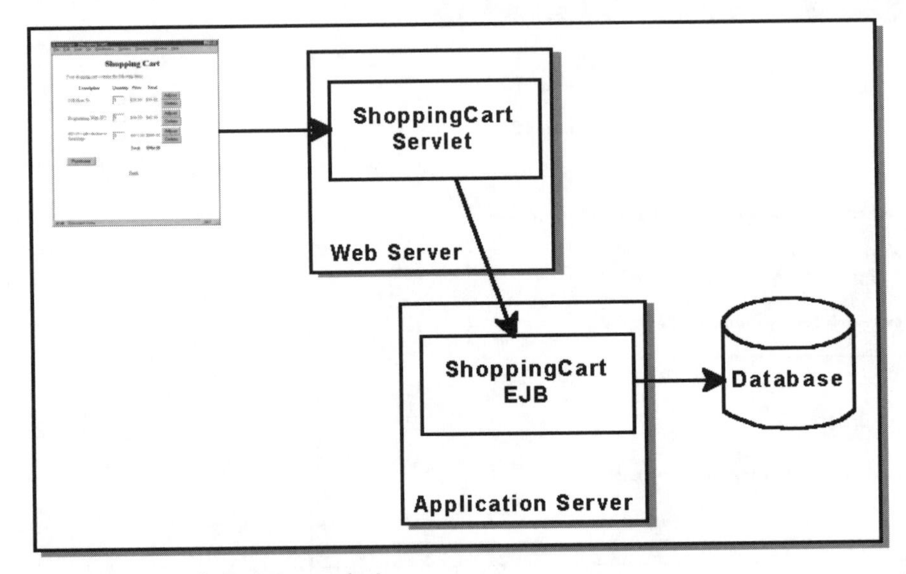

Figure 24.3 Shopping cart design.

implementation of the site without changing the interface code. For example, we could reimplement the EJB to use CyberCash and Oracle Financials rather than a simple two-table database without changing the shopping cart servlets or the JavaServer Pages.

Overall, the design for the online store demonstrates separation of functionality into components such as the ad rotator and search servlet as well as the shopping cart EJB. The example also shows how different network protocols can be combined— HTTP to the servlet, RMI to the Enterprise JavaBean. Finally, the example shows how several technologies can be linked into one application.

JMS Implementation

MiniJMS is a small implementation of the major functionality in the Java Messaging Service. Our design was partially dictated by the requirement that we implement a client library based on the JMS interfaces. We did not, however, rely on the server-side JMS interface; instead, we used this opportunity to demonstrate a Pure Java server implementation. Messaging is usually implemented via a central server. We used this basic design, setting up connections between each client and the central server via RMI. The server also interacts with the client by publishing objects into a JNDI context. These objects represent the connection factories and destinations defined in the JMS specification.

The server has connections to each running client and to a database for storing persistent messages. Our design relies on serialization to actually save the messages, but the database is used to keep track of the serialized objects and the acknowledged state for each client. This entire architecture is pictured in Figure 24.4. Although the code for

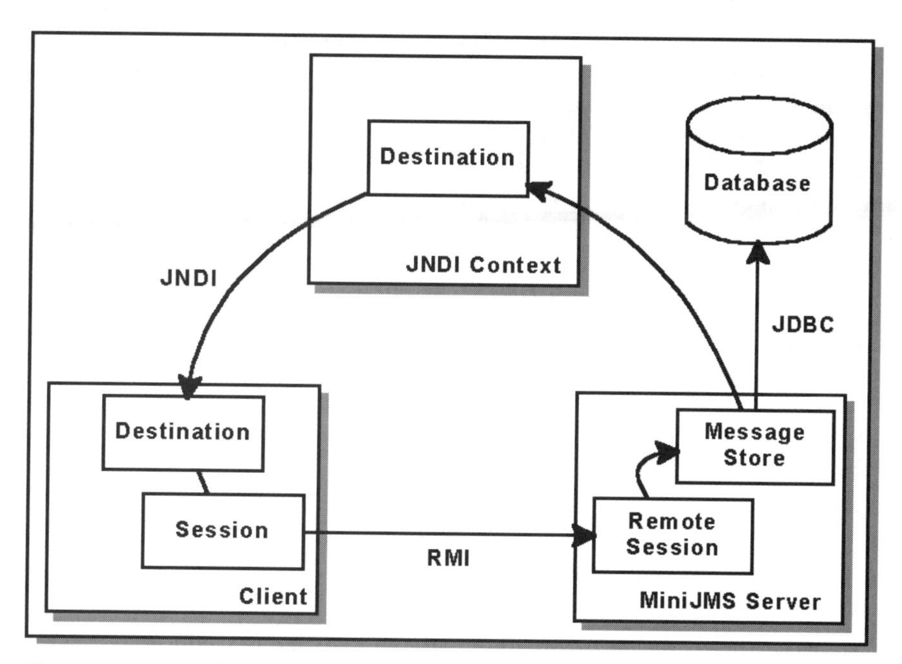

Figure 24.4 MiniJMS architecture.

MiniJMS is longer than the code for the online store and it uses as many technologies, the motivations and design decisions were somewhat easier. Networking implied RMI, persistence implied JDBC, and the JMS specification demands JNDI support.

Guidelines

Having programmed Java since its initial release and written hundreds of programs ranging from 20 lines to 50,000 lines, we have created a number of basic guidelines for enterprise Java development. These guidelines by no means constitute a complete list. Every program has its own idiosyncrasies and every programmer his or her own talents, design styles, and coding preferences. However, we do hope that these guidelines provide a good starting point for your own development projects. As you read them, please note that we have not always applied these rules in our examples. Often, generality and flexibility increase complexity, and we have always tried to err toward readability instead of functionality in putting together the examples for this book.

- **Use properties and resource bundles to define all of the strings in your applications.** This will help in two main ways. First, resource bundles make it easier to internationalize applications in this global economy. Second, it's a lot easier to change a misspelled word in a text file than it is in a Java file that has to be recompiled each time it is changed. As an add-on to this guideline, consider using the java.text package to format data, as we have done in several examples in this book. This takes the burden to parse formats off you and simplifies the localization procedures for your application.
- **Extending the previous guideline, use properties files to define strings that represent connection information, SQL, or configuration information.** Using properties files allows you to reconfigure an application without recompiling it. You could even reconfigure an application on a client by changing the properties file without having to change the code on the client machine or redeploy it. One excellent use of this technique is to list in a properties file the Actions in a JFC program or some other object that encapsulates functionality. The application can load these objects by name from the file when launched. Adding functionality in this case is as simple as implementing the one object and altering the properties file. The loading code and remainder of the application can be left unchanged.
- **Try to use generic SQL or store SQL in properties.** Many developers use one database for development and another for deployment, due to the expense of enterprise-level databases. Even if the databases are from the same vendor, you may want to tweak the SQL on deployment. In short, expect the SQL, database, and driver to change to some degree, and plan for it.
- **Be paranoid.** Use try-catch blocks whenever there is a reasonable possibility for an exception. On the flip side of this guideline, use exceptions from library-type code to notify the application that an error occurred. This will usually be clearer than a bunch of if-else statements.
- **Be very careful writing multithreaded code and realize that you may miss a possible deadlock condition in testing.** Use synchronization when necessary,

but don't just use it willy-nilly. Even in the newest interpreters, synchronized methods take more time than non-synchronized ones. Moreover, they can offer a false sense of security. Some data needs better-planned protection than method-level locks provide, so consider all of your shared data carefully. We highly recommend buying a book on Java threads programming if you haven't already, just to familiarize yourself with the world of multiple-threaded programming.

- **Don't trust the client when it comes to security.** Check all of the input into an EJB, servlet, JSP, or message receiver. Especially don't allow the client to trigger a potentially harmful operation, such as allowing it to run a program by submitting data to a servlet.
- **Rely on standards for security; avoid inventing your own security procedures.** If you do invent your own, make sure to open them to peer review for thorough testing. Sun and its partners are constantly improving and testing the standard Java security mechanisms. Rather than try to duplicate their efforts, participate in their peer review process and make Java secure for everyone.
- **Compartmentalize code for servlets and enterprise beans the same way you would the objects in a program.** In other words, use one servlet for one type of functionality, or one bean for one business area. Don't create a "kitchen sink" servlet, bean, or any Java object. Balance this rule with a desire to hide implementation and try to provide very powerful enterprise beans that have 5 to 15 methods that can hide the complexity of the server implementation from the client. For example, implement the e-commerce for a site in a bean that provides buy, sell, check credit, and other functionality into a few clear methods. But don't have this same bean search the Web site or anything like that. This type of macro-object design should facilitate reuse in your company's projects.
- **Design for extensibility.** One way to do this is to use properties files to define code to load. Others include encapsulating functionality into objects such as beans and servlets. Users, managers, and the marketing department will always want new, better, more features. Expecting this at the beginning makes life easier in the middle of a project. However, on very small, targeted projects, don't waste time building extensible code. If you could rewrite the code three times in the time it takes to design an extensible version, and you plan to write it only once, you probably don't need the flexible design. You can also use components to promote extensibility.
- **Protect grouped operations with transactions.** This is the tried-and-true mechanism for ensuring that operations perform atomically. Use it.
- **Choose your server providers carefully.** Think about the features they support, their compliance with Java standards, and the additional services they provide. This applies to all of the servers mentioned in this book, including but not limited to database servers, transaction monitors, messaging servers, application servers, JNDI providers such as LDAP, Web servers, and CORBA ORBs. Weigh the functionality against the provider's experience and track record. For example, just because some providers can write a transaction monitor that supports JTA or JTS, that doesn't mean that they are good at it or understand the subtleties. A great example of this, from a totally different programming area, is the

use of WindRiver Systems' real-time operating system on the Mars rover. An error occurred in the application code on the rover while it was on Mars. But WindRiver, having a great deal of experience with real-time systems, had planned for that type of error and included support for dynamically updating the code. Not only were the programmers able to leverage the tools provided by WindRiver's experience, but they were also able to use an important, but little used, feature to fix the problem. A less professional system provider may not have had the insight to include the feature or the tools.

- **Utilize each server to its fullest, both for resources and functionality.** Take advantage of database optimizations that increase performance, rely on application server connection pools, and optimize message delivery with your JMS provider. All of the enterprise technologies rely on providers. These providers, once chosen, can play a central role in creating a high-performance enterprise application.
- **Rely on standards for enterprise interfaces.** When possible, use the agreed-upon standard rather than a particular provider's extensions. In several cases over the past three years, these extensions have been discontinued in favor of a standard API. The last thing you want is to finish a yearlong project just in time to have the server provider change its interface on you.
- **Choose your virtual machine provider and server operating system with care.** Recent performance tests have shown a great improvement in Java performance, but they also show a wide difference between implementations when it comes to performance. In some cases, faster computers actually run Java more slowly because of the VM implementation.
- **Familiarize yourself with your virtual machine.** The Windows VM that comes with the JDK, for example, provides flags for defining the maximum memory size and whether or not to use a just-in-time compiler. Many server applications may require more memory than the default and will need to be run with adjusted parameters. Other VMs may provide special parameters as well. In a 24x7 environment, the VM is as important a part of your application as the enterprise API providers that you choose.
- **Plan for firewall tunneling in Internet applications.** Expect the client to use a proxy server that requires you to access the server via a servlet or HTTP gateway. RMI already supports this, but you will need to make sure that the gateway is installed. JMS providers may or may not provide a gateway for their product, and JNDI may not work across this boundary. Always consider the possibility of a servlet that acts as a gateway to your server program. If possible, make this servlet optional to clients inside the firewall.
- **Don't get caught up in the version madness.** It takes time to deploy an application, and you should expect to use the same version of an interface for at least a year, unless there is a specific reason for changing. New versions of all of the enterprise technologies will probably be announced in the next 12 months. Don't race to the new version just because it's there, and don't wait for the next version before implementing your project. For the time being, Java APIs are like buying a computer. Sure, a new one will be out soon, but if you always wait to buy the

latest and greatest, you'll never get the project done. Combine this with the previous guideline as well, because sometimes it is better to wait a month or two for the standard rather than take the proprietary version today. Many of the enterprise APIs will have updates designed to help library implementers and service providers. Although these updates indirectly help you, you will often be able to simply update the server without changing your code.

- **Write 100-percent Pure Java code whenever possible.** This code is more portable and easier to maintain. If performance is an issue, research other VMs. Recent tests show Java is comparable to C and C++ in a lot of cases and, when taking into account the savings in memory management code, can reduce resource usage.
- **Read a lot.** One source can't cover everything. That includes the documentation, the specifications, examples, tutorials, this book, and other books. Enterprise computing is complex; don't underestimate the value of more information.
- **Test everything, a lot, and then test it again.**

Hopefully, these guidelines will help you with your enterprise development. If you have other suggestions, please forward them to the authors for inclusion in future publications.

Summary

In the past two years, Java has grown from an interesting way to make cool Web pages to a powerful language for developing enterprise applications. As Java moves from the client to the server, there will certainly be hiccups, problems, and evolving standards. There will also be new, innovative applications that leverage Java and the portable environment it provides—applications such as developer tools that can be used to create both the client and server, databases that can be replicated across the enterprise and even into a personal digital assistant, televisions that run the same code a computer does, and houses that notify an EJB when their internal temperature changes.

The enterprise Java technologies such as servlets, Enterprise JavaBeans, and the Java Messaging Service are the first steps in bringing Java to the corporate network for application developers and network administrators. Combined with Java on the client, personal Java, and embedded Java, these technologies are designed to form the foundation for future enterprise development.

A Four-Tier Online Store

This chapter and Chapter 26, "MiniJMS: A Java Messaging Service Provider," include large examples that combine a number of the technologies discussed in this book. This chapter uses Enterprise JavaBeans, JDBC, servlets, and JavaServer Pages to create an online store. An online store was chosen for this example because it is familiar, but these concepts and techniques apply equally well to other enterprise applications. The primary goals for this example are:

- To provide an example that integrates multiple Enterprise Java frameworks
- To trade performance for simplicity in implementation, where necessary
- To provide an example that is complex enough to challenge readers and test their understanding of the concepts discussed in this book

The root of these goals is to provide a large, real-world example of how enterprise APIs are used. Of course, including a complete, large-enterprise application is beyond the scope of this book. In fact, this example contains about 2,000 lines of code in 20 classes, making it rather large to include in this chapter. As a result, the entire example is not included in text but is available on the CD-ROM. The key code for this example is included and described in this chapter.

Basic Design

The user's experience for this online store is similar to the simple version created in Chapter 11, "A JavaServer Page Online Store." When users first enter the store, they are presented with a welcome page, pictured in Figure 25.1. This page displays a list of the categories from which a user can choose, as well as a form for searching the site and the option of viewing the shopping cart. At the top of the page is a clickable advertisement.

If the user chooses a category, he is presented with a list of items for that category. This page also displays an advertisement at the top, as pictured in Figure 25.2.

Both the list of categories and list of products for each category are generated dynamically based on the directory structure of the store Web site. The list of products is related to the HTML files in a category directory, and the list of categories is related to the category directories in the store's root directory. JavaServer Pages are used to generate these dynamic lists. Advertisements are presented using the AdRotatorServlet. This is an enhanced version of the servlet discussed in previous chapters.

Upon selecting an item, the user is presented with information about the item and the option to add it to the shopping cart. There is also an option to view the cart without adding an item. An example of these item pages is pictured in Figure 25.3. The test items pages have one shortfall—that is, they do not contain a link back to their cate-

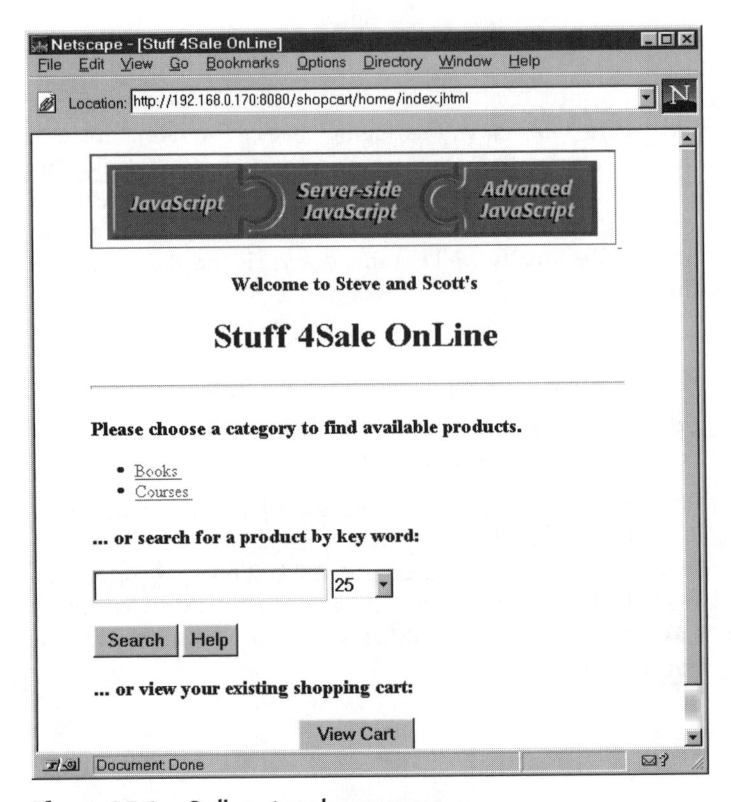

Figure 25.1 Online store home page.

Figure 25.2 A category page.

gory pages. This link could be added easily in a commercial deployment. Otherwise, these are basically the sorts of pages that you see at online stores today.

By either choosing to add the item to the cart or view the cart, the shopper initiates the ShoppingCart servlet that displays the current cart. The cart displays a list of the current items, their quantities, and prices, as pictured in Figure 25.4. At this point, the shopper can attempt to purchase the items, adjust the quantity of an item, or delete an item from the cart. A link is also provided that returns the user to the page he was on before initiating the cart servlet.

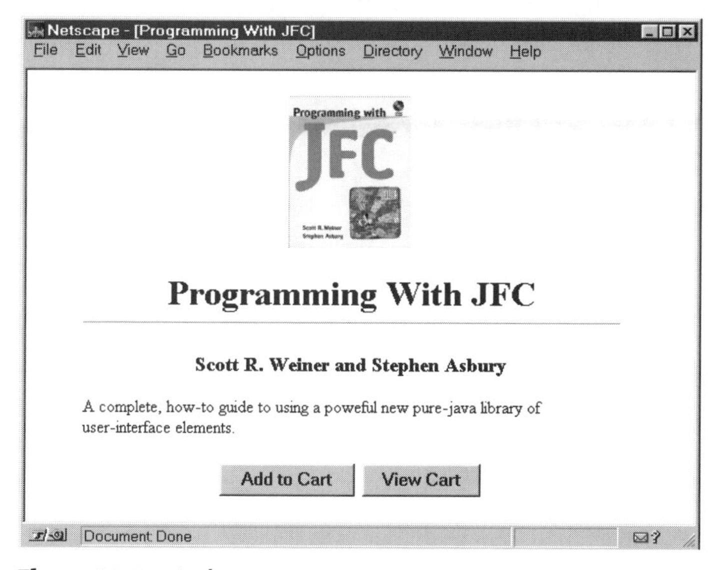

Figure 25.3 An item page.

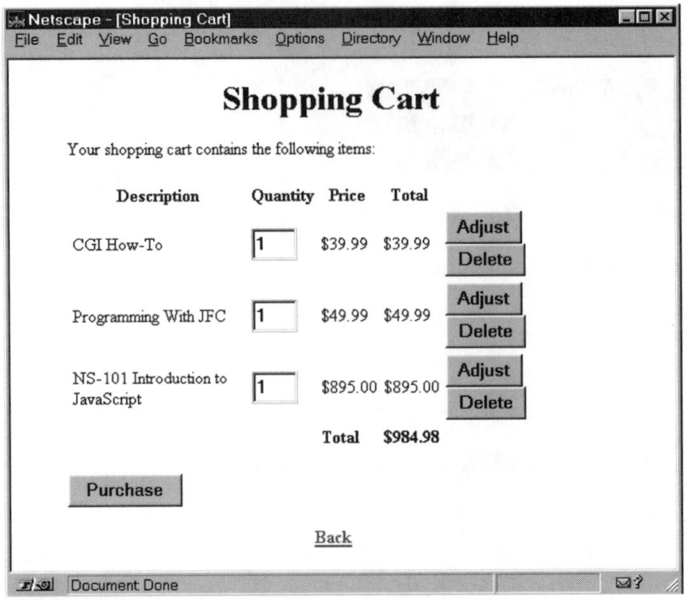

Figure 25.4 The shopping cart and its contents.

If the shopper chooses to purchase the items in the cart, the shopping cart servlet contacts an Enterprise JavaBean and confirms the availability and price of the items. Based on the bean's response, the servlet displays a confirmation page, pictured in Figure 25.5. The confirmation page highlights any problems with the order and displays a field for the user to enter his confirmation password.

Confirming the purchase tells the Shopping Cart servlet to again contact the ShoppingCart bean, this time requesting the purchase. If the purchase is successful, the servlet notifies the user with the page pictured in Figure 25.6.

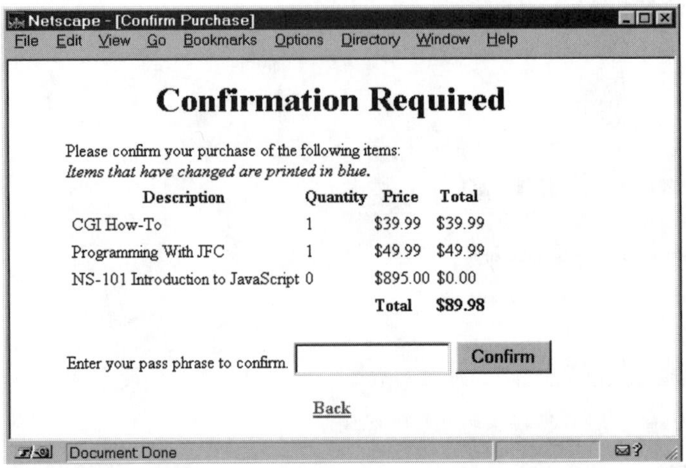

Figure 25.5 Confirmation page.

Figure 25.6 Purchase Confirmed page.

If an error occurs in the ShoppingCartServlet at any point, an error page is sent to the shopper. For example, this error may indicate insufficient credit to make a purchase.

The shopping cart EJB that supports the ShoppingCartServlet uses JDBC to talk to a database. This database contains the store's inventory as well as the registered shoppers and their credit limits. The bean acts as the interface to this database and implements all of the JDBC code used to implement the store.

The front page also contains a form that the shopper can use to search for a product. The searching is implemented using the HTMLSearchServlet discussed in Chapter 8, "A Servlet-Based Search Engine." The search engine displays a list of links to relevant pages. (For a more detailed discussion of the search engine, please refer to Chapter 8.)

One example report is included with this example. This report is implemented using a servlet called InventoryServlet. When requested, the InventoryServlet contacts the ShoppingCartBean to retrieve a list of the current products in inventory. This list is displayed to the client in tabular form, including the description, quantity, and price of the item as well as the current sales figures for each item. An example page from the InventoryServlet is pictured in Figure 25.7.

This example builds on a number of the examples used in other chapters. As a result, code has not been repeated here unless it changed significantly. Other chapters are referenced where appropriate so that you can find the code when needed. The entire code for this example is available, in one directory, on the CD-ROM.

The code for this example is organized into a single directory containing two packages. These packages are shopcart.ejbs and shopcart.servlets, and they contain the EJB and servlet code, respectively.

The Shopping Cart EJB

All of the actual purchasing in this example is managed by a single Enterprise JavaBean called ShoppingCartBean. The interface for this bean, called ShoppingCart, defines the methods used by servlets or other clients to access the inventory and credit databases. To keep this example manageable, the schema for this database is fairly simple. There are two tables: INVENTORY and CUSTOMERS. INVENTORY contains four columns, described in Table 25.1.

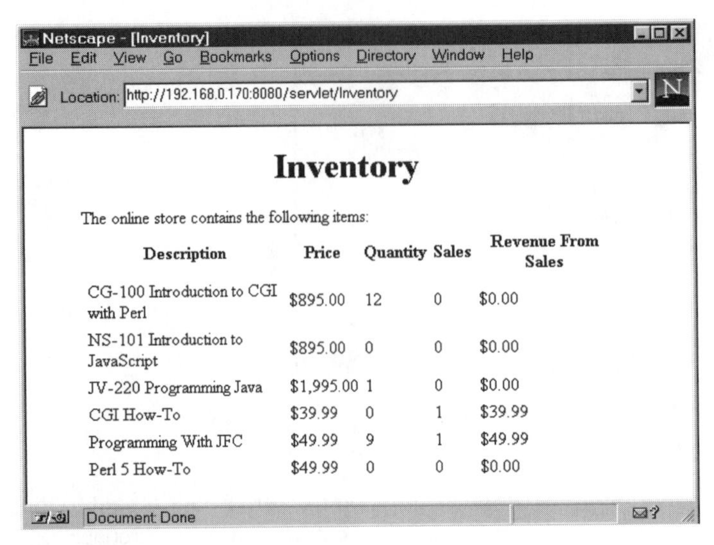

Figure 25.7 Inventory report.

CUSTOMERS contains three columns, described in Table 25.2.

The customer's name is used for identification to confirm a purchase. Applications could also include a password for this identification, although this password could be part of the servlet's environment, the JNDI context, or some other aspect of the design.

Notice that no mechanism is provided in this example for the customer to pay the bill, thus decreasing the credit used. Implementing this feature is very similar to the other features discussed, so it was not included. However, in a deployed online store, be sure to include that feature or the customers may get ornery.

Table 25.1 INVENTORY Table Description

COLUMN	DESCRIPTION
`ITEM_DESC`	The name of the item, used by clients to identify the item.
`PRICE`	The price per unit.
`QUANTITY`	The number of available units.
`SALES`	The total number of units sold.

Table 25.2 CUSTOMERS Table Description

COLUMN	DESCRIPTION
`CUST_NAME`	The customer's name/ID.
`CREDIT_LIMIT`	The total credit available to the customer.
`CREDIT_USED`	The amount of credit used by this customer.

ShoppingCart

The shopping cart bean is a stateful session bean. This means that when the servlet is talking to it, the servlet always uses the same bean until it disconnects. By using a stateful bean, the servlet is able to add items serially, make a purchase, and request the confirmed items, without the bean changing.

The bean itself stores a list of the items added and manipulates this list based on the contents of the database. All of the methods for adding items and retrieving them are defined in the ShoppingCart interface, as shown here:

```
package shopcart.ejbs;

import javax.ejb.*;
import java.rmi.RemoteException;
import java.rmi.Remote;
import java.util.*;

import shopcart.ejbs.*;

public interface ShoppingCart extends EJBObject, Remote
{
    public ShoppingCartItem addItem(ShoppingCartItem item)
     throws RemoteException;

    public boolean deleteItem(ShoppingCartItem item)
     throws RemoteException;

    public boolean purchaseCart(String user)
         throws BadCreditException,RemoteException;

    public ShoppingCartItem[] getItems() throws RemoteException;

    public Object[] getInventory() throws RemoteException;
}
```

Both the bean and its clients use ShoppingCartItem objects to represent items in the cart. These objects store a description, quantity, and price and can calculate their total value as quantity*price. The implementation for this data object is as follows:

```
package shopcart.ejbs;

import java.io.*;

public class ShoppingCartItem
implements Serializable
{
    public String desc;
    public double price;
    public int quantity;
    public int sales;
```

```
    public ShoppingCartItem(String s,double p,int q)
    {
        desc = s;
        price = p;
        quantity = q;
    }

    public double getTotal()
    {
        return quantity*price;
    }
}
```

ShoppingCartItems are marked Serializable so that they can be passed by value into the RMI calls made by the servlet to communicate with the enterprise bean.

ShoppingCartHome

The home interface for the ShoppingCartBean contains a single method, which follows. This method creates a cart bean, given a name. For this example, the name is used only for testing purposes. In a commercial application, you might use a name and password to identify the user or define database access.

```
package shopcart.ejbs;

import javax.ejb.*;
import java.rmi.RemoteException;
import containercart.*;

public interface ShoppingCartHome extends EJBHome
{
    ShoppingCart create(String name)
     throws CreateException, RemoteException;
}
```

Like all EJB home interfaces, ShoppingCartHome extends EJBHome, and the create methods throw RemoteExceptions and CreateExceptions.

ShoppingCartBean

The ShoppingCart interface is implemented in this example by the class ShoppingCartBean. This bean provides access to the database via a JDBC connection. The JDBC connection is configured using properties defined during deployment. These properties are listed in Table 25.3. The bean uses instance variables to store the values of these properties for use in any method.

For testing purposes, the shopping cart bean uses the DebugLog class discussed in Chapter 7, "Programming Servlets," to keep a log of errors and important changes in state. (Refer back to Chapter 7 for more information on this powerful debugging tool.)

Table 25.3 ShoppingCartBean Configuration Properties

PROPERTY	DESCRIPTION
`User`	The database user's name (optional).
`Password`	The database password (optional).
`url`	The URL for the database.
`Driver`	The JDBC Driver class used by the bean to contact the database.
`Logserver`	The IP address for the computer running the DebugLog's server. If this value is not set, debug messages are ignored.

Items currently in a cart are stored in a hash table. The key for the table is the item's description and the value is a ShoppingCartItem object. The following code begins the implementation for the ShoppingCartBean class. This code is continued until its completion. Comments and discussion have been added as regular text throughout to describe the major blocks of code.

```
package shopcart.ejbs;

//Imports removed to save space

public class ShoppingCartBean implements SessionBean
{
    protected DebugLog logger;

    public Hashtable items;
    public String cartName;
    public String url = null;
    public String user=null;
    public String password=null;
    public String driver=null;
    public String logServer=null;
```

This EJB doesn't do anything on Activate, but it closes the log if removed or passivated. Messages to the log are encapsulated in the method logToServer, a discussion of which follows. This method reconnects the DebugLog appropriately.

```
    public void ejbActivate()
    {
    }

    public void ejbRemove()
    {
        try
        {
            logger.closeLog();
            logger = null;
        }
```

```
        catch(Exception exp)
        {
        }
    }

    public void ejbPassivate()
    {
        try
        {
            logger.closeLog();
            logger = null;
        }
        catch(Exception exp)
        {
        }
    }
```

When the SessionContext is provided to the bean via the method setSessionContext, it caches all of its configuration properties in instance variables.

```
    public void setSessionContext(SessionContext ctx)
    {
        Properties env = ctx.getEnvironment();

        user = env.getProperty("user");
        password = env.getProperty("password");
        url = env.getProperty("url");
        driver = env.getProperty("driver");
        logServer = env.getProperty("logserver");
    }
```

The home interface requires a bean to be created using a name. This name is logged to the debug log in the ejbCreate method, as follows. The create method also instantiates the hash table that the bean uses to store shopping cart items or clears it if one is already assigned.

```
    public void ejbCreate(String nm)
    {
        cartName = nm;

        if(items == null) items = new Hashtable();
        else items.clear();

        logToServer("Created bean: "+cartName);
    }
```

The ShoppingCartBean's first remote method is addItem. This method takes a shopping cart item and adds it to the bean, logging the addition to the debug log. Each time an item is added, the bean connects to the database to check and update the item's availability and price before adding the item to its items hash table. Although this reconnecting may seem like overkill, it really isn't. The Application Server hosting the bean is actually storing a pool of database connections. When the bean "connects," it is really getting a connection from this pool. If your EJB host doesn't support connection pooling, make this connection in ejbActivate and close it in ejbPassivate to save the connection time. With pooling, open and close the connection as needed, making it available to other beans in the interim.

Because a shopper might add the same item twice, check the database only the first time. Subsequent additions change only the quantity field in the ShoppingCartItem object. The complete implementation for addItem is included below. The primary code for adding items appears in boldface type.

```
public ShoppingCartItem addItem(ShoppingCartItem item)
{
    ShoppingCartItem test=null;
    ResultSet rs=null;
    Statement statement=null;
    ShoppingCartItem retVal = null;
    Connection conn=null;
    double curPrice;
    int curQuantity;

    if(items == null) items = new Hashtable();

    logToServer("Adding item: "+item);

    if(item != null)
        test = (ShoppingCartItem) items.get(item.desc);

    if(test == null)
    {
        try
        {
            conn = connectToDB();

            statement = conn.createStatement();
            rs =
             statement.executeQuery("select * from inventory"
                                    +" where item_desc="
                                    +"\'"+item.desc+"\'");

            //Only take the first one
            if(rs.next())
            {
                curPrice = item.price;

                //reset price from DB
                item.price = rs.getDouble("PRICE");

                curQuantity = rs.getInt("QUANTITY");
```

```
                    logToServer("Adding "+item.desc
                                   +" at price "+item.price);

                    if(curQuantity < item.quantity)
                        item.quantity = curQuantity;

                    items.put(item.desc,item);

                    retVal = item;
                }
                else
                {
                    logToServer("Item "+item.desc
                                   +" not in database.");
                }
            }
            catch(Exception exp)
            {
                logToServer(exp.toString());
                retVal = null;
            }
            finally
            {
                try
                {
                    if(rs!=null) rs.close();
                    if(statement != null) statement.close();
                    if(conn!=null) conn.close();
                }
                catch(Exception exp)
                {
                    logToServer(exp.toString());
                }
            }
        }
        else
        {
            test.quantity+=item.quantity;

            retVal = test;
        }

        return retVal;
    }
```

The bean's client can request a list of the current contents using the method getItems, defined as follows. This method returns the ShoppingCartItems stored in the items hash table.

```
    public ShoppingCartItem[] getItems()
    {
```

```
        Enumeration keys;
        ShoppingCartItem[] retVal=null;
        int i=0;

        if(items != null)
        {
            retVal = new ShoppingCartItem[items.size()];

            keys=items.keys();

            while(keys.hasMoreElements())
            {
                retVal[i] = (ShoppingCartItem)
                            items.get(keys.nextElement());
                i++;
            }
        }
        return retVal;
    }
```

Clients may also want to delete an item using the method deleteItem. Deleting an item updates the quantity of the associated ShoppingCartItem. If the ShoppingCart-Item's quantity goes to 0, the object is removed from the items hash table. The definition for deleteItem is:

```
    public boolean deleteItem(ShoppingCartItem item)
    {
        ShoppingCartItem test=null;
        boolean retVal = false;

        if((items != null)&&(item != null))
            test = (ShoppingCartItem) items.get(item.desc);

        if(test != null)
        {
            test.quantity-=item.quantity;

            if(test.quantity <= 0) items.remove(test.desc);

            retVal = true;
        }

        return retVal;
    }
```

Clients tell the bean to execute a purchase with the method purchaseCart. This method performs a number of database checks to make sure that the specified user has the necessary credit to make the purchase, that the items are available, and finally, that the user's credit information is updated to reflect the purchase. This method is provided here, with discussions inserted at major operations.

```
public boolean purchaseCart(String user)
throws Exception, BadCreditException
{
    boolean retVal = false;
    ShoppingCartItem curItem;
    Enumeration cursor;
    ResultSet rs=null;
    Statement statement=null;
    Connection conn=null;
    double curPrice;
    int curQuantity, curSales;
    double total=0;
    double max, used;

    if(items == null) return false;

    logToServer("Purchasing items for: "+user);

    try
    {
```

Next, the purchaseCart method connects to the database. This connection will be closed at the end of the method. The connectToDB method is an internal method discussed later in the chapter.

```
        conn = connectToDB();

        statement = conn.createStatement();
```

The first check required to make a purchase is to get the customer's maximum and used credit. These values will be used to determine whether the purchase can be made. An exception is thrown if the database access fails. The available credit is calculated by looking at the limit and subtracting the amount used. This available credit is stored in the local variable max.

```
        rs = statement.executeQuery("select * from customers"
                                   +" where CUST_NAME="
                                   +"\'"+user+"\'");

        if(rs.next())
        {
            used = rs.getDouble("CREDIT_USED");
            max = rs.getDouble("CREDIT_LIMIT")
                        - used;
        }
        else
        {
            throw new Exception("Trigger failure, no credit.");
        }
```

Next, the purchaseCart method updates the list of items being purchased, making sure that they are still available and the price is correct. An exception is thrown to notify the caller whether the items have changed in the database. While the items are processing, the bean calculates the total price of the purchase and stores it in the variable total.

```
cursor = items.elements();

while(cursor.hasMoreElements())
{

    curItem = (ShoppingCartItem) cursor.nextElement();
    statement = conn.createStatement();
    rs =
      statement.executeQuery("select * from inventory"
                    +" where item_desc="
                    +"\'"+curItem.desc+"\'");

    //Only take the first one
    if(rs.next())
    {
        curPrice = curItem.price;

        //reset price from DB
        curItem.price = rs.getDouble("PRICE");

        curQuantity = rs.getInt("QUANTITY");

        if((curQuantity < curItem.quantity)
                ||(curPrice != curItem.price))
        {
            throw new Exception("Trigger failure,"
                            + " bad q/p.");
        }

        total += curItem.getTotal();
    }
    else
    {
        throw
         new Exception("Trigger failure item"
                       + " not in DB.");
    }
}
```

Now check the customer's credit. If the customer's credit doesn't cover the purchase, throw a BadCreditException. This is a custom exception that is propagated to the caller.

```
//make sure there is enough credit
if(total > max)
```

```
{
    throw new BadCreditException(max);
}
```

If the user's credit is okay, update the CUSTOMERS table to reflect the purchase by increasing the CREDIT_USED column.

```
//update the user's credit
statement.executeUpdate("update customers set "
                                +"credit_used="
                                + (total+used)
                                +" where cust_name="
                                +"\'"+user+"\'");
```

Next, update the inventory to reflect the purchase. Subtract the purchased items from the QUANTITY column and add them to the SALES column.

```
//update the inventory
cursor = items.elements();

while(cursor.hasMoreElements())
{

    curItem = (ShoppingCartItem) cursor.nextElement();

    rs = statement.executeQuery("select * from "
                            +"inventory"
                            +" where item_desc="
                            +"\'"+curItem.desc+"\'");

    //Only take the first one
    if(rs.next())
    {
        curQuantity = rs.getInt("QUANTITY");
        curSales = rs.getInt("SALES");

        statement.executeUpdate("update inventory "
                        +"set quantity="
                        + (curQuantity-curItem.quantity)
                        +" , sales="
                        + (curSales+curItem.quantity)
                        +" where item_desc="
                        +"\'"+curItem.desc+"\'");
    }
    else
    {
        throw new Exception("Trigger failure item"
                            +" not in DB.");
    }
}
```

```
            retVal = true;
        }
        catch(BadCreditException exp)
        {
            logToServer(exp.toString());
            throw exp;
        }
        catch(Exception exp)
        {
            logToServer(exp.toString());
            retVal = false;
        }
```

Close the database connection in a finally block to ensure that regardless of the exceptions thrown by the purchase process, the database connection is returned to the pool.

```
        finally
        {
            try
            {
                if(rs!=null) rs.close();
                if(statement != null) statement.close();
                if(conn!=null) conn.close();
            }
            catch(Exception exp)
            {
                logToServer(exp.toString());
            }
        }

        return retVal;
    }
```

That concludes the purchaseCart method. The next method in ShoppingCartBean is a convenience method that connects the DebugLogger to the server, if necessary, and logs a message to it.

```
    protected void logToServer(String str)
    {
        if(logger == null)
        {
            try
            {
                logger = new DebugLog();
                logger.logTo(logServer);
            }
            catch(Exception exp)
            {
            }
        }
```

```
        logger.log(str);
    }
```

The servlet that displays a report of the INVENTORY table uses the ShoppingCart-Bean's getInventory method to get the list of available items. In a larger application with more reports, you might want to use separate EJBs for the reports rather than including them in an existing one. This is included in this example to simplify the learning process.

The getInventory method, defined as follows, connects to the database and retrieves all of the available items. Information from each row in the database is used to create a ShoppingCartItem object. These objects are temporarily stored in a vector. Once all the items are read from the database, the vector is converted to an array, and the array is returned to the caller. Finally, the database connection is closed.

```
    public Object[] getInventory()
    {
        Vector items;
        Object[] retVal=null;
        ShoppingCartItem curItem;
        double price;
        int quantity;
        int sales;
        String desc;
        ResultSet rs=null;
        Statement statement=null;
        Connection conn=null;

        items = new Vector();

        try
        {
            conn = connectToDB();

            statement = conn.createStatement();
            rs = statement.executeQuery("select * from inventory");

            //Only take the first one
            while(rs.next())
            {
                price = rs.getDouble("PRICE");
                quantity = rs.getInt("QUANTITY");
                sales = rs.getInt("SALES");
                desc = rs.getString("ITEM_DESC");

                curItem = new ShoppingCartItem(desc,price,quantity);
                curItem.sales = sales;

                items.addElement(curItem);
            }
```

```
            retVal = new Object[items.size()];
            items.copyInto(retVal);
        }
        catch(Exception exp)
        {
            logToServer(exp.toString());
            retVal = null;
        }
        finally
        {
            try
            {
                if(rs!=null) rs.close();
                if(statement != null) statement.close();
                if(conn!=null) conn.close();
            }
            catch(Exception exp)
            {
                logToServer(exp.toString());
            }
        }

        return retVal;
    }
```

For convenience, the ShoppingCartBean has a method called connectToDB that makes the database connection and returns it. The information for the connection is based on the configuration parameters. Remember that in an Application Server, this connection process is probably loaded via an existing connection from a pool rather than by actually making a new connection to the database. The complete definition of connectToDB is included here:

```
    protected Connection connectToDB()
    {
        Connection retVal = null;

        try
        {
            Class.forName(driver);

            retVal = DriverManager.getConnection(url,user,password);
        }
        catch(Exception exp)
        {
            retVal = null;
            logToServer(exp.toString());
        }

        return retVal;
    }
}
```

As you can see, the ShoppingCartBean provides a great deal of functionality and integrates the JDBC interfaces with Enterprise JavaBeans.

NOTE When using BEA WebLogic and possibly other servers, you are not able to use file system persistence for Entity beans while using JDBC calls in the same beans due to a problem with processing in the transactional models. Check the documentation on your EJB host for details.

JavaServer Pages and HTML

The online store contains two types of JavaServer Pages and one type of regular HTML page. The first type of JSP is the site's home page. The second type is the category page. All of the product pages are static HTML. The decision to use JSP or HTML is based on the resource usage. An online store might feature hundreds of products, and to have hundreds of JSP-generated servlets might take up too many server resources. Static pages do not use the same resources and don't take any server resources, beyond caches, when just sitting on disk. As a result, regular HTML is a low resource and, it turns out, a fast solution for pages, so we have maximized its usage. In a site with hundreds of categories, you might want to use static pages for the categories as well.

The other architecture that many sites use in this situation is a single JSP, servlet, or CGI script that retrieves data from the database and dynamically creates all of the pages. In some respects, this is the most flexible mechanism, but it does require the most processing per page.

The static page and completely dynamic design can also be combined by creating a program that generates pages from the database and stores them on disk. The site administrator could run this program nightly so that the site is static throughout the day but can change on a daily basis. This compromise reduces the processing per page and reduces the up-to-the-second nature of the pages, while still maintaining some of the advantages of dynamic pages.

The main page for the online store is implemented in a JHTML page called index.jhtml. The majority of the page is static HTML; only the list of available categories and the advertisement are updated with each request. The advertisement is handled by the AdLinkRotatorServlet, a discussion of which follows. When displayed, the index.jhtml page looks like the Web page pictured in Figure 25.8.

To find the available categories, this page looks at its current directory and assumes that all subdirectories represent categories. The name of the directory is treated as the category name. The highlighted code that follows contains the Java that reads the current directory and displays the list of categories. The list is initialized only once—when the page is first loaded. The list of categories is stored in a vector called categories, defined in the <java type=class> tag at the bottom of the JHTML file. One possible improvement to this model is to have the page recheck the directory for updates on a regular schedule.

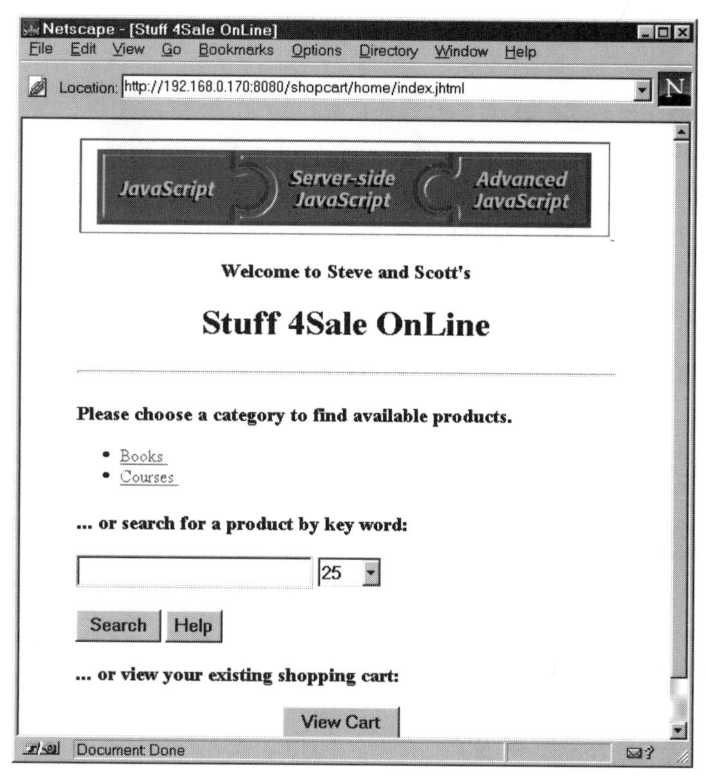

Figure 25.8 Index.jhtml.

```
<HTML>
<HEAD>
<TITLE>
Stuff 4Sale OnLine
</TITLE>
</HEAD>
<BODY TEXT="#000000" BGCOLOR="#FFFFFF" LINK="#FF0000" VLINK="#800080">
<CENTER>
<TABLE WIDTH=500 BORDER=0>
<TR>
<TD>

<CENTER>
<servlet
    code="shopcart.servlets.AdLinkRotatorServlet"
    imagedir="C:\\servers\\JavaWebServer1.1\\public_html\\shopcart\\ads"
    imageroot="/shopcart/ads"
    logserver="192.168.0.172">
</servlet>
<BR>
<H3>Welcome to Steve and Scott's</H3>
<H1>Stuff 4Sale OnLine</H1>
```

```
<HR>
</CENTER>

<H3>Please choose a category to find available products.</H3>
<UL>
<java>
    int i,max;
    String uri = request.getRequestURI();
    int ind;

    if(categories == null)
    {
        initCategories(request.getRealPath(uri));
    }

    max = categories.size();
        //Clean off the file name from the requestURI

    ind = uri.lastIndexOf("/");

    if(ind != (uri.length()-1))
    {
        uri = uri.substring(0,ind);
    }

    for(i=0;i<max;i++)
    {
</java>
    <LI>
    <A HREF="'uri+"/"+categories.elementAt(i)+"/index.jhtml"'">
    <java type=print>categories.elementAt(i)</java>
    </A>
    <BR>
<java>
    }
</java>
</UL>
</TD>
</TR>
<TR>
<TD>
<H3>... or search for a product by key word:</H3>
<FORM METHOD=GET
ACTION="/servlet/HTMLSearchServlet/shopcart/home">
<INPUT NAME="query" VALUE="" SIZE=25>
<SELECT NAME="maxhits" SIZE=1>
<OPTION VALUE="25">25
<OPTION VALUE="50">50
<OPTION VALUE="100">100
</SELECT>
<BR><BR>
```

```
<INPUT TYPE="Submit" NAME="submit" VALUE="Search">
<INPUT TYPE="Submit" NAME="submit" VALUE="Help">
</FORM>

<H3>... or view your existing shopping cart:</H3>
<CENTER>
<H2>
<FORM ACTION="/servlet/ShoppingCartServlet">
<INPUT TYPE="HIDDEN" NAME="action" VALUE="view">
<INPUT TYPE="SUBMIT" VALUE="View Cart">
</FORM>
</H2>
</CENTER>
</TD>
</TR>
</TABLE>
</CENTER>
</BODY>
</HTML>

<java type=class>
    Vector categories;
    String docRoot;

    public void initCategories(String rt)
    {
        File rootDir=null;
        String[] files;
        int i,max;
        File curFile;

        docRoot = rt;

        categories = new Vector();

        try
        {
            rootDir = new File(docRoot);

            if(!rootDir.isDirectory())
                rootDir = new File(rootDir.getParent());

            if((rootDir!=null) && rootDir.exists())
            {
                files = rootDir.list();

                max = files.length;

                for(i=0;i<max;i++)
                {
                    curFile = new File(rootDir,files[i]);
```

```
                    if(curFile.exists()
                                && curFile.isDirectory())
                    {
                        categories.addElement(files[i]);
                    }
                }
            }
        }
        catch(Exception exp)
        {
            categories.removeAllElements();
        }
    }
</java>
```

When the user selects a category, the link takes her to the directory associated with the category and to the index.jhtml file that the directory contains. This index.jhtml file is the home page for a category and is also a JHTML page.

Like the store's home page, the category pages dynamically display a list. In this case, the list contains the items in the category. To create the list, the category page looks at the available files. An example of one of these pages is pictured in Figure 25.9.

Although the implementation for these pages refers to different classes, the code is nearly identical to the example in Chapter 11, "A JavaServer Page Online Store." Rather than reproduce that code here, we direct you to the example in that chapter for details on the category page code.

The items for the store each has its own HTML pages. These pages should include buttons to add the item to the shopper's cart and view the current contents of the cart, such as the one pictured in Figure 25.10.

The HTML for this page follows. It contains two forms, which appear in boldface type; these forms target the ShoppingCartServlet discussed in the next section. This

Figure 25.9 A category page.

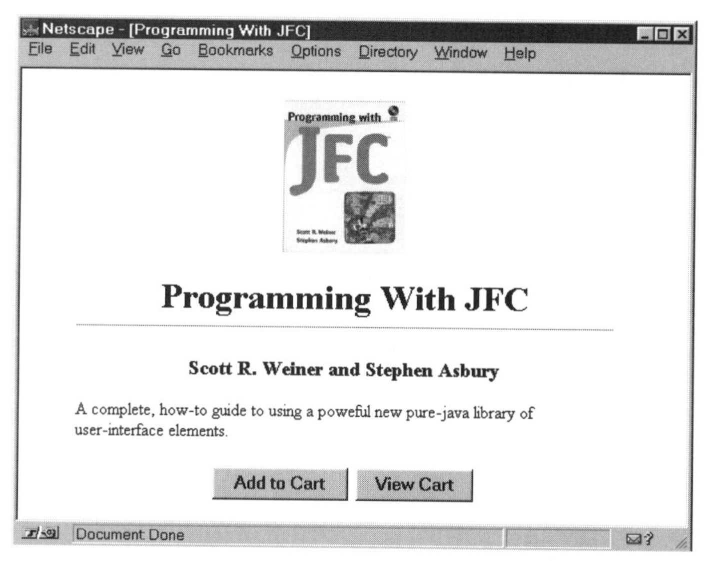

Figure 25.10 A product page.

servlet manages the client's shopping cart. The forms use hidden fields to pass information about the product to the servlet, the quantity being ordered, the expected price, and the action that the servlet should take. In the case of the view action, no item information is required.

```
<HTML>
<HEAD>
   <TITLE>Programming With JFC</TITLE>
</HEAD>
<BODY TEXT="#000000" BGCOLOR="#FFFFFF"
 LINK="#FF0000" VLINK="#800080">
 
<CENTER><TABLE BORDER=0 WIDTH="500" >
<TR>
<TD>
<CENTER><IMG SRC="./jfc.gif" NOSAVE HEIGHT=140 WIDTH=112> </CENTER>

<CENTER>
<H1>
Programming With JFC<BR>

<HR SIZE=1 NOSHADE WIDTH="100%">
</H1></CENTER>

<CENTER>
<H3>
Scott R. Weiner and Stephen Asbury</H3></CENTER>
A complete, how-to guide to using a powerful new pure-Java library of
user-interface elements.
```

```
<BR><BR>
<CENTER>
<TABLE WIDTH="50%">
<TR>
<TD>
<H2>
<FORM ACTION="/servlet/ShoppingCartServlet">
<INPUT TYPE="HIDDEN" NAME="item"
    VALUE="Programming With JFC">
<INPUT TYPE="HIDDEN" NAME="quantity" VALUE="1">
<INPUT TYPE="HIDDEN" NAME="price" VALUE="49.99">
<INPUT TYPE="HIDDEN" NAME="action" VALUE="add">
<INPUT TYPE="SUBMIT" VALUE="Add to Cart">
</FORM>
</H2>
</TD>
<TD>
<H2>
<FORM ACTION="/servlet/ShoppingCartServlet">
<INPUT TYPE="HIDDEN" NAME="action" VALUE="view">
<INPUT TYPE="SUBMIT" VALUE="View Cart">
</FORM>
</H2>
</TD>
</TR>
</TABLE>
</CENTER>
</TD>
</TR>
</TABLE></CENTER>
 
</BODY>
</HTML>
```

All of the item pages in this example use the same format as this one, changing only their description of the item and the hidden information passed to the servlet.

Servlets

This example relies directly on four servlets. The AdRotatorServlet is used to display ads. The HTMLSearchServlet is used to make the store searchable. The ShoppingCart-Servlet is used to manage the shopping cart, and the InventoryServlet can be used to check inventory.

AdRotator

The AdRotatorServlet used in this example is an improved version of the one from Chapter 11, "A JavaServer Page Online Store." This version uses a configuration file to

Table 25.4 AdRotatorServlet Initialization Parameters

PARAMETER	DESCRIPTION
`Imagedir`	The absolute path on the server containing the images and ads.txt file.
`Imageroot`	The URL relative to the root directory on the Web server in which the images are contained.
`logserver`	The IP address to which the server logs debug messages.

define the ad images and the links associated with them. When the servlet is called, it outputs an image link in HTML that displays the image and references the configured link. The example configuration file is:

```
http://www.pri.com/html/courses/path_javascript.html javascript.gif
http://www.pri.com/html/online_courses/ profile.gif
```

This file should be named ads.txt and placed in a directory along with the images specified. When the servlet is initialized, it retrieves its ads directory from the configuration parameter and reads the ads.txt file looking for link-image pairs. These pairs are stored in a vector as AdFileEntry objects that associate the link and image. The servlet also keeps track of a current index; each time the service method is called, the servlet displays the current ad and increments the index.

This servlet requires three initialization parameters, described in Table 25.4.

The init method reads these parameters and uses them to create the list of available ads. This code appears in boldface type in the following example. If there is no ads.txt file, the servlet looks for images instead. These will be displayed without links, because none were defined. This makes the servlet flexible because it can display both read-only and linked advertisements. The complete code for AdRotatorServlet is included here. First, let's look at the class definition and init method:

```
package shopcart.servlets;

//imports removed to save space

import DebugLog;

public class AdLinkRotatorServlet extends GenericServlet
implements SingleThreadModel
{
    protected Vector ads;
    protected int curIndex;
    protected String imageURL;
    protected DebugLog logger;

    public void init(ServletConfig config) throws ServletException
    {
        String imageDirName;
```

```
String logServer;
File imageDir=null;
File adSpec=null;

super.init(config);

curIndex = 0;
ads = new Vector();
imageDirName = getInitParameter("imagedir");
imageURL = getInitParameter("imageroot");
logServer = getInitParameter("logserver");

logger = new DebugLog();
logger.logTo(logServer);

try
{
    if(imageDirName != null)
    imageDir = new File(imageDirName);

    if(imageDir != null)
     adSpec = new File(imageDir,"ads.txt");

    logger.log("Looking for adspec at: "+adSpec);

    //Try to load the ads from a specification file
    if((adSpec != null)&& adSpec.exists())
    {
        try
        {
            FileReader fileIn = new FileReader(adSpec);
            BufferedReader bufIn =
                          new BufferedReader(fileIn);
            String curLine;
            int index;
            String link,fileName;
            AdFileEntry newEntry;

            while((curLine = bufIn.readLine()) != null)
            {
                index = curLine.indexOf(" ");

                if(index > 0)
                {
                    link = curLine.substring(0,index);
                    fileName = curLine.substring(index+1);

                    newEntry =
                     new AdFileEntry(link,fileName);
```

```
                        ads.addElement(newEntry);
                    }
                }

                bufIn.close();
            }
            catch(Exception exp)
            {
                logger.log("Invalid ad spec. file.");
                ads.removeAllElements();
            }
        }

        //If no spec file, or a bad one, just show ads
        if((ads.size()==0)
            && (imageDir!=null)
            && imageDir.exists()
            && imageDir.isDirectory())
        {
            String[] files;
            int i,max;

            files = imageDir.list();

            max = files.length;

            for(i=0;i<max;i++)
            {
                ads.addElement(
                        new AdFileEntry(null,files[i]));
            }
        }
        else if(ads.size()==0)
        {
            logger.log("Cannot find image dir: "+imageDirName);
        }
    }
    catch(Exception exp)
    {
        logger.log(exp);
    }
}
```

The AdRotatorServlet's service method, which follows, outputs the HTML for a link an or image, depending on the existence of the ads.txt file. The image displayed is based on the current index stored in the curIndex instance variable. At the end of the method, this index is incremented and the modulo operator is used to make sure that the index doesn't exceed the number of available ads. For example, if there are 10 ads and the current index is 9, it will be 0 the next time the service method is called.

The location for the image is relative to the initialization parameter imageroot, as stored in the imageURL instance variable. This ensures that the servlet outputs the correct link, regardless of its relationship to the images directory.

```
public void service(ServletRequest request,
                    ServletResponse response)
                    throws IOException,ServletException
{
    AdFileEntry curEntry;
    ServletOutputStream out=null;
    int len;

    try
    {
        out = response.getOutputStream();
        len = ads.size();

        if(len>0)
        {
            curEntry = (AdFileEntry) ads.elementAt(curIndex);

            if(curEntry.link != null)
            {
                out.print("<A HREF=\"");
                out.print(curEntry.link);
                out.println("\">");
            }

            out.print("<IMG SRC=");
            out.print(imageURL);
            out.print("/");
            out.print(curEntry.fileName);
            out.println(">");

            if(curEntry.link != null)
            {
                out.println("</A>");
            }

            curIndex= (curIndex+1)%len;
        }
        else
        {
            //Print a comment to HTML for testing
            out.println("<!--No ads.-->");
        }
    }
    catch(Exception exp)
    {
        logger.log(exp);
    }
```

```
        }
    }
```

The AdFileEntry objects used by the AdRotator simply store a link-file name pair that is used to output the ads:

```
class AdFileEntry
{
    public String link;
    public String fileName;

    public AdFileEntry(String l,String file)
    {
        link = l;
        fileName = file;
    }
}
```

For testing purposes, this servlet prints a comment to the HTML, indicating that no ads are available if none are available. This comment is not viewed by the user.

Searching

The HTMLSearchServlet used to search the online store is the same one described in detail in Chapter 8, "A Servlet-Based Search Engine." (Please refer to that chapter for details on the search servlet and the indexing engine behind it.) For this example, a copy of the servlet was made in the shopcart.servlets package. The code for the servlet and the HTML for the help and error pages remain virtually the same.

ShoppingCart Servlet

The ShoppingCart servlet represents the core of our online store. The servlet stores items in the shopper's session until a purchase is requested. During normal requests, the servlet displays its contents to the user with forms for editing the contents. Upon receiving a purchase request, the servlet contacts the ShoppingCart bean and checks the pricing and availability of the items before displaying a confirmation page. If the user confirms the purchase, the servlet again contacts the bean and makes the purchase request. If the request succeeds, the user is told. If it fails, the user is notified.

This servlet supports four input parameters, listed in Table 25.5. These parameters are passed to the servlet by the client. In this implementation, these are often part of hidden fields in a form that displays a button the user can press to purchase items or view the cart.

The servlet also depends on a number of initialization parameters, listed in Table 25.6. These are used to define the servlet's relationship with the ShoppingCartBean and the DebugLog.

The servlet uses these parameters to create a JNDI context, DebugLog, and ShoppingCartHome, all stored in instance variables. The servlet also maintains a NumberFormat object that is used to output any currency values. The entire code for

Table 25.5 ShoppingCartServlet Input Parameters

PARAMETER	DESCRIPTION
`action`	Add, adjust, delete, or view.
`item`	A text description of the item.
`price`	The item's expected price.
`quantity`	The number to affect.
`confirmed`	Set internally when the user confirms a purchase.

Table 25.6 ShoppingCartServlet Initialization Parameters

PARAMETER	DESCRIPTION
`url`	The URL for the JNDI provider.
`user`	The JNDI user.
`password`	The JNDI password.
`logserver`	The IP address for the debug log server.
`ShoppingCartHome`	The JNDI key for the shopping cart bean home.

the ShoppingCartServlet follows; regular text is used to break the discussion into reasonable pieces. First are the class definition and instance variables:

```
package shopcart.servlets;

//Imports removed to save space

public class ShoppingCartServlet extends HttpServlet
implements SingleThreadModel
{
    protected Context ctx;
    protected ShoppingCartHome home;
    protected DebugLog logger;
    protected NumberFormat formatter;
```

The servlet's init method uses another internal method called findHome to load the JNDI context. It also initializes the NumberFormat and DebugLog for messages.

```
    public void init(ServletConfig config) throws ServletException
    {
        super.init(config);

        String logServer;

        logServer = getInitParameter("logserver");
```

```
        logger = new DebugLog();
        logger.logTo(logServer);

        formatter = NumberFormat.getCurrencyInstance();

        findHome();
    }
```

The findHome method uses the internal method getInitialContext to create a JNDI context. This context is used to look up the ShoppingCartHome object based on the ShoppingCartHome initialization parameter.

```
    protected void findHome()
    {
        try
        {
            String homeName;

            homeName = getInitParameter("ShoppingCartHome");

            ctx = getInitialContext();

            if(ctx != null)
                home = (ShoppingCartHome) ctx.lookup(homeName);
        }
        catch(Exception exp)
        {
            ctx = null;
            home = null;
        }
    }
```

The getInitialContext method uses the initialization parameters to create a JNDI context. We have hard-coded the BEA WebLogic context for this example. You could also read it from initialization parameters.

```
    protected Context getInitialContext() throws Exception
    {
        Properties p = new Properties();
        String url = null;
        String user=null;
        String password=null;

        url = getInitParameter("url");
        user = getInitParameter("user");
        password = getInitParameter("password");

        p.put(Context.INITIAL_CONTEXT_FACTORY,
                "weblogic.jndi.T3InitialContextFactory");

        if(url != null)
```

```
            p.put(Context.PROVIDER_URL, url);
        else
            p.put(Context.PROVIDER_URL, "t3://localhost:7001");

        if (user != null)
        {
            p.put(Context.SECURITY_PRINCIPAL, user);

            if (password == null) password = "";

            p.put(Context.SECURITY_CREDENTIALS, password);
        }

        return new InitialContext(p);
    }
```

Because the ShoppingCartServlet supports a number of possible actions, the doGet method is quite lengthy. The discussion for this method is broken into sections, associated with the code being discussed.

The first block of code in doGet declares the local variables. Some of these variables are used temporarily during loops. Others hold information such as the current contents of the cart or the PrintWriter with which to send data to the response.

```
    public void doGet(HttpServletRequest request, HttpServletResponse
response)
    throws ServletException, IOException
    {
        HttpSession session; //The current session
        String cartName; //The name to use for the cart
        ShoppingCart cart=null; //The EJB
        Hashtable items; //The current list of items
        ShoppingCartItem item; //Used to iterate the list of items
        PrintWriter out; //The responses PrintWriter
        String action; //Which action was requested
        double price=0.0; //Temp variable
        int quantity=0; //Temp variable
        String desc=null; //Temp variable
        String errorMessage = null; //Temp variable
        String requestURL; // The URL used to request the servlet
        String referer; // URL for the page that made the request
        boolean outputCart = true; //Temp variable
```

The servlet stores the current items for a shopper in her session. A session is created for the shopper or retrieved for use throughout the method. The servlet also gets a copy of its URL, which is used as the target for forms that may be output dynamically. All of the pages displayed by the servlet include a link back to the page that initially contacted the servlet, if possible. The URL for the page that contacted the servlet should be stored in the Referer header field. Once the servlet gets this value, it includes it in the dynamic forms it creates. This allows the user to interact with the servlet, possibly creating numerous pages, and still have a link back to the original contact point.

Because the servlet overrides the actual referer with the original referer, the servlet's version and input parameter is checked first. Only if that parameter is unavailable does the servlet check the header fields.

```
session = request.getSession(true);
requestURL = HttpUtils.getRequestURL(request).toString();

//See if we are reloading first
referer = request.getParameter("referer");

//Then look for the refering page
if(referer == null)
    referer = request.getHeader("Referer");
```

The servlet expects to write HTML, and it tells the response so. The PrintWriter for the response is cached out in the local variable for later use.

```
response.setContentType("text/html");
out = response.getWriter();
```

The shopper's current items are stored in a hash table in the client session under the name "shoppingcart.items." This value is reused if it exists or created the first time the client initiates this method.

```
items = (Hashtable) session.getValue("shoppingcart.items");

if(items==null)
{
    session.putValue("shoppingcart.items",new Hashtable());

    items =
      (Hashtable) session.getValue("shoppingcart.items");
}
```

The current request for the servlet is stored in the "action" input parameter. This value is used to determine the servlet's response. For some requests, the description, price, and quantity associated with the request are also included. All of these values are cached in local variables. The description value is used as a flag to indicate whether an item is selected. If an error occurs, this value is set to null.

Throughout the doGet method, the errorMessage variable is used to hold an errorMessage. The servlet assumes that if this variable is non-null, an error occurred and it should display the appropriate notification to the user.

```
action = request.getParameter("action");

try
{
    desc = request.getParameter("item");
    price = (new
Double(request.getParameter("price"))).doubleValue();
```

```
            quantity =
Integer.parseInt(request.getParameter("quantity"));
        }
        catch(Exception exp)
        {
            //reset
            desc = null;
            errorMessage = "No item specified.";
        }
```

Next, the servlet checks to see which action was called. If the view action is called or the purchase action is used, the description can be null, so the servlet resets the errorMessage variable.

```
        if("view".equalsIgnoreCase(action)
            ||"purchase".equalsIgnoreCase(action))
        {
            errorMessage = null;
        }
```

If errorMessage is not null, doGet skips to the end, where the message will be displayed to the user.

```
        if(errorMessage != null)
        {
            //do nothing, but go to end
        }
```

If this is an add request, the servlet checks to see whether the user already ordered this item. In this case, the item's quantity is updated. When a new item is added to the cart, a ShoppingCartItem is created and added to the items hash table. Any exceptions are caught, and the errorMessage variable is set.

```
        else if("add".equalsIgnoreCase(action))
        {
            item = new ShoppingCartItem(desc,price,quantity);

            try
            {
                logger.log("Adding item: "+item);

                item = (ShoppingCartItem) items.get(desc);

                if(item == null)
                {
                    item =
                        new ShoppingCartItem(desc,price,quantity);
                    items.put(desc,item);
                }
                else
                {
```

```
                item.price = price;
                item.quantity += quantity;
            }
        }
        catch(Exception exp)
        {
            logger.log(exp);
            errorMessage = "Unable to add item(s).";
        }
    }
```

The adjust action tells the servlet to adjust the quantity of an item. This results in an error if the item is not in the session already. However, the servlet does not remove the item from the session, so the user could readjust a 0 value back to a positive one. Again, exceptions are caught and the error message is set.

```
    else if("adjust".equalsIgnoreCase(action))
    {
        item = new ShoppingCartItem(desc,price,quantity);

        try
        {
            item = (ShoppingCartItem) items.get(desc);

            if(item != null)
            {
                item.quantity = quantity;
            }
            else
            {
                errorMessage =
                  "Item(s) was not contained in the cart.";
            };
        }
        catch(Exception exp)
        {
            logger.log(exp);
            errorMessage = "Unable to adjust item(s).";
        }
    }
```

The delete action is similar to adjust except that it totally removes an item from the cart if the adjustment results in zero items of a particular type.

```
    else if("delete".equalsIgnoreCase(action))
    {
        item = new ShoppingCartItem(desc,price,quantity);

        try
        {item = (ShoppingCartItem) items.get(desc);
```

```
            if(item != null)
            {
                if(item.quantity > quantity)
                {
                    item.quantity -= quantity;
                }
                else
                {
                    items.remove(desc);
                }
            }
            else
            {
                errorMessage =
                  "Item(s) was not contained in the cart.";
            }
        }
        catch(Exception exp)
        {
            logger.log(exp);
            errorMessage = "Unable to remove item(s).";
        }
    }
```

Perhaps the most complex action is the purchase one. This action attempts to contact the ShoppingCart EJB and initiate a purchase. Purchasing is a two-step process. First, the servlet creates a list of items to confirm and checks them with the bean before displaying the confirmed items to the shopper. If the shopper confirms the purchase, the confirmed items are bought and the shopper is notified. The first time a purchase request is made, the servlet creates the confirmed item list and stores it in the client session with the name "shoppingcart.itemsToConfirm." The confirmation page sets the input parameter to confirmed, telling the servlet to perform the purchase. If this flag is set and no items appear in the session for confirmation, the errorMessage is set. The value of this parameter is the contents of a text field that the user fills in with her confirmation ID.

The code for contacting the EJB appears in boldface type in the following sample. To identify the shopping cart, the servlet uses the REMOTE_USER property, if possible. This is set if the user has authenticated with the Web server. Otherwise, the session ID is used.

The code for outputting the pages also appears in boldface type. In this case, output is managed by other methods discussed later.

```
    else if("purchase".equalsIgnoreCase(action))
    {
        Hashtable confirmedItems;

        confirmedItems = (Hashtable)
           session.getValue("shoppingcart.itemsToConfirm");

        //Try to use the remote user login
```

```
cartName = request.getRemoteUser();

if(cartName == null)
{
    session = request.getSession(true);

    if(session != null) cartName = session.getId();
}

if(home == null) findHome();

//Get the EJB shopping cart
if((home != null)&&(cartName != null))
{
    try
    {
        cart = home.create(cartName);
    }
    catch(Exception ex)
    {
        //perhaps home is gone, reset
        home = null;
        ctx = null;

        logger.log(ex);
    }
}

if(cart == null)
{
    errorMessage = "Unable to load cart.";
}
else
{
    logger.log("Cart: "+cart);
}

if(request.getParameter("confirmed")!=null)
{
    if(confirmedItems == null)
    {
        errorMessage =
         "No items confirmed for purchase.";
    }
    else
    {
        String user = request.getParameter("confirmed");
        doPurchase(confirmedItems,cart,items
                        ,user,out,requestURL,referer);
        outputCart = false;
    }
```

```
        }
        else
        {
            outputConfirm(items,cart,session
                            ,out,requestURL,referer);

            outputCart = false;
        }
    }
```

All other actions are treated as a request to view the cart, as indicated by the trailing else statement.

```
    else
    {
        //do nothing, just view
    }
```

Unless the confirm pages, purchase page, or an error occurred, the cart is displayed. If the errorMessage variable is set, a page displaying this message is sent to the client. This check is performed by the following if-else statement:

```
    if(outputCart && (errorMessage==null))
    {
        outputCart(items,out,requestURL,referer);
    }
    else if(errorMessage!=null)
    {
        outputErrorMessage(out,errorMessage,referer);
    }
}
```

The outputErrorMessage method is used to send an error message to the client. This method takes the PrintWriter, the message, and the URL of the referring page as arguments and outputs HTML.

```
protected void outputErrorMessage(PrintWriter out
                                  ,String errorMessage
                                  ,String referer)
{
    out.println("<HTML>");
    out.println("<HEAD>");
    out.println("<TITLE>");
    out.println("Shopping Cart");
    out.println("</TITLE>");
    out.println("</HEAD>");
    out.println("<BODY TEXT=\"#000000\" BGCOLOR=\"#FFFFFF\"");
    out.println(" LINK=\"#FF0000\" VLINK=\"#800080\">");
    out.println("<CENTER>");
    out.println("<TABLE WIDTH=500 BORDER=0>");
```

```
        out.println("<TR>");
        out.println("<TD>");

        out.println(errorMessage);

        if((referer!=null)&&(referer.length()>0))
        {
            out.print("<CENTER><H4><A HREF=\"");
            out.print(referer);
            out.print("\">Back</A></H4></CENTER>");
        }

        out.println("</TD>");
        out.println("</TR>");
        out.println("</TABLE>");
        out.println("</CENTER>");
        out.println("</BODY>");
        out.println("</HTML>");
        out.close();
    }
```

The ouputCart method takes the hash table containing the cart, the PrintWriter, the URL for the servlet, and the URL for the referring page as arguments. This method outputs the cart as a table, pictured in Figure 25.11, with text fields for adjusting the quantity of an item and buttons to initiate an adjustment or deletion. There is also a button to initiate a purchase.

Figure 25.11 A shopping cart page.

As the items are output, a running total of their cost is maintained. This total is displayed in the final row of the table. The actual code for outputting an item is contained in the next method, called outputItem. The requestURL argument is used by this method to assign the ACTION attribute for the forms.

The main code for this method is highlighted to separate it from the simple output of HTML. Like the error message page, this one contains a link back to the referer if one is provided.

```
protected void outputCart(Hashtable cart
                          ,PrintWriter out
                          ,String requestURL
                          ,String referer)
{
    ShoppingCartItem item;
    Enumeration items;
    float total=0;

    items = cart.elements();

    out.println("<HTML>");
    out.println("<HEAD>");
    out.println("<TITLE>");
    out.println("Shopping Cart");
    out.println("</TITLE>");
    out.println("</HEAD>");
    out.println("<BODY TEXT=\"#000000\" BGCOLOR=\"#FFFFFF\"");
    out.println(" LINK=\"#FF0000\" VLINK=\"#800080\">");
    out.println("<CENTER>");
    out.println("<TABLE WIDTH=500 BORDER=0>");
    out.println("<TR>");
    out.println("<TD>");

    out.println("<CENTER><H1>Shopping Cart</H1></CENTER>");
    out.println("Your shopping cart contains the following
items:<BR>");
    out.println("<TABLE>");
    out.println("<TR>");
    out.println("<TH>Description</TH>");
    out.println("<TH>Quantity</TH>");
    out.println("<TH>Price</TH>");
    out.println("<TH>Total</TH>");
    out.println("<TH></TH>");
    out.println("</TR>");

    while((items!=null)&&(items.hasMoreElements()))
    {
        item = (ShoppingCartItem) items.nextElement();

        outputItem(item,out,requestURL,referer);

        total += item.getTotal();
```

```
        }

        out.println("<TR>");
        out.println("<TD></TD>");
        out.println("<TD></TD>");
        out.println("<TD><B>Total</B></TD>");
        out.print("<TD><B>");
        out.print(formatter.format(total));
        out.println("</B></TD>");
        out.println("<TD></TD>");
        out.println("</TR>");

        out.println("</TABLE>");

        out.println("<BR><P ALIGN=Right>");
        out.print("<FORM ACTION=\"");
        out.print(requestURL);
        out.println("\" METHOD=\"GET\">");

        out.println("<INPUT TYPE=\"SUBMIT\" NAME=\"action\"
VALUE=\"Purchase\">");

        out.println("</FORM>");
        out.println("</P>");

        if((referer!=null)&&(referer.length()>0))
        {
            out.print("<CENTER><H4><A HREF=\"");
            out.print(referer);
            out.print("?referer=");
            out.print(referer);
            out.println("\">Back</A></H4></CENTER>");
        }

        out.println("</TD>");
        out.println("</TR>");
        out.println("</TABLE>");
        out.println("</CENTER>");
        out.println("</BODY>");
        out.println("</HTML>");
        out.close();
    }
```

The outputItem method outputs a form containing a single HTML table row. This row includes the description, price, and quantity for a ShoppingCartItem as well as the total price for all of the items of this type ordered. Hidden fields are used when necessary to pass data back to the servlet. The value of the Submit button is used to tell the servlet which action is being requested between delete and adjust.

```
    protected void outputItem(ShoppingCartItem item
                              ,PrintWriter out
```

```
                              ,String act
                              ,String referer)
    {
        out.print("<FORM ACTION=\"");
        out.print(act);
        out.println("\" METHOD=\"GET\">");
        out.println("<TR>");
        out.print("<TD>");
        out.print(item.desc);
        out.println("</TD>");
        out.print("<TD><INPUT TYPE=\"TEXT\" "
                  +"NAME=\"quantity\" VALUE=\"");
        out.print(item.quantity);
        out.println("\" SIZE=3></TD>");
        out.print("<TD>");
        out.print(formatter.format(item.price));
        out.println("</TD>");
        out.print("<TD>");
        out.print(formatter.format(item.getTotal()));
        out.println("</TD>");

        //Output the change form buttons and hidden fields
        out.println("<TD>");

        out.print("<INPUT TYPE=\"HIDDEN\" NAME=\"item\" VALUE=\"");
        out.print(item.desc);
        out.println("\">");
        out.print("<INPUT TYPE=\"HIDDEN\" NAME=\"price\" VALUE=\"");
        out.print(item.price);
        out.println("\">");
        out.print("<INPUT TYPE=\"HIDDEN\" "
                      +"NAME=\"referer\" VALUE=\"");
        out.print(referer);
        out.println("\">");

        out.println("<INPUT TYPE=\"SUBMIT\" "
                      +"NAME=\"action\" VALUE=\"Adjust\">");
        out.println("<INPUT TYPE=\"SUBMIT\" "
                      +"NAME=\"action\" VALUE=\"Delete\">");

        out.println("</TD>");

        out.println("</TR>");

        out.println("</FORM>");
    }
```

The confirmation page displays the items confirmed by the EJB, highlighting the ones that have changed in price or quantity from the items requested. Items may change price if their Web page is out of date. The quantity will change based on availability. These changes are determined by asking the ShoppingCart bean, passed as an argument, to add an item. The bean returns the same item, with the price and quantity adjusted. These adjusted values are placed in the session under the name "shoppingcart.itemsToConfirm." This page also contains a form for the user to enter a confirmation password. In this example, the confirmation password should correspond to a name in the database.

```
protected void outputConfirm(Hashtable items
                            ,ShoppingCart cart
                            ,HttpSession session
                            ,PrintWriter out
                            ,String requestURL
                            ,String referer)
{
    ShoppingCartItem item;
    ShoppingCartItem curItem;
    Enumeration curItems;
    Hashtable itemsToConfirm;
    float total=0;

    curItems = items.elements();

    itemsToConfirm = new Hashtable();
    session.putValue("shoppingcart.itemsToConfirm"
                    ,itemsToConfirm);

    out.println("<HTML>");
    out.println("<HEAD>");
    out.println("<TITLE>");
    out.println("Confirm Purchase");
    out.println("</TITLE>");
    out.println("</HEAD>");
    out.println("<BODY TEXT=\"#000000\" BGCOLOR=\"#FFFFFF\"");
    out.println(" LINK=\"#FF0000\" VLINK=\"#800080\">");
    out.println("<CENTER>");
    out.println("<TABLE WIDTH=500 BORDER=0>");
    out.println("<TR>");
    out.println("<TD>");

    out.println("<CENTER><H1>Confirmation "
                      +"Required</H1></CENTER>");
    out.print("Please confirm your purchase of");
    out.println(" the following items:<BR>");
    out.print("<EM>Items that have changed are printed");
    out.println(" in blue.</EM>");
    out.println("<TABLE>");
    out.println("<TR>");
    out.println("<TH>Description</TH>");
    out.println("<TH>Quantity</TH>");
    out.println("<TH>Price</TH>");
    out.println("<TH>Total</TH>");
    out.println("</TR>");
```

```
while((curItems!=null)&&(curItems.hasMoreElements()))
{
    curItem = (ShoppingCartItem) curItems.nextElement();

    try
    {
        item = cart.addItem(curItem);

        curItem.price = item.price;
        curItem.quantity = item.quantity;

        itemsToConfirm.put(item.desc,item);
    }
    catch(Exception exp)
    {
        item = new ShoppingCartItem("err",0,0);
    }

    out.println("<TR>");
    out.print("<TD>");
    out.print(item.desc);
    out.println("</TD>");
    out.print("<TD>");

    if(item.quantity != curItem.quantity)
        out.print("<FONT COLOR=\"#0033FF\">");

    out.print(item.quantity);

    if(item.quantity != curItem.quantity)
        out.print("</FONT>");

    out.println("</TD>");
    out.print("<TD>");

    if(item.price != curItem.price)
        out.print("<FONT COLOR=\"#0033FF\">");

    out.print(formatter.format(item.price));

    if(item.price != curItem.price)
        out.print("</FONT>");

    out.println("</TD>");
    out.print("<TD>");
    out.print(formatter.format(item.getTotal()));
    out.println("</TD>");
    out.println("</TR>");

    total += item.getTotal();
}
```

```
        out.println("<TR>");
        out.println("<TD></TD>");
        out.println("<TD></TD>");
        out.println("<TD><B>Total</B></TD>");
        out.print("<TD><B>");
        out.print(formatter.format(total));
        out.println("</B></TD>");
        out.println("</TR>");

        out.println("</TABLE>");

        out.println("<BR>");
        out.print("<FORM ACTION=\"");
        out.print(requestURL);
        out.println("\" METHOD=\"GET\">");
        out.println("Enter your pass phrase to confirm.");
        out.println("<INPUT TYPE=\"TEXT\" ");
        out.println("NAME=\"confirmed\" SIZE=16>");
        out.println("<INPUT TYPE=\"HIDDEN\" ");
        out.println("NAME=\"action\" VALUE=\"purchase\">");
        out.println("<INPUT TYPE=\"SUBMIT\" ");
        out.println("NAME=\"submit\" VALUE=\"Confirm\">");

        out.println("</FORM>");

        if((referer!=null)&&(referer.length()>0))
        {
            out.print("<CENTER><H4><A HREF=\"");
            out.print(referer);
            out.print("?referer=");
            out.print(referer);
            out.println("\">Back</A></H4></CENTER>");
        }

        out.println("</TD>");
        out.println("</TR>");
        out.println("</TABLE>");
        out.println("</CENTER>");
        out.println("</BODY>");
        out.println("</HTML>");
        out.close();
    }
```

A call to doPurchase is made from the doGet method when a purchase is requested, and the user id is assigned by the confirmation page. First, doPurchase adds the requested items to the cart. These are the confirmed items, not the user's original requests. If the items are added successfully, the bean is asked to purchase its items. This request either succeeds or throws an exception. If the exception is a BadCreditException, an appropriate message is displayed; otherwise, an error message is sent to the user. Finally, if no errors occurred, the servlet displays a page listing the purchased items with a link back to the online store's home page.

Because the purchase has occurred, the shopping cart is cleaned out so that the client can begin shopping anew.

```
protected void doPurchase(Hashtable items
                          ,ShoppingCart cart
                          ,Hashtable oldCartItems
                          ,String user
                          ,PrintWriter out
                          ,String requestURL
                          ,String referer)
{
    ShoppingCartItem item;
    ShoppingCartItem curItem;
    ShoppingCartItem cartItems[]=null;
    int i,max=0;
    Enumeration curItems;
    float total=0;
    boolean failed=false;
    boolean badCredit=false;

    curItems = items.elements();
    try
    {
        while((curItems!=null)&&(curItems.hasMoreElements()))
        {
            curItem = (ShoppingCartItem) curItems.nextElement();
            cart.addItem(curItem);
        }
    }
    catch(Exception exp)
    {
        failed = true;
    }

    if(!failed)
    {
        try
        {
            if(!cart.purchaseCart(user)) failed = true;
        }
        catch(BadCreditException exp)
        {
            failed = true;
            badCredit = true;
        }
        catch(Exception exp)
        {
            failed = true;
        }
    }
```

```
if(failed)
{
    if(badCredit)
    {
        outputErrorMessage(out
            ,"You do not have enough credit"
                +" to make this purchase."
            ,referer);
    }
    else
    {
        outputErrorMessage(out
            ,"Server failure, unable to purchase items."
            ,referer);
    }

    return;
}

out.println("<HTML>");
out.println("<HEAD>");
out.println("<TITLE>");
out.println("Purchase Confirmed");
out.println("</TITLE>");
out.println("</HEAD>");
out.println("<BODY TEXT=\"#000000\" BGCOLOR=\"#FFFFFF\"");
out.println(" LINK=\"#FF0000\" VLINK=\"#800080\">");
out.println("<CENTER>");
out.println("<TABLE WIDTH=500 BORDER=0>");
out.println("<TR>");
out.println("<TD>");

out.println("<CENTER><H1>Purchase Confirmed</H1></CENTER>");
out.print("Thank you for your purchase of the ");
out.println("following items:<BR>");
out.println("<TABLE>");
out.println("<TR>");
out.println("<TH>Description</TH>");
out.println("<TH>Quantity</TH>");
out.println("<TH>Price</TH>");
out.println("<TH>Total</TH>");
out.println("</TR>");

try
{
    cartItems = cart.getItems();
}
catch(Exception exp)
{
}
```

```
if(cartItems != null) max = cartItems.length;

for(i=0;i<max;i++)
{
    curItem = cartItems[i];

    if(curItem.quantity > 0)
    {
        out.println("<TR>");
        out.print("<TD>");
        out.print(curItem.desc);
        out.println("</TD>");
        out.print("<TD>");
        out.print(curItem.quantity);
        out.println("</TD>");
        out.print("<TD>");
        out.print(formatter.format(curItem.price));
        out.println("</TD>");
        out.print("<TD>");
        out.print(formatter.format(curItem.getTotal()));
        out.println("</TD>");
        out.println("</TR>");

        total += curItem.getTotal();
    }
}

out.println("<TR>");
out.println("<TD></TD>");
out.println("<TD></TD>");
out.println("<TD><B>Total</B></TD>");
out.print("<TD><B>");
out.print(formatter.format(total));
out.println("</B></TD>");
out.println("</TR>");

out.println("</TABLE>");

if((referer!=null)&&(referer.length()>0))
{
    out.print("<CENTER><H4><A HREF=\"");
    out.print("/shopcart/home/index.jhtml");
    out.println("\">Back To Store Front</A></H4></CENTER>");
}

out.println("</TD>");
out.println("</TR>");
out.println("</TABLE>");
out.println("</CENTER>");
out.println("</BODY>");
out.println("</HTML>");
```

```
        out.close();

        //reset the cart
        oldCartItems.clear();
    }
}
```

This servlet is rather long because of the HTML it contains. We have kept the code together in this example to make it easier to understand. In a larger commercial version of the same servlet, rather than add any more features, a store requiring more actions might consider breaking the responsibility for managing the cart into several servlets. This would make it easier for the programmer to maintain the site.

Inventory Report

The final servlet in this example is called Inventory Servlet. This servlet uses the ShoppingCart bean to retrieve the current inventory and display it. All of the code from this servlet should look familiar to you after reading the description of the ShoppingCartServlet.

```
package shopcart.servlets;

//imports removed to save space

public class InventoryServlet extends HttpServlet
implements SingleThreadModel
{
    protected Context ctx;
    protected ShoppingCartHome home;
    protected DebugLog logger;
    protected NumberFormat formatter;
```

The init methods sets up the connection to the debug server and the ShoppingCartHome.

```
    public void init(ServletConfig config) throws ServletException
    {
        super.init(config);

        String logServer;

        logServer = getInitParameter("logserver");

        logger = new DebugLog();
        logger.logTo(logServer);

        formatter = NumberFormat.getCurrencyInstance();

        findHome();
    }
```

The findHome method uses getInitialContext to access JNDI. Using the context, findHome looks up the ShoppingCartHome object that will create ShoppingCarts for the servlet. The same initialization parameters used by the ShoppingCartServlet are used by the InventoryServlet to create its context. Of course, each servlet must be configured separately.

```
protected void findHome()
{
    try
    {
        String homeName;

        homeName = getInitParameter("ShoppingCartHome");

        ctx = getInitialContext();

        if(ctx != null)
            home = (ShoppingCartHome) ctx.lookup(homeName);
    }
    catch(Exception exp)
    {
        ctx = null;
        home = null;
    }
}

protected Context getInitialContext() throws Exception
{
    Properties p = new Properties();
    String url = null;
    String user=null;
    String password=null;

    url = getInitParameter("url");
    user = getInitParameter("user");
    password = getInitParameter("password");

    p.put(Context.INITIAL_CONTEXT_FACTORY,
            "weblogic.jndi.T3InitialContextFactory");

    if(url != null)
        p.put(Context.PROVIDER_URL, url);
    else
        p.put(Context.PROVIDER_URL, "t3://localhost:7001");

    if (user != null)
    {
        p.put(Context.SECURITY_PRINCIPAL, user);

        if (password == null) password = "";
```

```
            p.put(Context.SECURITY_CREDENTIALS, password);
        }

        return new InitialContext(p);
    }
```

The doGet method contacts the ShoppingCart EJB, gets the inventory, and displays it in an HTML table. Each item is displayed in its own row, with the total sales included by item.

```
    public void doGet(HttpServletRequest request
                    , HttpServletResponse response)
    throws ServletException, IOException
    {
        ShoppingCartItem curItem;
        Object items[]=null;
        int i,max=0;
        String cartName;
        ShoppingCart cart=null;
        PrintWriter out;
        HttpSession session;

        //Try to use the remote user login
        cartName = request.getRemoteUser();

        if(cartName == null)
        {
            session = request.getSession(true);

            if(session != null) cartName = session.getId();
        }

        if(home == null) findHome();

        //Get the EJB shopping cart
        if((home != null)&&(cartName != null))
        {
            try
            {
                cart = home.create(cartName);
            }
            catch(Exception ex)
            {
                //perhaps home is gone, reset
                home = null;
                ctx = null;

                logger.log(ex);
            }
        }
```

```
response.setContentType("text/html");
out = response.getWriter();

out.println("<HTML>");
out.println("<HEAD>");
out.println("<TITLE>");
out.println("Inventory");
out.println("</TITLE>");
out.println("</HEAD>");
out.println("<BODY TEXT=\"#000000\" BGCOLOR=\"#FFFFFF\"");
out.println(" LINK=\"#FF0000\" VLINK=\"#800080\">");
out.println("<CENTER>");
out.println("<TABLE WIDTH=500 BORDER=0>");
out.println("<TR>");
out.println("<TD>");

out.println("<CENTER><H1>Inventory</H1></CENTER>");
out.println("The online store contains the"
                +" following items:<BR>");
out.println("<TABLE>");
out.println("<TR>");
out.println("<TH>Description</TH>");
out.println("<TH>Price</TH>");
out.println("<TH>Quantity</TH>");
out.println("<TH>Sales</TH>");
out.println("<TH>Revenue From Sales</TH>");
out.println("</TR>");

if(cart != null) items = cart.getInventory();

if(items != null) max = items.length;

for(i=0;i<max;i++)
{
    curItem = (ShoppingCartItem)items[i];

    out.println("<TR>");
    out.print("<TD>");
    out.print(curItem.desc);
    out.println("</TD>");
    out.print("<TD>");
    out.print(formatter.format(curItem.price));
    out.println("</TD>");
    out.print("<TD>");
    out.print(curItem.quantity);
    out.println("</TD>");
    out.print("<TD>");
    out.print(curItem.sales);
    out.println("</TD>");
    out.print("<TD>");
```

```
                out.print(formatter.format(curItem.price
                                        *curItem.sales));
                out.println("</TD>");
                out.println("</TR>");
            }

            out.println("</TABLE>");

            out.println("</TD>");
            out.println("</TR>");
            out.println("</TABLE>");
            out.println("</CENTER>");
            out.println("</BODY>");
            out.println("</HTML>");
            out.close();
        }
    }
```

This example shows how a servlet can act as a report engine, generating HTML from the database and included calculated values.

Building and Running the Store

In order to run the online store example, you need to create a database for it. A class called shopcart.BuildDB is included on the CD-ROM and takes a URL, driver, name, and password as command-line arguments. These values are then used to build the database. A Microsoft Access database file is included on the CD-ROM for use with this example as well. In this case, create an ODBC data source for it.

Next, the servlets must be installed, and the parameters discussed in this chapter must be configured.

Finally, install the ShoppingCart EJB. A script called build.bat is available on the CD-ROM. The NT script builds the source code and copies the .class files to the specified directory. This batch file also runs the BEA WebLogic deployment tools and EJB compiler on the bean. A deploymentDescriptor.txt file is included to support this automated deployment. If you are using another EJB host, please refer to that host's documentation to determine the steps required to load the ShoppingCartBean.

The ShoppingCartBean expects its JDBC information to be provided as environmental properties. With the BEA WebLogic server, we actually created a pool in the weblogic.properties file. To create the pool, the two entries were added to the properties file. The first entry is long, so the \ character is used to indicate that it continues for several lines. The second entry fits on a single line.

```
weblogic.jdbc.connectionPool.CartPool=\
       url=jdbc:odbc:Cart,\
       driver=sun.jdbc.odbc.JdbcOdbcDriver,\
       initialCapacity=1,\
       maxCapacity=2,\
```

```
        capacityIncrement=1,\
        props=user=none;password=none;server=none

# Add an ACL for the connection pool:
weblogic.allow.reserve.weblogic.jdbc.connectionPool.CartPool=guest
```

This pool refers to the ODBC data source. The bean is configured to use BEA WebLogic's JTS JDBC driver. This driver fronts the connection messages and supports the use of connection pools. It also supports any JTS calls that are used within the EJB. In our WebLogic deployment descriptor, the following lines are used to make this assignment:

```
driver       weblogic.jdbc.jts.Driver
url          jdbc:weblogic:jts:CartPool
logserver    192.168.0.170
```

Finally, the CD-ROM contains a manifest file for use in creating the EJB jar file.

Once you get the servlets, database, and bean installed, you can access the store with a Web browser by going to the stores home page index.jhtml. You may also want to access the InventoryServlet directly to keep an eye on the database as you make purchases. Check the BuildDB script for information on who is a registered customer and how much credit customers have. These values are stored in static arrays that you can edit as needed before building the database.

Summary

This example combined a number of the frameworks discussed in this book. Servlets and JavaServer Pages were used to display information to the user. Enterprise JavaBeans were used to implement the business logic, and JBDC was used to access a database. Communication between the servlets and EJB was managed via JNDI. As you may have guessed, most enterprise applications use a number of technologies. Almost all of the enterprise APIs are designed to rely on JNDI as the finding and naming API. All database access is managed with JDBC, and most enterprise applications use databases.

Some of the main lessons we hope you learn from this example are:

- **Pay special attention during the design stage to the mechanism that you choose for creating Web pages.** Are you using dynamic pages for everything, even if you don't need to? Depending on your resources, this may be okay, but it does cost Web server time and possibly database time, and that means money. Of course, some sites have to use dynamic HTML, and they should. In this case, use servlets or JSPs that fall into specific categories. For example, this store could have used three servlets for the Web pages: one for the home page, one for category pages, and one for all of the item pages. This keeps the server from having to load too many servlets, and it possibly allows some caching in the servlet's instance variables.

- **In the "Do as we say, not as we do" category: Don't put too much responsibility on a single object.** In a larger program, we would not have made the ShoppingCartBean handle the inventory request. This should be handled by another bean. The ShoppingCartServlet could also be split into separate servlets for displaying the cart, confirming the cart, and making the purchase. In this case, we split servlets to improve maintenance, but this choice should be balanced against resource usage. We broke these guidelines for educational purposes, but that doesn't mean you should, too.
- **Maximize the advantages of an Application Server.** The ShoppingCart bean uses the server's connection pools, allowing it to minimize the database connection times and optimize resource usage.
- **Reuse servlets and beans across applications when possible.** We duplicated the search servlet to make this example self-contained, but we could have easily referenced the existing one. The same is true of the AdRotatorServlet. In large installations, think about grouping a single type of functionality into a single servlet or bean. Reuse the functionality on this scale, taking advantage of the already tested nature of the installation and code.

The next chapter discusses another large example. This one, called MiniJMS, is a partial implementation of the JMS specification. In the same way that the example in this chapter used servlets and EJBs, MiniJMS uses JNDI, JDBC, RMI, and JMS, combining them into a complete, integrated example.

MiniJMS: A Java Messaging Service Provider

This chapter describes the implementation of MiniJMS, a JMS service provider used to test the examples presented in Chapter 20, "Programming with the Java Messaging Service," and Chapter 21, "A JMS-Based Alarm System." This service provider is by no means a complete, commercial messaging solution, but it does provide an example of a multitier enterprise application.

Our primary goals for MiniJMS are as follows:

- Provide an example that integrates multiple Enterprise Java frameworks
- Support enough of the JMS specification to run interesting and educational examples
- Trade performance for simplicity in implementation, where necessary
- Provide an example that is complex enough to challenge readers and test their understanding of the concepts discussed in this book
- Demonstrate the construction of a multithreaded server in Java

The root of these goals is to provide a large, real-world example of how the enterprise APIs are used. Of course, including a complete, large enterprise application is beyond the scope of this book. In fact, this example contains about 5,000 lines of code in 35 classes, making it rather large to include in this chapter. As a result, the entire example is not included in text, but it is available on the CD-ROM that accompanies this book. The key code for this example is described in the chapter.

MiniJMS relies on several enterprise APIs. First and foremost, it implements part of the JMS. This implementation relies on JNDI for finding resources, RMI for network connections, and JDBC for message persistence.

NOTE **Because a basic level of knowledge about the API is assumed in this chapter's discussions, you should read or at least skim Chapter 20, "Programming with the Java Messaging Service," to familiarize yourself with the JMS API if you have not already done so.**

MiniJMS implements the majority of the JMS API, but it is not intended for commercial use. It does not currently support distributed use, in the sense that the JNDI service provider, the file system context, used doesn't support networked operation. This implementation also doesn't support the message selectors and is not designed to plug into an application server or use distributed transactions.

Despite these limitations, MiniJMS does provide an example of a JMS provider that uses server-based message management. It provides persistent messaging, saving messages into a JDBC database and the file system. Also, MiniJMS provides an easy testing ground for understanding and testing JMS applications. On top of this, MiniJMS implements both the messaging models defined by JMS, even though this is not required by the specification.

Basic Design

JMS breaks messaging into two models: point-to-point and publish-subscribe. MiniJMS minimized the differences between these models as much as possible to centralize code. However, this centralization does add a small amount to the complexity of the core objects, because they do double duty by supporting both models.

The design for MiniJMS is split into three layers and two packages. The first layer provides the client interfaces specified in JMS. The second layer is a set of Remote interfaces for the RMI objects provided by the server. The third and final layer is the server itself. The relationship among these layers is pictured in Figure 26.1.

The server code is organized into the minijmsserver package; the remaining two layers are part of the minijms package.

Client/Server Interface

MiniJMS defines three Remote interfaces for communication between the client and the server. These interfaces are listed in Table 26.1.

The RemoteMiniServer interface, as shown in the following code, is implemented by the root object that is registered with RMI for access by the client. This object does not take up real resources on the server and is accessed for use by the client to create connections. This interface is also used to define the name MiniJMSServer, used by the server to bind with the RMI registry.

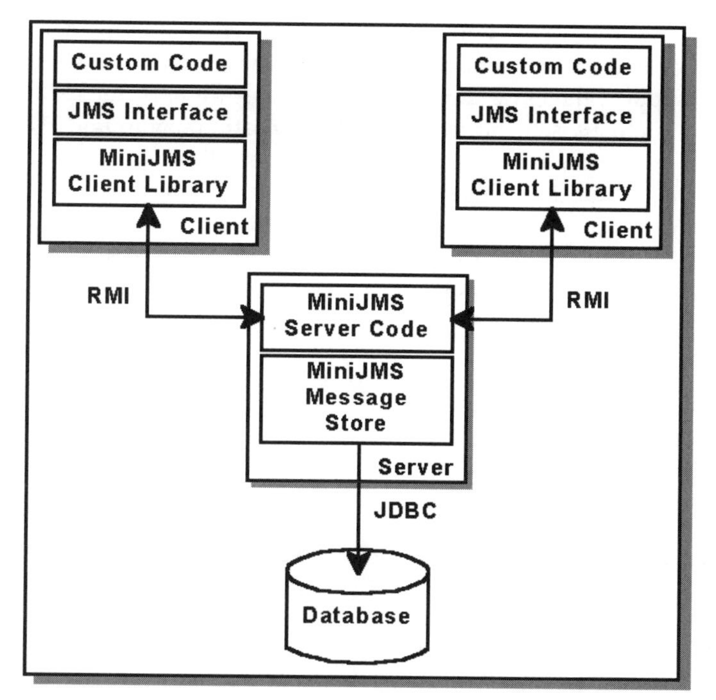

Figure 26.1 MiniJMS design.

```
public interface RemoteMiniServer extends java.rmi.Remote
{
    public final static String SERVER_NAME="MiniJMSServer";

    //Uses the client machine if id is null
    RemoteMiniConnection openConnection(String clientId)
     throws RemoteException,JMSException;
}
```

Table 26.1 Client/Server Interfaces

INTERFACE	DESCRIPTION
`RemoteMiniServer`	The basic interface between the client and server used to create connections.
`RemoteMiniConnection`	Fundamental connection interface used to create client ids and sessions.
`RemoteMiniSession`	The interface between a session on the client and its representation on the server.
`MiniClientSession`	Defines the interface implemented by the client for notifications from the server.

Connections to the server are represented on the server by objects that implement RemoteMiniConnection, included in the next batch of code. These objects take up server resources and thus support the close method. Connections are used to create client identifiers that the system uses to tag each client application/computer. By default, the client's IP address is used. This causes all of the applications on that machine to share some of the resources and messages in the server. In other words, if two applications on the same computer use the same id, they will share the messages for a particular destination. Clients can change this behavior by specifying a username when creating the connection. DurableTopicSubscribers also bypass this default by using their name to register for messages.

```
public interface RemoteMiniConnection extends java.rmi.Remote
{
    public String getClientId()
     throws RemoteException;

    public RemoteMiniConnection close()
     throws RemoteException, JMSException;//should return null

    //Tracks sessions and closes on close.
    public RemoteMiniSession createSession()
     throws RemoteException, JMSException;
}
```

The connection's main job is to create sessions. Notice that the connection interface doesn't include all of the methods in javax.jms.Connection. Many of these methods are handled on the client. Only the minimal necessary information travels to the server. Because sessions represent message processors, they have been broken into the client and server portions for better code management.

RemoteMiniSession defines a number of methods. These methods are listed in Table 26.2. Many represent the associated methods in the javax.jms.Session interface and are used by the client's session object to notify the server of a requested function.

Table 26.2 RemoteMiniSession Methods

METHOD	DESCRIPTION
`public void setTransacted(boolean tf) throws RemoteException, JMSException;`	Tells the remote session whether it is transacted.
`public RemoteMiniSession close() throws RemoteException, JMSException;`	Closes the remote session, freeing resources.
`public Queue createQueue(String queueName) throws RemoteException, JMSException;`	Creates a new queue with the provided name or throws an exception if the queue exists.

Table 26.2 *Continued*

METHOD	DESCRIPTION
`public Topic createTopic(String topicName) throws RemoteException, JMSException;`	Creates a new topic with the provided name or throws an exception if the topic exists.
`public void deleteDestination(String name) throws RemoteException, JMSException;`	Deletes a destination from the system, ultimately deleting all of the messages associated with the destination.
`public void send(Message message) throws RemoteException, JMSException;`	Sends a message to the MiniJMS server.
`public void setClient(MiniClientSession client)throws RemoteException, JMSException;`	Passes the client session to the server for notification of messages being received.
`public void commit() throws RemoteException,JMSException;`	Commits the received and sent messages. (See Chapter 20, "Programming with the Java Messaging Service," for a discussion on commit, rollback, and recover.)
`public void rollback() throws RemoteException,JMSException;`	Rolls back the session's transactions.
`public void recover() throws RemoteException,JMSException;`	Recovers the session's transaction.
`public void acknowledge(Destination d, String name) throws RemoteException,JMSException;`	Acknowledges the messages for a specific destination and name. This name might be the username that was passed to create the connection.
`public void registerFor(Destination dest, boolean durable, String name) throws RemoteException, JMSException;`	Internal method used to tell the server that the session has created a consumer for a particular destination. The name of the consumer is provided, and a flag indicates whether it is durable.
`public void unregisterFor(Destination dest,String name) throws RemoteException, JMSException;`	Tells the server that a consumer was closed, possibly stopping further delivery of messages with this destination to this client, if no more consumers remain.

Notice that one of the remote session's methods is used to create a relationship between the server and the client. The setClient method takes a MiniClientSession as an argument. MiniClientSession is an interface, defined in the following code, implemented by the Session object used by the client. This interface defines the single addMessage method used by the server to notify the client of messages being sent to it.

```
public interface MiniClientSession extends java.rmi.Remote
{
    public void addMessage(Message m)
            throws RemoteException;
}
```

The methods in this interface are the key protocol between the client and the server. The concepts of registering for a destination, sending, and receiving are used extensively in the client library.

The Client Library

All of the code that a JMS client needs is provided in the minijms package. This includes all of the classes with which the client interacts as specified by the JMS specification. The generic versions of these classes and their relationships with each other are pictured in Figure 26.2.

Figure 26.2 does not show the specific classes for managing queues and topics; instead, the complete mapping between the specification and MiniJMS is described in Table 26.3. This table hints at one of the design techniques used in MiniJMS to simplify the code. In several cases, more than one of the JMS types are implemented by a single MiniJMS class. For example, MiniDestination implements Destination, Queue, and Topic.

The message types are not included in this table; they are discussed later in this chapter. Basically, MiniJMS implements each message type in its own class.

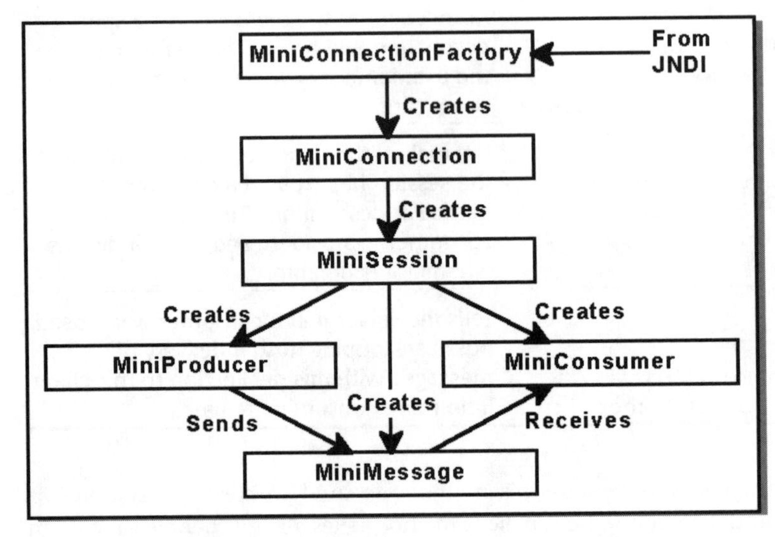

Figure 26.2 MiniJMS Client classes.

Table 26.3 MiniJMS Client Classes

JMS INTERFACE	MINIJMS CLASS
Destination	MiniDestination
ConnectionFactory	MiniConnectionFactory
Connection	MiniConnection
Session	MiniSession
MessageConsumer	MiniConsumer
MessageProducer	MiniProducer
Message	MiniMessage
ConnectionMetaData	MiniJMSConnectionMetaData
Queue	MiniDestination
QueueConnectionFactory	MiniQueueConnectionFactory
QueueConnection	MiniQueueConnection
QueueSession	MiniQueueSession
QueueSender	MiniProducer
QueueReceiver	MiniConsumer
TemporaryQueue	MiniTempDestination
Topic	MiniDestination
TopicConnectionFactory	MiniTopicConnectionFactory
TopicConnection	MiniTopicConnection
TopicSession	MiniTopicSession
TopicPublisher	MiniProducer
TopicSubscriber	MiniConsumer
TemporaryTopic	MiniTempDestination

Both destinations and messages are entity-type objects that represent data but don't perform any real operations. These two objects are discussed before the remaining client libraries to provide a foundation for the discussion.

MiniDestination

MiniDestination objects are used to represent destinations in the MiniJMS system. A Mini-Destination, as defined by the following code, can be a queue or a topic. The object keeps a flag indicating which type it should be treated as. Aside from storing a name and this isQueue flag, the destination's only other method is the getReference method, defined in Referenceable, used to allow the destination to be bound into a JNDI context. (Support for JNDI is discussed in more detail at the end of this section on the client library.)

```
package minijms;

//Import statements removed to save space.

public class MiniDestination
 implements Destination, Topic, Queue, Serializable, Referenceable
{
    protected String name;
    protected boolean isQ;

    public MiniDestination(String name, boolean isQueue)
    {
        this.name = name;
        isQ = isQueue;
    }

    public int hashCode()
    {
        return name.hashCode();
    }

    public boolean equals(Object o)
    {
        boolean retVal = false;

        if(o instanceof MiniDestination)
        {
            if((name!=null)&& name.equals(o.toString()))
            {
                if(((MiniDestination)o).isQueue()
                    ==isQueue()) retVal = true;
            }
        }

        return retVal;
    }

    public String toString()
    {
        return name;
    }

    public boolean isQueue()
    {
        return isQ;
    }
```

```
    public java.lang.String getTopicName()
     throws JMSException
    {
        if(!isQ)
            return name;
        else
            throw new JMSException();
    }

    public java.lang.String getQueueName()
     throws JMSException
    {
        if(isQ)
            return name;
        else
            throw new JMSException();
    }

    public Reference getReference()
                       throws NamingException
    {
        Reference retVal;

        retVal = new Reference(MiniDestination.class.getName()
                       ,new StringRefAddr("name",name)
                       ,MiniDestinationFactory.class.getName()
                       ,null);

        retVal.add(new StringRefAddr("isQueue"
                  ,(isQ?"true":"false")));

        return retVal;
    }
}
```

MiniDestination also implements Serializable so that it can be passed around in RMI messages or saved to disk.

The MiniJMSServer uses destinations as keys in hash tables and searches for them in vectors. To make this searching correct, both the hash code and equals methods are defined to ensure that two destinations are equal if they have the same name and isQueue flag.

MiniMessage

Messages in the MiniJMS system are all represented by a MiniMessage object or an instance of a subclass of MiniMessage. This class has a lot of code, the majority of which is accessor methods for the header fields. The code for these methods follows. One addition made to the regular header fields is that messages keep track of their session. This connection is used to implement the acknowledge message. MiniMessages uses the property JMS_MSG_NUM to test equality with other messages. MiniMessage implements Message and it implements Serializable, so it can be passed as part of an RMI message.

Here is the code that defines MiniMessage; some discussion has been inserted to clarify various portions of the class definition and some repetitive code has been left out, although it is included on the CD-ROM:

```
package minijms;

//Import statements removed to save space.

public class MiniMessage
 implements Message,Serializable
{
    protected String messageId;
    protected long timeStamp;
    protected String corrId;
    protected Destination replyTo;
    protected Destination destination;
    protected String type;
    protected int deliveryMode;
    protected long expiration;
    protected int priority;
    protected boolean redelivered;
    protected Hashtable properties;
    transient protected MiniSession session;

    public MiniMessage()
    {
        deliveryMode = Message.DEFAULT_DELIVERY_MODE;
        priority = Message.DEFAULT_PRIORITY;
        expiration = Message.DEFAULT_TIME_TO_LIVE;
        type="Message";

        properties = new Hashtable();
    }

    public boolean equals(Object o)
    {
        boolean retVal = false;
        String numKey;

        try
        {
            if(o instanceof Message)
            {
                Message msg = (Message) o;

                numKey = MiniJMSMessageStore.MSG_NUM;

                if(msg.propertyExists(numKey)
```

```
                    && propertyExists(numKey))
                {
                    if(getLongProperty(numKey)
                        == msg.getLongProperty(numKey))
                    {
                        retVal = true;
                    }
                }
            }
        }
        catch(Exception exp)
        {
            retVal = false;
        }

        return retVal;
    }

    public void setMiniSession(MiniSession s)
    {
        session = s;
    }

    public MiniSession getMiniSession()
    {
        return session;
    }

    public void acknowledge() throws JMSException
    {
        if((session != null)
            &&(session.getAckMode()
                ==Session.CLIENT_ACKNOWLEDGE))
        {
            session.acknowledge(destination);
        }
        else
        {
            throw new JMSException();
        }
    }

    public void clearBody() throws JMSException
    {
        //do nothing in generic case;
    }

    public String getJMSMessageID() throws JMSException
    {
        return messageId;
    }
```

```
public void setJMSMessageID(String id) throws JMSException
{
    messageId = id;
}

public long getJMSTimestamp() throws JMSException
{
    return timeStamp;
}

public void setJMSTimestamp(long timestamp) throws JMSException
{
    timeStamp = timestamp;
}

public byte [] getJMSCorrelationIDAsBytes() throws JMSException
{
    byte[] retVal = null;

    if(corrId != null)
        retVal = corrId.getBytes();

    return retVal;
}

public void setJMSCorrelationIDAsBytes(byte[] correlationID)
    throws JMSException
{
    corrId = new String(correlationID);
}

public void setJMSCorrelationID(String correlationID)
  throws JMSException
{
    corrId = correlationID;
}

public String getJMSCorrelationID() throws JMSException
{
    return corrId;
}

public Destination getJMSReplyTo() throws JMSException
{
    return replyTo;
}

public void setJMSReplyTo(Destination replyTo)
  throws JMSException
{
    this.replyTo = replyTo;
```

```
}

public Destination getJMSDestination() throws JMSException
{
    return destination;
}

public void setJMSDestination(Destination destination)
  throws JMSException
{
    this.destination = destination;
}

public int getJMSDeliveryMode() throws JMSException
{
    return deliveryMode;
}

public void setJMSDeliveryMode(int deliveryMode)
  throws JMSException
{
    this.deliveryMode = deliveryMode;
}

public boolean getJMSRedelivered() throws JMSException
{
    return redelivered;
}

public void setJMSRedelivered(boolean redelivered)
  throws JMSException
{
    this.redelivered = redelivered;
}

public String getJMSType() throws JMSException
{
    return type;
}

public void setJMSType(String type) throws JMSException
{
    this.type = type;
}

public long getJMSExpiration() throws JMSException
{
    return expiration;
}

public void setJMSExpiration(long expiration)
```

```
        throws JMSException
    {
        this.expiration = expiration;
    }

    public int getJMSPriority() throws JMSException
    {
        return priority;
    }

    public void setJMSPriority(int priority) throws JMSException
    {
        this.priority = priority;
    }
```

The remaining code in MiniMessage is used to manage the priorities. All the priorities are stored in a hash table called properties. A set of convenience methods are provided to convert the objects in the hash table to the appropriate types. For example, the method floatFor takes an object and, if the object is a String or Float, returns a float value. Otherwise, an exception is thrown. These methods are used by the MiniMessage subclasses such as MiniMapMessage to implement all of the data type conversions specified in the JMS documentation. The clearProperties, getPropertyNames, and propertyExists methods simply forward the request to the properties hash table. Only a sample of the properties methods is shown here; the remainder are available on the CD-ROM because the entire class has about 570 lines, too many to include here in a valuable way.

```
    public void clearProperties() throws JMSException
    {
        properties.clear();
    }

    public boolean propertyExists(String name) throws JMSException
    {
        return properties.containsKey(name);
    }

    public Enumeration getPropertyNames() throws JMSException
    {
        return properties.keys();
    }

    public boolean getBooleanProperty(String name)
        throws JMSException
    {
        return booleanFor(properties.get(name));
    }

    public byte getByteProperty(String name) throws JMSException
    {
```

```
        return byteFor(properties.get(name));
    }

    ... Code removed to save space ...

    public String getStringProperty(String name) throws JMSException
    {
        return stringFor(properties.get(name));
    }

    public Object getObjectProperty(String name) throws JMSException
    {
        return objectFor(properties.get(name));
    }

    public void setBooleanProperty(String name, boolean value)
            throws MessageNotWriteableException, JMSException
    {
        properties.put(name,new Boolean(value));
    }

    public void setByteProperty(String name, byte value)
            throws MessageNotWriteableException, JMSException
    {
        properties.put(name,new Byte(value));
    }


    ... Code removed to save space ...

    public void setStringProperty(String name, String value)
            throws MessageNotWriteableException, JMSException
    {
        properties.put(name,value);
    }

    public void setObjectProperty(String name, Object value)
            throws MessageNotWriteableException, JMSException
    {
        properties.put(name,value);
    }

    public boolean booleanFor(Object o) throws JMSException
    {
        if(o == null) throw new NullPointerException("No value.");

        if(o instanceof Boolean)
        {
            return ((Boolean)o).booleanValue();
        }
        else if(o instanceof String)
```

```
        {
            return Boolean.valueOf((String)o).booleanValue();
        }
        else
        {
            throw new JMSException("Bad Type");
        }
    }

    ... Code removed to save space ...

    public int intFor(Object o) throws JMSException
    {
        if(o == null) throw new NullPointerException("No value.");

        if(o instanceof Integer)
        {
            return ((Integer)o).intValue();
        }
        else if(o instanceof Short)
        {
            return ((Short)o).intValue();
        }
        else if(o instanceof Byte)
        {
            return ((Byte)o).intValue();
        }
        else if(o instanceof String)
        {
            return Integer.valueOf((String)o).intValue();
        }
        else
        {
            throw new JMSException("Bad Type");
        }
    }

    public String stringFor(Object o) throws JMSException
    {
        if(o == null) throw new NullPointerException("No value.");

        return o.toString();
    }

    public Object objectFor(Object o) throws JMSException
    {
        if(o == null) throw new NullPointerException("No value.");

        return o;
    }
```

```
    public byte[] bytesFor(Object o) throws JMSException
    {
        if(o == null) throw new NullPointerException("No value.");

        if(!(o instanceof byte[]))
         throw new JMSException("Bad Type");

        return ((byte[])o);
    }
}
```

Notice that the methods for converting values all accept strings as possible input, and the stringFor method converts any object to a string.

MiniJMS provides implementations of the message subtypes. These implementations are called MiniTextMessage, MiniMapMessage, MiniObjectMessage, MiniStreamMessage, and MiniBytesMessage. The stream and bytes messages are in no way optimized and do not support reading arbitrary bytes from the message. However, they should be sufficient for testing.

MiniConnectionFactory

The first real working class in MiniJMS is the MiniConnectionFactory. This class acts as the superclass for the MiniQueueConnectionFactory and the MiniTopicConnection-Factory. Basically, a factory keeps track of the URL to the server, as shown in this snapshot of the MiniConnectFactory.java file:

```
package minijms;

//Import statements removed to save space.

public class MiniConnectionFactory
 implements Serializable
{
    protected String url;

    public MiniConnectionFactory(String serverURL)
    {
        url = serverURL;
    }

    public String getURL()
    {
        return url;
    }
}
```

The subclasses for MiniConnectionFactory implements Referenceable, so they can be bound to a JNDI context. MiniConnectionFactory implements only Serializable, making it and its subclasses available for RMI messaging.

MiniConnection

The connections in MiniJMS extend the MiniConnection class. This class provides the core functionality for a connection to the MiniJMS server. In particular, the connection keeps track of username, password, client ID, and ExceptionListener for connections. MiniConnection also implements the code that creates a connection to the RMI server and stores a list of the connections sessions. The following code is taken from the MiniConnection.java file and includes discussions that indicate major functionality of the MiniConnection class:

```
package minijms;

//Import statements removed to save space.

public class MiniConnection implements javax.jms.Connection
{
    protected RemoteMiniServer server;
    protected RemoteMiniConnection remote;
    protected String user;
    protected String password;
    protected String clientId;
    protected ExceptionListener elistener;
    protected Vector sessions;

    public MiniConnection(String url,String name,String pass)
        throws JMSException
    {
        user = name;
        password = pass;
        sessions = new Vector();

        try
        {
            server = (RemoteMiniServer) Naming.lookup(url);
            remote = server.openConnection(user);
            clientId = remote.getClientId();

            if(remote==null) throw new Exception(url);
        }
        catch(Exception exp)
        {
            throw
            new JMSException("Failed to connect to server: "
                                +exp.toString());
        }
    }
```

The client ID for a connection defaults to the IP address of the client or the username. This value is used to determine to whom messages are delivered. All of the connections with the same client ID are treated as equivalent by the server and share the messages sent to it. The client ID is actually assigned by the server, so changing it involves reconnecting to the server, closing the existing connection in the process. As you can see from the following definition of getClientID and setClientID, changing the client ID causes the connection to reconnect to the server with the new value.

```
public String getClientID() throws JMSException
{
    return clientId;
}

public void setClientID(String id) throws JMSException
{
    try
    {
        if(remote != null)
        {
            remote = remote.close();
        }
    }
    catch(Exception exp)
    {
    }

    clientId = id;

    try
    {
        remote = server.openConnection(clientId);
    }
    catch(Exception exp)
    {
        throw new JMSException(exp.toString());
    }
}
```

MiniJMSConnectionMetaData implements the ConnectionMetaData interface. Because this information is mainly about the version of the provider, the code is not included in the book, but it is available on the CD-ROM.

```
public ConnectionMetaData getMetaData() throws JMSException
{
    return new MiniJMSConnectionMetaData();
}
```

The ExceptionListener is notified when bad errors occur. Currently, MiniJMS does not notify this listener anywhere, but the code is included here to perform the notification.

```
public void setExceptionListener(ExceptionListener listener)
{
    elistener = listener;
```

```
    }

    public void notifyListener(JMSException exp)
    {
        if(elistener != null)
        {
            elistener.onException(exp);
        }
    }
```

When a subclass of MiniConnection creates a session, it adds the session to the list of sessions being managed for this connection. Sessions remove themselves from the list when closed.

```
    public void addSession(MiniSession s)
    {
        synchronized(sessions)
        {
            if(!sessions.contains(s))
            {
                sessions.addElement(s);
            }
        }
    }

    public void removeSession(MiniSession s)
    {
        synchronized(sessions)
        {
            if(!sessions.contains(s))
            {
                sessions.removeElement(s);
            }
        }
    }
```

Starting a connection tells the sessions in that connection to resume. Currently, this feature is not implemented in the session objects.

```
    public void start() throws JMSException
    {
        synchronized(sessions)
        {
            int i,max;
            MiniSession session;

            max = sessions.size();

            for(i=0;i<max;i++)
            {
                session = (MiniSession) sessions.elementAt(i);
```

```
                session.resume();
            }
        }
    }
```

Stopping a connection tells the sessions in that connection to suspend. Currently, this feature is not implemented in the session objects.

```
    public void stop() throws JMSException
    {
        synchronized(sessions)
        {
            int i,max;
            MiniSession session;

            max = sessions.size();

            for(i=0;i<max;i++)
            {
                session = (MiniSession) sessions.elementAt(i);
                session.suspend();
            }
        }
    }
```

Closing a MiniConnection closes the sessions that it is managing and notifies the server that the connection should be closed. This frees up resources on the server.

```
    public void close() throws JMSException
    {
        try
        {
            synchronized(sessions)
            {
                int i,max;
                MiniSession session;

                max = sessions.size();

                for(i=0;i<max;i++)
                {
                    session = (MiniSession) sessions.elementAt(i);
                    session.close();
                }

                sessions.removeAllElements();
            }

            if(remote != null) remote = remote.close();
        }
        catch(Exception exp)
```

```
            {
                throw new JMSException(exp.toString());
            }
        }
    }
```

As you can see, connections have a close relationship with their sessions in this design. This relationship is transparent to the programmer using the JMS interfaces.

MiniSession

Perhaps the heart of the MiniJMS client implementation is the MiniSession class. This class defines the core behaviors of sending and receiving messages. Each MiniSession contains a reference to a RemoteMiniSession. This reference is used to communicate with the MiniJMS server. The MiniSession registers with the remote session as an RMI object. When messages arrive for this session on the server, the remote session sends them to the client using the addMessage message as defined in the ClientMiniSession interface. In order for the session to support RMI, it extends UnicastRemoteObject as discussed in Chapter 13, "Introduction to Java RMI," and the MiniSession constructor is declared to possibly throw RemoteExceptions.

Messages for a session are organized into a hash table that groups messages by destination. Message listeners registered with consumers are also tracked by the session in a hash table that groups them by destination.

```
package minijms;

//Imports removed to save space.

public abstract class MiniSession extends UnicastRemoteObject
 implements Session, MiniClientSession
{
    protected boolean transacted;
    protected int ackMode;
    protected MessageListener listener;
    protected RemoteMiniSession session;
    protected MiniConnection conn;
    protected Hashtable messagesForDest;
    protected Hashtable listenerForDest;
    protected Random rand;

    public MiniSession(boolean transacted,
                       int ackMode)
      throws RemoteException
    {
        this.ackMode = ackMode;
        this.transacted = transacted;

        messagesForDest = new Hashtable();
        listenerForDest = new Hashtable();
```

```
        rand = new Random();
    }
```

While the MiniSessions constructor creates the basic resources, it is up to the connection that creates a MiniSession to provide it with the RemoteMiniSession reference. This reference is obtained from the RemoteMiniConnection to which a MiniConnection has a reference.

```
public void setRemote(RemoteMiniSession r)
    throws JMSException
{
    session = r;

    if(session == null)
        throw new JMSException("Failed to connect.");

    try
    {
        if(transacted) session.setTransacted(true);
        session.setClient(this);
    }
    catch(Exception exp)
    {
        throw new JMSException("Failed to connect.");
    }
}

public RemoteMiniSession getRemote()
{
    return session;
}
```

MiniSessions keep track of their connection, acknowledgment mode, and whether or not they are transacted.

```
public void setConnection(MiniConnection c)
{
    conn = c;
}

//Used by messages to determine if ack should
//do anything.
int getAckMode()
{
    return ackMode;
}

public boolean getTransacted() throws JMSException
{
    return transacted;
}
```

Normally, a session uses its connection's client ID. If for any reason this fails, a random number is used.

```
public String getClientID()
    throws JMSException
{
    if(conn != null) return conn.getClientID();
    else return String.valueOf(rand.nextInt());
}
```

Sessions are expected to create the message that a client will send. MiniSession provides access to all of the message types, as specified in the JMS specification. When a client wants to send a message, it uses the session to create it.

```
public BytesMessage createBytesMessage() throws JMSException
{
    return new MiniStreamMessage();
}

public MapMessage createMapMessage() throws JMSException
{
    return new MiniMapMessage();
}

public Message createMessage() throws JMSException
{
    return new MiniMessage();
}

public ObjectMessage createObjectMessage() throws JMSException
{
    return new MiniObjectMessage();
}

public ObjectMessage createObjectMessage(Serializable object)
   throws JMSException
{
    return new MiniObjectMessage(object);
}

public StreamMessage createStreamMessage() throws JMSException
{
    return new MiniStreamMessage();
}

public TextMessage createTextMessage() throws JMSException
{
    return new MiniTextMessage();
}

public TextMessage createTextMessage(StringBuffer stringBuffer)
```

```
throws JMSException
    {
        return new MiniTextMessage(stringBuffer);
    }
```

MiniSession provides a simple interface to MessageProducers in the MiniJMS library for sending messages. The send method forwards the message to the Remote-MiniSession on the server.

```
public void send(Message message)
             throws JMSException
{
    try
    {
        session.send(message);
    }
    catch(JMSException exp)
    {
        throw exp;
    }
    catch(Exception exp)
    {
        throw new JMSException(exp.toString());
    }
}
```

Commit, recover, and rollback are also forwarded to the server for processing.

```
public void commit() throws JMSException
{
    try
    {
        session.commit();
    }
    catch(JMSException exp)
    {
        throw exp;
    }
    catch(Exception exp)
    {
        throw new JMSException("No remote connection.");
    }
}

public void rollback() throws JMSException
{
    try
    {
        session.rollback();
    }
    catch(JMSException exp)
```

```
        {
            throw exp;
        }
        catch(Exception exp)
        {
            throw new JMSException("No remote connection.");
        }
    }

    public void recover() throws JMSException
    {
        try
        {
            session.recover();
        }
        catch(JMSException exp)
        {
            throw exp;
        }
        catch(Exception exp)
        {
            throw new JMSException("No remote connection.");
        }
    }
```

When a session is closed using the close method defined here, it stops polling the server for messages, notifies the server that it will close, and removes itself from its connection.

```
    public void close() throws JMSException
    {
        try
        {
            if(session != null)
            {
                checker.stop();
                session = session.close();
                conn.removeSession(this);
            }
        }
        catch(JMSException exp)
        {
            throw exp;
        }
        catch(Exception exp)
        {
            throw new JMSException("No remote connection.");
        }
    }
```

MiniSessions provide a number of methods for acknowledgment, included in the following code. Remember that a client acknowledges a destination, not a particular message. This means that all of the messages that have been received by this session for the specified destination will be acknowledged. The session actually provides a version of acknowledgment that uses a name. This name is normally the client ID, but it can be different if a durable subscriber is used with the TopicSession. Ultimately, requests to acknowledge are forwarded to the server.

```
public void acknowledge(Destination d) throws JMSException
{
    acknowledge(d,getClientID());
}

public void acknowledge(Destination d,String name)
                          throws JMSException
{
    try
    {
        session.acknowledge(d,name);
    }
    catch(JMSException exp)
    {
        throw exp;
    }
    catch(Exception exp)
    {
        throw new JMSException("No remote connection.");
    }
}
```

The session manages a MessageListener. If this listener is assigned, it will be the only object to receive messages for this session. This is an advanced part of the API and is not intended for use by normal clients.

```
public MessageListener getMessageListener() throws JMSException
{
    return listener;
}

public void setMessageListener(MessageListener lst)
                                 throws JMSException
{
    this.listener = lst;
}
```

The MiniSession also keeps track of all of its consumers' MessageListeners. These listeners are associated with a particular destination and, in the case of a durable topic subscriber, have a unique name. When a listener is assigned to a destination, it shares all of the messages for its session and the destination, based on its name. When a consumer is assigned a listener, it registers it with the consumer's session using addMessageListenerFor.

MiniSession keeps track of listeners in vectors that are stored in a hash table. The hash table relates destinations to listeners. The vector stores the listeners for the destination.

Due to the persistent nature of messaging with JMS, a listener may be "owed" messages that were sent before it was registered. The MiniSession tries to assign these messages immediately on registration. The messageForNoWait method is discussed below; basically, it tries to find message that are readily available and doesn't wait for contact with the server.

Synchronization is used to protect the hash table of listeners.

```
public void addMessageListenerFor(MessageListener lst
                                 ,Destination dest
                                 ,String name)
                                  throws JMSException
{
    Vector listeners;

    synchronized(listenerForDest)
    {
        listeners = (Vector) listenerForDest.get(dest);

        if(listeners == null)
        {
            listeners = new Vector();
            listenerForDest.put(dest,listeners);
        }

        listeners.addElement(lst);

        //update listener with outstanding messages
        Message msg;

        try
        {
            while((msg = messageForNoWait(dest,name))!=null)
            {
                lst.onMessage(msg);
            }
        }
        catch(Exception ignore)
        {
        }
    }
}
```

When a message listener is removed from a message consumer or the consumer is closed, the consumer object notifies the session of this change with removeMessageListenerFor. This method removes the listener from the listenerForDest hash table.

```
public void removeMessageListenerFor(MessageListener lst
                                     ,Destination dest)
                                      throws JMSException
{
    Vector listeners;

    if((dest == null)||(lst==null)) return;

    synchronized(listenerForDest)
    {
        listeners = (Vector) listenerForDest.get(dest);

        if(listeners != null)
        {
            listeners.removeElement(lst);
        }
    }
}
```

Consumers provide three methods for accessing messages. In MiniJMS, these messages are forwarded to the session. The first method, messageFor, takes a name and destination. It tries to find a message for that name and destination in a local store without going to the server. In fact, none of the messageFor methods accesses the server. Messages are received asynchronously from the server using RMI. As messages arrive at the client, they are stored in a hash table. MessageFor checks this hash table with the method getMessageFor. If no message is available, it waits for one using normal thread waiting. The thread that is adding messages to the messagesForDest hash table calls notifyAll to wake up any waiting threads and give them a shot at the messages.

Again, synchronization is used to protect the local message store.

```
public Message messageFor(Destination dest,String name)
    throws Exception
{
    Message msg=null;

    synchronized(messagesForDest)
    {
        while(msg == null)
        {
            try
            {
                msg = getMessageFor(dest,name);

                if(msg != null) break;

                messagesForDest.wait();
            }
            catch(Exception exp)
            {
```

```
                }
            }
        }

        return msg;
    }
```

The second version of messageFor also takes a time-out and does not wait beyond the time-out for a message. We actually broke the waiting into several stages to make sure that any accidental notifications will not cause the method to return. This method returns only when the actual time passed exceeds the time-out or a message is available.

```
    public Message messageFor(Destination dest,long timeout,String name)
        throws Exception
    {
        Message msg=null;
        long now,start;

        start = System.currentTimeMillis();

        synchronized(messagesForDest)
        {
            while(msg == null)
            {
                try
                {
                    msg = getMessageFor(dest,name);

                    if(msg != null) break;

                    messagesForDest.wait(timeout/10);
                }
                catch(Exception exp)
                {
                }

                now = System.currentTimeMillis();
                if((now-start)>timeout) break;
            }
        }

        return msg;
    }
```

The messageForNoWait method checks for a message and if none is available in the local store, returns null. This is a very quick check and doesn't wait on the server in any way.

```
    public Message messageForNoWait(Destination dest,String name)
        throws Exception
    {
```

```
        Message msg=null;

        synchronized(messagesForDest)
        {
            msg = getMessageFor(dest,name);
        }

        return msg;
    }
```

Internally, a MiniSession uses the method getMessageFor to get messages from the local store. This method assumes that the caller synchronized the MessageForDest hash table to protect it. Messages in the local store are organized into two hash tables. The first stores hash-table values based on destinations as keys. These hash-table values in turn store vectors of messages based on name keys. In the simple case in which point-to-point messaging is used, there will probably be only one name registered for a destination, so the second hash table stores only one item. This is overkill, but it makes the code support both messaging styles, without alteration.

If an appropriate message is available when getMessageFor is called, it is returned. The session also acknowledges the message if it is not in client acknowledgment mode.

```
    protected Message getMessageFor(Destination dest,String name)
        throws JMSException
    {
        Message msg=null;
        Vector messages=null;
        Hashtable msgsByName;

        try
        {
            if(name == null) name = getClientID();

            msgsByName = (Hashtable) messagesForDest.get(dest);

            if(msgsByName!=null)
               messages = (Vector) msgsByName.get(name);

            if((messages != null)&&(messages.size()>0))
            {
                msg = (Message) messages.elementAt(0);
                messages.removeElementAt(0);

                if(ackMode != Session.CLIENT_ACKNOWLEDGE)
                {
                    acknowledge(dest,name);
                }
            }
        }
        catch(Exception exp)
        {
```

```
            throw new JMSException(exp.toString());
        }

        return msg;
    }
```

At the heart of a client's MiniSession is the addMessage method. This method is called by the remote session using RMI. The addMessagemethod distributes messages using these steps.

First, if the session has a MessageListener, it receives all messages. Second, if a MessageListener is available for the message, it is notified. If multiple listeners are registered for the same destination and name, one is chosen randomly according to the JMS specification.

If no listeners are available, messages are stored in the messagesForDest hash table, making them available to clients using the receive methods. Note that a client can't register a listener with the name "joe" on the destination "tmp" and try to retrieve messages for the same destination with the same name using a receive message in the Consumer. These two models are mutually exclusive on a name-destinations basis. When the messagesForDest table is used, it is told to notify threads waiting on it after the new message is added.

The addMessage method synchronizes calls to message listeners, in the sense that they will receive the onMessage call only from a single thread. Like the getMessageFor method, addMessage automatically acknowledges messages, unless configured not to, when they are delivered.

```
    public void addMessage(Message msg)
        throws RemoteException
    {
        Destination dest;
        Vector messages;
        Vector listeners;
        MessageListener lst=null;
        Hashtable msgsByName;
        String name=null;

        if(msg != null)
        {
            try
            {
                lst = null;
                name = null;
                msgsByName = null;
                listeners = null;
                dest = null;
                messages = null;

                try
                {
                name =
                msg.getStringProperty(MiniJMSMessageStore.REG_NAME);
                }
```

```
catch(Exception e)
{
    name = null;
}

dest = msg.getJMSDestination();

if((dest != null)&&(listener==null))
{
    synchronized(listenerForDest)
    {
        listeners =
            (Vector) listenerForDest.get(dest);

        //Pick one at random.
        if((listeners != null)
             &&(listeners.size()>0))
        {
            int i;
            int size = listeners.size();

            if(size>1)
                i = Math.abs(rand.nextInt())
                    % listeners.size();
            else
                i = 0;

            lst = (MessageListener)
                listeners.elementAt(i);
        }
    }

    if(lst != null)
    {
        lst.onMessage(msg);

        if(ackMode != Session.CLIENT_ACKNOWLEDGE)
        {
            acknowledge(dest);
        }
    }
    else
    {
        synchronized(messagesForDest)
        {
            if(name == null) name = getClientID();

            msgsByName = (Hashtable)
                          messagesForDest.get(dest);

            if(msgsByName==null)
            {
```

```
                        msgsByName = new Hashtable();
                        messagesForDest.put(dest
                                            ,msgsByName);
                    }

                    messages = (Vector)
                            msgsByName.get(name);

                    if(messages == null)
                    {
                        messages = new Vector();
                        msgsByName.put(name,messages);
                    }

                    messages.addElement(msg);

                    messagesForDest.notifyAll();
                }
            }
        }
        else if(listener != null)
        {
            listener.onMessage(msg);

            if(ackMode != Session.CLIENT_ACKNOWLEDGE)
            {
                acknowledge(dest);
            }
        }
    }
    catch(Exception exp)
    {
    }
  }
}
```

The MiniSession provides access to the server for deleting temporary destinations. The same method, shown below, is used for temporary queues and topics.

```
public void deleteTemporary(MiniTempDestination q)
    throws JMSException
{
    try
    {
        session.deleteDestination(q.toString());
    }
    catch(Exception exp)
    {
        throw new JMSException(exp.toString());
    }
}
```

One of the design mechanisms behind MiniJMS is the concept of a client registering for messages on a particular destination with a particular name. The server code uses this registration to begin checking for messages on that destination and passes them on to the client. Registrations can be durable or transient. By default, QueueReceivers use durable registrations, as do durable TopicSubscribers. Normal TopicSubscribers are transient. The main difference between durable and transient is that the server will store up messages for a durable subscriber and will not for a transient subscriber.

A number of methods, defined in the following code, are provided to the MiniJMS client classes for registering with the session. All of these result in a call to the MiniRemoteSession.

```
public void registerFor(Destination dest)
    throws JMSException
{
    registerFor(dest,true,conn.getClientID());
}

public void registerFor(Destination dest,String name)
    throws JMSException
{
    registerFor(dest,true,name);
}

public void registerFor(Destination dest,boolean durable)
    throws JMSException
{
    registerFor(dest,durable,conn.getClientID());
}

public void registerFor(Destination dest
                        , boolean durable,String name)
    throws JMSException
{
    try
    {
        session.registerFor(dest,true,name);
    }
    catch(Exception exp)
    {
        throw new JMSException(exp.toString());
    }
}

public void unregisterFor(Destination dest)
    throws JMSException
{
    unregisterFor(dest,conn.getClientID());
}

public void unregisterFor(Destination dest,String name)
```

```
        throws JMSException
    {
        try
        {
            session.unregisterFor(dest,name);
        }
        catch(Exception exp)
        {
            throw new JMSException(exp.toString());
        }
    }
```

When a connection is told to stop and start, it sends suspend and resume to the sessions. Currently, these messages are ignored.

```
    public void suspend()
    {
    }

    public void resume()
    {
    }
}
```

MiniSession is the key element in the client implementation for MiniJMS. Make sure that you are comfortable with its implementation and purpose before continuing with the material in this chapter.

MiniConsumer

Rather than implement separate consumers for the two messaging models, MiniJMS implements a single consumer that supports both. MiniConsumer is a MessageConsumer, TopicSubscriber, and QueueReceiver. Because MiniDestinations are both queues and topics, the consumer can use a single destination object to represent its associated destination.

A MiniConsumer tracks its session, a MessageListener, its destination, selector, and registered name. This name is the same one used to register with the session and will default to the connection's ClientID. The Boolean variable noLocal is used by the consumer to remember if it should ignore messages from the connection that it is attached to; currently, MiniJMS ignores the value of this flag. The Boolean variable unregOnClose is used by the consumer to remember whether it is durable or not. If this value is true, the consumer will unregister with the server when it is closed.

NOTE **MiniJMS does not support selectors or the noLocal feature.**

```
package minijms;

//Imports removed to save space.
```

```
public class MiniConsumer
 implements MessageConsumer
 , TopicSubscriber, QueueReceiver
{
    protected MessageListener listener;
    protected MiniSession session;
    protected MiniDestination dest;
    protected String selector;
    protected boolean noLocal;
    protected boolean unregOnClose;
    protected String regName;

    public MiniConsumer(MiniSession session
                          ,MiniDestination dest)
    {
        this.session = session;
        this.dest = dest;
        noLocal = false;
        unregOnClose = false;
    }
```

When a MiniConsumer is closed, it notifies the session in two ways. First, if it is a non-durable consumer, it unregisters its destination. Second, by setting its MessageListener to null, MiniConsumer tells the session to remove the MessageListener from its list.

```
    public void close()
      throws JMSException
    {
        if(unregOnClose) session.unregisterFor(dest);
        setMessageListener(null);
    }
```

The following accessors are provided for the message selector, registered name, and MessageListener.

```
    public String getMessageSelector() throws JMSException
    {
        return selector;
    }

    public void setMessageSelector(String s)
     throws JMSException
    {
        selector = s;
    }

    public MessageListener getMessageListener()
     throws JMSException
    {
        return listener;
    }
```

```
public void setMessageListener(MessageListener lst)
    throws JMSException
{
    if(listener != null)
    {
        session.removeMessageListenerFor(listener,dest);
    }

    listener = lst;

    if(listener != null)
        session.addMessageListenerFor(listener,dest,regName);
}

public String getRegName()
{
    return regName;
}

public void setRegName(String name)
{
    regName = name;
}

protected void setNoLocal(boolean b)
{
    noLocal = b;
}

public boolean getNoLocal() throws JMSException
{
    return noLocal;
}
```

Consumers provide three methods for receiving messages directly, defined as follows. These methods call the equivalent methods in the MiniSession object.

```
public Message receive()
 throws JMSException
{
    Message retVal = null;

    try
    {
        retVal = session.messageFor(dest,regName);
    }
    catch(JMSException exp)
    {
        throw exp;
    }
    catch(Exception exp)
```

```
        {
            throw new JMSException("No remote connection.");
        }

        return retVal;
    }

    public Message receive(long timeOut)
     throws JMSException
    {
        Message retVal = null;

        try
        {
            retVal = session.messageFor(dest,timeOut,regName);
        }
        catch(Exception exp)
        {
            throw new JMSException("No remote connection.");
        }

        return retVal;
    }

    public Message receiveNoWait()
     throws JMSException
    {
        Message retVal = null;

        try
        {
            retVal = session.messageForNoWait(dest,regName);
        }
        catch(JMSException exp)
        {
            throw exp;
        }
        catch(Exception exp)
        {
            throw new JMSException("No remote connection.");
        }

        return retVal;
    }
```

TopicSubscribers and QueueReceivers both provide type-specific access to their destination. The MiniConsumer implements both methods, as shown here, and throws an exception if the wrong one is used.

```
    public Queue getQueue() throws JMSException
    {
```

```
        if(dest.isQueue()) return dest;
        else throw new JMSException();
    }

    public Topic getTopic() throws JMSException
    {
        if(!dest.isQueue()) return dest;
        else throw new JMSException();
    }

    public void setUnregisterOnClose(boolean tf)
    {
        unregOnClose=tf;
    }
}
```

As you can see, the consumer in MiniJMS is mainly a front for the session, providing the basic information required to specify the destination and name for requests.

MiniProducer

Like the MiniConsumer, the MiniProducer implements all three of the producer interfaces: MessageProducer, TopicPublisher, and QueueSender. The producer keeps a reference to its session for performing the actual message sending. Configuration parameters for a producer include the default delivery mode, default priority, and default timeToLive for messages. Flags are used to indicate whether a message ID and time stamp are required for each message sent.

The MiniProducer is associated with a destination and keeps track of this destination in an instance variable.

Creating a MiniProducer initializes the instance variables, for which accessor methods are provided. The following code provides a snapshot of the MiniProducer.java file and contains embedded discussions for the interesting features in the MiniProducer class.

```
package minijms;

//Imports removed to save space.

public class MiniProducer
 implements MessageProducer,TopicPublisher,QueueSender
{
    protected MiniSession session;
    protected boolean disableMsgId;
    protected boolean disableTimestamp;
    protected int mode; //default mode
    protected int priority; //default priority
    protected int time; //default timeToLive
    protected MiniDestination dest;

    public MiniProducer(MiniSession session
```

```
                          ,MiniDestination dest)
    {
        this.session = session;
        this.dest = dest;

        disableMsgId = false;
        disableTimestamp = false;

        //default mode is not a correct value
        mode = DeliveryMode.PERSISTENT;

        priority = 4;
        time = Message.DEFAULT_TIME_TO_LIVE;
    }

    public void setDisableMessageID(boolean value)
     throws JMSException
    {
        disableMsgId = value;
    }

    public boolean getDisableMessageID()
     throws JMSException
    {
        return disableMsgId;
    }

    public void setDisableMessageTimestamp(boolean value)
     throws JMSException
    {
        disableTimestamp = value;
    }

    public boolean getDisableMessageTimestamp()
     throws JMSException
    {
        return disableTimestamp;
    }

    public void setDeliveryMode(int deliveryMode)
     throws JMSException
    {
        mode = deliveryMode;
    }

    public int getDeliveryMode() throws JMSException
    {
        return mode;
    }

    public void setPriority(int p) throws JMSException
```

```
{
    priority = p;
}

public int getPriority() throws JMSException
{
    return priority;
}

public void setTimeToLive(int timeToLive) throws JMSException
{
    time = timeToLive;
}

public int getTimeToLive() throws JMSException
{
    return time;
}
```

Closing a MiniProducer doesn't do anything because it doesn't require any server resources.

```
public void close() throws JMSException
{
}
```

Like the MiniConsumer, a MiniProducer provides access to its destination as either a queue or topic, throwing an exception if the wrong method is used.

```
public Queue getQueue() throws JMSException
{
    if(dest.isQueue()) return dest;
    else throw new JMSException();
}

public Topic getTopic() throws JMSException
{
    if(!dest.isQueue()) return dest;
    else throw new JMSException();
}
```

QueueSender defines four methods for sending messages. MiniProducer implements all four but relies on a single method for the actual send. The first three methods listed here simply call the fourth method, using default values where appropriate.

```
public void send(Message message)
 throws JMSException
{
    if(message != null)
    {
        send(getQueue(), message, mode
```

```
                , priority, time);
        }
        else
        {
            throw new JMSException("Null Message.");
        }
    }

    public void send(Message message,
              int deliveryMode, int pri,
               long timeToLive) throws JMSException
    {
        if(message != null)
        {
            send(getQueue(),message, deliveryMode
                ,pri,timeToLive);
        }
        else
        {
            throw new JMSException("Null Message.");
        }
    }

    public void send(Queue queue, Message message)
     throws JMSException
    {
        if((message != null)&&(queue!=null))
        {
            send(queue, message, mode
                , priority, time);
        }
        else
        {
            throw new JMSException("Null Message.");
        }
    }
```

The final send method is the most versatile. This method configures the messages header, using the flags provided. If the message has a timeToLive, the expiration time is set to the current time plus this value. If time stamps are enabled, one is set; if message IDs are enabled, one is assigned. Once configured, the producers session is told to send the message.

```
    public void send(Queue queue, Message message,
              int deliveryMode, int pri,
               long timeToLive) throws JMSException
    {
        long now = System.currentTimeMillis();

        if((message != null)&&(queue!=null))
        {
```

```
            if(session == null)
                throw new JMSException("No Session");

            message.setJMSDestination(queue);
            message.setJMSPriority(pri);
            message.setJMSDeliveryMode(deliveryMode);

            if(timeToLive <= 0)
                message.setJMSExpiration(0);
            else
                message.setJMSExpiration(now + timeToLive);

            if(!disableTimestamp)
            {
                message.setJMSMessageID(createId());
            }

            if(!disableTimestamp)
            {
                message.setJMSTimestamp(now);
            }

            session.send(message);
        }
        else
        {
            throw new JMSException("Null Message.");
        }
    }
```

TopicPublishers also provide a number of methods for sending messages to a topic. Again, these methods, listed below, are implemented in terms of the most generic form.

```
    public void publish(Message message)
     throws JMSException
    {
        if(message != null)
        {
            publish(getTopic(), message, mode
                , priority, time);
        }
        else
        {
            throw new JMSException("Null Message.");
        }
    }

    public void publish(Message message,
                int deliveryMode, int pri,
                 long timeToLive) throws JMSException
    {
```

```
        if(message != null)
        {
            publish(getTopic(),message, deliveryMode
                ,pri,timeToLive);
        }
        else
        {
            throw new JMSException("Null Message.");
        }
    }

    public void publish(Topic topic, Message message)
     throws JMSException
    {
        if((message != null)&&(topic!=null))
        {
            publish(topic, message, mode
                , priority, time);
        }
        else
        {
            throw new JMSException("Null Message.");
        }
    }
```

The final publish method is the most versatile. This method configures the messages header, using the flags provided. If the message has a timeToLive, the expiration time is set to the current time plus this value. If time stamps are enabled, one is set; if message IDs are enabled, one is assigned. Once configured, the producers session is told to send the message.

```
    public void publish(Topic topic, Message message,
              int deliveryMode, int pri,
               long timeToLive) throws JMSException
    {
        long now = System.currentTimeMillis();

        if((message != null)&&(topic!=null))
        {
            if(session == null)
                throw new JMSException("No Session");

            message.setJMSDestination(topic);
            message.setJMSPriority(pri);
            message.setJMSDeliveryMode(deliveryMode);

            if(timeToLive <= 0)
                message.setJMSExpiration(0);
            else
                message.setJMSExpiration(now + timeToLive);
```

```
                if(!disableTimestamp)
                {
                    message.setJMSMessageID(createId());
                }

                if(!disableTimestamp)
                {
                    message.setJMSTimestamp(now);
                }

                session.send(message);
            }
            else
            {
                throw new JMSException("Null Message.");
            }
        }
```

If message IDs are enabled, they are created using the client's IP address, the current time, and the client ID. This should ensure uniqueness across all clients in the system. In the worst case, a random number is used. Because JMS specifies that all Message IDs start with "ID:," that convention is used in the definition of createID as listed here.

```
        protected String createId()
        {
            String retVal;
            try
            {
                InetAddress here = InetAddress.getLocalHost();

                retVal = "ID:"+System.currentTimeMillis()
                                +here.getHostAddress()
                                +session.getClientID();
            }
            catch(Exception exp)
            {
                retVal =  "ID:"+System.currentTimeMillis()+Math.random();
            }
            return retVal;
        }
    }
```

That concludes the generic client classes for MiniJMS. Subclasses of MiniConnectionFactory, MiniConnection, and MiniSession are provided for the two messaging models defined in JMS.

In order to support point-to-point messaging, MiniJMS implements three classes. MiniQueueConnectionFactory extends MiniConnectionFactory and defines a QueueConnectionFactory. MiniQueueConnection extends MiniConnection and implements QueueConnection. MiniQueueSession extends MiniSession and implements QueueSession.

In order to support publish-subscribe messaging, MiniJMS implements three different classes. MiniTopicConnectionFactory extends MiniConnectionFactory and defines a TopicConnectionFactory. MiniTopicConnection extends MiniConnection and implements TopicConnection. MiniTopicSession extends MiniSession and implements TopicSession.

Rather than include the code for these specific classes here, we refer you to the CD-ROM. Basically, all of the model-specific classes are used to create other model-specific classes. Ultimately, the session classes create MessageConsumers and MessageProducers configured appropriately for their messaging model.

NOTE **MiniJMS does not support QueueBrowsers, so the MiniQueueSession will throw exceptions if they are requested.**

MiniJMS—and JMS in general—relies heavily on JNDI for establishing the relationship between the client and server. The next section discusses how MiniJMS supports JNDI.

JNDI Support

The JMS specification refers to destinations and ConnectionFactories as administered objects. In other words, they are objects that are bound to a JNDI context for access by a client. In general, clients do not create queues and topics. Instead, they look them up. The same is true for ConnectionFactories. This makes the JMS client able to change JMS providers without changing code, because the connection factory acts as the root for all of the other objects created.

Both the MiniQueueConnectionFactory and MiniTopicConnectionFactory classes implement Serializable and Referenceable to allow them to be bound into a JNDI context. MiniDestination, as you have seen, also implements this interface. Because the implementation for all of these classes is very similar, only one, MiniDestination, is shown here. The other examples are provided on the CD-ROM.

First the MiniDestination class states that it implements Referenceable. Next it implements the getReference method. The MiniJMS implementation creates a StringRefAddr that takes the name of the destination. Another reference is used for the isQueue value of the MiniDestination object. A custom ObjectFactory called MiniDestinationFactory is provided to perform the actual creation of objects removed from the context.

```
public Reference getReference()
                        throws NamingException
    {
        Reference retVal;

        retVal = new Reference(MiniDestination.class.getName()
         ,new StringRefAddr("name",name)
         ,MiniDestinationFactory.class.getName()
         ,null);

        retVal.add(new StringRefAddr("isQueue"
```

```
                                        ,(isQ?"true":"false")));

        return retVal;
    }
```

When a MiniDestination is bound into JNDI, it is asked for this reference. The JNDI provider stores the reference, including the to string addresses.

When a client looks up the destination, a MiniDestinationFactory is created and is asked to create the object that is being requested from the available information. The method getObjectInstance, defined in the javax.naming.spi.ObjectFactory interface, is called on the object factory to ask it to create the new object. This method is provided information about the object, such as the name it is bound under, the context, the context's environment, and an arbitrary informational object. This informational object for MiniDestinationFactory contains the reference created by the destination before it was bound.

MiniDestinationFactory uses the reference to recreate the MiniDestination and return it.

```
package minijms;

//Imports removed to save space.

public class MiniDestinationFactory
 implements ObjectFactory
{

    public Object getObjectInstance(
                  Object info,
                  Name name,
                  Context nameCtx,
                  Hashtable environment)
                  throws Exception
    {
        MiniDestination retVal = null;

        if(info instanceof Reference)
        {
            Reference ref = (Reference) info;
            RefAddr nameA;
            RefAddr isQA;
            String destName,isQ;
            boolean isQueue;

            nameA = ref.get("name");
            isQA = ref.get("isQueue");

            if((nameA != null)&&(isQA != null))
            {
                destName = (String) nameA.getContent();
                isQ = (String) isQA.getContent();
```

```
                isQueue = Boolean.valueOf(isQ).booleanValue();
                retVal = new MiniDestination(destName,isQueue);
            }
        }

        return retVal;
    }

}
```

To consolidate the creation of the initial JNDI context in MiniJMS clients and make it easy to configure, the provided examples do two things. First, they use properties files to define their context information. Second, a class called MiniJMSUtils is created that creates a context from a properties file. MiniJMSUtils installs the RMI security manager and updates the RMI classpath, saving the example that step in the code. Currently, the RMI class path is set to the current directory, but this could be configured in the properties file as well. Applets will not be able to change this system property, but they do not need to, so the exception thrown by the setProperties method is caught and ignored.

The properties file that configures the MiniJMSUtils JNDI connection contains two entries for the example code. These entries configure the initial factory to the File-SystemContext service provider and set the root directory for the context. In fact, the reference-supporting version of the file system context factory is used to support the binding of destinations and connection factories.

```
java.naming.factory.initial
        =com.sun.jndi.fscontext.RefFSContextFactory
java.naming.provider.url=file:///temp/jndistore
```

The code for MiniJMSUtils, which follows, is basically a recipe for loading a properties file, reading it, and using the properties to create an initial context for JNDI lookups. The properties file is specified by a file name. The file must be in the class path to be found.

```
package minijms;

import minijms.*;
import minijmsserver.*;
import javax.jms.*;
import javax.naming.*;
import java.io.*;
import java.rmi.*;
import java.util.*;

public class MiniJMSUtils
{
    public static Properties properties;
    public static Context context;

    public static void init(String propsFile)
```

```
        throws Exception
    {
        // Create and install a security manager
        SecurityManager mng;
        InputStream propsIn;
        Properties sysProps;

        mng = new RMISecurityManager();
        System.setSecurityManager(mng);

        //Update the system props for class loading;
        //fails for an applet but that's okay.
        try
        {
            sysProps = System.getProperties();
            sysProps.put("java.rmi.server.codebase"
                    ,"file:/"
                    + sysProps.getProperty("user.dir")
                    +"/");
            System.setProperties(sysProps);
        }
        catch(Exception ignore)
        {
        }

        //Load the properties file.
        propsIn
         = ClassLoader.getSystemResourceAsStream(propsFile);
        properties = new Properties();
        properties.load(propsIn);Properties p = new Properties();

        String user=properties.getProperty("java.naming.user");
        String password
               =properties.getProperty("java.naming.password");
        InitialContext retVal = null;

        p.put(Context.INITIAL_CONTEXT_FACTORY,
            properties.getProperty("java.naming.factory.initial"));

        p.put(Context.PROVIDER_URL
            , properties.getProperty("java.naming.provider.url"));

        if (user != null)
        {
            p.put(Context.SECURITY_PRINCIPAL, user);

            if (password == null) password = "";

            p.put(Context.SECURITY_CREDENTIALS, password);
        }
```

```
            context = new InitialContext(p);
        }
    }
```

The properties and context static variables are public and provide easy access to a program. The following examples all initialize the MiniJMSUtils class and use its variables to get to the JNDI context. This context is then used to access destinations or connection factories by name. Although this utility is included in the minijms package, it doesn't rely on any minijms code beyond the import statements, so you could use it with other JMS providers or JNDI providers.

This concludes the discussion on the MiniJMS client library. The server is discussed next, including code for accessing a database with JDBC, binding JNDI objects, adding the object factories discussed here to the JNDI context, and implementing the remote interfaces discussed in preceding sections.

The Server

The MiniJMS server provides a number of services. It implements the remote interfaces, supporting persistent messaging organized into queues and topics. It also registers the necessary objects in a JNDI context for use by the client. Finally, it maintains a database of messages for durable, nonaccessible clients.

The Message Store

At the heart of the server is the MiniJMSMessageStore class. This object defines the storage scheme for messages in the MiniJMS system. Messages that are marked as persistent are maintained in a database using JDBC. Actually, messages are stored on disk, and their paths are stored in the database. This separation is provided for JBDC drivers that do not correctly support binary data. All messages are held in memory for the destinations to which they will be delivered. However, if no running sessions have registered an interest in a message, it is not stored in memory, meaning that non-persistent messages in which no client is interested are ignored.

The schema for the MiniJMSMessageStore's database contains three tables. These tables and their columns are listed in Tables 26.4 through 26.6. The messages table, shown in Table 26.4, stores information about the persistent messages that are sent, including their destinations and a reference to their locations on disk. This reference is relative to a root directory configured in the server's properties file. The destinations table, shown in Table 26.5, contains the available destinations. The ack table, shown in Table 26.6, is keeps track of the last acknowledged message for a particular client and a particular destination.

The message store has some of the same features in the client code as the MiniSession. It organizes the registered listeners and messages into hash tables for distribution. The actual distribution is handled by the session's remote counterpart, which will be discussed in a moment. As well as storing messages, the message store is responsible for initializing the JNDI context with the available destinations. These destinations are stored in the store's database.

Table 26.4 Messages Table

COLUMN	DESCRIPTION
MSG_NUM	The message's unique number, assigned by the message store.
MSG_ID	The message's unique identifier.
DESTINATION	The name of the destination to which the message was sent.
CONTENT	The name of the file containing the serialized version of the message.

Table 26.5 Destinations Table

COLUMN	DESCRIPTION
NAME	The destination's name.
ISQUEUE	Either "true" or "false," indicating whether the destination is a queue. If it is not, it is a topic.

Table 26.6 Ack Table

COLUMN	DESCRIPTION
MSG_NUM	The number for the last message acknowledged.
DESTINATION	The destination to which this entry corresponds.
NAME	The name with which the consumer registered.

The MiniJMSMessageStore's instance variables hold the current messages, the context and properties files used to configure the store, a connection to a database, a statement for that connection, the directory name for the directory that stores the serialized messages, and a counter used to determine the unique numbers for messages. There are also static variables that define the names for two MiniJMS-defined message properties. These properties, JMS_MSG_NUM and JMS_REG_NAME, store the message number and registered name associated with a message. The message number is used in the database; the registered name associates a message with a particular MiniConsumer on the client.

The code for MiniJMSMessageStore follows, with embedded discussions that highlight the major features of the class.

```
package minijmsserver;

//Imports removed to save space.

public class MiniJMSMessageStore
{
    protected Hashtable destinations;
```

```
protected Hashtable messages;
protected Properties props;
protected java.sql.Connection conn;
protected java.sql.Statement statement;
protected Context context;
protected String objDir;
protected long curId;

public final static String MSG_NUM="JMS_MSG_NUM";
public final static String REG_NAME="JMS_REG_NAME";
```

The constructor for MiniJMSMessage store is a great example of how multiple technologies can be combined. Configuration information is stored in a properties file. This information is used to create a JNDI context. A JDBC database connection is created using the same properties file, and the contents of the DESTINATION table from the database are used to load MiniDestination objects into the JNDI context. The constructor even registers the MiniDestinationFactory with the JNDI context so that the destinations can be bound appropriately and autonomously. In just 30 or so lines of code properties, JNDI and JDBC are combined to create a unified whole.

The JMS specification says that a JMS provider should provide tools for administrating queues and topics. Although no specific tools are provided by JNDI, they can easily be created using the RemoteMiniSession interface or by simply inserting destinations into the message store's database and restarting the server.

The objDir variable initialized in the constructor, as defined here, refers to the directory that contains the serialized message objects referenced in the database.

```
public MiniJMSMessageStore(String propsFile)
    throws JMSException
{
    String url = null;
    String user=null;
    String password=null;
    String driver=null;
    java.sql.ResultSet rs;
    boolean isQ;
    String name;
    MiniDestination dest;

    curId = System.currentTimeMillis();

    destinations = new Hashtable();
    messages = new Hashtable();

    try
    {
        MiniJMSUtils.init(propsFile);
        context = MiniJMSUtils.context;
        props = MiniJMSUtils.properties;

        context.addToEnvironment(Context.OBJECT_FACTORIES,
```

```
                            "minijms.MiniDestinationFactory");


        url = props.getProperty("db_url");
        user = props.getProperty("db_user");
        password = props.getProperty("db_password");
        driver = props.getProperty("db_driver");
        objDir = props.getProperty("object_directory");

        if((context == null)
            ||(url == null)||(driver == null)
            ||(objDir==null))
        {
            throw
            new JMSException("Unable to connect to store.");
        }

        File dir = new File(objDir);
        if(!dir.exists()) dir.mkdirs();

        Class.forName(driver);

        conn = DriverManager.getConnection(url,user,password);
        conn.setAutoCommit(false);

        statement = conn.createStatement();

        rs =
        statement.executeQuery("select * from destinations");

        while(rs.next())
        {
            name = rs.getString("name");
            isQ =
        Boolean.valueOf(rs.getString("isqueue")).booleanValue();

            dest = new MiniDestination(name,isQ);

            Vector sessions = new Vector();

            destinations.put(name,sessions);
            context.rebind(name,dest);
        }

        rs.close();
    }
    catch(JMSException ex)
    {
        throw ex;
    }
    catch(Exception exp)
    {
```

```
            throw new JMSException(exp.toString());
        }
    }
```

Closing the message store frees up its JNDI context and JDBC connection. To ensure that close is called, the finalize method is implemented to call it.

```
    public void close()
    {
        try
        {
            context.close();
            statement.close();
            conn.close();
        }
        catch(Exception exp)
        {
        }
    }

    public Context getJNDIContext()
    {
        return context;
    }

    public void finalize()
    {
        close();
    }
```

The nextId method returns the next message number based on the order it is called and the creation time of the message store, as initialized in the constructor.

```
    protected long nextId()
    {
        return curId++;
    }
```

The message store is ultimately responsible for creating queues and topics. Before a destination can be created, the store checks that it does not already exist. Trying to create a queue or topic that already exists produces an exception. If the destination is created successfully, its information is inserted into the database, making it persistent. The new destination is bound into the JNDI context for access by other MiniJMS clients. The store also initializes a vector to store any registered sessions listening to the new destination and stores it in the destination's hash table.

```
    public Queue createQueue(String queueName)
     throws JMSException
    {
        Queue retVal;
```

```
        synchronized(destinations)
        {
            Object test = null;

            if(queueName!= null)
                test = destinations.get(queueName);

            if(test==null)
            {
                Vector sessions = new Vector();

                destinations.put(queueName,sessions);

                try
                {
                    statement.executeUpdate("insert into "
                                            +"destinations "
                                            +"values(\'"
                                            +queueName
                                            +"\',\'true\')");

                    retVal = new MiniDestination(queueName,true);

                    context.rebind(queueName,retVal);

                    conn.commit();
                }
                catch(Exception exp)
                {
                    try
                    {
                        conn.rollback();
                    }
                    catch(Exception ignore)
                    {
                    }

                    throw new JMSException(exp.toString());
                }
            }
            else
            {
                throw new JMSException(queueName+" exists.");
            }
        }

        return retVal;
    }

    public Topic createTopic(String topicName)
     throws JMSException
```

```
    {
        Topic retVal;

        synchronized(destinations)
        {
            Object test = destinations.get(topicName);

            if(test==null)
            {
                Vector sessions = new Vector();

                destinations.put(topicName,sessions);

                try
                {
                    statement.executeUpdate("insert into "
                                        +"destinations "
                                        +"values(\'"
                                        +topicName
                                        +"\',\'false\')");

                    retVal = new MiniDestination(topicName,false);

                    context.rebind(topicName,retVal);

                    conn.commit();
                }
                catch(Exception exp)
                {
                    try
                    {
                        conn.rollback();
                    }
                    catch(Exception ignore)
                    {
                    }
                    throw new JMSException(exp.toString());
                }
            }
            else
            {
                throw new JMSException(topicName+" exists.");
            }
        }

        return retVal;
    }
```

Deleting a destination using the deleteDestination method listed below is trickier than creating one. First, the destination must exist. Next, all of the messages for the destination must be removed from the database. In the process, all of the serialized messages referenced in the database must be removed. Then the entry in the DESTINATION table of the database is removed, and finally all of the acknowledgment records related to the destination are removed before the destination is removed from the destination's hash table.

```
public void deleteDestination(String destName)
 throws JMSException
{
    synchronized(destinations)
    {
        Object test = destinations.get(destName);
        ResultSet rs;
        File file;
        String content;

        if(test!=null)
        {
            try
            {
                //Delete messages from disk.
                rs = statement.executeQuery("select * from "
                                        +"messages "
                                        +"where destination=\'"
                                        +destName
                                        +"\'");

                while(rs.next())
                {
                    content = rs.getString("content");

                    file = new File(objDir,content);

                    if(file.exists()) file.delete();
                }

                rs.close();

                //Delete destination.
                statement.executeUpdate("delete from "
                                    +"destinations "
                                    +"where name=\'"
                                    +destName
                                    +"\'");

                //Delete acknowledgements.
                statement.executeUpdate("delete from "
                                    +"ack "
                                    +"where DESTINATION=\'"
                                    +destName
                                    +"\'");
```

```
                    //Delete all messages.
                    statement.executeUpdate("delete from "
                                +"messages "
                                +"where destination=\'"
                                + destName
                                +"\'");

                    conn.commit();
                }
                catch(Exception exp)
                {
                    try
                    {
                        conn.rollback();
                    }
                    catch(Exception ignore)
                    {
                    }
                    throw new JMSException(exp.toString());
                }

                destinations.remove(destName);
            }
        }
    }
```

A request for a message by a session results in a call to nextMessageFor in the message store on the server. This method checks for messages based on the ClientID or name used by the session. If a message has been cached for that id, it is tested to see if it has expired. If there is an unexpired message, it is returned. Otherwise, if there are messages but the current one has expired, null is returned. In case no messages are currently being held for an id, this method calls wait, pausing the requesting thread until it is notified of a message. The nextMessageFor method, listed here, is called by the RemoteMiniSession in a thread that loops checking for messages. In the case of an expired message, the loop calls this method again immediately after the null return value. Only when no messages are waiting delivery will the wait method be called, pausing the sessions polling thread.

```
    //Returns null if no message to get.
    public Message nextMessageFor(String id)
        throws JMSException
    {
        Vector msgs;
        Message retVal = null;
        long now,expires;

        msgs = (Vector) messages.get(id);

        if(msgs != null)
        {
```

```
            synchronized(msgs)
            {
                now = System.currentTimeMillis();

                if(msgs.size()>0)
                {
                    retVal = (Message) msgs.elementAt(0);
                    msgs.removeElementAt(0);

                    expires = retVal.getJMSExpiration();

                    if((expires > 0)&&(expires<now))
                    {
                        retVal = null;
                    }
                }
                else
                {
                    try
                    {
                        msgs.wait();
                    }
                    catch(Exception ignore)
                    {
                    }
                }
            }
        }

        return retVal;
    }
```

When the store is told to send a message, it does a number of things. The messages destination name is retrieved. Then the destinations hash table is queried for any sessions registered for the destination. The message is assigned a message number. If the message is persistent, it is saved to disk and a record indicating its location is stored in the databases MESSAGES table. Finally, if any sessions are registered listeners for the message's destination, a copy of the message is added to their vector of waiting messages. For durable subscriptions and queue receivers, these messages may be stored, even if the client is not running.

The session registration is stored in a RegPair object that includes the client id and the name of the registration/subscription. Messages delivered to a sessions queue are tagged with the registered name in case multiple subscriptions are using the same session. The complete code for send is listed here:

```
    public void send(Message message)
                throws JMSException
    {
        try
        {
```

```
String qname
    = message.getJMSDestination().toString();
Vector sessions
    = (Vector) destinations.get(qname);
int i,max;
RegPair pair;
String msgId=null;
long msgNum = nextId();
String content;
String insert;
Message toSend;

try
{
    msgId = message.getJMSMessageID();
}
catch(Exception e)
{
    msgId = "";
}

//Update the message table first.
try
{
    message.setLongProperty(MSG_NUM,msgNum);


    if(message.getJMSDeliveryMode()
        ==DeliveryMode.PERSISTENT)
    {
        content = messageToFile(message,msgNum);

        if(content == null)
            throw new JMSException("Null Content");

        insert = "insert into "
                    +"messages "
                    +"values("
                    +msgNum
                    +",\'"
                    +msgId
                    +"\',\'"
                    + qname
                    +"\',\'"
                    + content
                    +"\')";

        statement.executeUpdate(insert);
    }
}
catch(Exception exp)
```

```
        {
            throw new JMSException(exp.toString());
        }

        if(sessions == null)
        {
            conn.commit();
            return;
        }

        synchronized(sessions)
        {
            max = sessions.size();

            for(i=0;i<max;i++)
            {
                pair = (RegPair) sessions.elementAt(i);

                Vector msgs = (Vector) messages.get(pair.id);

                if(msgs == null)
                {
                    msgs = new Vector();
                    messages.put(pair.id,messages);
                }

                synchronized(msgs)
                {
                    toSend = copyMessage(message);
                    toSend.setStringProperty(REG_NAME
                                            ,pair.name);

                    msgs.addElement(toSend);
                    msgs.notifyAll();
                }
            }
        }

        conn.commit();
    }
    catch(Exception exp)
    {
        try
        {
            conn.rollback();
        }
        catch(Exception ignore)
        {
        }
        exp.printStackTrace();
```

```
            throw new JMSException(exp.toString());
        }
    }
```

Sessions acknowledge destinations by name and id using the acknowledge method shown here. This acknowledgment results in an entry in the ack table of the database. The previous entry is deleted before the new one is added.

```
    public void acknowledge(Destination d,String id, long msgNum)
        throws JMSException
    {
        //Update the message table first.
        try
        {
            String qname
                = d.toString();

            statement.executeUpdate("delete from "
                                    +"ack "
                                    +"where destination=\'"
                                    + qname
                                    +"\' and name=\'"
                                    + id
                                    +"\'");

            statement.executeUpdate("insert into "
                                    +"ack "
                                    +"values(\'"
                                    + msgNum
                                    +"\',\'"
                                    + qname
                                    +"\',\'"
                                    + id
                                    +"\')");
            conn.commit();
        }
        catch(Exception exp)
        {
            try
            {
                conn.rollback();
            }
            catch(Exception ignore)
            {
            }
            throw new JMSException(exp.toString());
        }
    }
```

Sessions rely heavily on the concept of registration to tell the message store that they are running and want to receive messages. Registration is performed by name and client ID on a destination-by-destination basis. When a session makes a registration, it is added to the list of sessions for that destination using the ID and name. A vector is also created for the client ID if one does not already exist. This vector shares all of the pending messages for a session regardless of the name used to register for them.

Registrations are stored using RegPair objects. These objects hold an id and name. RegPair implements hashCode and equals to ensure that two pairs with the same name and id are equal. As always, thread synchronization is used to protect the shared sessions' vector for a destination.

The registerFor method, included here, also performs another key task related to JMS messaging. If the client registering for messages is doing so from a persistent queue, that client is sent all of the messages from the queue after the client's last acknowledgment. The same is true for durable topic subscribers. However, queue receivers that have never acknowledged messages receive all of the previous messages, while a durable subscriber does not receive any messages sent before its initial registration. Once registered, both receive messages sent while they are disconnected from the server when they reconnect and register for them.

Non-durable subscribers and new subscribers have a new entry placed in the ack table on registration so that if a durable subscriber reconnects it gets missed messages.

```
public void registerFor(Destination dest
                        ,String id
                        ,String name)
    throws JMSException
{
    String qname = dest.toString();
    Vector sessions
        = (Vector) destinations.get(qname);
    RegPair pair = new RegPair();

    pair.id = id;
    pair.name = name;

    if(sessions==null)
    {
        sessions = new Vector();

        destinations.put(qname,sessions);
    }

    synchronized(sessions)
    {
        if(! sessions.contains(pair))
        {
            sessions.addElement(pair);
        }
    }

    Vector msgs = (Vector) messages.get(pair.id);
```

```
if(msgs == null)
{
    msgs = new Vector();
    messages.put(pair.id,msgs);
}

try
{
    ResultSet rs;
    long maxAck=-1;

    rs = statement.executeQuery("select * from "
                                +"ack"
                                +" where destination=\'"
                                +qname
                                +"\' and name=\'"
                                +name
                                +"\'");

    if(rs.next())
    {
        maxAck = rs.getLong("msg_num");
    }
    else
    {
        if(dest instanceof MiniDestination)
        {
            if(((MiniDestination)dest).isQueue())
            {
                maxAck = 0;
            }
        }
        else if(dest instanceof Queue)
        {
            maxAck = 0;
        }
        else
        {
            maxAck = -1;
        }
    }

    rs.close();

    //Don't back-fill totally new subscribers.
    //Do back-fill queue receivers.
    if(maxAck>=0)
    {
        String content;
        Message msg;
        int i,max;
```

```
                long msgNum;

                //And get missed messages.
                rs = statement.executeQuery("select * from "
                                        +"messages "
                                        +"where destination=\'"
                                        +qname
                                        +"\' and msg_num>"
                                        +maxAck
                                        +" order by msg_num asc");

                while(rs.next())
                {
                    content = rs.getString("content");
                    msgNum = rs.getLong("msg_num");

                    msg = messageFromFile(content);

                    if(msg != null)
                    {
                        if(!msg.propertyExists(MSG_NUM))
                            msg.setLongProperty(MSG_NUM,msgNum);

                        //Make sure the message isn't already
                        //waiting for delivery.
                        if(!msgs.contains(msg))
                            msgs.addElement(msg);
                    }
                }

                rs.close();
            }
            else
            {
                //Get this client in the list.
                acknowledge(dest,name,curId-1);
            }

            conn.commit();
        }
        catch(Exception exp)
        {
            exp.printStackTrace();

            try
            {
                conn.rollback();
            }
            catch(Exception e)
            {
            }
```

```
        }
    }
```

When a session unregisters for a destination, using the unregisterFor method shown here it is saying that it doesn't plan to retrieve messages for that destination any more. This results in the session being removed from the destination's list of registered sessions and removes the clients acknowledgment entry from the ack database table. If the client reregisters, it will be treated as a new registration, as discussed previously.

```
    public void unregisterFor(Destination dest
                              ,String id
                              ,String name)
                             throws JMSException
    {
        String qname = dest.toString();
        Vector sessions
            = (Vector) destinations.get(qname);
        RegPair pair;

        if(sessions!=null)
        {
            pair = new RegPair();
            pair.id = id;
            pair.name = name;

            sessions.removeElement(pair);

            try
            {
                statement.executeUpdate("delete from "
                                    +"ACK "
                                    +"where destination=\'"
                                    + qname
                                    +"\' and name=\'"
                                    + name
                                    +"\'");
                conn.commit();
            }
            catch(Exception exp)
            {
                try
                {
                    conn.rollback();
                }
                catch(Exception ignore)
                {
                }
                throw new JMSException(exp.toString());
            }
        }
        else
```

```
        {
            throw new JMSException("Not registered.");
        }
    }
```

The message store implements three internal methods for managing messages. The first method saves a message to disk. The second loads a message from disk. Both expect the message to be stored in the objDir, with a name equal to their message number followed by ".ser." For example, message number 1 is in 1.ser under the objDir directory. The final method copies a message by serializing it in memory and then unserializing a copy. Copying is used to ensure that the messages in memory for each session, id, and name are not shared and can have their header fields or properties manipulated as needed.

```
    protected String messageToFile(Message m,long msgNum)
    {
        String retVal = null;
        FileOutputStream fileOut;
        BufferedOutputStream bufOut;
        ObjectOutputStream objOut;
        File file;
        String fileName;

        if(m==null) return retVal;

        try
        {
            fileName = msgNum+".ser";
            file = new File(objDir,fileName);
            fileOut = new FileOutputStream(file);
            bufOut = new BufferedOutputStream(fileOut);
            objOut = new ObjectOutputStream(bufOut);

            objOut.writeObject(m);

            objOut.close();

            retVal = fileName;
        }
        catch(Exception exp)
        {
            exp.printStackTrace();
            retVal = null;
        }

        return retVal;
    }

    protected Message messageFromFile(String s)
    {
```

```
        Message retVal = null;
        FileInputStream fileIn;
        BufferedInputStream bufIn;
        ObjectInputStream objIn;
        File file;

        if(s==null) return retVal;

        try
        {
            file = new File(objDir,s);

            if(!file.exists())
                file = new File(s);

            fileIn = new FileInputStream(file);
            bufIn = new BufferedInputStream(fileIn);
            objIn = new ObjectInputStream(bufIn);

            retVal = (Message) objIn.readObject();

            objIn.close();
        }
        catch(Exception exp)
        {
            retVal = null;
        }

        return retVal;
    }

    protected Message copyMessage(Message m)
    {
        Message retVal = m;
        ByteArrayOutputStream byteOut;
        BufferedOutputStream bufOut;
        ObjectOutputStream objOut;
        ByteArrayInputStream byteIn;
        BufferedInputStream bufIn;
        ObjectInputStream objIn;

        try
        {
            byteOut = new ByteArrayOutputStream();
            bufOut = new BufferedOutputStream(byteOut);
            objOut = new ObjectOutputStream(bufOut);

            objOut.writeObject(m);

            objOut.close();
```

```
                byteIn =
                  new ByteArrayInputStream(byteOut.toByteArray());
                bufIn = new BufferedInputStream(byteIn);
                objIn = new ObjectInputStream(bufIn);

                retVal = (Message) objIn.readObject();

                objIn.close();
            }
            catch(Exception exp)
            {
                retVal = m;
            }

            return retVal;
        }
    }
```

As you can see, the message store represents a lot of code and ties together several enterprise frameworks. By changing the store implementation, MiniJMS can alter its persistence mechanism or support other JMS specifications and versions.

The Remote Server Objects

The object that the client initially connects to using RMI is an instance of MiniJMSServerImp, which implements the RemoteMiniServer interface. This object is used to create objects that implement the RemoteMiniConnection interface. These connections are implemented in the class RemoteMiniConnectionImp. Both classes extend the UnicastRemoteObject interface and are provided on the CD-ROM. The only non-obvious aspect of either object is that the remote connection keeps track of the sessions it creates and closes them when it closes, in the same way as the MiniConnection object does.

The RemoteMiniSession implementation, called RemoteMiniSessionImp, is far more complex than the server or connection and requires some in-depth discussion. The code for RemoteMiniSessionImp is included here, with discussions inserted as needed to clarify various techniques and concepts.

This remote session uses a vector called toSend to store messages that it has been told to send but hasn't sent. This vector is used when the session is running in transacted mode. As messages are sent to the client, they are stored in vectors contained in the histories hash table. These histories are used to implement rollback and recover.

Temporary destinations need to be cleaned up when a session closes, so they are stored in a vector called unregOnClose. The session also keeps a flag indicating whether it is transacted, a reference to the message store, its client ID, and a reference to the thread that it uses to poll for new messages in the store.

The constructor for RemoteMiniSessionImp initializes all of these variables, including the thread. However, the thread is initially suspended because no destinations have been registered for. When a destination is registered, the thread begins polling for messages.

```
package minijmsserver;

//Imports removed to save space.

public class RemoteMiniSessionImp
 extends UnicastRemoteObject
 implements RemoteMiniSession, Runnable, Unreferenced
{
    protected Vector toSend;
    protected Vector unregOnClose;
    protected Hashtable histories;
    protected boolean transacted;
    protected MiniJMSMessageStore store;
    protected Thread checker;
    protected String clientId;
    protected MiniClientSession client;

    public RemoteMiniSessionImp(MiniJMSMessageStore s, String id)
        throws RemoteException
    {
        store = s;
        clientId = id;
        unregOnClose = new Vector();
        toSend = new Vector();
        histories = new Hashtable();
        checker = new Thread(this);
        checker.start();
        checker.suspend();
    }
```

The setClient method is used by the MiniSession to tell its remote session to whom to send messages. Shown here, this method simply stores the client's reference in the client instance variable.

```
    public void setClient(MiniClientSession c)
    {
        client = c;
    }
```

Internally, the remote session uses the addMessage method to notify the client of new messages using RMI and the MiniClientSession interface. Messages being sent are added to a history vector in case the client doesn't acknowledge it and calls recover or the session is in transaction mode and is rolled back.

```
    public synchronized void addMessage(Message msg)
    {
        if(client != null)
        {
            try
            {
                client.addMessage(msg);
```

```
                Vector history = historyFor(msg);

                if(history != null) history.addElement(msg);
            }
            catch(Exception exp)
            {
            }
        }
    }
```

The session can be transacted or rely on normal acknowledgments. The client will send the setTransacted message to the server to indicate whether transactions should be used.

```
public void setTransacted(boolean tf)
  throws RemoteException, JMSException
{
    transacted = tf;
}
```

Because the remote session uses resources, it should be closed when not in use. Normally, the client sends the close message, but the session also implements unreferenced, from the Unreferenced interface. This is called if the remote object has no more RMI clients. Unreferencing the session causes it to close.

```
public void unreferenced()
{
    try
    {
        close();
    }
    catch(Exception ignore)
    {
    }
}
```

Closing the session using the close method stops the thread used to poll the message store. Then, if it is transacted, the session rolls back in case there is an uncommitted transaction. Finally, all temporary subscriptions are unregistered with the store. Temporary destinations are also deleted from the store.

```
public RemoteMiniSession close()
 throws RemoteException, JMSException
{
    try
    {
        Object[] unreg;
        Destination dest;

        checker.stop();

        if(transacted)//rollback the uncommited trans
```

```
                rollback();

            int i,max;

            max = unregOnClose.size();

            for(i=0;i<max;i++)
            {
                unreg = (Object[]) unregOnClose.elementAt(i);

                dest = (Destination)unreg[0];

                unregisterFor(dest,(String)unreg[1]);

                if((dest instanceof TemporaryTopic)
                    ||(dest instanceof TemporaryQueue))
                {
                    store.deleteDestination(dest.toString());
                }
            }
        }
        catch(Exception ignore)
        {
        }

        return null;
    }
```

The remote session provides an interface, listed here, for the client to the store for creating queues, topics, and deleting destinations. All exceptions are simply passed through from the store to the client.

```
    //Throws an exception if one exists.
    public Queue createQueue(String queueName)
     throws RemoteException, JMSException
    {
        return store.createQueue(queueName);
    }

    //Throws an exception if one exists.
    public Topic createTopic(String queueName)
     throws RemoteException, JMSException
    {
        return store.createTopic(queueName);
    }

    public void deleteDestination(String queueName)
     throws RemoteException, JMSException
    {
        store.deleteDestination(queueName);
    }
```

When a session is asked to send a message, it either stores the message for sending or sends it, depending on its transacted state. Non-transacted sessions send immediately. Transacted sessions delay sending until the commit method is called.

```
public void send(Message message)
            throws RemoteException, JMSException
{
    if(transacted)
    {
        synchronized(toSend)
        {
            toSend.addElement(message);
        }
    }
    else
    {
        reallySend(message);
    }
}
```

Really sending a message, using the reallySend method, involves passing it to the message store. Any exceptions are converted to JMS exceptions to comply with the JMS specification.

```
protected void reallySend(Message message)
    throws JMSException
{
    try
    {
        //Send message to store.
        //May use persistant store if appropriate.
        store.send(message);
    }
    catch(JMSException exp)
    {
        throw exp;
    }
    catch(Exception exp)
    {
        throw new JMSException("Failed to send message.");
    }
}
```

Committing a transacted remote session causes it to send any messages in the toSend vector. The session also clears out the histories vectors and acknowledges the messages in them; only the message with the highest number is acknowledged. Committing a non-transacted session has no effect. The complete code for commit is listed here:

```
public void commit() throws JMSException
{
```

```
if(!transacted) return;

int i,max;
Message msg;
long num=-1;

try
{
    synchronized(toSend)
    {
        max = toSend.size();

        for(i=0;i<max;i++)
        {
            msg = (Message) toSend.elementAt(i);
            reallySend(msg);
        }

        toSend.removeAllElements();
    }

    synchronized(histories)
    {
        Enumeration cursor = histories.keys();
        Vector history;
        HistoryPair pair;

        while(cursor.hasMoreElements())
        {
            pair = (HistoryPair) cursor.nextElement();
            history = (Vector) histories.get(pair);

            max = history.size();

            for(i=0;i<max;i++)
            {
                msg = (Message) history.elementAt(i);

                if(msg.propertyExists(
                    MiniJMSMessageStore.MSG_NUM))
                {
                    num = Math.max(num
                            ,msg.getLongProperty(
                              MiniJMSMessageStore.MSG_NUM));
                }
            }

            history.removeAllElements();

            //Acknowledge as a whole when transacted.
            if(num>0)
```

```
                    store.acknowledge(pair.destination
                  ,pair.name,num);
                }
            }
        }
        catch(Exception exp)
        {
            throw new JMSException(exp.toString());
        }
    }
```

Rolling back a transacted session removes all of the pending sends in the toSend vector and calls the internal method reallyRecover, discussed here. Recover calls the same method with a different argument. This argument tells the session whether the recovered messages should be marked as redelivered.

```
    public void rollback() throws JMSException
    {
        if(!transacted) return;
        toSend.removeAllElements();//throw away sends
        reallyRecover(false);
    }

    public void recover() throws JMSException
    {
        if(transacted) return;
        else reallyRecover(true);
    }
```

Both rollback and recover call the reallyRecover method listed here. This method takes messages from the histories vectors and resends them using addMessage. This causes them to be redelivered if the client is still available.

```
    //tf == true -> mark redelivered
    protected void reallyRecover(boolean tf) throws JMSException
    {
        try
        {
            synchronized(histories)
            {
                Enumeration cursor = histories.keys();
                Vector history;
                Destination d;
                int i,max;
                Message msg;
                HistoryPair pair;
                String name;

                while(cursor.hasMoreElements())
                {
```

```
                    pair = (HistoryPair) cursor.nextElement();
                    history = (Vector) histories.get(pair);

                    d = pair.destination;
                    name = pair.name;

                    max = history.size();

                    for(i=0;i<max;i++)
                    {
                        msg = (Message) history.elementAt(i);

                        if(tf) msg.setJMSRedelivered(true);

                        addMessage(msg);
                    }

                    history.removeAllElements();
                }
            }
        }
        catch(Exception exp)
        {
            throw new JMSException("Failed to recover completely.");
        }
    }
```

Clients send the acknowledge method, as defined below, to the server to indicate receipt. Acknowledging a destination uses the histories vectors to determine the last message sent to the client and notifies the message store with the largest message number received.

```
    public void acknowledge(Destination d,String name)
     throws JMSException
    {
        if(transacted) return;

        Vector history = historyFor(d,name);
        Message m =null;
        long num;

        if(history.size()>0) m = (Message) history.lastElement();

        try
        {
            if((m!=null)
                &&(m.propertyExists(MiniJMSMessageStore.MSG_NUM)))
            {
                num =
                 m.getLongProperty(MiniJMSMessageStore.MSG_NUM);
```

```
                store.acknowledge(d,name,num);
                history.removeAllElements();
            }
        }
        catch(Exception exp)
        {
            throw new JMSException(exp.toString());
        }
    }
```

The history vectors are stored by name and destination. The session implements two internal methods for getting the history based on a message or a destination and name. These methods are listed here:

```
protected Vector historyFor(Message m)
{
    Destination d=null;
    String name=null;

    try
    {
        d = m.getJMSDestination();

        name =
         m.getStringProperty(MiniJMSMessageStore.REG_NAME);
    }
    catch(Exception exp)
    {
        name = null;
    }

    if(name == null) name = clientId;

    return historyFor(d,name);
}

protected Vector historyFor(Destination d,String name)
{
    Vector retVal=null;
    HistoryPair pair;

    if((d==null)||(name==null)) return null;

    synchronized(histories)
    {
        pair = new HistoryPair();
        pair.destination = d;
        pair.name = name;

        retVal = (Vector) histories.get(pair);
```

```
            if(retVal == null)
            {
                retVal = new Vector();
                histories.put(pair,retVal);
            }
        }

        return retVal;
    }
```

When a client session registers for messages to a particular destination, the remote session is told. The registerFor method, shown here, takes the destination, a name to register with, and a flag indicating if the registration is durable and should last beyond the close method. Temporary destinations are treated as non-durable, even if the flag is true. This method also resumes the sessions polling thread because it now has at least one destination that may receive messages in the message store.

```
    public void registerFor(Destination dest
                            ,boolean durable,String name)
        throws RemoteException,JMSException
    {
        try
        {
            store.registerFor(dest,clientId,name);

            //Always unregister for temporary items.
            if(!durable || (dest instanceof TemporaryTopic)
                    ||(dest instanceof TemporaryQueue))
            {
                Object[] unreg = new Object[2];

                unreg[0] = dest;
                unreg[1] = name;
                unregOnClose.addElement(unreg);
            }

            checker.resume();
        }
        catch(JMSException exp)
        {
            throw exp;
        }
        catch(Exception exp)
        {
            throw new JMSException(exp.toString());
        }
    }
```

Unregistering for a destination is passed directly to the store using the sessions client ID and the provided name.

```
    public void unregisterFor(Destination dest,String name)
        throws RemoteException,JMSException
    {
        try
        {
            store.unregisterFor(dest,clientId,name);
        }
        catch(JMSException exp)
        {
            throw exp;
        }
        catch(Exception exp)
        {
            throw new JMSException(exp.toString());
        }
    }
```

The run method, listed here, defines the code executed by the session's polling thread. As implemented, run simply checks the store for messages and calls addMessage to send them to the client.

```
    public void run()
    {
        while(store != null)
        {
            Message next;

            try
            {
                next = store.nextMessageFor(clientId);

                if(next != null) addMessage(next);
            }
            catch(Exception ignore)
            {
            }
        }
    }
}
```

In the same way that the MiniSession is the workhorse on the client, the RemoteMiniSessionImp, combined with the message store, are the workhorses on the server. RemoteMiniSessionImp demonstrates how objects that represent client connections can be used to implement a multithreaded server.

The Server: MiniJMS

The server itself is implemented in a small class called MiniJMS, listed here. This class contains only a main method. The server must be run with an IP address on the command line, indicating the machine containing the server's rmiregistery. For example, you might run it using:

```
> java minijmsserver.MiniJMS 192.168.0.172
```

The main method creates the message store using a hard-coded properties file discussed here. The store creates the JNDI context into which the server binds a TopicConnectionFactory and a QueueConnectionFactory. The ObjectFactories for these two classes are also provided to the JNDI context.

Finally, the server creates the MiniJMSServerImp object and binds it to the RMI registry. At this point, the server is running and waiting for connections. Notice that the connection factories bound into JNDI use the same server IP as the RMI registry, allowing the server to potentially register with another computer. However, the file system context used in this example doesn't support this type of access, so you would need to use another provider like LDAP to make the MiniJMS server a distributed application.

The server prints message to the console indicating its status during each stage of initialization.

```
package minijmsserver;

//Imports removed to save space.

public class MiniJMS
{
    public static void main(String args[])
    {
        MiniJMSServerImp server;
        MiniJMSMessageStore store;
        Context context;
        String serverURL=null;

        System.setErr(System.out);

        try
        {
            if(args.length>0)
            {
                serverURL = "//"+args[0]+"/"
                                +MiniJMSServer.SERVER_NAME;
            }
            else
            {
                System.out.println("No Server Specified.");
                System.exit(0);
            }

            System.out.println("Creating store.");
            store = new MiniJMSMessageStore("minijmsserver/"
                            +"minijmsserver.properties");
```

```
                System.out.println("Created store.");

                System.out.println("Creating server.");
                server = new MiniJMSServerImp(store);
                System.out.println("Created server.");

                System.out.println("Binding factories to context.");
                context = store.getJNDIContext();

                context.addToEnvironment(Context.OBJECT_FACTORIES,
                                   "minijms.MiniTConnFactoryFactory");

                context.addToEnvironment(Context.OBJECT_FACTORIES,
                                   "minijms.MiniQConnFactoryFactory");

                context.rebind("QueueConnectionFactory"
                    ,new MiniQueueConnectionFactory(serverURL));

                context.rebind("TopicConnectionFactory"
                    ,new MiniTopicConnectionFactory(serverURL));

                System.out.println("Bound factories to context.");

                System.out.println("Starting to bind server.");

                Naming.rebind(serverURL, server);

                System.out.println("Mini JMS bound in registry");
            }
            catch (Exception e)
            {
                System.out.println("Mini JMS: "
                                    + e.getMessage());
                e.printStackTrace();
                System.exit(0);
            }
        }
    }
```

The properties file used by the server defines the database connection information, the directory that the store will use to store messages, and the JNDI connection information.

```
db_url=jdbc:odbc:MiniJMS
db_driver=sun.jdbc.odbc.JdbcOdbcDriver

object_directory=c:\\temp\\objects

java.naming.factory.initial=\
                        com.sun.jndi.fscontext.RefFSContextFactory

java.naming.provider.url=file:///temp/jndistore
```

MiniJMSMessageStore supports a username and password for the database connection information, but they are not used in this example.

Building and Running MiniJMS

MiniJMS, in the default configuration, relies on an ODBC data source called MiniJMS. The CD-ROM includes a Microsoft Access database file that contains the data for this database, or you can use the minijmsserver.BuildDB script to create a database using a different database vendor. Simply alter the script or create a different one that generates the database schema discussed in the section on the MiniJMSMessageStore. You will also need to create a directory called c:/temp/jndistore for use by the JNDI file system context.

In order to compile and use MiniJMS, install the JMS libraries on your computer. These are in a package called javax.jms. You will also need the JNDI libraries discussed in Chapter 5, "Using JNDI," and the file system JNDI service provider. All of these libraries can be obtained from the CD-ROM or the JavaSoft Web site at www.javasoft.com. All of these libraries must appear in your class path.

Several small batch files are included in the chapter_26 directory of the CD-ROM; they build the minijms and minijmsserver packages as well as run rmic on the three remote objects, MiniJMSServerImp, RemoteMiniConnectionImp, and RemoteMiniSessionImp. The script build.bat also builds the database and creates a jar file called minijms.jar that is used by the examples in Chapter 20, "Programming with the Java Messaging Service." Once created, your client can use this jar file to get access to the MiniJMS classes.

Running JMS is a three-step process. First, make sure that all of the library files are in your class path. Next, start the RMI registry. The registry must have access to the minijms classes, so you may want to put the minijms.jar file in your class path. Then start the MiniJMS server. This server is called minijmsserver.MiniJMS and takes a single command-line argument containing the IP address of the local host. This address is used to find the RMI registry. For example, you might enter:

```
> java -nojit minijmsserver.MiniJMS 192.168.0.172
```

Notice that due to a bug in some versions of the JDK that causes errors when using RMI, the just-in-time compiler is not used. You may not need to take this precaution with your installation.

Use the examples in Chapter 20 to test MiniJMS and see it in action.

Summary

MiniJMS is a large application that ties together several Enterprise frameworks, including JNDI, JDBC, and RMI. The main take-home points from this example are as follows:

- Use properties files when possible. This allows easier reconfiguration of the program.

- Use JNDI to access objects whose implementation should be hidden from the programmer. MiniJMS uses JNDI to register the destinations and connection factories, allowing the programmer to access these objects without knowing their implementation details or actual class names.
- Use JDBC for database access and try to use generic SQL to make porting between databases easier. MiniJMS uses basic SQL, although the build script for Microsoft Access does use the currency field for message numbers, because longs are not supported. However, the client is unaware of this "hack."
- Recognize that JNDI providers may have limited functionality and the choice of provider can play an important role in your implementation or deployment. For example, the file system provider we used prevents the client from accessing the JNDI context unless the client and server share a file system.
- Recognize that JDBC drivers can also limit your implementation. The JDBC-ODBC driver, with Access, prevents the efficient storage of serialized objects in the database, causing us to store them on disk.
- Considering that MiniJMS is only an example program, realize that enterprise applications are large and can take a lot of time to write and test. Of course, you probably knew that already! This bullet is for your boss, who disagrees with you and wants it tomorrow, bug-free.
- Rely on thread synchronization to protect shared resources, keeping in mind that you may not be able to protect something with only synchronized methods. For example, when we read messages, we both retrieve and remove them. If we relied on synchronized messages, another thread could perform an operation between the retrieve and remove. Synchronizing a block of code protects against this type of interference.

All in all, there are many lessons to learn from this example. Not all are listed here, but hopefully this example, the one in Chapter 25, "A Four-Tier Online Store," and all of the others from this book provide a great start for you on your journey into Java enterprise programming.

JDBC Information

DBMetaData Methods

Table A.1 DatabaseMetaData Methods for Retrieving Database Information

boolean **allProceduresAreCallable**()	Determine if all the procedures returned by getProcedures() can be called by the current user.
boolean **allTablesAreSelectable**()	Determine if all the tables returned by getTable() can be accessed, or selected by the current user.
boolean **dataDefinitionCauses TransactionCommit**()	Determine if this data source commits the transaction after executing a data definition statement.
boolean **dataDefinitionIgnored InTransactions**()	Determine if data definition statements are ignored in a transaction.
boolean **doesMaxRowSizeIncludeBlobs**()	Determine if this data source consider max row size to include max size for Binary Large Objects (BLObs)?
ResultSet **getCatalogs**()	Get the catalog names available in this data source.
String **getCatalogSeparator**()	Returns the separator between catalog and table name.
String **getCatalogTerm**()	Get the data source vendor's preferred term for "catalog".

Continues

Table A.1 DatabaseMetaData Methods for Retrieving Database Information *(Continued)*

`ResultSet` **`getColumnPrivileges(`** `String catalog, String schema, String table,String columnNamePattern)`	Get a description of the access rights for a table's columns.
`ResultSet` **`getColumns(`** `String catalog, String schemaPattern, String tableNamePattern, String columnNamePattern)`	Get a list of table columns available in a catalog.
`ResultSet` **`getCrossReference(`** `String primaryCatalog, String primarySchema, String primaryTable, String foreignCatalog, String foreignSchema, String foreignTable)`	Get a description of the foreign key columns in the foreign key table that references the primary key columns of the primary key table.
`String` **`getDatabaseProductName`**`()`	Return the name of this database product.
`String` **`getDatabaseProductVersion`**`()`	Return the version of this database product.
`int` **`getDefaultTransactionIsolation`**`()`	Determine the database's default transaction isolation level? The values are define in defined in java.sql.Connection: TRANSACTION_NONE - Transactions are not supported. TRANSACTION_READ_COMMITTED - Dirty reads are prevented; non-repeatable reads and phantom reads can occur. TRANSACTION_READ_UNCOMMITTED - Dirty reads, non-repeatable reads and phantom reads can occur. TRANSACTION_REPEATABLE_READ - Dirty reads and non-repeatable reads are prevented; phantom reads can occur. TRANSACTION_SERIALIZABLE - Dirty reads, non-repeatable reads and phantom reads are prevented.
`int` **`getDriverMajorVersion`**`()`	Determine the JDBC driver's major version number.
`int` **`getDriverMinorVersion`**`()`	Determine the JDBC driver's minor version number.
`String` **`getDriverName`**`()`	Determine the name of this JDBC driver.
`String` **`getDriverVersion`**`()`	Determine the version of this JDBC driver.
`ResultSet` **`getExportedKeys`** `(String catalog, String schema, String table)`	Get a description of the foreign key columns that reference a table's primary key columns.
`String` **`getExtraNameCharacters`**`()`	Get the characters that can be used in unquoted identifier names (those beyond a-z, A-Z, 0-9 and _).
`String` **`getIdentifierQuoteString`**`()`	Determine the string used to quote SQL identifiers.
`ResultSet` **`getImportedKeys`** `(String catalog, String schema, String table)`	Get a description of the primary key columns that are referenced by a table's foreign key columns.

Table A.1 *(Continued)*

`ResultSet` **`getIndexInfo(`**
`String catalog,`
`String schema,`
`String table,`
`boolean unique,`
`boolean approximate)`
	Get a description of a table's indices.

`int` **`getMaxBinaryLiteralLength`**`()`	Determine how many hexadecimal characters you can have in an inline binary literal.
`int` **`getMaxCatalogNameLength`**`()`	Determine the maximum length of a catalog name.
`int` **`getMaxCharLiteralLength`**`()`	Determine the max length for a character literal.
`int` **`getMaxColumnNameLength`**`()`	Determine the limit on column name length.
`int` **`getMaxColumnsInGroupBy`**`()`	Determine the maximum number of columns in a GROUP BY clause.
`int` **`getMaxColumnsInIndex`**`()`	Determine the maximum number of columns allowed in an index.
`int` **`getMaxColumnsInOrderBy`**`()`	Determine the maximum number of columns in an ORDER BY clause.
`int` **`getMaxColumnsInSelect`**`()`	Determine the maximum number of columns in a SELECT list.
`int` **`getMaxColumnsInTable`**`()`	Determine the maximum number of columns in a table.
`int` **`getMaxConnections`**`()`	Determine how many active connections you can have at a time to this database.
`int` **`getMaxCursorNameLength`**`()`	Determine the maximum cursor name length.
`int` **`getMaxIndexLength`**`()`	Determine the maximum length of an index in bytes.
`int` **`getMaxProcedureNameLength`**`()`	Determine the maximum length of a procedure name.
`int` **`getMaxRowSize`**`()`	Determine the maximum length of a row.
`int` **`getMaxSchemaNameLength`**`()`	Determine the maximum length allowed for a schema name.
`int` **`getMaxStatementLength`**`()`	Determine the maximum length of an SQL statement.
`int` **`getMaxStatements`**`()`	Determine how many active statements can be open at one time to this database.
`int` **`getMaxTableNameLength`**`()`	Determine the maximum length of a table name.
`int` **`getMaxTablesInSelect`**`()`	Determine the maximum number of tables in a SELECT statement.
`int` **`getMaxUserNameLength`**`()`	Determine the maximum length of a user name.
`String` **`getNumericFunctions`**`()`	Get a comma-separated list of math functions in this database.

`ResultSet`
`getPrimaryKeys``(String catalog,`
`String schema,`
`String table)`
	Get a description of a table's primary key columns.

`ResultSet` **`getProcedureColumns(`**
`String catalog,`
`String schemaPattern,`
`String procedureNamePattern,`
`String columnNamePattern)`
	Get a description of a catalog's stored procedure parameters and result columns.

Continues

Table A.1 DatabaseMetaData Methods for Retrieving Database Information *(Continued)*

ResultSet **getProcedures(** String catalog, String schemaPattern, String procedureNamePattern)	Get a description of stored procedures available in a catalog.
String **getProcedureTerm**()	Determine the database vendor's preferred term for "procedure".
ResultSet **getSchemas**()	Get the schema names available in this database.
String **getSchemaTerm**()	Determine the database vendor's preferred term for "schema".
String **getSearchStringEscape**()	This is the string that can be used to escape '_' or '%' in the string pattern style catalog search parameters.
String **getSQLKeywords**()	Get a comma-separated list of data source SQL keywords that are NOT also SQL92 keywords.
String **getStringFunctions**()	Get a comma-separated list of string functions.
String **getSystemFunctions**()	Get a comma-separated list of system functions.
ResultSet **getTablePrivileges(** String catalog, String schemaPattern, String tableNamePattern)	Get a description of the access rights for each table available in a catalog.
ResultSet **getTables(** String catalog, String schemaPattern, String tableNamePattern, String[] types)	Get a description of tables available in a catalog.
ResultSet **getTableTypes**()	Get the table types available.
String **getTimeDateFunctions**()	Get a comma-separated list of time and date functions.
ResultSet **getTypeInfo**()	Get a description of all the standard SQL types supported by this database.
String **getURL**()	Determine the URL for this database.
String **getUserName**()	What's our user name as known to the database.
ResultSet **getVersionColumns(** String catalog, String schema, String table)	Get a description of a table's columns that are automatically updated when any value in a row is updated.
Boolean **isCatalogAtStart**()	Determine if a catalog appear at the start of a qualified table name. (Otherwise it appears at the end)
Boolean **isReadOnly**()	Determine if the data source is in read-only mode.
Boolean **nullPlusNonNullIsNull**()	Determine if concatenations between NULL and non-NULL values NULL. A JDBC-Compliant driver always returns true.
Boolean **nullsAreSortedAtEnd**()	Determine if NULL values sorted at the end regardless of sort order.
Boolean **nullsAreSortedAtStart**()	Determine if NULL values sorted at the start regardless of sort order.
Boolean **nullsAreSortedHigh**()	Determine if NULL values sorted high.
Boolean **nullsAreSortedLow**()	Determine if NULL values sorted low.
Boolean **storesLowerCaseIdentifiers**()	Determine if the database treat mixed case unquoted SQL identifiers as case insensitive and store them in lower case.

Table A.1 *(Continued)*

Boolean **storesLowerCaseQuotedIdentifiers**()	Determine if the database treat mixed case quoted SQL identifiers as case insensitive and store them in lower case.
Boolean **storesMixedCaseIdentifiers**()	Determine if the database treat mixed case unquoted SQL identifiers as case insensitive and store them in mixed case.
Boolean **storesMixedCaseQuotedIdentifiers**()	Determine if the database treat mixed case quoted SQL identifiers as case insensitive and store them in mixed case.
Boolean **storesUpperCaseIdentifiers**()	Determine if the database treat mixed case unquoted SQL identifiers as case insensitive and store them in upper case.
Boolean **storesUpperCaseQuotedIdentifiers**()	Determine if the database treat mixed case quoted SQL identifiers as case insensitive and store them in upper case.
Boolean **supportsAlterTableWithAddColumn**()	Determine if add column is supported with ALTER TABLE.
Boolean **supportsAlterTableWithDropColumn**()	Determine if drop column is supported with ALTER TABLE.
Boolean **supportsANSI92EntryLevelSQL**()	Determine if the ANSI92 entry level SQL grammar is supported. This is required for JavaSoft's JDBC Compliance.
Boolean **supportsANSI92FullSQL**()	Determine if the ANSI92 full SQL grammar is supported.
Boolean **supportsANSI92IntermediateSQL**()	Determine if the ANSI92 intermediate SQL grammar is supported.
boolean **supportsCatalogsInDataManipulation**()	Determine if a catalog name be used in a data manipulation statement.
boolean **supportsCatalogsInIndexDefinitions**()	Determine if a catalog name can be used in an index definition statement.
Boolean **supportsCatalogsInPrivilegeDefinitions**()	Determine if a catalog name can be used in a privilege definition statement.
Boolean **supportsCatalogsInProcedureCalls**()	Determine if a catalog name can be used in a procedure call statement.
Boolean **supportsCatalogsInTableDefinitions**()	Determine if a catalog name can be used in a table definition statement.
Boolean **supportsColumnAliasing**()	Determine if column aliasing is supported.
boolean **supportsConvert**()	Determine if the CONVERT function between SQL types is supported.
boolean **supportsConvert**(int fromType, int toType)	Determine if CONVERT is supported for the supported SQL types.

Continues

Table A.1 DatabaseMetaData Methods for Retrieving Database Information *(Continued)*

boolean **supportsCoreSQLGrammar**()	Determine if the ODBC Core SQL grammar is supported.
boolean **supportsCorrelatedSubqueries**()	Determine if correlated subqueries are supported. A JDBC-Compliant driver returns true.
Boolean **supportsDataDefinition AndDataManipulationTransactions**()	Determine if both data definition and data manipulation statements within a transaction are supported.
Boolean **supportsDataManipulation TransactionsOnly**()	Determine if only data manipulation statements within a transaction are supported.
Boolean **supportsDifferent TableCorrelationNames**()	Determine if table correlation names are supported. If so, are they restricted to be different from the names of the tables?
Boolean **supportsExpressionsInOrderBy**()	Determine if expressions in ORDER BY lists are supported.
boolean **supportsExtendedSQLGrammar**()	Determine if the ODBC Extended SQL grammar is supported.
boolean **supportsFullOuterJoins**()	Determine if full nested outer joins are supported.
boolean **supportsGroupBy**()	Determine if the GROUP BY clause is supported.
boolean **supportsGroupByBeyondSelect**()	Determine if a GROUP BY clause can add columns not in the SELECT provided all the columns in the SELECT are specified.
boolean **supportsGroupByUnrelated**()	Determine if a GROUP BY clause can use columns not in the SELECT.
Boolean **supportsIntegrity EnhancementFacility**()	Determine if the SQL Integrity Enhancement Facility is supported.
Boolean **supportsLikeEscapeClause**()	Determine if the escape character in LIKE clauses supported. A JDBC-Compliant driver returns true.
Boolean **supportsLimitedOuterJoins**()	Determine if there is limited support for outer joins.
boolean **supportsMinimumSQLGrammar**()	Determine if the ODBC Minimum SQL grammar is supported. All JDBC-Compliant drivers must return true.
boolean **supportsMixedCaseIdentifiers**()	Determine if the database treats mixed case, unquoted SQL identifiers as case sensitive and as a result stores them in mixed case. A JDBC-Compliant driver will return false.
Boolean **supportsMixedCase QuotedIdentifiers**() return true.	Determine if the database treats mixed case, quoted SQL identifiers as case sensitive and as a result store them in mixed case. A JDBC-Compliant driver will
boolean **supportsMultipleResultSets**()	Determine if multiple ResultSets from a single execute is supported.
Boolean **supportsMultipleTransactions**()	Determine if multiple transactions can be opened at once, on different connections.
Boolean **supportsNonNullableColumns**()	Determine if columns be defined as non-nullable. A JDBC-Compliant driver returns true.

Table A.1 *(Continued)*

Boolean **supportsOpenCursorsAcrossCommit**()	Determine if cursors remain open across commits.
Boolean **supportsOpenCursorsAcrossRollback**()	Determine if cursors remain open across rollbacks.
Boolean **supportsOpenStatementsAcrossCommit**()	Determine if statements remain open across commits.
Boolean **supportsOpenStatements AcrossRollback**()	Determine if statements remain open across rollbacks.
boolean **supportsOrderByUnrelated**()	Determine if a n "ORDER BY" clause use columns not in the SELECT.
boolean **supportsOuterJoins**()	Determine if outer join are supported.
Boolean **supportsPositionedDelete**()	Determine if positioned DELETE statements are supported.
Boolean **supportsPositionedUpdate**()	Determine if positioned UPDATE statements are supported.
Boolean **supportsSchemas InDataManipulation**()	Determine if a schema name can be used in a data manipulation statement.
Boolean **supportsSchemas InIndexDefinitions**()	Determine if a schema name can be used in an index definition statement.
Boolean **supportsSchemas InPrivilegeDefinitions**()	Determine if a schema name can be used in a privilege definition statement.
boolean **supportsSchemas InProcedureCalls**()	Determine if a schema name can be used in a procedure call statement.
Boolean **supportsSchemas InTableDefinitions**()	Determine if a schema name can be used in a table definition statement.
boolean **supportsSelectForUpdate**()	Determine if SELECT for UPDATE is supported.
Boolean **supportsStoredProcedures**()	Determine if stored procedure calls can use the stored procedure escape syntax.
Boolean **supportsSubqueries InComparisons**()	Determine if subqueries in comparison expressions supported. A JDBC-Compliant driver returns true.
Boolean **supportsSubqueriesInExists**()	Determine if subqueries in 'exists' expressions are supported. A JDBC-Compliant driver returns true.
Boolean **supportsSubqueriesInIns**()	Determine if subqueries in 'in' statements are supported. A JDBC-Compliant driver returns true.
boolean **supportsSubqueries InQuantifieds**()	Determine if subqueries in quantified expressions are supported. A JDBC-Compliant driver returns true.
boolean **supportsTableCorrelationNames**()	Determine if table correlation names are supported. A JDBC-Compliant driver returns true.
Boolean **supportsTransaction IsolationLevel(** int level)	Determine if the database supports the given transaction isolation level.

Continues

Table A.1 DatabaseMetaData Methods for Retrieving Database Information *(Continued)*

boolean **supportsTransactions**()	Determine if transactions are supported. If they are not, the isolation level is TRANSACTION_NONE.
boolean **supportsUnion**()	Determine if UNION is supported.
Boolean **supportsUnionAll**()	Determine if UNION ALL is supported.
Boolean **usesLocalFilePerTable**()	Determine if the database uses a file for each table.
Boolean **usesLocalFiles**()	Determine if the database stores tables in a local file.

JDBC 2.0 Enhancements to DatabaseMetaData

Table A.2 JDBC 2.0 DatabaseMetaData Methods

METHOD	USE
Class **getClass**(String catalog, String schema, String className)	Get the Java class object corresponding to a specific user-defined type with type JAVA_OBJECT.
Connection **getConnection**()	Get the Connection object that produced this metadata object.
ResultSet **getUDTs**(String catalog, String schemaPattern, String typeNamePattern, int[] types)	Get a description of the user-defined types defined in a schema.
Boolean **rowChangesAreDetected**(int type)	Determine whether or not a result set can detect that a row has been changed by anyone.
boolean **rowChangesAreVisible**(int type)	Determine whether or not a TYPE_STATIC or TYPE_KEYSET result set can see the row changes that it makes.
Boolean **supportsBatchUpdates**()	Determine if the driver supports batch updates. Return true if the driver supports batch updates.
Boolean **supportsResultSetConcurrency**(int concurrency)	Determine if the database supports the given type of result set concurrency.
boolean **supportsResultSetType**(int type)	Determine if the database supports the given result set type.

JDBC Driver Vendors

Table A.3 Available JDBC Drivers

VENDOR	DATA SOURCE SUPPORTED
Agave Software Design	Oracle, Sybase, Informix, others via ODBC
Altera Software	Altera SQL Server
Asgard Software	Unisys A series DMSII database
Caribou Lake Software	Ingres

Table A.3 *(Continued)*

VENDOR	DATA SOURCE SUPPORTED
Cloudscape	JBMS
Connect Software	Sybase, MS SQL Server, Informix
Ensodex, Inc.	Several through ODBC
IBM	IBM DB2 Version 2
IBM	DB2 for OS/400
GWE Technologies	Mysql
GIE Dyade	RMI Bridge for remote access to JDBC drivers
Hit Software	DB2, DB2/400
IDS Software	Oracle, Sybase, MS SQL Server, MS Access, Informix, Watcom, and others via ODBC
I-Kinetics, Inc.	Oracle, Informix, Sybase, and others via ODBC
Imaginary	mSQL
InterBase	InterBase
InterSoft	Essentia
Intersolv	DB2, Ingres, Informix, Oracle, Microsoft SQL Server, Sybase 10/11
JavaSoft	Several dozen through ODBC drivers
KonaSoft, Inc.	Sybase, Oracle, Informix, SQL Anywhere
Liberty Integration Software	Most PICK flavors including VMARK, Unidata, General Automation, PICK systems
NetAway	Oracle, Informix, Sybase, MS SQL Server, DB2, others via ODBC
OpenLink	Oracle, Informix, Sybase, MS SQL Server, CA-Ingres, Progress, Unify, PostgreSQL, Solid, and others via ODBC.
Oracle Corporation	Oracle
SAS Institute Inc.	SAS, and via SAS/ACCESS, Oracle, Informix, Ingres, and ADABAS
SCO	Informix, Oracle, Ingres, Sybase, Interbase
Simba Technologies, Inc.	Oracle, Sybase, MS SQL
Solid Information Technology	Solid Server
Sybase, Inc.	Sybase SQL Server, SQL Anywhere, Sybase IQ, Replication Server and more than 25 enterprise and legacy database servers via Sybase
OmniCONNECT Symantec	Oracle, Sybase, MS SQL Server, MS Access, Watcom and others via ODBC
Trifox, Inc.	ADABAS, DB2, Informix, Ingres, Oracle, Rdb, SQL Server, Sybase, and legacy systems via GENESIS.
Visigenic	Several dozen through ODBC drivers
WebLogic	Oracle, Sybase, MS SQL Server, Several dozen through ODBC drivers
XDB Systems, Inc.	Many databases through ODBC
Yard Software GmbH	YARD-SQL Database

What's on the CD-ROM?

The CD-ROM included with this book contains all of the source code demonstrated in this book, as well as several other example programs and resources. To make the CD-ROM easier to use, it is indexed via an HTML file. This file appears in the root directory, and is named index.htm. Simply open this file in a browser, and follow the links to find examples, resources, and last minute news or information.

The example programs are available directly from the CD-ROM in the directory ejava_examples and in the zip file ejava_ex.zip. We have provided the zip file for developers on operating systems that will not copy the long file names correctly from the CD-ROM. Inside the ejava_examples directory are a set of sub-directories named for the chapters in the book. These chapter directories contain directories for each example in that chapter. For example:

```
ejava_examples/chapter_13/class_loading
```

contains the example on using the codebase to control class loading in RMI. Inside the ejava_examples directory there is also an index.html file that contains a list of links to the HTML descriptions for each chapter's examples.

Keep in mind that some of the examples discussed in the book are not included line for line to save space. In these cases, the complete code is provided on the CD-ROM.

The CD-ROM also contains a number of applications, RFCs and libraries, that can be used to run the provided examples, including :

- BEA WebLogic Application Server (formerly called Tengah)

- JBMS 1.5 Evaluation version from Cloudscape, Inc., a pure Java database engine with an included JDBC driver
- Java 2 and the Servlet Development Kit version 2.0
- Eliza code
- RFC 1766
- RFC 2254

Please refer to the CD-ROM for the exact details on using these applications.

What Is Freeware / Shareware?

Freeware is software that is distributed by disk, through BBS systems and the Internet free. There is no charge for using it, and can be distributed freely as long as the use it is put to follows the license agreement included with it.

Shareware (also known as user supported software) is a revolutionary means of distributing software created by individuals or companies too small to make inroads into the more conventional retail distribution networks . The authors of Shareware retain all rights to the software under the copyright laws while still allowing free distribution. This gives the user the chance to freely obtain and try out software to see if it fits his needs. Shareware should not be confused with Public Domain software even though they are often obtained from the same sources.

If you continue to use Shareware after trying it out, you are expected to register your use with the author and pay a registration fee. What you get in return depends on the author, but may include a printed manual, free updates, telephone support, etc.

The CD-ROM contains two demonstration applications, the BEA Weblogic Application Server and JBMS, that are available for your testing for a limited time. Like Shareware you must pay for these applications if you intend to use them beyond the demonstration time period.

Hardware Requirements

Of course the primary requirement for using the CD-ROM is a CD-ROM drive. To use the JDK and JFC you will also need to meet their installation requirements which include:

- 50 MB of available disk space (if you include the source code, documentation and JavaSoft examples)
- 16 MB of RAM although more is always better.

The examples from the book are under 10 MB including source, compiled files and other resources. You can run these from the CD-ROM or copy them to your hard disk so that you can change them to try out the various techniques.

Other resources on the CD-ROM include specific information regarding their requirements.

Since enterprise applications require a number of applications to be running, the actual requirements for a developer to use these examples will vary. However, the authors developed all of the examples on Pentium based computers with 32–80 MB of RAM. You will also need a network connection to access supporting applications, documents and libraries that are available from the Internet.

Installing the Software

You can either use the examples from this book directly from the CD-ROM or copy the examples to your hard disk. To copy the examples:

1. Place the CD-ROM into your CD-ROM drive.
2. Copy the ejava_examples directory from the CD-ROM to your hard disk or open the ejava_ex.zip file and extract it to your hard disk.

Use the zip file to unpack the examples if you are on a computer that does not recognize the long file names on the CD-ROM. To test whether or not your system supports these file names, open several of the ejava_examples sub-directories and inspect the file names. All source code files should end in ".java" and compiled files should end in ".class".

Using the Software

Refer to the appropriate chapter for information on running the examples in this book. Remember that many of the examples require supporting applications or hosts. For example, servlets require a Web server, and Enterprise JavaBeans require a host. The chapters that discuss each technology also describe the deployment issues for using them. We have also tried to provide directions on the CD-ROM, in the HTML guides to help you determine which applications or hosts you need for each chapter.

User Assistance and Information

If you find any problems in the examples included on the CD-ROM please contact the authors using the links provided on the index.htm page to access the web site for errata and other issues.

The software accompanying this book is being provided as is without warranty or support of any kind. Should you require basic installation assistance, or if your media is defective, please call our product support number at (212) 850-6194 weekdays between 9 AM and 4 PM Eastern Standard Time. Or, we can be reached via e-mail at: **wprtusw@wiley.com**.

To place additional orders or to request information about other Wiley products, please call (800) 879-4539.

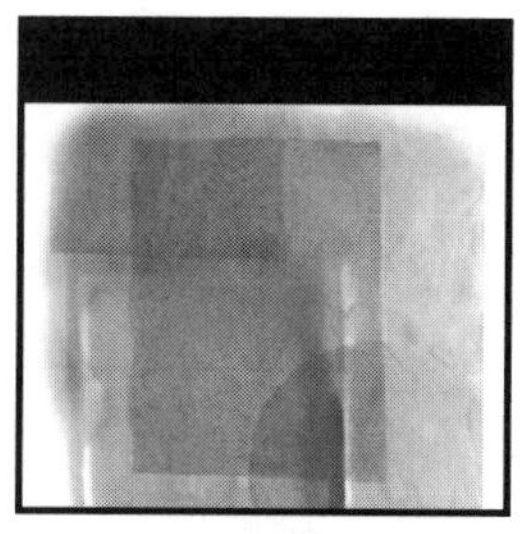

INDEX

S

Java™ Development Kit Version 1.1.x and Java Servlet Development Kit 2.0 Combined Binary Code License

This binary code license ("License") contains rights and restrictions associated with use of the accompanying software and documentation ("Software"). Read the License carefully before installing the Software. By installing the Software you agree to the terms and conditions of this License.

1. **Limited License Grant.** Sun grants to you ("Licensee") a non-exclusive, non-transferable limited license to use the Software without fee for evaluation of the Software and for development of Java™ applets and applications. Licensee may make one archival copy of the Software and may re-distribute complete, unmodified copies of the Software to software developers within Licensee's organization to avoid unnecessary download time, provided that this License conspicuously appear with all copies of the Software. Except for the foregoing and the distribution rights authorized for the servlet classes specified in Section 2 below, Licensee may not re-distribute the Software in whole or in part, either separately or included with a product. Refer to the Java Runtime Environment Version 1.1 binary code license (http://java.sun.com/products/JDK/1.1/index.html) for the availability of runtime code which may be distributed with Java compatible applets and applications.
2. **License to Distribute Servlet Classes.** Licensee is granted a royalty-free right to reproduce and distribute the servlet classes contained in the Software identified therein as "Sun.Servlet.*," "Javax.Servlet.*" or "Jsdk.Doc.Apidoc.*" ("Servlet Classes") provided that Licensee: (i) distributes the Servlet Classes complete and unmodified only as part of, and for the sole purpose of running, Licensee's Java compatible servlets ("Servlets"); (ii) does not distribute additional software intended to replace any component(s) of the Servlet Classes; (iii) agrees to incorporate the most current version of the Software that was available from Sun no later than 180 days prior to each production release of the Servlet; (iv) does not remove or alter any proprietary legends or notices contained in the Servlet Classes; (v) includes the provisions of Sections 4, 5, 6, 7, 9 and 10 in Licensee's license agreement for the Program; and (vi) agrees to indemnify, hold harmless, and defend Sun and its licensors from and against any claims or lawsuits, including attorney's fees, that arise or result from the use or distribution of the Program.
3. **Java Platform Interface.** Licensee may not modify the Java Platform Interface ("JPI", identified as classes contained within the "java" package or any subpackages of the "java" package), by creating additional classes within the JPI or otherwise causing the addition to or modification of the classes in the JPI. In the event that Licensee creates any Java-related API and distributes such API to others for applet or application development, Licensee must promptly publish an accurate specification for such API for free use by all developers of Java-based software.

4. **Restrictions.** Software is confidential copyrighted information of Sun and title to all copies is retained by Sun and/or its licensors. Licensee shall not modify, decompile, disassemble, decrypt, extract, or otherwise reverse engineer Software. Software may not be leased, assigned, or sublicensed, in whole or in part. Software is not designed or intended for use in on-line control of aircraft, air traffic, aircraft navigation or aircraft communications; or in the design, construction, operation or maintenance of any nuclear facility. Licensee warrants that it will not use or redistribute the Software for such purposes.
5. **Trademarks and Logos.** This License does not authorize Licensee to use any Sun name, trademark or logo. Licensee acknowledges that Sun owns the Java trademark and all Java-related trademarks, logos and icons including the Coffee Cup and Duke ("Java Marks") and agrees to: (i) comply with the Java Trademark Guidelines at http://java.com/trademarks.html; (ii) not do anything harmful to or inconsistent with Sun's rights in the Java Marks; and (iii) assist Sun in protecting those rights, including assigning to Sun any rights acquired by Licensee in any Java Mark.
6. **Disclaimer of Warranty.** Software is provided "AS IS," without a warranty of any kind. ALL EXPRESS OR IMPLIED REPRESENTATIONS AND WARRANTIES, INCLUDING ANY IMPLIED WARRANTY OF MERCHANTABILITY, FITNESS FOR A PARTICULAR PURPOSE OR NON-INFRINGEMENT, ARE HEREBY EXCLUDED.
7. **Limitation of Liability.** SUN AND ITS LICENSORS SHALL NOT BE LIABLE FOR ANY DAMAGES SUFFERED BY LICENSEE OR ANY THIRD PARTY AS A RESULT OF USING OR DISTRIBUTING SOFTWARE. IN NO EVENT WILL SUN OR ITS LICENSORS BE LIABLE FOR ANY LOST REVENUE, PROFIT OR DATA, OR FOR DIRECT, INDIRECT, SPECIAL, CONSEQUENTIAL, INCIDENTAL OR PUNITIVE DAMAGES, HOWEVER CAUSED AND REGARDLESS OF THE THEORY OF LIABILITY, ARISING OUT OF THE USE OF OR INABILITY TO USE SOFTWARE, EVEN IF SUN HAS BEEN ADVISED OF THE POSSIBILITY OF SUCH DAMAGES.
8. **Termination.** Licensee may terminate this License at any time by destroying all copies of Software. This License will terminate immediately without notice from Sun if Licensee fails to comply with any provision of this License. Upon such termination, Licensee must destroy all copies of Software.
9. Export Regulations. Software, including technical data, is subject to U.S. export control laws, including the U.S. Export Administration Act and its associated regulations, and may be subject to export or import regulations in other countries. Licensee agrees to comply strictly with all such regulations and acknowledges that it has the responsibility to obtain licenses to export, re-export, or import Software. Software may not be downloaded, or otherwise exported or re-exported (i) into, or to a national or resident of, Cuba, Iraq, Iran, North Korea, Libya, Sudan, Syria or any country to which the U.S. has embargoed goods; or (ii) to anyone on the U.S. Treasury Department's list of Specially Designated Nations or the U.S. Commerce Department's Table of Denial Orders.

10. **Restricted Rights.** Use, duplication or disclosure by the United States government is subject to the restrictions as set forth in the Rights in Technical Data and Computer Software Clauses in DFARS 252.227-7013(c) (1) (ii) and FAR 52.227-19(c) (2) as applicable.
11. **Governing Law.** Any action related to this License will be governed by California law and controlling U.S. federal law. No choice of law rules of any jurisdiction will apply.
12. **Severability.** If any of the above provisions are held to be in violation of applicable law, void, or unenforceable in any jurisdiction, then such provisions are herewith waived to the extent necessary for the License to be otherwise enforceable in such jurisdiction.However, if in Sun's opinion deletion of any provisions of the License by operation of this paragraph unreasonably compromises the rights or increase the liabilities of Sun or its licensors, Sun reserves the right to terminate the License and refund the fee paid by Licensee, if any, as Licensee's sole and exclusive remedy.

CUSTOMER NOTE: IF THIS BOOK IS ACCOMPANIED BY SOFTWARE, PLEASE READ THE FOLLOWING BEFORE OPENING THE PACKAGE.

This software contains files to help you utilize the models described in the accompanying book. By opening the package, you are agreeing to be bound by the following agreement:

Java 2 and SDK 1.2

JMBS 1.3

To use this CD-ROM, your system must meet the following requirements:

RAM. 16MB or more

Hard Drive Space. 50 MB

Peripherals. CD-ROM drive; Web browser in order to navigate CD-ROM contents.